Agriculture and Rural Areas Approaching the Twenty-first Century

CHALLENGES FOR AGRICULTURAL ECONOMICS

Agriculture and Rural Areas Approaching the Twenty-first Century

CHALLENGES FOR AGRICULTURAL ECONOMICS

EDITED BY

R. J. Hildreth
Kathryn L. Lipton
Kenneth C. Clayton
Carl C. O'Connor

IOWA STATE UNIVERSITY PRESS / AMES

Kenneth C. Clayton is Director, National Economics Division, Economic Research Service, United States Department of Agriculture, Washington, D.C. R. J. Hildreth is Managing Director, the Farm Foundation, Oak Brook, Illinois. Kathryn L. Lipton is Economics Editor, *National Food Review*, and Staff Economist, Office of the Director, National Economics Division, Economic Research Service, United States Department of Agriculture, Washington, D.C. Carl O'Connor is Professor and Marketing Economist, Department of Agricultural and Resource Economics, Oregon State University, Corvallis, Oregon.

©1988 Iowa State University Press, Ames, Iowa 50010
All rights reserved

Composed by Iowa State University Press from editor-provided disks

Printed in the United States of America

First edition, 1988

Library of Congress Cataloging-in-Publication Data

Agriculture and rural areas approaching the twenty-first century: challenges for agricultural economics / edited by R. J. Hildreth . . . [et al.].—1st ed.
    p.   cm.
    Based on material presented at an American Agricultural Economics Association (AAEA) conference held Aug. 7–9, 1985, in Ames, Iowa.
    Includes index.
    ISBN 0–8138–0043–9
    1. Agriculture—Economic aspects—United States—Congresses.   2. Agricultural innovations—United States—Congresses.   3. Farm management—United States—Congresses.   I. Hildreth, R. J. (Roland J.)   II. American Agricultural Economics Association.
HD1755.A39 1988
388.1′0973—dc19   87–31861
                                                            CIP

CONTENTS

PREFACE

AS the twentieth century draws to a close, agriculture, the food system, and rural communities face a rapidly changing and at times bewildering array of problems.

The emergence of a well-integrated, international economy opens new problems and opportunities for farmers and rural people at the same time that it imposes constraints on policymakers and limits certain choices. The effects of high real interest rates and high dollar value on agriculture, the food system, and rural communities clearly demonstrate the importance of the fiscal and monetary policy. Rapidly changing communication technology coupled with the computer revolution and its widespread acceptance have brought us into the information age and created enormous new opportunities, while at the same time creating the potential for serious social problems. Breakthroughs in biotechnology promise another technological revolution, opening new vistas while at the same time requiring potentially serious adjustments. The interface between rural and urban communities is undergoing rapid change as the economics of industry and its location shift. Political and social changes promise to transform the relationships among members of society and how we govern ourselves.

This proceedings is based on material presented at an American Agricultural Economics Association (AAEA) conference, "Agriculture and Rural Areas Approaching the Twenty-first Century: Challenges for Agricultural Economics," held August 7–9, 1985, in Ames, Iowa, following the association's seventy-fifth annual meeting. It seemed particularly appropriate at this anniversary for a profession that has prided itself on meeting the challenges of the past to identify the challenges facing agriculture and rural areas in the twenty-first century.

The purpose of the conference and of this proceedings is to help the profession of agricultural economics better serve during this period of rapid transition. The papers presented seek to redefine the issues we face as a profession and to point the way to a sharper, more relevant set of priority issues by (1) characterizing the changing state of agriculture and the rural

ix

community; (2) assaying the changing state of economic logic and quantitative methods; (3) exploring how the analysis of problems of agriculture and the rural community can make a contribution to improvements in logic, data, and methods; and (4) identifying and defining significant problems of agriculture and the rural community and the issues needing attention by agricultural economics research, teaching, and extension.

There is clearly a need for establishing new program thrusts, strengthening and improving existing programs, and reallocating resources, both within the profession of agricultural economics and between agricultural economics and other agricultural fields. It will be difficult for agricultural economics topics to be included in competitive and special grants programs unless there is a clear definition of the issues demanding priority. More generally, a sense of priority and relevance is needed if adequate funding is to be available for the profession's programs in the future. Furthermore, a sense of priority and relevance will assist individual agricultural economists in allocation of their time and energy to topics that are challenging as well as in the national interest.

Appreciation goes to the AAEA Committee on Issues and Priorities for the years of planning that went into the conference and to the Cooperative State Research Service/USDA, and the Economic Research Service/USDA for financial support of the conference and this proceedings.

R. J. Hildreth
Chairman, AAEA Committee on
Issues and Priorities

Agriculture and Rural Areas Approaching the Twenty-first Century

CHALLENGES FOR AGRICULTURAL ECONOMICS

An Overview: Agricultural Economics at a Crossroads

EMERY N. CASTLE and R. J. HILDRETH

> Are, in fact, our associations doing their jobs well? In certain respects — publishing journals, providing communication, and running meetings — they will prove most adept. In others — evaluating the future of their professions, identifying employment prospects for students, explaining their needs to Washington — their performance is episodic. Some do well; others poorly. If science is to play an increasingly important role in modern society, then the associations that de Tocqueville predicted would be so important to a democracy must constantly prove their effectiveness. We scientists should both contribute to and demand performance from our professional societies.
>
> DANIEL E. KASHLAND, JR.
> *Science,* 23 August 1985

WHATEVER else may be said about agricultural economics as a profession and the American Agricultural Economics Association as a professional society, it certainly must be granted that they are willing to engage in self-examination to better evaluate their future and to explain their needs to others. This volume reports the results of one such examination, but it is far from an isolated example. The citations in the papers attest to a long tradition of introspection on the part of at least many members of the profession. But the papers and discussions reported on here reflect an intensity of concern that is worthy of note. The fact that the conference was held in the summer of 1985, when the agricultural sector was experiencing great distress, may have contributed to the feeling of urgency that seemed to prevail. Also, it was the seventy-fifth anniversary of the association, which undoubtedly encouraged reflection and introspection. In any event, a genuine effort was made to discover if agricultural economics is as socially useful as it might be.

Emery N. Castle is Chairman, Economics Core Program, Oregon State University, Corvallis. R. J. Hildreth is Managing Director of the Farm Foundation, Oak Brook, Illinois.

3

The bulk of the discussion centered on three main themes:

• What is the nature of the social and economic environment likely to prevail for the remainder of this century and at the beginning of the next?
• What social problems will exist on which agricultural economists might work?
• What theories, tools, and data will agricultural economists need?

Even though most papers and discussions concentrated on one of the above themes, almost all covered more than one and some addressed all three. Agricultural economists predominated at the conference, but, by design of the conference planners, representatives of many other interests participated as well. Administrators, government and foundation officials, scholars from several other disciplines, and industry people gave papers and engaged in the discussions. By design, the conference covered research, teaching, extension education, and public service. Also by design, the field of agricultural production and marketing, the agricultural industry, food and agricultural policy, international agriculture, human capital and the rural community were all considered appropriate fields of study for agricultural economists.

The purpose of this overview is to extract from the papers, the formal discussion of the papers, and the participant involvement those ideas considered to be of the greatest importance to the profession. No attempt has been made to identify the source of the ideas expressed. Such an overview cannot capture the essence of each paper; that is not its purpose. Rather than to repeat and duplicate, the objective here is to extend, synthesize, and integrate that which was written and said.

The Social and Economic Environment

No attempt was made to predict the future in detail or to forge a consensus of what the future is likely to be. Nevertheless, it became clear that many of the participants expected certain trends to continue and new developments to occur that would affect their working environment or the working environment of their students. The conference planners intended that the conference be of relevance to the immediate future. While this was accomplished, the planning period of most conference participants seemed to be the remainder of this century and in some cases the first decade of the next century.

The forces of change that have transformed the relations among nations since World War II have not yet run their course. The presence of different ideologies in the world, nuclear weapons, and nations at various stages of development establish the basis for even greater change in the future. Agriculture and food will continue to play a major role in international relations and in development. Also, the discovery of new knowledge will continue to create and recognize the resources available for food and fiber use.

There will continue to be a human capital as well as a commodity dimension to the role of agricultural and natural resources in economic development. Those concerned with U.S. agriculture will need to know about international trade possibilities for domestically produced commodities. Certainly this will include how such commodity flows will be influenced by U.S. economic performance and government policies, as well as economic performance and government policies in other countries. It is clear that agricultural economists will be in demand in other countries as well. Some will be educated in the United States and will be natives of this country. Others will not be natives, and the capacity of many developing countries to educate their own people will certainly improve. This trend will place a higher value on the ability to acquire knowledge about global geography, history, politics, and economics.

The mutual dependence of the urban and the rural will become more pronounced. Much of the uncertainty affecting agriculture and rural areas will stem from unpredictable shocks that have their origin in other countries, in the urban economy, or in government. Even as new technology permits better adaption to conditions in nature, many exogenous social forces of importance to agriculture and rural areas will continue to be unpredictable. But it should not be assumed that the urban society has only undesirable shocks up its sleeve. In the United States the income from off-farm employment has been a stabilizing force in farm family income. Thus, a major part of the social adjustment of agriculture will involve a better understanding of global events and the interface between the rural and urban society. By drawing on such knowledge it may be possible to develop strategies that will permit rural America to draw new strength from the larger economy. Not only will the external economy serve as a market for the commodities to be sold but a place where human capital may be developed and, when in excess, marketed. There was skepticism at the conference that international trade would provide a rapidly growing outlet for U.S. farm commodities. While growth is foreseen it is not expected to be spectacular.

Fiscal difficulties being experienced by the U.S. government were recognized as a major secular influence on the agriculture of the nation. One manifestation is that pressure exists to contain the costs of farm programs at the federal level and, indirectly, provide impetus to the decentralization of government. The growth of state and local government may well have enormous implications for agricultural economists. Federal funding for agricultural research always has been of great importance, but as state funding becomes of relatively greater importance, state problems relative to national problems will undoubtedly be emphasized more in such research. Unless foundations or special appropriations are forthcoming for work on national problems, they may go unresearched. Without appropriate regional coordination there are likely to be gaps in research (where states hope to borrow results from other states) at the same time there is duplication of effort in neighboring states. Capacity for the analysis of public policy issues at the national level may not be maintained.

Decentralized government may be expected to reflect the interests of local constituencies. Because nonfarmers outnumber farmers in most rural communities, local government will have need for the analysis of problems that are neither farm nor agriculture specific. The agricultural economics profession may need to face again the question that it faced 75 years ago — will it be agricultural economics, narrowly interpreted, or will it be a profession concerned with a broad range of rural economic issues?

The assumption, sometimes explicit but often implicit, that the quality of life would constantly change both domestically and internationally, was encountered again and again. The feeling prevailed that incomes generally would rise, but this general optimism was tempered by the expectation that there would continue to be regional poverty as, for example, in parts of Africa. Furthermore, it was recognized that even in those societies where average per capita incomes were rising, there would be people and regions that would be bypassed, at least temporarily. No doubt the reason for the general optimism was the belief that certain fundamental lessons of economic development have been learned. Investment in improving the human agent and in the discovery of knowledge has come to be viewed as a cause rather than a result of economic development. Further, the knowledge already available has laid a foundation for technology that promises to change both agriculture and the larger society even more in the future than it has in the past. Biotechnology and electronics provide both promise and potential. In one case, the potential of vastly increasing agricultural output exists; in the other, the cost of recording and transmitting information has dropped enormously with great increases in the analytical capability of the farm and resource manager. The implications for the management of firms, both farm and nonfarm, are enormous. Farm management, perhaps the oldest area in agriculture economics, appears to be in the midst of an enormous revolution. Both the way decisions are made as well as the structure of the industry is experiencing dramatic change.

With improved incomes, people will become increasingly concerned with these nonmarketed goods and services that enter their consumption functions. Environmental quality can be expected to influence agriculture even more in the future than it has in the past. An affluent society is unlikely to tolerate siltation of streams or the misuse of chemicals, when the production of foodstuffs is so inexpensive as measured by the percentage of income that goes for this purpose. How the agricultural industry accommodates these larger social objectives will become an increasingly important part of agricultural policy.

There was no evidence that the conference participants expected that the real cost of agricultural products in the Unites States would reverse their long-run declining trend. But neither did the participants seem to believe the percentage of income spent on food in the United States would decline as dramatically in the future as it has in the past. The expectation also prevailed that agriculture would continue to become more efficient worldwide and that average global incomes will rise. This will create a growing world demand for agricultural products and there will be increased trade. But the growth in demand for U.S. agricultural exports will not be at the spectacular levels of the 1970s. Furthermore, food deficits will trouble some regions of the world—parts of Africa, Asia, and Latin America. Thus, human resource development and the discovery of knowledge for the purpose of improving food production, distribution, and consumption will continue to be a need for some time to come.

What Are the Problems?

In a separate document, opportunities for agricultural economists in research, teaching, and extension education will be identified, based on the conference results. There will be no attempt here to provide such a list or to prescribe an agenda of activity, but rather to identify the fundamental trends affecting the field with the objective of providing a contemporary description of the domain of agricultural economics.

A dominant impression created by the conference is the vital nature of the field and its enormous importance to our social system, to agriculture, and to institutions that serve all America. The adjustments are indeed great that will be faced by those segments of our society concerned with agriculture and rural areas. No other group or body of thought addresses this range of issues in such a comprehensive way as does agricultural economics. The profession has every reason to be proud of its mission.

But if the mission of agricultural economics is worthy, its agenda is indeed ambitious. For example, world economic development, international trade, and macroeconomics are all major areas of study within economics and integral to agricultural and resource economics. Yet to understand the complexities of agricultural policy, operating as it does in an international arena and in an urban-oriented economy, requires the sophisticated use of these concepts. The physical interdependency of agriculture with other segments of society in the use of land, water, and the atmosphere brings issues of environmental policy to the fore. And, as has been noted, many rural communities have long since lost their primarily agricultural orientation and a host of policy issues have arisen that are outside traditional agricultural economics. Agricultural business firm management (traditionally farm management and marketing) will draw on business management, finance, and psychology as well as production economics.

One, then, is driven to the conclusion that at least two main branches of agricultural economics may well emerge in the period ahead and it is not clear if the important literature of each can be mastered by one person. One branch will be concerned with the adaptation of agricultural firms and businesses in an increasingly uncertain world. This field of study usually will take certain conditions as given — the international arena, macroeconomic policy, and domestic policy related to agriculture. Knowledge about these areas will be of great value because they will do much to affect the profitability and survival of agricultural firms. But the main focus of this body of study will be on the adaptation of agricultural firms to these exogenous forces. The study of firm management will include traditional production economics theory, but additional emphasis will be placed on decision making under uncertainty. The acquisition and processing of information will be a major area of interest. Not the least of the uncertainty will be the rapidity and profitability of technical and institutional change.

The other main branch of agricultural economics will relate to the public policies that affect agriculture and rural people. As used here, "policies" pertain to the social mechanisms that relate agriculture and rural people to the remainder of the national and international economy. These social mechanisms define the entitlements that will prevail under different circumstances and conditions. They will include, but will not be limited to, such issues as exchange rates, investment in agricultural knowledge and human capital, capital gains taxation, air quality standards, land use controls, and water law.

The role of technology in economic decision making and the impact of technology on policy could possibly link the two branches of thought described. Technical change is having an enormous effect on the way farms are organized and managed. Much technical change is output-increasing with enormous implications for public policy. Agricultural economics can take pride in its pioneering work on technical change. Even though the existing literature on technical change may provide an excellent base for future work, the emerging problems associated with technical change may be very different from those experienced in the past. Certainly there will be a limit as to what agricultural economists can accomplish working independently on this subject. To really penetrate deeply into such a subject will require the insights of many disciplines.

It follows that there will be a wide range of subjects studied and that many different approaches will be followed. What, if anything, will unify agricultural economics? If the profession is to remain a cohesive group it will be because one or both of the following conditions will prevail.

• There will be concern about those activities that require space or are rural in orientation. This will include but will not necessarily be limited to farming and agriculture.

• There will be generally accepted methodologies or approaches to problem solving.

What Theories, Tools, and Data Will Agricultural Economists Need?

With an exploding range of problems confronting the professional workers in agricultural economics, it is not surprising that concern would be expressed with the tools of their craft. Their distinctive approach was fashioned in an earlier era; its essentials were: (1) mastery, skilled use, and often the formulation and testing of economic theory; (2) the application of a wide range of quantitative techniques; and, (3) the extensive use of real-world information as data about the economy generally, the agricultural industry, resources, and agricultural firms. This information was often but not always in quantitative terms.

When the essentials of this traditional approach are pondered, it is recognized that it is not just that particular problems have changed. Economics as a discipline has undergone a major transformation. Quantitative techniques have become much more formal and have increased in number. The capacity to process numerical information has grown enormously, but the data on many aspects of agriculture and rural life has declined in availability and quality. These developments are more likely to rupture the unity of agricultural economics than the changed range of problems on which agricultural economists will work.

The profession of economics may well be approaching a crisis. The usefulness of much that is called economics is being called into question by those inside as well as outside the profession. Part of the dissatisfaction stems from the trivial nature of some of the problems that are investigated. Some allege the reason this is so is that the highly formal and abstract models used do not have general applicability. In other instances it is argued that real-world examples are chosen to illustrate a method or an approach rather than a method or an approach having been developed to investigate a real-world problem of condition.

Similar criticisms have been made of much quantitative work in agricultural economics. Many of the early agricultural economists helped develop quantitative techniques to investigate problems in their field. As econometrics and operations research techniques became more complex, it became more and more time consuming just to master their essentials. When a great amount of time has been invested in such techniques, it is quite natural for an applied worker to search for real-world problems to which they might be applied. It is not surprising that the results are different than when the problem preceded the technique.

Paradoxically, both the quantity and quality of data have declined even as theoretical models and quantitative techniques have become more powerful. The reasons for this are several but three stand out. One is that data collection efforts have been reduced at the federal level, partly as a result of budget reductions. Another is that the concepts underlying much of the data that are collected have become obsolete because of economic change. Still another is that economics researchers may have less concern about the quality of their data than they once did, because their attention has been focused on the intricate nature of the economic and quantitative models rather than on the need to obtain results relevant to the solution of real-world problems.

These concerns have led some in the profession to suggest that a crossroads has been reached similar in many ways to the situation that existed when the profession was founded. At the time one group argued for a pragmatic orientation that would have utilized economics as one, but only one, of several disciplines of value to the study of rural America. However, the approach chosen was to maintain very close ties with economics, indeed, agricultural economics was viewed as a field of study within economics. The argument is now advanced that other disciplines and approaches are more useful to the solution of particular problems than searching the economics literature for a particular model that may seem to be relevant to the problem being investigated. Nevertheless, there are those who hope the traditional approach will be maintained and that even more emphasis will be placed on the corpus of economics by agricultural economists. There are many variations of these alternate positions including the argument that agricultural economists misapply economics or use obsolete theory. This approach would encourage agricultural economists to be more careful in their use of economic concepts.

Another point of view often expressed has been present in both economics and agricultural economics for several decades. This is the argument, held frequently by "institutionalists" (although not by them exclusively) that the normative presuppositions embedded in classical and neoclassical economics direct attention away from important problems. According to this point of view much economic analysis takes the distribution of wealth and entitlements as given, even though it is over such matters that conflicts arise and policy is made. To the extent that economics and agricultural economics ignore such issues, it is bound to be irrelevant to much that is important in public policy.

Teaching, Extension, and Research

Conference participants addressed all of these activities in their deliberations. Not only were papers devoted to these activities, but they were often discussed in the papers on substantive problems. Certainly both the conference planners as well as the participants recognized the importance of all three functions and that each will change as this century ends and the next one begins.

The traditional unity of the three functions will be subjected to increasing stress. Greater sophistication in research will necessarily mean that research results will need to be interpreted carefully, both in the sense that one will need to know how the results were obtained as well as to know how they may be used in decision making.

There may have been a tendency of the conference participants to neglect education and teaching relative to research and extension. Teaching was perhaps viewed too narrowly rather than as an integral part of the total educational process. If the educational process generally, not necessarily just that part of the educational process limited to the schools and colleges of agriculture, functions well, there will be much greater capacity to use the results of research than would otherwise be the case.

Given the rapid rate of change foreseen by the conference participants in technology, institutions, and global development, the useful life of narrowly technical and vocational information will be shortened. Conversely, the enduring value of knowledge about fundamental natural science processes as well as international considerations will be enhanced. Undergraduate work in agriculture should provide an opportunity for a truly liberal education. What other professional study provides a greater opportunity to learn something about natural science, social science, and the humanities? However, it is not clear that this opportunity is being fully reflected in the curricula in agriculture.

One of the great challenges facing extension work is definition of audience and clientele. If the broad view is taken of rural America, the possible audience for extension economics encompasses federal, state, and local government officials, large commercial farmers, and smaller part-time farmers. While a broad range of public service work will undoubtedly be undertaken nationally, particular extension programs will need to choose carefully among a great many alternatives.

An overriding impression that emerged from the conference with respect to research was that the issues debated and discussed were of real-world importance as well as of academic interest. The apparent willingness of the profession to accept a pluralistic approach in research may be recognition that the real-world urgency and difficulty of the problems make it important that more than one approach be tried. We conclude that it is very important for agricultural economists to get outside the classrooms and research establishments and make direct observations of economic conditions. Researchers need to know firsthand of the real-world conditions their data presumably measure and represent. In the long run this may lead to an improvement in the quality of the data; in the short run it will result in such data being used with greater sensitivity and understanding.

Whither Agricultural Economics?

As the conference drew to a close, one had a sense of optimism and new dedication. This was in the face of the realization that the range of problems was exploding, and that there is lack of agreement on how those problems should be investigated, what should be taught to students, and how public service should be focused. Perhaps this stemmed from a recognition and an acceptance of diversity within the profession.

It has become clear that some agricultural economists and some academic departments of agricultural economics will become more pragmatic. They will draw on a wider range of disciplines than they have in the past. Others will remain close to economics in the belief that greater disciplinary depth will yield the greatest returns over time. Members of both groups are expressing concern about the quality and availability of data and recognize that an empirical orientation combined with theory and intellectual constructs are essential to improved social service.

There continue to be those who argue that institutional economics can make a constructive contribution. They believe that a systematic concern with the rules of the game are a more relevant focus of investigation and such an understanding will help specify the kinds of information that should be collected.

Again, the profession seems willing to accommodate this approach even as some express skepticism as to the amount of substantive knowledge that has been produced by this kind of activity.

Whether optimism is justified may well depend on the emergence of theories of broad scope in agricultural economics. To date, progress in the field often has followed the seminal thinking of a few key people. These are the people who were acutely aware of the social problems of agriculture and rural areas. They generalized and extended the methods of economics and quantitative analysis so that the real-world problems could be better addressed. The history of thought does not provide a reliable guide as to how and when these intellectual giants will emerge. But the necessary condition is that both a social and an intellectual problem must exist; certainly this conference demonstrated that both prevail in rural America and in agricultural and resource economics.

1

The Changing Role of Agricultural Economics

ORVILLE G. BENTLEY

Creative institutions are essential to the conduct of our daily affairs. They are symbols of collective efforts, reflecting the capacities and the personal commitments of the people who created them. To make a lasting contribution, a professional society should be an agent for the intellectual development and continued growth of its membership. Moreover, it should provide continuity and a sense of belonging. Much has been achieved, yet much remains to be done. It is in that framework that I am sure the American Agricultural Economics Association approaches its future.

Over the years it has been my privilege to have worked with many talented and dedicated people. Among them were outstanding leaders prominent in the history of your Association — Ray Penn, Don Paarlberg, Earl Butz, Earl Heady, Carroll Bottom, Joe Ackerman, Emery Castle, and of course your Nobel laureate, the world-renowned Theodore Schultz. But there were many more. I recall with affection the commitment and support that I received from the department heads of Agricultural Economics at Ohio State University, South Dakota State University, the University of Illinois, and program leaders from the Economic Research Service and the private sector.

In addition, there is a long list of distinguished scholars from your profession who have advised on program activities and served as outstanding members of various committees that I have been privileged to chair.

But however pleasant it is to reminisce about the past, the challenge is to look ahead, and a seventy-fifth anniversary is an appropriate time to do so.

It is quite unnecessary to say to this group that "agricultural is going

---

Orville G. Bentley is Assistant Secretary for Science and Education, USDA, Washington, D.C.

through another transition." The changes are far-reaching, with implications for agricultural policy, agricultural credit, shifts in production trends and consumer demands, resource allocations, competition for world markets, and a sharp increase in the availability of new technologies that will likely bring profound changes to the food and fiber system from production through utilization. Moreover, as change takes place in the agricultural sector, the obvious linkage to the economy in general will occur, with spin-offs leading to changes in the political, social, and international sectors.

Unfortunately, and perhaps fortunately, there are no easy prescriptions or foolproof models to suggest a risk-free course of action for the future. The demands on the intellectual and professional leadership of the food and agricultural system will be great in the years ahead. Sound thinking, incisive and penetrating analyses, and intellectual rigor will be at a premium as we face the difficult choices among policy options and economic production and marketing strategies.

These tough decisions will spell challenge to the agricultural economics profession, especially for the young men and women who will carry leadership responsibilities in the future. We will all have to devise new approaches to problem solving, drawing heavily from every resource available. In fact, the multidisciplinary approach will likely be more the modus operandi of the future than it has been in the past. You have the training and experience to look at issues in a comprehensive manner, a skill of tremendous use to decision makers in agriculture, whether it be at the farm level or by national policy leaders.

As teachers, research scholars, and extension education specialists, our particular responsibility is for developments in science and education in both the public and private sectors. Our challenge is to develop a team effort, mobilizing the best talent possible to answer the pressing questions that lie ahead for the clientele we serve. This means we are talking about universities, government-supported scientists and educators, and the leadership from all sectors of private industry.

Because of our particular responsibility, it seems that the matter of planning and projecting future directions for science and education takes on added significance. One of the prime reasons for this statement is that the potential changes that can be brought about as a result of developments in biotechnology and the application of new developments in molecular biology to agriculture will bring a series of changes comparable to those that we experienced through the development of hybrid seeds, improved rations for livestock and poultry, and the introduction of the chemical age in the early post–World War II era.

Now, what about our institutions?

There is no doubt that our research and educational institutions will make adjustments based on their appraisal of academic needs and new breakthroughs in science. Moreover, interaction with the clientele these institutions serve will guide program directions in research, extension education, and teaching. But as these demands for research and education grow while facing budget restraints, the planning process takes on added significance.

The reason for this can be described in various ways. The common jargon these days is to talk in terms of "strategic planning," which is, in fact, an exercise in looking at long-range goals and directions that institutions are going to take. The process itself is important to the esprit de corps of the staff in research and educational institutions.

But the benefits go far beyond the institutional context. In a highly decentralized federal-state research system there is a need to develop a broad consensus on issues and to set priorities for allocating resources to agreed-upon program objectives. While we say it often, we must continue to recognize that the federal-state system derives its strength and vitality in part from its diversity and flexibility. Yet this very strength makes it more difficult to develop a conceptual framework for programs that result in a rigorous approach to solving problems and to define future directions for our activities.

This diversity is greatly increased on a national and international scale. Hence, there is a critical need for building a program consensus that has substantial input from the grass roots level.

The system is complex and sometimes difficult to understand, even for those who are a part of it, whether they are at the institutional level, or think of themselves as individuals on the scientific or administrative level.

Planning is critical to developing understanding at the national level, both in the executive branch and in the Congress. It calls for a continuing effort on the part of the leadership in our system, whether at the university, the agricultural experiment station, the cooperative extension service, or at the national program level.

There are pragmatic reasons for planning and program evaluation efforts that fall outside the development of both "tactical" and "strategic" plans. Not everyone is concerned with the work of the individual institutions or with activities such as those carried out by the Joint Council on Food and Agricultural Sciences or the Users Advisory Board. But, whether from the public or private sector, each of you contributes in your own way, primarily through identifying problems, the committing resources, utilizing the expertise of scientists in research and extension programs, and teaching students at the graduate and undergraduate levels.

It is axiomatic that change is a part of progress. Yet it is sometimes difficult for us to recognize the magnitude of outside forces having a profound effect on developments likely to occur within the agricultural system.

A complete list of changing conditions that will influence developments in agriculture would be very long, but such a list would include these considerations:

1. Profitability in the agricultural sector. With falling exports, lower land values, and high interest rates relative to inflation, the nation's farm sector is experiencing a very difficult time.
2. Water quality and management. Thirty-four states have identified agricultural nonpoint source pollution as a major cause of water contamination. In the arid west, water management issues have reached a critical stage.
3. Opportunities in biotechnology. The potential payoffs of this research are considerable and include possible breakthroughs such as pest- and drought-resistant plants, plants that produce their own fertilizer, and vaccines that simulate the natural immunity of animals.
4. Trained personnel. Changing issues and opportunities in agriculture require new skills (e.g., molecular biology and systems analysis) and expanded appreciation of our interconnected world.
5. Diet and health issues. Diet, nutrition standards, and physical well-being are pervasive points of discussion among the U.S. citizenry. Improved linkage between changing human nutrition requirements and productive research could have great payoffs for the agricultural industry.

These five items are the top priority issues recently identified by the Joint Council on Food and Agricultural Sciences for fiscal year 1987. The Council prepares an annual priorities report as a guide for those policy-makers who develop the federal budget and for others in science and education who seek guidance concerning important national problems facing the food and agricultural system. A longer look at the most urgent problems needing solutions is presented in the five-year plan. The Council is working on an update of that plan now.

Input for the annual priorities report is received from a broad spectrum of performers and users of agricultural research. Members of the Joint Council represent land-grant universities, etc., and they obtain input from organizations that represent the many components of this decentralized system.

These priorities are having an influence on decisions made in Washington, at least in areas where they are compatible with administrative and congressional policy preferences. The funding of the competitive grants program in fiscal year 1985 is an example of this impact.

Agricultural economics has a prominent place in the five priorities identified for fiscal year 1987. The profitability issue needs a major input of ideas from your profession. What are the implications of current market and financial trends on the future farm economy in the United States (e.g., options for farmers, characteristics of successful operators, and consequences of less government involvement)?

At the May 1985 meeting of the Joint Council, Michael D. Boehlje, Iowa State University, Leo E. Lucas, the University of Nebraska, and Harold D. Guither, University of Illinois/Economic Research Service, discussed what is being done at this time and some options for the future. The good work being done by these people and others should be continued and expanded.

Another dimension of the declining profit picture is identifying alternative opportunities for farmers who must find another line of work (i.e., training needs, other business opportunities, relocation, etc.).

With regard to water quality, what are the most efficient ways to reduce nonpoint pollution and use scarce irrigation water, given the technology now available?

Biotechnology developments will require that we examine the potential impact of new technologies on the demand and supply situation, industry structure, government programs, and community stability to insure a smooth transition from one set of practices and interactions to another. Robert J. Kalter, Cornell University, recently completed an assessment of the bovine growth hormone on the dairy industry. The results of the study will provide invaluable insights for establishing dairy policy at the national and state levels.

Skilled personnel demands will require the agricultural economics profession to advise state and federal administrators of research and education programs on the training needed by future economists. Are current curricula keeping pace with changes occurring in the international arena? Should there be more emphasis on integrating social and biological sciences? Which combination of skills can best address emerging issues?

Changing patterns of food consumption are having significant impacts on agriculture. Predicting changing food-buying habits is always a risky proposition, but having more advance knowledge of these trends would give farmers, processors, and marketers more time to adjust their operations.

One theme that permeates needed economic analysis is its anticipatory character. Agricultural economists have done an outstanding job at improving the decision-making process at the firm level, but more help is needed by government decision makers in anticipating future events. In addition to the Joint Council priorities, we need help in:

1. Examining the consequences of regulatory trends. What are the costs to the agricultural industry of more restricted use of herbicides, pesticides, and fertilizers?

2. Determining the advantages and disadvantages of U.S. agriculture being the early adopters of technologies derived from biotechnology research (e.g., impacts on competitive status, per-unit costs, community stability, etc.).

3. What are the likely impacts of closer collaboration between universities and federal labs with the private sector on the development of new technologies (i.e., exclusive licenses)?

The suggested agenda for agricultural economics is rather extensive. The logical question is: Where do the resources come from to tackle these important issues?

I feel the profession must take the lead in demonstrating the necessary role of agricultural economics in improving the competitive position of U.S. agriculture by addressing the questions: (1) how does agricultural economics speed up the technology-adoption process? (2) how do profitable farming enterprises benefit the U.S. economy? (3) why should we improve our understanding of world production and trade trends?

These and related questions need answers. Policymakers and their staffs in Washington are generally two to three generations removed from agriculture. Your programs address the broader social issues of the day, but few people outside agriculture are fully informed about the issues and problems in agriculture. You need to show how the results of your programs can make a difference and why they need to be integrated with the biological and physical sciences.

To demonstrate that you are responsible managers, both pluses and minuses should be presented in program plans. As past initiatives phase down (e.g., energy research), be willing to share with outside groups how resources are being allocated to current priority areas.

When preparing plans, do not react directly to critics. Examine their concerns in a constructive way and incorporate them into a forward-looking package. The agricultural economics profession has a proud history that has served the country well. When looking ahead, be positive and explain what can be done with X amount of resources. The approach must be holistic and not appear self-serving. To gain the attention of busy people I would strongly urge that you establish priorities. Without a priority list there is no easy way to decide among a multitude of legitimate needs.

In contrast to controlled economies, such as in the USSR, U.S. farmers operate as free, independent businessmen, controlling their means of production, making their own decisions, and receiving the results of their own labor and management abilities. Helping these independent farmers make the best decisions possible, given the circumstances facing them, has been a major contribution of the agricultural economist. To continue your fine work you need to show how economic studies can help the farm community and government policymakers make better decisions in the future.

In preparation for the 1985 Farm Bill, the Economic Research Service and several agricultural economists at universities prepared 20 background papers. This information was the primary foundation for the Administration's proposed 1985 Farm Bill. Similar contributions will be made in the future. Be prepared to demonstrate the nature of these future studies in clear and concise language so that the informed layman can understand. We must move out of our inner circle of professional friends to obtain the support of the community at large. Without this broadened understanding, additional financial support will be increasingly difficult to obtain.

2

Approaching the Twenty-first Century: Lessons from History

WAYNE D. RASMUSSEN

Can there be lessons from history? "The past is prologue" graces the facade of the National Archives in Washington, while the statement "He who ignores the lessons of history is doomed to repeat his mistakes," has, in varying versions, become part of our folklore. But then Henry Ford said flatly, "History is bunk."

History is, simply, a branch of knowledge that records and explains past events. The historian explains how we got from some time and some place in the past to some subsequent time and place. Much history can be and is quantified, although historians generally express themselves through narrative writing. Few historians would ever say that history repeats itself, but we do say that a knowledge of the reasons for our past successes and failures may help us avoid mistakes today.

In this paper, I outline the historian's approach to problems, suggest areas in which a knowledge of the past may help us understand some of today's problems, discuss one such problem in greater depth, and conclude with a note or two regarding the twenty-first century.

The Historical Approach

The historian must identify and define a researchable problem, collect all relevant available data, analyze the data to determine what really happened and why it happened, and then reach a conclusion. This conclusion should, in my opinion, be helpful in understanding a present-day problem.

Wayne D. Rasmussen is retired as Chief of the Agriculture and Rural History Branch of the Agriculture and Rural Economics Division of the Economic Research Service (USDA), Washington, D.C.

One distinctive feature in historical research is that the historian must examine all the evidence before reaching a conclusion as to what happened and why. This contrasts with economic research, where the researcher develops a theory, collects evidence to be used in testing the theory, and, using or devising an appropriate model, determines whether the theory is accurate or at least reasonable. The economist may use this theory to predict future movements of the economy or to point out the results of alternative courses of action. The historian, in contrast, may relate the past to the present, but the accepted standard is to stop short of looking into the future and not recommend a course of action.

The historian, in looking at all of the evidence surrounding an issue, tends to take a broad, impartial view. Although two historians might and often do offer somewhat different interpretations as to why events happened or actions were taken, the facts upon which these interpretations are based should be essentially the same. The true historian may not look for and offer only evidence that supports a predetermined point of view. While the strength of the historian is a comprehensive, unbiased (insofar as possible) view, the need to assemble all possible evidence regarding an issue may cause the historian to delay writing his account and reaching his conclusions. As critics may say, the historian does not finally complete his work until he has had an opportunity to study a manuscript hidden in an inaccessible monastery in Tibet.

Perspective on Today's Problems

The federal historian brings historical perspective to bear on current problems. This perspective should be accurate, impartial, and useful as background to all involved in a policy argument.

During the mid-1980s, future price-support programs and strengthening farm credit became the focus of national attention. Farm prices were going down while the general economy was prospering and farm foreclosures (particularly in the Midwest) were increasing. Many proposals were made with respect to price supports, but, at least from the point of history, few if any were new.

Proposals were made, for example, for rigid production controls. In 1621, when Virginia faced a tobacco surplus, the government limited production to 1000 plants of nine leaves each per head of a family or per laborer. This stringent limitation failed to limit production to demand and prices continued to slump. Finally in 1631, Virginia law provided that no tobacco could be sold for less than six pence per pound under penalty of imprisonment. These and other attempts at controlling production and prices failed, but they encouraged production in Maryland and North

Carolina (Gray 1933, 1:260–61). These experiences do not necessarily mean that rigid production controls or price fixing nearly four centuries later would fail as they did in Virginia, but they at least suggest some problems to avoid.

During the mid-1980s, a number of proposals were made to differentiate between needed production and surplus production or between production for domestic and for foreign sales by issuing certificates representing different levels of price support, often related to different markets. Such certificates were part of the McNary-Haugen acts passed by the Congress in 1926 and 1927 and vetoed by President Calvin Coolidge. In the 1960s and early 1970s, certificate programs were authorized by Congress and were used for wheat and feed grains (Bowers 1984, 23–28).

Questions regarding the original purposes of the Federal Farm Loan Act and other legislation eventually consolidated in the Federal Farm Loan Act can be answered in part by studying the hearings and the *Congressional Record*. However, the need for land banks was first brought to national attention by the Country Life Commission of 1908 (Country Life Commission 1975). A year later, the National Monetary Commission, also appointed by President Roosevelt, presented a detailed report on the German rural credit system. In 1912, President William Howard Taft outlined the need for national land banks (Taft 1912, 3–7). These reports provide some of the philosophic background of the present-day Farm Credit Administration and are useful for understanding problems of half-a-century later.

These examples indicate that historical perspective is often helpful in understanding and acting upon current problems. Even more important, historical perspective may assist in the analysis of long-range questions, those that began as much as a century ago and will almost certainly be with us in the twenty-first century. It might now be helpful to turn to a problem that relates to the structure and future of agriculture in even a more fundamental way.

The USDA–Land-Grant University System

The USDA–Land-Grant University System began in 1862 at a time when farmers comprised 53 percent of the work force and produced 42 percent of the gross national product (GNP). Farmers now comprise about 3.2 percent of the work force and produce 2.3 percent of the GNP. Approximately 125,000 farms produce half the value of total farm production. Yet in total, the farm and food system is one of the largest sectors of the economy, and it has long provided the American people with a reliable supply of safe food at modest cost.

The institutions making up the USDA–Land-Grant University System, the Department of Agriculture, and the land-grant universities with their Colleges of Agriculture, Experiment Stations, and Extension Services have been major forces in helping farmers achieve a productivity never before experienced by humankind. But can these institutions meet the challenges of the future?

The question is not new. Agricultural economists have been raising it for at least a quarter of a century. In 1962, James T. Bonnen wrote: "We now face the urgent necessity to adjust the System to new functions in a new and rapidly changing environment" (Bonnen 1962, 1279). A few years later, following up on this theme, Bonnen (1965, 1123) wrote:

> The Land-Grant–USDA System is losing its dedication to the welfare of the entire rural community. . . . evidence of mutually destructive behavior is to be found in the relationships of practically all rural institutions: the colleges, the USDA, local rural community organizations both public and private, and the myriad of organizations that attempt to represent the various interests of the farmer, including the agricultural committees of Congress.

Two decades later the situation appeared no better. Bonnen argued that the system was growing disfunctional with no evidence suggesting a reversal of this failure. Indeed, "one must assume a continued erosion in the interlinkage and coherence of agricultural institutions. The tension-ridden but once close relationships of the colleges and the USDA will no doubt go on deteriorating, as their goals continued to diverge" (Bonnen 1983, 963).

Bonnen was not the only agricultural economist to express concern one time or another over this apparent problem. At times Glenn Johnson, R. J. Hildreth, Edward Schuh, Harold Breimyer, Lyle Schertz, and others have addressed the problem. The future of the USDA–Land-Grant University System is also related to the functions of the system. While James Bonnen has written that "the land-grant idea is probably the one original educational idea of this society," he has also said that "the function of a university is not to provide society with what it wants, but what it needs" (Bonnen 1962, 1291). In considering how the agricultural economist relates to the goals of the system, R. J. Hildreth (1965, 1503) wrote: "The real need, it seems to me, is for better training in economics and methodology in order that these tools may be applied with deeper understanding and greater insight, and thus more proficiently and more purposefully, to relevant problems." A few years later Glenn Johnson (1971, 728) wrote: "Our knowledge-producing and teaching institutions are under sharp criticism and pressure. Many students question whether our universities and nonuniversity research institutions are properly related to the issues and problems of our time."

As we move toward the next century, will the USDA–Land-Grant University System find a new vitality or will the institutions break apart and be absorbed by others that are more relevant to the needs of the American people? A brief historical review might help us better understand how the system got to where it is today and thus better understand where it may be going in the future.

Origins of the System

The land-grant universities and the Department of Agriculture were born in controversy. Both had been urged for many years as supports for family farms. Many Southerners saw these institutions as ways of encouraging western settlement by nonslaveholding farmers and thus as a method of increasing Northern over Southern political influence. Thus it was not until the South had withdrawn from the Union that the laws could be passed. However, when the war was over, all of the Southern states accepted the terms of the land-grant act, while the Department worked to meet the needs of Southern farmers.

Nevertheless, opposition to the agricultural colleges and the Department continued. Many farmers and farm organizations charged that the new colleges taught courses that had nothing to do with agriculture and that the young people attending the colleges were encouraged to go into other occupations than farming. There was truth to both charges. Most college courses contained little material of immediate use to farmers, mainly because there was no real body of knowledge available to be taught. It was not until the colleges began to establish experiment stations and passage of the Hatch Experiment Station Act in 1887 that it became possible to develop courses relevant to agriculture in the individual States (Marcus 1985).

Even after the experiment stations were in operation, many farmers doubted the usefulness of what they were doing, and state legislatures generally were slow to appropriate funds adequate to undertake meaningful experiments. The colleges and experiment stations needed to do something that would help the farmer, that would be highly visible, and that would meet a felt need. The testing of fertilizers was an obvious place to start, particularly in the South where farmers dependent on fertilizer for the production of cotton and tobacco were all too frequently defrauded by unscrupulous manufacturers and salesmen. The North Carolina Experiment Station, established in 1877, had its beginnings in fertilizer testing. By the turn of the century, 30 states had adopted laws regulating the sale of fertilizers. And within the same period, many stations began inspecting nursery stock (Porter 1979, 84–85).

The development of a test for measuring the quantity of fat in milk is another example of a station meeting an immediate farm need. In 1890, Stephen M. Babcock of the Wisconsin Agricultural Experiment Station announced his famous test, saying that it was not patented. This contribution to the dairy industry aided in developing confidence in the experiment stations at a time when their future was still uncertain.

The Department of Agriculture faced some of the same problems. As late as 1881, the chairman of the House Committee on Agriculture stated, "Sooner or later the work of the department should be closed," and he proposed that action be taken immediately (Baker 1963, 28). However, like the experiment stations, the Department began to meet some major needs of American agriculture. In 1888, scientists undertook work on Texas cattle fever. By 1890, they had definitely established that the fever was spread from animal to animal by the cattle tick and had proposed methods for its control, an achievement that won support for the Department. Within a few years, under the leadership of James Wilson, the Department was on its way to becoming one of the world's greatest research institutions and was building a strong relationship with the land-grant colleges. In 1906, Congress doubled federal funds available to the state experiment stations and directed the Department's Office of Experiment Stations to give closer supervision to the projects supported by these funds. While this could have led to strains between the Department and the stations, such was not the result, perhaps because Secretary Wilson and one of his two assistant secretaries had been directors of experiment stations and his other assistant secretary had helped establish and govern a station.

Tensions within the System

The Office of Experiment Stations had been established in the Department in 1888, in accordance with the Hatch Experiment Station Act, to administer the funds granted to the states for their individual stations. From the beginning, the directors of the office saw it as having a coordinating rather than a directing function. Later, this same relationship developed with respect to the Extension Service. However, the relationship between the Department and the land-grant institutions was threatened when a series of New Deal farm acts led the Department to deal directly with farmers on a number of issues. At first, in handling the programs established by the Agricultural Adjustment Act of 1933, the Department called upon the state extension services to sign up the farmers and be responsible for the program on the local level. For the most part the extension services and agricultural colleges responded to the crisis situation, but other programs soon followed the acreage adjustment and price-support activities. Many extension services feared that instead of being advisors to farmers, the county agents would become advocates and administrators of a number of complex and controversial USDA programs (Saloutos 1982, 47, 243–45).

The conflicts came to a head over the soil conservation programs. The extension services had long carried on educational programs in this area and felt that they should be given the responsibility for the new activities. However, the administrator of the Soil Conservation Service (SCS), Hugh H. Bennett, campaigned vigorously for an SCS assistance program that would go directly to landowners and won the support of Secretary of Agriculture Henry A. Wallace for this approach. Although the controversy continued into the 1950s, relations between SCS and Extension have improved over the past 25 years (Simms 1970, 116–29). Generally, the land-grant institutions and the USDA have achieved a reasonable working relationship with regard to the action programs. In some instances this may seem to be an "arms' length" or "uneasy truce" relationship, and particular actions on one side or the other may lead to controversy. For example, the recent decision by the Department to phase out the field staff of the Economic Research Service led to protests from a number of the land-grant institutions. However, the present situation whereby the entire system is either under attack or sees its influence eroding calls for mutual support if the individual units are to survive.

The System in Transition

Farm and food programs are under attack from outside critics and from sources within the agricultural community. Such critics as Rachel Carson, in her book *Silent Spring* (1962), and Jim Hightower, in *Hard Tomatoes, Hard Times* (1973), argued that the USDA–Land-Grant University System concentrated too narrowly on plants, animals, soils, farm prices, and commercial farmers, neglecting the problems of small farmers, rural communities, and consumers. The so-called hunger lobby argues that the system does not give enough attention to hungry people in this nation and in other parts of the world. Yet when the USDA–Land-Grant University System turns its attention to some of these broader issues, representatives of organizations concerned with commercial agriculture argue that the purpose of the system is to serve the needs of farmers and the food chain (Ruttan 1982, 76–83).

The farm economy today is closely tied to the general and international economies. Approximately every third acre of U.S. grain production is exported, and the rate of exchange affects every midwestern farmer. Economists argue that general monetary and fiscal prices have more impact on farm income than do traditional farm price and income policies. The

USDA–Land-Grant University–Agricultural Committees of the Congress triumvirate no longer dominates national agricultural policy as it once did. The Department of State, the Department of the Treasury, the Department of Defense, the Office of Management and Budget, and the White House are concerned one way or another with farm exports and the costs of food. The Department of Health and Human Services is concerned with food stamps and the health and safety of food, the Environmental Protection Agency checks on food safety, and the Department of Transportation is involved with moving grain from where it is grown to ports where it may be shipped overseas.

With the widespread involvement in agriculture by so many policymakers, there are a number of pressing questions facing the USDA–Land-Grant University System in which an understanding of the historical background may help in their resolutions. A key question is who should be served by the system. When the institutions were established in 1862, they were to serve farmers, who were enough of the population that serving farm interests might be seen as serving national interests. Today, if the agricultural colleges and the USDA try to limit their activities to supporting farmers and related industries, they may find themselves, as they have historically, with a continuing decline in basic support. Some economists argue that the institutions must broaden their support bases by becoming more involved in the food chain all the way through distribution and consumption. Another possibility is to look toward greater involvement with the rural population. In any case, understanding the evolution of the problem should help in its solution.

For a century the USDA–Land-Grant University System had the lead role in agriculture and food programs. But the growth in interrelationships between agriculture and the rest of the economy, the declining number of farmers, and the importance of agriculture in international trade has raised the question as to whether the system should have the lead role. As mentioned previously, many federal agencies are intervening in agricultural policy and various special interest groups are influencing national policy. Today, many policy decisions respecting farming affect the welfare of the entire nation. Some critics say that views within the system are so narrow that the system should not be permitted to make these decisions. As these conflicts continue, much time and energy is lost fighting for influence. Again, knowledge of the origins of these conflicts could contribute to their resolution.

Science and education as carried out by the land-grant universities and the Department, including agricultural economics, have also been attacked in recent years for lack of innovative lines of research, emphasis upon application of science and technology rather than upon basic research, and too much concern with industry-oriented research (Rasmussen and Hildreth 1984, 4). Other critics have said that research and extension is directed primarily at large commercial farms, with little attention to small or moderate-sized farms, and with no concern over the piling up of surpluses. Critics argue that more of the federal research money should be handled outside the system and that more research should be diverted to non-land-grant universities. Actually, this has been happening for about 20 years and the results are difficult to measure. However, a number of studies have shown that public funds invested in research by the land grant universities and the USDA have had a payoff in production far surpassing that of any other public investment. If these studies are accurate and there is no reason to believe that they are not, one must ask why the public, through Congress and the Administration of whichever political party, press for reductions in public research funds. It is possible that agricultural research has been so successful that the public takes it for granted. The public may need a lesson in history that humankind, including even Americans, has not always had a sure supply of healthful food at reasonable cost.

Even if the public becomes aware of the payoff from agricultural research there is still a problem of who should do what. All public institutions are under pressure, and probably rightly so, to conduct relevant research. But even within that framework, should the USDA–Land-Grant University System concentrate on basic research and leave its application to the private sector? This question has a long historical background that should be known to every person making these decisions (Hadwiger 1982, 201–2).

Related to the question of basic and applied research is that of how and to whom agricultural technology is to be delivered. The county agent, at the end of the Extension Service's delivery system, has traditionally conveyed scientific and technologic information to the farmer. Although they have been criticized (much like the rest of the system) for not always reaching all of the poor and disadvantaged farmers, recent studies indicate that they have been effective in dealing with a majority of farmers. Nevertheless, if the system stops short of practical applications of the research it carries out, leaving that to the private sector, the county agent may fall behind with the knowledge that farmers need. The agent could possibly be replaced by the representatives of private industry—the fertilizer dealer, the machinery dealer, the seed supplier, etc. However, farmers might find it costly to be deprived of the balanced judgement that the county agent has traditionally provided (Feller et al. 1984, 5:119–32).

Scientific research and agricultural education are not the only traditional responsibilities of the USDA and the land-grant universities that are being challenged. For 50 years, this system has been charged with major responsibilities for soil and water conservation, farm credit, farm price and income policy, small community and rural development, food distribution, and food safety. But many of these responsibilities are eroding. The Farm Credit Administration, which was part of the USDA from 1939 to 1943, is now an independent agency. The Commodity Futures Trading Commission became independent in 1974. The Food and Drug Administration, which originated in USDA, is now in the Department of Health and Human Services. Proposals for transferring other functions, particularly relating to food distribution and forestry, are made regularly.

A somewhat different situation, but one which is quite relevant, has arisen regarding the agricultural responsibilities of the land-grant universities. In many of the major land-grant universities, the number of students, the number of faculty, and the funds devoted to agriculture are substantially less than those devoted to the arts and sciences, a situation far different from that prior to World War II. Although some institutions are reporting increasing enrollments in agriculture, the problem is still serious. Declining enrollments in agriculture will lead to a decline in public support.

Historically, the system has faced a number of serious problems. How these were solved may give some indication as to how to meet the present situation. In the past, the land-grant universities and the USDA have, in general, expanded the scope of the problems with which they dealt and thus attracted a broader support for their programs. Now, the system is being pushed, over some strong objections, in the direction of accommodating the nation's interest in food as well as farming. If this is indeed the future, then the system's supporters will include the consumer as well as the producer, the urban resident as well as the farmer. If new support is not found, the USDA will be abolished, with its functions dispersed to other agencies; Colleges of Agriculture will lose their identities, with their courses of instruction being merged into those of the Colleges of Arts and Sciences and Engineering. History does not repeat itself, or does it?

That Look Ahead

It is the year 2010. The American Agricultural Economics Association, the Farm Foundation, and the Economic Research Service are sponsoring a national symposium on the problems facing American agriculture. Four key questions have been selected as of overriding importance to the future of American agriculture. They are: (1) How can we save the family farm? (2) What should be the levels of farm price supports from 2010 to 2014? (3) How should the farm credit system be strengthened? and (4) What is the future of the USDA–Land-Grant University System?

References

Baker, G. L., W. D. Rasmussen, V. Wiser, and J. M. Porter. 1963. *Century of Service.* Washington, D.C.: USDA.

Bonnen, J. T. 1962. Some Observations on the Organizational Nature of a Great Technological Payoff. *Am. J. Agric. Econ.* 44:1279–94.

_____. 1965. Present and Prospective Policy Problems of U.S. Agriculture: As Viewed By An Economist. *Am. J. Agric. Econ.* 47:1116–29.

_____. 1983. Historical Sources of U.S. Agricultural Productivity: Implications for R & D Policy and Social Science Research. *Am. J. Agric. Econ.* 65:958–66.

Bowers, D. E., W. D. Rasmussen, and G. L. Baker. 1984. History of Agricultural Price-Support and Adjustment Programs, 1933–84. Agric. Inf. Bul. 485. Washington, D.C.: USDA.

Carson, R. 1962. *Silent Spring.* Boston: Houghton Mifflin.

Country Life Commission. 1975. Report. In *Agriculture in the United States: A Documentary History,* ed. W. D. Rasmussen, vol. 2, 1860–1906. New York: Random House.

Feller, I. L. Kaltreider, P. Madden, D. Moore, and L. Sims. 1984. *The Agricultural Technology Delivery System.* 5 vols. University Park: Institute for Policy Research and Evaluation, Pennsylvania State Univ.

Gray, L. C. 1933. *History of Agriculture in the Southern United States to 1860.* Vols. 1 and 2. Washington, D.C.: Carnegie Inst.

Hadwiger, D. 1982. *The Politics of Agricultural Research.* Lincoln: Univ. of Nebraska Press.

Hightower, J. 1973. *Hard Tomatoes, Hard Times: A Report of the Agribusiness Accountability Project on the Failure of the American Land Grant College Complex.* Cambridge, Mass.: Schenkman.

Hildreth, R. J. 1965. Have We Gone Too Far? *J. Farm Econ.* 47:1497–1503.

Johnson, G. L. 1971. The Quest for Relevance in Agricultural Economics. *Am. J. Agric. Econ.* 53:728–39.

Marcus, A. I. 1985. *Agricultural Science and the Quest for Legitimacy.* Ames: Iowa State Univ. Press.

Porter, J. M. 1979. Experiment Stations in the South, 1877–1940. *Agric. History* 53:84–101.

Rasmussen, W. D. and R. J. Hildreth. 1984. *The USDA-Land Grant University System in Transition.* East Lansing: Cooperative Extension Service, Michigan State Univ.

Ruttan, V. 1982. *Agricultural Research Policy.* Minneapolis: Univ. of Minnesota Press.

Saloutos, T. 1982. *The American Farmer and the New Deal.* Ames: Iowa State Univ. Press.

Simms, D. H. 1970. *The Soil Conservation Service.* New York: Praeger.

Taft, W. H. 1912. Preliminary Report on Land and Agricultural Credit in Europe. 62d Cong., 3d Sess., Senate Document No. 967.

3

The Continued Political Power of Agricultural Interests

CHRISTOPHER K. LEMAN and ROBERT L. PAARLBERG

Over most of this century, U.S. agricultural interests enjoyed a well-deserved reputation for power in the public policy arena. In recent decades, however, a suspicion has grown that organized agricultural interests are losing power to interests from beyond the farm sector. Traditional farm-commodity programs have come under attack; labor, consumer, and environmental groups have entered the farm policy debate; the 1977 and 1981 farm bills passed by the narrowest of margins; and farm exports have on several occasions been suspended, either in deference to domestic consumers or in the interest of foreign policy. Regulatory laws were passed in the 1970s that for the first time did not exempt agriculture, and federal courts issued decisions regarding regulation and western land and water that were widely lamented by farmers.

Here we test these suspicions by examining the political power of farm interests in four leading farm policy issue areas: (1) commodity programs; (2) international farm trade; (3) regulation; and (4) western land and water. In each of these four areas, we find that organized agricultural

Christopher K. Leman is Assistant Professor at the Graduate School of Public Affairs, University of Washington, Seattle. When this was written, Leman was also an Associate at the Center for International Affairs at Harvard University and a Resident Fellow in Food and Agricultural Policy at Resources for the Future. Robert L. Paarlberg currently holds those positions, as well as Associate Professor of Political Science at Wellesley College. For comments on an earlier draft or other assistance, appreciation is extended to James E. Anderson, Margaret Andrews, Jeffrey M. Berry, James T. Bonnen, William P. Browne, Cris Coffin, Kenneth D. Frederick, Don Hadwiger, Charles M. Hardin, Gary Keith, Carl F. Myers, Glenn Nelson, Robert H. Nelson, Henry Peskin, Frank Popper, Peter Rowland, R. Neil Sampson, Fred Sanderson, Rachel Sarko, Gregory S. Schell, Ross B. Talbot, and Richard Wahl.

interests retain significant political power. At the same time, this continued power over narrowly defined "farm policy" sometimes does little to protect the modern farm sector from sudden changes in the larger policy environment.

In one sense, the continued political power of organized agricultural interests should not be a surprise. American politics has long been characterized by relatively strong sectoral interest groups, owing to the weakness of national parties and especially to the division of federal power between Congress and the executive branch (Schattschneider 1942; Key 1961). Despite some recent recovery of presidential powers (now that a decade has passed since the post-Watergate weakening of the presidency), the rest of the executive branch—certainly the Agriculture Department—remains resistant to direction from above, and Congress remains fiercely independent. Congress in the past dozen years has been marked by weakened party leadership, erosion of the seniority system, and a proliferation of relatively autonomous committees, subcommittees, and caucuses. Interest groups of all kinds have exploited the situation, becoming more numerous and more specialized, making larger campaign contributions and mobilizing more expert advice on their behalf (King 1978, 1983). Other things equal, organized agricultural interests should be sharing in these political gains.

However, other things are not equal. The share of the U.S. population living on farms stands today at less than 3 percent, and continues its relentless decline. Farming no longer dominates rural areas either physically or economically as it once did. The number of counties with agriculture as their main source of income has decreased from about 2000 in the 1950s to only 700 by the 1970s—just one-fifth of the nation's total (Castle and Goldstein 1984). This demographic decline would seem enough by itself to require some parallel decline in the political power of agricultural interests.

But farming still enjoys a relatively prosperous and populous base from which to seek political power. The average net worth of full-time farmers in the United States (as of January 1, 1984) was $790,000, or roughly six times the average net worth of all American households. Even with a steady decrease in numbers since the 1930s, over two million U.S. farms remain. These farm numbers compare with only several companies that manufacture automobiles, 127 that produce aluminum, 3900 that manufacture computers, and 5700 that operate sawmills. In fact, farms represent nearly one-quarter of all the nation's businesses (Dun's Marketing Services 1985). Moreover, the number of holders of agricultural land has declined little in decades, still totalling about four million (Boxley forthcoming; Geisler et al. 1983). Farms are in every state (hence in the constituency of every U.S. senator) and in an unusually large number of congressional and state legislative districts (Rowland and Dubnick 1982). Dairy farms alone number roughly 200,000 and are found in 70 percent of all congressional districts. With such significant political resources still at their disposal, farm sector interests are in fact still able to exercise considerable power.

Commodity Programs

The legislative struggle that takes place every four years to reauthorize federal farm-commodity programs is one important litmus of the political power of organized agricultural interests. It appeared for a time in the 1970s that these interests were losing their strength, since they were unable to preserve legislated commodity programs based upon traditionally rigid concepts such as "parity." The Agriculture Act of 1970, followed by the farm bills of 1973 and 1977, moved commodity programs away from rigid price supports toward more flexible "deficiency payment" mechanisms that appeared to allow for greater "market orientation." Some concluded from these legislative events that the long-predicted demise of the commodity programs was at last underway.

It was not unreasonable to expect this demise in the 1970s, since the share of the U.S. population living on farms had decreased far below the 25 percent share of the 1930s, when federal commodity programs were first enacted. Mandatory census adjustments and a 1962 court-ordered redistricting of state legislatures had also cut into the political overrepresentation of rural districts in Congress. Rural districts, which had constituted 83 percent of an absolute majority of the U.S. House of Representatives as late as 1966, fell to only 60 percent of a majority by 1973 (Destler 1980, 31). In 1973, for the first time, farm-state legislators seeking to reauthorize commodity programs had found it necessary to join in an awkward coalition with backers of organized labor and consumer interests. From evidence such as this, astute observers like James T. Bonnen (1980, 317) concluded, "There is no longer a stable or viable political coalition for the support of food and agriculture legislation."

When an even more "market-oriented" farm bill, the Agriculture and Food Act of 1981, then passed the House of Representatives by a spare margin of just one vote (205–203), the predicted demise of commodity programs seemed assured. One political scientist concluded from the difficult legislative history of this "uncommonly austere" legislation that "the future of federal farm programs remains in doubt" (Peters 1982, 169–70). Three economists with experience on Capitol Hill warned that "the 1981 farm bill could be the last omnibus farm legislation" (Infanger et al. 1983, 9).

From the vantage point of 1985, these judgments must now be reconsidered. The programs set in place by the 1981 farm bill proved to be anything but "austere," and the prospect that those generous programs will be reauthorized now seems overwhelming. Commodity program outlays during the first four years of the Reagan administration totalled $53 billion, a 228-percent increase compared to the $16 billion spent during the preceding Carter years. Total farm and farm income program outlays in 1982 were equal to only 1.6 percent of all U.S. budget outlays, compared to a somewhat larger 2.7 percent share in 1960. But total current dollar outlays had meanwhile increased tenfold (Spitze and Brewer 1985). In fact, a 1984 report by the Congressional Budget Office found that in relation to its size, the agricultural sector receives more federal support than any other major economic sector (U.S. Congressional Budget Office 1984).[1] The ability of a shrinking community of farmers to lay claim to a sizeable share of these much larger federal budget outlays is strong evidence that the political power of the farm community remains largely intact.

This continued power of agricultural interests stems in part from the logic of collective political action. Although consumer groups can claim to represent a larger share of the voting public, they find it more difficult to organize and to mobilize their numbers, since the marginal incentive for any one individual to participate is still not very strong (Olson 1982, 1; Berry 1982). Consumer groups have also relied significantly over the years on alliances with labor unions, but these unions have pursued consumer issues only episodically, and are themselves now losing membership and power. The smaller relative size of the farm sector affords relatively good opportunities for political organization. Even as farmers diminish in number they face not only a greater incentive but also a greater opportunity to organize, as the reward to individual farmers of contributing to collective political action becomes more obvious. Also, while farm numbers have declined, total farm wealth has increased, so more funds have become available for the deployment of experts, lobbyists, and political contributions (Browne 1982). Opposition from consumer and environmental groups has in some cases energized farm groups to defend their interests more effectively (Guth 1978). The multiplication of agricultural pressure groups horizontally into particular commodities and vertically into agribusiness and trading interests might seem a source of fragmentation, but the group leaders and their allies within parallel congressional subcommittee structures have generally been able to forge a consensus, at least for the purpose of defending traditional commodity programs.

The power of farm interests to secure generous commodity program benefits stems as well from the perceived need for such benefits. Whenever the commercial health of the farm sector goes into a cyclical decline as it did after 1981, political support for aid to farms goes up and commodity program outlays automatically grow larger. One reason political support for farms appeared to be faltering during the years prior to 1981 was that the farm sector had less need for such support. During the decade of the 1970s, the overall rate of return to investment equity in farm production assets increased to a remarkably prosperous 12.5 percent, up from only 6.8 percent during the previous decade (National Planning Association 1984, 42). In 1973, average farm family income actually exceeded that of the nonfarm sector. Agriculture was winning what really mattered, so it could afford to lose ground to nonagricultural interests in the struggle to control commodity programs. Nonagricultural interests led by consumers, labor organizations, and environmentalists found themselves less advantaged at this point, and intervened in the farm policymaking process simply to protect themselves. They scored a number of apparent political victories in the process, but without denying the farm coalition much of lasting political significance. When early in the 1980s commercial and financial conditions in the farm sector once more turned downward, the farm coalition responded by redoubling its attention to the preservation of commodity programs and was able to reestablish its traditional claim to compensatory relief from the public sector.

It is now possible to extend this analysis to include the outcome of the 1985 farm bill debate. From the opening phase of that debate, organized agricultural interests showed a remarkable ability to deflect the Reagan administration from its planned attack on expensive farm-commodity programs. To the distress of budget-cutters in the executive branch, Congress spent the first two months of its 1985 session debating measures that would have actually increased farm spending. A handful of farm-belt senators defied both the White House and the Senate majority leadership by launching an emotional campaign to increase farm-debt relief, paralyzing the normal business in Congress for nearly six weeks. The financial crisis in the farm sector was making it impossible to consider significant cutbacks in commodity programs. A poll taken in late January had revealed that 65 percent of the U.S. adult population thought it a "bad idea" to spend less on farm aid so as to reduce the budget deficit. Sensing its political advantage, the farm coalition pushed through a $2.5 billion farm credit bill that would have provided an expensive advance on commodity loans to grain and cotton farmers. The president quickly vetoed this measure, but remained powerless to return the debate to his own original objective of commodity program reductions.

By the time final congressional action was taken on the re-authorization of commodity programs, the impetus of reform had all but disappeared. By a wide bipartisan majority vote of 282 to 141, the House of Representatives passed a new farm bill in October 1985, which froze target prices at high existing levels. Not even the Republican-controlled Senate could block this effort to preserve generous income supports. The result was a new farm bill that cost a record $25.8 billion in fiscal year 1986, its first year of operation.

At this point a larger political question must be asked. How significant is this demonstrated ability of the farm coalition to continue to secure generous commodity program benefits whenever the farm sector finds itself under stress? The relative potency of traditional commodity programs has been diminished by the increased indebtedness of the farm sector, by its more complete integration into the rest of the U.S. economy, and also by that sector's increased sensitivity to foreign trade. The commodity programs, designed to support and to stabilize U.S. farm product prices, are no longer the most powerful means in this new environment to provide well-targeted relief to agriculture. The debt-to-income ratio on today's average farm is ten times as high as it was 35 years ago, making commodity price fluctuations less important than interest rate fluctuations for many farmers today (Boehlje 1984, 237). Relatively self-sufficient as recently as 50 years ago, when commodity programs were first enacted, farmers now purchase nearly 60 percent of everything they use, making them also more sensitive to input costs (such as for equipment or energy) and to price levels in the wider economy, neither of which the commodity programs can hope to control. The increasing importance of off-farm income has also increased the sensitivity of the farm sector to conditions in the overall economy, further reducing the potency of commodity programs. (Nelson 1984, 698). Today's farms are also more dependent on exports and therefore more sensitive to fluctuating conditions in the larger world economy. In this environment, U.S. domestic commodity programs can easily be swamped by adverse foreign exchange rate fluctuations, or by a turnaround in global financial conditions. Trying to offset a loss of farm export earnings exclusively through domestic commodity program manipulation (e.g., by raising domestic prices and cutting production) can only invite a further loss of world market share.

The experience of the 1980s is instructive in this regard. Despite a fivefold increase in yearly commodity price-support spending by the federal government between 1981 and 1983, real net farm income still declined by nearly half (Duncan and Drabenstott 1984, 32). The 1983 Payment-in-Kind (PIK) program alone transferred an average of $12,000 per farm to the agricultural sector, yet did little to relieve the stress of many heavily indebted farmers.

What indebted farmers needed much more than high commodity prices was a reduction in real interest rates. Interest expenses as a percentage of total production expenses in the farm sector had doubled by 1982 compared to a dozen years earlier, due to a sudden turnaround in U.S. monetary policy and in economic conditions worldwide (Paarlberg et al.

1984, 82). So long as real interest rates remained high, little could be done for financially stressed farmers through commodity program manipulations. Each percentage point drop in the average rate of interest on outstanding farm debt translates automatically into a $2 billion decrease in farm production expenses (Paarlberg et al. 1984, 82). The most obvious way to reduce interest rates without reflating the economy would be to cut federal budget deficits. By one estimate, a federal deficit reduction of about $150 billion between 1984 and 1989 would do enough, by way of lowering interest rates and dollar exchange rates, to increase annual net farm income (other things being equal) between 25 percent and 60 percent – or $6.4 billion to $15.4 billion (Galston 1985, 39). To accomplish as much through traditional commodity programs in the absence of an interest rate reduction would be prohibitively expensive to taxpayers; it would also be inequitable, since these programs are so poorly targeted. The largest one percent of all farms capture roughly one-fifth of all program payments. USDA figures reveal that in 1984 only 17 percent of federal farm income subsidies went to farmers defined to be under financial stress because of heavy debt.

If traditional commodity programs prove inadequate to protect agriculture from larger problems (such as macroeconomic shocks), should organized agriculturalists spend less time defending commodity programs and more time lobbying the Federal Reserve Board or the Treasury Department, in hopes of turning fundamental U.S. macroeconomic policies more to agriculture's advantage? Prior to the adoption of the commodity programs, farmers were deeply concerned about such questions as monetary and tariff policy, and they even enjoyed some modest influence over policy outcomes (Benedict 1953). But the organized agricultural interests of today, which represent a much smaller share of the total population, might find it difficult to exercise power beyond their own sector of the economy. Too much of their power over farm policy comes from their disproportionate representation within the agriculture committees of the Congress, and from their privileged client status within the Department of Agriculture. They would enjoy neither of these advantages beyond the narrowly defined food and farm-policy arena. Their continuing grip over commodity policy has also derived, to some extent, from their specialized understanding of the farm sector and from their exclusive command over the arcane language and details of farm programs. This sort of influence is entirely useless in nonfarm-policy settings. Agriculturalists command respect when food and farm programs are at issue, but their views might be dismissed and their influence might be diluted to nothing in political battles over defense spending, tax incentives for the oil and gas industry, or social security reform. If agriculturalists were to retarget their scarce political resources away from farm sector policies and toward the pursuit of a macroeconomic policy objective such as deficit reduction, they might find themselves talking perfect economic sense, but exercising no measurable influence.

Recognizing this unhappy political reality, organized agricultural interests will probably continue, in times of farm sector distress, to seek public policy relief through manipulation of the less potent instruments under their control (such as commodity programs). As has been shown, however, these programs are no longer the solution they once were. Even if these programs can be enlarged, they will continue to be swamped by macroeconomic shocks from beyond the farm sector. And in the meantime, the costs, the inequities, and the distortions associated with the enlargement of these programs could even make them politically intolerable to critical elements of the farm coalition itself. Since 1981, in part due to commodity program distortions, farm bloc unity has come under a new strain. Two agricultural interest groups not previously prominent in commodity policy debates, the agribusiness sector and the livestock producer association, have recently assumed a higher profile, hoping to block any continuation of existing farm policies that might lead to a replay of the 1983 PIK program, which took one-third of U.S. cropland out of production, increased feed costs to livestock producers, and reduced the sales of agribusiness companies both at home and abroad. The PIK program, plus the 1983 decision to encourage the slaughter of dairy cattle by paying farmers to reduce dairy production, brought the National Cattlemen's Association, the National Pork Producers Council, and the National Broiler Council into an alliance for the first time, with the American Farm Bureau Federation, milk processors, and consumer groups, in opposition to the status quo in domestic commodity programs. The continued political power of organized agricultural interests to preserve traditional commodity programs is therefore a dubious solution to the larger difficulties now facing the U.S. farm sector.

International Farm Trade

The continued power of organized agricultural interest also deserves to be recognized, and then qualified, in the area of international farm trade. Here, as with commodity programs, the power of agriculturalists to control narrow farm trade actions has been largely preserved. But the significance of such actions, in a larger policy context, has measurably declined.

A decade ago it was fashionable to suspect that farm interests were losing control over narrowly defined farm trade policy, to domestic consumer interests and to the concerns of foreign policy. Under organized pressure from consumer interests, in the mid-1970s, a remarkable sequence of executive actions was taken to restrain farm exports—a soybean embargo in 1973, followed by a brief suspension of additional grain sales to the Soviet Union in 1974, followed by an even more significant grain sale suspension to the Soviet Union and to Poland in 1975. President Nixon had given an apparent endorsement to this new drift in U.S. farm trade policy in 1973, when he explained that "in allocating the products of America's farms between markets abroad and those in the United States, we must put the American consumer first" (Destler 1980, 50–59). Foreign policy concerns also seemed to have eclipsed agriculture. Despite his own earlier pledge not to use the "food weapon," President Jimmy Carter shocked agriculturalists in January 1980 by placing a partial suspension on grain and other farm sales to the Soviet Union, officially invoking reasons of foreign policy and national security to "punish" the Soviets for their recent invasion of Afghanistan.

In retrospect, these events were not indicative of any decline in the power of farm interests. They were, instead, temporary byproducts of a farm export environment that otherwise could hardly have been more favorable to U.S. agriculture. During the decade of the 1970s, U.S. farm exports were not being constrained by U.S. policy; they were at last being more effectively promoted. Thanks in part to two devaluations of the dollar, plus an end to shipping restrictions on U.S. farm sales to the Soviet Union, exports suddenly took off. The U.S. balance of trade in agricultural products, which had stood at only $1.9 billion in 1971, increased to $9.3 billion in 1973, and reached a stunning $25 billion by the end of the decade.

It should not have been surprising that this surge in farm exports would call forth a defensive political reaction from domestic consumer groups, who felt their interests momentarily at risk. During the first six months of 1973, as this remarkable farm-export surge was getting under way, the index of consumer prices for food in the United States rose by a politically intolerable 15 percent. Increased foreign demand was only one cause of higher domestic food prices, but domestic consumer advocates and cost-of-living watchdogs were nonetheless able, in the context of the times, to seize upon farm exports as a convenient political scapegoat and to demand some marginal export restraints.

But agricultural interests were also quick to fight back. In 1975, midwestern grain interests were successful in forcing President Ford to lift his brief suspension of farm sales to the Soviet Union and to negotiate a long-term agreement that guaranteed minimum sales of at least 6 million tons a year for at least the next five years. Then in 1977 these same interests were able to insert into U.S. farm legislation a little-noticed "embargo insurance" provision, which required the Secretary of Agriculture to move commodity loan rates all the way up to 90 percent of parity in the event of any future export suspension undertaken for reasons of tight domestic food supplies.

The purpose of this legislation was not so much to ensure compensation in the event of a renewed farm export suspension, as to prevent such a suspension by making it too expensive for the president to contemplate (Paarlberg 1985, 130).

Agriculturalists were surprised by the 1980 grain embargo, which escaped coverage under their "insurance" scheme because it had been undertaken for reasons of foreign policy and national security, rather than to protect consumers under circumstances of tight domestic supplies. But the larger impact of the 1980 embargo decision was an even more dramatic reassertion of exclusive agricultural control over farm trade policy. The initial reaction of farm interests was to insist upon adequate financial compensation for as long as the embargo remained in place. The compensation they received cost the federal government an estimated $3.4 billion for fiscal year 1980 alone (U.S. Library of Congress 1981, 5–6). Considering the fact that U.S. grain exports worldwide continued to expand throughout the period of this partial and ineffective embargo, this was generous compensation indeed.

In 1981, U.S. agriculturalists then went on to use their considerable political muscle to hold President Reagan to his campaign promise to lift the embargo, overcoming determined opposition from the Secretary of State and most of the rest of the foreign policy community in the process. Sales to the Soviet Union were resumed and negotiations on a new long-term agreement were initiated (with the State Department no longer the lead agency), despite an intensifying crisis in Poland and the otherwise unyielding cold war attitudes of the Reagan administration. To placate domestic farm interests, Reagan made the conscious decision to treat agriculture as an exception, and to separate farm trade from the conduct of the rest of his foreign policy. Farm trade policy decisions were taken by Reagan's Cabinet Council on Food and Agriculture, where the views of the State Department were not given equal standing (Haig 1984, 82).

Not even the declaration of martial law in Poland, in December 1981, was enough to alter the new wide-open farm-export sales policies of the Reagan administration. Despite an imposition of economic trade sanctions in every other product area (including high-technology products, computers, and oil and gas equipment), U.S. grain sales to the Soviet Union were permitted to continue, and were even encouraged to expand. The president announced unambiguously that "the granary door is open" (U.S. Department of State 1984, 4). The use of this double standard for agriculture during the Polish sanctions crisis even brought harsh criticism of Reagan from U.S. allies in western Europe, who were being pressured to make no exceptions in their own Soviet sales restrictions. Far from sacrificing U.S. farm exports to the interests of foreign policy, Reagan in 1982 was doing precisely the opposite.

Organized agricultural interests had seen to it that he would have little choice in the matter. Those interests had earlier inserted a new embargo insurance provision in the 1981 farm bill, which specified that producers would have to be compensated at 100 percent of parity in the event of any future foreign policy embargo that singled out agricultural products. This provision, with its multibillion dollar budgetary implications, was by itself enough to discourage any reimposition of a selective farm product embargo. But later in 1982, agriculturalists went farther, inserting an even more potent "contract sanctity" provision into the Commodity Futures Trading Act, which obliged the president to allow contracted farm sales to continue even in the event of a declared across-the-board embargo. And in 1983, U.S. farm-export interests once again showed their enormous influence over farm sales by securing a new long-term farm trade agreement with the Soviet Union. Under the terms of this agreement, which will run through 1988, guaranteed "embargo-proof" Soviet access to the U.S. market was increased by 50 percent (Paarlberg 1985, 134–136).

In light of these more recent actions, it is difficult to argue that organized agricultural interests have lost control over farm trade policy, either to consumers or to foreign policy officials. As with commodity programs, their political control had only been temporarily challenged, at a time when prices were so high and exports growing so rapidly that the farm sector did not need much public policy protection. As soon as prices fell and U.S. farm exports stopped growing, the dominance of agriculturalists in the farm trade policy arena was firmly reasserted.

As with domestic commodity programs, however, the policy control agriculturalists were able to reassert over farm trade was by no means adequate to ensure the desired result. Control over farm trade policy has been fully established, consumer and foreign policy advocates have been shouldered aside, and public expenditures for farm-export promotion have grown, but the U.S. share of international farm exports has nonetheless fallen into a steady decline. Narrowly defined farm trade policies, no less than narrowly defined commodity policies, have been swamped by adverse macroeconomic effects that narrow farm sector policy remedies are powerless to control.

The rapid growth of U.S. farm exports during the 1970s was largely a consequence of record income growth among importing countries, sustained in many instances through easy credit plus a favorable downward realignment of dollar exchange rates. When the world economy fell into both a deep recession and a severe liquidity crisis after 1981, and when dollar exchange rates began to soar following a dramatic turnaround in U.S. monetary policy, there was little that narrowly defined U.S. farm-export policies could do to repair the damage. Between 1981 and 1985, USDA authorizations for the Public Law 480 food aid program increased from $1.4 billion to $2.3 billion, and authorizations for commercial export credit programs increased from $1.9 billion to $5.3 billion, but the volume and the value and the market share of U.S. farm exports nonetheless declined (National Commission on Agricultural Trade and Export Policy 1985, 79). Between 1981 and 1983, the total value of U.S. farm exports fell by 17 percent.

In their frustration, organized agricultural interests used their narrow power over farm-export policy to secure even more ambitious export promotion policies, including in 1985 a three-year $2 billion "in-kind" export subsidy program. But even if it worked perfectly (and export subsidy programs never do, least of all those that flood markets with "in-kind" surplus commodity payments), this program could not hope to increase the total value of U.S. farm exports by more than 2 percent. Farm trade policy could not offset the more potent impact of macroeconomic policy. By one calculation, U.S. farm exports had been falling automatically by 16 percent in response to every 20 percent increase in the exchange rate of the dollar abroad. According to Jim Longmire and Art Morey (1983, 21), "macroeconomic factors have had, and will have, a much greater impact on U.S. farm program stocks, farm exports, and agricultural prices than many of the more direct export subsidy arrangements currently in place or under consideration."

Not even a downward adjustment in domestic commodity loan rates would be enough in this new macroeconomic environment to restore export growth. The upward float of dollar exchange rates had become volatile enough to swamp such isolated domestic farm price adjustments. Between 1980 and 1983, the U.S. domestic price of corn, adjusted for inflation, actually fell by 5 percent. But due to higher dollar exchange rates, the price for U.S. corn paid by foreign customers increased by 35 to 40 percent, wiping out foreign sales.

So the ability of farm interests to control narrowly defined farm issues emerges once again as an inadequate source of policy protection for the farm sector. Control over traditional farm trade policy instruments — ranging from export restrictions to export subsidies — does not translate neatly into export growth. The policy variables most important to export growth lie well beyond the traditional farm-policy arena. They include not only U.S. macroeconomic policy (which can drive up exchange rates), but also U.S. industrial trade policy and U.S. international finance and assistance policy (which can alter the purchasing power of U.S. farm trade customers abroad). No matter how powerful agriculturalists might be within the narrow policy arena of farm trade, they cannot hope to exert decisive influence over these larger international economic policy questions. Nor would it be entirely sufficient if they could do so. Just as U.S. farm policy can be swamped by nonfarm policy, so can the actions of the

United States be swamped, within the larger world economy, by the offsetting policy actions of other governments or by the autonomous actions of the international private sector.

This being the case, U.S. agricultural interests will have to plan on a farm trade policy environment that continues to administer periodic shocks to the U.S. farm sector. Farm interests will not be able to eliminate these shocks by redeploying their power to control all of U.S. foreign economic policy, nor will they be able to offset the full impact of these shocks through a more ambitious manipulation of narrowly defined farm trade or domestic commodity policies. They will make a larger contribution instead by using their well-established power within the farm sector to help promote farm programs, farm structures, and farm financing and marketing mechanisms better suited to absorbing the impact of these shocks.

Regulation

Early federal regulation of the farm sector was largely economic in nature and was generally welcomed by agricultural interests. Beginning with the Meat Inspection Act and the Pure Food and Drug Act (both passed in 1906) many laws have enhanced the market for agricultural products by regulating the safety, purity, grading, and labeling of agricultural products. Often this regulation has publicly funded a service that otherwise would have had to be provided privately (Nadel 1971; Hinich and Staelin 1980). Some farm commodity programs also operate through regulation, called "marketing orders." The operation of these various instances of government regulation has been so consistent with the economic interests of farmers that Theodore J. Lowi (1979, 68–69) has argued, "Agriculture is that field of American government where the distinction between public and private has come closest to being eliminated. . . . Agriculture has emerged as a largely self-governing federal estate within the federal structure of the United States."

Recent decades, however, have brought an increase in federal regulation for broader social purposes, especially environmental and occupational ones, that are less consistent with the immediate economic interest of farm operators (Bardach and Kagan 1982). The rise of such regulation in the 1970s seemed to be compromising the farm sector's traditional autonomy. New laws like the Occupational Safety and Health Act of 1970, the Water Pollution Control Act Amendments of 1972 (amended and renamed in 1977 the Clean Water Act), and the Federal Insecticide, Fungicide, and Rodenticide Act (FIFRA) of 1972, among others, did not exempt agriculture as had earlier laws regarding transportation, labor, and social security.

Federal court decisions soon increased the sting to farmers of each of these new environmental laws.

Farm groups were not active in the initial debates on some of these laws, and it is possible that if they had been, the laws would have contained provisions limiting the regulation of farms (Kramer 1979, 209–10). However, once the laws were passed, farm groups quickly mobilized to secure this same result. Over half of the lobbyists employed by the general farm organizations are now assigned to regulatory questions (Bonnen 1984). As a result of these farm lobby efforts, the new regulatory laws have now been amended and their implementation has been weakened, leaving farms once again less firmly regulated overall than any other major sector of the U.S. economy.

Federal pesticide legislation had to affect farms, because they account for more than 70 percent of the nation's pesticide use (U.S. Environmental Protection Agency 1984, 2–8). Some farm states had taken the initiative in regulating pesticides, in the hope that by discouraging misuse they would forestall federal efforts to ban use of pesticides entirely (Manley and Hadwiger 1982). FIFRA did transfer jurisdiction over pesticides from the Department of Agriculture to the Environmental Protection Agency (EPA) in 1972, but Congress rejected the Nixon administration's proposal to require permits for the use of particularly dangerous pesticides. Subsequent amendments to FIFRA and administrative actions delegated significant responsibilities in pesticide regulation to the state departments of agriculture, such as in whether to register a substance for "special local needs," when to grant exceptions to these rules, and how to license restricted-use applicators. Despite the transfer of pesticide regulation from USDA to EPA, lower-level administration by the states has left the law quite loose in application (Rowland and Marz 1982).

Farm uses of pesticides have often been the last to be prohibited. In 1979, for example, although EPA ordered an emergency suspension of the use of the herbicides 2,4,5-T and Silvex in forestry and most other uses, it continued to allow them in certain range and crop uses, suspending them there only in the mid-1980s, and only when demand had declined. The use of pesticides on public lands has sometimes been more heavily regulated than on private lands, as in 1972 when EPA prohibited the use on federal lands of 1080, an anticoyote poison that is still widely used on private grazing lands. However, after years of protest by ranchers, the agency in 1985 again authorized limited use of 1080 on federal lands.

Sediment, nutrients (especially from fertilizers and livestock waste), chemicals (especially pesticides), and naturally occurring elements (including salt and metals) in agricultural runoff can pollute lakes, streams, and groundwater. In fact, farms supply more than half of the nation's loadings of phosphorus, nitrogen, and sediment, among other pollutants (U.S. Environmental Protection Agency 1984, 1–14). Water pollution controls were greatly tightened in principle in the 1972 water pollution amendments, which required permits for point sources of pollution and for alterations in wetlands. The law established a state-run process for areawide "208" plans regarding point and nonpoint sources, but for nonpoint sources there was no requirement for permits or other enforcement. The law applied as much to farms as to other sources of water pollution, but a series of actions by Congress and by Republican and Democratic administrations alike reduced its impact on farms (Radosevich and Skogerboe 1978, 96–104). Under pressure from farm groups, the Nixon administration EPA quickly exempted from the permit requirement the outfalls from irrigation operations of less than 3000 acres and livestock operations with less than 1000 head (silvicultural activities were also exempted).

EPA emphasized point and urban sources in the "208" plans, while stressing that the states should regulate nonpoint sources on a voluntary basis and make use of the existing soil and water conservation districts and the Soil Conservation Service, an approach also preferred by the Office of Management and Budget, which discouraged new spending. Most states were only too happy to take this loose approach, as locally generated nonpoint pollution was often not a major problem within their borders, imposing its greatest costs on other states downstream. Even a state like Iowa with considerable concern about water quality did not force landowners to adopt a practice without governmental sharing of the cost, and cost-sharing funds for this purpose were virtually nil (Crosson and Brubaker 1982, 167).

In 1975, federal cases brought by the Natural Resources Defense Council led courts to order a change in this selective approach. One decision forced EPA to include nonpoint and rural sources in the "208" plans; as a result the agency adopted regulations requiring that these plans identify "best management practices" for agricultural lands. Another court decision struck down EPA's exemptions of small irrigators and feedlots from the requirement for a permit. EPA began to design a system of general permits for such cases, while encouraging outraged irrigators to amend the law if they did not want to be covered (Anderson 1977). Few such permits were ever issued, because in the Clean Water Act of 1977, Congress declared irrigation outfalls, no matter how large and concentrated, to be nonpoint sources, and no longer to be subject to permits. In the debate on this legislation, efforts to strengthen the nonpoint program by requiring the states to enforce "best management practices" were turned back by a coalition of agricultural and timber interests. And when a third major court decision in 1975 had expanded the number of wetlands whose alteration required a permit, Congress in 1977 narrowly rejected an effort to loosen the regulation of wetlands, but exempted many agricultural and silvicultural activities from the existing constraints. Whereas federal constraints on industrial and municipal pollution (much of which was from point sources) remained strong and were even strengthened in some ways by the Clean Water Act, regulation of agricultural pollution was not strengthened, and, although already weak, was weakened still further. The only real action was establishment of the Rural Clean Water Program, under which the federal government would share the cost of improvements voluntarily installed by farmers.

The 1977 legislation left considerable discretion to EPA in how to deal with nonpoint water pollution. As under Presidents Nixon and Ford, EPA's leadership during the Carter administration was preoccupied with other programs, and put little staff or budget into nonpoint questions, while placing a high priority on maintaining good relations with farm groups. As a former EPA official from the period recalled in a 1985 interview with one of the authors, "You'd have farmer Brown mad at you, and all those tractors surrounding your building." Thus in 1978, EPA decided to approve state "208" plans that had no provision for mandatory enforcement so long as a voluntary approach could be shown to be effective (U.S. Environmental Protection Agency 1978). State water quality officials who had labored for consensus with agricultural interests on acceptance of some mandatory controls saw their efforts disintegrate; one accuses EPA of having "welched" on earlier requirements (Heft 1985). In Ohio, for example, where the legislature was debating a water quality law, news of EPA's policy was quickly followed by legislative action denying water quality regulators any enforcement authority for agricultural sediment. The 1987 renewal of the Clean Water Act, passed over President Reagan's veto, continued to show a pattern of success of agricultural interests. Although a Senate subcommittee in 1983 had approved a bill requiring the states to have enforcement authority for nonpoint sources and denying federal commodity payments to farmers who pollute, these provisions were respectively defeated or weakened at the committee level.

In a few cases, water pollution from farming has encountered overwhelming opposition. An example is wildlife refuges, which generally are wetlands and hence can be particularly damaged by irrigation runoff. In 1985, the U.S. Department of the Interior decided to shut down the runoff into the Kesterson National Wildlife Refuge from 40,000 acres irrigated from projects of the Bureau of Reclamation in California's San Joaquin Valley. The case was unusual in that the critical pollutant at Kesterson was selenium, an unusually strong poison that was killing or pitifully malforming birds. Moreover, groundwater quality was threatened, prompting the state Water Resources Board to declare the refuge a toxic dump and order the federal government to clean it. Further sharpening the issue at Kesterson was that like many other wildlife refuges, it is covered by the Migratory

Bird Treaty Act, which reflects international obligations and is enforced by criminal penalties. Very few instances of agricultural runoff are likely to encounter so powerful a combination of restraints.[2]

Other forms of environmental regulation have tended to be applied more lightly to farm areas. The Clean Air Act has had less impact on farms than on most other economic sectors. Even a politically potent regulatory effort like that regarding hazardous waste has not always been pressed as successfully on farms. Much recent regulation has focused on concentrated disposal sites rather than on-site hazardous waste, much of which is located on farms.

In contrast to their reservations about regulation, farm groups have been very supportive of the voluntary approach traditionally taken in federal soil conservation programs. Yet some of the most popular features of these programs have hampered them in reducing erosion. Financial and technical assistance have been spread rather evenly, although the erosion problem was never uniform and has shifted over the years. Moreover, this assistance has entirely missed those erosive lands whose owners do not want assistance, and it has sometimes promoted production at the expense of conservation (Leman 1982). Repeated efforts by various presidents to cut back or retarget the Agricultural Conservation Program and the Soil Conservation Service have been only partially successful, even in times of governmentwide budgetary retrenchment.

Farmers' resistance to mandatory approaches meant that for more than 50 years, few soil conservation practices were required even as a condition for a farm's participation in federal agricultural adjustment programs. This remarkable situation was changed when the 1985 farm bill moved to tie this participation to prohibitions on "sodbusting" and "swampbusting," and to a requirement for conservation compliance. Environmental groups played a crucial role in passage of these provisions. But passage was assured only because, in contrast to the tight regulation of air and water pollution, pesticides, and hazardous waste that was successfully resisted by farmers, the farmers found the changes in soil conservation policy relatively unthreatening as evidenced by polls and the position of farm groups and members of the congressional farm bloc. To the extent that, as they are implemented in the coming years, these measures (especially the swampbuster and conservation compliance) prove unpopular among farmers, they are likely to be modified accordingly.

Resistance in farm areas has also reduced the reach of the Occupational Safety and Health Act of 1970. For example, the 1977 and subsequent annual appropriations acts have totally exempted from the 1970 law all farms with ten employees or less — an exemption that other small businesses enjoy only if they have a better-than-average safety record. The regulations implementing the law exempt all farms from certain "general industry" standards, including an obligation to communicate to employees information about possible exposure to hazardous chemicals and to assure them access to records on their exposure to such chemicals and on other medical conditions. Another exemption is from the requirement that workers be provided toilets and fresh water. Only after repeated court orders did the Occupational Safety and Health Administration (OSHA) review the field sanitation issue, deciding in 1985 to continue the exemption.[3]

Aside from such formal exceptions, federal and state administration of safety and health regulations has been looser regarding farm work. For example, with the development of pesticides that degrade more quickly in the soil but are more toxic, field workers are facing new dangers that regulators have yet to address (Wasserstrom and Wiles 1985). Whereas the exposure to pesticides of all other workers is regulated by OSHA, that of farm workers is regulated by EPA, which has less authority in the workplace and is required under FIFRA to rely on state administration. Many state workers' compensation laws do not apply to farm workers.

The Fair Labor Standards Act of 1938 was first extended to farm work in 1967, although it still exempts small farms; the only other small businesses exempted are retail or service establishments. Other farm employees not covered include all those in the range production of livestock and some that are paid on a piece-rate basis.[4] No farm employer, no matter how large, is subject to the requirement to pay overtime. The age at which child labor is prohibited is lower than in other economic sectors; under certain circumstances, children as young as ten years old can legally be employed. State laws on minimum wages and overtime frequently exempt agricultural concerns. Until 1978, federal legislation on unemployment insurance did not cover agriculture; today small farms remain exempt. Agricultural employers are exempt from paying social security taxes for some infrequent workers.

Agricultural workers have always been exempted from the provisions of the National Labor Relations Act of 1935. In the 1960s and early 1970s the nation was gripped with controversy over a national boycott of table grapes called by the United Farm Workers of America (UFWA) and backed by nonagricultural unions. In California the campaign helped produce in California an Agricultural Labor Relations Act recognizing the right of farm workers to bargain collectively. However, in the past decade the drive to unionize farm workers has declined nationwide. UFWA has been able to win a contract in only one other state besides California (Florida), and it has been frustrated enough by administration of the California law to initiate a new boycott in 1984. This boycott seems to have been considerably less successful than the earlier one, perhaps reflecting the weakening position of labor in American politics.

An important regulatory trend at the state and local level is zoning to limit and direct the development of rural land, requiring that much of it be kept in agricultural or silvicultural uses. Although these laws have appreciably curtailed the farmer's traditional option to sell land to developers, they have been applied loosely enough to allow the continuation of substantial development of rural land. In the process, the owners or operators of agricultural land have received substantial concessions, including "right-to-farm" laws, tax breaks, purchases of development rights, and generous loans.

With some exceptions, regulation for environmental quality and occupational safety is considerably looser on farms than it is in other economic sectors. Public interest groups have not made as many criticisms of this situation as would seem warranted. Industries and municipalities that are more tightly regulated have also publicly had few complaints.

Western Land and Water

In the first three cases examined, the involvement of government in agriculture has been limited to financial payments, trade restrictions, or regulation. In the West, however, government—especially the federal government—also owns lands that are commercially grazed (or logged), and it builds or operates projects that supply water for irrigation. In doing so, it once more pays special heed to the continued political power of farm interests.

Livestock interests have long named the terms under which they use federal grazing lands, enjoying most of the benefits of ownership with few of its responsibilities. Despite the rise of competing land uses and groups, the ranchers' power remains impressive, based particularly in recent years on pleas about their difficult financial situation. Bitter opposition has slowed decades of effort by the federal land agencies to reduce permitted grazing levels; since 1980, by use of language in the appropriations acts requiring that any reduction by the Bureau of Land Management (BLM) of 10 percent or more not be made until administrative appeals by permittees have been acted upon—a process that can take up to two years. Some ranchers have also long resisted federal restrictions informally by grazing more livestock than officially permitted. Livestock interests have repeatedly turned back fee increases, such as by 1978 legislation that established a formula based on "ability to pay," under which the fee has actually fallen in recent years to $1.35 per animal unit month (1985), about one-fifth the estimated fair market value (U.S. Department of Agriculture 1985). Congress is now considering proposals to make this formula permanent. In 1982, the Reagan administration proposed to sell off tens of millions of acres of federal lands, especially those for grazing; opposition came from many quarters, but contributing to the withdrawal of the proposal was that the ranchers made it clear that they preferred their existing permits to having the opportunity to purchase the lands (Leman 1984). Even so, the administration gave ranchers more power over the public grazing lands through actions to allow them to own water rights there (Schmidt 1983). Environmental activism has particularly focused on public lands. The timber industry has felt the brunt of this pressure in restrictions on how logging can be conducted and in the banning of logging entirely from some federal lands through their addition to the National Wilderness Preservation System. In 1974, a federal court upset ranchers by agreeing with the Natural Resources Defense Council that BLM must prepare environmental impact statements under the National Environmental Policy Act on its decisions to issue grazing permits. However, as this effort has proceeded, only moderate reductions have been made in the amount of grazing allowed. Grazing is the only commodity use that has continued largely unabated in wilderness areas; ranchers have had to accept restrictions in construction and vehicle use, but they have not been prevented from operating as have loggers and miners. Generally, ranchers have not faced as much environmental opposition as have the latter groups; in fact they have allied with environmental groups on such issues as restricting strip mining, requiring that mined lands be reclaimed, and blocking federal eminent domain needed for the construction of coal slurry pipelines. Without support from environmental groups, ranchers who own the land's surface probably would not have gained the right to veto plans to mine federally owned subsurface coal (through the Surface Mining Control and Reclamation Act of 1977).

Some would see a decline in the power of the farm interests in the fact that no major new federal reclamation projects have been authorized or started since 1976. However, this falloff is more apparent than real, because Congress previously had authorized a large backlog of projects that persists today. Also, many federal projects that are already in operation have gained authorization for much additional construction, and starts have continued in recent years. States have become primary defenders of irrigators in their search for public works solutions to pollution problems (e.g., projects to increase water supplies or control salinity in soil and runoff) that otherwise must be solved by retiring federally irrigated acreage from production (Howe 1980, 27). State-financed water projects, such as those in California and Texas, are becoming more common, with irrigation being a prominent purpose.

More important than how much more water will become available through construction is how the water from existing projects will be allocated. Although environmentalists are concerned about allocation, their concern is not as uncompromising as was their opposition to the projects before they were constructed, nor is it as automatically contrary to the wishes of irrigators. As western economies and political patterns evolve, irrigators face demands from municipal and industrial water users, while legal and political changes increase the water needs of fisheries (for the maintenance of a minimum stream flow) and Indian tribes. Already the total acreage under irrigation in the Southwest has begun to decline. But the key question in this transition is at what rate farmers will lose water and under what terms; the outcomes are generally proving agreeable to the irrigators (Ingram 1982). More than 85 percent of the West's water consumption, an impressive proportion by any measure, is for irrigation, and even with the reductions that are in prospect it will remain high (Frederick 1982). Despite the ongoing expiration of their long-term contracts for the water from federal reclamation projects, irrigators are often getting preferential treatment in obtaining new contracts over the objections of other users who are willing to pay more for it. Transfers of water out of irrigation have generally produced compensations for farmers, such as construction to help them subsist on less water of poorer quality, or generous financial compensation. As the competition for water has intensified, the state government's role in regulating water rights has become more important. State water law favors those with an early claim, many of whom are farmers. In cases where new procedures are being established, as in groundwater, farmers seem to be holding their own (Ingram 1982, 139–42; Andrews and Fairfax 1984).

The two great purposes of the Reclamation Act of 1902 were to settle large parts of the arid West and to promote farming by small, local operators. The first purpose was impressively achieved, largely through massive subsidies to the farmer. Although the projects supposedly were to pay for themselves through fees for the water, in fact repayment was with no interest. Congress repeatedly lengthened the repayment period and set the payments according to farmers' "ability to pay," and various other legislative or administrative measures reduced their burden still further (Campbell 1984). By 1977, only about 19 percent of the real project costs of agricultural water supply projects had yet been repaid (North and Neely 1977).

The second purpose of the Reclamation Act — to provide water from the federal projects only to small landholdings farmed by local residents — was far less faithfully observed. When large landholders within reach of the new projects initially withheld land from sale, amendments in 1914 and 1926 to the Reclamation Act required the recipients of federal water who had lands in excess of the allowable total to sell them in amounts that would distribute the land more equally. However, Congress exempted several projects (e.g., the Big Thompson project in Colorado) from this requirement, and when the supporters of other projects were unable to obtain a similar change in the law, they obtained administrative rulings that had the same effect (e.g., for the Imperial Valley project in California) or pressed the Bureau of Reclamation not to enforce the law (e.g., in the Salt River project in Arizona and the Central Valley project in California).

In 1976, a federal court ordered the Department of the Interior to end many of these abuses and to enforce the Reclamation Act's acreage limitation provisions. However, political pressures immediately arose to legalize many of the previous infractions via the Reclamation Reform Act of 1982, which along with some features distasteful to large irrigators secured gains that their predecessors only dreamed of. The legislation increased to 960 acres the size of farms that would receive project water at subsidized rates, and allowed farms whose holdings were in excess of this amount to receive water while charging them for its full cost. The residency requirement was entirely eliminated. In addition, the 1982 amendments specifically exempted several major projects (e.g., the Central Arizona project, the Big Thompson project, and Army Corps of Engineers irrigation projects in California), so that excess acreage there continued to receive subsidized water with no requirement that the excess land be sold or that the full cost of the water be paid.

Western ranchers and irrigators alike have had considerable success in influencing federal and state authorities. As Maass and Anderson (1978, 274) find in their study of irrigation and politics in the United States and Spain, "unified local interests can use or manipulate governmental institutions to achieve their purposes." They observe:

> The most powerful conclusion that emerges from the case studies is the extent to which water users have controlled their own destinies as farmers, the extent to which the farmers of each community, acting collectively, have determined both the procedures for distributing a limited water supply and the resolution of conflicts with other groups over the development of additional supplies. (p. 366)

Conclusions

The continuing decline in the numbers of farms and farmers may have reduced the overall political power of the farm sector, but it has also reduced the cost to taxpayers of aiding those that remain in farming, therefore reducing the quantity of power needed by farmers to remain sovereign in their own domain. When measured on a per-farmer basis, aid to agriculture has been on the rise rather than in decline. At least in proportion to their numbers, farmers are stronger than ever. Farm commodity policy continues to be written largely within the farm sector. Agriculturalists have secured farm trade policies that are often at variance with the general thrust of U.S. foreign policy. They have obtained unusually favorable treatment in environmental and occupational regulation, and they have maintained excellent terms for themselves in the management of western federal land and water.

Agricultural interests also seem to be benefiting from the Reagan-era devolution of power from the federal government to lower levels. For example, farmers long preferred to keep regulation at the state level, hoping to forestall stricter federal intervention. Even where strong federal laws exist, the delegation of important responsibilities to the states has helped moderate their impact, as in water quality and pesticides. State departments of agriculture, which have long been closely responsive to farmers, have often been given a major role in administering federal programs that affect them.

With the help of some new allies, including environmental groups, agricultural interests have generally preserved their ability to assert sovereignty in those areas that most closely affect them. More strongly perhaps than any other private landowners, farmers have insisted that property rights entitle them to freedom from government control. Their desire for a voluntary approach has meant that regulatory laws have been written, amended, and administered in ways that often have treated farmers more permissively than other groups. Even when the federal government helps farmers with loans and commodity payments, there is a hesitation to apply strict conditions on this help, despite the fact that federal payments to those in other sectors have long been used to enforce environmental, civil rights, and other requirements (Advisory Commission on Intergovernmental Relations 1984). Even with federally owned lands and water projects, farmers and ranchers have successfully invoked traditions favoring local sovereignty. One thoughtful observer has written, "Farm and conservation policy are so drenched in this hands-off rhetoric that we tend to forget it is an artifact of politics, not an inviolable principle of law" (Cook 1985, 106).

Considering the extent of public investment in the private farm sector, and the fact that public and private agricultural lands encompass most of the country's area and consume much of its water, it is impressive that regulatory sovereignty within the farm sector has received so little challenge. Yet agriculture is enough of an underpinning of the rural economy and landscape that concern for its survival will continue to convince many of its need for sovereignty. And in any case, the diversity and geographic extensiveness of farming will hamper any public policy that does not rely significantly on the voluntary cooperation of farmers. Resistance by agriculturalists has no doubt saved federal regulators and land and water agencies from adopting some policies that would never have worked. But special treatment needs to be recognized as such, so that its social costs can be more carefully and consciously evaluated. The argument for special treatment may be justified in some instances but in others it may compromise a legitimate policy goal deserving of national support.

Can agriculturalists be judged powerful even though their numbers continued to decline? In fact, the rate at which farmers leave agriculture has little apparent connection to the political power of the "farm coalition." During the 1950s and 1960s, despite the supposed strength of that coalition, farm numbers declined by approximately 3 percent a year. During the middle to late 1970s, although the farm coalition was supposed to be losing power, this rate of decline actually slowed to under 1 percent. Now in the mid-1980s, under adverse macroeconomic conditions, farm disappearances are perhaps catching up to where they might have been if the earlier trend had been maintained (Riemenschneider 1985).

Some agriculturalists will not feel powerful unless they can bring this long-term trend to a total halt. But others will realize that resource adjustment, including the flow of some jobs out of agriculture, is a key to farm sector prosperity. Smoothing the necessary movement of resources in and out of agriculture, so as to reduce the social and economic costs that accompany this adjustment process, would be a more worthy goal of farm policy and a more worthy test of the political power of farm interests. Because of their demonstrated power over policy within the farm sector, agriculturalists ought to be well positioned to pass this test. Their first step might be to revise or dismantle some existing policies that have at times disrupted the adjustment process within the farm sector.

U.S. grains policies conspicuously disrupted the process of cyclical adjustment during the mid-1970s, both at the beginning and at the end of the market upturn that was then taking place. Those policies aggravated instability, first by restraining production, subsidizing exports, and dumping stocks too quickly into a tightening market, and then by encouraging farmers to borrow and to expand just as the market was about to go slack (Gardner 1981, 104). Government farm payments, which ought to be counter-cyclical, actually made net farm income less stable between 1976 and 1981 than it otherwise would have been (Tweeten 1983, 928).

More recently, it has been the growth of highly leveraged farming, with reduced liquid assets, that has disrupted adjustment under conditions of cyclical downturn. It may be time to reconsider those federal farm policies that have encouraged this sort of farming, including commodity programs rewarding land acquisition by paying out benefits "per bushel" of production, poorly targeted subsidized farm credits (especially economic emergency and disaster loans), and a variety of tax rules sheltering those who purchase land. Future research would do well to examine the extent to which existing farm programs postpone and therefore disrupt adjustment processes that would be difficult enough without such programs. The existence of such programs, authored by powerful farm interests, raises a final point. The bias favoring large farmers in some of these existing programs is not an accident. It reflects a considerable inequality of political power within the farm sector. The emphasis throughout this analysis has been upon the political power of the U.S. farm sector as a whole, in opposition to nonfarm interests. An equally important research question would be to identify those within the farm sector who control the exercise of this power. If the farm sector is like any other, it would not be surprising to find those who already have the greatest resources (the most money and the most land) exercising this power on their own behalf, while trying to disguise their advantage behind populist endorsements of "family farming." It is somewhat surprising that political leaders in the nonfarm sector and also the national broadcast media have so often taken this populist rhetoric at face value.

It will always be less contentious among agriculturalists to look away from concentrations of power within the farm sector, to look away from the distortions in farm program benefits that grow out of those power concentrations, and to focus instead upon the more unifying theme of aggregate farm sector strength in opposition to the rest of the economy. That is what we have done here. Having found aggregate farm sector strength to be largely undiminished, we now suggest moving the debate forward to examine the distribution of public benefits that derives from that strength.

Notes

1. This figure includes federal support for research and education, another longstanding instance of support for agriculture that continues at high levels relative to other economic sectors.

2. Also notable about the Kesterson situation was that although the Department initially decided to deny federal water to 40,000 acres, an agreement was reached under which the local irrigation district would receive an extension allowing it to undertake various measures to stem the pollution without removing the land from production, and thus continue to receive the water.

3. In announcing the decision, Secretary of Labor William E. Brock said that if the states did not make sufficient progress in adopting their own regulations in the following eighteen months, the exemption of agriculture from the federal standard would end. About a third of the states (including leading agricultural states like California, Florida, and Texas) now require some form of sanitation facilities for field workers; these regulations are generally not as strict as the proposed federal standard. In February 1987, a Federal appeals court panel ordered Brock to implement a nationwide Federal standard. The Administration was expected

to appeal this decision to the Supreme Court, and the matter was not concluded at this writing.
    4. In one unusual instance, agriculture is regulated more tightly than other industries via the Migrant and Seasonal Agricultural Worker Protection Act of 1983, a successor to the Farm Contractor Registration Act of 1963, which was not strongly enforced (Emerson 1982).

References

Advisory Commission on Intergovernmental Relations. 1984. *Regulatory Federalism: Policy, Process, Impact, and Reform.* Washington, D.C.: GPO.

Anderson, K. 1977. The EPA General Permit Program. In *Irrigation Flow Quality Management: Proceedings of a National Conference,* ed. J. P. Law and G. V. Skogerboe. Fort Collins: Colorado State Univ.

Andrews, B. T., and S. K. Fairfax. 1984. Groundwater and Intergovernmental Relations in the Southern San Joaquin Valley of California: What Are All These Cooks Doing to the Broth? *Univ. of Colo. Law Rev.* 55:145–271.

Bardach, E., and R. A. Kagan, eds. 1982. *Social Regulation: Strategies for Reform.* San Francisco: Institute for Contemporary Studies.

Benedict, M. R. 1953. *Farm Policies of the United States, 1790-1950: A Study of their Origins and Development.* New York: Twentieth Century Fund.

Berry, J. M. 1982. Consumers and the Hunger Lobby. In *Food Policy and Farm Programs*, ed. D. F. Hadwiger and R. B. Talbot. Proceedings of the Academy of Political Science 34:68–78.

Boehlje, M. 1984. Agricultural Policy and Financial Stress. In *Agriculture, Stability, and Growth. Reports from a Public Policy Study of the Curry Foundation,* 237–40. New York: Associated Faculty Press.

Bonnen, J. T. 1980. Observations on the Changing Nature of National Agricultural Policy Decision Processes, 1956-76. In *Farmers, Bureaucrats, and Middlemen: Historical Perspectives on American Agriculture,* ed. T. H. Peterson, 309–42. Washington, D.C.: Howard Univ. Press.

_____. 1984. U.S. Agriculture, Instability, and National Political Institutions: The Shift from Representative to Participatory Democracy. In *United States Agricultural Policies for 1985 and Beyond.* Tucson: Univ. of Arizona and Resources for the Future.

Boxley, R. F. Forthcoming. Farmland Ownership and the Distribution of Land Earnings. Washington, D.C.: USDA, ERS.

Browne, W. P. 1982. Farm Organizations and Agribusiness. In *Food Policy and Farm Programs,* ed. D. F. Hadwiger and R. B. Talbot. Proceedings of the Academy of Political Sciences 34:198–211.

Campbell, D. C. 1984. The Pick-Sloan Program: A Case of Bureaucratic Economic Power. *J. Econ. Issues* 18:449–56.

Castle, E. N., and M. Goldstein. 1984. Income Distribution, Poverty, Natural Resources, and Public Policies: Conceptual and Research Issues. Rural Development, Poverty, and Natural Resources. Workshop Paper Series. Washington, D.C.: Resources for the Future.

Cook, K. 1985. Commentary: Agricultural Nonpoint Pollution Control: A Time for Sticks? *J. Soil and Water Cons.* 40:105–6.

Crosson, P. R., and S. Brubaker. 1982. Resource and Environmental Effects of U.S.

Agriculture. Washington, D.C.: Resources for the Future.

Destler, I. M. 1980. *Making Foreign Economic Policy.* Washington, D.C.: Brookings Inst.

Duncan, M., and M. Drabenstott. 1984. Another Troubled Year for U.S. Agriculture. *Econ. Rev.* 30–41.

Dun's Marketing Services, 1985. *Standard Industrial Classification Statistics.* New York: Dun and Bradstreet.

Emerson, R. D. 1982. Farm Labor In the United States. In *Agriculture, Change, and Human Values,* ed. R. Haynes and R. Lanier. Gainesville: Univ. of Florida.

Frederick, K. D., with J. C. Hanson. 1982. *Water for Western Agriculture.* Washington, D.C.: Resources for the Future.

Galston, W. A. 1985. *A Tough Row to Hoe: The 1985 Farm Bill and Beyond.* Washington, D.C.: Roosevelt Center for American Policy Studies.

Gardner, B. L. 1981. *The Governing of Agriculture.* Lawrence: Regents Press of Kansas.

Geisler, C. C., N. L. Bills, J. R. Kloppenburg, Jr., and W. F. Waters. 1983. The Structure of Agricultural Landownerships in the United States, 1946 and 1978. Search: Agriculture 26. Ithaca: Cornell University.

Guth, J. L. 1978. Consumer Organizations and Federal Dairy Policy. In *The New Politics of Food,* ed. D. F. Hadwiger and W. P. Browne, 123–27. Lexington, Mass.: Lexington Books.

Haig, A. M. 1984. *Caveat: Realism, Reagan, and Foreign Policy.* New York: Macmillan.

Heft, F. 1985. Letter to the Editor. *J. Soil and Water Cons.* 40:178–79.

Hinich, M. J., and R. Staelin. 1980. *Consumer Protection Legislation and the U.S. Food Industry.* New York: Pergamon.

Howe, C. W. 1980. The Coming Conflicts over Water. In *Western Water Resources: Coming Problems and the Policy Alternatives.* Boulder: Westview Press.

Infanger, C. L., W. C. Bailey, and D. R. Dyer. 1983. Agricultural Policy in Austerity: The Making of the 1981 Farm Bill. *Am. J. Agric. Econ.* 65:1–9.

Ingram, H. 1982. Water Rights in the Western States. In *Food Policy and Farm Programs,* ed. D. F. Hadwiger and R. B. Talbot. Proceedings of the Academy of Political Science 34:134–43.

Key, V. O. 1961. *Public Opinion and American Democracy.* New York: Knopf.

King, A. O., ed. 1978. *The New American Political System.* Washington, D.C.: American Enterprise Inst.

_____. 1983. *Both Ends of the Avenue: The Presidency, the Executive Branch, and Congress in the 1980s.* Washington, D.C.: American Enterprise Inst.

Kramer, J. 1979. Agriculture's Role in Government Decisions. In *Consensus and Conflict in U.S. Agriculture: Perspectives from the National Farm Summit,* ed. B. L. Gardner and J. W. Richardson. College Station: Texas A & M Univ. Press.

Leman, C. K. 1982. Political Dilemmas in Evaluating and Budgeting Soil Conservation Programs: The RCA Process. In *Soil Conservation Policy, Institutions, and Incentives.* ed. H. Halcrow et al. Ankeny, Iowa: Soil Conservation Society of America.

_____. 1984. The Revolution of the Saints: The Ideology of Privatization and Its Consequences for the Public Lands. In *Selling the Federal Forests,* ed. A. E. Gamache. Seattle: Univ. of Washington.

Longmire, J., and A. Morey. 1983. Strong Dollar Dampens Demand for U.S. Farm

Exports. Washington, D.C.: USDA, ERS-IED.

Lowi, T. J. 1979. *The End of Liberalism: The Second Republic of the United States.* Rev. ed. New York: W. W. Norton.

Maass, A., and R. L. Anderson. 1978. . . . *And the Desert Shall Rejoice: Conflict, Growth and Justice in Arid Environments.* Cambridge, Mass.: MIT Press.

Manley, A. L., and D. F. Hadwiger. 1982. Taking 'Cides: The Controversy over Agricultural Chemicals. In *Farmers, Bureaucrats, and Middlemen: Historical Perspectives on American Agriculture,* ed. T. H. Peterson, 200–21. Washington, D.C.: Howard Univ. Press.

Nadel, M. V. 1971. *The Politics of Consumer Protection.* Indianapolis: Bobbs-Merrill.

National Commission on Agricultural Trade and Export Policy. 1985. Interim Report to the President and Congress. Washington, D.C.: GPO.

National Planning Association. 1984. State of American Agriculture. Washington, D.C.

National Safety Council. 1984. Work Injury and Illness Rates. Washington, D.C.

Nelson, G. L. 1984. Elements of a Paradigm for Rural Development. *Am. J. Agric. Econ.* 66:694–700.

North, R. M., and W. P. Neely. 1977. A Model for Achieving Consistency for Cost-sharing in Water Resource Programs. *Water Res. Bull.* 13:572–80.

Olson, M. 1982. *The Rise and Decline of Nations: Economic Growth, Stagflation, and Social Rigidities.* New Haven: Yale Univ. Press.

Paarlberg, P. L., A. J. Webb, A. Morey, and J. A. Sharples. 1984. Impacts of Policy on U.S. Agricultural Trade. Washington, D.C.: USDA, ERS-IED.

Paarlberg, R. L. 1985. *Food Trade and Foreign Policy.* Ithaca, N.Y.: Cornell Univ. Press.

Peters, J. C. 1982. The 1981 Farm Bill. In *Food Policy and Farm Programs,* ed. D. F. Hadwiger and R. A. Talbot. Proceedings of the Academy of Political Science 34:157–73.

Radosevich, G. E., and G. V. Skogerboe. 1978. Achieving Irrigation Return Flow Quality Control through Improved Legal Systems. Report to the Environmental Protection Agency, no. 600/2-78-184.

Riemenschneider, C. 1985. Redressing the Farm Problem: More Aid Would Not Have Worked. *New York Times,* March 10.

Rowland, C. K., and M. Dubnick. 1982. Decentralization of Agriculture. In *Food Policy and Farm Programs.* ed. D. F. Hadwiger and R. A. Talbot. Proceedings of the Academy of Political Science 34:212–22.

Rowland, C. K., and R. Marz. 1982. Gresham's Law: The Regulatory Analogy. *Policy Stud. Rev.* 1:572–81.

Schattschneider, E. E. 1942. *Party Government.* New York: Holt, Rinehart and Winston.

Schmidt, W. E. 1983. U.S. May Lose Control of Western Rangeland. *New York Times,* February 14.

Spitze, R. G. F., and J. A. Brewer. 1985. Treasury Costs of U.S. Agricultural and Food Policy. Illinois Agricultural Economics Staff Paper 85 E-318. Champaign-Urbana: Univ. of Illinois.

Tweeten, L. 1983. Economic Instability in Agriculture: The Contributions of Prices, Government Programs and Exports. *Am. J. Agric. Econ.* 65:922–31.

U.S. Congressional Budget Office. 1984. *Federal Support of U.S. Business.* Washington, D.C.: GPO.

U.S. Department of Agriculture, Forest Service and Department of the Interior,

Bureau of Land Management. 1985. *1985 Grazing Fee Review and Evaluation.* Washington, D.C.: GPO.

U.S. Department of State. 1984. U.S. Foreign Policy and Agricultural Trade. Current Policy no. 535. Washington, D.C.

U.S. Environmental Protection Agency. 1978. Regulatory Programs for Nonpoint Source Control. Revised Program Guidance Memorandum No. 31. Washington, D.C.: EPA.

_____. 1984. Nonpoint Source Pollution in the U.S. Washington, D.C.

U.S. Library of Congress. 1981. Agriculture: U.S. Embargo for Agricultural Exports to USSR. Library of Congress Issue Brief IB80025. Washington, D.C.

Wasserstrom, R., and R. Wiles. 1985. *Field Duty: U.S. Farm Workers and Pesticide Safety.* Washington, D.C.: World Resources Inst.

4

The Social Environment of Agriculture and Rural Areas

DON A. DILLMAN

The topic that I have been asked to address is the identification of issues that agricultural economists should and can work on from the perspective of my discipline as we approach the twenty-first century. This task is a somewhat disconcerting one. For most of the last ten years a portion of my time has been devoted to a rather large and multidisciplinary project that concerns developing solutions to soil erosion problems in the Pacific Northwest. Frequently, scientists from the 12 disciplines meet and discuss what research should be done. More than once, I have been told by scientists from other disciplines exactly what I should be doing.

In our most recent annual meeting, one of the biological scientists looked me straight in the eye and said, "What I want to know from you is what is the matter with the farmers? They know that erosion is a problem. I know that if they would simply use the practices we have already developed that the problem would be solved. What your project should do is tell us exactly how to get farmers to do what they already should have been doing." His suggestion is not exactly what I wanted to hear even if it was in the spirit of multidisciplinary cooperation. What scientists from one discipline expect of those in another is often quite different from the views of those within that discipline. Knowing how I have sometimes reacted to other people trying to define the sociological research agenda, I am, appropriately I think, a bit gun-shy about suggesting what your research agenda should be. Nonetheless, there is merit in sociologists and economists attempting to influence one another's research agendas. Recently I served on

Don A. Dillman is Professor of Sociology and Rural Sociology and Director of the Social and Economic Sciences Research Center at Washington State University, Pullman. Portions of this paper are based in part upon previous works of the author (1985, 1986) and are reproduced here by permission of the Rural Sociological Society.

a thesis committee of an agricultural economics student who was studying the economics associated with the adoption of no-till drills, an enormous machine that can cost $180,000 and requires a very large tractor to pull it across the steep Palouse hills of eastern Washington. The student had completed summarizing a very long chapter with a considerable number of equations, most of which I did not understand, and I asked him for a two sentence conclusion. His response was simple and direct, "I cannot for the life of me figure out any economic reason whatsoever for using a no-till drill. The only reason that I can suggest for why many farmers are using them is the status they get out of it in their community." In two sentences he provided one of the most succinct arguments I had heard for a sociologist to be studying the development of no-till drills.

I can also recall sitting on sociology thesis committees when I looked at the small predictive power of regression equations filled with attitude scales, belief scales, measures of social status, and other sociological variables, which together explained perhaps 8 percent of the variance in the dependent variable. Occasionally in these meetings I have pondered whether a simple economic variable might have doubled the explained variance and then some. Unfortunately, I suspect sociologists are as much at a loss on how to construct and use such measures as economists might be on measuring some traditional sociological variables.

Against this background of concerns I would like to identify some emerging social issues that strike this sociologist as in need of investigation by social scientists concerned with rural and agricultural issues. I will begin by commenting very briefly about the nature of sociology and the kinds of variables that a sociological perspective encourages one to consider. Second, I will set a context for the discussion of emerging issues by looking historically at the kinds of forces affecting rural America throughout this century and how that has led to certain kinds of issues being investigated. Third, I will comment on a fundamental transition that I believe is now occurring in American society, our entry into the information age, which poses new issues for investigation. Finally, I will develop several information age related issues that I believe both economists and sociologists need to be considering during this period of rapid transition we are experiencing in agriculture and rural areas of the United States. Hopefully, it will be a time when we are actively influencing one another's research agendas.

A Sociological Perspective on Human Behavior

As a sociologist I have a perspective on human behavior that results in my being concerned about particular variables. Within sociology there is a wide variety of theoretical perspectives on behavior. However, there are also some commonalities that give coherence to the discipline and tend to set it apart from the other social sciences. Sociology came into existence as a discipline because of the hypothesis that social interactions and the institutional structures that flow from those interactions are significant determinants of human behavior. By understanding who interacts with whom, under what conditions they interact, and the sources of rules that govern that interaction, we may gain an ability to explain individual and group behavior.

If a sociologist were asked to list the concepts most important to the discipline, I expect that such a list would usually include: role, role conflict, norm, deviance, institution, community, status, social power, culture, primary group, peer group, relative deprivation, alienation, formal organization, social exchange, prestige, and several dozen other concepts. If one were to examine carefully the concepts I have listed here, one would find that each deals with some aspect of how people interact with one another. These concepts have been central to the contributions made by rural sociologists to the study of rural issues throughout this century.

Three Eras of Change and Social Organization

Since the early 1900s American society has gone through two eras of significant social change, and it is now entering a third era that has profound implications for how society is organized and the social arrangements that govern the use of available technology. Agriculture, rural people, and our colleges of agriculture will be greatly influenced by our movement into this era. The first era (Figure 4.1) can be described as the community control era, which persisted as a dominant force until the 1940s (Kolb and Brunner 1935). The second era is that of the mass society, which has been dominant during the last 40 years, but whose influence is rapidly declining (Warren 1972). The third era is the "information age" that is rapidly developing and will dominate the social and technological organization of society and the world as we reach the turn of the century (Dillman 1983, 1985). The social issues facing rural America are not unique to agricultural and rural areas; they are a reflection of these major forces at work in the larger society and world.

Figure 4.1 shows that 1985 was an especially perplexing time for agriculture and rural communities when the forces of all three eras persisted to some degree. A result is that quite different definitions of what the social issues faced in agriculture are and what should be done about them persist. I will describe these three eras and then use them as a context for describing a number of important social issues we will face as we draw ever closer to the twenty-first century.

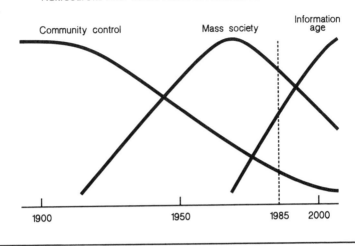

Fig. 4.1. Strength of three eras of social and economic change in the United States by year

THE COMMUNITY CONTROL ERA. At one time in the United States, community was a geographic place where people could and typically did go about the rounds of their daily lives, having all or nearly all of their needs met. Most people's lives were pretty much confined to the community in which they lived, and community was a powerful controlling force in their daily affairs.

One of the nation's earliest rural sociologists, Charles Galpin, is remembered partly for his novel way of identifying community boundaries (Galpin 1915). He used road turnings (i.e., the indentations of wheel tracks at road intersections), which typically went in both directions near the center of these natural communities and only one way near the periphery, to identify social boundaries. These indentations in the summer dust, which turned to trenches in the winter mud, were the communication lines over which nearly every connection with the outside world was made, whether the carrying of produce to sell, the delivery of medical care, or the bringing of religious instruction. The destination for these road turnings was most often the village center where the search for information or products was turned over to somebody else who served as a broker with a somewhat more distant source where another brokerage transaction connected the need to an even more distant part of society.

A particular kind of behavior was associated with these rural communities, which had a small population size, a low density of population, much homogeneity (most residents were family-size farmers), and a low rate of population turnover (Dillman 1979a). The behavior was different than that typically found in large cities. For example, when a farmer borrowed a hand corn sheller or wagon the borrower did not just say he needed to use it. He usually felt obligated to say why it was needed and perhaps why he did not borrow it from the other neighbor like the last time he needed one.

Small rural communities had an overlapping institutional structure. The people seen in church were the same people that were seen when one went shopping, and whose children went to school with your children. The nature of these communities forced people to lead consistent lives. In many rural communities, if one liked to drink beer on Saturday night then that person was not allowed to teach Sunday school on Sunday morning. The simple question of "What will the neighbors think?" had as much of a controlling influence on behavior as the fear of getting arrested has today. The threat of juvenile delinquency could often be handled more effectively by threatening to tell the father of the offending youth's girlfriend than by the threat of jail.

In the community control era, the family farm, whereby a family owned the enterprise, provided most of the labor, and made most of the management decisions, dominated agriculture. If one were to list the social issues connected to the community control era, one would start with the disadvantaged status of being rural, having a lower level of living and poorer access to schools and medical care. Bringing about change in people's lives meant overcoming some very powerful community norms and having a great deal of patience. If we had held a meeting to discuss social issues affecting farmers in the 1920s and 1930s, I think we would have spent a lot of time talking about farming as a way of life. We would have also discussed the difficulties of bringing about the acceptance of better technology being produced by the land-grant colleges, which was deemed essential to producing a better quality of life for rural people.

It is against this background that some of the research issues traditionally pursued by rural sociologists made considerable sense. One of the most significant areas of research inquiry has been the diffusion of innovations. An often quoted finding from this research is the fact that the diffusion of hybrid seed corn took some 14 years before virtually everyone was using it. Subsequent research showed a striking pattern whereby communities had a few innovators who tried it first while others waited to see what happened. A second group, that is the early adopters, tried the innovation only after they saw that it had worked for the innovators. Then came the intriguing aspect. The majority looked not to the innovators for guidance but to those who had adopted somewhat later. There was a hierarchy of influence of one set of people influencing a later set who then influenced those who adopted last. Communities were tightly knit systems with an internal organization that innovation had to penetrate over a lengthy diffusion period.

The essence of rural communities in which one had a nearly complete investment of one's life had a considerable effect on the rate of change in the community control era of the early part of this century. Important research was directed towards understanding these social aspects of behavior.

THE MASS SOCIETY. The mid-twentieth century witnessed an assault on tightly knit neighborhoods and communities on nearly every front. Automobiles, paved roads, and telephones expanded the size of the population aggregate within which people went about their daily interactions. The telephone expanded and speeded up interactions. Greater societal wealth made possible unprecedented travel opportunities. The rise in national corporations assured a regular turnover of local managers with whom less mobile segments of the population did business.

The expansion of diverse educational opportunities and military experiences brought rural people into contact with other sections of the country and other countries of the world to an unprecedented degree. The entry of women into the labor force in large numbers brought still other interactions that were not community bound. Television and other media of the mass society bombarded the countryside with the same programs and advertisements received in New York and San Francisco. The mass media produced homogeneity throughout the society.

The mass society also placed emphasis on building large hierarchies. In corporations as well as social service agencies, local representatives reported to regional representatives and so on up the corporate ladder. The arm of the federal government was increasingly felt in all aspects of American life from education to transportation.

Communities as arenas for action were opened to outside influences. Whether on educational issues or health concerns, decisions were likely to be made outside the boundaries of communities, with little consideration given to the effects of those decisions on other community institutions.

The mass society produced the best of times as well as the worst of times for rural people. There was a concerted effort to bring farmers into the mainstream of society, putting them on a par with urban people by providing the means for making a higher level of living, electricity, and even piped water. The avenue for accomplishing that was to help farmers adopt new technologies that would enable them to run larger farming operations and be more productive. Farmers who achieved higher incomes not only bought televisions, but via the mass media they learned to want the same things that urban people wanted: new cars, vacations, and modern homes.

One of the main social issues of this era, although I am not sure it was perceived as such, was that a tremendous number of farmers had to leave farming. In 1951, some 220,000 farmers left agriculture; by 1961, the number had dropped to 138,000 per year, in comparison to the approximately 30,000 a year now leaving agriculture. I recall that in one southern Iowa county in 1960 there were one-third fewer farmers living there than had been the case in 1950.

Another aspect of the mass society was the specialization that occurred in agriculture. The Farmers' Home Administration no longer required farmers in some areas of the country to have a few dairy cows to provide a small cash flow. Specialization witnessed the rise of national and very powerful commodity organizations from the wheat, corn, and soybean producer groups to the national wool growers. The major effect of this change was to orient farmers more and more toward national concerns in their area of financial interest, just as it was happening in other areas of American life. Also, in the mass society farmers began borrowing money to a much greater degree, emulating procedures that were bringing massive wealth to America's largest corporations. In retrospect the mass society was a pleasant era. Societal wealth increased tremendously. The exit of farmers from agriculture was a concern, but not nearly what it might have been considering that most of them quickly became better off financially. If not them, then certainly their children improved their material well-being. In the mass society, the concern with social issues was not nearly so great as I sense it will become as we move further into the next era, the information age.

THE INFORMATION AGE. We are now experiencing an astonishing revolution in the ability to organize, store, retrieve, and transmit information. The essence of the information age is massive increases in

1. The speed by which communication may occur between one place and another;
2. The amount of information that can be transmitted from one point to another;
3. The fidelity of long-distance communications;
4. Miniaturization of computer and communication technologies;
5. The ability to send as well as receive information from virtually any point on earth;
6. The relative importance of telecommunicated messages compared to transactions requiring physical movement as determinants of human behavior;
7. The ability to select from data banks the precise information for making decisions;

8. The ability through artificial intelligence to conceptualize problems and possible solutions and ways beyond individual human capabilities;

9. The relative importance of information versus labor and energy in the production of goods and services;

10. The rate of potential change and who interacts with whom for what purpose; and

11. The development of information-intensive products through biotechnology and other research (Dillman 1985).

It is important to ask what the changes I have just outlined might mean in practical terms. Let me project ahead to a hypothetical dairy farmer in the year 2000. These changes could mean making daily assessments of individual production, feed consumption, and cost records for herds of genetically manufactured cows, each of which is too large to be allowed out of the milking shed. It could mean sending and receiving production records to or from anywhere on earth by instant electronic command rather than mail or personal visit. It could also mean the capability for video communication with European dairy farmers more easily, more quickly, and at no more cost than once was required to take a vehicle to a neighboring farm home, facilitated by instantaneous computer translation of languages. It could mean receiving national and worldwide narrowcast TV programs tailored to the needs of dairy farmers complete with feedback potential for instant referenda, all at a very low cost. It could mean easily locating, sorting, and identifying from massive data files the information needed to make a decision using voice rather than keyboard commands. It could also mean through use of artificial intelligence the designing of an entirely new way to house, feed, milk, and care for cows. It takes into account everything from the micro farm climate to farmer temperament, with the best solution being unique to each farmer.

Farfetched? Perhaps! However, one wonders if that scenario is any less plausible than the following scenario might have seemed to the dairy farmer's grandfather in the community control era of the 1920s: a single farmer milks 100 cows by himself, six at a time as they pass a through a small milking room when it is each cow's turn. While being milked she receives an exact ration of grain that depends upon how many pounds of milk were produced by her the preceding week. Cows are bred to bulls that have never been closer than several hundred miles to the farm, let alone the individual cow. A few "prize" cows were born to mothers who were not actually their real mothers; each of the cows is one of a hundred or so of their genetic mother's offspring. In addition, all of each day's production is hauled away in a single container, sold at a price set by government policy with a significant portion of each day's production ending up in government storage. This scenario is no longer a future possibility; it is a reality of the 1980s. Even this description is a bit out-of-date. I recently visited a new milk facility where cows wore electronic recognition tags so that the average of the last five milkings could be displayed to the operator and in which the teatcups of the milking machine were automatically removed without the aid of an attendant. The manure was being processed and recycled for bedding.

We are shifting from an industrial society to one in which most effort goes into and most value is produced by information processing activities (Pool 1983b). Information is being substituted to some degree for time, labor, and energy in the production of goods and services (Hawken 1985). Examples of the shift toward substituting information for energy and time exists in nearly all segments of society, including secretarial work, operation of air and rural transportation, industrial robots, conservation tillage, poultry production, agricultural pest management, etc.

By one calculation the information sector of society has shifted from one-twentieth of the work force in 1870 to about one-third in 1950 to one-half at present (Cleveland 1985). Some 90 percent of the new jobs created from 1970 to 1980 have been described as information or service activities (Naisbitt 1982). Further, the value added to economic output by information work has increased from $300 to $5000 (in 1958 purchasing power) per worker between 1900 and 1975 (Jansen 1983).

Accurately perceiving what a full-fledged information age will be like is probably beyond our most imaginative capabilities. When Gutenberg invented the moveable type mold it is doubtful he could have envisioned the universality of daily newspapers, stock prices, and weather forecasts, or even why they might come into existence. Indeed, one could imagine that Gutenberg's invention had its detractors who saw it as a novel idea but not something that could completely replace copying manuscripts by hand. Most innovations, whether printing press, auto, or airplane, have little or no initial advantage over other technologies at first, and they are decidedly noneconomic. The earliest automobiles were slower than horses, far less reliable, completely unusable on muddy roads, and certainly not to be bought if it meant selling your horse. The real advantage of new technologies comes after one technology is linked to another and new capabilities are developed producing unforeseen demands for unforeseen products.

I have yet to meet a person who feels his checkbook can be balanced more quickly and with less effort on his personal computer than can be done manually. Not until software got beyond the checkbook balancing stage to graphing of monthly expenditures and creating income tax data did the advantages become apparent. Clear-cut advantages are only beginning to accrue to most information age technologies. There is an abundance of ideas of what breakthroughs might take place in agriculture, from biotechnological innovations to farm equipment. Recently I attended an industry meeting sponsored by a manufacturer of no-till drills. I was extremely impressed that the areas they seemed most to focus on were spray technology, which could be controlled far better by computer than it is by the present mechanical means, and, secondly, by fertilizer placement. The demonstration of seeds responding better if different kinds of fertilizers were placed in different locales in relation to the seed raises interesting possibilities about the kind of "intelligent" drill that might work best in the future.

It is commonly predicted that one of the most common tools of the future will be individual computers or microprocessors that come as an integral part of each machine, dedicated to a particular function much as the electrical motor is today. We have barely begun to see the kinds of ways in which information substitutes for energy and labor in the production of goods and services. When one considers the incredibly large number of scientists living in today's world, compared to all previous times, and the tremendous investment in research now occurring in most of the industrialized country, there seems little doubt that we are in the midst of a revolution with dramatic implications for all of us.

Our movement into the information age underlies many issues in need of investigation by rural social scientists.

The Issues

DEVELOPMENT OF AN INFORMATION INFRASTRUCTURE FOR RURAL AMERICA. Not since the development of the telephone has a technological change provided so much potential for overcoming the friction of rural space. The social and economic future of rural America will be greatly influenced by the extent to which a functioning rural information infrastructure is put into place. There are five essential components of that infrastructure. First, the telecommunications capability for rapidly sending and receiving large quantities of information is an important feature of the rural information infrastructure. Telecommunications is to the information age what highways and railroads were to the industrial age. However, it would be a mistake to think of the future telecommunications capabilities as simply a beefed-up version of today's rural telephone systems or most communities' cable television systems. The rural telephone system in the United States evolved as a hierarchical geographic structure. Local subscribers were connected by means of a two-wire loop to the nearest exchange, which was connected by coaxial cable to nearby exchanges and a toll exchange on the long-distance network. The toll exchanges were connected by cable or microwave (and more recently satellite) to distant locations where the process to local subscribers was reversed (Pool 1980).

The ends of the network, especially those ends going into rural areas where precedence was given to achieving broad coverage at the expense of quality (e.g., party lines), had very little capacity. The use of fiberoptics in appropriate combination with satellites and digital switching gives a low-cost, broad-band capability from one end of the telephone system to another. The potential result is a very high-quality and capacity transmission from one point to any other point.

The second essential aspect of the rural information infrastructure is the ability to use the network signals that become available. This requires the acquisition of equipment for receiving, sending, and using telecommunicated information. The standard home system of the future has been described as including a video phone with conference capability, an intelligent computer with electronic mail terminal, multichannel, two-way optic fiber cable with feedback controls, and a video recorder and player (Pool 1980). The cost of this equipment by the year 2000 is estimated by Pool to be about the same as for an automobile. Whereas the buy-in to the agricultural and early industrial ages was a strong back and willingness to work, the buy-ins to the information age are the ability to purchase communication devices and skills to use them.

A third part of the information age technology infrastructure is the use of information technologies that come embodied in the tools and materials one uses to produce goods and services for the competitive market. Such products range from microprocessors that serve as guidance systems to farm equipment (e.g., moisture and depth sensors on no-till grain drills) to the products of biotechnology research (e.g., new plants, animals, or other organisms) (Rosenblum 1983).

A fourth essential part of the information infrastructure is a system for rapid delivery of goods and services (Jansen 1983). Inasmuch as a driving force behind the development of an information age is the desire to substitute information for energy, this aspect of an information social structure may seem surprising. However, the critical parts of the economic work place will likely consist of components that cannot be repaired on site, if at all. Another driving force of the information age is substitution of the ability to locate something for having capital tied up in inventories near where parts or supplies are needed. A positive correlation between use of long-distance telephone and travel has been noted by Pool (1980). It can also be noted that the 24-hour delivery of products by Federal Express and others from nearly anywhere to anywhere else in the United States was ushered in by the information age rather than out.

The fifth essential component of the rural information infrastructure is people having the capability to effectively use those technologies (Nora and Minc 1980). That will require motivation for learning new skills. Whether rural Americans accept the challenge of learning these skills is no less important to the success of the information age than the development of the technologies themselves. Learning to be productive in the use of information technologies will likely require much more than taking something out of a box and plugging it in, providing yet another basis for new inequalities.

Traditionally, rural Americans have been slower than urbanites to adopt many technologies. The telephone is an interesting partial exception, the diffusion of which apparently grew more rapidly in prosperous rural areas than some urban ones (Pool 1983a). The potential for overcoming the disadvantages of rural distance may also be a compelling reason for speeding up the adoption of information technologies. Certainly, one of the research priorities for the social sciences is to study who adopts what information technology for what reasons and who does not with what consequences. In addition to the examination of differences between rural and urban people, differences within rural America must be examined. It is important to know whether rural America becomes a land of information "haves and have nots."

WHO WILL LIVE IN RURAL PLACES? Few questions are more fundamental to understanding the impacts of the information age on rural America than the question of who will live there. Will rural places grow or decline? Will the composition of the rural population be drastically altered? Such questions are multifaceted and complex. They involve consideration of the inherent centralizing and decentralizing effects of information technologies, the inherent appeal of living in rural locations, the possible evolution of new forms of work organizations, and the changing importance of agriculture and other kinds of employment in the larger economy. They also involve consideration of the products of biotechnology.

It has been argued that information technologies are neither inherently centralizing or decentralizing for society (Mandeville 1983). Simply because the cost and quality of effective two-way telecommunications may no longer depend on distance does not mean that where one lives will make little difference in one's ability to earn a livelihood. Much would seem to depend upon the extent to which telecommunication is truly substituted for physical movement of people. Goddard has noted that when travel is easier, telecommunications increase, but when it becomes harder, telecommunications decrease (Goddard 1980). He then goes on to suggest that the increased use of telecommunications may generate more travel than that for which it substitutes. But large segments of society have yet to experience high-quality, low-cost, two-way communications so as to learn whether the relationship holds as it did in the past for telephonic communications.

One of the most widely discussed potentials for the information age is the development of the so-called electronic cottage whereby increasing numbers of people work at home rather than commute to an office or manufacturing plant (Toffler 1980; Nilles 1982; Salomon and Salomon 1984; Pratt 1984). In theory one could telecommunicate with equal effectiveness to New York City from a home in Montana as one could from a New Jersey suburb. Telecommunicating will be advantageous to many employers because of savings in office space and the ability to use more part-time and lower-salaried employees.

Among employees, telecommunicating has many supporters, including those who like to set their own hours, prefer being able to mix work with other responsibilities (e.g., child care), and dislike commuting. Telecommunicating also has its detractors, including those who feel employees miss out on learning and promotion opportunities because of not being seen or exposed to normal office interactions. Unions and others also look critically at the electronic cottage as potentially a new kind of sweat shop where children and others could be forced to work long hours (Mattera 1983).

A carefully reasoned analysis of telecommunicating by Salomon and Salomon (1984) raises a number of critical questions about the contribution of the work place to the formation of one's social identity and the likelihood of increased tension in one's home if the occupant's work is centered there. They conclude that the individual is called upon to carry much of the nonmonetary costs of telecommunicating while most of the benefits go to the firm. They also note that people vary widely in their acceptance of telecommunicating.

Working entirely at one's home is only one form of telecommunicating, and perhaps the one of lesser importance. There is also a form whereby an employee spends some days working at home and other days at work, thus overcoming the problem of being out of touch with opportunities offered by interaction in an office. Should significant numbers of employees be able to reduce the days of commuting to an office, it seems likely the commuting ring around major metropolitan areas would be expanded. Telecommunicating may also be enhanced by the difficulty of finding and maintaining employment opportunities for both adults in two-career families and by the shift towards an aging population. The electronic cottage may provide an opportunity to tap work skills of older segments of the population to whom part-time work without a commute could be quite attractive.

If the electronic cottage becomes a reality, will that encourage a resurgence of growth in rural places? The answer appears unclear. Rural sociologists have repeatedly shown that people, if they had their druthers, would live in more rural locations than they presently do (Zuiches 1982; Dillman 1979b). Recent Gallup polls show no decline in such preferences. If people spend a greater portion of their daily activities in their homes, it seems likely that greater effort will be made to realize one's residential preferences. Toffler has noted the societal trend toward greater presumptive activity, that is, producing more of one's own goods from garden vegetables to housing additions (Toffler 1980). Rural settings are associated with more space and fewer restrictions on the kinds of presumptive activities that are possible.

Many of the people who currently hold a preference for rural living and have acted accordingly, during the renewal of rural population growth in the 1970s, spent their formative years in small communities. It may be that their previous experience in rural communities is a factor drawing them back in their later years. We are now in a period of history in which most adults have spent their formative years in suburbs. It is not clear whether their preferences will be the same as the generation that preceded them. However, work by Fuguitt and Zuiches (1975) has shown that although a residence-of-birth effect on preferences exists, it is less than the effect of one's present place of residence.

Apart from the electronic cottage, it is important to know whether industrial plants will be increasingly attracted to rural America or away from it. The telecommunications revolution, which might enable existing industries to move toward the less expensive rural labor markets, has already encouraged them to simply skip over rural America in favor of even less expensive labor markets in distant countries (Hobbs 1983). Another important question is whether the many labor-intensive industries that moved to rural America during the last decade might pick up and move once more to another country.

CHANGES IN FARM OPERATIONS. Last spring I followed development of the farm crisis with considerable interest and, at one point, I posed the question of what would happen if a significant number of family-size farmers were forced out of agriculture in the near future. The stimulus for this exercise was the work of the USDA-ERS (1985), which suggested that 123,000 of the 678,000 farm units in the $50,000 to $500,000 gross income per year category, which is about as close as one might get to a definition of a family-size farm, were insolvent or getting close to bankruptcy. Farms in this category comprise 28 percent of the total number of the U.S. farms that produce 57 percent of the sales.

At first, I dealt with four traditional categories of farms that might replace them: limited resource farmers, part-time farmers, other family farms, and corporate farms. It did not seem likely that any of these types of farms would undergo substantial expansion. This is not the period for limited resource farmers; besides being economically insignificant, the attitudes that undergird the back-to-the-country movement of the 1960s and 1970s are not very prevalent among young people today. Part-time farming as an interim solution seemed reasonable; it allows one to preserve a lifestyle and a place of residence. However, in the long run it does not seem like it will be very important in terms of overall production.

It seemed reasonable that some family farmers who did not buy land would decide that the price is now affordable and therefore invest. However, if they stayed out of the market in the 1970s when people were optimistic about exports, one wonders what the basis would be for their sudden motivation to start buying land. It is also difficult to envision a great expansion in corporate farming. In the past, farming has not lent itself to centralized corporate decision-making structures, and it is difficult to understand why a large corporation would invest heavily in land, thereby immobilizing a large amount of capital. Once land is owned, something needs to be done with it.

It was at this point that I asked myself if perhaps the issue was being considered in an inappropriate way. I was attempting to deal with a new set of problems in a situation not previously faced by agriculture by using pretty traditional concepts. A time of great change such as we are now in (i.e., with rapid development of an interdependent world economy, less governmental involvement to stabilize agriculture, declining land values, and the rapid emergence of new technologies) might be a time for the development of new ways of farming.

In times past, the renter has usually been subordinate to the owner (e.g., accepting all the farming risk with cash rents). Renters have often had to search exceedingly hard to find suitable land to rent. Might we be seeing the beginning of a period in which the power relationship reverses, and owners have to struggle to find renters? A new breed of "farm operators" might emerge who find it possible to rent their labor and their machinery at a fixed price to a landlord who must then take all the risk, thus turning the concept of cash rent upside down.

It also seems possible that we might see an evolution toward franchise farming. Recently I was told of a company that would contract with a farmer to feed hogs, providing him with feeder pigs, feed, antibiotics, vaccines, and a protocol for their application. In turn, the farmer would furnish the land, buildings, and labor to raise the just-weaned pigs to market weight. When ready for market the corporation would retake possession of the pigs and give the farmer a fixed price per head as payment for raising them. Franchise farming seems a distinct possibility for several commodities. One wonders if the development through biotechnology of new and different crop varieties for which the patent rights are owned by corporations might also lead to franchising.

Whatever else can be said about a family-farm agriculture with farmland being owned and managed by those who provide the labor, it provided considerable certainty that the land in a particular community was going to be planted and harvested year after year. This situation provided for considerable community stability even if in some instances it was at a near-poverty level.

When a separation occurs among who owns the land, who does the actual farming, and who owns the components of the production process, new possibilities emerge. An example of this combination of attributes might occur if a corporation owns a superior strain of a biologically engineered crop variety that they license to a farmer who owns the machinery, who then contracts to farm someone else's land.

Under this situation conditions no longer exist that virtually mandate the production of crops in a given locale, even when it is expected to be unprofitable. The corporation that owns the plant varieties may conclude it is more profitable to grow them in another area of the country where weather conditions are more favorable, or even in another country where labor costs are lower.

It seems possible that animal production might move from one area of a country to another where less inclement weather is more favorable to low-cost production. The dairy industry is a case in point.

Under conditions of surplus production, which seem likely to prevail in the coming decades, one even wonders if state experiment stations may find themselves pitted against one another to produce small advantages for their area of the country in an effort to prevent movement of production from one place to another. Work on frost-free organisms suggests that possibility.

One can envision significant dislocations in who produces what and where as a result of changes in (1) the structure of agriculture production; (2) the continuation or even an increase in our ability to produce agriculture surpluses; and (3) the development of new means of producing high yielding crops. Such changes may have tremendous social consequences for states and regions that lose out in the competition. Agriculture may be entering an era of competition for production that was once preserved for industrial plants—an era of chasing tractors instead of smoke stacks.

CHANGES IN MUTUAL SUPPORT AMONG FARMERS AND FARM GROUPS. Interaction with other people establishes our identities, gives us feelings of self-worth, influences our values and beliefs, and establishes norms that constrain our behavior in ways that make group life possible. It is unclear what changes generated by the information age might bring to people's normal interaction patterns. Possibilities exist for more interactions with machines, of a long-distance nature, of high quality, and using more of our sensory abilities. Among the unanswered questions are these: Will machine interaction substitute for human interaction or simply create more desire for it? Will attention to the interactive programming of narrowcast media (targeting programming to relatively small groups), whether electronic church or voluntary interest group, influence identity so that we become estranged from people in physical proximity to us? When new people move into a community, will telecommunications with long-distance friends slow down the normal integration processes? Will people's allegiances be drawn out of the community so that creating groups to get action on local problems will be more difficult? A discussion of who interacts with whom may give the appearance of being a topic that could only be of interest to sociologists and not very important; however, I believe it underlies one of the most troubling issues that will face agricultural people in the coming decade.

The agricultural sector has always found it difficult to face the overproduction issue, partly because of the cultural heritage associated with the community control era. Greg Easterbrook (1985) has made this point:

> One of the cultural differences between farmers and city folks is that farmers live in places where everybody is in pretty much the same line of work. Everybody is either a farmer or provides a service that farmers need. Imagine if advertising executives had to live in complexes populated entirely by other advertising executives and could have only advertising executives for friends. Would they be so aggressive about stealing business? To be true capitalists, farmers would have to view their neighbors as their arch enemies so they compensate by viewing farming itself—the act of working the fields, not as selling the finished product—as their purpose and keeping everybody going as a political challenge. This thinking reflects a kindness and communal purpose we admire in rural life. It also makes for too many farmers.

In recent years, I have heard a great deal about how difficult it is to get farm groups together to resolve farm issues. People often spoke as if it were just a matter of time until these groups would realize their common predicament. If the structural changes I have described do in fact occur, if the number of farmers continues to dwindle, if the institutions that served them tend to disappear from rural communities, if the specialization by commodity continues to increase, it will be increasingly difficult to bring agricultural groups together to deal with common concerns.

The grass roots sentiments of looking out for their neighbors will also likely decline. This in itself suggests greater difficulties in representing agriculture to Congress and the American public as a single issue of great concern.

MAINTAINING INSTITUTIONS THAT SERVE RURAL AMERICA. There is much reason for concern that rural America might soon become a wasteland of decaying institutions. Indeed, it is already happening. As middle-sized farmers disappear, many of the remaining businesses along main street are going with them. The tremendous land devaluation now in process is making it more difficult for local governments to remain solvent and maintain services. However, this weakening of rural institutions is happening at precisely the time that the new information technologies suggest an evolution towards quite different community institutions.

The development of the electronic cottage whereby people commute to work electronically and the linkages of one's productive work to national networks may draw the most important interactions associated with work away from one's community of residence. Direct deposit of money to where it will command the most return and other services may bypass local communities not to mention states and regions of the country. Direct purchase of customized products and services from electronic video catalogs may bypass today's regional shopping plazas as well as branch catalog stores and what little remains on main street. The electronic church that passes the collection plate electronically and immediately gives individual response to prayers of participants may make the exhortation of TV pastors seem quaint, making it even more difficult to maintain the steeples and stained glass of the remaining local churches. Application of artificial intelligence to the diagnosis of medical problems may make locally based medical practitioners little more than service representatives of modern medicine. The potential exists for nearly any educational aspiration to be satisfied but only by reaching beyond nearby communities. The process of bypassing local organizations and dealing directly with the centralized providers of services has been called *disintermediation* (Hawken 1985). No one knows whether the geographically unbounded electronic transactions of the information age will destroy the institutional structures of locality, but it is an issue that clearly needs to be examined.

One of the most distressing social changes faced by many rural communities near the end of the community control era was the consolidation of schools in order to have large enough numbers of students in each school. As the farm population declines further in the midwestern states, the specter of another round of school consolidations becomes evident. One might ask, why not connect three to five students per school together electronically to provide a high school physics or calculus class of appropriate size? One of the most important implications of the information age is that development of new institutional arrangements need not rely on the combining of contiguous geographic areas. Students in high schools that are too small to warrant a physics class in any section of the state might be hooked together as easily as those in adjoining school districts.

Present institutional structures involve transactions among people who give time and financial support in return for services to the community. Institutional services are also articulated with one another so that the full range of community needs are met. It is not clear to me how one elicits attention to necessarily local problems, from street lights to swimming pools, when the source of people's livelihood and needs in all areas of life are increasingly individually focused on suppliers of jobs and services in distant places.

This issue extends even, and perhaps especially, to the structure of information public utilities. The idea of national information utilities that can provide answers to all questions is in many respects a very seductive one. Yet, to what extent can national data banks, even those augmented with artificial intelligence, possess the answers to local problems?

For the past several years, I have been involved in research on conservation tillage as a means of controlling soil erosion. I am impressed by how erosion control techniques vary from one region of the country to another, and the great extent to which farmers perform the role of innovators and testers of new conservation tillage methods. The solution to soil erosion control is probably an evolving one, and it will likely result from a combination of general information and local adaptation. The building of local facilities from research parks to handball courts also requires a combination of standard information and local information. Any effort to build national data networks must, I think, consider how local knowledge can be combined with general knowledge. Unless the structure of the information utilities provides for local input and adaptation, I fear that their use will be quite limited.

One of the challenges of the information age will be to achieve input as well as output at all levels of information utilities (Morentz and Robinson 1983). That task could become especially difficult if other institutions that serve rural America are being weakened by the information age and if rural America lacks the political clout to make it happen.

One of the most fundamental questions to be addressed about the information age is how the institutions that give predictability and order to life become restructured to support the existence of an information society. It means a lot more than individuals having an economically productive role. It means generating commitment to the institutions themselves so that alienation is minimized, conflicts can be resolved, and the collective good can be realized.

Conclusion

The United States is entering a new era, the information age, which will greatly affect the issues that need to be researched by both economists and sociologists as we near the twenty-first century. Among these issues are the development of a rural information infrastructure, concerns about who will live in rural places, changes in who operates America's farms and the conditions under which they are operated, a likely decline of mutual support among the remaining farmers, and the maintenance of institutions that serve agricultural and rural America.

These issues are not discrete ones that lend themselves to compartmentalization by discipline. Understanding the impacts of information technologies on rural people, places, and institutions is a challenge for all social scientists who are concerned about the future of rural America. I hope we accept that challenge.

References

Cleveland, Harlan. 1985. The Twilight of Heirarchy Speculations on the Global Information Society. *Public Admin. Rev.* 45(1):85–95.

Dillman, D. A. 1979a. Down a One-way Road. In *The American Heritage and the Rural Community,* ed. Donald H. Bishop, 107. Pullman: Washington State Univ.

_____. 1979b. Residential Preferences, Quality of Life, and the Population Turnaround. *Am. J. Agric. Econ.* 61:960–66.

_____. 1983. Rural North America in the Information Society: An Invitation to the 1984 RSS Meeting. *The Rural Sociologist* 3:345–57.

_____. 1985. Social Impacts of Information Technologies on Rural North America. *Rural Sociol.* 50:1–26.

_____. 1986. Cooperative Extension at the Beginning of the 21st Century. *The Rural Sociologist* 6:102–19.

Easterbrook, G. 1985. Making Sense of Agriculture. *Atl. Mon.* 256(July): 63–78.

Fuguitt, G. V., and J. J. Zuiches. 1975. Residential Preferences and Population Distribution. *Demogr.* 12:491–504.

Galpin, C. J. 1915. The Social Anatomy of an Agricultural Community. Research Bulletin No. 34. Madison: Univ. of Wisconsin.

Goddard, J. B. 1980. Technology Forecasting in a Spacial Context. *Futures* 12:90–105.

Hawken, P. 1985. *The Next Economy.* New York: Holt, Rinehart, and Winston.

Hobbs, D. 1983. What Is Information in an Information Age: Implications for Equality. Address presented at the Von Tungeln Symposium, Department of Sociology and Anthropology. Ames: Iowa State Univ.

Jansen, T. B. 1983. Information Technology: The Need for Social Experiments. *Technol. Forecasting and Soc. Change* 23:325–52.

Kolb, J. H., and E. deS. Brunner. 1935. *A Study of Rural Society.* Cambridge, Mass.: Riverside Press.

Mandeville, T. 1983. The Spatial Effects of Information Technology. *Futures* 15:65–72.

Mattera, P. 1983. Home Computer Sweatshops. *The Nation* 236(April):390–92.

Morentz, J. W., Jr., and S. R. Robinson. 1983. Report of Rural Community Group. Proceedings of Information Needs for Modern Agriculture Symposium, 30–35. Lincoln: Central AGNET.

Naisbitt, J. 1982. *Megatrends: Ten New Directions Transforming Our Lives.* New York: Warner.

Nilles, J. 1982. Teleworking: Working Closer to Home. *Technol.* 2(April):56–62.

Nora, S., and A. Minc. 1980. Computerizing Society. *Society* 4:25–30.

Pool, I. deS. 1980. Communication Technology and Land Use. *Ann. Am. Acad. Polit. and Soc. Sci.* 451:1–12.

_____. 1983a. Forecasting the Telephone: A Retrospective Technology Assessment. Norwood, N.J.: ABLEX Publishing Corporation.

_____.1983b. Tracking the Flow of Information. *Science* 221:609–13.

Pratt, J. H. 1984. Home Teleworking: A Study of its Pioneers. *Technol. Forecasting and Soc. Change* 25:1–14.

Rosenblum, J. W., ed. 1983. *Agriculture in the 21st Century.* New York: John Wiley & Sons.

Salomon, I., and M. Salomon. 1984. Telecommunicating: The Employee's Perspective. *Technol. Forecasting and Soc. Change* 25:15–28.

Toffler, A. 1980. *The Third Wave.* New York: William Morrow.

U.S. Department of Agriculture. 1985. The Current Financial Condition of Farmers and Farm Lenders. Agricultural Information Bulletin No. 490. Washington, D.C.: USDA, ERS.

Warren, R. 1972. *The Community in America.* 2d ed. Chicago: Rand McNally.

Zuiches, J. 1982. Residential Preferences. In *Rural Society in the U.S.: Issues for the 1980s,* ed. D. Dillman and D. Hobbs, 247–55. Boulder: Westview Press.

5

Technological Innovations with Implications for Agricultural Economics

GLENN L. JOHNSON

Technology is one of the four driving forces in agricultural growth and development. The others include: (1) institutional improvements, including the institutions of concern to students of international trade and monetary arrangements; (2) development of human capacity (capital); and (3) growth in bio/physical as contrasted to human capital. In the short run, agricultural production, consumption, and investment respond to relative prices. In the longer pull, changes in productive capacity and welfare originate largely in these four factors.

My assignment is to concentrate on technological innovation and on the implications that technological change has for the discipline of agricultural economics. If I neglect food and agricultural policy or trade and international monetary issues, it is because time and space are limited, and there are other concurrent papers and discussions on these topics. Similarly, I tend to avoid topics covered in subsequent papers and discussions, such as natural resources and the environment, developments in economics not germane to the study of technology, the politics of agriculture, institutional change, and the social environment, except as related to technical change, macroeconomics, and human capital. This means that I will concentrate on technological change as I believe our organizers intended, and the challenges it poses for us in the first part of the next century. Inevitably, this involves a great deal of production economics, albeit in a broad sense.

Glenn L. Johnson is Professor of Agricultural Economics at Michigan State University, East Lansing. This paper has benefited from the criticisms and suggestions of James Fisher, Neil Harl, Theodore Hullar, Ronald Knutson, James Oehmke, and James Tiedje. The author, of course, remains responsible for its present content.

82

More specifically, my objectives and assignment are to (1) provide a summary of current and prospective patterns of technological change in agriculture; (2) focus critically on concepts, theories, techniques, and approaches used by agricultural economists in studying technical change; and finally (3) summarize needed contributions from agricultural economists.

Prospective Summary of Technological Changes

In this summary, I draw on materials which Sylvan Wittwer and I have presented elsewhere (Johnson and Wittwer 1984) and two national productivity conferences, one on crops (Brown et al. 1975) and the other on livestock (Pond et al. 1980). These reports, in turn, drew on the extensive literature generated by agricultural research administrators; technology analysts such as Schultz, Ruttan, Evenson, Eddleman, and Sundquist; and many other individuals, and such science related agencies as the National Academy of Sciences (NAS), the National Science Foundation (NSF), Experiment Station Committee on Organization and Policy (ESCOP), the international research institutes, the Agricultural Research Service (ARS), the Economic Research Service (ERS), and other agencies. Many appropriate references are listed in Johnson and Wittwer (1984).

Cellular molecular biology—genetic engineering—has become a buzzword among people concerned with high agricultural technology. It does hold high promise in many areas but has not yet replaced conventional plant breeding and conventional work on improving livestock. To date the major contributions have been in livestock, particularly in the production of biologicals for controlling livestock diseases and growth. The advances that have occurred have to do with the simpler life processes for the generation of antibiotics, hormones, and other substances previously producible mainly by using live, whole animals. Massive genetic reconstruction of whole animals is still something for the future; for the most part, the same is true for massive reconstructions of whole plants through molecular microbiology.

Electronics is having its impacts, some of which are very practical. New and better sensors are being coupled to controls for irrigation, planting, fertilization, pesticide application, and a large number of other operations. Electronics are also introducing major advances in the managerial control of production and marketing systems. The stress is on data storage, manipulation, and improvement of information systems. Improved electronics are also having impacts on the structure of agriculture and agricultural business. Ability to manage contracts for the production of primary products, processed products, and various marketing services is being vastly increased. These changes have potential for restructuring agribusiness and the control of agribusinesses over the producers of primary products. The role of the price mechanism in regulating production and consumption and allocating resources may substantially change in the decades ahead. A substantial substitution of both private and public electronic controls for the allocative functions of the market mechanism may take place. As such electronic capability arises, important issues will be created for persons concerned about the structure of agriculture and agribusiness in relation to government. Agricultural sectors and subsectors may be controlled somewhat like the divisions of General Motors, with prices playing much different roles than at present.

Advances in agricultural engineering will continue to be important. The prospects are that the level of living of the American labor force will continue to rise and that labor will continue to get more expensive. If this is so, it will be increasingly important to save labor. "Nonrecreational" stoop labor of commercial (as contrasted to hobby) farms will be almost entirely eliminated from agriculture by early in the next century, though some hobby farms, like golf courses, will use labor intensively. The labor-saving technologies of the future will also be required to save fossil energy. Electronic controls will be important in doing this. Engineering procedures to complement and make it possible to farm the more fragile soils that will have to be farmed in the future will be important. Also, water-saving irrigation systems will be needed. There will be continued advances in food storage, processing, and product enhancement in both agribusiness and farming. In food processing, marketing, and distribution, labor- and energy-saving technologies will be increasingly required.

There will continue to be heavy emphasis on chemicals and biologicals but with much more careful consideration to dangers of contaminating the food chain and polluting the environment. Fertilizers along with chemical and biological disease, pest, and other controls will be needed to meet the increasing demand for food over the decades ahead.

Further efforts and accomplishments can be anticipated in the general area of integrated pest management. While success today in developing totally integrated pest management schemes has been meager, substantial progress has been made on partially integrated schemes and more can be anticipated. The situation is more analogous to research on cancer than on infantile paralysis. There is not likely to be a Salk vaccinelike breakthrough in integrated pest management; instead, it is more likely that slow incremental, somewhat sporadic progress will take place similar to that being attained in cancer research. Nonetheless, the importance of protecting the food chain from contamination and the environment from pollution is likely to keep the integrated pest management effort going.

Projections for American agriculture indicate that international competition in commodity markets, possible energy shortages and foreign exchange needs to buy energy, demands for improved world and U.S. diets, and population growth make it advantageous for the United States to develop capacity to double agricultural production in the next half-century or so. I stress, in this connection, that capacity to produce is not the same as actual production. The greater capacity to produce generated by technological research increases production only when knowledge of the technology is distributed to producers and the inputs for production (seeds, plants, machines, chemicals, etc.) in which technology is imbedded are produced, distributed, purchased, and actually used by producers. I realize the importance of, but do not have time to discuss, the short- and long-run tendency of market-controlled farm economies to outproduce effective demand at product prices that do not cover expenditures and investments. This tendency exists regardless of technology levels, as the depressed nature of agriculture in less developed countries attests, and regardless of the presence of governmental production controls and price supports, as our own 1920s attest with their remarkable similarity to the present situation (Johnson and Quance 1972; Johnson 1984a). Presumably, this policy issue will be considered in a concurrent session on food and agricultural policy.

There can be no doubt about the short-run adverse effects of U.S. fiscal deficits and consequences of high interest rates and a strong dollar on U.S. exports and the welfare of U.S. farmers. International monetary developments and the trading policies of U.S. trading partners are also important. The strength of the dollar is likely to be short-lived. Our trade deficits are not likely to be sustained for long without bringing on other difficulties, some of which will be intolerable.

In the next 20 to 50 years, monetary/fiscal and trade considerations are not likely to reduce the need for expanded U.S. agricultural production. Though the time lag from basic disciplinary research (only part of which is of known relevance and only part of which turns out to be relevant) to the adoption of economically viable technology is shortening, it is often much more than 15 years. For example, I am still awaiting fulfillment of the expectations that my biological science and chemistry professors generated within me in the late 1930s about the possibility of improving photosynthesis and even replacing it with chemical engineering. Regardless of these short-term economic, political, and social considerations and of the long- and short-run tendencies to outproduce effective demand, we will need to continue to improve our technology in the decades ahead. Despite the importance of technology, we should never trust that technological advances alone will get expanded output or that overproduction, surpluses, and farmer distress can be eliminated and overproduction controlled by retraining technological research and cutting budgets for such research.

In the report cited earlier, Johnson and Wittwer (1984) found it to be nationally advantageous to strive for a 60 percent increase in capacity by

2010 and a 100 percent increase by 2030. But, capacity to produce and use of such capacity are two different things. We can always decide to make or not make the investments and expenditures needed to convert capacity into actual production on the basis of farm management, marketing, and policy studies provided we have the technology available. To have such capacity by 2030 requires an average annual growth rate of 2 percent in capacity per year. To convert such capacity into use would require cropping an additional 50 to 60 million acres by 2030. We would also need to be able to crop more intensely, to produce much higher crop yields, and to use more productive livestock. Constraints on land, water, and energy use would require an ability to shift agricultural production systems to more reliance on science and technology, greater human skills to handle high technology, improved institutions and policies, a much expanded and improved capital base, and greater entrepreneurial and managerial skills. As in recent decades, these four factors will continue to be the four prime movers for agricultural advance. What we will actually need to produce is, of course, much more difficult to ascertain than is the need for the capacity.

Required Kinds of Research

The agricultural research required to secure the discussed increases in capacity and to indicate how much of this capacity to use may be classified in three categories.

PROBLEM-SOLVING RESEARCH. Problem-solving (PS) research is designed to solve specific problems on farms, for industries, for governments, or in homes. Of necessity, it is multidisciplinary across the social as well as the biological and physical sciences. PS research will continue to be essential and of increasing importance, though specific problems are difficult to foresee for very far into the future.

SUBJECT MATTER RESEARCH. Subject matter (SM) research produces information on subjects important to groups of farmers, consumers, and others facing important sets of problems. SM research generates knowledge relevant for solving problems in the set but must ordinarily be supplemented by other information to solve any single problem in the set. It is also multidisciplinary. SM research in agriculture is done mainly in the USDA (ARS and ERS) and agricultural college departments.

DISCIPLINARY OR BASIC RESEARCH. Disciplinary (DISC) or basic research is becoming increasingly important for food and agriculture. DISC research is that designed to improve the theories, techniques, and basic measurements of a particular academic discipline such as chemistry or economics. It may or may not be of known relevance for solving a particular practical problem.

It seems worthwhile to indicate that there has been a clear increase in the relative importance of DISC or basic research in the bio/physical sciences insofar as agricultural technology is concerned and that this trend should be expected to continue. Basic advances in these disciplines are of increasing importance to the research and development (R & D) efforts of the industries (both farm and nonfarm) engaged in providing "high-tech" inputs to agriculture. This development, however, does not mean that multidisciplinary PS and SM efforts on the applied end of the research spectrum are decreasing in absolute importance though they are probably decreasing in relative importance. Thus, there seems to be no basis for concluding that the high technologies now being attained in agriculture justify diminished attention to either the private or the public sector multidisciplinary SM and PS research and extension efforts to which agricultural economists make such substantial contributions. There is certainly some evidence that high technology is increasing the relative as well as absolute importance of research on such multidisciplinary subjects as fossil energy; environmental degradation; contamination of the food chain with growth hormones, carcinogens, and bacteria or viruses immune to antibiotics fed to livestock; environmental pollution; and other questions and problems growing out of high technology. Schmid (forthcoming) and others conclude that industry does that which is advantageous to it but neglects needed research where its benefits can easily escape private appropriation. There is a further legitimate public concern in those instances where the private firms find it so easy to appropriate gains that they become polluters and contaminators. Conversely, it is not always possible for entrepreneurs to capture enough of the benefits to make public R & D and problem-solving research unnecessary. Thus, there seems to be little ground for believing that the increasing relative importance of high technology will reduce the amount of R & D and multidisciplinary SM and PS efforts needed in the public versus the private sector.

Approaches Used in Analyzing Technical Change

Our tools and approaches for analyzing technical change will require considerable improvement in the decades ahead. In this section I consider needed improvements for

1. Analyzing the interrelationships among technical, institutional, and human change in doing policy analyses and developmental studies;

2. Studying technology assessment and values;
3. Relating technology assessment to private and public risk bearing and chance taking;
4. Studying agro-ethics of technical change;
5. Defining technical change;
6. Studying the origin of technology;
7. Understanding the distribution and adoption of technology;
8. Analyzing changes in efficiency;
9. Properly using duality theory;
10. Conducting holistic multidisciplinary studies of technical change;
11. Understanding relationships among farm management, farming systems research, and technological development; and
12. Understanding relationships among markets, food systems research, and technological change. It is important that our tools for analyzing technical change be in good shape if we are to appropriately benefit from and avoid the damages of technological change.

INTERRELATIONSHIPS. There is an important interdependency in generating growth among changes in technology, institutions, human capacity (human capital), and ordinary bio/physical capital (Bonnen 1985). A better understanding of the interrelationships of these driving forces is needed in setting agricultural science policy and in managing the further development of both less and more developed agricultural economies.

One hesitates to use the word complementarity in considering the interrelationships among these driving forces because such usage implies an unrealistic macro agricultural production function with technical change, institutional improvements, human development, and bio/physical capital as inputs. Though I am a production economist and for that reason, perhaps, carry production functions around as something of a security blanket, I am unwilling to stretch the concept of a production function that far.

It is probably best to investigate these interrelationships by treating all four of the driving forces as individually essential but largely insufficient to generate significant advances in agricultural sectors without assistance from the other three. Whether we think of complementarity or of essentiality and sufficiency, it is difficult to determine the contributions of any one of these four given no changes in the other three. If all four are inadequate and one is improved, little progress follows. If three are more than adequate and one is deficient, improvements in the deficient one make it possible to benefit from all four and to mistakenly attribute the resultant gain to which all four contribute to only one, such as technical research or education or improved markets and policies or a credit program.

The difficulty experienced in estimating returns to one of the three independent of the other two is increased by the problems encountered in quantifying technological advance, institutional improvement, and human development. I believe that this is a fundamental difficulty in technology assessment and agricultural science policy studies whether we look at efforts of the Office of Technology Assessment or at the appraisals of technological advance and studies of human capital formation and institutional change carried out by such agricultural economists as Zvi Griliches, T. W. Schultz, Vernon Ruttan, and a number of others.

When Ed Schuh and I tried to estimate the contributions that social sciences could make to agricultural production by improving institutions and human development for the World Food and Nutrition Study (National Academy of Sciences 1977), we found that the bio/physical sciences had, in effect, claimed for technological advance all of the gains that could be attained when the institutional, human skill, and capital prerequisites are in place and only technological advance is added. There was, in effect, nothing left of the pie to be claimed for social science research on institutions and human development when technologies are available but institutions and human skills are deficient.

There are many examples of instances where important technological advances produce nothing because of the lack of institutional infrastructure and poor policies. One of the most important in my experience was the development of improved palm oil varieties in Nigeria. Nigeria taxed palm oil so heavily that these varieties were never used in Nigeria. By contrast, Malaysia used the new varieties effectively to become a primary producer of palm oil because the country had policies and institutions amenable to exploiting the new West African varieties, which could outproduce wild varieties six to one under experimental conditions and probably three to one under commercial plantation conditions. Similarly, there are many readily available technologies in the developed western world that simply cannot be used in many African countries because of the inadequate investments in human capital and the defective policies and institutions of such countries. By contrast, there is the extremely rapid ready use of such technologies in Taiwan and South Korea, which have both the human capital investments and the institutional structures to encourage introduction and utilization.

This relationship of technological advance to institutional improvements and human capital formation to growth in bio/physical capital and development is so close that agricultural economists should stress the proportions in which the four are required in the industry, firm, or country. It is more important to get together packages of the four in appropriate proportions than it is to spend time trying to estimate their separate contributions. Though I know that academicians and administrators like to be able to prove there are handsome separate payoffs for whatever they specialize in among the four in their research, extension, and advisory efforts, I doubt our ability to produce accurate estimates. I believe it is more honest and more strategic to note the interrelationships and to spend our time creating appropriate packages than it is to argue about the separate productivity of essentially interdependent activities.

The bio/physical capital that carries technological change has an important interrelationship with the other three forces; however, the relationship of this force to the others is different than those among the other three. Bio/physical capital is produced, saved, and invested partially as a consequence of having the technology, the institutional infrastructure, and the human capacity in place to create it. This makes bio/physical capital growth, in part a *sequential* consequence of the other three. Though this is also partially true of human capital, it appears more true for bio/physical capital. New technologies do not affect production until they have been converted into the factors of production that must be produced, saved or purchased, and utilized by farmers, agribusinessmen, and homemakers before output is affected. Bio/physical capital—like technological advance, institutional improvement, and human development—is essential but insufficient. When we consider its sufficiency as well as its essentiality, the fact that bio/physical capital is a *sequential* consequence of the other three causes it to bear a different relationship to them than if it were simply a *concurrent* fourth necessary but insufficient condition. In our science policy and developmental analyses, agricultural economists have not done very well in handling the necessity and insufficiency of the other three. Much work remains to be done before we will adequately understand the interrelationships among these four driving forces for agricultural change.

TECHNOLOGY ASSESSMENT AND VALUES. Technological assessment is necessarily a multidisciplinary subject matter or problem-solving exercise that generally involves evaluation. For these two reasons, attempts to do technology assessment as a specialized disciplinary exercise in economics, without attention to values, are bound to be inadequate. At the problem-solving level, technology assessment necessarily involves value as well as value-free information, as both are necessary in producing prescriptions as to "what ought or ought not" to be done or "what ought or ought not have been done" with respect to technology. Subject matter research on new technology that has as its objective the accumulation or generation of a body of multidisciplinary knowledge useful to a rather well-defined set of decision makers facing a rather well-defined set of problems. Conceivably, such research can omit value considerations; however, this is typically not true because the word "assessment" in the phrase "technology assessment" is virtually synonymous with the word "evaluative"—it implies prescription or problem solving. Some of the values of concern to technology assessors are monetary as when they consider prices, incomes, and expenditures, but others are nonmonetary as when they consider the health and aesthetic consequences of food chain contamination and environmental degradation.

Thus, much technology assessment analysis requires investigation of value consequences of alternative scenarios to see more clearly who is hurt and benefitted by technological advance in what way, when, and where. When the value consequences of alternative scenarios are discussed iteratively and interactively with decision makers and persons affected by their decisions, much can be learned about the nonmonetary and monetary values involved, as well as more about the positivistic characteristics of requirements and consequences of alternative technologies (Rossmiller 1978). This subject is considered further in the next section on agro-ethics.

AGRO-ETHICS. In at least eight major conferences held in recent years, philosophers and agriculturalists have considered ethical questions concerning the impacts of technological change on the food chain, the environment, life-styles, hunger, and the structure of U.S. and world agriculture. Prior to this meeting, Gene Wunderlich conducted a supplemental session on agro-ethics. Last February, the University of Florida, Texas A & M University, and Michigan State University sponsored a conference on agro-ethics to develop teaching materials for use in the undergraduate teaching programs. Currently, the National Agriculture and Natural Resources Curriculum Project is attempting to improve undergraduate education in the agricultural sciences by developing teaching materials on the general subject of ethical and public policy aspects of domestic and international agricultural systems. This project is sponsored by the American Association of State Colleges of Agriculture and Renewable Resources as well as by the National Association of State Universities and Land-Grant Colleges. In general economics and in agricultural economics there is an increasing concern with the need to do objective research on values and on policy prescriptions. This section expands on what has been stated about the value dimensions of research on technology assessment.

In setting agricultural science policy and in doing technology assessment research, agricultural economists use the maximizing calculus of economics to define optima and to predict the consequences of technological change and its regulation. Defining these optima requires knowledge of values—monetary or nonmonetary and intrinsic or in exchange. Both prescriptive and predictive use of the optima defined by use of the economic calculus is enhanced by more accurate knowledge of values.

The philosophy of logical positivism conditions and guides much of the work of the biological and physical scientists and, unfortunately, technology assessors. This philosophic view is also important in economics (Keynes 1963; Robbins 1932; Friedman 1953; Johnson forthcoming b).

Logical positivists reject the possibility of there being objective descriptive knowledge of the values that conditions, situations, and things "really have." Logical positivists accept and help generate knowledge about who values what, how much, and countenance the conversion of limited kinds of such knowledge into prescriptions via the techniques of Pareto-optimality and Myrdal's (1944, Appendix II) "conditional normativism." However, logical positivists part ways with technology assessors who attempt to describe "real values" as opposed to what values are assigned to what by whom. Yet, it is essential that technology assessors go beyond "who assigns what value to what" to deal with "what really has value" if they are to be objective, useful appraisers in technologies that hurt some persons in order to benefit others. For example, it is not enough to view cancer caused by contaminants as unobjectively and emotionally bad when cancer can be objectively described as "really possessing" the characteristic of badness. It is also to be noted that without such knowledge, we cannot recommend that externalities of technologies be internalized through non-Pareto, non-market interventions of governments or others with power to control and change the ownership of rights and privileges. In this instance, interpersonally valid cardinal knowledge of values (welfare) is required (Arrow 1963; Reder 1948). Objective as contrasted to emotional technology assessment requires that agricultural economists go beyond logical positivism, Pareto-optimality, and conditional normativism to the objective study of what really has value. I do not have time to go into what is involved in such studies and should not because I have gone into this matter at length elsewhere (Johnson 1960, 1976, 1977, 1980, 1982a, 1983b, 1984b, forthcoming b; Johnson and Zerby 1973; Johnson and Brown 1980). There is a very active literature these days on research methodology for economists. Further, certain competent philosophers, political scientists, and legal theorists have attained substantial command over economic theory, particularly when expressed axiomatically and mathematically (Harsanyi 1982; McCloskey 1983; McClennen 1983; Sagoff 1985). The inadequacies of Pareto-optimality, utilitarianism, benefit/cost computations, the concept of efficiency, and the difficulties encountered in analyzing trade-offs between equality and production are being examined carefully. New logical ground is being broken but description is being neglected. Wunderlich's preconference meeting on such issues as part of agro-ethics was excellently organized. All of economics, not just resource economics, is entering a state of methodological and philosophic flux. Bromley's paper for this postconference session also deals with these methodological and philosophic issues as do papers by Barkely, Deaton and Weber, and Tweeten.

TECHNOLOGY ASSESSMENT AND RISK. Agricultural economists have substantial capacity and responsibility for assessing the risks involved in creating and adopting new technologies. This involves assessing both (1) the values of gains and losses that may result; and (2) the badness of paranoia attached to running risks of losses and the goodness of experiencing chances for gains.

Severe social, environmental, nutritional, health, and other losses can result from the use of some new agricultural technologies. For some years now the expected utility E(u) hypothesis has been used so extensively that many agricultural economists cannot consider the risk of loss without turning to that analysis (Halter and Dean 1971; Schoemaker 1982; Tversky and Kahneman 1981). There are a number of difficulties involved in using the E(u) hypothesis to analyze the risks associated with technical change. That analysis postulates cardinal knowledge of values (utilities) but does not postulate their interpersonal validity. As new technologies confer benefits on some, often at the expense of imposing losses on others, interpersonally valid utility or welfare measurements are required. This makes it necessary for us to go beyond the usual E(u) analysis to measure, in an interpersonally valid manner, the values of the losses and gains resulting from use of technology before we make non-Pareto-optimal policy prescriptions.

Another fundamental difficulty involved in using the E(u) hypothesis to analyze risk has to do with the concepts of risk preference and aversion. What is typically called risk aversion by expected utility analysts has to do with the shape of a person's utility function for wealth but not with the badness (paranoia) some experience in taking risks. Similarly, what is typically called risk preference has to do with the shape of an individual's utility function for increase in wealth and income but not with the goodness (joy and pleasure) others experience when taking chances for gains. Many, but fortunately not all, E(u) analysts follow the very questionable practice of labeling persons who have increasing marginal utility for gains in income and wealth *risk preferrers* and those with increasing marginal disutility for losses in wealth and income *risk averters*. This practice is questionable because the E(u) analysis does not deal with how a person whose utility for increases in income and wealth is affected by the risks they take in order to get more of them. Similarly, it does not deal with how a person's disutility for losses in income and wealth is affected by taking the risks. This shortcoming is recognized in the current literature by Robison and Fleisher (1983), Johnson (forthcoming a), and Harsanyi (1982, 54).

In the future assessments of risky technology advances, we will require improvement in our ability to measure values (welfare) in an interpersonally valid way and to deal with the fear some have of taking chances as well as with the utility some derive from running risks or taking chances. Most E(u) analysts and many theorists expect populations of people to be risk averse in the sense of having a utility function for income and wealth that decreases at an increasing rate for losses and increases at a decreasing rate with increases in income and wealth. This conclusion stands in stark contrast to the ability of the State of Michigan to sell lottery and lotto tickets. Michiganders seem to fall in one of the following categories: (1) they have utility functions that increase at increasing rates with gains in income and increases in wealth; (2) they extract a great deal of pleasure from playing lottery games; *or* (3) they do not make their decisions on the basis of the E(u) analysis. In any event, their behavior is inconsistent with the "risk aversion" commonly postulated by the limited E(u) analysis. To date little attention has been given to applying the E(u) analysis (and alternatives thereto) to public choices in policy analyses of risky new technologies. Professional and public paranoia is particularly apparent with respect to nuclear power, food chain contamination, environmental degradation, groundwater pollution, and income distribution effects of new technologies. This paranoia and its converse, the joy and pleasure experienced when gambling with new technology for gains, requires that policy analysts get beyond what E(u) analysts commonly call risk aversion and preference in public assessment of the risks of adopting new technologies.

APPROPRIATE DEFINITIONS OF NEW TECHNOLOGY. Our analyses of new technology are hampered by the definitions of technological change that we employ. A number of economists in their disciplinary specialization have defined a technological advance as an event that changes the parameters of a production function. For instance, Ruttan and Hayami (forthcoming) state "we regard technological change as any change in production coefficients resulting from the purposeful resource-using activity directed to the development of new knowledge embodied in designs, materials, and organization." One difficulty with such definitions of technical change is that they are highly specialized in economics and, within economics, on using the concept of a production function. Another difficulty is that technological change may introduce new factors of production not included in estimated production functions except as conditioning factors fixed in zero quantities. Such definitions have the additional disadvantage of distracting the analyst away from acquiring concrete knowledge of the chains of events and processes whereby disciplinary scientists make the basic discoveries used by R & D workers or inventors to create new factors of production which, in turn, have to be produced, marketed, financed, and purchased by farmers and, finally, used in production.

I believe there are substantial advantages in defining a technological advance as occurring with the discovery of a new factor of production (Johnson 1958). The new factor of production can, itself, be a new intermediate input between the production process and previously used factors of production (e.g., the herringbone milking parlor invented by Australians shortly after World War II). It is made of conventional inputs — concrete, steel, pipes, milking machines, and wood — but is nonetheless a new intermediate input between such primary traditional inputs and the production of milking and feeding services which are, themselves, also intermediate to the final process of producing milk in the biological systems of cows. My definition has the advantage of specifically identifying what new factors of production are important. This, in turn, focuses our attention on (1) the advantages and disadvantages to a farmer of using or investing in the new factor; and (2) what is involved in producing, distributing, and encouraging proper use of it. A subsequent section of this paper gives more attention to analysis of the distribution and adoption of technology.

In my own work, I have gone so far as to state that a technological change has occurred even if the new technology is used in zero amounts, provided the manager involved has learned about and analyzed the new technology carefully enough to conclude that the optimum amount to use is zero. The technological change process is complete as soon as a manager knows enough about a technology to decide on the optimum amount to use of the new input or capital item carrying it; the fact that the optimum amount may turn out to be zero rather than some positive quantity does not make any conceptual difference. Zero is a perfectly good number. If, after the initial adoption of a new technology in zero or any other larger amount, it "pays" to change the initial quantity because of price changes, such changes can be regarded as an economic rather than a technological change.

ORIGINS OF TECHNOLOGICAL CHANGE. Policymakers who desire to encourage or discourage the creation of particular new technologies need to understand their origins. The development of the induced technological change hypothesis (ITCH) (Binswanger and Ruttan 1978; Ruttan and Hayami forthcoming) has been an important step forward in the ability of applied economists to explain the origins of technical change. ITCH, however, does not fully explain the origins of technological change. In addition to originating with the maximizing activities of basic researchers, R & D workers, inventors, and entrepreneurs, technological change has complex origins in the chance events, insights, inspirations, social pressures, habits, and curiosities of many people in the long chain of processes between basic disciplinary research at one extreme and applied research to invent and develop new bio/physical inputs at the other extreme. The hypotheses that actors in this stream are motivated by gain makes a substantial contribution, but the fuller understanding of the process we still need seems to require multidisciplinary (sociological, psychological, and other) as well as economic investigations of science.

ANALYSIS OF TECHNICAL AND ECONOMIC EFFICIENCY. Bio/physical scientists and some economists persist in trying to distinguish between adjustments in production that always have a net advantage because they are technical and those that pay because of value (sometimes price) relationships. The former are referred to as technically efficient and the latter as economically efficient adjustments. Advantageous adjustments, of course, depend on (1) technical possibilities and (2) the values of inputs, products, wastes, and pollutants or contaminants. This section indicates some of the difficulties with these formulations which need to be resolved in the years ahead to improve our analyses of efficiency.

In recent decades, the idea of a frontier production function has gained much currency and is now widely considered in general economics literature (Farrell 1957; McFadden 1978; Kopp and Smith 1980) and in the more theoretical literature produced by agricultural economists (Timmer 1970). This literature suffers from lack of attention to the economics of shifting among subproduction functions of more general production functions through investments and disinvestments. Misspecification and misaggregation of inputs and outputs also creates problems. The difficulties are both empirical and theoretical, with the theoretical ones being the more crucial.

A carefully specified subproduction function indicates which factors of production are variable, which are fixed and at what levels, and which vary at random to generate unexplained residuals. Also, when inputs and/ or outputs are aggregated into categories, a carefully specified production function will deal with input and product categories "sufficiently homogenous for purposes at hand."

A rigorously specified stochastic production or subfunction will have both interior and exterior points due to chance variations in the variables randomly generating the unexplained residuals. As Schmidt and Knox-Lovell (1977) and others point out, it does not make empirical or theoretical sense to fit a production function so that all chance variations in output become points interior to or on the fitted function.

When one makes observations of a panel of firms, one may also encounter firms that do not conform stochastically to the specification of what factors are fixed at what level (i.e., inputs specified to be fixed may actually vary nonstochastically from firm to firm). Such "wild card" observations may, of course, be either inliers or outliers to the subfunction one seeks to estimate, depending on whether the failure to conform to specifications is an input deficiency or excess. An observed firm will be an inlier if one of the so-called fixed variables is nonstochastically present in smaller amounts than specified. Conversely, it will be an outlier if one of the supposedly fixed inputs is nonstochastically present in larger amounts than specified. Of course, it makes no sense to fit a production function so as to make these outliers into inliers and treat the result as if the offending inputs are present in less than the "specified" amounts. What is needed is (1) to restrict observations to firms meeting the specified conditions, which eliminates such inlying and outlying firms from the panel before fitting the function; or (2) to observe the offending inputs and then fit a more complete function that treats them as variable inputs. Input and output aggregation errors also create similar problems.

When economists are careless in their specifications and aggregations and, hence, observe interior points to production functions, they sometimes regard the firms represented by interior points as technologically inefficient. Then they presume that it is always "technically" advantageous for such firms to move to the isoquant for their level of output and that, having gotten to the isoquant, they should then make an "economic adjustment" to move along the isoquant to the line of least cost combination and subsequently from there to the high profit point. The movement to the isoquant is said to involve the attainment of "technological efficiency" while the movement around the isoquant is regarded as the attainment of "price efficiency."

It should be sufficient to point out that there are many instances in which it will not pay to move an inlier to an isoquant because the deficiency in the factor of production that causes the firm to be an inlier cannot be advantageously corrected. What is fixed and variable can be endogenously specified as a result of Clark Edwards's (1959) mathematical treatment of resource fixity (and, hence, variability) as endogenous. Though some (notably Johnson and Pasour 1981, 1982) seem slow to realize it, Edwards's formulation is based fundamentally upon the employment of the internal opportunity cost concept with respect to unspecialized durables fixed for the firm as a whole but reallocatable within the firm (see also Johnson 1982b; Johnson and Quance 1972). Clark's formulation also takes into account off-farm opportunity cost or salvage value for resources being disposed of and the off-farm opportunity cost or acquisition cost for resources being acquired.

If the marginal value productivity of a limiting input causing a firm to be an inlier does not justify acquisition of more of that input, the firm is on a different subproduction function than is being estimated. Clark Edwards's formulation indicates that it can be endogenously more advantageous for a firm to remain on an apparent interior point than it is to move to the isoquant on the subfunction the analyst is trying to estimate. In such instances it is simply uneconomic to change; clearly what is regarded as "technically efficient" is uneconomic. In all instances in which it is "technically" advantageous to move an inlier to the isoquant, it must also be economically advantageous to do so (i.e., it is necessary that the additional amount of the deficient input be procurable at a cost less than or equal to what would be justified by its expected marginal value productivity). If this is not thought to be true, a maximizing rational entrepreneur will not make the expenditure or investment. If only advantageous changes are made, then technical and economic efficiency cannot be distinguished. Similarly, there may be outlier firms to a specified production function. Sometimes it is not advantageous to dispose of the additional amounts of inputs that make these firms outliers, in which case outliers are not moved. Again, technical and economic efficiency cannot be distinguished.

In this connection, Frank Knight (1933) noted long ago the tenuous nature of the distinction between technical and economic efficiency:

> The correct definition of efficiency is the ratio, not between "output" and "input" but between useful *output* and total output or input. Hence efficiency, even in the simplest energy transformation, is meaningless without a measure of usefulness or value. In any attempt to understand economic efficiency, the notion of value is more obviously crucial since most economic problems are concerned with a number of kinds both of outlay and of return, and there is no conceivable way of making comparisons without first reducing all the factors to terms of a common measure.

More recently, Kenneth Boulding (1981) made a similar point:

> . . . it is very important to recognize that all significant efficiency concepts rest on human valuations and that efficiency concepts which are based on purely physical inputs and outputs may not be significant in human terms, or at least their significance has yet to be evaluated. All efficiency concepts involve a ratio of output to input in a process. The more output per unit of input, the more efficient we suppose it to be. The significance of the efficiency concept, however, depends on the significance of the outputs and inputs in terms of human valuations.

In the decade ahead we will need to do better research than we have been doing to understand the roles of technology changes and value changes (including prices) and efficiency.

THE CREATION, DISTRIBUTION, AND ADOPTION OF TECHNOLOGY. Diffusion theory, though often used by sociologists, communication researchers, and administrators, has severe deficiencies in explaining the spread and use of technology, though it must be credited with having added important multidisciplinary dimensions to the study of the distribution and adoption of new technology. The induced technological change hypothesis (ITCH) previously discussed has helped correct these deficiencies by adding a crucial economic dimension. ITCH analysts have added an emphasis on the advantages and disadvantages of creating the expendable inputs and capital items that carry new technologies.

In analyzing the process of replacing horses with tractors in the U.S. agricultural sector from the mid-1920s to the 1950s, one must analyze a process whereby farmers disinvested in horses and invested in tractors. Investment and disinvestment theories, therefore, are important in understanding what went on. The disinvestment in horses and the investment in tractors shifted farmers from one subfunction to another of the overall production function that existed *after* the invention of the tractor. Such shifts in subproduction functions as a result of investments and disinvestments can be treated endogenously in economic theory. Failure to do so leaves static theory bereft of ability to analyze investments and disinvestments.

A theory that shifts endogenously from one subfunction to another no longer generates a unique set of cost and demand structures. To understand the replacement of horses with tractors and what this did to the supply functions for agricultural products and to the demand for factors of production, it is necessary to understand when farmers find it advantageous to shift from one subproduction function to another. Clark Edwards's (1959) approach mentioned earlier for determining endogenously which subproduction function is most economic has been extended by Alan Baquet (1979). Baquet refined the user cost concepts considered by Keynes (1963) and Arthur Lewis (1949) for use in determining the optimum amount of services to extract from durables whether the durables carry old or new technology. Each subproduction function for producing services from durables generates a different set of cost structures and a different set of demands for the variable factors of production used in generating the services. For the most part, our analyses of technological change are inadequate in this respect. This inadequacy relates to the following discussion.

EMPIRICAL PROBLEMS WITH NEEDED EXTENSIONS OF DUALITY THEORY. Considerable empirical difficulty attends the use of duality to relate product supply and input demand functions to macro- and semi-macro-production functions for sectors, regions, and countries. This difficulty is particularly acute for macro-production functions for aggregation of outputs, but it is important even for whole-farm functions for multiple product farms. Stage II for well-behaved production functions generates a unique structure of marginal and total and average fixed-, variable-, and total-cost functions (seven in all) and a unique set of demand functions for the factors of production. This has been long known and is currently rigorously proven as part of what is known as duality theory. Unfortunately, present versions of duality theory are (1) theoretically incomplete and (2) often dangerously extended in empirical work to apply to industry and sector production functions.

The theoretical incompleteness was touched upon in the previous section. When entrepreneurs find it advantageous to shift from one subproduction function to another, duality theory, as now developed, does not deal endogenously with such shifts. What appears to be needed is an extension of duality theory to include Clark Edwards's (1959) endogenization of investments and disinvestments and further developed by Alan Baquet (1979) to include a new, more complete treatment of the user costs involved in changing the amount of services extracted from fixed durables.

There is also an empirical concern about duality. If valid national and industrial production functions can be estimated (or even only postulated to exist), demand and cost or supply functions can be developed for them. In this connection, it is important to realize that production function analysts of individual farm enterprises and farms know that it is extremely difficult to overcome the aggregation problems encountered in estimating whole-farm production functions for complex farm businesses producing several products. I, for one, remember the difficulties I encountered trying to fit a whole-farm value productivity function to data from a panel of west Kentucky farmers engaged in the production of beef cattle, forage, corn, strawberries, popcorn, and dark (snuff) tobacco. These several products were produced with the same and different resources at different times of the year, sometimes in competition with each other (in which case opportunity costs were important) and sometimes not. It was simply impossible to aggregate these products to permit estimation of a reliable single, whole-farm production function. Similar difficulties were encountered in fitting value productivity functions to whole-farm data for multiple product farms in the northwestern part of Michigan's lower peninsula. Some of these farms had fruit enterprises, and most of them engaged in general livestock and crop farming as well. The fruit enterprises were so different from the crop and livestock enterprises that it was impossible to aggregate them together. The difficulty was avoided by eliminating the fruit enterprise from the farm accounts and fitting the function only to the closely related feed crop and livestock residual. Christoph Beringer (1956) fitted more than one enterprise production function to data from complex western Illinois farms instead of fitting a single whole-farm function. He classified the enterprises of these complex farms into grain, forage, and fat stock categories. Farms with dairy and poultry enterprises were excluded. By so disaggregating, he was able to fit meaningful separate enterprise production functions but was unable to fit reliable whole-farm production functions. These three experiences account for the dismay with which I view agricultural sector and industrial macro-production functions and the associated uses of duality theory, factor shares, and lagged adjustment coefficients in studying the effect of technology change on the national and industrial demand functions for factors of production and on national and industrial supply functions for agricultural products. I believe that empirical aggregation and misspecification problems for both outputs and inputs are usually too great for duality and factor share computations to be trustworthy sources of supply and demand functions at national and industrial levels.

Fortunately, this concern about the empirical validity of such estimates does not create severe, insurmountable theoretical difficulties. National and industrial production functions are not essential parts of neoclassical supply and demand theory. In production economics, product supply and input demand functions can be derived from the consequences of resources owners working with identifiable enterprise production functions or identifiable consumption functions at individual firm levels. Basically, what I question is transferring the use of duality from empirically valid enterprise production functions within a firm to empirically questionable macro-production functions. This empirical question is, of course, a different question than the one raised concerning the need to extend duality theory to deal with the economics of investing and disinvesting and, hence, with the economics of shifting from one subproduction function to another within a larger but empirically valid production function.

IMPORTANCE OF HOLISTIC MULTIDISCIPLINARY STUDIES OF TECHNICAL CHANGE. McCloskey (1983) has made the general case for holistic as contrasted to highly specialized "modernistic" research. His arguments are relevant for studies of technological change. The theories relevant for the study of technological change are, therefore, drawn from many disciplines other than economics. What McCloskey argues is that specialization on the theories and empirical techniques of one discipline (economics) to the exclusion of the others is less productive than a more holistic approach that also draws upon the theories and empirical knowledge of the other relevant disciplines. Still further, he has argued, along with Howard Bowen (1982), that this multidisciplinarity often involves the humanities and other social sciences dealing with values and prescriptions. Again, we reach the earlier conclusions about the need to study values.

In technological studies, there is a need for the analysis of scenarios involving the consequence of alternative science policies and technologies (Johnson, forthcoming c). Projective and simulative models to analyze such scenarios are sometimes rejected by those unsympathetic to quantification and large models. Also, as models for studying technical change are necessarily multidisciplinary, such models are also sometimes rejected by persons with strong interests in and preferences favoring more specialized disciplinary research.

In this connection, it is important to distinguish between size of models and the multidisciplinarity essential for effective technology assessment. Multidisciplinary models may or may not be large. Similarly, highly specialized economic models may be very large. Multidisciplinarity seems essential in developing the projection and simulation models required to assess alternative technology scenarios. In general, specialized models, whether large or small and whether constructed by economists, biological scientists, sociologists, or humanists, are inadequate. Conversely, multidisciplinary models typically beat specialized disciplinary models, large or small. The important point to make is that the complex models needed in dealing with technological change are multidisciplinary and complex.

Farm management, marketing, and policy studies of technical change reflect the need for holistic multidisciplinary views of technology. Farm management emerged out of the bio/physical agricultural sciences. Dairy science expanded into dairy management. Beef science and agronomy evolved into beef and crop management. These different kinds of enterprise management eventually grew into general farm management. At a later date, production economists such as myself specialized farm management so much on production economics that it lost its multidisciplinary complexity and, hence, its strength for purposes of doing relevant subject matter and problem-solving research (Johnson 1957). Marketing, too, is multidisciplinary in this same sense although here, perhaps, the relationship to institutional change has, traditionally, been more important than the relationship to technical change. Now, however, technological advances in the marketing process and distribution of agricultural products are at least as rapid as those in the production of primary products; hence, the multidisciplinarity of marketing also involves the relationship between marketing and technological change.

When farm management became unduly specialized on economics and lost its relevance, a farming systems approach emerged to partially replace it and to make up for the deficiencies of farm management as a subpart of production economics (Johnson 1982c). Farming systems research now plays an important role in agricultural R & D and in inventing activities that create technical change. Marketing analysts have paid attention to structure, conduct, and performance studies in recent years, and this is a plus because this approach is fairly multidisciplinary. This approach plus attention to the multidisciplinary relationships between technology and marketing may make it unnecessary for traditional marketing to disappear and be replaced by food systems analysis. Instead, traditional marketing can grow and change so that it need not disappear to be replaced by a successor—food systems analysis.

Needed Contributions of Agricultural Economists for Technological Change

Agricultural economists do (1) research, (2) extension work, (3) resident instruction, (4) advising and consulting, and (5) administrative work in government and assist or serve as entrepreneurs in private enterprises. Much of this work involves technological change.

RESEARCH RESPONSIBILITIES. On the research front, agricultural economists have much work to do to improve their theories and quantitative techniques for use in contributing to subject matter and problem-solving research involving technology.

With respect to *disciplinary economic research,* we previously indicated some of the things that need to be done. To summarize, we need a better view of the complementary or other interrelationships among technical, institutional, and human change. We need to understand better how the three are related to growth in bio/physical capital. We have noted the inadequacies of our risk analysis and the need to get beyond the expected utility hypothesis. We have especially stressed the need for research on agro-ethics, the need to better define new technology, and the need to deal with the various origins of technical change. We have seen the inadequacies of our theories concerning the distribution and adoption of new technology. Our researchers need to remedy these deficiencies by extending duality theory to include the endogenous determination of asset fixity and variability or, alternatively, investment and disinvestment. Serious questions exist about the empirical validity of macro-production functions and duality, which should be addressed by our more disciplinary workers. Similarly, the idea of frontier production functions is questionable as is the distinction between technical and economic efficiency. These questions should be investigated by agricultural economists and the underlying theory improved. We have seen something about the importance of holistic multidisciplinary research on technical change. More attention to holistic approaches will probably increase their respectability while revealing the deficiencies of the currently more respected modernistic research on technical change.

Switching to *subject matter research,* agricultural economists have much to contribute. Subject matter research involving technological change is multidisciplinary. My own participation on multidisciplinary teams has been particularly gratifying; however, I have been hampered by the deficiencies of general economics as discussed above. Still further, I have been hampered by our inability (and by positivistic rejection of the possibility) to do objective research on the values that conditions, situations, and things "really have." Agricultural economists will particularly need to research the impacts of technological change in the subject matter areas of farm management, land or resource economics, marketing, environmental studies, and policies. Changes in both production and electronic information and control technologies will have important impacts. The former will change supply, demand, and scale relationships in farming and agribusiness. They will also have impacts on land and water resources and, more generally, on the total environment. The latter will have great impacts on the management and operation of farms and agribusiness and, hence, on the structure of both agrarian and urban communities.

Policy studies for agriculture will need to consider the welfare impacts of changing technologies on the structures of our society as a whole, our agribusinesses including recreation and nonfarm natural industries, as well as our farming sector (Johnson 1983a, 1984b).

Problem-solving research involving technological change will continue to be important for the work of agricultural economists. Such research will need to be done in both the public and private sectors to support extension programs and to provide for and protect the interests of the public in the creation, use, and exploitation of new technologies. Because practical problems are volatile and ephemeral, it is difficult to indicate with any precision what they will be in the decades ahead. In general, they will be closely related to the foreseeable kinds of subject matter research outlined in the previous section.

EXTENSION WORK AND TECHNICAL CHANGE. Extension workers are seldom concerned with disciplinary questions. Instead, their technological concerns are mainly with (1) the dissemination of multidisciplinary subject matter research of relevance in considering problems involving new technology and (2) the solution of practical problems involving new technology. As there is really little difference between subject matter and problem-solving investigations done by extension workers, on one hand, and the subject matter and problem-solving research work done by researchers, on the other, the previous discussions of subject matter and problem-solving research are quite applicable to extension work. It is important to note that if researchers can restrain their disdain for subject matter and problem-solving research, they can often bring greater disciplinary excellence to bear on subjects and problem solving than can many extension workers. This can help, provided the disciplinary researchers remember to cooperate with researchers from other disciplines and to accord respectability to subject matter and problem-solving research and extension. Cooperation with extension workers has the advantage of making disciplinary researchers more relevant and of helping to keep their subject matter and problem solving better focused on the practical, private and social problems.

TEACHING AND TECHNICAL CHANGE. I turn now to teaching, with particular attention to the graduate teaching of agricultural economics (Fienup and Riley 1980; Johnson 1983b). Disciplinary excellence is required, not only in economics but in the ancillary disciplines of economics — mathematics, statistics, philosophy, logic, etc. But, that is not the end of the matter. The graduate training of agricultural economics should inculcate a respect for multidisciplinarity and research on values and prescriptions if agricultural economists are to be trained to do adequate subject matter and problem-solving work on technological change.

At the undergraduate level, it must be recognized that a relatively low percentage of our students will have research careers, and that many of them are headed for decision-making and administrative careers in agribusiness and in government. Clearly, if they are to be called agricultural economists they should have disciplinary knowledge of economics, but they need not receive substantial training in doing disciplinary research. That can be left for graduate study if they become graduate students. At the undergraduate level, they need to be taught to (1) respect multidisciplinary approaches to problem solving; (2) respect subject matter research; (3) understand the nature of value knowledge and of procedures for converting value-free and value knowledge into prescriptions; and (4) understand the importance for agriculture of the interrelationships among technical, institutional, and human change and capital growth.

CONSULTING AND ADVISING. Those agricultural economists who are engaged in consulting and advising are, in effect, more specialized extension workers though they often work on private account as both short- or long-term staff members. Again, the emphasis is on the practical (on subject matter and on problem solving). Multidisciplinarity and attention to the values and prescriptions as well as to value-free knowledge is important for consulting and advising on technical change.

ADMINISTRATORS AND ENTREPRENEURS. Public administrators and private entrepreneurs can be regarded as more or less permanently employed consultants and advisors who bear even greater responsibility than consultants and advisors for the decisions they make and influence. Their emphasis is more on problem solving and less on subject matter than the interests of consultants, advisors, and extension workers. As problem solvers, value knowledge is as important as value-free knowledge and the stress is almost wholly on the prescriptive. The technical dimensions of the practical problems they address will be important but not predictably more or less important than the institutional, human, and capital growth dimensions.

References

Arrow, K. J. 1963. *Social Choice and Individual Values.* 2d ed. New York: John Wiley & Sons.
Baquet, A. E. 1979. A Theory of Investment and Disinvestment Including Optimal Lives, Maintenance, and Usage Rates for Durables. Ph.D. diss., Michigan State Univ.

Beringer, C. 1956. Problems in Finding a Method to Estimate Marginal Value Productivities for Input and Investment Categories on Multiple-Enterprise Farms. In *Resource Productivity, Returns to Scale, and Farm Size,* 106–13. Ames: Iowa State College Press.

Binswanger, H. P., and V. W. Ruttan, eds. 1978. *Induced Innovation: Technology, Institutions, and Development.* Baltimore: Johns Hopkins Univ. Press.

Bonnen, J. T. 1985. United States Agrarian Development: Transforming Human Capital and Institutions. In *United States-Mexico Relations: Agriculture and Rural Development.* Stanford: Stanford Univ. Press.

Boulding, K. 1981. Evolutionary Economics. Beverly Hills: Sage Publications.

Bowen, H. R. 1982. *The State of the Nation and the Agenda for Higher Education.* San Francisco: Jossey-Bass.

Brown, A. W. A., T. C. Byerly, M. Bitts, and A. San Pietro, eds. 1975. Crop Productivity—Research Imperatives. Proceedings of an International Conference, Oct. 20–24, 1975, Boyne Highlands, Mich.

Edwards, C. 1959. Resource Fixity and Farm Organization. *J. Farm Econ.* 41:747–59.

Farrell, M. J. 1957. The Measurement of Productive Efficiency. *J. Royal Stat. Soc.* 120:253–81.

Fienup, D. F., and H. M. Riley. 1980. *Training Agricultural Economists for Work in International Development.* New York: Agricultural Development Council.

Friedman, M. 1953. *Essays in Positive Economics.* Chicago: Univ. of Chicago Press.

Halter, A. N., and G. W. Dean. 1971. *Decisions Under Uncertainty with Research Applications.* Cincinnati: South-Western Publishing.

Harsanyi, J. C. 1982. Mortality and the Theory of Rational Behaviour. In *Utilitarianism and Beyond,* ed. A. Sen and B. Williams. Cambridge: Cambridge Univ. Press.

Johnson, G. L. 1957. Agricultural Economics, Production Economics, and the Field of Farm Management. *J. Farm Econ.* 38:441–50.

———. 1958. Supply Functions—Some Facts and Notions. In *Agricultural Adjustment Problems in a Growing Economy,* ed. E. O. Heady et al. Ames: Iowa State College Press.

———. 1960. Value Problems in Farm Management. *Agric. Econ. J.* 14:13–31.

———. 1976. Philosophical Foundations: Problems, Knowledge, and Solutions. Agricultural Change and Economic Method. *Eur. Rev. Agric. Econ.* 3:207–34.

———. 1977. Contributions of Economists to a Rational Decision-making Process in the Field of Agricultural Policy. In *Decision Making and Agriculture,* ed. T. Dams and K. E. Hunt, 592–608. Oxford: Oxford Agricultural Economics Inst.

———. 1980. Ethical Issues and Energy Policies. In *Increasing Understanding of Public Problems and Policies—1980,* Proceedings of the 30th National Public Policy Education Conference, Vail, Colorado.

———. 1982a. Agro-Ethics: Extension, Research, and Teaching. *South. J. Agric. Econ.* 14:1–10.

———. 1982b. An Opportunity Cost View of Fixed Asset Theory and the Overproduction Trap: Comment. *Am. J. Agric. Econ.* 64:773–75.

———. 1982c. Small Farms in a Changing World. In *Small Farms in a Changing World: Prospects for the Eighties,* 7–28. Manhattan: Kansas State Univ., Paper No. 2.

_____. 1983a. Synoptic View. In *Growth and Equity in Agricultural Development,* ed. A. Maunder and K. Ohkawa, 592–608. England: Gower Publ. Co. Ltd.

_____. 1983b. The Relevance of U.S. Graduate Curricula in Agricultural Economics for the Training of Foreign Students. *Am. J. Agric. Econ.* 65:1142–48.

_____. 1984a. Toward the Twenty-first Century: U.S. Agriculture in an Unstable World Economy: Discussion. *Am. J. Agric. Econ.* 66:597–98.

_____. 1984b. Ethics, Economics, Energy, and Food Conversion Systems. In *Food and Energy Resources,* ed. D. Pimentel and C. W. Hall, 147–180. Orlando: Academic Press, Inc.

_____. Forthcoming a. Risk Aversion vs. Aversion for Losses and Risk Preference vs. Preference for Gain. In *Annals of Agricultural Sciences,* Series G. Warsaw: Polish Academy of Sciences.

_____. Forthcoming b. Economics and Ethics. In *Centennial Review,* 24th Annual Centennial Review Lecture. East Lansing: Michigan State Univ.

_____. Forthcoming c. Holistic Modeling of Multidisciplinary Subject Matter and Problematic Domains. In *Systems Economics,* ed. D. G. Miles. Ames: Iowa State Univ. Press.

Johnson, G. L., and J. Brown. 1980. An Evaluation of the Normative and Prescriptive Content of the Department of Energy Mid-term Energy Forecasting System (MEFS) and the Texas National Energy Modeling Project (TNEMP). In *Texas National Energy Modeling Project: An Experience in Large-Scale Model Transfer and Evaluation,* Part III, ed. M. L. Holloway. Austin: Texas Energy and Natural Resources Advisory Council.

Johnson, G. L. and L. Quance. 1972. *The Overproduction Trap in U.S. Agriculture.* Baltimore: Johns Hopkins Univ. Press.

Johnson, G. L., and S. H. Wittwer. 1984. Agricultural Technology Until 2030: Prospects, Priorities, and Policies. Agricultural Experiment Station Special Report 12. East Lansing: Michigan State Univ.

Johnson, G. L., and L. Zerby. 1973. What Economists Do About Values—Case Studies of Their Answers to Questions They Don't Dare Ask. East Lansing: Dept. of Agric. Econ., Michigan State Univ.

Johnson, M. A., and E. C. Pasour, Jr. 1981. An Opportunity Cost View of Fixed Asset Theory and the Overproduction Trap. *Am. J. Agric. Econ.* 63:1–7.

_____. 1982. An Opportunity Cost View of Fixed Asset Theory and the Overproduction Trap: Reply. *Am. J. Agric. Econ.* 64:776–77.

Keynes, J. M. 1963. *Scope and Method of Political Economy.* London: Macmillan.

Knight, F. H. 1933. *The Economic Organization.* Chicago: Univ. of Chicago Press.

Kopp, R. J., and V. K. Smith. 1980. Frontier Production Function Estimates for Steam Electric Generation: A Comparative Analysis. *South. Econ. J.* 46:1049–59.

Lewis, W. A. 1949. *Overhead Costs.* London: Allen and Unwin.

McClennen, E. F. 1983. Rational Choice and Public Policy: A Critical Survey. *Social Theory and Practice* 9:335–79.

McCloskey, D. N. 1983. The Rhetoric of Economics. *J. Econ. Lit.* 21:481–517.

McFadden, D. 1978. Cost, Revenue, and Profit Functions. In *Production Economics: A Dual Approach to Theory and Applications,* ed. M. Fuss and D. McFadden. Amsterdam: North Holland Publishing.

Myrdal, G. 1944. *The American Dilemma.* New York: Harper Brothers.

National Academy of Sciences. 1977. *World Food and Nutrition Study: The Potential Contributions of Research.* Washington, D. C.: Commission on International Relations, National Research Council.

Pond, W. G., R. A. Merkel, L. D. McGilliard, and V. J. Rhodes, eds. 1980. *Animal Agriculture: Research to Meet Human Needs in the 21st Century.* Boulder: Westview Press.

Reder, M. W. 1948. *Studies in the Theory of Welfare Economics.* New York: Columbia Univ. Press.

Robbins, L. 1932. *An Essay on the Nature and Significance of Economic Science.* London: Macmillan.

Robison, L., and B. Fleisher. 1983. Risk: Can We Model What We Can't Define or Measure? In *Risk Management Strategies for Agricultural Production Firms,* Proceedings of a seminar held March 28–30, 1983 in San Antonio, Texas.

Rossmiller, G. E., ed. 1978. *Agricultural Sector Planning: A General System Simulation Approach.* Agricultural Sector Analysis and Simulation Projects. East Lansing: Dept. of Agric. Econ., Michigan State Univ.

Ruttan, V. W., and Y. Hayami. Forthcoming. Induced Technological Change in Agriculture. Proceedings of a Workshop Developing a Framework for Assessing Future Changes in Agricultural Productivity held July 16–18, 1984.

Sagoff, M. 1985. Values and Preferences. College Park: Center for Philosophy and Public Policy, Univ. of Maryland.

Schmid, A. Forthcoming. Property Rights in Seeds and Micro-Organisms. In *Public Policy and the Physical Environment,* ed. R. K. Godwin and H. Ingram. Greenwich, Conn.: JAI Press.

Schmidt, P., and C. A. Knox-Lovell. 1977. Estimating Technical and Allocative Inefficiency Relative to Stochastic Production and Cost Frontiers. Econometrics Workshop Paper No. 7702. East Lansing: Dept. of Econ., Michigan State Univ.

Schoemaker, P. J. H. 1982. The Expected Utility Model: Its Variants, Purposes, Evidence, and Limitations. *J. Econ. Lit.* 20:529–63.

Timmer, P. C. 1970. On Measuring Technical Efficiency. *Food Research Institute Studies in Agricultural Economics, Trade, and Development* 9:99–171.

Tversky, A., and D. Kahneman. 1981. The Framing of Decisions and the Psychology of Choice. *Science* 211:453–58.

Technological Innovations with Implications for Agricultural Economics: **A Discussion**

NEIL E. HARL

In general I have little disagreement with Professor Johnson's paper. Agricultural economists have come to expect a high level of professional competence in his writings and this paper is no exception. I am particularly impressed with his emphasis on the point that "The theories relevant for the study of technological change are . . . drawn from many disciplines other than economics." Indeed, I struggled with some aspects of that problem area in my presidential address to the American Agricultural Economics Association in 1983 (Harl 1983, 849–50).

In traditional fashion, therefore, I have elected to focus on several areas that are not covered in the paper or are dealt with only tangentially.

Resource Adjustment

The title of Professor Johnson's paper, "Technological Innovation with Implications for Agricultural Economics," suggests a breadth of approach that is consistent with reality. In keeping with the conventional wisdom that knowledge is increasing at a rate that bears some resemblance to an exponential growth curve, agriculture will be a participant in a technology growth process producing what promises to be the greatest period of technological growth since the dawn of civilization. That is, unless agriculture is nudged into the technological backwater with attention directed elsewhere, and that hardly seems likely. Certainly the economic gains from technology in agriculture promise to be nontrivial. Yet one of the issues for agricultural economists is the extent to which technology is driven by the promise of economic gain and the position of the agricultural sector vis-à-vis other sectors in affording opportunities for gains from technological developments.

PROBLEMS OF ECONOMIC ADJUSTMENT. With much of the new technology likely to be output-increasing or cost-decreasing in nature, or both, one major implication for agriculture is almost certain to be massive and con-

Neil E. Harl is Charles F. Curtiss Distinguished Professor in Agriculture and Professor of Economics, Iowa State University, Ames, and member of the Iowa Bar.

tinuing resource adjustment. In fact, matters of resource adjustment as technological developments occur are likely to constitute large and continuing challenges for the agricultural sector. It is well to keep in mind that agriculture is heading into the coming era with

1. A chronic capacity on the part of U.S. agriculture to overproduce at prevailing price relationships;

2. A staggering debt load for U.S. agriculture in absolute terms, in relation to farm income and with respect to assets for those most heavily indebted;

3. Falling farmland values in the United States, Canada, and in several other food-producing regions of the world, in line with the realities of high real interest rates, the ineffectiveness of the demand for food in some areas of the world and the realities of international trade;

4. An enormous debt burden for much of the Third World, which is likely to dampen for some time the demand for food to upgrade diets and to assure a minimum level of diet;

5. Shifts in preferences for food as dietary concerns assume a greater role in shaping the demands for food; and

6. Striking increases in levels of food production in several major food-producing regions of the world in recent years in such countries as the People's Republic of China where institutional change has played a major role, and in countries such as Brazil and Argentina where capital availability has made it possible to bring large areas of previously uncultivated land into production.

Certainly concern about overproduction and food demand would suggest caution in assuming, as has been generally believed for much of the past half-century, that agriculture will grow out of its problem of overproduction and will need to "strive for a 60 percent increase in capacity by 2010 and a 100 percent increase by 2030." (Johnson, 85–86). The expectations generated by such statements may be as difficult to sustain in the future as they have in the past for U.S. agriculture.

Even with the deepening concern about productivity in the agricultural sector, particularly loss of productivity because of soil erosion, new technology coupled with further change in institutions to provide greater economic incentives for producers (such as in the USSR) seem almost certain, before the end of this century, to provoke enormously significant resource adjustments in agriculture worldwide.

One likely result of new technology in agriculture is an increase in production from a given amount of inputs. Thus, the level of utilization of some inputs may decline; use may be made of lower quality inputs; or the level of inputs could remain constant with production levels increasing. The adjustment process promises to be particularly protracted for land as a production input. With increases in productivity and in light of the price and income inelasticity of demand for primary food products, continuing pressure on land values appears highly probable. Marginal lands for areas impacted by new technology would be expected to shift to lower uses on the value scale. If the societal interest is in maintaining a level of agricultural output, attention would be expected to focus on reductions in levels of inputs or use of lower quality inputs in production. This could permit some easing of concern about soil conservation, for example, if an increase in production per acre of land under cultivation were to occur as a result of technological developments. If the national interest is in maintaining a particular level of production, the public interest would be well served with investment in research in new technologies with the potential for reducing the utilization level for inputs of greater present value than the present value of the research investment.

Without a doubt, the adjustment problems stemming from or induced by technological developments are likely to pose for agricultural economics and agricultural economists opportunities for research and extension activity unparalleled in modern time.

WHO BENEFITS FROM NEW TECHNOLOGIES? A related question involves the issue of who ultimately benefits from new technology and in what proportions—farmers, consumers, input suppliers, or output processors. In many instances, consumers tend to be the major beneficiaries in the long run, with more output at a lower price. In a market characterized by highly elastic demand or by a rapid growth in demand, producers may retain a relatively large share of the gains from technical change. However, in a market characterized by relatively inelastic demand and by slow growth in demand, as is typically the case with food in high-income countries, most of the gains from technical change are passed along to consumers in the form of lower product prices. Only early adopters gain under competitive market conditions. Perhaps consumers do not yet understand that it is in their best economic interest to support subsidized research in areas of new technology in agriculture and to support institutional change such as tax inducements to increase the capital stock in agriculture and thus to increase production levels.

A related problem area of concern in both research and extension is the importance of anticipating technological change as investments are made. If major problems are to be avoided, expectations of investors need to be modified, based upon the best available information about anticipated change. It is likely in technical change that part of the existing capital stock will be reduced in productivity and, hence, in value. A major effort could be justified in developing and refining models of projected technological change with accompanying estimates of economic impact. In fact, elsewhere I have suggested that major efforts be made to assess the economic and social effects of developments of biotechnology after a development has a reasonable probability of being introduced (Harl 1984, 21).

Impact on Third World Economies

Professor Johnson's paper does not recognize the potential for differential economic impacts from new technologies between and among nations on the basis of stage or level of development. This promises to be an area of particular importance for agricultural economics because of the amount of international trade in agricultural commodities.

New technology may affect price and quality competition for products internationally. That is one compelling reason for the United States to press ahead relentlessly with research. A loss of comparative advantage could have far-reaching effects upon the balance of trade and upon domestic income levels.

Viewed from the standpoint of the Third World, the prospects for breakthroughs in new technologies hold both threats and promises. The matter of limited capability to carry on research, the limited capability of Third World countries to exploit technological developments, and the question of access to technological breakthroughs in the First World pose substantial economic obstacles to Third World nations. Moreover, adjustment problems in the Third World could be substantial. Anticipating the effects of new technologies is especially important in that developments are likely to have a direct impact on more economic sectors than the Green Revolution.

One of the significant problems faced by the Third World is the lack of an institutional framework for the development and diffusion of new technologies, especially the new biotechnologies. Certainly there exists a challenge to construct institutional arrangements appropriate for the circumstances of a particular country. The lack of strong public sector institutional structures poses quite different problems than is the case in developed countries. Quite clearly, the need exists for developing possible approaches to building Third World capacity to deal with the impact of new technology.

Without continued significant emphasis on technologies such as biotechnology in Third World countries, the terms of trade for many internationally traded commodities could deteriorate for Third World countries over the next several years. Stated bluntly, countries with a strong scientific base could raid the Third World gene pool, tilt production relationships in favor of the developed world, and sell the resulting products back to the Third World. Access of Third World countries to new technologies may be vital for their continued economic development. Land-grant universities with their unique linkage to Third World countries and their involvement in developing the new technologies may be the best hope for bridging the transfer of new technologies to the Third World in usable form.

Process of Adjustment

For all of the effects discussed thus far, market forces will be activated as new technologies are introduced and disseminated. For the category of effects from the introduction of new technologies, a major research and extension contribution may be to (1) provide additional insight into the relative productivity of funds targeted toward maintaining or enhancing productivity in agriculture; (2) anticipate the effects of adjustments likely to be caused by the introduction of new technologies; (3) quantify the adjustments anticipated; (4) provide needed insights into the redirection and redeployment of resources; and, in some instances (5) ease the economic pain from adjustment by appropriate compensation. As Ruttan (1972) notes, the economic gains from increases in productivity are diffused broadly and the costs should be borne broadly.

For colleges and universities the adjustments may create strained relationships with some of the traditional support groups for research and extension. The adjustments will affect input suppliers and, in some instances, output processors. In some cases, the adjustments may be modest and permit a gradual adaptation to a new economic order. In others, the effects may cause considerable economic trauma. As one example of the problems that may arise, land-grant universities have engaged in a unique division of labor in plant breeding with breeding carried on in the state agricultural experiment stations that release seedstock to seed companies in the private sector. Seed varieties that are the products of substantial capital and human expenditures by publicly funded scientists and facilities will focus attention on the problems of protecting adequately the public interest.

It is not too early to begin educational efforts to sensitize individuals to the potential gains and losses that may result from research in technology.

Implications for Resource Allocation

Although not of immediate importance to agricultural economics but of strong secondary importance is the likely impact of expectations about new technologies on public resource allocation including resource allocation within universities. Perceptions about a high potential payoff from technological development appear likely to influence resource allocation within particular areas of scientific inquiry, between areas of inquiry, and, to a degree, between research and other functions within institutions carrying on research in areas likely to produce technological development with large positive economic consequences. The potential problems amenable to research attention range from compensation levels for professional-level personnel to problems of conflict of public interest as relationships between research programs and private industry become more intimate and intense.

Relative Costs of Labor and Capital

Professor Johnson considers briefly the relative cost of labor as a factor influencing the generation of new technology. If expectations are that labor will have a high and rising cost and capital will be relatively cheap, it should be reasonably expected that capital will substitute for labor, including capital expenditures for research in areas likely to produce technological developments that substitute capital for labor and capital expenditures for implementation of short-term spin-offs from research. On the other hand, perceptions that capital cost will be high and labor cost plateauing or declining could have a quite different effect. Wide swings in the real cost of capital within the past decade underscore the potential importance of this variable. One could, of course, hypothesize that the current costs of labor and capital are relatively unimportant under an assumption that investment behavior with respect to research is a long-run phenomenon. If indeed that is true, a long-term trend toward greater cost per unit of labor with less relative change expected in the cost per unit of capital appears to be a prospect.

Relationship to Institutional Change

Recognition by Professor Johnson that "technological advance is closely related to institutional improvements and the development of human capital" (Johnson, 90) is highly appropriate. However, the discussion obscures the duality of the problem: (1) the relationship between institutional arrangements and productivity, quite apart from new technology, and (2) the relationships between technological advance and institutional arrangements. Certainly one can find no clearer example of the former than the changes in institutional rules in China since 1978 and the substantial increases in productivity that have followed.

References

Harl, N. E. 1983. Agricultural Economics: Challenges to the Profession. *Am. J. Agric. Econ.* 65:845–54.

Harl, N. E. 1984. University/Industry Relations—Problems and Promise. Paper presented at the annual meeting of the American Association for the Advancement of Science, New York, May 28.

Ruttan, V. W. 1972. *Agricultural Research Policy*. Minneapolis: Univ. of Minnesota Press.

Technological Innovations with Implications for Agricultural Economists: **A Discussion**

RONALD D. KNUTSON

Professor Johnson's paper looks at technological change primarily from the perspective of a production economist. My comments are primarily from a research and extension policy perspective. The biotechnology and information revolution has major implications for policy regarding agricultural research and extension—implications that potentially surpass the mechanical revolution of the 1930 to 1950 period and the chemical revolution of the 1950 to 1980 period. It is my impression that Professor Johnson vastly underestimates these implications.

The Johnson paper makes many points that invite reaction and comment. My comments are limited to three central points: (1) the potentially profound impact that biotechnology and information technology may have on the structure of agriculture and its implications for the agricultural research and extension system; (2) the need for reevaluation of the role of agricultural research and extension in the biotechnology and information

Ronald D. Knutson is Professor and Extension Economist in the Agricultural and Food Policy Center, Department of Agricultural Economics, Texas A & M University, College Station.

Many of the ideas and implications discussed in this paper were developed during work on the Office of Technology Assessment study of the relationship between technology, farm structure, and public policy. The author benefited greatly from discussions with Michael J. Phillips, B. R. Adelman, Edward G. Smith, James Richardson, and many others. The views expressed here are those of the author.

technology era; and (3) some observations on how extension work can be most effectively accomplished in the biotechnology and information technology era.

Technology and Structure

When combined with the current financial crisis in agriculture, rapid biotechnological and information-technological change could be the final nail in the coffin of moderate size farms. This is the case for three primary reasons:

1. Technical and pecuniary economies of size throughout agriculture are becoming increasingly apparent (Smith 1982; Buxton 1985; Office of Technology Assessment 1985; Cooke 1985). Biotechnology and information technology are likely to further exaggerate the economic advantages of large-scale (and integrated) farms.

2. Technology adoption is not structurally neutral. Small and moderate size farms tend to lag in the adoption of new technology (Office of Technology Assessment 1985; Buxton 1985). While most small farms do not depend on farm income for their survival, moderate size farms tend to be operated by full-time farmers. Early adopters (large farms) reap the benefits of technological change to the detriment of the laggers (Cochrane 1958).

3. Biotechnology and information technology tend to be demonstrably more complex than most technological changes of the past. As indicated by Johnson, these new technologies create the need for complex farming systems. For example, the use of bovine growth hormone (BGH) to increase milk output per cow is not just a matter of a daily BGH injection; it requires a new mix of feed inputs including changes in the management function. Moderate size farms are less likely to be prepared to make such changes on a timely basis.

The demise of moderate size farms and the appearance of a bimodal farm structure have profound implications for agriculture, agribusiness, rural communities, and the land-grant universities (Office of Technology Assessment 1985). The development of an industrialized agriculture will diminish the need for the traditional local agribusiness structure of input suppliers, country banks, and marketing firms. In the process local communities will either dry up and/or have a clientele that is limited largely to part-time farmers. Large-scale farms will do their business in major agribusiness centers. Identifying those centers will be a key to agribusiness development in the future.

As this process of industrialization occurs, there will be a transformation in the agriculture component of the land-grant university system. While in the past agriculture schools have had an open, public service orientation, they will increasingly be transformed to the more closed, private service orientation of engineering and business schools. In the process, agricultural extension in all probability will shift to a survival mode emphasizing service to the needs of part-time farmers, urban gardeners, 4-H, and family living. Such potentialities, while seldom discussed in public, are nonetheless real—even today.

Administration of Research and Extension

In all probability, private-sector investment in agricultural research now exceeds public-sector investment (Office of Technology Assessment 1985). Since the enactment of the Plant Variety Protection Act in 1970 and the *Diamond* v. *Chakrabarty* decision in 1980, private-sector investment in agricultural research has tripled. Therefore, surprise can logically be raised about the assertion by Johnson that only minor adjustments may be needed in the mix of publicly supported research and extension. Surely, the granting of private-sector property rights and a tripling of private-sector investment relative to public-sector investment in agricultural research has major implications for the nature of the agricultural research and extension production function, related isoquants, cost functions, and price ratio, if not for the social welfare function upon which public-sector decisions are (or should be) based (Evenson 1983).

For example, consider the following illustrations:

• The biotechnology and information technology era has the potential for creating a series of "have" and "have not" universities. The "have" universities will be those that are (have been) able to attract substantial private-sector support, such as the University of California, Washington University, Cornell, and Stanford. Note that some of these universities are not land-grant universities. Lacking basic research talent, the problem-solving research base of the "have not" universities deteriorates. Likewise extension scientists do not have ready access to the high-technology research results.

• Inherent in the conference of private property rights is the potential for, if not the likelihood of, monopolistic pricing of the products of both public- and private-sector research. This occurs because both public- and private-sector research output will be patented and sold through the private sector on an exclusive basis. As a result, taxpayers who finance public-sector research in effect will be taxed twice—once when they pay for the research and once again when they purchase the products of research (whether intermediate inputs or final consumer goods). This process of "double taxation" could result in serious questions being raised about the logic of preferential treatment of publicly supported agricultural research, even though the real price of food may be falling.

From such illustrations, it can be seen that the research and extension administration process is not business as usual—much as our deans and directors might want our legislators to believe that nothing has changed. Agricultural research policy changes have thrown our land-grant university administrators into direct competition with one another for the support of the private sector, to become a "have" university. While "codes of conduct" have been developed among the land-grant administrators to protect the public interest, these codes are at best fragile in the competitive contest for scientific manpower, status, and even survival.

Extension Reactions

If these observations on the potential impact of biotechnology and information technology are anywhere near accurate, there are profound implications for how extension goes about its business. As previously indicated, the initial question facing extension administrators involves clientele. One might get the impression from the preceding comments that moderate size farms can just as well be written off. That is not my point. It does need to be recognized that moderate size farms are in very serious trouble, but not necessarily doomed.

Since the agriculture component of land-grant universities has a special public responsibility, they also have an obligation to give moderate size farms every opportunity to survive through the creation and transfer of new technology. For extension that responsibility is particularly great, since its unique public responsibility is technology transfer, and lags in technology adoption appear to be an important cause of moderate size farms' competitive problems. The 1985 farm bill contains several provisions that would mandate the targeting of research and extension programs toward the problems of moderate size farms. University administrators naturally cringe at such meddling by the Congress in "their business."

Studies of the structural neutrality issue suggest that, except possibly for some agricultural engineering projects, research has not necessarily been biased toward large-scale farming (White 1985). However, since one of the effects of the biotechnology and information technology era is to make the management function more complex, agricultural economists bear a special responsibility to develop management systems suited to moderate size farms. Such management systems must include farm production, marketing, and financial management components in a farming systems context. The development of such systems cannot be left to the extension farm management specialists nor to traditional farm management researchers. It must be interdisciplinary both within agricultural economics departments (management, marketing, and finance) and across departments (economics, business, entomology, plant science, animal science, etc.). Insightful leadership will be required to develop such farming systems for moderate size farms. Additionally, agricultural economists in the public sector are in all probability the only ones that would develop such moderate size farming systems. Private agribusiness firms will develop and implement farming systems for large-scale farms.

How will extension deliver such farming systems to moderate size farms? For that matter, how will extension deliver all forms of complex biotechnology and information technology to moderate size farms? Questions are arising as to whether county agents are equipped to perform the technology transfer function on future technology. It is sometimes suggested that many county agents may already be technologically obsolete. This question is not limited to county agents; it arises with regard to individuals within the agricultural economics profession as well. Some suggest that the county agent's role has changed from an educator to a facilitator of education, with specialists doing the educating. Questions then arise as to whether it is possible to justify the current county agent structure, education requirements, and salary levels for a meeting organizer. These are agonizing issues, but they are ones that must be faced head-on.

One other trend within extension is troubling. It relates to a perceived tendency of extension specialists to isolate themselves from researchers and to develop their own research base. The complaint is often made by extension specialists that "No research is being done that is relevant to my program." A logical response to such a complaint is "How long has it been since you talked to a researcher about your needs or attempted to find out what research is being done in the department?" My own experience suggests that much relevant research is going unused (on a timely basis) or unfostered because of a growing lack of communication between research and extension.

At least one caveat is warranted. As agricultural experiment station research moves toward the more basic side of the basic-applied continuum, limitations on research funds suggest that extension may need to become more involved in highly applied forms of research such as new biotech product testing or the development of software computer packages. Maybe there is a need to dust off the old Berkeley model where extension economists such as Farrell and Thor were serving the applied research as well as the extension needs of their constituents in the fields of marketing and policy. Additionally, better communication between research and extension clearly is needed.

Concluding Remarks

It can be seen that my remarks on technology issues run in very different directions than those of Professor Johnson. They also run in a different direction than those of research policy experts such as Ruttan (1982). This difference in approach serves to emphasize how broad and fertile biotechnology and information technology issues are for agriculturalists.

References

Buxton, B. 1985. *Economic, Policy, and Technology Factors Affecting Herd Size and Regional Location of U.S. Milk Production.* Washington, D.C.: Office of Technology Assessment.

Cochrane, W. W. 1958. *Farm Prices: Myth and Reality.* Minneapolis: Univ. of Minnesota Press.

Cooke, S. C. 1985. *Size Economies and Comparative Advantage in the Production of Corn, Soybeans, Wheat, Rice, and Cotton in Various Areas of the United States.* Washington, D.C.: Office of Technology Assessment.

Diamond v. Chakrabarty. 1980. 447 U.S. 303.

Evenson, R. E. 1983. Intelligent Property Rights and Agribusiness Research and Development: Implications for the Public Agricultural Research System. *Am. J. Agric. Econ.* 65:967–75.

Ruttan, V. 1982. *Agricultural Research Policy.* Minneapolis: Univ. of Minnesota Press.

Smith, E. G. 1982. Economic Impact of Current and Alternative Farm Programs on Farm Structure in the Southern High Plains. Ph.D. diss., Texas A & M Univ., College Station.

Smith, E. G., J. W. Richardson, and R. D. Knutson. 1984. *Cost and Pecuniary Economies in Cotton Production and Marketing: A Study of Texas Southern High Plains Cotton Producers.* College Station: Texas Agricultural Experiment Station.

U.S. Congress. Office of Technology Assessment. 1985. *Technology, Public Policy, and the Changing Structure of Agriculture: A Special Report for the 1985 Farm Bill.* Washington, D.C.: GPO.

White, F. C. 1985. Economic Impact of Agricultural Research and Extension. *Technology, Public Policy, and the Changing Structure of Agriculture.* Office of Technology Assessment. Washington, D.C.: GPO.

6

Domestic Food and Agricultural Policy Research Directions

LUTHER TWEETEN

No statement could better summarize nor sober what I am about to attempt than the words of T. W. Schultz (1964, 1004):

> A particular profession can become obsolete. We, too, are subject to these risks. Thus it should be salutary, now and then, to remove our workday blinders and look at our approach to agricultural economics, the problems on our research agenda, the tools we use, and the way we are organized. Yet I marvel at how often we do this and how little of it is conducive to any beneficial results.

Schultz's caveat notwithstanding, I proceed recognizing that domestic food and agricultural research priorities must be designed not for the emotions and wants of the past or present but for perceived needs of the future. To help in that design is the purpose of this paper.

The first section of this paper is mostly descriptive economics; it summarizes and synthesizes what we think we know or would like to know about the economic structure and problems of food and agriculture. The second section deals with prescriptive economics; given the economic problems and structure of agriculture, what are the implications of alternative public policies to alleviate economic ills? A central theme here is that our prescriptive economics has been narrow and underutilized.

Emphasis herein is on agricultural rather than food policy. Policy issues regarding macroeconomic policies, international trade, and resource economics are discussed elsewhere and are treated only peripherally in this

Luther Tweeten is Regents Professor, Department of Agricultural Economics, Oklahoma State University, Stillwater. Comments of Filmore Bender, Bruce Bullock, Don Paarlberg, Daryll Ray, and other reviewers were very helpful. Of course, the author is solely responsible for shortcomings of this paper.

paper. The scope of agricultural policy as treated herein closely follows that employed by Brandow (1977) in "Policy for Commercial Agriculture." Although attention is on research, what I say also has implications for teaching and extension. Before suggesting broad research thrusts and selected specific research priorities, I will briefly outline the past and prospective economic environment for food and agricultural policy and for research.

Descriptive Overview

This section describes the economic environment for food and agricultural policy, and reviews trends in aggregate supply and demand. It also contains a synthesis to explain emerging agricultural problems—a synthesis contrasted with that advanced four decades ago by T. W. Schultz. Data and analysis gaps are noted. The tough philosophical and methodological questions await the later section on prescriptive economics, however.

PAST AND PROSPECTIVE ECONOMIC TRENDS. The political-economic environment for food and agriculture and, hence, also for research priorities depends heavily on whether the future is dominated by abundance and a depressed agricultural economy or by shortage and high food prices. In the former environment, economic issues of farmers predominate. In the latter environment, economic issues of food and consumers predominate.

Predictions for the future are rooted in the past. The food and agricultural economy has been dominated by protracted periods of unfavorable or favorable conditions, the latter often associated with wars. For example, farmers generally experienced "hard times" from the end of the Civil War to 1896, with both the 1870s and 1880s punctuated by bursts of economic panic and farm protest movements (Tweeten 1979). Farmers blamed railroads, grain exchanges, banks, the gold standard, and middlemen for their problems.

Then followed 25 years of generally favorable times for farmers. The hard times that returned in the 1920s got worse in the 1930s. Relief was attempted through cooperative input purchases and marketing and through modest commodity stock acquisitions by the Federal Farm Board. By the early 1930s these timid approaches were swamped by events. In 1933, a major government role in supporting farm prices and incomes emerged that has remained to this day. Prosperity returned to the farm from 1941 to the mid-1950s and again from 1973 to 1980.

Several conclusions can be drawn from past experience. Periods of farm distress or prosperity, though sometimes extended, may be getting shorter. Agriculture is unstable because it depends on the unpredictable forces of nature. But the long-term periods of farm recession and prosperity were "man-made." Low prices in the 1870s and 1880s stemmed from a conscious public decision to open new lands, which increased production. Tight money supply and deflation were also factors, but so little was known of the theory or application of monetary policy that it would be hard to blame damage to the farming economy on money conspiracy.

High tariffs and failure to maintain money supply helped to make the 1920s and 1930s more unfavorable than they needed to be. Rapid advances in productivity (largely a product of prior private and public investments in agricultural research, extension, and education) played a key role in the economic difficulties of farmers in the 1950s and 1960s. Soviet grain purchases helped to bring farm prosperity from 1973 to 1980.

Erratic and overly expansionary monetary policies (aggravated by the energy crisis) in the late 1970s caused inflation. Tight monetary policy to restrain inflation brought nationwide recession in 1981 and 1982. High real interest and exchange rates since 1982, stemming partly from high structural federal deficits, continue the litany of farm economic ills caused by man rather than by nature.

Commodity programs probably helped to reduce variation in farm and food prices since 1933, but commodity programs did not serve long-term goals such as raising net farm income, alleviating poverty, preserving the family farm, or conserving the soil (Tweeten 1984; Batie 1983). In summary, the nation has a spotty record of economic policy to reduce economic shocks to agriculture or to alleviate the consequences. It is easy to believe that with appropriate economic policy research and education the nation could do better.

In looking to the future, it is cautioned that forecasters tend to be captive to current circumstances. When times are unfavorable, the tendency is to project pessimism. When times are favorable, the tendency is to project optimism. Simply expecting current conditions to continue for the indefinite future has always been incorrect. Given these uncertainties, economic research, like food and agricultural policy itself, must be designed for all seasons.

Recent studies (O'Brien 1984; Resources for the Future 1984) anticipate slightly faster rates of increase in supply than in demand for food and other farm products for the next decade or two. This implies declining real farm prices in the United States and the world. No *strong* downward trend in real farm prices is projected, but there will be considerable variation around the long-term trend. Although real food prices will rise temporarily from time to time, and world food crises will appear on rare occasions, the world's capacity to produce food will not be challenged. Food problems will be severe in some regions, especially Africa, however.

UNDERSTANDING THE CAUSES OF FARM PROBLEMS. Agricultural economists have invested intellectual capital in understanding the economic structure of agriculture and thereby the problems of low prices and incomes,
instability, and poverty. Because it was the clearest and most comprehensive
statement of its time and because many economists built on his work, T. W.
Schultz's (1945) synthesis of four decades ago is worth repeating. The principal elements were:

1. New technology and public resource development (e.g., irrigation
projects) caused farm productivity to increase and caused a substitution of
capital for farm labor.

2. The competitive structure of the farming industry made it inevitable that farmers would adopt new technology. High fixed costs relative to
variable costs meant that farmers tended to keep farms in full production
even when prices were well below full costs of production. Profitable and
productive new capital inputs were introduced even when excessive land
and labor were committed to agriculture.

3. Demand for farm output increased slowly. A major reason was the
low income elasticity of demand.

4. Because supply persistently advanced relative to demand for farm
output, the result was "chronic disequilibrium adverse to agriculture."

5. Agriculture was constantly burdened with excess labor and lower
earnings than in the nonfarm sector because labor mobility was impeded by
lack of education and skills, poor health, lack of knowledge of nonfarm
job opportunities, racial discrimination, employment barriers of organized
labor, and government regulation.

6. The agricultural economy was unstable. Agriculture's economic
structure made it especially sensitive to instability in the industrial
economy. Schultz predicted that chronic surpluses were likely to put in their
appearance between 1947 and 1950.

His predictions left much to be desired, but Schultz's synthesis provided hypotheses for research for a decade and more. Times have changed,
however, and a new synthesis must form the basis for understanding farm
problems.

Productivity has indeed continued to expand farm output. Capital
continues to substitute for labor and the farming industry continues to
adopt new technology when it is profitable to do so. But on the whole,
demand has expanded at nearly the same rate as productivity since 1945. It
is quite a coincidence that aggregate farm input volume was exactly the
same in 1984 as when Schultz published his book in 1945 (Council of
Economic Advisors 1985, 340). The best single predictor of long-term

trends in real farm prices has been the change in real cost of production brought about by productivity gains in agriculture.

Some excess labor remains in agriculture but farm population had nearly stabilized by 1980. Farm income per capita adjusted for tax advantages, the farm way of life, and for cost of living no longer chronically lags income per capita of nonfarmers.

Studies (Tweeten 1979; 1983b, 924) indicate that long-term demand and supply of farm commodities are elastic. This elasticity is one reason why commercial agriculture does not display long-term tendencies to low income or low rates of return.

A large reservoir of excess labor in agriculture no longer exists but excess labor remains a problem on many midsize and small farms. Ability of the nonfarm sector to assimilate labor from agriculture is no longer in doubt; the excess is a small portion indeed of the nonfarm labor force. Schooling and other human resource investments in farm people have dramatically improved in the past four decades. Still, human resource and poverty problems on farms have diminished much less rapidly than our economic research and education on those problems. Poverty characterizes an estimated 20 percent of farm families. Rural areas, after resurgence in the 1970s, once again lag behind urban areas in employment and population growth. Given that farm families depend on nonfarm sources for two-thirds of their income, it is surprising that rural development policy research and education have been allowed to fall into disrepair and obscurity.

A principal remaining characterization by Schultz is instability in agriculture. Short-run demand and supply tend to be inelastic, making farm prices and incomes highly sensitive to shocks from nature and man.

In summary, the following features characterize today's agricultural economy:

1. Inelastic short-run demand and supply make farm prices and incomes highly sensitive to shocks to either supply or demand.

2. Elastic long-run demand and supply give agriculture capabilities to adjust over time to productivity advances, even if supply outruns demand for farm output by the fairly narrow margins anticipated for the next two decades.

3. Agriculture continues to be buffeted by forces of nature and public policy. Because of heavy dependence on off-farm and export earnings, agriculture is now influenced by macroeconomic policies more through resource input and commodity export markets than through domestic commodity demand. It is less buffeted by business cycles than in the past but more buffeted by inflation cycles and other man-made forces of macroeconomic and trade policies. Financial stress and cash-flow problems can

persist for several years while resources earn less than their acquisition cost but more than their salvage value.

4. Agriculture is characterized by high capital investment per worker (twice the rate for industry as a whole), by net debtorship (farmers owe others $100 for each $23 owed to farmers), and by dependence on exports. Each of these factors makes agriculture especially sensitive to macroeconomic and trade policies that influence real interest and exchange rates. Heavy reliance on real estate assets also makes the farming industry sensitive to cash-flow problems caused by inflation. Inflation also causes cost-price problems because, other things being equal, input prices rise more quickly than product prices (Tweeten 1983a).

5. Agriculture is a heterogenous industry not easily classified, but three farm types stand out for policy purposes. One is large farms with annual sales of $200,000 or more. Many of these are larger-than-family-size, use sophisticated management and marketing techniques to cope with cash-flow and instability problems, realize resource returns at least comparable to returns on similar resources in the nonfarm sector, and have income and wealth well above that of the average consumer or taxpayer. Such farms account for only 5 percent of all farms but for half of farm output.

A second type of farm is the part-time small farm with sales under $40,000 per year. Such farms are inefficient as measured by opportunity cost of resources but survive and even thrive by using off-farm income to pay for consuming a farm way of life, by using tax features to write off farm losses against nonfarm income, and by using publicly subsidized community services. Part-time small farms have consistently favorable total income and are rarely in poverty. Small farms account for only 13 percent of farm output (sales) and for about 70 percent of all farms.

Between these farms are midsized family farms with sales of $40,000 to $200,000 per year. Traditionally the backbone of agriculture and rural communities, these farms have fallen on hard times. On the average, they are less efficient than large farms (although averages deceive) and have less off-farm income than small farms to cope with cash-flow and instability problems. In the face of narrow profit margins and large capital requirements to form an economic unit, midsize family farms refinanced each generation find it more and more difficult to compete with small part-time farms and with large farms. They are declining not only in numbers but also in share of all farms and output. They lobby heavily for commodity programs.

A research agenda cannot be established and economic problems of agriculture cannot be understood without recognizing the above configuration of farms. Adequately sized, well-managed farms tend to be near economic equilibrium as measured by resource returns. Smaller farms accept low returns because farming is partly a consumption good. It follows that if large farms are breaking even and if other farms are not covering all resource costs, then rates of return will be below opportunity costs on the average for the farming industry, despite no disequilibrium in the sense of incentives for resources to shift elsewhere. Also, if a large proportion of farm income comes as capital gain as is normal in an inflationary economy and if the family farm must save and invest a large portion of income to control assets, then current rates of return on assets will be low and cash-flow problems severe even in a well-functioning farm economy. Thus alleged major farm problems of today are equilibrium problems in contrast to disequilibrium labor problems of Schultz's day.

SOME RESEARCH SUGGESTIONS. Many of the above features of the economic landscape are only dimly known. They must be regarded as unrejected hypotheses suitable for further testing. Data and analysis to promote understanding are often weak. A surfeit of farm data for national income accounts obscures the dearth of data to measure personal income by farm type and size. Much more needs to be known of the macroeconomic impacts of federal tax policies on agriculture, particularly of the tendency for the investment tax credit, rapid depreciation allowance, and interest write-offs to increase capital use and output, substitute capital for labor, speed the demise of family farms, and create excess capacity. Resource costs per unit of output along with other measures of production and market economies of size by commodity remain elusive or unavailable.

The profession is not in agreement on fundamental issues such as the capacity of the farming industry to adjust to changes in supply and demand, the impact of price supports and supply controls on farm exports, and the benefits and costs of an export cartel or other institutional interventions to create more "orderly" markets in agriculture. Also at issue is the impact of macroeconomic policies on farm-export demand. More reliable estimates of supply and demand parameters can narrow the range of disagreement among economists, farmers, and the public at large over such issues. More reliable parameters can also improve predictions of econometric models.

Much disagreement persists over the magnitude of basic parameters such as the elasticity of demand and supply—particularly long-run elasticities. The profession seems to favor precise estimates of an incorrect concept to less precise estimates of the correct concept. Estimates of the demand for farm output (Tweeten 1967) including export demand were largely ignored for several years. The profession instead relied on the low-price elasticity of domestic food demand to measure the relationship between price and aggregate demand. One result was surprise at the large impact of high support prices and value of the dollar on demand in the 1980s. The profession has used precise short-run supply elasticities to gauge supply response over long-run periods. Long-run estimates were available (Tweeten and Quance 1969) but some (Brandow 1977) even doubted whether long-run supply response had any meaning. One result was failure to foresee the long-term impact of government supports on excess capacity and slippage in commodity programs. For example, the wheat allotment base went from 53 million acres in 1975 to 93 million acres in 1985. Voluntary acreage diversion programs are supposed to raise income because they not only provide a direct payment but they presumably reduce output to bring higher prices and receipts working against an inelastic demand. However, wheat acreage harvested may have been greater in 1985 with a 30 percent diversion program than had there been no wheat program since 1975.

Some basic data series have been neglected. Aggregate productivity and yield trend data are limited, subject to major revision, or diminished in usefulness for analysis because of unavailability of data to adjust for weather. The rate of productivity growth in farm output per unit of conventional inputs was reported as summarized in Table 6.1.

Table 6.1.   Rate of productivity growth in farm output per unit of conventional inputs

	Published in:	
	1982	1985
Period	(Annual rate of increase %)	
1949–59	2.05	1.95
1959–69	1.70	1.75
1969–79	1.45	1.78

Source: Council of Economic Advisors 1985 and earlier issues.

Given demand for farm output increasing nearly 2 percent per year, the first set of data suggested falling rates of productivity advances and a bright future for farm prices and receipts in the 1980s if past trends continued. The revised numbers gave less reason for optimism.

Some basic data are not collected or published by the Economic Research Service but would be especially helpful. As noted above, one is a weather index. Another is an index of excess or reserve farm production capacity, defined as expected production in excess of market utilization at current prices with normal weather. Such excess capacity exists because the government diverts production from markets with supply control, stock accumulation, and export subsidies. At some lower price, the market would clear. Of interest is not only the extent of reserve capacity and in what commodities it is concentrated, but what conditions would eliminate the reserve.

Pressing concerns in food and nutrition economics include the impact of alternative provisions for food stamp and welfare programs on nutrition of target groups. Of interest also is the impact on national health and on farmers' economic welfare of alternative measures, including nutritional guidelines, to improve diets. What are the costs and benefits of food protection and safety regulations to producers and consumers? These issues are not pursued in depth here; additional detail is provided elsewhere (U.S. Department of Agriculture 1985, 22, 23).

The data and research agenda could go on, but the time has come to attend to more philosophical issues. The above synthesis constitutes an economic setting and descriptive paradigm. The challenge is to analyze the implications of this synthesis for public policy.

Prescriptive Economics

In public policy economics, researchers choose issues judged to be important to taxpayers, farmers, consumers, policymakers, and to themselves and the profession. I will make a case that domestic food and agricultural policy has been hampered by (1) an overly narrow conceptual paradigm, (2) misguided notions of who is our clientele, and (3) overspecialization. These factors influence prescriptive economics, which I defined as the analysis of options by economists to help policymakers and society decide what is the appropriate policy response to increase well-being of society confronted by economic issues such as posed in the previous section.

Our profession has sought intellectual integrity through a welfare economics paradigm defining the bounds of scientific inquiry. That paradigm for the most part has judged prescriptive economics as defined above to be unworthy because it is allegedly normative in the sense of being based on economists' value judgments of what ought to be. Instead, the argument goes, public policy economists ought to specify alternative means to reach ends given by the political system. The argument contends that economists are not to specify ends because they cannot measure utility and because, even if they could measure utility, it is the political system that must specify ends and make policy decisions.

In defending prescriptive economics, I will make a case for the following propositions:

1. Prescriptive economics need not be normative.
2. The old welfare economics of pareto optimality and political sys-

tem sovereignty is an inadequate guide to setting the research and education agenda in the economics of public policy.

3. The new welfare economics of promoting efficiency while dealing with equity questions through actual or potential compensation is also an inadequate guide to set a research and education agenda.

4. The profession needs to get on with the task of estimating a social welfare function for use in economic analysis and in setting the research agenda for public policy economics. Public policy economics needs to present options to improve well-being for society as a whole rather than only for farmers, taxpayers, or consumers. That requires specification of a social welfare function as objective and free as possible of value judgments of researchers.

PRESCRIPTIVE ECONOMICS NEED NOT BE NORMATIVE. It is traditional to divide economics into normative and positive dimensions. *Normative* has been used to define the economics of "what ought to be," hence advocacy of positions grounded on value judgments of researchers rather than on facts and logic, or the promotion of allocations dictated by some arbitrarily established norm such as profit maximization. *Positive* economics on the other hand deals with "what is," avoids value judgments regarding goodness or badness, avoids advocacy, and only specifies alternatives to obtain objectives or ends specified by the political process.

First, let us dispose of the concept of normative in its narrowest form. It is often defined as that part of economics that deals with goodness or badness. Presumably everything economists do is judged by someone to be useful (good). All economics is normative by this definition, and the terms positive and normative are best dropped here in favor of the terms descriptive and prescriptive economics. Without advocacy, *prescriptive* economics specifies alternative means to achieve ends such as greater income or well-being of farmers, taxpayers, consumers, and society. As Johnson and Quance (1972, 45) note, prescriptive economics can be objective in that the researcher subjects concepts to tests of consistency, clarity, and workability.

The prescriptive economics called for here is not normative in the sense of advocacy of either means or ends that are no more than value judgments of researchers. But descriptive economics raises the issue of what and whose ends are to be served and what alternatives are to be analyzed. Economics is commonly defined as the science of allocating scarce means among competing ends to satisfy those ends as fully as possible. Proximate ends may be food, leisure, income, or employment. At a higher level, the ends may be equity and efficiency. The ultimate end is variously called well-being, satisfaction, utility, or absence of pain. References to "pursuit of happiness" or other terms for well-being in national documents, ubiquitous pronouncements by politicians, and statements by individuals all point to well-being of people as the ultimate goal of an economic system. Economic theory is built around rational pursuit of utility by people. Johnson and Quance (1972, 21) state that "the U.S. farmer operates, in substantial part, as a profit and/or utility maximizer or a loss and/or disutility minimizer." The point is that public policy economists determining means to improve well-being of society are engaged in the positivistic economics of "what is" or "what could be" rather than the normative economics of "what ought to be." Alternatively, prescriptive economics may be viewed as "what if" or "if-then" propositions: "If society wishes to improve well-being, then the following options are means to that end." At issue is not whether individuals and society as a whole are trying to improve well-being; instead, the issue is how economists can help them in their quest.

INADEQUACY OF PARETO OPTIMALITY AND POLITICAL SYSTEM SOVEREIGNTY. Most of us were brought up to accept Robbinsonian wisdom that "Economics is not concerned with ends *as such*. It is concerned with ends in so far as they affect the disposition of means" (Robbins 1935, 30). Robbins's statement of positivistic economics leaves to the economist the role of specifying the implications of alternative means to reach ends given by the political process. The price system too is to be subservient to the ultimate sovereign, the political process. Summarizing the Robbinsonian role for the economist, I (Tweeten 1979, 526) stated some years ago:

> He is to be a "social" engineer concerned with specifying alternative ways of reaching given goals. He is to be concerned with "what is," not with the normative economics of "what ought to be." For economics to be an objective science, the economist must not make value judgments that entail interpersonal comparisons of utility. He cannot take sides in policies that make some worse off, others better off. He can be a technician but not an advocate. In the role of economist, he can be an adviser but not a politician. He can maintain a political dialogue only as long as politicians are asking the questions.

R. G. F. Spitze (1983, 240) advances a similar theme. His position is that economists should not substitute their values for those of an ever-changing society. It is difficult to fault that position. But he then goes on to imply that the political process expresses preferences of society.

Economists working for a private firm or individual quite properly might show one person how to aggrandize himself at the expense of society. But publicly employed economists are hired by the public at large to show alternative means to improve the well-being of society. It is usually possible to make some individual or group better off by making someone worse off. But it is rarely possible to make someone better off without making someone else worse off. Maximizing income for farmers or any other one group will not do in public policy. Well-being must consider trade-offs and, hence, ultimately must consider the welfare of society as a whole.

Acceptance of the political process as the expression of the ends of society is to accept a flawed and biased social welfare function. The political process is fragmented and distorted. Public policy economists salaried by tax dollars are not doing their job if they restrict their analysis only to alternative means to reach goals specified by farmers, agribusiness firms, consumers, taxpayers, Congressman X, or by the political process.

This conclusion must not confuse roles of government and science. Government legislates. Economic science informs. The decision process is best informed when economists specify implications of a full range of ends. Public policy economics also informs indirectly: Research, education, and extension inform the public, which in turn influences government through public opinion and the vote. Public policy economists who solely wait for government to specify the research and education menu contribute to government failure, an inevitable consequence of an uninformed public and a selectively informed government.

INADEQUACY OF THE NEW WELFARE ECONOMICS OF EFFICIENCY. Gardner (1984, 62) takes issue with Spitze's fundamentally conservative

> . . . "quietism," whose essential feature is acceptance of policies as they exist based on a presumption that what a democratically elected government decides in matters of farm policy represents legitimate and appropriate public choice that, whatever criticisms we may make of it from an economist's viewpoint, cannot be objectively claimed inferior to any alternative.

Gardner escapes from the Robbinsonian trap only to fall into the confines of new welfare economics. It has been fashionable under the "new welfare economics" to argue that policies can be recommended if economic efficiency is improved so that gainers can compensate losers. Gardner (1981, 73) advances prescriptive economics by showing income redistributions among taxpayers, producers, and consumers, as well as changes in national income as measured by net social cost under alternative policy interventions. He does not wait for the political process to request such information.

For such classical welfare analysis to guide policy decisions that assure improving well-being of society, winners must compensate losers with transfers that do not distort incentives for efficiency. Because any kind of compensation, let alone nondistorting transfers, is generally impractical, two options are open: (1) pursue efficiency without regard to the distribution of gains and losses, or (2) estimate a social welfare function giving weight to equity and efficiency so that these components may be aggregated and options compared for their contribution to well-being. Gardner selects (1) and rejects (2). In his (1984, 49) words:

> The main sustained attempt to provide an objective "public in-terest" ground for the critique of policy, arising from compensation principles in welfare economics, fizzles out with the practical impossi-bility of nondistorting transfers. This throws us back, analytically, on the social welfare function. Unless we know it, there is little we can criticize, and we don't know it.

By ruling out compensation or redistribution of income because such policies reduce economic efficiency, Gardner joins other economists in a trap which is a variant of new welfare economics. By implicitly holding that efficiency is of infinite value and equity is of no value, economists can pursue allocations to raise efficiency without regard to equity. That leaves economics of little or no help to policymakers in confronting the great issues of our time, such as how large a safety net to provide farmers or anyone else, how to provide distributive justice, and how to estimate welfare trade-offs between economic efficiency and equity.

Public policy economists seeking to avoid social welfare functions, marginal utility of income, and aggregate well-being fall victim to inconsis-tency at best and hypocrisy at worst. Brandow (1977, 271) is forthright in siding with the angels: "This reviewer refuses to aggregate utilities indis-criminately." Fortunately, this principle did not constrain his professional activity. He repeatedly used aggregate economic measures such as income to indicate well-being. By implicitly assuming the dollar provided the same utility to each recipient, he was also making the value judgment that a dollar of food or income to the poor and starving created exactly as much well-being as a dollar of food or income to the rich and obese. Another frequent value judgment is that society should transfer income to the poor. Either value judgment would appear to violate Brandow's stricture against aggregating utilities indiscriminately.

Neoclassical economists proffer strategies that increase income without regard to distribution while other social scientists proffer strategies to equalize income distribution without regard to economic growth. Neo-classical economists render to equity the same obscurity that other social scientists render to economic efficiency. Dividing economics into economic efficiency and equity domains and then throwing away equity solves little. Surely, the profession can do better. Even crude quantification of marginal utilities of income would elevate analysis.

TOWARD A SOCIAL WELFARE FUNCTION. Part of the baggage economists find difficult to discard is the proposition that utility is neither measurable nor additive. Utility can be measured although not without error. Conventional economic yardsticks such as costs, returns, and income also cannot be measured without error. Because of inevitable aggregation error, a purist would have to reject all aggregate economic variables used to formulate public policy. The issue is not whether utility can be measured and added, but whether it can be measured and added with sufficient validity to provide a tool for improving public policy analysis and decisions.

In recent years advancements have been made on several fronts in estimating utility or social welfare functions. Psychologists and sociologists have made progress in specifying the domains of quality of life (well-being) and the reliability of attitudinal scales to measure quality of life. I view some results (Harper and Tweeten 1977; Tweeten and Mlay 1985) as promising. Income and other explanatory variables used to predict individual well-being measured by socio-psychological scales give results useful for judging group, but not necessarily individual, utility. But utility estimates for a high-income group versus a low-income group often suffice for public policy analysis. In this sense, utility measurement is simpler in public policy economics than in farm management. Errors tend to average out when predicting group utility but not when predicting individual utility.

Three arguments in the utility function on which increasing information is available are the foremost candidates for inclusion in the social welfare function. These are income mean, variance, and distribution. Such a function provides information on mean-variance trade-offs and equity-efficiency trade-offs. Calculating a socially optimal income level, variance, and distribution also requires specification of technical possibilities. Optimal trade-offs between income mean and variance recognize that greater income security tends to reduce mean income but that society is willing to trade off some mean income to obtain greater security. Optimal trade-offs between income level and distribution recognize that a more equal income distribution among society tends to reduce incentives along with aggregate income, but that society is willing to forego some aggregate income to obtain greater equity.

USE OF DESCRIPTIVE VERSUS UTILITARIAN PRESCRIPTIVE ECONOMICS. Contrasts between prescriptive economics and descriptive economics were summarized in Table 6.2. Neither approach needs to be normative. The prescriptive approach does not say that utility ought to be a major end of society; it recognizes that it *is* the major end of society. Prescriptive economics then goes on to prescribe allocations consistent with the goal of maximizing utility or any other goal of society such as income equality, maximum income growth, or minimum unemployment. These prescriptions are held out as positivistic options to voters and others who make decisions. No advocacy need take place. Policymakers are free to choose

Table 6.2. Contrasts between prescriptive and descriptive economics

Item	Prescriptive economics	Descriptive economics
Orientation	Economics of what could be. Goal- or ends-oriented. Prescriptions, "if-then" statements: If the objective is X, then here is prescription to achieve X.	Economics of what is or what will be. Need not explicitly specify a goal or end.
Role of economic theory	Competitive model is tautology for optimal allocation.	Competitive model provides hypotheses.
Test of economic theory	Ability to prescribe allocation to increase well-being or other ends. Theory useful to extent real world does not resemble its prescriptions.	Ability to predict reality. Theory useful to extent real world resembles its predictions.
Algorithm models	Optimization. Models must be structurally sound.	Error minimization. Need not have strong theoretical or structural base if predict outcomes well.

the utility maximizing solution or any other solution, including those that serve special interest groups.

A major difference between prescriptive and descriptive economics is in the use of theory. Purely descriptive economists view the real world, note that it little resembles perfect competition, and declare the competitive model irrelevant. Prescriptive economists viewing the real world also note that it does not resemble perfect competition, but they view the competitive model allocations as a useful norm to judge performance of the real world. After adjusting for risk and for the costs of information and of making adjustments, prescriptive economics may indicate that it may be difficult to improve on the economic performance of a particular market that does not display the perfectly competitive structure. Policy measures to improve efficiency by atomizing an industry may entail greater costs than the measures would add to income. Whereas descriptive economics views the test of a theory as its ability to predict the real world, prescriptive economics views the allocations of the theoretical competitive model as a useful yardstick not only to measure real world performance but also to prescribe allocations to improve well-being. Competitive theory is useful, therefore, precisely to the extent the model does not resemble the real world. For example, a diagnostic device (model) to test automobile engines for malfunction would be of little value if all engines were perfect in structure and performance.

For prescriptive purposes, the competitive model is a tautology specifying marginal conditions that must hold to optimize utility. The optimal allocation conditions to maximize well-being apply equally to a barter, socialist, or market economy. The price system is not required. In theory, administered allocations could bring about the ideal outcome. In practice, the price system may come closer but a diagnostic device is needed to compare performance of the market versus the public sector. Efficient market performance does not necessarily require perfect information, perfect mobility, or large numbers of buyers and sellers. Of course, there must be some predictive element in prescriptive economics. That is, it must be possible to say with some reliability or predictability that the allocation calculated to increase well-being will in fact do so if carried through.

Prescriptive economics may utilize optimization tools in prescribing allocations to reach objectives specified. In contrast, in its purest form, descriptive economics may make no more use of optimization than to minimize error in extending a past trend to predict future outcomes.

Finally, prescriptive economics requires the highest standards of professionalism. Prescriptive economics is abundant today, practiced by laypersons and economists alike, but much of it is superficial and subjective. My call is to bring it "off the streets" and into professional circles where hypotheses can be tested and methods can be made as objective and scientific as possible. Only by applying the very best minds and tools and subjecting procedures to continuing professional scrutiny can utilitarian prescriptive economics be tested for consistency, clarity, and workability.

APPLYING PRESCRIPTIVE ECONOMICS TO FARM AND FOOD PROBLEMS. A typical list of farm problems would include economic instability, demise of the family farm, environmental degradations (soil erosion, chemical pollution, etc.), and poverty. Acute problems of financial stress and excess capacity might be viewed as another phase in the cyclical instability problem characterizing agriculture. Food and nutrition problems include the influence of commercial advertising on nutrition, the influence of nutrition on health and longevity, the influence of chemical additives or red meat consumption on health and nutrition, and the availability of food to "at risk" populations such as the poor and indigent.

A traditional positivistic response is to show what is likely to happen to farm income, food prices, and perhaps to government spending with and without various types of commodity programs to correct the above problems. The result is likely to be a strong implicit argument for continued commodity programs, because producers who would be made worse off by termination of commodity programs are in the best position to utilize such information to influence the political process to continue the programs. Economists using this approach become unintended advocates of commodity interests at the expense of consumers and taxpayers.

The Gardnerian neoclassical prescriptive response is to show the same results as above but to take the analysis a step further to estimate that gains to producers from government interventions are more than offset by losses to consumers and taxpayers (Gardner 1981, 73). The positivistic result is an implicit argument for discontinuing commodity programs because economic efficiency and national income would be raised.[1] Economists using this approach become unintended advocates of static economic efficiency at the expense of distributive justice and security.

The prescriptive positivistic methodology called for herein is to show all the information included in the above two approaches but to go one step further and place utility weights by income level on gains and losses of consumers, producers, and taxpayers. Net social benefit, the sum of utility gains and losses, might be positive or negative from long-run phase out of commodity programs depending not only on the level of national income but also on whether programs reduce variation in income and transfer income from high- to low-wealth groups.

The different welfare paradigms specify very different analysis of the poverty problem in agriculture. The conventional descriptive approach would tend to ignore poverty if the political process does not consider it to be a problem; Gardner's neoclassical analysis would treat it only so far as poverty represents foregone output from underinvestment in human capital. But the prescriptive utilitarian approach would estimate utility gains from transfers and other programs to alleviate poverty. Disincentive effects, of course, would be considered in the analysis. Voters and policymakers would be provided the information and they would decide what, if any, policy changes are appropriate. In short, the prescriptive approach potentially enables economics to address in as objective a manner as possible the major policy issues of our time. It recognizes that both the market and the political system fail; neither is capable of establishing a public policy research and education agenda serving the needs of society.

Miscellaneous Topics

Fragmentation and compartmentalization have characterized not only food and agricultural economic research and education but also policy processes. These and other criticisms of policy research and education are discussed below.

PROFESSIONAL CRITICISM: NOT ENOUGH POLICY RESEARCH? Criticism of farm policy economics research and education was muted in the early years of the profession, partly because the profession was thoroughly dominated by farm management and marketing economists unlikely to call for research and education outside their fields. However, some early criticism showed dismay over the modest amount of policy research relative to the severity of problems.

In 1926, the Social Science Research Council appointed an Advisory Committee on Research in Agricultural Economics. The committee consisted of H. C. Taylor, Northwestern, Chairman; J. D. Black, Minnesota; K. L. Butterfield, Michigan State; J. S. Davis, Stanford; L. C. Gray, Bureau of Agricultural Economics, U.S. Department of Agriculture; E. G. Nourse, Institute of Economics, Washington, D.C.; and G. F. Warren, Cornell. Their report on agricultural economics research (Witt n.d., 20–21) stated that

> . . . a rather large amount of this investigative work is concerned with questions of private efficiency or profit rather than public welfare or social economics. . . . There is danger that this work . . . be continued unduly as routine service instead of pressing on to further genuine researches of the more intricate or valuable type based upon and made possible by these earlier investigators.

In the 1930s, much research was directed at issues of tenure, credit, cooperatives, and marketing. Comparatively few studies by agricultural economists addressed macroeconomic and trade issues, although macroeconomic and trade policies in no small part caused the Great Depression. The lack of studies was partly the result of a widely held but incorrect belief that persists to this day: Agriculture could do nothing about macroeconomic policy; therefore, agricultural economists should direct research and education to other issues.

The tardy support for agricultural policy research was in part a belated recognition of the importance of public policy to agriculture. Equally as important may have been the view that policy economics was too controversial a topic in a field dominated by interest groups preferring that many policy issues be discretely veiled. In time, numbers of agricultural economists with backgrounds and interests in macroeconomic issues increased along with willingness of agricultural deans and experiment station directors to support agricultural policy research.

Although changes in category definitions obscure results, between 1966 and 1982 approximately a 10 percentage point shift in specialization occurred from microeconomic fields (e.g., farm management, firm marketing) to macroeconomic fields (e.g., agricultural policy, international trade and development) among numbers of the AAEA (Swanson 1984, 786). Still, agricultural price, income, and policy analysis accounted for only 13 percent of specializations.

TOO MUCH QUANTITATIVE EMPHASIS? At issue was not just the quantity of resources but the tools used to study the economics of agricultural and food policy. Some of the criticisms are perennial. For example, J. D. Black (1928, 28) argued that

> Just at the time when there is a trend elsewhere in the social and natural sciences away from the purely mathematical work . . . we agricultural economists are rushing headlong into it. . . . Less mathematics and more logic apparently need to be the watchword at the present moment if we are not to make ourselves ridiculous in the eyes of our fellow social sciences by our excesses in methodology.

Criticism continued. Three comments from 1984 alone convey the intensity of feeling:

> This commentary assumes that the profession currently may be mesmerized by its ability to work with quantitative techniques and the flirtation with these techniques may have caused a loss of sight of some important issues now facing U.S. farms and the broader agricultural industry. (Barkley 1984, 798)

> Academic agricultural economists now spend almost full time massaging their computers; policy problems rarely fit into their rigorous formulations. And those modern agricultural economists with a policy bent for the most part either work for a commodity trade association or are employed by a consulting firm which does contract work for those same trade associations or for other special interests. (Cochrane 1984, 41)

> What a growing segment of our profession seems bent on doing, in part, is decorating empty economic boxes, conceptual constructs so esoterically defined as to be empirically void and irrelevant to understanding the real world. (Madden 1984, 104)

Although some commentaries are more charitable (see Farrell 1981), one cannot help but be struck by the breadth and depth of the reaction of the profession to what is widely viewed as excesses in mathematical modeling. Related criticism also is directed at professional publications.

REFORMING THE PUBLICATION PROCESS. Our professional publications have received much criticism. Editors of the *American Journal of Agricultural Economics* are criticized for a review process that encourages narrow mathematical articles, because reviewers tend to accept authors' assumptions but carefully scrutinize for a logical flow from assumptions to conclusions. This favors the neat presentations in mathematical articles, however irrelevant the problem addressed and unrealistic the assumptions.

The review process works against substantive policy oriented articles because real-world policy analysis is seldom neat and clear-cut.

According to Schultz (1964, 1009),

> . . . most things that are published (in agricultural economics) are either not new, or they are very ephemeral. Models are virtually all a repetition of a few specialized analytical tricks and the empirical inferences based on them, when they are relevant to the real world, are short lived. There is a tendency, when perchance a seminal paper is submitted, for review editors to look upon it askance and play safe by recommending against its publication.

The situation has improved little two decades after Schultz's comment. Reforms are overdue. Editors need to give more weight to the importance of problems and conclusions in selecting articles. Perhaps publication of *Choices,* the magazine of applied agricultural economics, will resolve some problems.

NOT ENOUGH INTERDISCIPLINARY POLICY ECONOMICS? Farm debt stress in the 1980s traces mainly to failure of macroeconomic policies, which in turn traces to the decline in encompassing institutions (political parties, presidential and congressional leadership, etc.) that view public policy from the perspective of society rather than of narrow special interests. Similarly, many of the shortcomings of the public policy economics profession trace to the decline of an encompassing socioeconomic science. In an age of accumulated knowledge so vast each Ph.D. candidate can grasp only a part of it, specialization is inevitable. Compartmentalization attends specialization. A high price is paid in loss of a holistic paradigm at a time when policies and markets are ever more integrated in the real world and cannot be viewed in isolation.

A holistic approach to agricultural and food policy economics inevitably is multidisciplinary or interdisciplinary. Multidisciplinary interaction among researchers in various disciplines has long been a goal of economists but success stories are rare. On the other hand, large numbers of individual agricultural and food policy economists have performed distinguished interdisciplinary research utilizing disciplinary skills in agriculture, economics, and statistics combined in one individual.

Our profession has a long tradition of dabbling in political science. That is fitting, given the influence of political processes on economic outcomes. Conceptually, requirements for an optimal economic system and an optimal political system are similar. Political economic contributions of Harold Hoteling, Kenneth Arrow, Gordon Tullock, James Buchanan, and Mancur Olson (see Olson 1982) suggest that a principal force behind fragmented and short-sighted macroeconomic policies is the "democratization" of federal government processes at the expense of encompassing institutions (such as congressional leadership and political parties) seeking to act in the public interest. Proliferation of staffs of individual congressmen and senators relative to professional staffs of congressional offices and committees also reduces the power of encompassing organizations to act in the public interest. Glenn Nelson (1983, 901) notes the tendency for agricultural and food policy decisions to be made increasingly by those outside the U.S. Department of Agriculture. A problem is that much of the federal analytical expertise needed to appraise implications of alternative policies rests in the U.S. Department of Agriculture. Separation of decisions from staff expertise compromises opportunities for sound decisions.

In short, agricultural economists traditionally have had an interdisciplinary focus (i.e., agricultural economists also acting as political scientists or statisticians) rather than a multidisciplinary focus (i. e., agricultural economists working with political scientists or statisticians). The prescriptive economics called for herein requires more interdisciplinary and multidisciplinary work in other fields basic to understanding the economics of agriculture. Such fields include sociology and psychology. Without economics, other social "sciences" tend toward populism. Without other social sciences, economics tends toward engineering and is unable to confront today's major socioeconomic issues. I see no alternative to adding more time to Ph.D. programs and greater use of postdoctoral programs to broaden our overspecialized profession.

Summary and Conclusions

Our predictive economics is often flawed. Agricultural economists tend to project current circumstances into the foreseeable future. Yet neither boom nor bust persists. History has consistently sided neither with the Cassandras nor with the Pollyannas. Economic analysis and public policies must be designed for all seasons.

A large reservoir of excess labor in agriculture no longer exists but redundant labor remains a problem on many midsize and small farms. Ability of the nonfarm sector to assimilate labor from agriculture is no longer in doubt — the excess is a small portion indeed of the nonfarm labor force. Schooling and other human resource investments in farm people have drastically improved in the past four decades. Nonetheless, some problems remain despite their obscurity in research. Poverty characterizes an estimated 20 percent of farm families but poverty is given little attention in data systems, in policy research, or in farm policy debate and legislation.

Rural areas, after resurgence in the 1970s, once again lag behind urban areas in employment and population growth. Given that farm families depend on nonfarm sources for nearly two-thirds of their income, it is surprising that rural development research has been allowed to fade into near obscurity.

Our base of data and parameters continues to be inadequate. Improving on the base would improve econometric models and address basic issues such as the capacity of agriculture to adjust to shocks in demand and supply.

The political-economic environment for agricultural and food policy formulation has changed radically over the years. Economic research and education too often have mirrored the fragmented political system, responding to and affirming special pleadings of interest groups. Food and agricultural policy economists employed by the public are expected to serve the public interest. The profession cannot do that if it sets its research agenda based on goals and ends articulated by special-interest groups. Both the market and the political process are flawed in their ability to specify ends or goals required for prescriptive research and education in the public interest.

Our welfare economics paradigm has not served the profession well. It has tended to favor the status quo and special interest groups. To service the wider interests of society, economists need to begin work on the professional equivalent of placing a man on the moon—specifying a social welfare function. That does not mean turning professional interest away from problems of food and agriculture. It just means that we work with food and agricultural problems in the context of the welfare of society as a whole.

Prescriptive economics turns us from descriptions of "what is" to hypotheses of "what could be." Analytical depth and professional oversight is essential to avoid tendencies for prescriptive economics to rely on speculation and value judgments.

This is no call to replace democratic political processes by the dictates of a computer model programmed to prescribe utility-maximizing solutions. Society through democratic political processes will continue to make decisions of what, when, and how to allocate; often the decision will be to allow the price system to allocate. I only call for adding an estimated utility-increasing option to the conventional income and employment-increasing options of which voters and other decision makers are informed through education. The procedure would reduce opportunities for special interests to control the research, education, and political agenda. Professionalism is the ability to rise above special interests that see economists as tools for rationalizing special favors at the expense of society.

Note

1. Questions have been raised about the validity of classical cardinal welfare analysis, particularly whether static inefficiency estimated from economic distortions are reflected in dynamic real world income performance. Empirical results from Agarwalla (1983) for 31 developing countries indicated that countries with greatest economic distortions had the least economic growth in the 1970s. Nonetheless, more conceptual and applied research is needed on the relationship between market interventions and dynamic economic efficiency.

References

Agarwala, R. 1983. Price Distortions and Growth in Developing Countries. Working Paper No. 575. Washington, D.C.: The World Bank.

Barkley, P. W. 1984. Rethinking the Mainstream. *Am. J. Agric. Econ.* 66:798–801.

Batie, S. S. 1983. Resource Policy in the Future. In *Farm and Food Policy,* ed. M. Hammig and H. Harris, 94–107. Clemson, S.C.: College of Agricultural Science, Clemson Univ.

Black, J. D. 1928. Research in the Prices of Farm Products. *J. Farm Econ.* 10:66.

Brandow, G.E. 1977. Policy for Commercial Agriculture, 1945-1971. In *A Survey of Agricultural Economics Literature,* ed. L. Martin, 209–92. Minneapolis: Univ. of Minnesota Press.

Cochrane, W. W. 1984. Agricultural Policy in the United States – A Long View. In *Benjamin H. Hibbard Memorial Lecture Series,* 1–45. Madison: Dept. of Agric. Econ., Univ. of Wisconsin.

Council of Economic Advisors. 1985. Economic Report of the President. Washington, D.C.: GPO.

Farrell, K. 1981. Using Models in Policy Formulation: Commentary. In *Modeling Agriculture for Policy Analysis in the 1980s,* 175–78. Kansas City, Mo.: Federal Reserve Bank.

Gardner, B. 1981. *The Governing of Agriculture.* Lawrence: The Regents Press of Kansas.

————. 1984. Flaws of the Market as Regulator of Agriculture: The Lack of Policy Implications. In *Benjamin H. Hibbard Memorial Lecture Series,* 47–65. Madison: Dept. of Agric. Econ., Univ. of Wisconsin.

Harper, W., and L. Tweeten. 1977. Socio-psychological Measures of Quality of Rural Life: A Proxy for Measuring the Marginal Utility of Income. *Am. J. Agric. Econ.* 59:1000–05.

Johnson, G. L., and C. L. Quance. 1972. *The Overproduction Trap in U.S. Agriculture.* Baltimore: Johns Hopkins Univ. Press.

Madden, J. P. 1984. Discussion: What To Do With Those Empty Economic Boxes. In *Economics of Farm Size,* 104–8. Ames: Center for Agricultural and Rural Development, Iowa State University.

Nelson, G. L. 1983. A Critique of Executive Branch Decision-making Processes. *Am. J. Agric. Econ.* 65:901–7.

O'Brien, P. 1984. World Market Trends and Prospects: Implications for U.S. Agricultural Policy. In *Agriculture, Stability, and Growth,* 1–62. Port Washington, New York: Associated Faculty Press.

Olson, M. 1982. *The Rise and Decline of Nations.* New Haven: Yale Univ. Press.

Resources for the Future. 1984. Feeding a Hungry World. *Resources* 76:1–20.

Robbins, L. 1935. An Essay on the Nature and Significance of Economic Science. 2d ed. London: Macmillan.

Schultz, T. W. 1945. *Agriculture in an Unstable Economy.* New York: McGraw-Hill.

_____. 1964. Changing Relevance of Agricultural Economics. *J. Farm Econ.* 46:1004–14.

Spitze, R. G. F. 1983. Comments for the Panel. In *Farm and Food Policy,* ed. M. Hammig and H. Harris, 237–40. Clemson, S.C.: College of Agricultural Science, Clemson Univ.

Swanson, E. R. 1984. The Mainstream in Agricultural Economics Research. *Am. J. Agric. Econ.* 66:782–92.

Tweeten, L. 1967. The Demand for U.S. Farm Output. *Food Res. Inst. Stud.* 7:343–69.

_____. 1979. *Foundations of Farm Policy.* Lincoln: Univ. of Nebraska Press.

_____. 1983a. Impact of Federal Fiscal-Monetary Policy on Farm Structure. *South. J. Agric. Econ.* 15:61–68.

_____. 1983b. Economic Instability in Agriculture: The Contributions of Prices, Government Programs, and Exports. *Am. J. Agric. Econ.* 65:922–31.

_____. 1984. Causes and Consequences of Structural Change in the Farming Industry. Report No. 207. Washington, D.C.: National Planning Association.

Tweeten, L., and G. Mlay. 1985. Marginal Utility of Income Estimated and Applied to Economic Problems in Agriculture. Agricultural Policy Analysis Project Paper B-21. Stillwater: Dept. of Agric. Econ., Oklahoma State Univ. Mimeo.

Tweeten, L., and C. L. Quance. 1969. Positivistic Measures of Aggregate Supply Elasticities: Some New Approaches. *Am. J. Agric. Econ.* 51:342–52.

U.S. Department of Agriculture. 1985. Economic Research Service in Transition. Washington, D.C.: USDA.

Witt, Lawrence. Date unknown. Historical Highlights and Developments in Agricultural Economics. East Lansing: Dept. of Agric. Econ., Michigan State Univ. Unpublished manuscript.

Domestic Food and Agricultural Policy Research Directions: A **Discussion**

FILMORE E. BENDER

Each of the individuals who accepted the responsibility of preparing a paper for this conference has undertaken a serious professional challenge. I believe that Dr. Tweeten has presented a number of important concerns that will continue to occupy the profession for some time.

He begins by providing a very brief summary of some of the recent events in the farm sector. He refreshes our memory concerning the succinct statement presented by T. W. Schultz regarding the underlying factors that led to agriculture's problems in the 1930s, 1940s, and 1950s. Dr. Tweeten proceeds to provide an updated list of features that characterize today's agricultural economy. I believe that one of the most important points made by Dr. Tweeten is to contrast the situation examined by Schultz in 1945 when the agricultural sector was characterized by excess resources, especially labor, with the current situation, which Dr. Tweeten describes as being an equilibrium.

A recent Office of Technology Assessment (OTA) report (1985) indicates that farms in excess of $200,000 a year in gross sales represent 5.4 percent of all farms but generate more than 50 percent of total cash receipts and more than 80 percent of net farm income. These farms dominate the commercial agricultural scene, but it is the midsized family farms with sales of $40,000 to $200,000 per year that appear to dominate the political scene. This background information leads Dr. Tweeten to suggest certain areas of research he feels will be fruitful.

Dr. Tweeten feels that much more needs to be known of the macroeconomic impacts of federal tax policies on agriculture. I believe that he has not stressed this need as strongly as it should be. If one of the concerns of agricultural research is on resource use in the agricultural sector, it is readily apparent that income tax laws have a far greater impact on decisions regarding the activities of large farms than reading the literature in agricultural economics would imply. It is my judgment that the changes in federal income tax laws in 1981 had a greater impact on agricultural activities than did the farm bill of 1981. I am not asking that this hypothesis be tested. I am only saying that to the degree the profession is concerned about

Filmore E. Bender is Associate Director, Maryland Agricultural Experiment Station, University of Maryland, College Park.

resource allocation and resource use in commercial agriculture, a far greater emphasis on income tax laws and credit arrangements needs to be integrated into the research agenda.

I was deeply disturbed by Dr. Tweeten's discussion concerning prescriptive economics. It appears to me that he has set positive economics up as a "straw man" to be knocked down and replaced with prescriptive economics. As Friedman (1953, 4–5) stated:

> Positive economics is in principle independent of any particular ethical position or normative judgments. . . . Normative economics and the art of economics, on the other hand, cannot be independent of positive economics. Any policy conclusion necessarily rests on a prediction about the consequences of doing one thing rather than another, a prediction that must be based — implicitly or explicitly — on positive economics. There is not, of course, a one-to-one relation between policy conclusions and the conclusions of positive economics; if there were, there would be no separate normative science. Two individuals may agree on the consequences of a particular piece of legislation. One may regard them as desirable on balance and so favor the legislation; the other, as undesirable and so oppose the legislation.

In other words, I see little that distinguishes prescriptive economics as described by Dr. Tweeten from positive economics as described by Dr. Friedman. Nevertheless, what Dr. Tweeten says with regard to the role of public policy economists salaried by tax dollars is important (i.e., they must not restrict their analysis only to alternative means to reach the goals specified by farmers, agribusiness firms, consumers, taxpayers, or any other special interest group). However, this is far more difficult to implement than it is to discuss. In general, public policy economists are paid because some special interest group has felt that its needs could and would be served by supporting such research. In fact, these groups often feel betrayed when research results contrary to their interests are published.

It takes a great deal of courage on the part of the individual scientist as well as the research administrators to pursue research on unpopular topics and more importantly to publish the results of that research. Dr. Tweeten suggests that a solution is to pursue work on the definition and quantification of the social welfare function. Intuitively each of us makes some trade-off between efficiency and equity in policy judgments. Dr. Tweeten's call to quantify these judgments is not new. In 1944, Von Neumann and Morgenstern (1953) indicated that economics should deal with cardinal utility. But even without cardinal measures of utility, Dr. Tweeten suggests that the profession could use the mean and distribution of income when weighing the alternatives of efficiency versus equity.

In large measure, the current debate over income tax reform is a debate concerning the benefits to society that accrue through increased investment, innovation, and economic activity when incomes are not heavily taxed versus the equity gain to society from a highly progressive income tax. Admittedly, given the current tax laws with various deductions and write-offs, one might question how progressive the current structure is. Nevertheless, it is society's stated intention that the current income tax structure would provide some redistribution of income.

In the last section of his paper, Dr. Tweeten touches on a number of different topics without going into great depth on any of them. I feel that some elaboration would be desirable in certain cases. Dr. Tweeten indicates that there is not enough policy research currently underway. I would take this one step further by suggesting that the most important agricultural policy established by the United States was the conscious decision to invest in teaching, research, and extension in agriculture.

The Morrill Act of 1862, the Hatch Act of 1887, and the Smith-Lever Act of 1914 resulted in an enormous public investment in agriculture. This public investment has transformed American agriculture in ways that were completely unanticipated. Consequently, one of the major agricultural policy variables in the United States today is the dollars devoted to research and extension in agriculture. In spite of this, agricultural policy analysts tend to focus attention on price supports and other more narrowly focused aspects of agricultural policy. I fully acknowledge the very long lead times involved in research concerning public investment in agriculture. I am also aware of the outstanding research that has been done on the benefits from agricultural research and extension expenditures. What I am saying is that this research is not integrated into or considered to be a part of the body of research dealing with agricultural policy, and yet it should be.

For the more than 20 years that I have been involved with agricultural economics as a profession, I have been hearing repeated calls to engage in more multidisciplinary and interdisciplinary research. As an administrator I am fully cognizant of the importance of holistic approaches to major problems. Every effort is made at the University of Maryland to encourage teams of researchers to address problems of importance. However, as a scientist I remember participating in a large number of both interdisciplinary and multidisciplinary research efforts. There were periods extending for several months or even several years when I found myself associating more often with food scientists or agricultural engineers than I did with my fellow economists or agricultural economists. It would be overstating it to say that I felt an "identity crisis," but from time to time I did feel a need to retool myself as an agricultural economist and to reenter the mainstream of my primary profession. It takes an individual of superior intellectual ability and supreme self-confidence to engage in both interdisciplinary and multidisciplinary research. When identified, these individuals should be cultivated, nurtured, and encouraged to blossom. I believe that a major challenge for research administrators will be to provide the correct incentives for scientists to participate in multidisciplinary research.

I was interested in Dr. Tweeten's suggestion that a way to broaden the experience of our scientists is to encourage postdoctoral experiences. What I have observed as an agricultural administrator is that postdoctorals blossom and flourish in those disciplines that are facing a glut of new scientists. Consequently, it appears to me that during those periods when there are more new Ph.D.s entering the profession than there are vacancies, we should encourage postdoctorals both as a practical solution to the employment problem and as a mechanism for expanding the horizons of the young professional. However, when market conditions are tight and there is more than one vacancy for every new Ph.D., we must turn our attention to other means of broadening the scientific experience of an individual. Most universities encourage sabbatical leaves. Many corporations have adopted similar policies for their professionals. With individuals enjoying productive professional careers that span more than 40 years, we must expect and encourage continuing retraining and retooling. I believe that we will see far greater emphasis on retraining of our professionals in the future than we have observed in the past.

In summary, Dr. Tweeten has given us much to consider. I believe that the insight he offers by suggesting that current agricultural problems should be viewed within the context of an equilibrium in contrast to the problem of 40 years ago, which were quite rightly viewed in the context of a disequilibrium, is of major importance. I can only echo his call for a greater emphasis on agricultural policy research. I wish to modify this charge by indicating that among these policy topic areas are: (1) the impact of teaching, research, and extension expenditures in support of agriculture, (2) the income tax and credit arrangements in which agriculture functions, and (3) the other macro- and international trade policies that have an impact on agriculture.

References

Friedman, M. 1953. *Essays in Positive Economics.* Chicago: Univ. of Chicago Press.

U.S. Congress. Office of Technology Assessment. 1985. *Technology, Public Policy, and the Changing Structure of American Agriculture: A Special Report for the 1985 Farm Bill.* Washington, D.C.: GPO.

Von Neumann, J., and O. Morgenstern. 1953. *Theory of Games and Economic Behavior.* Princeton: Princeton Univ. Press.

Domestic Food and Agricultural Policy Research Directions: A Discussion

J. BRUCE BULLOCK

I find myself in complete agreement with the first part of Dr. Tweeten's paper. In fact, I commend him for a stimulating paper up to the point that he suggests that estimation of the social welfare function be the top priority for agricultural policy research.

I am surprised that Dr. Tweeten has placed so much emphasis on the need for agricultural policy researchers to specify the social welfare function. I would favor some expansion of research on specifying a social welfare function as an academic exercise. However, I cannot get excited about making this the focus of all agricultural policy research.

If you think the jokes about economists being unable to agree on a conclusion are bad now, you haven't seen anything until we begin debating about the arguments, mathematical form, and coefficients of the social welfare function.

First of all, equity—like beauty—is in the eye of the beholder. Whose definition of equity are we going to use in specifying the function?

Secondly, how can we expect agricultural economists to agree on the coefficients of the social welfare function, when as a profession we cannot agree on whether the export demand for U.S. agricultural products is elastic or inelastic or whether an increase in the value of the dollar relative to other currencies has a negative or a neutral impact on the demand for U.S. farm exports, *ceteris paribus*.

I agree with Dr. Tweeten that economic efficiency criteria by themselves are an inadequate basis for policy decisions. Agricultural policy research can and should provide information about the nature and magnitude of the distributional impacts of policy alternatives. However, it seems to me we can achieve much of what he is proposing without trying to specify the social welfare function.

One of our roles as academic agricultural economists is to function as society's thinkers. That will sometimes require that we think about and discuss the unthinkable. We have a responsibility to cause the public and policymakers to "ask the right questions" as they define and implement

J. Bruce Bullock is Professor and Chairman, Department of Agricultural Economics, University of Missouri, Columbia.

agricultural policy. However, before we can cause the public and policy-makers to ask the right questions, we have to be asking ourselves the right questions.

We can start by raising at least four basic questions and forcing ourselves to go beyond the rhetoric of the questions and focus on the economics of the issues.

First, what is the economic rationale for having any type of government farm program in the United States as we enter the last 15 years of the twentieth century? Is the U.S. food supply in some type of danger that can be rebuffed by farm programs?

It is one thing to justify farm family welfare programs when farm families account for 25 percent of the population and have incomes that are only about 50 percent of their urban counterpart. It is quite a different task to justify farm family welfare programs when less than two percent of the population are dependent on farming for their family income and this portion of the population is on average wealthier than their urban counterparts.

Second, what is the farm problem in 1985? There has been much discussion about details of alternative farm programs, but there has been almost no discussion of the problem to be solved by the farm programs. How can we meaningfully define and evaluate alternative farm policies and programs without a clear definition of the farm problem? Is the 1985 farm problem identical to the farm problem that existed in 1933? If not, how do we justify farm programs in 1985 that are only slight modifications of programs designed and implemented 50 years ago?

Third, how will the technological developments that are expected to come out of the biological science laboratories over the next five to ten years alter the farm problem and the economic justification for even having farm programs? Both economists and policymakers have been very short-sighted in analysis and discussion of farm programs. Longer-run perspectives are needed.

Fourth, are the theoretical concepts and analytical models we use to evaluate policy alternatives an appropriate representation of the agricultural sector? Dr. Tweeten pointed out the major structural changes that have occurred in U.S. agriculture. However, we have not thought through implications for how this changed structure might alter the way we can interpret data. For example, what is the meaning of a supply elasticity estimate derived from aggregate data when 90 percent of the output is produced by 30 percent of the producers and the marginal cost curve of these producers is substantially below the cost curve of the 70 percent of producers that produce only 10 percent of the output? In this kind of situation, the intersection of the supply and demand curve does not define a market equilibrium. However, the whole foundation of our economic analysis of policy alternatives is based on the definition of market equilibrium being defined by the intersection of supply and demand.

Key Research Needs

There is a long list of agricultural policy research needs that I think have higher priority than specification of a social welfare function. Moreover, they would need to be addressed, even if we had a social welfare function specified.

The following list of agricultural research issues and questions certainly does not include all items that should be placed on the research agenda.

1. We need to improve our understanding of the impacts of macroeconomic policy on the agricultural sector. And, of equal importance, we must improve our understanding of the sensitivity of the macroeconomy to various types of developments in agriculture.

Conventional wisdom of the farmer is that the economic performance of the entire economy rises and falls with changes in net farm income. What empirical evidence do we have to support or disprove this? We, as a profession, have been quite reluctant to educate agricultural producers about the magnitude of the farm income multiplier in the national income equation. We can no longer ignore this relationship if we are going to fulfill our role as public supported policy analysts.

In response to demands that some types of government programs be developed to ameliorate the adverse impacts of the current financial stress in agriculture, former Budget Director David Stockman demanded information and analysis demonstrating that ignoring the agricultural finance problems would have a significant impact on GNP, employment, interest rates, and the national debt. Our profession was in poor shape to respond to that quite legitimate request for information and analysis. Existing econometric models have not been designed to effectively address these types of questions.

2. What changes, if any, in the mechanisms and institutions we have for financing agriculture are required to work out of current financial difficulties and avoid a repeat of the current situation in the future? How are we to finance agricultural production in the future?

3. What are the implications for land prices and land-ownership distribution if commodity prices are allowed to move to world market clearing levels? The shadow price of much of the lower-quality land is probably

close to zero at current commodity prices. The problem is that in many situations there are several hundred dollars of debt held against that land. What kinds of policies and institutions are appropriate for dealing with these types of adjustments?

4. What types of changes in property rights are required to achieve desired levels of soil and water conservation? What are the economic and political consequences of these changes? What types of mechanisms and institutions would be appropriate for achieving those objectives?

What are the most effective mechanisms and institutions for dealing with the instability of agriculture? Instability is often listed as a major problem for agriculture. Is U.S. agriculture unstable? If so, why? What do we mean by instability?

Dr. Tweeten states that "agriculture is unstable because it depends on unpredictable forces of nature." I think a much more appropriate statement would be that investment in agricultural production activities is risky because of uncertainties about weather and about changes in demand.

These uncertainties are a characteristic of the environment within which the agricultural sector operates. These uncertainties need not be a source of instability of investment in agricultural production. Whatever instability there is in U.S. agricultural investment is generated by the naive way agricultural producers interpret short-run changes in prices.

In view of this, we need to develop mechanisms to help agricultural producers and policymakers distinguish short-run deviations about the trend from longer-term movements along the trend or substantial changes in the trend itself. We should be encouraging the development of mechanisms and institutions that generate information about longer-term perspectives on agricultural markets and provide both producers and consumers with mechanisms to manage the risk associated with the uncertainties inherent in agricultural production processes.

For example, extension of futures markets two to three years into the future would be an important contribution to this process. Because of our inability to forecast the future with accuracy, we tend to underestimate the contribution that systematic forecasting can make to decision making in a world of uncertainty.

5. Ray Bessler talked 20 years ago about the problem of nonadditivity of agricultural economics research. The problem still exists. Because of the nonadditivity of much of our research, we have developed limited capacity to provide the kind of information needed to define and evaluate policy alternatives.

As we examine the research priorities and try to identify the resource needs to support an appropriate agricultural policy research program, I suggest that we give some consideration to an idea that has been discussed by North Central Department Chairs about a network of agricultural policy research centers across the country (Seitz 1985).

The purpose of this network would be to develop a research and information system that captures our composite knowledge about how the agricultural sector functions and how it interrelates with other sectors of the U.S. and world economy. The network would maintain this knowledge in an operational form that would enable us to (1) provide analysis of alternative policies; (2) evaluate the probable immediate and dynamic impacts of exogenous shocks to the agricultural sector; and (3) project the future under most likely and alternative scenarios.

This network of centers can best be thought of as a set of laboratories for policy analysis. These laboratories would be staffed on a continuing basis with a team of scientists specializing in a given area of expertise. Resources would be provided to maintain a comprehensive data base to allow access to powerful computational facilities and to assure adequate operating support. This well-supported team of scientists would conduct in-depth analysis of policy alternatives and their consequences. Over time, these laboratories would refine and expand their data bases, the sophistication of their modeling efforts, and the range of alternatives considered. They could analyze both the micro and the macro aspects of policy decisions. The analysis would be based on state-of-the-art, quantitative models of the economic system that would allow projections of a broad range of impacts of policy alternatives on a wide range of affected constituencies. The resources and continuity would allow specification of comprehensive analytical models that would simultaneously deal with "all" of the important variables. As supercomputers become more accessible, the potential gains from the development of such models will be enhanced.

In addition to being able to provide the in-depth analyses, such laboratories should be structured to respond more quickly and fully to policy questions than is possible when a new study must be generated to address each request for information. The individuals involved in the development and operation of these models would rapidly gain adequate experience to be able to contribute to the judgmental assessment that is imperative, regardless of the quality of the quantitative analysis. These laboratories would provide the ideal setting for the training of graduate students and other young scientists preparing for a career in academia or public service.

One of the major roles of such laboratories would be to provide the information necessary to make more informed decisions in the public sector. Policy prescriptions emanating from individuals, interest groups, politicians, etc., could be analyzed on a timely basis to ascertain their indirect or secondary, as well as their direct and immediate, impacts. At the same time, these models would provide a substantially enhanced knowledge base to support improved extension programs reaching directly out to citizens. An important role of the laboratory staff would be the development of educational materials that could be utilized to enhance the regional or state extension programs.

In addition to a series of laboratories focused on specific topics, it is important that a means of tying them together be developed. Data maintenance, scenario development, coordination of analysis, and coordination of materials for extension programming could all be accomplished through an umbrella organization comprised of representatives of each of the laboratories. This organization would also need to determine the conditions under which an institution would "qualify" to participate in this coordinated effort.

For a long time we have been underinvesting in agricultural policy research. Moreover, much of the research that has been developed is nonadditive. A coordinated network of policy research centers would provide the basis for correcting that situation. It would also provide a mechanism for demonstrating that sound economic analysis is a necessary input to effective development of U.S. farm policy.

Reference

Seitz, W. D. 1985. Agricultural Policy Analysis: A Federal-State Partnership for the Challenge Ahead. Illinois Agricultural Economics Staff Paper No. 85E-323. Champaign: University of Illinois.

Domestic Food and Agricultural Policy Research Directions: A Discussion

DON PAARLBERG

Luther Tweeten's paper is comprehensive and clearly written, and I find myself in substantial agreement with most of it.

There is, however, one point on which we differ. It concerns what Tweeten calls prescriptive economics, a recasting of what most of us know as normative economics. I shall confine myself to that point.

Tweeten's definition of prescriptive economics is "the analysis of options by economists to help policymakers and society decide what is the appropriate policy response to increase well-being of society confronted by economic issues."

It is not entirely clear from the paper whether prescriptive economics is seen as prescribing a course of action (which would seem to be the case, given the meaning of the word) or whether it means simply analyzing alternative courses of action as to their economic consequences. Maybe it is some of both. Tweeten wants us to get on with estimating a social welfare function and doing our analysis with regard to such a function.

I have grave misgivings about the ability of economists to prescribe agricultural policy actions or to estimate a social welfare function. Policy decisions are concerned with economics, about which we know considerable. But they are also concerned with social acceptability, about which we know little, and with ethical considerations, about which our professional knowledge is not significantly greater than zero. Our model, though we are often reluctant to admit it, is economic man, that mythical self-seeking creature who lacks awareness of social justice and who is impervious to public opinion.

This narrowness has been increasing. The rigorous discipline we now call economics was once broader, named political economy. The training of our young people embraces less and less of our sister social sciences. How then can we feel qualified to prescribe public policy? We would not want the National Council of Churches to prescribe public policy, nor would we want the Rural Sociological Society to be the architect thereof. Neither should we, as agricultural economists, arrogate this role to ourselves.

Don Paarlberg is Professor Emeritus, Department of Agricultural Economics, Purdue University, West Lafayette, Indiana.

However imperfect it may be, the integration of economics and social and ethical aspects of farm and food policy is (and should be) in the hands of elected public officials.

Our task, as I see it, is to do our economic analysis as carefully as we can and to lay it before the people and their elected representatives. We thus educate those of the public that are open to new knowledge, service those elected representatives who want our evaluation, and trouble the consciences of those who do not.

We are not qualified to prescribe. We *are* qualified to inject into the decision arena the economic parameters of various options. We are competent regarding maybe one-third of the input leading to public policy decisions. We are not competent to advise regarding the entire 100 percent. Some of the most inept farm policy proposals I have seen during 16 years in public service came from agricultural economists. Typically these were wholly in accord with economic criteria but oblivious to other social disciplines. Politically, they were nonstarters.

Tweeten discusses the difficulty of making value judgments. We strain ourselves to avoid value judgments. The most obvious effort to do so is found in our embracing of Pareto optimality, whereby we can support decisions making some people better off if we see to it that no one is worse off. This may satisfy the urge for professional purity, but it is of little use to the policymaker. There may have been some Pareto-optimal decisions during my term in the public service, but if so they could probably be counted on the fingers of one hand.

Actually there is no escape from value judgments. Our profession is founded on them. I list a few:

- That efficiency should be the sole criterion for decision making;
- That people are concerned only with maximizing their incomes; and
- That the utility of income should be excluded from the principle of diminishing returns.

Tweeten says (and here I agree with him completely) that as publicly employed economists we should be concerned with the general public as well as with the specific interests of farm people. We have the capability to assess the economic consequences for nonfarm people of actions intended to help farmers. We have not always done so. We have not adequately considered the economic consequences for farm laborers and agribusiness firms of reducing cotton acreage. We have not considered the economic effect of milk price supports on food costs of low-income consumers. We have not until recently studied the differential effects of payment programs on large and small farmers. With a few notable exceptions, we have slighted soil and water conservation and rural poverty. Our studies of commodity programs have often assumed highly inelastic coefficients of supply and demand (long-run as well as short-run) despite growing evidence that this is not the case. Most of these shortcomings, in my judgment, come as a result of special solicitude for the agricultural elite.

If we apply our efforts to the economic aspects of farm and food policy and expand these in some of the neglected areas I have mentioned, there is little need to invade the turf of other social disciplines. Agenda changes of this kind would improve our performance far more, I think, than prescribing solutions that concern areas beyond our competence.

7

Issues in World Agriculture
– a U.S. Perspective

JOHN W. MELLOR

The purpose of this paper is to define the major issues in world agriculture subject to the analytical tools of agricultural economics. World agricultural issues are defined as issues that arise outside the United States but that affect the concerns and interests of the United States.

A U.S. perspective is taken in this paper for three reasons. First, as each issue in world agriculture can be seen from many perspectives, each of which gives a different view of the importance of the issues' elements and courses of action and perhaps even producing a different final assessment, it is best to state the perspective adopted explicitly at the outset. Second, since this paper is being done for the American Agricultural Economics Association, it seems appropriate to adopt the dominant perspective of that group. Third, because American agriculture is large and because trade is important to the prospects of American agriculture and the global concerns of the United States, the perspective of the United States is of considerable interest to other groups.

Because the range of issues in world agriculture is immense, analysis is facilitated by classifying the issues so that their interactions are emphasized. I therefore divide the issues into three categories:

International Food Flows. International food flows are extraordinarily large by past standards, growing rapidly, and moving largely and increasingly from the developed to the developing countries of the world. These phenomena are recent and ill-understood. Policy has not as yet fully adjusted to them. The flows are mostly commercial, but noncommercial

John W. Mellor is Director of the International Food Policy Research Institute in Washington, D.C.

flows of food aid are large, controversial, and their relation to commercial flows are also poorly understood.

Global Poverty. Massive numbers of people exist in such abject poverty that they do not even receive enough energy to live an active, healthy life. Such poverty is concentrated in the developing countries of the world, and there is a widely perceived need in developed countries to lift people out of such poverty and malnutrition and an unarticulated belief that it is possible to do so. Thus, the global poverty problem is also construed as a U.S. problem.

Unequal Distribution of Human Capital. The extraordinarily unequal incidence of human capital in the world is the basis of inequalities in development and of the concentration of poverty. Redressing this inequality would increase the prosperity of all nations, including the United States, while the means for redressing this inequality lie substantially with the United States. Hence, this problem too may be construed as a U.S. problem.

For each of these issues I will touch upon the implications for research, extension, and teaching. I will attempt to show the importance of each of the issues and to show how each issue is related to the other. I will attempt as I go to diagnose gaps in knowledge in these three areas and to define the research needs. The paper will treat both extension and teaching, but will emphasize research since once that need is clear, the other two fall rather easily into line.

International Food Flows

THE BASIC ISSUES. Net imports of basic food staples into the developing countries (excluding China), rose from an annual average of 8 million tons between 1966 and 1970, to 27 million tons from 1976 to 1980, and to about 50 million tons in 1984. By projecting production and consumption, Leonardo Paulino (1986) depicts that flow as increasing to between 75 and 80 million tons by the year 2000. Although some countries in the Third World are significant net exporters, they are few. Conversely, most developed countries have become net exporters of basic food staples. Thus there has been a dramatic increase in net exports from developed to developing countries. This increase is the product of structural changes in demand and supply conditions that are a natural and logical product of specific stages of economic development.

As development gets underway, the growth of basic food staple production tends to accelerate. Since the processes for accelerating growth are basically those that shift the supply function outward, and since shifting the supply function in turn depends largely on processes of complex institutional changes that require rapid expansion of supplies of trained people and the institutional structures that support them, these processes are necessarily slow. In the meantime, development increases the incomes of low-income people, who have high marginal propensities to spend on food. In fact, at this stage, when marginal propensities to spend on food are high, the processes of agricultural growth with strong employment multipliers tend to increase demand rapidly even as supply increases (Mellor 1976). The result is that demand tends to shift much more rapidly than supply, causing net imports to increase rapidly. This tendency is documented in Paulino and Bachman (1979) and in Paulino (1986), particularly for the countries for which basic food staples production is growing rapidly. Conversely, once the development process has neared its apogee, the shifting of the supply function tends to become institutionalized and hence supply continues to grow rapidly. In the meantime, marginal propensities to spend on food decline sharply. As a result, as incomes increase supply tends to shift much more rapidly than demand, creating exportable surpluses. A peculiarity of the present situation in the world is that massive areas and numbers of people are in each of these two stages: the one with a tendency to increase exports rapidly and the other with a tendency to increase imports rapidly. Since food trade, although massive by past standards, is still a small proportion of total food production, it becomes difficult to predict trade balances and net pressures on prices since small differences in the rates at which supply and demand shift in these large blocks of countries will have large effects on the volume of trade and prices.

In the mid-1980s, with the economic slowdown in world demand, shifts in demand in developing countries have been slowed. Shifts in supply, which are subject to much longer-term phenomena, have continued to be relatively rapid. The latter has also been somewhat true of the developed countries. The product has been tremendous downward pressure on international prices. The appearance of that pressure is, of course, greatly exaggerated in the largest exporter, the United States, because of increase in the valuation of the dollar which has causes largely outside of agriculture. A look at the late 1960s and the early to mid-1970s, when world development was moving quickly, suggests that there was modest upward pressure on real food prices. Since the processes of economic development and rising resource productivity are now somewhat endogenous in developing countries it would not be surprising to find that global food supply and demand balances were coming to resemble those of the late 1960s and early 1970s, with once again mild net upward pressure on food prices. For that to happen, an acceleration in technological change associated with the new biology would have to be overbalanced by widespread accelerated growth in the high potential growth countries of Asia and Latin America.

Third World countries represent the dynamic aspect of future import demand. Of course in the last decade or so the Soviet Union has also been a major and rapidly growing importer. In this context it is useful to see the Soviet Union as a late-stage developing country. Marginal propensities to spend on food are still quite high in the Soviet Union, partly because incomes are low and perhaps partly because of the low availability of nonfood goods and services. Long before the developing countries, the Soviet Union will begin to decrease its marginal propensity to spend on food and will gradually import less. In fact, the period of explosive growth rate of supply in the Soviet Union has been considerably more rapid than in Western Europe. The real difference in the trade flows is caused by demand.

It is notable that the import demand of developing countries grows explosively when livestock consumption grows substantially and consumes a significant proportion of total basic food staples. In the early stages of development, livestock production tends to be built primarily on waste and byproduct feeds. As the growth of livestock production accelerates, the supply of those types of feeds becomes highly inelastic and there is a switch to the much more elastic supply of food staples that can be used for human consumption. As that process accelerates, the proportion of basic food staples fed to livestock increases.

Since the demand for livestock products tends to remain elastic with the elasticity changing little as incomes rise, that demand tends to become the driving force in the demand for basic food staples. At that stage growth in demand may exceed the growth of domestic production significantly and therefore cause growth in imports to explode. The most dramatic case of this is Taiwan, which has increased its livestock feed as a proportion of total domestic utilization of cereals from 4 percent in 1960 to 1962 to about 50 percent in 1980 to 1982. Cereal imports now represent some 58 percent of total consumption of cereals (Sarma 1986). This is an extreme case, but illustrates the point well.

THE RESEARCH AGENDA. The agenda for research on international food flows develops naturally from the above exposition. While the broad outlines of global food flows are clear, the details are so unclear as to prejudice effective planning.

We need a detailed understanding of the temporal path of supply and demand balances in developing countries. It is possible that rather than the simple picture I depicted earlier, that when supply shifts first become substantial, based on basic agricultural research, that supply will move ahead of demand, providing an early exporting phase (Tsujii 1982). Then the employment multipliers derived from agricultural growth would gradually become more powerful, at which time demand would move ahead more rapidly, causing a shift to imports. All of this must be related closely to the progression in the livestock sector. We need careful studies of these matters to understand the timing of structural changes. The implications for agricultural exporters are immense (perhaps as much as tens of millions of tons of exports annually), with profound implications for domestic agricultural production policy in the developed countries.

We also need to more fully understand the relative importance of supply shifts and price responses in the developed countries. We now have a substantial literature and many polemics implying that the supply response to price in developed countries is large. There has been less discussion of the role of shifts in supply, how these relate to the diminishing weight of shifts in demand, what the implications are for aggregate exportable surpluses, and the interaction of those surpluses with price. One could provide many examples of the importance of this, but certainly the European Common Market is a prime case. There supply shifts are large, demand is essentially static, and prices are kept high. If European prices were brought down to equal world prices, would the response to price be large enough to overwhelm the continuing effect of the shifts in supply? How strong are these shifts in supply? What might be done to reduce them? Are they affected by prices? There is much speculation but little hard data on these complex questions. Indeed, we have polemics between neoclassicists and structuralists but little analysis of the interaction of the two types of forces. One could raise similar questions for North America.

As there is considerable uncertainty about supply shifts and price responses in both developed and developing countries, the question of what cost food production in developing countries should be pursued over what time span becomes complex. There can be little question that all developing countries must seek to shift supply through agricultural research, extension, infrastructure development, and input supply. The numbers of people in the basic agriculture and food sector is so large and capital is so constrained that it is nonsense to talk about these countries as having no comparative advantages in food. One can also make the case that large areas in virtually every country have a comparative advantage in pursuing technological improvements in agriculture and in obtaining a rapid rate of growth from that technological advance. That is not the issue. The issue comes from expensive capital investments in agriculture for land reclamation and irrigation. How much can be spent on these in view of future world food supply balances and the implicit price situation? There are clearly projects and programs in developing countries with rates of return that are low with any reasonable estimate of future prices. When appeal is made to price incentives in developing countries in the context of structural processes that take decades to foment, what price regime and hence what cost regime do we have in mind? The implications that alternative policies have for the major exporters are large. Careful empirical studies on this set of questions is needed.

We need to analyze much more carefully the appropriate commodity composition of trade in the future. This has several components. There is the whole issue of cereals trade. Clearly cereal flows from the developed to the developing countries will grow for several decades. How much will they grow? At what price? What should be done to encourage them? What other issues need to be raised? There is also a complex set of issues surrounding the trade of labor-intensive agricultural commodities. This would include much of livestock production and fruits and vegetables. How much comparative advantage and specialization can there be among Third World countries and hence how rapidly can intra–Third World trade in these commodities grow? Furthermore, what should the long-term comparative advantage be for these commodities in trade between developed and developing countries? At the most simplistic level, could the developed countries sell much more cereal if they were willing to import more livestock products, fruits, and vegetables? How does this vary among developed countries? What are the implications for the European community's expansion? What are the implications for the location of fertilizer production and other capital-intensive industries?

Finally, the mechanics of trade processes need to be better understood, particularly the relationship between state and private institutions and how they affect demand, supply, and prices.

TEACHING IMPLICATIONS. As our knowledge of these issues grows, it obviously needs to be conveyed to the current electorate in the United States through extension programs and to the future electorate through teaching programs. There needs to be an emphasis first on the simple issue of the interlocking of economies in the world and of the tremendous importance of the Third World to U.S. agriculture. The effort at selling foreign aid on the basis of poverty alleviation, particularly in the 1970s, created a clear misimpression among the electorate in the United States. The developing countries are in general no longer poverty-stricken countries with no economic relevance to the United States. They are beginning to develop rapidly. Their poverty problems are, of course, immense, but they are diminishing in the context of rapid real and potential growth. We need to understand that and then see how it affects commercial exports.

Global Poverty

THE BASIC ISSUES. Most of the poor are in the developing countries. We can say further that the poverty that cannot be met by modest redistribution of income within national boundaries lies in the Third World countries. For example, in the United States poverty is not normally defined to include more than 10 to 15 percent of the population. Incomes below the poverty line in the United States could be raised above it by redistribution of a modest proportion of total national income. That cannot be said of developing countries. In most developing countries it would be difficult to define a poverty line that included 40 percent of the population, and that line would be considerably lower than one that included only 5 to 10 percent of the population in developed countries.

This raises an important philosophical issue. To what extent is concern for poverty constrained by national boundaries? When we ask the Rawlsian question of fairness and justice (Rawls 1971), do we assume that we would be plunked down as citizens of the United States of America, or is our random placement in the world to include all countries and people? I suspect that in answering the Rawlesian question we in effect open the possibility of being plunked down anywhere, but put the probability of coming down in the United States considerably higher than the proportion of the United States population to that of the rest of the world. Thus the philosophical issue is rather complex. Let me assume, however, that Americans think of themselves as having some concern with the probability of landing in the poverty-stricken classes in developing countries. We then see in the name of fairness and justice a philosophical basis for a U.S. concern and a U.S. interest in dealing with poverty in Third World countries.

One should distinguish clearly between a long-run solution to poverty in developing countries and its short-run mitigation. The long-run solution is development. If one is concerned with poverty in developing countries and wishes to deal with it through development, one necessarily advocates a policy that puts the primary emphasis of public policy on developing agriculture and then deriving linkage and multiplier effects from agricultural growth that stimulate the growth of other sectors of the economy (Mellor 1976). This growth pattern has a high employment content and can induce high rates of growth quickly. It is reasonable to think that once a country has developed minimal institutional structures and a body of trained personnel that it can eliminate most poverty, (i.e., getting it down to U.S. proportions within 15 to 25 years (Mellor 1976; Mellor and Mudahar 1974).

There is also the possibility that poverty can be mitigated in the short run. That obviously must be done by redistribution. As far as the developing countries are concerned and because of their low average incomes, we have to think substantially in terms of redistribution from the developed countries. Foreign assistance to deal with the long-term problem and dealing with the short-term problem should be distinguished here. The short-term problem shows itself most particularly in the inadequate intake of basic energy sources. In other words, it is largely a food problem. Thus we are talking about moving quantities of food beyond what the market moves from surplus-producing developed countries to developing countries with food deficits. This has to be done in a way that does not excessively depress domestic prices in the receiving countries; after all, one does not want to obstruct the long-term solution to the problem. Avoiding a price depressing effect is simply done when the objective is to reduce poverty because one wants to see to it that food enters the hands of people with high marginal propensities to consume it, precisely because they are very poor. There are two major vehicles for achieving this. One is through increased employment of the poor and the other is through subsidies decreasing the price of food. In each case the objective is to increase food consumption.

THE RESEARCH AGENDA. The research agenda for dealing with the long-term problem of poverty includes research on what agriculture needs to develop with particular emphasis on agricultural research and how to optimize it, input supply and how to maximize its rate of growth, and development of infrastructure. All of this involves issues I will take up in the third part of this paper. Research is also required on how to maximize the growth of employment with an agricultural strategy. This requires work on the linkages and multipliers between agricultural growth and nonagricultural growth and how they may be attained most effectively. We need a good deal more description of those processes and then analysis of the policy needs.

The research agenda for short-term needs is quite straightforward. We first need more research on how to increase employment as supplies of food increase. Second, we need to learn more about food subsidies and how they can be best operated when food is transferred internationally. In this context we need much more research on food aid since that would presumably be the primary vehicle for transferring food from developed to developing countries to mitigate poverty.

TEACHING IMPLICATIONS. Teaching in the United States on global poverty has two dimensions: (1) enabling people to comprehend the problem and (2) making it possible to understand the role of food in growth and poverty reduction and its relation to developed-country agricultural policy.

Teaching on the first dimension needs to attend to three issues: (1) the philosophical issue of national or global responsibility for poverty, (2) the relationships between long-term reduction of poverty and development strategy and between agricultural employment policies and functions and poverty reduction, and (3) the time required to reduce poverty in countries in different stages of growth.

Food aid deserves special emphasis in teaching programs because it can be so important to U.S. agriculture and because of the complexity of its relationship to poverty reduction in developing countries. Emphasis needs to be given to the differences in the demand elasticities of countries and income groups and to policies that can ensure that increments to demand in developing countries match additions to supply from food aid.

Unequal Distribution of Human Capital

THE BASIC ISSUES. There is an extraordinary disproportion of human capital between the developed countries and the developing countries. Indeed, it is not an oversimplification to say that is the root of the differences in development. The basic issue here is to what extent is it in the interest of the developed countries to use their disproportionate share of human capital to redress the imbalance and how can they do it? Obviously, if it is believed that development of developing countries will be advantageous to the developed countries, then they should show interest in this issue. It is probably fair to say that this is the essential issue of foreign aid. After all, we know that pure capital transfers have low rates of return in developing countries precisely because of the scarcity of human capital. This is not to say that only human capital should be transferred, but one should see the basic relationship between human capital and the returns to other forms of capital.

While I have stated this issue in general terms, it is of particular importance for agriculture. Agriculture needs a vast set of complex institutions if it is to improve. They must be staffed by highly trained people. This ranges all the way from the enormous number of people with advanced degrees needed in the agricultural research systems to the large number of people with college degrees to run large numbers of other institutions.

The emphasis given to different levels of training raises complex issues. Emphasis has recently been put on primary school education. In a number of African countries that emphasis has been from the point of view of what development requires. Related to this is how to transfer human capital at the various levels of education. This transfer is probably easier to make at the higher levels than at the lower. This means that the proportion of foreign assistance from developed countries at each level may not be the optimum for the country assisted. The relationships between the number of people trained and the institutions built to receive them are complicated; one cannot change without change in the other.

THE RESEARCH AGENDA. Probably the most important issue in the human capital research agenda is the proportion of expenditures allotted to the different levels of education. Nearly all countries expend a lot on education.

That is probably politically determined, so that research on what the overall expenditures should be would probably have little influence. The proportion given to each level is probably somewhat politically determined as well, but the results of research would be more likely to influence the process.

There is much research that needs to be done on the role of technical assistance in development (i.e., on transfers of human capital from developed to developing countries). How do land-grant colleges affect the process on increasing the human capital of developing countries? What are the institutional arrangements needed for the process? How can expatriates be useful? In what proportion should expatriates help build institutions and should people be trained abroad?

TEACHING IMPLICATIONS. There is a tremendous need to develop awareness that human capital transfers to developing countries are needed so that the institutions in the United States can be tuned better to this purpose. Beyond that, there is a need to teach the relation between technical assistance and the development of human capital in developing countries.

Finally, teaching the relation between human capital, development, poverty alleviation, and international food trade ties together the three elements of this essay and tells us much about the global economy in which we will live for the next few decades.

References

Mellor, J. W. 1976. *The Economics of Growth—A Strategy for India and the Developing World.* Ithaca, N.Y.: Cornell Univ. Press.

Mellor, J. W., and M. S. Mudahar. 1974. Stimulating a Developing Economy with Modernizing Agricultural Sector: Implications for Employment and Economic Growth. USAID Technological Change in Agriculture Project Occasional Paper No. 76. Ithaca, N.Y.: Cornell University.

Paulino, L. 1986. Food in the Third World: Past Trends and Projections to 2000. Research Report 52. Washington, D.C.: International Food Policy Research Inst.

Paulino, L., and K. Bachman. 1979. Rapid Food Production Growth in Selected Developing Countries: A Comparative Analysis of Underlying Trends, 1961–1976. Research Report 11. Washington, D.C.: International Food Policy Research Inst.

Rawls, J. 1971. *A Theory of Justice.* Cambridge, Mass.: Harvard Univ. Press.

Sarma, J. S. 1986. Cereal Feed Use in the Third World: Past Trends and Projections to 1990 and 2000. Research Report 57. Washington, D.C.: International Food Policy Research Inst.

Tsujii, H. 1982. *Comparison of Rice Policies Between Thailand, Taiwan, and Japan: An Evolutionary Model and Current Policies.* Kyoto: Kyoto Univ. Press.

Issues in World Agriculture
– a U.S. Perspective: **A Discussion**

PAUL R. JOHNSON

I only have a sketch of a paper on which to comment, but I believe that the fleshing out of that sketch will not materially affect any comments that I might make.

I am pleased that Mellor for the most part is taking the long view of the rural problems that he sees. The television pictures of Ethiopia show us a crisis in food distribution, but that is not an issue in world agriculture that economists have much to say about. Mellor addresses three basic topics: international food flows, global poverty, and unequal distribution of human capital.

The title of this paper and the nature of the topic led me to go back and leaf through another treatment of this topic that is now 40 years old. *Food for the World* (Schultz 1945) contains papers and discussions from a conference about world agricultural problems as seen by the participants as the United States was coming out of World War II. The issues have not changed since 1945. The problems seen then concerned food supply, population changes, quality of nutrition, and incomes of farmers. All of these issues are involved in Mellor's three areas of concern. The main difference in concerns of the two studies is that the discussion of poverty in the earlier study included U.S. poverty, both rural and urban. Neither kind of poverty is pervasive in this country today. Otherwise, the discussions sound very much alike.

International trade in food was discussed in the earlier study. Much of the discussion would be familiar today. The world then was coming out of the Depression and a world war, both of which inhibit international trade. The participants in the earlier study recognized that the poorest countries would be net food importers as Engel's Law tells us. Mellor's point that developing countries can increase production but increase consumption even more, so that food imports increase, is certainly as valid today as it was then.

In 1945, the U.S. price support program prompted T. W. Schultz to observe, "We are in the process of evolving an agricultural policy that can have only one ultimate result in respect to foreign trade, and that is to get us out of it altogether" (Schultz 1945, 199). In my judgment that quote is

Paul R. Johnson is Professor of Economics, North Carolina State University, Department of Economics and Business, Raleigh.

true today also. Mellor is certainly correct when he points out that the recent appreciation of the dollar makes things worse for U.S. exports. However, that is an exacerbating factor for U.S. prices that are kept high by price supports. All of the U.S. agricultural export problems are not due to macro policies extraneous to the agricultural sector.

Two other concerns for the international trade section of the paper are dealing with state traders and governmental interference in both importing and exporting countries. The first Mellor mentions via his discussion of Russia as an importer. It seems to me that the institutional setting for trade is going to vary by country and setting is crucial for analysis of problems. The future flow of food from the United States to developing countries, both commercial and concessional sales, is going to depend on the policies being pursued by the importing country. I realize that a paper such as this has to deal in generalities. Maybe the role of a commentator is to point out that things may not be as simple as they seem, even though the author knows this full well.

The other two topics of the paper, poverty and human capital, are so intertwined they can hardly be separated. Mellor recognizes this in his introductory comments. Again, I am pleased that the author recognizes the long-run nature of the poverty problem. You cannot make short-run redistribution of wealth if you do not have any. I remind you of the 1945 discussion of poverty in the United States in the 1930s and contrast that with today. Countries that are so poor that poverty can be measured by some caloric shortfall may be helped by some redistribution of food from richer countries. But as Mellor warns, doing this and at the same time avoiding depressing food prices in the recipient countries is a tricky thing indeed.

Curing poverty is, of course, the essence of development. Developmental economics is not my field. However, my occasional forays into this thicket have convinced me that governmental economic policies in general have hurt rather than helped find the cure. Even a country as agriculturally developed as Brazil is operating with a whole array of taxes, subsidies, exchange rates, and other devices that vary over time and commodities. Whatever the basis of each of these wedges is, their presence inhibits the changing use of and growth in the resource base of the country involved.

In Mellor's view the unequal distribution of human capital seems to be a problem for the United States and the developed countries. I see a role for some transfer here, but I have to ask who was the donor of human capital for Japan, Taiwan, and Singapore.

In summary, the paper points to some interesting problems that will continue to plague world agriculture and thereby the United States. The author was not expected to have solutions, so this broad overview of problems gives us an excellent status report on a never-ending problem.

Reference

Schultz, T. W., ed. 1945. *Food for the World.* Chicago: Univ. of Chicago Press.

Issues in World Agriculture
– a Third World Perspective: **A Discussion**

ALAIN DE JANVRY

John Mellor has identified several priority issues for research and teaching on world agriculture, taking for this purpose a U.S. perspective, namely, one that gives primacy to the issues that are of greater concern and interest to this country. Among the plethora of alternatives, he chose to single out three: (1) the growing importance of agricultural trade and the mutual benefits that it can bring to both the United States and the Third World, in particular under the form of increased demand for U.S. food exports resulting from healthy growth in the Third World and from investment decisions guided by comparative advantages; (2) the continued massiveness of poverty and deprivation in the Third World and the need to attack them, in the short run, via increased international food aid and in the long run, via agriculture-led economic growth; and (3) the lack of trained personnel and the need to assist human capital formation.

Our interests in world agricultural development cannot, however, only be confined to a U.S. perspective. Indeed, much of the research and training we do here on the subject is motivated by the direct interests of Third World nations in promoting economic growth and in enhancing social welfare. In the long run, there most likely exists a communality of interests between the United States and the Third World, since a more developed and equitable world is a source of opportunities for both greater economic exchanges and greater political stability. This was clearly demonstrated by the benefits for the United States of the economic reconstruction of Europe and Japan after World War II and by the new opportunities created by the economic takeoff in China, as well as by the loss of employ-

Alain de Janvry is Chairman, Department of Agricultural and Resource Economics, University of California, Berkeley.

ment in industry and effective demand for agriculture in the United States that resulted from economic recession and debt crisis in Latin America during the last five years. In the short run, however, there may well exist conflicts in economic gains between the United States and the Third World (i.e., the current debates on protectionism and commodity price stabilization); and our research and teaching may be dictated by the rightful interests of the poor in Third World countries.

I have chosen to discuss three issues in world agriculture that seem to me are at the heart of both the perpetuation of malnutrition and hunger in many less-developed countries (LDCs) and the farm income or public budget crisis in the United States and the European Economic Community. They are questions of food security, the politics of policy, and the implementation of structural reforms.

Food Security and Microeconomic Policies

What are the issues that will dominate world agriculture in the years to come? In the Third World, the dominant issue from a developmental standpoint will likely remain the continuing food crisis in Africa even beyond the current drought, the permanence of extensive malnutrition and hunger on the Indian subcontinent in spite of successful output growth, and the changing rules of access to food for countries (especially in Latin America and the Middle East) that have fallen into heavy food dependency and find reliance on imports compromised by unfavorable terms of trade, heavy debt burdens, and foreign exchange shortages. The mirror image in the United States and Europe of this difficult food situation in the Third World is a sluggish demand for exports, mounting production surpluses, farm income difficulties, and unbearably high public budgets to subsidize agricultural exports. As the Overseas Development Council (1984) recently expressed, the U.S. costs of Third World recession are such that "they lose, we lose."

An effective integrative approach to analyze these problems is that of food security. We define food security as access for all people and, at most time, to enough food to satisfy nutritional requirements. Food security is thus characterized by both a level and a variability in food intake (Reutlinger 1982). Level and variability of intake are, in turn, determined by the availability of food (domestic supply and imports) and by individual access (entitlements determined by control over productive resources, prices, and income) to food, both of which are stochastic.

Research on food security and the appropriate modeling for this purpose have to take us beyond the sterile debate on comparative advantages and trade versus food self-sufficiency. They also have to go beyond simple concerns with price stabilization using buffer stocks or variable tariffs to address the question of the level and stability of food entitlements for particular social groups. The gains from trade evidently cannot be neglected, but use of trade as an instrument of food security has to be an integral part of an explicit development strategy and must be complemented by other policy instruments to ensure food security for all segments of the population. Consequently the models used need to incorporate a detailed social disaggregation to evidence how the nutritional status of different social groups is differentially affected by specific policy instruments. These models must explain resource allocation in production, income (and especially wage) formation, and consumption patterns. They must also give a detailed specification of the foreign sector, of the substitutability in production and consumption between domestic and imported goods, of exchange rate determination, and of foreign exchange constraints. This is particularly important to trace out the impact on the poor of current stabilization policies.

With the coefficient of variation in international prices typically larger than that in domestic yields, modeling will show, for instance, that improving the food security of quasi-subsistence farmers is best obtained by policies that raise their mean income level, while that of the urban poor is best ensured by policies that reduce their vulnerability to food instability. As the degree of risk aversion increases, more reliance will be placed on domestic production than on trade in ensuring national food security by reallocating resources between food and cash (export) crops toward the former. In the long run, alternative styles of development, including redistribution of assets via structural reforms, the tightening of labor markets, and intersecting investment priorities, are key to food security. Successful economic growth in the Third World, based in particular on a broad-based model of agricultural-led industrial development, will raise consumers' income and induce a transition in consumption toward livestock products, stimulating the demand for imports of feed grains that can be supplied by U.S. producers (Paarlberg 1984).

Food security, analyzed in multisectoral, multimarket, and household models, is thus an effective research approach to the design of policies to cope with the two dominant problems of world agriculture today: permanence of malnutrition and hunger in the LDCs and lack of effective demand for farm exports in the more developed countries (MDCs).

The Politics of Policy

Government interventions in agriculture are pervasive and assume a large variety of forms. Not only do governments intervene in the distribution of public goods, such as technology and infrastructure, but they also enter actively into the mechanisms of price determination. These interventions have a wide variety of objectives such as stimulating production, enhancing farm incomes, stabilizing prices, improving the nutritional status of consumers, generating public revenues and foreign exchange earnings, and redistributing income among individuals, regions, and sectors. It is well known that these objectives are often contradictory and that use of price distortions as a policy instrument is thus loaded with political implications. It is because of these many contradictory functions of prices that most governments are reticent to leave the determination of prices to market forces and that many organized groups in civil society compete to acquire control over their determination.

In recent years a large amount of work has been done to identify the existence of price distortions and to trace out their consequences on resource allocation and social welfare. This includes, for instance, the many studies done at the World Bank (Scandizzo and Bruce 1980; Bale and Lutz 1979). Yet, very little is known of the determinants of these distortions and, hence, of how to endogenize government behavior in economic models. Clearly, identifying distortions and tracing out their consequences is not sufficient to recommend alternative policies if the determinants of the existence of these distortions are not known in the first place. Policy analysis needs to be complemented by political economy if policy recommendations are to be meaningful. Interesting advances for this purpose have been made in the theory of pressure groups, the theory of rent seeking, the theory of economic regulation and public choice, and the theory of the state. Yet, these frameworks are still insufficient to capture two important aspects of policymaking. One is the degree of relative autonomy of the state in decision making (what motivates governments to act in a crisis response or in a planning mode to sustain capital accumulation or preserve the legitimacy of class relations) and the constraints imposed on state behavior by fiscal, legitimacy, and administrative limits. The other is the complex, interactive process between electoral politics and bureaucratic behavior, on the one hand, and pressure group politics and lobbies' demands on the other.

While the importance of policy analysis has been well recognized in agricultural economics, policy without politics is not a useful exercise. Yet, few students of agricultural economics are trained in political economy of different vintages. Understanding political economy requires knowledge of the history of economic thought and of institutions. As with foreign languages, requirements in these fields, which were common at least in economics departments, have been dropped in many universities. Yet, new developments in political economy (interest group competition, theory of the state, capture theory, rent seeking and conflict resolution), as well as in the mathematical theory of games, bargaining, and contracts, will likely make it one of the hottest future topics in the profession. Since the role of government is so important in agriculture, agricultural economics should not miss the opportunity of being at the frontier of this important field. And since the role of the state is even greater in the Third World, development economists should be at the forefront of this area of knowledge.

Structural Reforms

Many evils of underdevelopment have their origins in structural deficiencies that either block economic growth (Africa) or allow for eventually rapid, if unstable, growth but bias the distribution of benefits toward the rich, resulting in a worsening distribution of income and few improvements in the status of the poor (Latin America and the Middle East). These structural deficiencies imply that unqualified application of neoclassical economics does not work (in particular because markets often fail or are seriously distorted, especially labor markets characterized by massive unemployment) or that, if it does, it leads to social consequences that are hardly acceptable to those preoccupied with the persistence of mass poverty (in particular because of dualism, extreme inequality in asset ownership, technological inadequacies, structural unemployment, social disarticulation, etc.). These structural specificities were at the heart of development economics and called for an active role of the state in managing a catching-up process (Hirschman 1981). This led to the important phase of import substitution industrialization that promoted rapid capital accumulation under protectionism and an active state. Subsequent disillusionment with the social consequences of rapid growth has led to the emergence in the 1970's of a "growth with equity" school that has recommended policies of redistribution before growth, redistribution with growth, basic needs, employment generation, agriculture-led development strategies, integrated rural development, and promotion of the informal sector.

In recent years, these structuralist schools have come under serious attack for their presumed excessive zeal in centralized planning, rationalization of government interventions, and tolerance for price distortions (Lal 1983). Development economics has been reduced to the strict application of neoclassical principles (open economy, balanced budget, and getting the prices right, including and especially the exchange rate) with a primary interest on the problems of international trade and finance.

This is a personal opinion, but I see this as a dangerous tendency that should be held in check. While the neoliberal criticism has been helpful in acknowledging the key roles of decision making by decentralized agents and of market-determined prices in guiding an efficient allocation of resources, structural change remains at the heart of development economics. These changes cannot be expected to occur as a sole by-product of economic growth, at least not with an acceptable time span. State interventions and structural reforms remain necessary. Recent reinterpretations of successful equitable growth in Taiwan and South Korea—the presumed archetypes of market-led neoliberal development—have, for instance, clearly demonstrated the active role of the state in promoting extensive redistribution of the land as a precondition for equitable growth, infant industry protectionism, incentives to labor-intensive exports, priorities to productivity-enhancing investments in agriculture, and promotion of human capital formation (Pack and Westphal 1985).

While historical experience and policy simulations give us some knowledge of what could be the expected consequences of different types of structural reforms, we still have little experience with their implementation. There is widespread agreement on the potential benefits of land reform, but the political and administrative difficulties of implementing it are stifling initiatives. It has been widely said that rural development programs must be managed in a decentralized, participatory, and adaptive fashion (Korten 1980), but successful examples are still largely nonexistent. Grass-root movements have been advocated as a powerful alternative approach to development, but we still largely miss a theory of how they can be promoted and how they can aggregate into something larger than isolated instances.

Teaching in these areas requires a close integration between theory and practice. Yet in recent years, stagnant foreign aid budgets and the politicalization of aid programs have reduced opportunities for long-term field involvement by U.S. academics. The result is a dangerous loss of expertise on development programs in U.S. universities, precisely when, as John Mellor pointed out, our universities should be increasingly involved in the formation of the human capital that will assume leadership in Third World structural reforms.

REFERENCES

Bale, M., and E. Lutz. 1979. Price Distortions in Agriculture and Their Effects: An International Comparison. Staff Working Paper No. 359. Washington, D.C.: The World Bank.

Hirschman, A. 1981. *Essays in Trespassing: Economics to Politics and Beyond.* Cambridge: Cambridge Univ. Press.

Korten, D. 1980. Community Organization and Rural Development: A Learning Process Approach. *Public Adm. Rev.* 40(5):480–512.

Lal, D. 1983. *The Poverty of "Development Economics."* London: Inst. of Economic Affairs.

Overseas Development Council. 1984. U.S. "Costs" of Third World Recession: They Lose, We Lose. *Policy Focus,* No. 2.

Paarlberg, R. 1984. U.S. Agriculture and Third World Development: Harmonies or

Disharmonies of Interest? In *Agriculture Stability and Growth: Toward a Cooperative Approach.* New York: Associated Faculty Press.

Pack, H., and L. Westphal. 1985. Industrial Strategy and Technological Change: Theory Versus Reality. Paper presented at the Conference on New Directions in Development Theory, Center for International Studies, MIT Cambridge.

Reutlinger, S. 1982. Policies for Food Security in Food-importing Developing Countries. In *Food Security: Theory, Policy, and Perspectives from Asia and the Pacific Rim.* Lexington, Mass.: Lexington Books.

Scandizzo, P., and C. Bruce. 1980. Methodologies for Measuring Agricultural Price Intervention Effects. Staff Working Paper No. 394. Washington, D.C.: The World Bank.

8

Quantitative Techniques

S. R. JOHNSON

Agricultural economists have had a key role in the development and application of quantitative techniques in economics and, more specifically, economic analysis. Since the initial experience with budgeting in farm management, time-series and statistical methods in commodity markets, and sector analysis during the 1930s, the importance of quantification and quantitative techniques to policy and decision analysis to a fuller understanding of the agricultural industry has been widely recognized.

Early applications and the development of quantitative techniques in agricultural economics were limited by two important factors: (1) the availability of data systems and, perhaps relatedly, (2) the cost and even technical feasibility of the required computations. Both of these barriers have been relaxed in important respects during the last 50 years. Data systems have been expanded and have become more timely based on an emerging computer technology. Also the theory in economics and agricultural economics has developed pointing to additional measurements required for economic analysis. Costs of computation have been reduced through more flexible computer software as well as advances in optimization theory and method. At the heart of many of the computations for quantitative applications is an optimization problem in parameter estimation and/or model solution.

The 1950s and early 1960s witnessed a rapid extension in applications of quantitative techniques. These developments were accompanied by and to an extent they led to advances in economic theory, computational methods, and improvements in the scope and quality of the data systems on the food and agricultural complex. During this period, agricultural econo-

S. R. Johnson is Professor of Economics and Administrator, Center of Agricultural and Rural Development, Iowa State University, Ames.

mists provided leadership in the development of quantitative techniques. Many of the techniques influencing research in other areas of economics and in management and the behavioral sciences had their origins in agricultural economics. Moreover, the research generating these advances was very much in phase with the current decision and policy issues in the agricultural and food complex. These policy issues included new production technologies, changes in the structure of agricultural and rural communities associated with a mass population exodus, governmental regulation of agricultural commodity markets and farm income, and, finally, an integration of domestic and world commodity markets.

Since the 1950s and early 1960s, the record of agricultural economists in the development and application of quantitative techniques has been less impressive. In some respects this is simply because the "action" in the area has become more widespread. Other specialized fields in economics, the other social sciences, and the management or decision sciences recognized the value of quantitative analysis. It is tempting to attribute the relinquishing of the leadership of agricultural economists in quantitative techniques to this "bigger pond" theory (i.e., the developments in agricultural economics are not as significant because many more disciplines and scientists are now involved).

But perhaps this is a generous interpretation of events. At the opposite extreme, one could argue that applications of quantitative techniques in agricultural economics had become more opportunistic and less innovative. Agricultural economists have been more satisfied with a role of applying quantitative methods developed in other branches of economics or other disciplines. In addition, these applications have not always addressed the major policy and decision issues of the agricultural and food complex. Finally, the use of imported techniques has not been as questioning or participated in as broadly as when the quantitative technologies grew out of the major policy and structural analysis questions of the day.

The foregoing observations have anticipated the two major themes of the paper. First, the discipline tends to exhibit leadership in the quantitative areas when the developments are themselves led by policy and decision problems important to food and agriculture. Second, to contribute to the advances in quantitative method, research must be questioning and the limitations of findings carefully communicated. When new quantitative methods are mechanical devices generated outside the discipline and applications and research are driven more by their availability than real policy and decision issues, the leadership role of the discipline and the value of the quantitative research is likely to be greatly diminished.

These propositions are not intended to detract from the importance of specialization and division of labor. Instead, they reflect an attitude or orientation of those involved in quantitative research. When quantitative research is undertaken for agriculture, the results are likely to be highly questioned and the techniques themselves more carefully evaluated. There are stakes for both the discipline and the industry in the results. Alternatively, when our research is directed more by outside influences and incentives to demonstrate puzzle-solving expertise and gadgetry, it is likely to become less original and to generate fewer advances in method.

Developments in Quantitative Techniques

Since the emergence of quantitative methods as important research tools in agricultural economics, there have been a number of significant developments. These developments or additions to the technology are reviewed to identify the major contributions to the quantitative modeling technology and to provide a perspective on why and how these techniques were developed and/or integrated into the existing agricultural economics research approaches.

The review of the major developments in modeling technology is undertaken more or less chronologically. This chronological approach is attractive since, in a number of cases, the techniques of technologies have built upon or developed in response to limitations of quantitative modeling approaches relative to important research issues and questions for agriculture.

MULTIVARIATE STATISTICAL ANALYSIS. Classical statistical methods found many early applications in agricultural economics. These advances could be seen as coincidental with developments in statistical method. Alternatively, the incentive for the development of multivariate statistical methods can be viewed as rooted in the decision problems critical to agriculture in the 1930s. Extensive government policies were initiated for regulating agricultural markets. Information to regulate the markets required new data systems and methods for summarizing these data relative to key behavioral parameters. In addition, important changes in technology, structure, and other features of the agricultural industry were accelerating in the 1930s. The associated data bases provided a fertile ground for development and refinement of multivariate statistical methods.

The leadership of agricultural economics in the development and application of multivariate methods is found, for example, in the works of Bean (1929), Moore (1914), Schultz (1938), Ezekiel (1930), and Working (1926). [See Judge (1977) for more detail.] By the 1950s, statistical laboratories, which were common in agricultural economics departments, developed specialized methods for estimating multivariate relationships that were then applied routinely in structural and policy analyses. Subsequently, these multivariate techniques have been refined, for example, in reflecting more accurately characteristics of data and methods of sampling, in merging sample and nonsample information, and in more fully incorporating restrictions from the theory.

BUDGETING AND LINEAR PROGRAMMING. It is difficult to separate budgeting and linear programming as quantitative techniques in agricultural economics. Both rely on linear input/output relationships. The major data bases for both are found in farm enterprise records, experimental data, and frequently, surveys identifying resource constraints. Both have been applied widely in farm management exercises. The applications of budgeting, in fact, provided a ready slot for linear programming methods once they became available.

Linear programming found wide application and development in agricultural economics in the 1950s. At first these applications were relatively narrow, for enterprise selection for different farm types (Heady 1952; Bradford and Johnson 1953; and Swanson 1956). However, as linear programming became more fully understood and in response to attempts to anticipate longer term agricultural adjustments, applications were made in regional economics, transportation, and in the studies of more integrated production and distribution systems. These methods were applied in analyzing natural resource decisions as well (e.g., Heady and Candler 1958).

Refinements of linear programming and applications of linear approximations to production functions have contributed to the development of more extensive models. These more extensive applications have been facilitated by improved optimization algorithms, more extensive resource data, cost-of-production surveys in agriculture, and other contributions to the information base on which the models reside. Not unimportantly, the technology adoption, industry structure change, natural resource issues, and related questions to which these early applications were made have persisted as important policy problems in agriculture.

STRUCTURAL ECONOMETRICS. The development of structural econometric methods occurred during a flurry of activity associated with the Cowles Commission in the early 1950s. Interestingly, a number of agricultural economists were involved (Judge 1977). To provide a complete list of the agricultural economists that had important roles in the development and early application of structural econometric methods would be difficult and certain to offend by omission [examples include Cromarty (1959), Fox (1953), Foote (1953), Kuznets (1955), and Tintner (1952)].

Structural or simultaneous equation methods have greatly influenced the quantitative modeling work in agriculture economics. Most of the large-scale sector commodity models used in forecasting and policy analysis incorporate the simultaneous methods at least in specification due to the necessity of observing data in aggregate time frames and/or the theory. Extensions of structural econometric modeling have included expansions of the scope and size of models, integrations of different forms of price determination processes (e.g., rational expectations), and, more recently, introductions of time-series methods (e.g., Fomby et al. 1984). As is the case with many quantitative techniques, available computer capacity and software limited early applications. Presently, highly efficient software for estimating and applying structural econometric methods is available.

SYSTEMS ANALYSIS. Partially in response to perceived inflexibilities in classical statistical, structural econometric, and optimization models, systems analysis has evolved as a widely utilized quantitative technique in agricultural economics. System models are eclectic in nature, providing opportunities for more direct introduction of subjective or personalized information (Johnson and Rausser 1977). In addition, they tend to be less dominated by prior information from the economic theory. These models evolved in the 1960s, a period when extensions of the scope of agricultural economics research were occurring. The extensions involved resources, ecology, development planning, and other areas where the scientific basis for policy was weak. In these situations, heuristic methods incorporating systems concepts were attractive. River base planning and other highly integrated systems models by Halter and Miller (1966), Halter et al. (1970), and their contemporaries are exemplary of these methods and the problems to which they were applied.

The attraction of quantitative modelers in agricultural economics to systems methods can be traced to four areas: (1) the development of flexible computer technologies for organizing and operating highly complex mathematical representations; (2) the extension of the scope of research in agricultural economics; (3) the inadequacies of the theory and, more generally, the scientific basis for addressing these problems; and (4) a dissatisfaction with the restrictive nature of many of the quantitative techniques widely applied by agricultural economists. The more technical of these reasons for the development of systems methods have to a large extent been eliminated by advances in estimation method, theory, data, and decision analysis (Johnson and Rausser 1977).

BAYESIAN ESTIMATION. Bayesian estimation methods have attractive theoretical foundations applicable to the decision and policy problems in agricultural economics. From a practical viewpoint, Bayesian methods provide for incorporation of prior information in the estimation of parameters of policy and decision models. In addition, the Bayesian framework is itself explicitly decision-theoretic. Although Bayesian methods rely on probabilistic foundations quite different from those supporting classical statistical methods, their implications for applications are relatively straightforward. Specifically, the approach provides for efficiently merging sample and non-sample information in estimation and decision contexts.

Although Bayesian methods can be extended to many multivariate problems typical in agricultural decision and policy analysis, applications are at present relatively limited (Zellner 1985 argues differently). This is largely because of the computational burdens for Bayesian estimation in multivariate contexts (Zellner 1971). At the same time, the more direct applications of Bayesian methods in decision analysis have been largely superseded by advances in decision making under uncertainty, which incorporate more realistic assumptions on utility functions. Thus, the Bayesian methods, although important potentially for application in agricultural economics, will likely await advances in computational methods. Some of the same factors that influenced the introduction and development of systems analysis methods in agricultural economics underlie the interest in and attraction of Bayesian methods for addressing agricultural decision and policy problems (Zellner 1985).

NONLINEAR OPTIMIZATION. Nonlinear optimization problems are prevalent in standard applications of economic theory. Thus, the development of computer capacity and software for solving these problems was greeted with wide application in agricultural economics. These applications tended to focus most directly on problems with the objective function for maximand nonlinear, but the technology or "constraint matrix" is linear. Examples include risk programming, spatial price equilibrium analysis, temporal price equilibrium analysis, regional planning, and others (Day and Sparling 1977). For brevity, under this heading are included other optimization methods that involve essentially nonlinear computations: integer programming, dynamic programming, and stochastic programming. Applications and refinements of mathematical programming in agricultural economics have been, in general, natural extensions of theory to applied work. This is particularly true for dynamic optimization, risk programming, and the analysis of spatial and temporal price equilibrium (Burt 1964; Judge and Takayama 1973).

TIME-SERIES METHODS. With the development of advanced computer software and increased capacity to solve nonlinear optimization problems, time-series methods have been applied more widely in agricultural economics. These modern time-series methods are an outgrowth of traditional trend analysis and related approaches to studying persistence (Box and Jenkins 1976). Processes, largely determined by the data, are projected using flexible models for characterizing past behavior. Both univariate and multivariate time-series methods are now available. A particular attraction of these methods is that they provide "good fits" in the sample. Moreover, if the structure that generated the sample observations is not disturbed, forecasts from time-series methods can be highly accurate.

Generally, time-series methods are applied for data from shorter time periods and where assumptions of structural consistency are plausible. Alternative methods are used to characterize persistent tendencies in the data, vector valued autoregressive processes, spectral analysis, and many others. These methods have been popularized subsequent to the publication of the classic by Box and Jenkins (1976). Applications of time-series methods in agricultural economics have been mainly for forecasting. Recently, these models have been integrated more fully into the estimation of structural models and forecasting in mixed contexts (Sims 1980).

CONTROL THEORY. Control theoretic methods are designed to capture the full dynamics of decision problems. The control theory ruberic, in fact, refers to the formulation of sufficiently broad optimization problems that permit conducting experiments within systems to provide better information on their structure as a basis for future policy decisions. In short, control theory represents an integrated framework for viewing the estimation and decision processes for standard policy and decision problems. Control theory has been applied for relatively standard agricultural policy problems; that is, traditional models have been reformulated. Then, control theory has been applied utilizing information from the decision sequence to update information of the system and thereby improve future performance. Like time-series analysis, most of the advances in control theory methods have occurred outside agricultural economics (Aoki 1975). However, the control theory approach represents a recent and attractive trend in integrating estimation and decision problems in a decision theory framework (Rausser and Freebairn 1974).

EXPERIMENTAL MODELING APPROACHES. Perhaps based on ideas from applications of systems analysis and simulation methods in agricultural economics, more heuristic quantitative modeling approaches are appearing. These approaches utilize sample and nonsample information and more adaptive decision processes. Applications of many of the large-scale econometric models incorporate these modeling techniques. Characteristic of these models is the use of heuristic techniques and other methods in developing their structures. This approach to the development of models has been examined recently by Leamer (1985).

In general, the approach calls for an expansion of the inferential methods traditionally used in evaluating models and estimators (McAleer et al. 1985). The approach can be viewed as emerging because of important limitations in the microfoundations of the aggregate economic theory and the associated "data mining" that characterizes much of the quantitative work in the area. For this reason, a high share of the information content of the models is from the data. How these models and methods should be evaluated is a problem to be discussed subsequently. Nevertheless, such modeling techniques are widely applied in agricultural economics.

New Developments

New developments in quantitative techniques in agricultural economics reflect a number of stimuli. As the review in the previous section indicated, these stimuli can be from the policy and decision problems in agricultural economics or from experiments with methods that have evolved outside the discipline. Here these potential developments of quantitative techniques are viewed in terms of issues, including areas of theory, inference and method, modeling technology, and policies and institutions. Thus, the stimuli range from extensions in the theory that permit alternative or advanced applications of quantitative techniques to different characterizations of policy problems and demands for information.

ISSUES FROM THE THEORY. The theoretical foundations for agricultural economics have been largely neoclassical until relatively recently, when advances in economic theory and a recognition of the limitations of neoclassical theory have prompted a number of developments with important potential for increasing the usefulness of agricultural economics research. Those that appear likely to emerge, influencing the direction of agricultural economics research, are indicated below along with cursory comments on how these developments have occurred and their potential influence on quantitative analysis in agricultural economics.

UNCERTAINTY AND RISK. A characteristic of many of the policy and decision problems in agricultural economics is the fact that decisions must be made when there are important sources of uncertainty about their outcomes. These uncertainties evolve from the competitive structure for the agricultural industry, the openness of domestic agricultural markets, the environment, changes in technology, and other factors. In short, for individual decision makers and those who organize and regulate agricultural commodity markets, there are important uncertainties.

Uncertainty in agricultural economics decision and policy analysis has been long recognized. Important advances have been made in better understanding the choice problem under uncertainty. However, there are results that deserve to be incorporated in agricultural economics research. These relate largely to the correspondence between decision making at the individual level and market responses, the microfoundations of agricultural price analysis. Many of the results for individual decisions under uncertainty incorporate relatively strong assumptions on the utility functions. Until these utility function restrictions are relaxed and the correspondence between individual level and aggregate level behavior is formalized, the value of these theories for applied work will be limited. However, the prevalence of uncertainty in agriculture suggests it will be an area of emphasis in future quantitative modeling.

DYNAMICS AND INTERNATIONAL DECISION MAKING. Like risk and uncertainty, dynamics and intertemporal decision-making problems occupy a prominent role in agricultural decision and policy analysis. Time frames for production of many agricultural commodities involve important lags. Many resource problems in agricultural economics have essentially dynamic physiological underpinnings. Finally, decisions in markets characterized by uncertainty are essentially forward looking, adding to the importance of appropriately characterizing dynamic structures.

These dynamic aspects of policy and decision problems in agricultural economics have long been recognized, especially in the natural resource area. Extensive dynamic models of exploitation of natural resources have been developed and applied. Although these models rely on relatively weak physiological foundations, they have been useful in indicating the intertemporal trade-offs for individuals and society.

Refinements in dynamic modeling methods that will make them more attractive for investigating agricultural decision and policy problems can be viewed in two areas. First, it is clear that the fundamental basis for dynamic decision making is presently relatively weak (i.e., the theory of intertemporal preferences). Applications of dynamic models utilize relatively simplistic temporal separability hypotheses. Second, the physiological basis for dynamic models is limited. Understanding these dimensions will involve further exploration of the dynamics of the physical systems. The fact that these dynamics are interactive with economic decision processes is a source of additional concern in the development of useful dynamic decision-making and policy models.

AGGREGATION. Many of the agricultural policy problems that are important currently and for the future involve aggregates. These aggregates are for countries, markets, industries, sectors, and other levels at which economic policies are formulated and applied. Unfortunately, the models applied in characterizing the behavior of these aggregates and formulating the policy problems frequently have limited microfoundations: the models are largely empirical in content and based on past trends and behaviors as characterized by approximate functional forms (Johnson 1981).

The experience with large-scale econometric and systems models has emphasized the importance of understanding better the foundations for the aggregate models. Also, it has suggested different ways of modeling the aggregates, using approximations recognizing more fully that the major source of information is empirical and such approximations are likely to change as external factors are altered and, importantly, with policies directed toward the aggregates (Leamer 1978). Adaptive estimation procedures and theories involving explicitly ideas of approximations will influence developments in this area.

ENDOGENIZATION OF POLICY CHOICE. Policy models can be viewed from two perspectives. From one extreme, models can be structural representations of the situations in which the policy decisions are to be made. In these models, various policy instruments and outcomes based on different decisions for these policy instruments are identified. Then the policy problem is formulated, and outcomes are provided based on presumed objective functions. At the other extreme is the idea of endogenization of policy choice — inferring on the basis of past behavior and from more primitive assumptions a decision framework for agents actually making the policy decisions. These models endogenize policy choices.

Methods of endogenizing policy choices have become increasingly interesting as the various levels of decision making in integrated agricultural markets have become more clearly recognized. Presently, methods of endogenizing policy choice are largely empirical; that is, simple approximate structures are developed. Within these structures, largely in terms of policy instruments, "weights" are identified. These weights reflect the policy behavior on the basis of past experience.

REGULATION. Concerns about the environment, endogenization of externalities, natural resources, and other factors point to the importance of better understanding the implications of regulation. Recently, the theory of regulation has expanded significantly, providing for more appropriate specifications of models designed to estimate producer and consumer behavior under different regulatory regimes and for evaluating the performance of regulated markets. Since many of the regulations of markets and individuals are designed to counter impacts of risk and uncertainty and to condition expectations, these developments have begun to be integrated with those on risk and uncertainty and expectations.

DUALITY AND MICROFOUNDATIONS. The duality theory results of the 1970s and 1980s provide a number of opportunities for extending economic models and empirical applications in decision and policy contexts. Essentially, duality methods have provided alternatives for measurements that can be utilized in better understanding individual and aggregate decision problems. Measurements required by dual formulations of traditional models are frequently more observable. This aspect of duality theory and the insights provided by the alternative formulations of what are essentially identical economic decision problems represent a major contribution to agricultural economics. Duality theory has provided the potential for revising and improving index numbers and other measures of economic performance and data collection, and, more generally, for a better understanding of the behavior of economic agents based on measurable outcomes of decision processes.

EXPECTATIONS AND RATIONALITY. Implications of rationality are important epistemologically as well as in formulations of standard decision problems. According to the rational expectations theory, expectations of individual agents should be modeled as if determined within the context of the framework represented by the economic model (Haltiwanger and Waldman 1985). Since rational expectations are essentially forward looking, the models must be based, for example, on data that are ultimately projectable. If not, highly complex models can be reduced to more simple models for purposes of understanding the behavior of economic agents, the epistemological implications of the rational expectations framework (Simon 1959).

Presently, rational expectations are beginning to be applied and evaluated in economic models. These applications have been relatively mechanical. The full epistemological implications of rational expectations have not been completely recognized or incorporated in the development of our models. Among these implications is the fact that highly complex models residing on external variables that cannot be accurately projected may perform no better than more simplified approximations of these models that reside on the projectable subset of the conditioning variables. Implications of this observation for model specification, a priori information from the theory and, in general, the applications of quantitative techniques are far reaching.

ISSUES OF INFERENCE AND METHOD. Perhaps the most unsettled area for developments in quantitative techniques in agricultural economics are in inference and method of estimation (Zellner 1985). Here, developments in statistics and related fields as well as in econometrics have been rapid in recent years. Many of the results are negative, in that developments show that existing approaches to estimation and inference that are highly empirical and heuristic in content have major limitations. In short, in most applied modeling, the rules applied for inference and evaluation of results are inconsistent with the methods used in deriving the results. This problem is evidenced in the flurry of recent articles pointing out the limitations of econometrics (Hendry 1980; Leamer 1983; McAleer et al. 1985; Zellner 1985).

PRETESTING. A common approach in quantitative modeling for agricultural decision and policy analysis involves a preliminary evaluation of alternative specifications with the same sample data. Frequently, alternative specifications are tried and eliminated based on qualitative responses inconsistent with perceived theory, the fit in the sample data, patterns in residuals, and other features. Then the final model is reported with inferential information consistent with the fact that it was the only specification evaluated.

Results available on pretesting show that the reporting inferences from such models involve great overstatement. In particular, the test statistics and other information lead those who use the results to conclusions that cannot be supported with the reliability advertised in the reported results. This characteristic of the research approach and the development of inferences in agricultural economics is probably the single most important contributor to the disappointment with applications of quantitative techniques. The pretesting results available demonstrate conclusively the drawbacks of this practice.

BIASED ESTIMATION AND PRIOR INFORMATION. A number of developments have been made that provide for incorporation of nonsample information in standard estimation and inferential problems (Fomby et al. 1984). These methods have been termed biased estimation, mixed estimation, and Bayesian estimation. In each, the approach is to introduce information in addition to that from the sample and estimate the parameters of interest more correctly. While these methods represent improvements over existing approaches to more ad hoc inclusions of prior information, they are not without problems. Problems of specifying precisely the reliability of the ultimate estimators are common (i.e., while there are good bases for introducing systematically the prior information, the impact of this prior information on the estimators is only qualitatively known). Exact distributions of the estimators are, in general, not available.

The unavailability of sampling distributions for biased estimators has probably influenced greatly the application of these methods in policy and decision contexts. However, in some cases they are highly attractive relative to existing approaches that depend on extensive data mining and pretesting. As the value of these methods is more fully understood and computational procedures for applications are more widely available, it is likely they will find their way more directly into decision and policy research.

DEPERSONALIZATION OF MODELS. Partly related to the practice of pretesting and experimentation in the empirical data for model specifications, many of the models utilized in the quantitative analysis of agricultural decision and policy problems are personalized (i.e., the priors on the particular model specifications are either very weak or highly identified with the individuals doing the research). This makes it difficult if not impossible for others to duplicate the research process. In this circumstance, the scientific basis for the findings is questionable. Inferences tend to be overstated, research results cannot be replicated, and, in general, the fundamental basis for scientific progress is absent. False signals on the reliability with which policies can be evaluated with the models are communicated.

HEURISTIC METHODS. Partly in response to the state of disarray that characterizes the current econometric and empirical or inferential work in agricultural economics and, more generally, in economics, interest has developed in alternative approaches. Much of this work has been identified with Leamer (1985). Generally, the theme in the literature on more heuristic methods to model specification and estimation emphasizes the fact that it is only necessary to represent results for what they are (Zellner 1985). Although this seems to be a decidedly simple concept, it is widely ignored in applications in agricultural economics and economics.

If models are developed from curve-fitting methods, why not say it? It is not surprising that such would be the case in aggregate level analysis. The reason has been anticipated in the discussion of issues from the theory. Specifically, the theoretical foundations for these aggregate relationships are limited. Thus, models with high empirical content are to be anticipated. Imposing classical or Bayesian inference methods with such heuristic modeling approaches begs the question. As mature scientists, we must recognize that progress in understanding economic structures and the value of results of research for nutrition and policy analysis depends ultimately on accurately communicating the quality of information.

ISSUES FROM MODELING TECHNOLOGY. The modeling technology related to computer developments and software will have broad future implications and applications of quantitative modeling techniques in agricultural economic research. In fact, the advances in computer technology and software for data-base management and model archiving provide valuable opportunities for improving the quality of quantitative models and the development of approaches to quantitative modeling that are more consistent with rules of scientific inquiry.

DISTRIBUTIVE PROCESSING. Distributive processing is occurring at an increasingly rapid pace in computer technology. Essentially, distributive processing means that more of the computations associated with applications of quantitative techniques can be conducted on a decentralized basis. Implications of distributive processing relate to the development of specialized versions of models, the transmission of data bases for use in differing contexts, and the development of approximations or simple versions of more complex models.

Much distributive processing occurs with computers of relatively small capacity. Thus, the more specialized models suggested must be economical in processing capacity requirements. The integration of distributed processing modes and the operation and development of decentralized versions of models that can be employed by specialized users is a theme that will receive much attention in quantitative work in agricultural economics and in other decision sciences as computer technology evolves.

LARGE-SCALE COMPUTERS. The developments of large-scale computers means that models of sizes that were in the past thought unfeasible can now be solved. Implications of this large-scale processing, however, may be limited for large-scale models of the type that have been available and utilized in agricultural economics in the past. Instead, the value of the large-scale computers may be more in artificial intelligence, heuristic modeling, and the use of models in alternative kinds of cognitive exercises.

These cognitive experiments tend to be extensive, must occur on a simultaneous basis, and, in general, are likely to use the large-scale computers more effectively than as simple problem-solving devices. One of the difficulties with large-scale models, as applied in the past and ones that are presently bumping against existing computer capacity, is that the data to support these models are relatively frail. In addition, the models as applied in the past require a great deal of hands-on development; they are highly labor intensive. The cognitive procedures, replacing the decisions made in the development of these large-scale models with computerized processes and systematic estimation methods, may therefore, contribute to the large-scale modeling activities, but these contributions will be through different modeling technologies.

DATA-BASE MANAGEMENT. Data-base management methods and, particularly, the software and hardware required for data-base management are improving. This provides for the opportunity of shared data bases, use of professional resources more efficiently, model archiving, and other practices that may contribute generally to making agricultural economics more scientific. The development of large-scale, high quality data bases that are widely accessible in the profession lowers the cost of quantitative analysis. Additionally, software and models that reside on these data bases or model management systems can be shared to increase the participation in work on quantitative models.

The availability of the data bases and model management systems make it possible for others to duplicate research results at low cost. This prospect is especially important given the frailty of the theory, especially for aggregate models. It is highly likely that in the near future researchers will have at their fingertips accurate and common data bases, the capacity to operate models developed by other researchers, and the opportunity to reproduce and extend existing results more efficiently. This will allow the discipline to concentrate more on the substantive aspects of quantitative techniques than on mechanical processes associated with data assembly and estimation.

ALTERNATIVE DATA SOURCES. The computer technology also has important implications for improved data. That is, the sheer volume of shorter time-frame data will not be an obstacle to analysis and archiving. In addition, through recording of transactions and integrations of these transactions into aggregates, the computer technology can provide new data sources. Examples include futures markets transactions, scanning systems, remote sensing, integrated financial data systems, monitoring of stream flow, and data on growth processes or simulators of plants. Available data, particularly for describing behaviors of economic and physical systems on a shorter time-frame basis, are likely to become more widely available.

ISSUES FROM POLICY AND INSTITUTIONS. The policy questions for agriculture and natural resources or the industry and/or clientele served by agricultural economics change depending on many factors. These factors have included changes in the political representation of agriculture, in integration of domestic and international commodity markets, in the ways that policies are developed and applied in regulating agriculture, in the technology for production, in information and dissemination, and, of course, in many others. The point is that the policy questions, the ways that policies are developed and applied, the decision framework for individual agents, and the institutions are under continual change. These changes have implications for future directions of agricultural research and the development of quantitative techniques to support this research.

RATIONAL DECISION MODELS. The rational-choice policy framework is one usually adopted by quantitative modelers in agricultural economics. Modelers view their job as delineating the policy options, evaluating these options, and then somehow communicating them for purposes of decision making. It is becoming increasingly clear that this approach to policy and decision modeling is limiting the value of agricultural economics research (Allison 1971; Johnson 1985). Theories, quantitative modeling techniques, and models that recognize more fully the nature of decision processes in the agricultural sector, and, more generally, the clients of agricultural economists must continue to be developed. The latter models recognize political and bureaucratic processes.

Implications of these observations for agricultural economic models are far reaching. They indicate that more comprehensive models should be formulated. In addition, performance measures for these models should not be only for agriculture or the agents for which the models are being developed; they may be important for political trade-offs as well. Perhaps this aspect of the policy modeling process has been most vividly demonstrated in the 1985 Farm Bill debate where the importance of organizational structures and frameworks in influencing policy choice and the political process for policy evaluation was clearly evident.

LINKAGES. Related to the above observations, the importance of linkages across sectors and across decision problems is being better recognized. As an example, in agricultural commodity models for domestic policy purposes the linkages between commodities are of importance in evaluating the performance of the policy and the incidence of benefits for different policy choices. On the other hand, at a commodity level, linkages across countries are increasingly important in establishing equilibrium prices and understanding movements in international commodity prices as affected by domestic policies, changes in supply and demand, and other factors. Generally these linkages among countries and commodity markets are relatively poorly understood. One of the reasons is the difference in time frames of models. Across countries, different growing seasons, different policy regimes, etc., must be accommodated. Across commodities, different physiological constraints for responses must be handled. In short, the integrated emphasis of policies and the interlocking of commodity markets through expanded information technology, lower transportation costs, wider scope trading, and other features are placing increased emphasis on an improved understanding of linkages.

BIOLOGICAL AND PHYSIOLOGICAL INFORMATION. Just as the computer technology is influencing research in agricultural economics, it is also having important impacts in the biological and physical sciences. An implication of the impact of computer technologies in the biological and physical sciences relates to the potential for incorporating more directly biological and physiological restrictions in economic modeling exercises. These restrictions are beginning to be evidenced in, for example, weather yield models that incorporate results of phenological simulation models for plants, livestock models that incorporate reproductive restrictions, shorter time-frame models that reflect transportation capacities, and other types of modeling enhancements. As these biological and physiological information bases become more available, it will be more important to adapt the quantitative techniques in agricultural economics to reflect them more directly.

TIME FRAMES. The technology for collecting improved and more timely data has significant implications for the time dimensions of models. As short time-frame data are available to decision makers and policy analysts, they will use them in making individual and aggregate decisions. Models that can reside on these data bases will then become important if economics and agricultural economics are to contribute to the policy process. What this implies is shorter time-frame models and an improved basis for understanding short-term decisions. Also, the availability of the shorter time-frame data bases implies that methods must be developed for merging the available time frames and/or aggregating across time.

The Future

Anticipating the future and future developments in quantitative techniques is obviously a dangerous enterprise. At the same time, there are themes in the evolution of quantitative techniques as applied in agricultural economics, computer technology, institutions, and other factors influencing the economic research agenda that suggest that speculations with a reasonable footing can be advanced. These are summarized in the form of a number of brief statements organized by short- and long-term implications. (The short-term speculations are derived largely from the discussion in the previous section.) In both discussions only a limited number of points are made. Clearly, extended laundry lists of future potential directions for quantitative modeling could be developed. The present list is limited and intended to indicate priorities for agricultural economics research.

SHORT-TERM IMPLICATIONS

COMPUTER TECHNOLOGY. Changes in computer technology that are already present and simply remain to be incorporated will influence client demands, data systems, model design, and the scope of quantitative models. The implication is for shorter time-frame models, models that can utilize distributed processing capabilities of clients, expanded data bases, models that can reflect the rapid information transfer, and models of scales that have not in the past been comprehensible (but perhaps which achieve this scale based on very different approaches to modeling emphasizing cognitive methods and artificial intelligence).

INFERENTIAL METHODS. The state of the art relative to applications of statistical methods in presenting findings in agricultural quantitative economic research is deplorable. Statistics are presented for estimators in, for example, linear statistical models that have nothing to do with the way the estimates were generated and their reliability. Somehow we seem to be bound to conventions for reporting and applying models that are not reflective of the results or the processes used to get them. If the models are largely empirical and derived from curve-fitting exercises, we should be clear about that in communicating them to the discipline. In the near future, quantitative modelers are going to have to address this problem directly if their results are to be taken seriously. More generally, it is difficult to advance the state of knowledge if the communication system between researchers includes unnecessary noise because of outmoded conventions for reporting results.

MICROFOUNDATIONS. Almost as important as the deplorable state that we find ourselves in for statistical inference is the status of the microfoundations for policy-level aggregate analysis in agricultural economics. Macroeconomic theory and policy have gone through a crisis related to microfoundations. Elements of the same crisis exist in sector and commodity market models used in agricultural economics. Simply put, we have almost no theoretical basis for most of the specifications used in commodity market and sector-wide analysis.

MODEL SCOPE. Until recently much of agricultural economics research has been oriented toward performance measures of importance to the agricultural sector or the perceived clients of the agricultural economics discipline. It is not clear, with the changing dimensions of policy and decision problems for agricultural economics related to the political constituencies and the international dimensions of commodity markets, if this narrow view of policy performance measures will continue to be valuable. Models of expanded scope must be developed to reflect multiple decision criteria and performance measures. However, this should not be interpreted to mean that we simply need larger models; more clever models that are smaller and reflect these dimensions are necessary. Of course when communicating outside the field, the transparency of the models becomes even more of an issue in their design.

LONG-TERM IMPLICATIONS. The long-term implications for quantitative techniques and their applications in agricultural economics are largely related to changes in the way quantitative modeling should be viewed and potential changes in the institutional setting in which these models will be developed.

EXPERIMENTAL LABORATORIES. To a large extent, laboratories for work in economics have been poorly equipped. The investigators in quantitative economic research in agricultural economics and in other areas of economics have operated very much on a hand-to-mouth basis. It will be recognized in the future that results developed from such superficial analyses have little value. One way to improve the basis for quantitative research is to organize the research so that it is more in phase with the major policy and decision issues in agricultural economics. This has the impact of broadening the participation in the research and making it possible to attract the resources required to do the research properly.

PARTICIPATION IN THE POLICY PROCESS. Participation in policy processes is broadening, meaning that the quantitative analysis for policy that is developed will be coming from different constituencies. The land-grant institutions need to recognize this theme of decentralization and initiate policy modeling and quantitative approaches to modeling reflective of this changed institutional setting. This means the development of research centers, investments in quantitative modeling for economics that are consistent with investments in the physical sciences for research, and, generally, the undertaking of quantitative modeling with the expectation of serious participation in the policy process.

INTERDISCIPLINARY WORK. Interdisciplinary research is widely overused and, unfortunately, in the past it frequently has found its level in the lowest common denominator of knowledge among the disciplines. However, with the expanding scope of research questions and the necessity for incorporating more science into models, interdisciplinary efforts will become increasingly important. This is especially true as the traditional clients for agricultural economics (farmers) diminish in number. Agricultural economists will become more interested in food policy, processing industries, natural resource problems, and other research areas that require policy models incorporating ideas and results from several disciplines.

Implications for the Discipline

By convention, agricultural economists are viewed as involved in research, teaching, extension, and/or public service activities. These missions are consistent with the land-grant institutions, the intellectual home of agricultural economics. In the present section, conjectures are offered on the implications of the observations made relative to quantitative modeling techniques for activities in these three areas of endeavor.

RESEARCH. Research budgets are limited. At the same time, a theme of the discussion indicates that more extended research investments need to be made in quantitative techniques and analysis. The implication is for a change in organization of research activity. Instead of agricultural economics units that attempt to do research in all areas, some specialization is likely to occur. The result will be research centers, cooperative ventures between departments and governmental agencies, and increased specialization within agricultural economics departments relative to research emphasis. These changes in the organization of research activities should help focus improved research on the important policy issues for agricultural economics and permit the kinds of extensive investigations necessary for useful quantitative research. A profession organized with a research structure similar to that in the physical sciences is implied if important progress is to be made in the development and application of quantitative techniques.

TEACHING. Teaching programs in agricultural economics are likely to become broader than in the past. The tendency to use narrow and mechanical approaches to problem solving in undergraduate and even graduate teaching in agricultural economics is perhaps more pronounced that in business schools. Individuals have been trained in techniques and approaches with a mentality dangerously close to that of trade schools (i.e., they understand the mechanics of how to do certain types of analyses but not very much about the methods themselves). The result of this overspecialization is beginning to be recognized in American business. It is important that agricultural economics anticipate this trend away from specialization. The implied change involves broader training for graduate and undergraduate students, emphasizing mechanics less and theory and basics more. Also, a deepening of the training seems appropriate. Post-doctoral positions, in-service training, and other methods adding to human capital are likely to become more commonplace. These opportunities for training also will be reflected in the adoption of new information dissemination technologies.

EXTENSION. The information dissemination technology probably has the most broad implications for extension. The traditional and current extension systems emphasizing personal information dissemination likely will not be much in evidence in the future. Major clients of the extension system require close contact with researchers or those who know the most about the policy problems and the quantitative analyses. This close contact is increasingly facilitated by the leverage possible with new information dissemination technology. Quantitative techniques can aid in substituting human and physical capital for labor in the delivery of information. These substitutions have important structural and technical implications for the way agricultural economics has organized itself in the extension area.

References

Allison, G. T. 1971. *Essence of Decision: Explaining the Cuban Missile Crisis.* Boston: Little, Brown & Co.

Aoki, M. 1975. *Optimal Control and Systems Theory in Dynamic Economic Analysis: A System-Theoretic Approach.* New York: American Elsevier.

Bean, L. H. 1929. The Farmers' Response to Price. *J. Farm Econ.* 11:368–85.

Box, G., and G. M. Jenkins. 1976. *Time Series Analysis: Forecasting and Control.* San Francisco: Holden-Day.

Bradford, L. A., and G. L. Johnson. 1953. *Farm Management Analysis.* New York: John Wiley & Sons.

Burt, O. R. 1964. Optimal Resource Use Over Time with an Application to Ground Water. *Manage. Sci.* 11:80–93.

Cromarty, W. A. 1959. An Econometric Model for United States Agriculture. *J. Am. Stat. Assoc.* 54:556–74.

Day, R., and E. Sparling. 1977. Optimization Methods in Agricultural and Resource Economics. In *A Survey of Agricultural Economics Literature,* vol. 2. Minneapolis: Univ. of Minnesota Press.

Ezekiel, M. 1930. *Methods of Correlation Analysis.* New York: John Wiley & Sons.

Fomby, T., R. C. Hill, and S. R. Johnson. 1984. *Advanced Econometric Methods.* New York: Springer-Verlag.

Foote, R. J. 1953. A Four Equation Model for the Feed-Livestock Economy and Its Endogenous Mechanisms. *J. Farm Econ.* 45:44–61.

Fox, K. A. 1953. An Analysis of Demand for Farm Products. Tech. Bull. No. 1081. Washington, D.C.: USDA.

Halter, A. N., M. L. Hayenga, and T. J. Manetsh. 1970. Simulating a Developing Agricultural Economy: Methodology and Planning Capability. *Am. J. Agric. Econ.* 52:272–84.

Halter, A. N., and S. S. Miller. 1966. River Basin Planning: A Simulation Approach. Agricultural Experiment Station, Spec. Rep. No. 24. Corvallis: Oregon State Univ.

Haltiwanger, J., and M. Waldman. 1985. Rational Expectations and the Limits of Rationality: An Analysis of Heterogeneity. *Am. Econ. Rev.* 75:326–40.

Heady, E. O. 1952. *Economics of Agricultural Production and Resource Use.* Englewood Cliffs, N.J.: Prentice-Hall.

Heady, E. O., and W. Candler. 1958. *Linear Programming Methods.* Ames: Iowa State Univ. Press.

Hendry, D. F. 1980. Econometrics: Alchemy or Science? *Econometrica* 47:387–406.

Johnson, S. R. 1981. Alternative Designs for Policy Models of the Agricultural Sector. In *Modeling Agriculture for Policy Analysis in the 1980's.* Kansas City: Federal Reserve Bank.

————. 1985. A Critique of Existing Models for Policy Analysis. In *Agricultural Sector Models for Policy Analysis,* ed. Z. A. Hassan and H. B. Huff. Ottawa, Canada: Agriculture Canada.

Johnson, S. R., and G. C. Rausser. 1977. Systems Analysis and Simulation: A Survey of Applications in Agricultural and Resource Economics. In *A Survey of Agricultural Economics Literature,* vol. 2. Minneapolis: Univ. of Minnesota Press.

Judge, G. G. 1977. Estimation and Statistical Inference in Economics. In *A Survey of Agricultural Economics Literature,* vol. 2. Minneapolis: Univ. of Minnesota Press.

Judge, G. G., and T. Takayama. 1973. *Studies in Economic Planning over Space and Time.* Amsterdam: North Holland.

Kuznets, G. 1955. A Survey of Econometric Results in Agriculture: Discussion. *J. Farm Econ.* 37:235–36.

Leamer, E. E. 1978. *Specification Searches.* New York: John Wiley & Sons.

_____. 1983. Let's Take the Con Out of Econometrics. *Am. Econ. Rev.* 73:31–43.

_____. 1985. Sensitivity Analyses Would Help. *Am. Econ. Rev.* 75:308–13.

McAleer, M., A. R. Pagan, and P. A. Volker. 1985. What will Take the Con Out of Econometrics? *Am. Econ. Rev.* 75:293–307.

Moore, H. L. 1914. *Economic Cycles: Their Law and Cause.* New York: Macmillan.

Rausser, G. C., and J. W. Freebairn. 1974. Approximate Adaptive Control Solutions to Beef Trade Policy. *Ann. Econ. Soc. Meas.* 3:177–203.

Schultz, H. 1938. *The Theory and Measurement of Demand.* Chicago: Univ. of Chicago Press.

Simon, H. 1959. Theories of Decision Making in Economics and Behavioral Science. *Am. Econ. Rev.* 49:253–83.

Sims, C. 1980. Macroeconomics and Reality. *Econometrica* 48:1–48.

Swanson, E. R. 1956. Determining Optimum Size of Business from Production Functions. In *Research Productivity, Returns to Scale, and Farm Size,* ed. E. O. Heady, G. L. Johnson, and L. S. Hardin. Ames: Iowa State Univ. Press.

Tintner, G. 1952. *Econometrics.* New York: John Wiley & Sons.

Working, E. J. 1926. What Do Statistical Demand Curves Show? *Q. J. Econ.* 41:212–35.

Zellner, A. 1971. *An Introduction to Bayesian Inference in Econometrics.* New York: John Wiley & Sons.

Zellner, A. 1985. Bayesian Econometrics. *Econometrica* 53:253–69.

Quantitative Techniques: A Discussion

DAVID A. BESSLER

Stan Johnson has provided us with a useful paper on quantitative techniques, surveying virtually all interesting (useful) techniques in use today and providing us with a thoughtful view of future developments. I find myself in agreement with almost all of his points; consequently, my discussion should be viewed as providing embellishment on his basic structure.

These comments focus on the future of econometric methods. My self-assessment is that I have no expertise in mathematical programming methods. My only comment is that as our computing capabilities progress, we will be able to consider more elegant nonlinear and nonparametric forms.

Within the ambit of econometric method, I see activity on at least three major fronts. First is research on structural versus nonstructural methods. I think we have just begun to understand what we mean by the word "structure" and the implications that various definitions of the word have for our econometric work. Depending on how we define the word, I see quite different requirements on data and method. Second, I see increased activity on diagnostic methods. We usually revert to asymtotic theory to justify the choice of a particular estimator, then apply it with small samples (e.g., we may estimate five or more coefficients with, say, 20 or 30 observations). Recent jack-knife-type methods (bootstrap) and explicit out-of-sample tests ought to be useful in gaining insights into the appropriateness of our particular applications. Finally, I see increased activity in formal and informal use of Bayesian techniques in econometric applications. Most of us are implicitly Bayesian when we "mine our data." Mere recognition of this point begs for explicit Bayesian specifications. Unfortunately, this is easier said than done. The requirements in terms of prior information are probably too taxing, except in all but the simplest specifications. Various instrumental methods will probably be used in the more complex modeling efforts. Within this last topic, I also put ex post sensitivity analysis. Extreme bound analysis, conducted on a tentatively accepted model, will probably occupy more time, and discussion of such will probably occupy more journal space.

David A. Bessler is Professor of Agricultural Economics at Texas A & M University, College Station.

The three topics outlined above are relevant to analysis of secondary data collected in an uncontrolled experiment. Such data are most prominent in econometrics; yet there is increased effort in experimental method (Smith 1982; Plott 1982). Such efforts get around most of the inference problems that nonexperimentalists face. However, experimental methods bring forth another set of problems, including relevance of the experiment and motivation of the experimental subject. While I see increased activity in experimental economics over the next 10 or 20 years, I have only done cursory reading in the area and would feel uncomfortable making explicit statements about its future.

Certainly, other topics in econometric methods not covered by Dr. Johnson or me will be important over the next two decades. I recommend *Handbook of Econometrics* (Griliches and Intrilligator 1984) as a good place to start in thinking about the future. *Advanced Econometric Methods* (Fromby et al. 1984, 553–601) has a nice section on future topics in econometrics.

Economic Structure

One point from the early works on econometric structure that seems to be ignored in agricultural economics is that structure is relative to the type of modification contemplated (Hurwicz 1962, 237). I often hear the criticism of recent vector autoregression (VAR) work not being structural. Because such work seeks to summarize the regularities in the historical data, it somehow ignores the true "structure." This interpretation of structure leads to the view, which I think is mistaken, that there is one proper econometric specification—that is, *the* "structural" specification.

An alternative view of "structural" defines it as that which remains fixed under a particular modification. Under this definition, a model is deemed structural relative to a particular set of interventions. The model builder must specify these at the outset. If, for example, one is interested in modeling interrelations among variables in the U.S. hog market, and is not particularly interested in taxing, subsidizing, or otherwise meddling in the market, then the moving average representation (MAR) can be viewed as a "structural" estimate of how variable j reacts to shocks in variable i at different lags (Bessler 1984).

Many structural representations that economists want to estimate may not be obtainable given usual sources of data. In particular, usual identification restrictions, used to obtain "the" structural specification are incredible—generally not believable. General equilibrium (Liu 1960), rational expectations (Sims 1980), and aggregation considerations (Geweke 1985; Theil 1954) all imply that zero-type restrictions are often not appropriate, in most cases leading to an underidentified econometric structure. The implications of these criticisms are that if we constrain ourselves to analysis of aggregate data observed in uncontrollable environments, then *at best* we can summarize the regularities in the historical data. The moving average representation provides a summary of these regularities. The MAR structure will generally not help us answer the question of what will happen when an unprecedented "structural change" occurs. To answer this question we need controlled observation (randomization). The results of Pratt and Schlaifer (1984) point us unambiguously in the experimental direction. Of course, certain economic questions cannot be put into experimental form. Here we are left with judgment (economic theory).

Rational expectations have been cited as a justification for *not* believing the identification restrictions used in standard econometric practice. The obvious question is then, why not estimate the model under rational expectations? The most obvious answer is that the general equilibrium and aggregation criticisms still hold. But, even if one ignores these, the standard practice is still often marred. In discussing how far one carries the rationality assumption, one is quickly led into an infinite regress of game theoretical models—how rational do I assume that you assume that I act? It is not all that clear to me that one can stop the process at some arbitrary round (see the recent book edited by Frydman and Phelps [1983]).

In discussing the Lucas and Sargent (1981) volume on rational expectations a year or so ago, Shiller (1984) notes the extensive research on people's abilities to forecast. In particular, we all use rules of thumb, heuristics, and other irrational devices to make judgments about the future (see Tversky and Kahneman 1974). How are we to interpret this agent-specific research? Should we ignore it by dismissing it as assumption testing (which of course Friedman recommends against)? Should we view it as evidence relevant to the dismissal of rational expectations? Or should we first forecast with rational expectations, note their poor forecasting ability, and then ask why? With respect to this last question, I have yet to see a rational expectations model outperform a simple, properly specified, univariate autoregression.

DIAGNOSTICS. Our usual approach in econometric analysis is to specify a model based on prior theory and apply an estimator that has desirable large sample (asymptotic) properties to a finite (small) set of data. The rationale for proceeding in this fashion is that it is a better justification than none. Small sample procedures are available and ought to be considered in econometric work.

First, I think we ought to seriously consider out-of-sample forecasting ability in model diagnosis. Further, we ought to hold tight to those specifications that forecast well, and tentatively reject those that do not. A major problem I see with current econometrics is that we have no mechanism for scientific progress. That is, we have no real test of a model, especially when we do lots of pretesting. The out-of-sample test sets up a competition between two or more alternatives and makes acceptance (tentative acceptance) dependent upon adequate forecasting ability. Here, we still may end up with many models if forecast errors are not significantly different between two models. But, at the very least, we know when to tentatively reject a specification.

One particularly appealing test for out-of-sample forecasting ability is the mean squared error (MSE) test of Rick Ashley (Ashley et al. 1980, 1149–68). The test has been around about five years or more, but I have only seen it used a couple of times. Other tests involving explicit decisions may be useful, although they generally run into the criticism that they are decision-specific. As such, it is difficult for the profession at large (scientific community) to hold any general opinion about the results.

When actual out-of-sample forecasting competitions are not possible, due to limited data or lack of a reasonable competitor, the "bootstrap" methods may be quite helpful (see Freedman 1984). Here one resamples the residuals from the initial (OLS, GLS, VAR) fit of a model and creates pseudo data, which can be reestimated to provide simulated distributions on the variation in parameter estimates. Freedman finds, for example, that standard errors calculated from the usual asymptotic formulas are often much smaller than the bootstrapped statistics, the associated implication being that the usual two-times-the-standard-error rule for t-statistics is much too low.

Given the rather ubiquitous nature of small-sample econometrics, I have recommended elsewhere that a small bootstrap program subroutine be included in all econometric software. Of course, there is no "free lunch" and the bootstrap can give misleading results if it is misapplied (Schenker [1985] provides an example in a recent paper).

BAYESIAN MODELS. Most of us have more or less strong prior beliefs on how variables interact in the markets we study. The Bayesian model of inference is, of course, quite appropriate for incorporating this information. Unfortunately, the Bayesian requirements are often too rich for more than simple prior specifications. Or, the lack of scientific consensus on where to put prior density precludes researchers from sticking their necks out. Instead, we are content to summarize what we think the data are saying. Unfortunately, our summaries are usually reflective of our prior beliefs (Leamer 1978).

Litterman (1979) has recently suggested a mechanical (instrumental) prior that treats each series of a multiple time series as a random walk. So the prior coefficient on the first lag of a particular series is centered on one, while coefficients of all other lags and on all other variables are centered on zero. A couple of forecasting studies show this prior to be promising (Kling and Bessler 1985). More informative priors (priors with different centers) may do an even better job of summarizing useful information.

Others suggest the use of a uniform distribution over minus and plus infinity. While the econometrics can be solved for such information, it is hard to see how we gain, relative to ordinary least squares (Zellner 1972, ch. 2).

I think intercourse between the researcher and the data is ultimately best handled through Bayes' theorem. Yet, practically speaking, I think we are very far from implementing all but rather simple models. As an alternative, we will probably see extended work on ex post simulations (extreme bound analysis, in Leamer's words). Here the research begins with an estimated model. Ranges on the estimated parameters are considered and the outcomes of simulations are reported. Believable results are then based on the believability of the simulations.

References

Ashley, R., C. Granger, and R. Schmalensee. 1980. Advertising and Aggregate Consumption: An Analysis of Causality. *Econometrica* 48:1149–68.

Bessler, D. 1984. An Analysis of Dynamic Economic Relationships: Results on U.S. Hog Market. *Can. J. Agric. Econ.* 32:109–24.

Freedman, D. 1984. Bootstrapping the Econometric Model. *J. Am. Stat. Assoc.* 79:135–39.

Fromby, T. B., R. C. Hill, and S. R. Johnson. 1984. *Advanced Econometric Methods.* New York: Springer-Verlag.

Frydman, R., and E. Phelps. 1983. Individual Forecasting and Aggregate Outcomes. In *Rational Expectations Examined.* Cambridge: Cambridge Univ. Press.

Geweke, J. 1985. Macroeconomic Modeling and the Representative Agents. *Am. Econ. Rev.* 75:206–10.

Griliches, Z., and M. Intrilligator, eds. 1984. *Handbook of Econometrics.* Amsterdam: North Holland.

Hurwicz, L. 1962. On the Structural Form of Interdependent Systems. In *Logic, Methodology, and Philosophy of Science,* ed. Nagel et al. Stanford: Stanford Univ. Press.

Kling, J., and D. Bessler. 1985. A Comparison of Multivariate Forecasting Procedures for Economic Time Series. *Int. J. of Forecasting* 1:5–24.

Leamer, E. 1978. *Specification Searches.* New York: John Wiley & Sons.

Litterman, R. 1979. Techniques for Forecasting with Vector Autoregressions. Unpublished, Ph.D. diss., Univ. of Minnesota.

Liu, T. C. 1960. Underidentification, Structural Estimation and Forecasting. *Econometrica* 28:855–65.

Lucas, R., and T. Sargent, eds. 1981. *Rational Expectations and Econometric Practice.* Minneapolis: Univ. of Minnesota Press.

Plott, C. 1982. Efficiency of Experimental Security Markets with Insider Information. *J. Pol. Econ.* 90:663–98.

Pratt, J., and R. Schlaifer. 1984. On the Discovery of Structure. *J. Am. Stat. Assoc.* 79:9–21.

Schenker, N. 1985. Qualms About Bootstrap Confidence Intervals. *J. Am. Stat. Assoc.* 80:360–61.

Shiller, R. 1984. Book Review on Lucas and Sargent. *J. Money, Credit, and Banking* 16:118–23.

Sims, C. 1980. Macroeconomics and Reality. *Econometrica* 48:1–48.

Smith, V. 1982. Microeconomic Systems As An Experimental Science. *Am. Econ. Rev.* 72:923–55.

Theil, J. 1954. *Linear Aggregation of Economic Relations.* Amsterdam: North Holland.

Tversky, A., and D. Kahneman. 1974. Judgment Under Uncertainty: Heuristics and Biases. *Science* 186:1124–31.

Zellner, A. 1972. *An Introduction to Bayesian Inference in Econometrics.* New York: John Wiley & Sons.

Quantitative Techniques: **A Discussion**

LESTER H. MYERS

These comments need to be prefaced with the observation that Professor Johnson has provided the profession with a comprehensive treatment that concisely identifies many of the concerns facing professionals who utilize quantitative techniques. As one reflects on the subject and, more precisely, on the paper itself, it is useful to keep the objectives of this session in mind. These are threefold: (1) the identification of critical unresolved research and instructional issues relating to quantitative techniques used in agricultural economics; (2) the development of some ideas relating to the relative importance of the identified issues; and (3) a discussion of the role of the agricultural economics profession in addressing and solving these problems.

Lester H. Myers is Chief of the Food Marketing and Consumption Economics Branch of the Commodity Economics Division, Economic Research Service, U.S. Department of Agriculture (USDA). Comments reflect the opinions of the author and are not meant to imply an official position or view of USDA.

With respect to the third objective, Professor Johnson implies that professionals involved in agricultural economics should be actively involved in developing the quantitative techniques needed to solve important policy and decision problems. He states that "when new quantitative methods are mechanical devices generated outside the discipline and applications are driven more by their availability than real policy and decision issues, the leadership role of the discipline and the value of quantitative research is likely to be greatly diminished."

Certainly, if the general practice is for the technique to determine the application rather than the problem characteristics determining the technique, one would question the "leadership" role of the discipline in the area of quantitative techniques and also its ability to approach problem solving in a rigorous, scientific way. However, this practice may occur in segments of the profession regardless of whether the techniques are developed within or outside the discipline. We are basically an applied science and need to be cognizant of the relevance of various techniques to the solution of particular problems. However, this need, by itself, does not dictate that the leadership role for developing quantitative techniques resides primarily within the discipline. It does imply that we communicate our understanding of the problems we need to solve to those who are "best" equipped to develop the technical advances in quantitative methods, be they in mathematics, statistics, mathematical economics, or any other discipline/subdiscipline.

A key role for the agricultural economist, and one that Professor Johnson obviously recognizes, is the identification of deficiencies in the ability of existing quantitative techniques to adequately address the unique characteristics of the applied problems we need to solve. To communicate these needs, however, the agricultural economist must be comfortable with a wide range of techniques and must be particularly cognizant of the underlying structures that generate the observed data. This has implications for the breadth and depth of training programs leading to Ph.D. degrees in agricultural economics.

Our ability to mechanically solve large-scale problems has, I think, been both useful and a hindrance to our ability to adequately train professionals. On the one hand, it has permitted the empirical solutions to problems that are more consistent in scope with "real world" conditions than was possible prior to the development of large-scale computers and sophisticated quantitative models. However, the resources needed to develop large models are often justified on the argument that the model, once developed, can be used to solve a wide variety of problems. Thus there would seem to be a built-in tendency toward trying to "fit" the problems to the available model framework, the very problem discussed by Professor Johnson. It can also encourage projects that "skip" some of the critical phases of the scientific method. Master's and Ph.D. research that constitutes a component part of a much larger research project may not adequately involve the student in the problem formulation and method determination phases of the research process.

Quite properly, Professor Johnson calls attention to the problem of "subjectivity" in the use of quantitative analysis—a process he refers to as the "personalization" of models. Ironically, we often associate objectivity with being an advantage of quantitative analyses and of results based on quantitative models. Obviously, subjective decisions are and must be made throughout the research process.

As mentioned in the paper, when subjective decisions are not fully defined in the reporting process, the research cannot be validated through duplication nor can it be accurately evaluated on the basis of the information presented. Unfortunately, in all too many cases the researchers themselves may not recognize the implicit subjectivity. As a profession, our credibility depends on the complete reporting of the research process. Thus, I think one of the critical problems facing us over the next several years is the development of reporting techniques that allow for the complete documentation of research involving large-scale quantitative models. The problems seem to be exacerbated by the limited budgets for experiment station publications and by competition for limited pages in refereed journals. Electronic data storage and dissemination techniques may provide the means to attack this problem. Still, much has to be done to develop a framework for using available hardware and software to improve the communication and research evaluation process.

Related to the subjectivity issue is the general lack of discipline exhibited in the use of theory and statistical techniques. I fully agree with Dr. Johnson's observation that we conduct and report statistical inference tests that are inappropriate. Also, there is a tendency to misuse economic theory. A rigorous theoretical framework for market behavior under modern conditions does not exist. We consistently rely on theories relating to the behavior of individual consumers or firms to empirically explain movements in observed data on economic aggregates. Models are then validated on the basis of how well the estimates conform to a priori expectations based on theories that are largely irrelevant. Clearly, a high priority within the profession should be the devotion of resources to the development of economic theories of markets as we observe them. This relates to quantitative methods because the development of those theories depends on being able to develop mathematical statements of market behavior and to formulate statistical estimation techniques that conform to the structural characteristics of the observed data. This is a "risky" area of work, and agricultural economists and administrators may have to develop modified criteria for measuring performance to attract the needed research resources.

Finally, I would like to briefly list several specific areas where I believe the profession will have to devote research priority over the coming years. Because of the comprehensive nature of the Johnson paper, the areas listed below tend to be embodied in comments within it.

1. The estimation of response parameters when participants within the economic system respond to economic information generated by the model itself. This would seem to be especially important to forecasting models. In a more general way, the problem relates to how economic agents assimilate, evaluate, and react to information. This is extremely important for model specification and also for providing input to public officials on the "value" of publicly collected and reported data.

2. The empirical specification and measurement of expectations. Johnson's comments on rational expectations are relevant to this area. Advances in economic theories of consumer and firm behavior will undoubtedly focus on intertemporal dynamics. Thus, specification of the expectation function is critical.

3. The development of methods for publicly documenting and reviewing analyses based on large-scale models. Several problems relate here. First, given tight publication budgets, how do we provide documentation of the "complete" research process? Second, the time required to adequately review studies using large-scale models and sophisticated quantitative techniques is not insignificant. Qualified reviewers need to be assured that they will be rewarded for time spent reviewing other work. Currently, those who are most qualified to be reviewers tend to perceive the opportunity costs to be quite high.

4. More training and emphasis on experimental methods and sampling techniques. Quantitative techniques usually require high-quality data. However, the profession has not placed equivalent emphasis on devoting professional efforts and research budgets to developing data series.

5. Techniques need to be developed to simplify the specification of large programming models so that more research time can be allocated to studying the underlying economic issues and less time to mechanical activities. An example of progress in this area is the World Bank's General Algebraic Modeling Language.

In summary, the paper by Professor Johnson has provided us with a comprehensive list of problems that need to be addressed over the next few decades. Positive efforts toward the solution of these problems will involve not only individual researchers, but university administrators, government officials, and the American Agricultural Economics Association as well. It is one thing to define priorities; it is another challenge to devise the incentive system that encourages the attraction of needed resources.

9

Resource and Environmental Economics: Knowledge, Discipline, and Problems

DANIEL W. BROMLEY

The Conceptual Challenge

Conventional resource economics recognizes problems as arising from market failure; it maintains a distinction between those things that contribute to efficiency as opposed to those things that are redistributive in nature; and it finds guidance in benefit-cost analysis where potential Pareto compensation gives license for change. In the best tradition of economics, resource economists seek to be regarded as objective scientists.

However, resource problems are entitlement, or initial endowment, problems, and as such welfare economics provides us with no unambiguous answer as to what should be done (Chipman and Moore 1978). As hard as we might wish it were not so, the resource economist inevitably confronts conflicts in which two or more parties are faced with unwanted and uncompensated costs, and where gains from trade are either difficult to negotiate, or are impossible. The existence of joint costs, a situation in which negative effects (spillovers) transcend the nominal boundaries of firms, is determined by an entitlement structure in which not all scarce and valuable factors of production or consumption are ownable. In such a legal environment, economic agents have adopted production and consumption plans that presume ownership of necessary factors.

Starting from this presumption of rights, resource economics is about the ability of certain parties to shift uncompensated costs onto others. The social problem concerns who is able to shift such costs? On whom are these

Daniel W. Bromley is Anderson-Bascom Professor and Chair, Department of Agricultural Economics, University of Wisconsin, Madison. I am particularly indebted to Emery Castle, Dick Norgaard, Alan Randall, Al Schmid, and Kathy Segerson for assistance on an earlier version.

costs shifted? Which kinds of costs are most often shifted to others? And, how can existing (and future) conflicts of this sort be resolved in a manner that is both equitable and not wasteful?

We understand that the status quo structure of entitlements defines a bundle of resource endowments, and that these entitlements also determine particular outcomes that may be regarded as efficient (Bromley 1982a, 1986; Samuels 1981). Some of these entitlements are legitimized by statutory or common law; others are presumptive in that they have yet to be addressed either legislatively or judicially. As economists we are invited into the policy arena to comment on possible changes in this status quo. This opportunity presents us with a difficult task. Of what significance, in economic terms, is the status quo? After all, it yields for us a constellation of prices that we will use in an economic analysis of change. But if the contemplated change is to show up as a different structure of entitlements – and most resource policy does precisely that – then the new entitlement structure will give rise to its own constellation of prices. Our science provides us with no basis for judging the status quo – except for the fiction of a perfect world without transaction costs. We are asked to evaluate an existing Edgeworthian economy against a hypothetical ideal; a fictional welfare frontier is posited and we are asked to contemplate an economy inside that frontier. In fact, the welfare frontier is never attainable in a world with transaction costs and we must ask about its relevance for policy. Indeed, ours is a world of efficiency loci and feasibility loci (Graaff 1967).

Graaff considers a particular point inside a welfare frontier whose coordinates represent the satisfaction enjoyed by members of society. A costless lump-sum redistribution of wealth by taxes and bounties will move society to a new point within the frontier. Repeated applications of such redistributions will trace out a family of points known as the efficiency locus – so labeled because it traces out a series of allocatively efficient points for various distributions of welfare. It is possible to consider one of these combinations as optimal only if the efficiency locus should happen to coincide with the welfare frontier. Graaff's efficiency locus is Bator's utility possibility frontier (Graaff 1967).

Graaff (1967, 76) differentiates the efficiency (or "actuality") locus from the welfare frontier by noting that the welfare frontier shows the best we can do, given tastes and techniques, in an institutional vacuum. The efficiency locus shows the best we can do if we take the existing institutional set-up as a datum. It describes the result of distributional changes (by lump-sum measures) within that framework.

Unfortunately, any notion of an economy in an institutional vacuum is as fictional as an economy without transaction costs. Hence, the idea that economic policy can do anything to move society to the welfare frontier is of little practical or theoretical meaning. Nor does it do anything for reality to talk of costless lump-sum redistributions. Instead, economic policy must be viewed against a matrix of attainability or feasibility. The feasibility locus indicates the political realities of making one person better off while holding the welfare of others at current levels. The feasibility locus does not exist because of lump-sum redistributions, nor does it presume the institutional setup to be given; it is inscribed in utility space by feasible institutional changes.

Through any point on a feasibility locus there passes an efficiency locus indicating the results of hypothetical lump-sum redistributions in the institutional arrangements corresponding to that point. To move along the feasibility locus via institutional change is to move from a point on one efficiency frontier to a point on another. Restated, the welfare frontier is an unattainable fiction; economic life is found on a feasibility locus; a particular point on a feasibility locus also coincides with a point on an efficiency locus; and to move along the feasibility locus is to jump from one efficiency locus to another.

While any number of studies exist regarding (1) the willingness to pay for certain environmental goods; (2) the costs of achieving certain environmental standards; and (3) the efficiency of creating markets for emissions, I believe that the central conceptual challenge to our profession is to develop an improved understanding of the matter of entitlements—not only their existence at any particular moment, but the more vexing problem of their modification in the face of "unacceptable" performance.

I will address three particular dimensions of the problem. The first concern will be with the resolution of joint-cost situations or with externality policy. The second concern, while related, will instead focus on the structure of entitlements that underlies situations of jointness. Finally I will discuss the matter of uncertainty as it influences natural resource policy and economics.

This treatment will not be in isolation from the kinds of resource problems that I believe we face, but the thrust of the discussion will be in the direction of the problems of resources to which economists might contribute. I have chosen this conceptual tack for several reasons. First, and possibly most importantly, it seems to me that the resource problems that loom on the horizon are of a sort that imply a different motivation for collective action than the conventional "market failure" rationale. Secondly, there is growing evidence that direct government involvement in certain domains of daily life entails its own form of failure called "nonmarket failure" (Wolf 1979). Third, the status quo structure of presumed entitlements governing many natural resource uses has a profound influence on the way that the choice problem is framed, and hence on the outcome that seems to be preferred. My final reason for this emphasis is that there appears to be a persistent failure of economists and policymakers to view resource problems through the same set of "lenses." It follows, therefore, that the preferred solutions for each of these two participants will differ. I regard it as essential that these different perspectives be understood by the theoreticians, by those who may work directly with citizens and decision makers on resource problems (e.g., extension specialists), and by the policy makers themselves.

Beyond Market Failure

The future success of resource economics as a policy science will depend, I believe, on the extent to which we are able to move beyond the well-known economics of Edgeworth into the much more complex economics of Pigou. This may seem surprising since Pigouvian thought is regarded as very much in the mainstream of resource economics. However, I suggest that the economics of Pigou has simply been appropriated by the Edgeworthians and has, for the most part, been used to motivate discussions about the optimal tax on offending activities.

By a fuller recognition of the Pigouvian economy I have in mind the concept of general economic welfare or the general well-being of the community. While resource economists tend to equate Pigou with a marginal tax to reconcile private and social benefits and costs, this casts Pigou in a rather more "marginalist" light than is justified. Pigou was concerned with the inextricable linkages among citizens, both contemporaneously but also intertemporally (Pigou 1962). This linking represents a certain jointness, and jointness of costs and benefits is the very essence of resource economics. But there is a more encompassing problem of jointness that does not seem to have received the attention it deserves.

The Edgeworthian economy, familiar to us all, is a world in which individual agents compete for private goods (i.e., for goods that are rivalrous in consumption). In the course of that consumption of private goods certain spillovers may occur thereby driving a wedge between private and social benefits. A similar story could be told about the Edgeworthian economy in input space for firms. This economy is one of private scarcity, functioning markets, and some externalities. We can imagine production possibility frontiers, social indifference curves, and discussions about Pareto-better moves. It is the stuff of contemporary resource economics.

By way of contrast, the essence of the Pigouvian economy is not bargaining over private goods with incidental side effects sometimes present. Instead, the Pigouvian economy is one of pervasive visitation of unwanted costs — costs that are either of a collective-consumption nature, or that are privately borne. In the Pigouvian economy people do not only come together to trade at the margin, balancing willingness (and ability) to pay against changing marginal increments to satisfaction. Instead, the Pigouvian world is one in which individuals (across both space as well as across generations) visit costs and benefits on others. The good Edgeworthian is inclined to view this visitation of costs as an aberration, believing that such events, when they are observed, can be corrected with "taxes and bounties." On the other hand, a modern Pigouvian would find numerous examples of instances in which joint costs are present.

In Pigou's time economists were beginning to see some of the side effects of modern technology, of crowded cities, and of unbridled individualization of economic life. Pigou was writing about the familiar technological externalities that went on to become the staple of economics textbooks—a smokey factory and a nearby laundry, a confectioner and the adjacent waiting room for a doctor, a sparking railroad and dry wheat fields. In each of those instances it was clear that the interest of the individuals so affected were incompatible.

Resource economics problems today are still dominated by the element of jointness. Problems of air quality, groundwater quantity and quality, energy exploration policies, coastal habitat problems, urban sprawl, wilderness designation and management, the management of other public lands, private forest land management, soil erosion, locally unwanted land uses (LULUs), surface water problems, marine fisheries, habitat/species preservation, mineral exploration, and the management of toxic and hazardous materials are all characterized by jointness.

This inextricable binding together of multiple interests in the ways in which natural resources are used and managed creates a special conceptual challenge to the resource economist, for the quite obvious reason that not all parties for whom these matters are of interest are able to enter consensual bargains to have their wishes expressed. The physical realities of many of these natural resource problems preclude the thoroughgoing individualization of ownership and control that is the essence of the Edgeworthian economy. Constantly to fall back on the Edgeworthian view of such matters seems to beg the ultimate questions of who has the socially sanctioned rights to undertake specific actions, who has the exposure to unwanted costs, and who must bear the burden of proof in order to be relieved of such costs, if relief is indeed warranted.

There is another difficulty with "market failure" as a motivating idea for recognizing a problem with the status quo. Some have correctly pointed out that a failure of existing market phenomena is no assurance that involvement by the state will make matters any better. Wolf (1979) writes of "non-market failure."

Dating from Pigou (and even Adam Smith, though his concerns in such matters are often ignored by his more zealous disciples), economists have understood that there is sometimes a divergence between private costs and social costs. Francis Bator (1958) seems to have popularized the concept of market failure with his classic article "The Anatomy of Market Failure." As a metaphor, market failure is convenient; like many metaphors it may have only limited analytical power.

Consider a world in which independent economic agents engage in a variety of activities, yet the actions of one hold uncompensated cost implications for another. If those costs are transmitted via the physical media rather than via the price mechanism we would consider them to be technological externalities. Conventional wisdom would recognize this as a problem of "market failure." We would say that there is a divergence between private costs and benefits and social costs and benefits.

There are two dominant views regarding the solution to this externality problem. One view is to tax the offending party an amount equal to the marginal social damages inflicted on others, thereby internalizing the offsite costs. Another view is to create an opportunity for the two incompatible uses to bargain over the joint costs. The first view is associated with Pigou, the latter with Coase.

The Pigouvian solution requires the involvement of an authority outside the two interacting firms, and this will usually mean the government. Of course even after the imposition of the optimal tax there will remain some actual physical interdependence (joint costs) but the "efficient" level of joint costs will have been realized by the tax. Coasian opposition to the strict application of Pigou's tax on the offending activity centered on the idea that joint costs indeed require two agents in close proximity; jointness is a function of the physical proximity of two incompatible activities. In other words, many externalities would not exist if the two parties would only keep their distance. Indeed, the current debate over acid-rain policy serves to remind us that the taller smokestacks have simply expanded the geographic region over which joint costs are experienced.

The Coasian solution was to recognize the dual nature of joint costs and to establish a situation where both parties might negotiate. The Coasian solution results in a situation where following this consensual bargaining there will remain some relations involving scarce resources that lie outside of this bargained solution — and that market forces, left to themselves, cannot internalize. Thanks to Buchanan and Stubblebine (1962), we now regard this situation as one of Pareto-irrelevant externalities.

If we are to follow the Coasian prescription, there are two possible outcomes. The first is one in which no bargain can be struck between the two incompatible uses and so the status quo remains unmodified. Demsetz (1967) would offer the observation that this absence of a bargained outcome is itself optimal and that therefore the status quo structure was optimal (by which he more correctly means efficient). Others would suggest that this outcome is simply an artifact of the status quo structure of presumptive rights that forced the victim of unwanted costs to approach the source of those costs to offer payment for relief (Bromley 1978a, 1978b, 1982a, 1986; Mishan 1974; Samuels 1971, 1981). The fact that there was no change may indeed be "efficient," but such a conclusion strips efficiency of much policy interest.

The other possible outcome is one in which the two parties indeed strike a bargain so that the victim pays the offending party to reduce off-site costs somewhat, or the emitter buys off the disutility of the victim. As above, there would remain some joint costs that were not part of the bargain; the externality would have been "optimally" internalized.

It seems safe to observe that a bargained outcome in the Coasian tradition is much less common than is the failure of the parties to reach some agreement, either because they did not try or because they tried and failed. Dahlman (1979) argues that this inability to move beyond a particular status quo outcome is a function of the existence of transaction costs. These costs are central to the concept of externalities. Indeed, Dahlman (1979, 143) notes that

> . . . it is not possible to specify any class of transaction costs that—
> given individual wealth-maximizing behavior under well-specified con-
> straints that include exchange costs—generate externalities that consti-
> tute deviations from an attainable optimum; second, that the concept
> of externalities—insofar as the word is intended to connote . . . the
> existence of an analytically proven market failure—is void of any posi-
> tive content but, on the contrary, simply constitutes a normative judg-
> ment about the role of government and the ability of markets to estab-
> lish mutually beneficial exchanges.

Dahlman's view is that the relevance of externalities (what I am here calling joint costs) is to be found in the existence of transaction costs; such impediments to bargaining are thus a necessary condition for the persistence of unwanted costs being visited on others. Notice that transaction costs are not necessary for the persistence of physical interdependence among economic agents, for even when costless bargaining occurs there remains physical interdependence that is "not worth" eliminating.

Dahlman suggests that there is no transaction cost that can generate a Pareto-relevant externality. Put somewhat differently, Pareto-relevant externalities cannot exist on the basis of transaction costs since those costs must exist in a model of the attainable optimum. It is the presence of transaction costs that prevent the attainment of the perfect Pigouvian world, and transaction costs are quite capable of rendering the Coasian world optimal as it stands—otherwise it would change. That is, the Pigouvian solution invokes the omniscient central controller who can view the world as a unified firm and so generate a schedule of taxes and bounties that will render all remaining technological externalities Pareto irrelevant. This is the Pigouvian Planner so denigrated by the Chicago School. In Coase's corner we see the Walrasian Auctioneer, the deus ex machina of competitive markets, attempting to iterate toward some equilibrium in which optimality will, by definition, be found. However, the presence of transaction costs implies that it may not be possible to move from the status quo—in which case things are considered (rather found, by definition) to be optimal.

But the Dahlman critique is precisely with these two stylized solutions to so-called "market failure" problems. The contemporary relevance of externalities and market failure is with reference to some Pareto optimum. Dahlman asks us to consider a properly specified (and well behaved) general equilibrium system, which for every initial endowment yields a unique general equilibrium price vector. Given current entitlements and so endowments, the economist is then able to specify a unique Pareto-optimal solution. Now, into this system admit externalities and let the Walrasian Auctioneer grind out the new equilibrium price vector.

In general, this new price vector and its associated allocation of resources will differ from that attained in the world without externalities. Hence, we conclude that externalities prevent the attainment of a Pareto optimum, and the accompanying distortion is considered to be bad; it is here that the solution of government is often invoked. Since a world with zero transaction costs is also a world without externalities (by definition), the first model from above is one without transaction costs. But the second model, with externalities, is the one with transaction costs. Indeed, it is the very existence of transaction costs that differentiate the two models.

Dahlman concludes that the conventional prescription of searching for the combination of taxes and bounties that will make the second model resemble the first (and using government as the vehicle for that process) is misdirected for the simple reason that the first model is not attainable; it is a scientific fiction. Another way of stating the same thing is to suggest that the search for Paretian perfection is a quest for a fictional target.

Dahlman suggests this problem is not unique to externality matters; the early concern with monopoly was judged against a world of perfect competition, which is the first model discussed above. More recently those concerned with market structure have adopted as a norm something called "workable competition." The literature on international trade measures current performance (in the presence of tariffs and certain barriers) against the perfect world (Krueger 1974). But how relevant is the perfect world of zero transaction costs when one is concerned with policy formulation? Dahlman (1979, 153) argues, "If we include costs of transacting in the constraints that describe the conditions under which economic agents perform their individual wealth maximization, we would then describe an attainable optimum, and this is the one we should use in judging optimality and welfare problems."

Cheung (1970) offers a variation on this same theme. He starts by questioning the very term "externality," preferring instead to focus on the nature of contracting among various interests to a resource conflict. Thus Cheung broadens the issue from one of the willingness to contract which is a function of transaction costs of interest to Dahlman, to the legitimacy to contract. Thus, there are two possible explanations for the persistence of joint costs: (1) the costs of delineating and enforcing the limits of exclusive rights are too high and so there is an absence of willingness to contract; or (2) contracts may not exist to define exclusivity because exclusive rights are not regarded as being legitimate.

Consider first the situation in which the various parties to a situation of joint costs have the legitimacy to contract and so the matter is simply one of the costs of arranging bargains. Here, the costs of forming exclusive rights to contract can be thought of in two stages. The first would be the costs of gathering information about the rights in question, the costs associated with bargaining over the nature of the emerging rights, and finally the costs of enforcing the contracts that have been arranged. These costs will vary according to the resource situation. For instance, on a high seas fishery the sheer dispersion of the various agents would make this aspect very expensive indeed. In the matter of intergenerational resource problems the costs are, of course, infinite. It is in this sense that the state, acting as an agent for yet unborn citizens, undertakes contracts on behalf of the future with those currently living. In contrast there are other resource situations where very few parties are involved, and in which contracting costs would be quite low.

If the contracting process has been successful, then the second stage is one in which existing exclusive rights are transferred over time. There are costs associated with this transfer process, just as there are costs associated with the original definition of exclusive rights. Cheung (1970) notes the income that can be derived from an exclusive right, or the gain from enforcing that right, depends on the existence of transferability in the marketplace; for without transfer the higher options may not be realized. Hence, the lower the costs of contracting for transfers the higher will be the gain of enforcing exclusivity. And the cost of enforcing exclusivity depends also on the existence of transfer and its associated costs.

Both stages then—establishment of exclusivity and the transfer of existing exclusive rights—entail transaction costs. The absence of exclusive rights can imply two quite different conditions. The first, just discussed, is that the costs of establishing exclusivity may exceed the perceived benefits attaching thereto. It is here that those who find compelling reasons for volitional exchange will advocate actions that have as their purpose the reduction of transaction costs, in a sense wishing to lower the barriers to individual contracting. But one cannot conclude that the existing situation is one of market failure; in the absence of a market, where it requires the purposeful actions of the state to permit the establishment of market processes (by lowering the transaction costs that now preclude a market), we would be hard pressed to label the status quo as a situation of "market failure" for the simple reason that no market exists. As others have commented, the absence of markets may itself be "optimal" on efficiency grounds (Demsetz 1967).

So we come to the nub of the matter, and that is the structure of entitlements that exist or are presumed to exist in situations of joint costs. That is, we must deal with Cheung's second category, which is the legitimacy of any particular negotiation over joint costs. And that legitimacy depends upon the structure of legal entitlements.

The Problem of Entitlements

Economists, who with evident satisfaction denounce political solutions to resource allocation problems on the ground that such procedures give inordinate weight to a few "influential special interests," are surprisingly uninterested in the observation that bargained (i.e., market) outcomes reflect the underlying wealth position of those able to make their interests effective with dollar "votes." The mention of this inconsistency is met with the glib reminder that political matters are quite outside of the powerful body of reasoning to which all informed economists subscribe. Yet economic analysis can only operate within a structure of resource endowments and wealth positions that define the choice domains over which individuals will (can) maximize.

There are really two levels of transactions in a society. The first is concerned with negotiations and bargains over the structure of choice sets. It is here that transactions take place over the "rules of the game." To deny this is an economic problem is to dismiss the very essence of how the second level of transactions will be circumscribed. For at this prior level of transactions there is a structure of endowments and entitlements; there is a demand for institutional change; there are costs of change as well as benefits; and there are certainly transaction costs.

But, as Arrow reminded us, there seems to be no unambiguous aggregating mechanism whereby the best outcome can be discerned. In the absence of this mechanism, indecisiveness seems to be the alternative to the more comfortable Newtonian order. For most of us the maximizing opportunities present in the second level of transactions prove irresistible to a science more at home with the calculus than with game theory.

The essence of the first level of transactions is negotiation for advantage — the determination of choice (or opportunity) sets. And those who are successful in having their interests (or claims) transformed into rights are thus assured of an income stream into the future; they have acquired property out of a mere claim. More correctly, they now have an entitlement that may be protected by a property rule, by a liability rule, or by inalienability (Bromley 1978b).

The ability of independent agents to undertake primary transactions over the nature of opportunity sets, or secondary transactions within opportunity sets, requires the prior acquiescence of the state. Recall that even in a democracy the citizens grant to the state (subject to procedural niceties) the power to control the process whereby opportunity sets will be defined, as well as to regulate behavior within those opportunity sets as individuals go about the business of daily living. These opportunity sets are defined by the institutional structure of the society under consideration. That is, entitlements (presumed or actual) derive from the institutional arrangements in place at any given moment.

What are the central concerns of the state as it contemplates the extension to individual entrepreneurs of a franchise to attempt to resolve joint costs? Some would suggest that the state, except in the rarest of circumstances, ought to define the conditions (including property entitlements) that will allow volitional exchange among parties to joint costs (Anderson 1982; Buchanan 1972; Coase 1960; Demsetz 1967). This preference is based on familiar arguments that bargained exchange among wealth-maximizing agents will produce the largest social dividend. But the franchise raises a number of concerns, particularly in those instances where uncertainty is present. Indeed the social legitimacy of contracts is intimately bound up with some collective sense (with the state acting as agents for the future) of the relative benefits and costs of individual contracts as opposed to some command solution to joint costs. There is also an equity question: victims of noxious wastes attempting to pay some large chemical company to take its refuse elsewhere. For the moment let us worry only about the "efficiency" effects.

The existence of joint costs presents the state with a necessary choice of attempting to force a resolution, or of leaving it to the parties to work out. I have elsewhere suggested that part of the choice is dependent upon the nature of those joint costs — is the situation one of mere nuisance or are health effects probable? Are the joint costs intermittent or constant? Are there significant third-party effects? Are transaction costs high and likely to remain so, or high and capable of being reduced? Is there a unique damage function? Are irreversibilities present (Bromley 1978b)? But there is another dimension to this choice and that is the potential costs of making the wrong decision.

When the state grants contracting rights to a variety of economic agents, it does so on the assurance that the social dividend will be thus enhanced, and that there is a small risk of immoderate losses. Of course not all societies grant this franchise so willingly, but in the market-oriented countries we find this to be quite prevalent. In such settings joint costs present a special dilemma; so much economic activity is organized through markets (or through market-like arrangements) that to do otherwise is seen as the exception. Good Coasians ask why it is that all joint-cost situations cannot be resolved through volitional bargains. Others offer good reasons why this will not be done, among them being the same reasons why a number of nonenvironmental relationships do not occur in markets (Okun 1975).

But having decided that volitional exchange is not the appropriate means for resolving problems of acid rain, groundwater contamination, soil erosion, wilderness preservation, hazardous wastes, and other prevalent joint-cost situations, the state is still faced with the problem of what to do. Consider the problem of acid rain. It is well understood that the large number of affected parties and the very great distances that separate all of them generally preclude a market-oriented solution from altering the status quo.

The electric utilities would suggest that they have a "right" to burn coal as they wish, and those who claim damages from such action should therefore bear the burden of proof — and the transaction costs — to alter the status quo. But this is not a situation of "market failure" since there is no market present; nor is it possible for a market to exist. Some, opposed to government activity with respect to acid rain, would like to suggest that the absence of a market is itself optimal — when the benefits of reducing acid deposition finally outweigh the costs of reducing coal emissions (including the transaction costs), then there will be a change. But this position cannot be taken seriously since the legal right to dump potentially harmful matter into the atmosphere has never been granted; current emitters merely have a presumptive right (privilege) while the alleged victims have no rights (Bromley 1982b).

On the other side of the argument, those who are opposed to any possible damages from acid deposition would claim that they have a "right" to be free of such costs; that is, they presume an entitlement structure. Indeed, the current debate is over the very nature of the presumed entitlement structure; the victims claiming that they have a "right" to be free from the real (or potential) damages, and the utilities claiming that they have a "right" to generate electricity the cheapest way possible until it is shown that the benefits of control exceed the costs.

This situation is familiar to resource economists; we encounter it in the domain of agricultural chemical use, in soil erosion debates, in concern for rural-urban land conversion, and in other conflicts where the status quo structure of behaviors result in joint costs. The choice problem can be rather paralyzing; in the absence of better information about the long-run implications of prevailing behaviors it may be "wasteful" to insist that such behaviors be altered. And yet it is always those benefiting from the status quo who will seek delays in government action, arguing that more information is required before a correct decision can be taken.

The proponents of change will base their case on the incidence of unwanted costs, while the proponents of the status quo will rest their defense on a benefit-cost analysis that shows the uncertain future benefits of emission reductions to be outweighed by the known and current costs of emission controls. The protagonists are making two quite different arguments. One party is saying joint costs (i.e., incidence) matters; the other is saying that there is yet no "market failure" and hence nothing should be done. Economists will usually feel more comfortable with the "market failure" position taken by the utilities since arguments on the incidence of costs and benefits are said to fall outside the domain of "objective science."

However, "market failure" alone cannot motivate a solution to this problem since there is no production possibility frontier that is everywhere superior to the one that we now occupy (Lang 1980; Mishan 1969). Nor is there a feasibility locus in utility space that is unambiguously superior to the one on which we find ourselves. The logic of "market failure" to motivate collective action in such conflicts founders upon an elusive target that assumes a world of perfectibility. There can be no failure from an attainable world on efficiency grounds since the status quo finds us on a feasibility locus defined by the technical and institutional realities around us (Graaff 1967). Of course there is a vector of taxes and bounties that will move us from the status quo, but those taxes and bounties are predicated upon moving us to a perfect (but unattainable) world. Market-celebrating economists are correct to reject government action, but for the wrong reason. Government action is not called for to solve efficiency problems since, given transaction costs, we are already on an efficiency frontier and a feasibility locus. But neither is it correct to claim therefore that "what exists is optimal."

What exists is simply a particular configuration of resource use and outputs that carries with it a vector of costs and benefits, both their magnitude as well as their incidence. And it is the incidence of costs and benefits that motivates public action. As Randall (1974) pointed out so well some time ago, the Coasians have themselves an ironic victory; by showing that the allocation of rights has no bearing on efficiency, it can be shown that problems of joint costs reduce to simple incidence problems. This, by the way, is what the "policymakers" have been telling us all along.

The primacy of cost incidence places special emphasis on the way in which the decision problem is formulated. Indeed, unlike efficiency analysis where we assume that the beneficiaries can compensate the losers from a particular policy choice and still retain a surplus (the Kaldor-Hicks condition) incidence analysis focuses immediately on potential winners and losers.

This issue has been discussed by Norgaard and Hall (1974). They show, using a consumption possibility frontier and a social indifference curve (which, unfortunately, they also refer to as a social welfare function), that transaction costs will differentially modify the consumption possibility frontier as between amenities and material goods. Indeed, depending upon the status quo structure of entitlements (i.e., whether polluters or victims are protected by a property rule), they show that two different output bundles are equally preferred by "society."

One output bundle, following from a restrictive entitlement on pollution, will have more amenities and fewer "material" goods than will another bundle arising from an entitlement structure that is permissive of pollution. Norgaard and Hall (1974, 255) conclude that the "composition of output is different even though society is indifferent to the state of the law."

Social indifference curves, as in the Norgaard and Hall (1974) analysis, can indeed reveal social indifference between alternative entitlement structures and the output bundles that follow logically from those structures. But it is a mistake to stop here, for social indifference curves simply aggregate over preferences in some mystical way ignoring that some members of society have very strong preferences for material goods, while others have very strong preferences for amenities. It is not incorrect to conclude that "society is indifferent" as between output bundle I and output bundle II, but it begs the central question of how individuals and groups with different interests in those two bundles will work to get their tastes given social sanction. And it is the social welfare function, not the social indifference curve, which reflects that aggregating process (Bromley and Bishop 1977; Mishan 1969).

It is the aggregating property of the social welfare function, indicating who counts, that is required before we can simply dismiss two quite inconsistent output bundles as equally preferred. For it should be clear that we can have either bundle I or bundle II, but not both. How will it be decided that we will have one over the other? Precisely by the primary transactions discussed above. It is here that the economic behavior to influence entitlements — and hence output bundles — will be carried out.

To understand that process, and hence to begin to move toward an analytical treatment of primary transactions, it would seem critical that we pay somewhat more attention to the ways in which individuals view the choices before them. To that we now turn.

The Framing of Decisions

The presumptive rights of the status quo define a particular decision environment and require that any action be judged against that benchmark. Invariably the choice is cast as one of acting now or waiting until more (or better) information is available. That this biases action in favor of the status quo ought to be obvious; it is always easy to protest that we do not know enough yet to be certain that any policy response would improve things. This attitude has been prevalent in debates over soil erosion, acid rain, hazardous materials, and nuclear power plants.

A benefit-cost analysis of policy choices would properly reckon the probabilities attached to alternative outcomes of pursuing a few distinct policy options. For instance, in the current debates over acid rain policy the options are usually cast in terms of percentage reductions in SO_2 (or NOx), and then one must speculate about the possible impacts on future damages from these alternatives. The concern in such policy is to provide decision makers with an array of choices and to urge adoption of that action with the highest associated expected value. There are, to be sure, several dimensions of risk in such choices.

The first is an engineering risk in that there may be some difficulty with various technological means of reducing SO_2 emissions; each particular technique carries with it an associated performance vector. The second dimension of risk is that a particular emissions regime may have associated with it a wide array of physical damage to lakes, trees, materials, and human health. Part of this problem is due to the lack of knowledge regarding transport of emissions; part is due to the transformation of emissions into undesirable chemicals that then damage valuable objects; and part is due to a lack of knowledge about the ultimate damage to a particular object from a specific dose of deposited chemicals. The third dimension of risk is a lack of good information regarding values that citizens will assign to the various resources potentially at risk by the continued deposition of acids.

Engineers are at work on the technical dimension; biologists are at work on the second dimension; and economists are at work on the third. And yet all of this research seems quite unfulfilling to a policymaker contemplating angry constituents, some wanting immediate action and others insisting that government stay out. One has the impression that policymakers want all of this information, yet they seem hesitant to accept those decisions that seem to make the most sense to the separate disciplines. Indeed, economists feel particularly frustrated about the policy outcomes (Brandl 1985; Buchanan and Tullock 1975).

The reasons, I submit, have to do with several dimensions of the choice process that we either do not understand or choose to ignore. The first of these, previously discussed at length, concerns the venerable distinction between doing what is "efficient" as opposed to making decisions on the basis of the incidence of costs and benefits. Politics is incidence, and so public policy is incidence policy.

The second dimension concerns the distinction between monetary and nonmonetary values. While in recent times there has been a greater political demand for the determination of monetary values with regard to amenities and recreational resources, there is still a great reluctance to base decisions on such monetary imputations. Such imputed values inform the decision process, but they will rarely drive it.

The final aspect of the decision process is that public decision makers seem disinclined to regard losses and gains symmetrically. That is, the "expected value" decision maker will choose the action that produces the greatest expected payoff, while the decision maker concerned with "minimizing maximum regret" will choose the action that promises the smallest expected opportunity loss. Under conventional treatments of risk analysis the expected payoff is but the obverse of the expected opportunity loss. However, this is a symmetry of theory that contradicts empirical reality.

Recent developments in the theory of risk analysis provide some promise for resource economists concerned with this critical problem of choice (Kahneman and Tversky 1979; Tversky and Kahneman 1981). In prospect theory one can find a richer arena in which to consider the complex decision problems of environmental policy. Prospect theory partitions the decision problem into two parts: (1) framing the actions, outcomes, and contingencies and (2) evaluating the choices to be made. The experiments of Kahneman and Tversky, along with those of a number of other researchers, confirm that people do not behave as expected utility theory predicts they would.

In an illustration of the "certainty effect," Kahneman and Tversky (1979) found that 80 percent of their respondents preferred a sure gain of 3000 to the choices of a 4000 gain with probability of 0.8 or a zero gain with probability of 0.2. The value of the sure thing is 3000 while the expected value of the gamble is 3200. Yet the sure thing was the dominant choice. When concerned with losses as opposed to gains, they found the opposite effect. That is, a sure loss of 3000 was preferred by only 8 percent of the respondents, while 92 percent preferred the gamble of a 4000 loss with probability 0.8, or a zero loss with probability of 0.2. In the positive domain the certainty effect contributes to risk aversion so that a sure gain is taken rather than a larger, but probable, gain. In the negative domain the certainty effect leads to risk-seeking preferences for a probable loss over a smaller, but certain, loss.

This distinction between the positive and negative domains is relevant for environmental policy because, unlike conventional investment analysis, here expenditures are being undertaken to protect against probable losses;

it is critical to understand that expected payoffs from productive investments differ from expected opportunity losses from failing to make defensive investments. Consider the choices studied by Kahneman and Tversky (1979). To keep the problem tractable let us assume away the uncertainty that relates to the biological dimension of acid rain. That is, assume that we present the policy maker with a fairly simple choice problem:

A. Do nothing about acid rain and suffer certain losses in habitat valued at 3000; or

B. Install engineering devices that precipitate out acid precursors. If this action is taken there are two possible outcomes:
   1. There is an 80 percent probability that the devices will not work and we will lose the cost of the devices plus the habitat for a total loss of 4000; or
   2. There is a 20 percent probability that the devices will work and our net losses, after paying for the devices, will be zero.

Here we have a decision problem very much like the one studied by Kahneman and Tversky. The value of the gamble in the Kahneman and Tversky experiment indicated that 92 percent of the respondents preferred option B (the control strategy in my example) to option A (do nothing about acid rain). Expected utility theory would predict that the respondents would prefer option A since it has the lowest expected-value loss. In fact, their respondents were risk seeking in the domain of losses in the hopes of hitting the 20 percent chance of no loss. It seems reasonable to suppose that this risk preference when facing losses would be even more pronounced when environmental resources are at stake.

In the above choices there was a sure loss if nothing was done and a fairly high probability of a loss if action were taken. In another experiment Kahneman and Tversky offered the following choices regarding possible losses:

A. 6000 with 45 percent chance, and zero with 55 percent chance; or
B. 3000 with 90 percent chance, and zero with 10 percent chance.

In both instances the value of the gamble is the same (an expected loss of 2700) and yet their respondents favored option A by 92 percent to 8 percent. If we again imagine this to be an acid rain problem, it is not hard to see that option A (some control strategy that still has only a near 50–50 chance of reducing losses) might be quite preferred even though its expected value is identical to the do-nothing option B.

By discussing prospect theory I am not suggesting that the public favors doing something about acid rain (though it may). The purpose here is to illustrate that risk aversion and risk seeking have been found to have different dimensions when choices involving gains are compared with choices involving losses. In a prospect offering gains of the same magnitudes as the above losses, Kahneman and Tversky obtained an exact reversal of the above findings; 80 percent of their respondents preferred a sure 3000 to an 80 percent chance at 4000, even though the expected value of the latter choice is greater.

Public policy is often characterized as a process of minimizing losses as opposed to actions that will maximize gains. For such objectives policymakers are often castigated as "irrational" or wasteful. Yet it may well be that the very essence of social policy is as found in the previous experiments. That is, we are willing to gamble to avoid certain losses, but we are risk averse in the domain of gains, preferring a certain gain to a chance at a much larger one.

Resource economics would seem to benefit from a more thorough consideration of prospect theory where this risk-seeking behavior to avoid losses could be given conceptual as well as empirical content. The Minimax Regret Decision Criterion from expected utility theory is one that addresses the difference between the payoff from the correct decision and the payoff from the actual decision. Because of the presence of irreversibilities in many resource choices, it is reasonable to suppose that most policymakers (just as with most respondents in the Kahneman and Tversky experiments) clearly reject the formal equality of the expected value of gains and losses and would choose a strategy that would minimize their maximum regret. While under conventional assumptions that seems equivalent to choosing so as to maximize expected benefits, prospect theory suggests otherwise.

On Knowledge, Disciplines, and Problems

I would suggest that there are three general phases in the evolution of natural resource economics. The first phase was concerned with the role of natural resources as factors of production. Economists began to build upon the Ricardian and Marshallian views of land and then to elaborate that to other naturally occurring assets. This "production phase" was cast in Edgeworthian terms, and the economic question was one of how to use natural resources efficiently. The assumption was required that such resources were definable in discrete units, and that property arrangements (entitlements) were not in doubt. Because these premises held for land, we soon saw land combined with capital, management, and labor as inputs to be adjusted following the principle of equimarginal returns.

The second phase in the evolution of resource economics was concerned with the general failure of market processes to allocate efficiently a variety of natural resources, including land. Resource economists then became concerned with the variety of remedial actions that might be taken to rectify the observed flaws in the systems of atomistic exchange. More often than not these flaws arose because of the physical nature of many resources that precluded their discrete demarcation and ownership. Economists dealt with taxes, subsidies, unitized firms, omniscient controllers, and Walrasian Auctioneers. This phase also coincided with an active federal effort to invest in natural resource projects (irrigation, transportation, recreation, hydroelectric production), and so benefit-cost analysis was frequently used to evaluate these actions.

The burden of this paper has been to argue that we are now on the threshold of a third phase in resource economics, one that will be primarily concerned with "situational conflicts" as opposed to general efficiency phenomena. It seems to me that confrontation and conflict will predominate among resource economics problems, and that the essence of that conflict will be over presumed (or actual) rights and duties on the part of those bearing joint costs. The legitimacy of existing resource uses will be challenged by those bearing unwanted costs, and the legitimacy of such challenges will be argued by those now well served by the status quo.

Resource economics will become more pragmatic, more concerned with problem solving, more empirical, and even more concerned with the development of concepts to address the emerging situational conflicts. I believe that we will be called upon to offer better conceptual guidance regarding the critical distinction between efficiency and social optimality. There are obvious inefficiencies that can be avoided in the design of bargaining arenas, as well as in the design of government programs that facilitate, induce, or require certain actions.

Federal programs will diminish in importance as we move away from irrigation and other large projects. Such programs will be replaced by local-level resource management, largely dominated by efforts to resolve problems of locally incompatible uses. Natural resource economics will become more explicitly, but conditionally, normative. However that will not threaten its standing as a science, for independent scientists can still assess outcomes within the conditional environment set down by the larger political context; one can certainly be objective about recording the incidence of costs and benefits, about explaining cause and effect, and about predicting alternative futures.

This evolution in problem focus and in methods can be understood as a logical extension of the long-term maturation in economic epistemology. Following the definitive review by Castle et al. (1981), we can identify three distinct lineages to the contemporary discipline of resource economics. The first vein traces its roots to the early rationalists, Descartes, von Leibniz, and Spinoza. The rationalists believed that reason alone, unaided by experience, was sufficient to understand the world around them and to arrive at basic truths about that world. Rationalism holds that one can logically deduce truth from "self-evident" premises; rationalism stands opposed to empiricism as a source of knowledge about the world, as well as on methods of verifying knowledge. Castle et al. follow the rationalists through classical and marginalist thought in economics, and on into welfare economics, which stands as an attempted synthesis of marginalist and collectivist ideas. It is the deductive, predictive, and standard-setting dimensions that differentiate the rationalists from others in the economic family; there is little interest in problem solving, rather the knowledge base itself is the theater of interest. This is referred to as the classical line of thought.

The second line of thought is said to be the positivists, with Francis Bacon standing as the intellectual father, and with Auguste Comte being given credit for its fullest development. Positivists were less interested in explaining phenomena than they were in simply describing the phenomena experienced. Unlike the classical lineage, the positivists were not as concerned with setting standards of performance such as improving national income. Rather, the positivists approved of a reasoned and theoretical approach to problems. Logical positivism is the latter-day version, with its attempt to model philosophy after mathematics and the natural sciences. It had as its purpose the transformation of philosophy from a speculative enquiry into an analytical one. The logical positivists believed that the meaning of a statement could only be determined by tests that applied empirical observations; it was scientific empiricism. The logical positivists maintained that statements that could not be confronted with empirical evidence were simply outside the pale of science, or more seriously, were without any meaning. Castle et al. (1981) regard its practitioners as inductive empiricists. George Warren of Cornell would be an early agricultural economist of the positivist school.

The third line of descent is referred to as the pragmatists, deriving from Veblen and the German historical school and having its philosophical roots in Peirce and Dewey. Methodologically the pragmatists were empiricists, though less systematically so than the positivists. Pragmatism is unashamedly problem oriented, and hence is explicitly normative, although it embraces theory in its formulations. Richard T. Ely, John R. Commons, Henry Taylor, Benjamin Hibbard, and George Wehrwein were early land economists of the pragmatist school at Wisconsin.

To summarize, the rationalists (on which much of neoclassical economics is based) were knowledge, not problem, oriented. They adhered to formal deductive systems of thought and were, for the most part, concerned with nonnormative prediction. The positivists were pure empiricists, were inductive, and were also interested in nonnormative prediction. In contrast to the rationalists, the positivists were less interested in knowledge for knowledge's sake. Finally, the pragmatists were principally problem oriented, strongly empirical, and explicitly normative.

Castle et al. (1981) maintain that these three lines merged during the 1920s to constitute land economics, which then evolved into what we now consider to be resource economics. But that merging cannot conceal the tensions that remain between a discipline that is pulled in one direction toward problem-solving work and in another direction toward knowledge-oriented work. In modern usage, this is the tension between "applied" and "basic" work.

The contemporary preoccupation of resource economists with respect to deductive versus inductive and "positive" versus "normative" can be understood as part of this struggle. The relevance of this for the current discussion is that it is the pull of "objectivity" that attracts resource economists to the "knowledge" side of the matter, while it is the desire to be relevant to important public policy issues that attracts us to the "problem" side.

Contemporary resource economics will be confronted by this choice with increasing frequency. The growth of scientific knowledge now allows, indeed, forces us to recognize causality in the world around us. Yet such certitude, or the relocation of the responsibility for events from the domain of "acts of God" to the domain of human action, brings with it the realization that something must be done. It is out of this causal link that liability is determined, and it is thus that the existence of joint costs becomes a policy variable.

In the absence of scientific knowledge about toxic chemicals, about cedar rust, about asbestos and lung problems, about soil erosion and off-site problems with fish and aquatic life, about coal dust and black-lung disease, and about mercury and brain functions, we would face a situation in which the victims simply accepted the status quo as inevitable. However, the role of new knowledge is to reduce the unexplained variation in the human condition and to permit the establishment of cause for unwanted circumstances. But, having linked seemingly unrelated events, it is then the policy problem to resolve the conflict.

That policy process will engage resource economists to the extent that we are willing and able to operate in a decision environment that is clearly political in nature. It would seem that our skills will be of increasing relevance in the domain of primary (as opposed to secondary) transactions as described earlier. This domain of political economy would take us back to the general origins of economics. It would also require that we acquire a deeper understanding of the theory of the state and the implications of that theory for economic decisions (Bromley 1976). In the absence of these changes in our perspective I worry that resource economics will become increasingly irrelevant to a world of political conflicts over joint costs.

References

Anderson, T. L. 1982. The New Resource Economics: Old Ideas and New Applications. *Am. J. Agric. Econ.* 64:928–34.

Bator, F. M. 1958. The Anatomy of Market Failure. *Q. J. Econ.* 72:351–79.

Brandl, J. E. 1985. Distilling Frenzy from Academic Scribbling: How Economics Influences Politicians. *J. Policy Anal. and Manage.* 4:344–53.

Bromley, D. W. 1976. Economics and Public Decisions: Roles of the State and Issues in Economic Evaluation. *J. Econ. Issues* 10:811–38.

_____. 1978a. Externalities, Extortion, and Efficiency: Comment. *Am. Econ. Rev.* 68:730–35.

_____. 1978b. Property Rules, Liability Rules, and Environmental Economics. *J. Econ. Issues* 12:43–60.

_____. 1982a. Land and Water Problems: An Institutional Perspective. *Am. J. Agric. Econ.* 64:834–44.

_____. 1982b. The Rights of Society versus the Rights of Landowners and Operators. In *Soil Conservation Policies, Institutions, and Incentives,* ed. H. G. Halcrow et al., Chap. 10. Ankeny, Iowa: Soil Conservation Society.

_____. 1986. Markets and Externalities. In *Natural Resource Economics: Policy Problems and Contemporary Analysis,* ed. D. W. Bromley. Hingham, Mass.: Kluwer-Nijhoff Publ.

Bromley, D. W., and R. C. Bishop. 1977. From Economic Theory to Fisheries Policy: Conceptual Problems and Management Prescriptions. In *Economic Impacts of Extended Fisheries Jurisdiction,* ed. L. G. Anderson, Chap. 15. Ann Arbor: Ann Arbor Science Publ.

Buchanan, J. M. 1972. Politics, Property and the Law: An Alternative Interpretation of *Miller et al.* v. *Schoene. J. Law and Econ.* 15:439–52.

Buchanan, J. M., and W. C. Stubblebine. 1962. Externality. *Economica* 29:371–84.

Buchanan, J. M., and G. Tullock. 1975. Polluters' Profits and Political Response: Direct Controls versus Taxes. *Am. Econ. Rev.* 65:139–47.

Castle, E. N., M. M. Kelso, J. B. Stevens, and H. H. Stoevener. 1981. Natural Resource Economics, 1946–1975. In *A Survey of Agricultural Economics Literature,* ed. L. Martin, vol. 3. Minneapolis: Univ. of Minnesota Press.

Cheung, S. N. S. 1970. The Structure of a Contract and the Theory of a Nonexclusive Resource. *J. Law and Econ.* 13:49–70.

Chipman, J. S., and J. C. Moore. 1978. The New Welfare Economics, 1939–1974. *Int. Econ. Rev.* 19:547–84.

Coase, R. 1960. The Problem of Social Cost. *J. Law and Econ.* 3:1–44.

Dahlman, C. J. 1979. The Problem of Externality. *J. Law and Econ.* 22:141–62.

Demsetz, H. 1967. Toward a Theory of Property Rights. *Am. Econ. Rev.* 57:347–59.

Graaff, J. deV. 1967. *Theoretical Welfare Economics.* London: Cambridge Univ. Press.

Kahneman, D., and A. Tversky. 1979. Prospect Theory: An Analysis of Decision under Risk. *Econometrica* 47:263–91.

Krueger, A. 1974. The Political Economy of the Rent-seeking Society. *Am. Econ. Rev.* 64:291–303.

Lang, M. G. 1980. Economic Efficiency and Policy Comparisons. *Am. J. Agric. Econ.* 62:772–77.

Mishan, E. J. 1969. *Welfare Economics: An Assessment.* Atlantic Highlands, N.J.: Humanities Press.

_____. 1974. The Economics of Disamenity. *Nat. Resour. J.* 14:55–86.

Norgaard, R. B., and D. C. Hall. 1974. Environmental Amenity Rights, Transactions Costs, and Technological Change. *J. Environ. Econ. and Manage.* 1:251–67.

Okun, A. M. 1975. *Equality and Efficiency: The Big Tradeoff.* Washington: Brookings Inst.

Pigou, A. C. 1962. *The Economics of Welfare.* London: Macmillan.

Randall, A. 1974. Coasian Externality Theory in a Policy Context. *Nat. Resour. J.* 14:35–54.

Samuels, W. 1971. The Interrelations Between Legal and Economic Processes. *J. Law and Econ.* 14:435–50.

_____. 1981. Welfare Economics, Power, and Property. In *Law and Economics.* ed. W. J. Samuels and A. A. Schmid. Boston: Martinus Nijhoff.

Tversky, A., and D. Kahneman. 1981. The Framing of Decisions and the Psychology of Choice. *Science.* 211:453–58.

Wolf, C., Jr. 1979. A Theory of Non-market Failure: Framework for Implementation Analysis. *J. Law and Econ.* 22:107–40.

Resource and Environmental Economics: A Discussion

ALAN RANDALL

Dan Bromley makes an eloquent case for a particular perspective on the challenges facing resource economics: a perspective that owes much to the institutionalist and land economics traditions. Several of the review panelists and discussion leaders are also individuals known to be sympathetic to these viewpoints. However, institutionalist and land economic perspectives are by no means dominant within the natural resource economics profession. Rather, I would identify the mainstream as basically neoclassical in its economics, although there are divisions between rational planners and public choice theorists when it comes to conceptualizing the role of government in natural resource systems. Further, a growing Austrian-individualist wing provides an increasingly effective counterbalance to the institutionalist land economics wing of the profession. After considering the cast of characters assembled on this program, I have decided that I am perhaps best placed to assume a heavy responsibility: that of representing the approximately 75 or 80 percent of practicing natural resource economists who

Alan Randall is Professor of Resource Economics and Environmental Policy, Department of Agricultural Economics and Rural Sociology at Ohio State University, Columbus.

would not identify themselves with the institutionalist land economics tradition. While I am not entirely comfortable in this role as representative of the mainstream and its right branch, I feel obligated to perform this service, which by default has fallen to me.

Bromley's basic premise is that resource economics is entering the third phase of its evolution. In this third phase, resource economics will move beyond the conventional concerns of efficiency and market failure to a more pragmatic consideration of the political economy of resource conflicts and the structure of entitlements (institutions) that legitimize particular outcomes. One can take this prediction as a fact statement and quarrel with it. On its face, the evidence that the mainstream concerns with efficiency and market failure are becoming ever more entrenched seems at least as strong as the evidence for Bromley's emerging third phase. As I survey the history of resource economics, Bromley's third phase looks to me much more like an earlier era: the second era (if one regards Ricardian classical land economics as era one) represented by Ely, Commons, and a subsequent generation of land economists. A mainstreamer may question whether Bromley is astutely predicting a new and developing orientation for resource economics, or merely hankering for a return to the concerns and methods of an earlier time.

One may wonder from whence comes the demand for the kind of knowledge that would be generated in Bromley's third phase. If we had a better understanding of the political economy of resource conflicts and the relationship between entitlements and outcomes, what would we do with that knowledge? While the rationalist tradition glorifies knowledge for its own sake, institutionalists tend to be a pragmatic lot. The pragmatic tradition values knowledge for its usefulness. A mainstreamer may well suspect that an institutionalist would value knowledge of these "third phase" things for the pragmatic purpose of manipulating entitlements and the outcomes of resource conflicts. That suspicion would make a mainstreamer uncomfortable.

One may also inquire about the production possibilities for that kind of knowledge. Speaking for myself, my instinctive sympathy with some institutionalist precepts has been tempered by frustration at the relatively little progress institutionalists have made in solving the scientific problems on their rather grandiose agenda.

About a decade into the life of the Coase theorem, when debates about the allocative symmetry of bribes, charges, and various liability rules were raging, it was commonplace to observe that, regardless of the detailed outcomes of these particular squabbles, Coase had at least "made the study of institutions respectable among economists." What that meant, I believe, was that Coase had laid the groundwork for the study of institutions by reductionist methods. Reductionist methods are very good for doing those things they can do, and reductionist approaches had been well worked out in other areas of economics. So, progress came quite rapidly in the reductionist study of institutions. Two problems remain however. First, the agenda for reductionist inquiry into institutional matters is much more restricted than is the institutionalist agenda. Second, it is this broader institutionalist agenda that remains resistant to analytical attack.

Having expressed some mainstream skepticism about Bromley's vision of the future of resource economics, I now briefly offer an alternative view on the challenges facing resource economists. I should preface these comments by complimenting Bromley on his interpretation of the notion of "challenges." Implicitly, Bromley rejected (as I do) the notion that the challenges facing resource economics amount to a laundry list of subject matter for applied research. Resource economists have been and still are both responsive and proactive in their choice of research topics. Public concerns that run the gamut from traditional land tenure problems to the environmental hazards engendered by modern organic chemistry and nuclear physics have claimed the attention of resource economists. I am regularly amazed by the breadth of topics that attract resource economists and the speed with which they turn their attention to emerging public concerns. On this point I might remind the reader that only a minority of resource economists work in the land-grant complex. While land-grant resource economists maintain good and regular communication with their colleagues in other parts of the universities and government agencies, the totality of the resource economics undertaking may have escaped the notice of some in the land-grant complex who are not resource economists. The last thing the resource economics profession needs is yet another list of topics for its attention.

Rather, I agree with Bromley's implicit position that the real challenges are those concerned with how to do better resource economics. Like Bromley, I will take an optimistic attitude. I will express my list of challenges as emerging trends in resource economics; the challenge is to make sure the trends actually emerge.

1. Resource economists are going to become even better economists. They will quickly adopt and apply new findings in the core of mainstream, reductionist economics. They will be receptive to emerging core areas such as game theory, and some among their number will continue to seek inspiration in the institutionalist and Austrian wings. Resource economists will not only adopt innovations in economics rapidly, they will continue contributing to the development of the mother discipline.

2. Resource economists will become more eclectic in methodology. With the breakdown of the logical empiricist consensus in philosophy of science and the increasing skepticism about reductionist methods, resource

economists will become receptive to alternative methodological approaches.

This prediction in no way contradicts the one preceding it. An expanding core of shared understanding is, I insist, compatible with increased methodological eclecticism.

3. The ethics of positivism, value freedom, and rational planning will become less compelling to resource economists. The emerging trends to see science as a form of rational discourse and to accept the notion that normative, value, and ethical issues are also legitimate subjects of rational discourse will broaden the subject matter of inquiry in resource economics and fundamentally change the manner in which we resource economists go about our business.

4. One implication of all this is that some resource economists will be more willing to see advocacy processes as legitimate contributors to the rational acquisition of knowledge and to a more open policy decision process. Thus, there will be some among us who will be more willing to see their contribution in advocacy terms. Some will be more willing to make their contribution to improved public decisions by helping various legitimate interests make their particular cases. While such a development would lead us far from rational planning concepts of how science might contribute to policy, I believe that neither science nor policy would be damaged by such a development.

Resource and Environmental Economics: A Discussion

A. ALLAN SCHMID

Bromley concludes that "resource problems are entitlement problems, and as such welfare economics provides us with no unambiguous answer as to what should be done." I am in complete agreement with Bromley's argument and the supporting literature. What is surprising is that it is still necessary for a paper oriented to the twenty-first century to spend so much time on this point. It seems doubtful that any more discussion will convince the disbelievers. But hope springs eternal, so Bromley once again critiques a value or entitlement presumptive welfare economics.

Part of the attraction and siren's song of welfare economics is that it allows the analyst to be authoritative and detached from the political process. You can pronounce on imbecile institutions without the necessity for compromise and political choice inputs. Also it allows tenure-seeking academics time-saving opportunity to develop deductive models with policy conclusions without the necessity of gathering much empirical data. You can denounce a policy as not reaching the optimum without having to engage in messy inference on the relation of who actually got what and the responsible particular instrumental policy.

If we did not need to beat the welfare economics horse for the benefit of future students, we would have more time to explore just how we might "focus on the incidence of costs and benefits from existing and possible actions." Bromley has put his finger on one important area—that of risk analysis. It would certainly be helpful to gather more observations in the spirit of Kahneman and Tversky, who describe how people actually make risky choices. The big problem is that different people have different risk attitudes. Thus, the institutional research question is whose risk preferences count under different decision rules. This would be more useful than an Olympian critique of a given institution as not producing an optimum (as if anyone knew what the optimum will be).

In many resource decisions, access to information is not equally available to all parties. We need to know more about how the rules of the game affect the production and distribution of information. Bromley asks "how entitlements determine burdens of proof" and we might add, what is ac-

A. Allan Schmid is professor, Department of Agricultural Economics, Michigan State University, East Lansing.

cepted as proof. Further, there will be some inevitable costs of being wrong. Different institutions affect the sharing of the eventual costs of mistakes.

Transaction costs are a major topic in the Bromley paper. He suggests as a major research and teaching topic "how entitlements determine transaction costs." This is part of a larger inquiry into how certain parties shift cost to others. Certainly entitlements can sometimes affect the size of transaction costs and thus the occurrence of trade when permitted. In other cases, property rights cannot affect the size of transaction costs, but they can affect the ensuing consequences. One application that I think is particularly important is in the context of exclusion costs. In this case, large groups whose members have small diffused benefits relative to the total cost of action (but whose total benefits exceed costs) are at a disadvantage relative to small groups with intense and concentrated interests. This inability to organize applies both to making market bids and to influencing government action.

We need carefully designed and controlled studies to compare whose preferences get expressed in both market and government even where high exclusion costs provide the opportunity of free ridership. This type of study requires an institutional theory that defines the relevant institutional (structural) variables in functional terms so that we are not confused by the particular nominal manifestation of it. This will allow the empirical testing of the impact of a particular kind of right by observation across a number of similar cases. This means resource economists should not overly differentiate their product so that they can learn from policy analysis more generally. For example, to understand how pollution rights work, we may have to study some nonnatural resource experience that has similar functional characteristics.

One of the keys to an empirical study of rights alternatives is to find institutional variation to compare. Often there simply is no variation within a state. This implies a major role for multistate coordinated studies. It also means that we need some contrived institutional change where researchers help design things such as the negative income tax experiment rather than relying on natural experiments. Researchers will need extension worker help here.

Further, institutional theory will have to carefully specify the situation character of goods that create human interdependence. The same right applied to a situation of high exclusion cost produces a different performance than it does in the case of high information costs, economies of scale, peak load characteristics, or whatever. Finally, we need to specify and control for noninstitutional and nonsituational characteristics. Where full experimental designs are not possible, model specification is vital.

I believe that the components of an institutional theory are in place to guide empirical research relating product situation, institutional structure, and performance (who gets what). The utility of this theory is not as a critique of welfare economics but to develop empirically testable relationships between rights alternatives and substantive performance. It complements and supplements rather than replaces conventional micro and macro theory. For example, the latter can be used to trace the effects of a reduction in pesticide use on the location of production, but it is institutional theory that relates whether a prohibition administered at the local or national level, etc., will actually result in changed pesticide use.

To predict what will actually happen with a rights change, policy analysis must go beyond theories of advantage to theories of behavior. Incorporation of behavioral science is critical. Learning and perception of alternatives affects actual individual choice. The design and implementation of policy to achieve a given performance requires tools to link psychology and economics.

What are the research implications of Hirsch's positional goods? They are intimately related to Bromley's insistence that many resource policy issues involve basic ownership decisions by public bodies. You cannot consider a market exchange until it is decided who is the owner that receives the bid of the nonowner. What do economists know about such conflict resolution after all of their years of devotion to Pareto-better change? Not much in my judgment. Yet, there are some resource economics themes we could build on. Students of land tenure have long alluded to the connection between land reform and productivity. Modern studies have bastardized this into how tenure arrangements affect what is considered the marginal input so that the optimal combination of resources with known marginal value products is reached. But, as Lester Thurow in his book *Dangerous Currents* (1983) suggests, labor's MVP is not a given, but is affected by motivation stemming from whether the worker feels fairly treated. This is one application of Hirsch's positional goods. Income distribution may not be independent of production. This is an empirical question deserving our attention. I would hypothesize that whether people think the game is fair has something to do with such things as opportunistic behavior in the context of the free rider problems noted before and how much we have to spend policing regulations. In short, income distribution may affect willing participation and this has measurable economic consequences.

The need for more involvement in conflict resolution has implications for extension work. Historically, extension was involved in the organization of co-ops, irrigation districts, and school district consolidation. Extension workers did not approach the participants with specifications of welfare-maximizing institutions, but rather they helped people make the necessary compromises and develop experience of trust and empathy, which we are learning is important in resolution of such situations as the prisoners dilemma. I suggest that we might begin by inspection and codification of this experience. In contrast, now academic reward seems biased toward elegant symbolic model building rather than participation in interactive problem solving. We seem satisfied to publish rather than to participate.

I will close with one further dimension of a useful policy science. It may need to include a management dimension rather than simply a policy analysis. We have invested more scholarly input into planning and evaluation than into execution and administration. This is as true for both farm and business management as for public firms. Many of us have answered the siren call of the central budget office doing cost-benefit analysis or reforming regulations rather than helping to make an operating agency work. I am beginning to think that we are too concerned with optimal choice of projects or rules and not enough concerned with making whatever is chosen work. People like Tom Peters are arguing in the private sector that the business school graduates with all their knowledge of take-over finance and discounted cash flows have ignored whether the sales clerk is keeping the customer happy. I suspect the same may apply in the public sector in the management of water, forest, etc.

Reference

Thurow, L. C. 1983. *Dangerous Currents, The State of Economics.* New York: Random House.

10

Developments in Economics of Importance to Agricultural Economics

RULON D. POPE

The title of this paper is indeed ambitious and far exceeds my abilities to synthesize. Nonetheless, it is hoped a very modest vehicle can be instrumental for stimulation of thought and discussion in this area.

Of necessity I will be very selective, and no attention will be devoted to referencing agricultural economics literature that might be directly or tangentially related to my assignment. It seems difficult to communicate even a small portion of the ideas in the literature. Consequently, I will concentrate on pointing to the literature and my impressions of its value.

By definition, the forecast is subjective. Interestingly, a very large debate in economics bears directly on this subject. If you or I were able to forecast which areas of economics will be important to agricultural economics, then entry should occur with the accompanied rents captured by early entrants. Certainly, my own rent-seeking behavior would prevent my telling you the truth free. Thus, my own behavior and the perfect markets literature might suggest that my forecast has little value.

Further, one might also inquire whether my forecast is adaptive or rational or any of the other plethora of methods used to "expect." For at least the adaptive case, present and lagged quantities are clearly important for the forecast. For this reason, the next section begins with a review of some recent changes in emphasis in economics. It should be stressed that these marginal changes do not indicate total productivity. Indeed, I suspect that rather accepted and standard models of demand and supply will con-

Rulon D. Pope is Professor of Economics at Brigham Young University, Provo, Utah, and Visiting Professor of Agricultural Economics at the University of Wisconsin, Madison.

tinue to be "bread-and-butter" tools for agricultural economists in the foreseeable future. Yet, I suspect one will also see significant refinements of such models (e.g., Varian 1984b).

The Recent Past

A simple and, it is hoped, useful way to assess changes in economic knowledge is to use the *Journal of Economic Literature* (*JEL*). One could use the surveys or an analysis of bibliographic entries or readership of particular journals. Consider the entries in Table 10.1, which are journal publications for the journals covered by the *JEL* for various broad areas of economics for two time periods, 1974 and 1984. Though one worries some about possible administrative changes and the sample periods, I believe the entries indicate the changes that have and are occurring for these broad categories.[1]

Microeconomic theory articles exceed those in macroeconomics (22, 23) but macroeconomics has had the largest growth rate. In other general areas, social choice and uncertainty and game theory (25, 26) have experienced a very rapid growth rate while general equilibrium theory has stagnated (21).

As to specific areas, the following had growth rates approaching 200 percent: selective areas of economic history (e.g., 44); capitalistic systems (51); defense economics (114); business cycles (131); construction and use of econometric models (212); economic and social data (220, 225); productivity and growth data (226, 227); banking theory and policy (310, 311, 312); public finance: fiscal policy (320); trade relations and policy (421, 422); international finance and aid (431, 433, 443); industrial organization and policy (611, 616); economics of public enterprises (614); industrial studies (630, 631, 632, 635, 636); rural economics and agricultural finance (714, 718); farm management, marketing, and agribusiness (715, 716); energy (723); labor studies (824, 825, 826, 831, 833); demographic economics (841); health economics (913); social security and aging (915, 918); crime (916); discrimination (917); and consumer and housing economics (921, 932).

Several areas declined. Among them are: growth, planning theory and policy (111, 113); developing country studies (121, 122, 123); forecasting (132); mathematical methods and models (213); international investment and capital markets (441); organization and decision theory (511); business and public administration (513); marketing and advertising, and accounting (531, 541); antitrust (612); agricultural supply and demand (711); land reform (717); manpower (811); welfare programs (911); education (912); urban economics and policy (931, 933); and regional economics (941).

Table 10.1. Research publications in the *Journal of Economic Literature*

Classification number	Classification title	1974	1984
11	General economics	152	84
12	Teaching of economics		New(40)
20	General economic theory	24	41
21	General equilibrium theory	63	87
22	Microeconomic theory	411	506
23	Macroeconomic theory	198	310
24	Welfare theory	238	211
25	Social choice, bureaucratic performance	70	225
26	Economics of uncertainty and information, game theory, and bargain theory		New(136)
27	Economics of centrally planned economies		New(88)
31	History of economic thought	162	264
36	Economic methodology	31	48
	Economic History		
41	General	33	19
42	North America	132	40
43	Ancient and medieval	7	12
44	Europe	64	161
45	Asia	23	17
46	Africa	4	4
47	Latin America and Caribbean	4	21
48	Oceania	18	10
50	Economic systems	1	10
51	Capitalist economic systems	51	168
52	Socialist and communist economic systems	138	103
53	Comparative economic systems	16	11
111	Economic growth theory and models	124	43
112	Economic development models and theories	115	174
113	Economic planning theory and policy	191	99
114	Economics of war, defense, and disarmament	18	41
121	Economic studies of developing countries	217	110
122	Economic studies of developed countries	67	40
123	Comparative studies (Developed and developing countries)	48	24
124	Economic studies of centrally planned economies		New(56)
131	Economic fluctuations	39	107
132	Economic forecasting and econometric models	119	104
133	General outlook and stabilization theories and policies	204	196
134	Inflation and deflation	166	251
211	Econometric and statistical methods and models	311	350
212	Construction, analysis, and use of econometric models	44	91
213	Mathematical methods and models	66	44
214	Computer programs	13	5
220	Economic and social statistical data and analysis	3	38
221	National income accounting	119	144
222	Input-output	31	31
223	Financial accounts	11	11
224	National wealth and balance sheets	12	14
225	Social indicators and social accounts	7	13
226	Productivity and growth: Theory and data	24	85
227	Prices	44	76
228	Regional statistics	6	10
229	Microdata	41	0

Source: Issues of the *Journal of Economic Literature,* 1974 and 1984.

240

Table 10.1. Research publications in the *Journal of Economic Literature* (cont'd.)

Classification number	Classification title	1974	1984
310	Domestic monetary and financial theory and institutions	0	16
311	Domestic monetary and financial theory and policy	331	546
312	Commercial banking	155	232
313	Capital markets	282	383
314	Financial intermediaries	58	51
315	Credit to business, consumer, etc.	71	74
320	Fiscal theory and policy, public finance	0	28
321	Fiscal theory and policy	198	260
322	National government expenditures and budgeting	58	95
323	National taxation and subsidies	213	309
324	State and local government finance	98	125
325	Intergovernmental finance relationships	25	34
400	International economics	0	20
411	International trade theory	139	163
420	Trade relations, commercial policy, international economic integration	0	21
421	Trade relations	111	245
422	Commercial policy	119	136
423	Economic integration	104	80
430	Balance of payments, international finance	0	3
431	Balance of payments, mechanisms of adjustment, exchange rates	170	333
432	International monetary arrangements	96	85
433	Private international lending	0	21
441	International investment and capital markets	65	54
442	International business	114	94
443	International aid	45	96
500	Administration, business finance, marketing, accounting	2	1
511	Organization and decision theory	94	57
512	Managerial economics	79	104
513	Business and public administration	101	56
514	Goals and objectives of firms	36	24
520	Business finance and investment	1	18
521	Business finance	128	128
522	Business investment	113	116
531	Marketing and advertising	149	90
541	Accounting	102	93
610	Industrial organization and public policy	1	1
611	Market structure: Industrial organization and corporate strategy	176	280
612	Public policy toward monopoly and competition	89	72
613	Public utility and government regulation of other industries in private sector	91	114
614	Public enterprises	10	73
615	Economics of transportation	86	107
616	Industrial policy		New(67)
621	Technological change, innovation, research and development	120	234
	Industry studies		
630	General	57	104
631	Manufacturing	217	353
632	Extractive industries	71	88
633	Distributive trades	36	32
634	Construction	10	21

Table 10.1. Research publications in the *Journal of Economic Literature* (cont'd.)

Classification number	Classification title	1974	1984
635	Service and related industries	147	262
636	Nonprofit industries: Theory and studies		New(8)
710	Agriculture	73	54
711	Agricultural supply and demand analysis	157	128
712	Agricultural situation and outlook	18	22
713	Agricultural policy, domestic and international	96	150
714	Agricultural finance	14	39
715	Agricultural marketing and agribusiness	32	69
716	Farm management, allocative efficiency	40	96
717	Land reform and land use	71	66
718	Rural economics	31	89
720	Natural resources	0	3
721	National resources	109	158
722	Conservation and pollution	133	119
723	Energy		New(252)
731	Economic geography	22	36
800	Manpower, labor, population	0	4
811	Manpower training and development	47	25
812	Occupation	41	55
813	Labor force	72	105
820	Labor markets, public policy	0	3
821	Theory of labor markets and leisure	141	241
822	Public policy, role of government	77	103
823	Labor mobility, national and international migration	59	56
824	Labor market studies, wages, employment	269	478
825	Labor productivity	44	73
826	Labor markets, demographic characteristics	25	66
830	Trade unions, collective bargaining, labor-management relations	0	10
831	Trade unions	42	116
832	Collective bargaining	52	68
833	Labor-management relations	42	91
841	Demographic economics	136	277
851	Human capital	96	60
910	Welfare health and education	0	15
911	General welfare programs	48	44
912	Economics of education	99	73
913	Economics of health	73	154
914	Economics of poverty	47	42
915	Social security	34	67
916	Economics of crime	24	72
917	Economics of minorities, economics of discrimination	94	162
918	Economics of aging	0	New(21)
921	Consumer economics, levels and standards of living	168	329
930	Urban economics	0	11
931	Urban economics and public policy	139	93
932	Housing economics	79	134
933	Urban transportation economics	31	16
941	Regional economics	330	249
Totals		11,353	15,374

In absolute terms, micro and macro theory, econometrics, money and capital markets international exchange rates and balance of payments, taxes and subsidies, manufacturing studies (and to a lesser extent, industrial organization), and labor and consumer studies all have entries exceeding 300 in 1984 and would seem to have an especially prominent place in economic inquiry.

In examining the given data, it seems that a few conclusions are in order. First, macroeconomic fields including money and international macro studies have boomed. Another high growth industry is demographics. As one peruses the titles of papers, apparently one of the driving forces behind this growth is the new family economics. Related growth fields involve labor policy, social security and aging, and health. Finally, industrial organization and industry studies have grown substantially. This latter group includes many studies from the *Journal of Law and Economics*. Finally, one sees reductions in many abstract fields of theory and more microbusiness-related activities such as business finance, marketing, accounting, and administration.

In nearly every case, I believe that it is clear that research has responded to data and social needs. For example, the emphasis on demographics, aging, saving and social security, and health seem to be linked to changes in fertility, gender changes in the labor market, changes in the number of cohorts in various age groups (such as overall aging) and the accompanying policy dilemmas regarding taxation and social security and the provision of health care. Similarly, the decline or stagnation of growth or general equilibrium theory may be due to a paucity of interesting disciplinary or social problems in these areas or the inability of the theory to provide meaningful insights (take your pick, I prefer the latter). On the other hand, game theory and uncertainty have ascended because they shed light on many observed behaviors. Therefore, I would maintain that in the long run, the theory (concepts) and measurement tools useful to agricultural economics will be those that are instrumental to understanding behavior.[2] Further, it is unclear whether one can look to the mother discipline to provide many management or administrative tools. These seem to fall on the other side in the demarcation between business and economics.

Rational Expectations and Efficient Markets

The rapid growth of articles devoted to macroeconomics and finance is traceable in many respects to a few economic events and intellectual stimuli. The stagflation of the 1970s, the apparent impotence of stabilization policies, and the move to floating exchange rates were key events. The intellectual genesis of the resurgence was due to work by Freidman, Muth, and Lucas, with the latter considered the dominant figure. Lucas (1981) created an equilibrium model of the business cycle based upon intertemporal substitution of labor when most heretofore business cycle models presumed disequilibrium. One result from Lucas's work is

$$y_t = y_p + be_t \tag{1}$$

where y_t is actual output and y_p is full employment output,[3] e_t is the forecast error by the public of the money stock, and b is a constant. Thus, money forecast errors can affect actual output but if the money stock is fully anticipated then there is no effect of money growth on real output.

Lucas's work has been extremely influential and I think a fair assessment of its import is given by Tobin (1981, 41) (no great fan of monetarism):

> The ideas of the second counter-revolution are too distinctive and too powerful to be lost in the shuffle. They are bound to shape whatever orthodoxy emerges. The durable ideas are more methodological than substantive-interally consistent derivations of rational expectations and rational behavior embodied in the structural equations of a general equilibrium macroeconomic model. These ideas are already being mobilized to explain the causes of informational imperfections, long-term contracts and other commitments, incompleteness of capital markets . . .

Thus, Tobin views this work as contributing mainly to methodology. Indeed, if anticipated policy has no real effects, one might guess that contracts overlapping through time and other institutional features regarding information might be important explanations of the business cycle (Fischer 1977). Thus, a new institutional economics has been spawned.

I would like to discuss the micro or price theoretic implications of Lucas's work. First, one must acknowledge that Lucas almost single-handedly, by including the concept in his work that was widely read, is responsible for the interest in rational expectations though Muth (1961) originally proposed the idea. An agricultural economic genealogy might be helpful. First, Nerlove (1958), improving on others' work, substantially altered agricultural economics by proposing and popularizing the adaptive expectations (and partial adjustment) models of supply and demand response. The profound impact of this contribution is documented by Askari and Cummings (1977). The research focuses on the right issue: decisions involve uncertainty and one must make these decisions by forecasting future states of nature. Yet anyone who has used these models knows of many inherent weaknesses, such as persistent biased expectations of price. Thus, in principle, the adaptive expectation method (with a cobweb as a special case) can lead to considerable stupidity on the part of economic agents. However, these methods have made a long and successful contribution in studying agricultural markets.

It is interesting that agricultural commodities were cases mentioned in the literature where rational expectations were seen as reasonable. To illustrate the basic notion, Muth (1961) posited that it was irrational for individuals to persist in beliefs that might not be consistent with the process generating the random variable (e.g., price). Thus, Muth posited as a positive economic proposition that the rationally expected price is the conditional expectation of the reduced form of an economical model. To illustrate, let demand be of the form

$$q_t = b_0 + b_1 p_t + b_2 y_t + e_t \tag{2}$$

where the b's are parameters, p_t is own price at time t, q is the corresponding quantity demanded, y_t is income, and e_t is an identical and independently distributed (IID) random disturbance. Supply is also conventionally defined by

$$q_t = c_0 + c_1 p_t + c_2 z_t + u_t \tag{3}$$

where p_t is an expected price at time $t-1$ that would occur at time t, the c's are parameters, z is an exogenous variable, and u_t is an IID disturbance. The rationally expected price is $E(p_t|I_{t-1})$ where I_{t-1} is the information available at $t-1$. Thus, since the model is assumed to contain all information,

$$_{t-1}p_t = [(c_0 - b_0) + c_2\,_{t-1}z_t - b_2\,_{t-1}y_t]/(b_1 - c_1) \tag{4}$$

where the double subscripts denote predicted values (Eckstein 1984). For example, $_{t-1}z_t$ is the predicted value of z given information available at $t-1$. Thus, rational expectations require that the market behaves as if it knows the parameters (b's and c's) as well as unbiased predictions of exogenous variables (z and y). Wallis (1980) and others have suggested that the exogenous variables could be predicted by time-series methods. Thus, rational expectations can be viewed as giving structure to distributed lag models in the exogenous variables.[4]

There have been many attacks on rational expectations including the criticism that the expectation in (4) should be based on an objective notion rather than on subjective distributions. A difficulty for researchers is that one is ultimately lead to explanations of market behavior in order to obtain expected price even if one wishes to study a region, state, or country. Rather than list all potential problems here, I think that as a concept Lucas and others have successfully launched it to supremacy (Sheffrin 1983). Expectations of the future should be forward looking and based upon the process that generates the random variable.

There is one issue that is particularly relevant for agricultural economists. Might the futures market form a rationally expected price thus destroying the need for all of the machinery indicated in (4)? Indeed, it would if (4) is the reduced form for the futures market at planting time. Arbitrage arguments may lead one to believe that this is so. Empirically, it seems that there is some evidence that the futures market does not contain any more predictive power than rationally expected prices (Sheffrin 1983), but this seems to beg the issue previously raised. Ultimately, this issue will be resolved by empirical work. However, a rational expectations model with inventories and government programs is substantially different than the one indicated, and there is every reason to suspect that the two expectations are different. In any event, it seems that rational expectations is and will continue to be an important research agenda in agricultural economics for some time.

THE LUCAS ECONOMETRIC CRITIQUE. A second contribution by Lucas that has relevance to agricultural economists deals with the stability of econometrically estimated parameters. The argument was first posed as a cost of adjustment model in which Lucas argues that all parameters in a distributed lag model really included prices and thus were not stable (Lucas 1981). In a more recent attack, the issue is raised more subtly and deals directly with dynamic policy. With rational expectations, expectations of, for example, price depend upon expected government policy. This is seen by interpreting weather as a government variable in equation (4). The actual future may not be known with certainty but suppose that the policy can be written as a mathematical rule with noise. For example, target price adjustments may be linearly related to the difference between income and some target income. In such a case, a change in the rule (parameters of the equation) will alter the coefficients of the supply equation, (3), because the form of expectations changes. Thus, existing parameter estimates could not be used to forecast the impact of a policy rule change. This criticism seems valid and, with the change in agricultural policy rules every few years, it may be especially relevant. It is hoped that acknowledging the validity of this criticism will cause policy analysts to build a more fundamentally consistent model of behavior under uncertainty or lead to research that demonstrates the Lucas criticism is not empirically very important.

EFFICIENT MARKETS. It is also clear that the rational expectations arguments have become intricately involved with the so-called efficient market hypothesis. Rational expectations are conditional expectations and are unbiased. Thus, they obey

$$p_t = {}_{t-1}p_t + e_t \tag{5}$$

where e_t is the random disturbance and the forecast is arbitrarily chosen as a one period ahead forecast. Thus, rational expectations resemble the random walk or martingale property of much of the weak form of Fama's (1980) efficient market tests. Fama has proposed further elaborations of the test embodied in (5) based upon additional and/or insider information (semistrong and strong forms of the efficient markets hypothesis).

Another issue studied by market theorists is whether market price could reveal all available information in the sense that it is a sufficient statistic for all information (Grossman 1978; Grossman and Stiglitz 1980). The general conclusion of this literature seems to be that when information is costly, the market price is not a sufficient statistic that can be observed by uninformed traders in order to make informed decisions. Further, the incentive to collect costly information exists such that an equilibrium without rents is obtained. It appears that this crucially hinges upon the types of uncertainty and requires that the number of uncertainties be greater than the number of markets (Allen 1981; Sheffrin 1983). In other cases, information gathering does not occur since one can likely costlessly observe price that is a sufficient statistic for all information held in the market.

The studies of markets by financial economists have, in my opinion, altered the course of economics. They have forced us to more carefully think about what it means for markets to be rational and informationally efficient (e.g., Roll 1984). What information is and does, its demand and supply components, and how it affects market outcomes is an important growing area, and its growth is in large part due to the developments in this field. This research has also spawned a more thoughtful consideration of market adjustments and how goods markets (e.g., inventories) might be different than markets for financial instruments. If many markets have the martingale or random walk property, there are extremely important implications for forecasting economic variables. For example, Hall (1978), using the efficient markets and rational expectations notion, argued that consumption in the United States was a random walk property. Empirical work has done little damage to this hypothesis. This implies that the best forecast of tomorrow's consumption is today's consumption. One need not build an elaborate intertemporal econometric model to explain the evolution of consumption. A similar careful analysis in agricultural economics for agricultural income, consumption, land values, etc., would prove informative.

Demographic Economics

A second growth area noted in Table 10.1 is demographic economics. A large subarea here is the new family economics, with demographics and labor also growing rapidly. This area is also intimately connected to the economics of consumption and probably Gary Becker or T. W. Schultz is considered to be associated with its genesis more than anyone else. Becker and his students have pushed economic research into new areas of behavior such as fertility, marriage, divorce, human capital, altruism, intergenerational transfers and the evolution of income and wealth, and many other activities of economic life. It is curious that the family as an economic institution had received so little economic study in light of its economic importance and the large amount of research by sociologists and other social scientists. Perhaps, it is due to so many nonmarket transactions within the family.

Since this literature is so broad, it is impossible for me to even give a sense of the important developments in each area. The recent book by Becker (1982) summarizes much of his thinking on the family. Examples of some of the questions studied by Becker are: Is labor to be specialized within or without the home? How is work to be divided between the sexes? Why are some societies monogamous while others are polygamous? Why do higher-income men in the United States marry at younger ages and have more stable marriages? Why have the urban and rural fertility differences been narrowing or eliminated in most countries of the world? How does fertility (quantity of children) interact with investment decisions in children? (These investments in quality might involve human and social capital and/or nutrition and health.) What is the relationship of inherited traits or family effects to the accumulation of wealth and income? How do taxes and bequests affect the rise and fall of families (with respect to income)? Why do family heads bequest at death when inter vivos giving is generally less costly given tax considerations? Might one see more sibling rivalry with regard to the distribution of family income rather than the generation of family income? That is, might siblings fight over parental giving but always pursue actions that maximize family income? How does altruistic behavior affect job choices by spouses?

Becker, using theoretical and empirical analyses, provides very interesting and compelling answers or conjectures to these questions. The framework is the economic model of the rational self-interested or altruistic man. Many have found this work lacking in insight or repulsive since the economic model is used to analyze many problems that have seemed beyond economic man [see Hannan (1982) and Ben-Porath (1982) for a review]. Yet, it seems to me that this exercise forces economists to consider more carefully data and explanations within the traditional province of sociologists and psychologists. (Perhaps the exchange between agricultural economists and rural sociologists will resemble an earlier time.) At this point, there seems little doubt that the economic model is a powerful descriptor of behavior. As the general economy, and much of the agricultural sector in particular, changes demographically (such as trends in off-farm work, fertility, and aging), these research issues are bound to become more important.

Related research in this area not only involves many interesting labor supply issues (e.g., mobility) but other consumer or household issues. For example, the effect of nutrition is an important related field (e.g., Pitt and Rosenzweig 1985). With the current famine conditions worldwide, this will no doubt grow in importance. Similarly, as policy debates involving distributional issues continue, it seems that agricultural economists will become more interested in issues of income and wealth distribution and accumulation.

The New Industrial Organization

Also apparent from Table 10.1 is the recent growth in industrial organization (IO). For some years, this was a substantial but modestly growing industry in economics. In the last decade, it seems to have gained considerable momentum. Also, it naturally includes many industry studies perhaps not thought to be IO. For example, much of the economics of regulation and law and economics belongs to this heading in the *JEL*. Further, many of the applications of experimental economics deal with these issues.

I will first mention an area I see as impressive and relevant. It is the contestable market theory associated with Baumol et al. (1982) and others. The basic claim of the theory is that the set of conditions that lead to efficient resource use are much less restrictive than previously thought. This requires that the notion of efficiency be stated and the one that seems most appropriate is the Ramsey (1927) notion of efficient pricing that, for example, utility is maximized subject to constraint (such as zero profit). Under a set of conditions, most notably costless reversible entry and a Nash-type reaction by incumbent firms, the Ramsey prices can be attained in many cases without regard to the number of players (even natural monopoly). Though the assumptions are strong, it gives one pause when concentration ratios are used for policy prescriptions or measures of monopoly power.

In many respects, this theory or its forerunners have involved significant advances in the theory of the multiproduct firm, whether competitive, monopoly, or whatever. For example, the papers on economies of scope by Panzar and Willig (1981) and Baily and Friedlander (1982) are, I believe, fundamental to agriculture.[5] For two outputs, A and B, and cost function C, the scope issue involves the comparison of $C(A,O) + C(O,B)$ and $C(A,B)$. Scope economies are shown to result from quasi-public inputs, that is, inputs that have the property that use in one output does not diminish the available inputs for use in other outputs.[6] Further, this literature establishes the relationship between scope economies and the existence of multiproduct firms. Why are Wisconsin dairy farms multiproduct when many in California are single product? What is needed is a careful integration of the certainty theory with scope economies and uncertainty. Secondly, the Ramsey second-best argument seems relevant for a wide range of agricultural issues. Perhaps one should define efficiency more broadly and look for optimally distorting agricultural policies.[7] This approach is prevalent in public finance in deriving optimal taxes (Atkinson and Stiglitz 1980).

There are also a host of industry issues that have been studied in this literature that seem not to have received similar attention in the agricultural sector. For example, it does not seem that agricultural economics has focused on contract theory as much as IO or law and economics. There has been scant attention paid by agricultural economists to share rental or lease arrangements (contracts) and the possibility that labor will shirk requiring incentive contracts or monitoring (the principal-agent problem). Yet, the ascendancy of shared ownership by labor, so-called direct marketing schemes (pyramidlike notions) franchises, bonuses (which resemble two-part tariffs), share land leasing, and other incentive-based contracts and hierarchies, indicate that this area is an important issue (e.g., Singh 1985).

Though agricultural economic literature has dealt extensively with agricultural commodity programs, there has not been a similar enthusiasm for other regulation issues and industry studies. One such area is the theory of rent seeking associated with Stigler (1971), Posner (1975), and Peltzman (1976). This literature argues that an industry group, (e.g., in agriculture) will expend resources in order to seek or maintain rents when expected benefits are not less than expected costs. Perhaps a corollary is that rents accrue most to politicians when a credible threat to a policy change is made (Mueller 1979). In any event, we need to sort out transfers from real reductions in welfare or rents (see Rausser 1982). Thus, the profession may have expended more energies developing the supply curve of milk rather than the supply of rent seeking by dairy associations. Hence we may know more about welfare triangles than we do about the overall welfare losses to society (and congressional voting behavior).[8]

Risk and Games

It is perhaps arbitrary that uncertainty is separately listed here, especially since we have already discussed expectations. As a theory, it is only a tool for understanding behavior. Yet, as noted in Table 10.1, risk theory seems to be a dominant force in the research agenda. Much behavior just cannot be understood without using some form of uncertainty theory (see e.g., Hey 1979).

Yet, in spite of the enormous impact of expected utility theory, the dominant theory, there is a groundswell of opposition beginning with psychologists and moving to economists. Most of the opposition to the theory comes not from the poor performance of the theory empirically in market settings but from experimental evidence that the axioms are systematically violated. The basic axioms are: the individual can order the set of distributions; the ordering is transitive; if distribution 1 is preferred to 2 is preferred to 3, then there exists a convex combination of 1 and 3 that is indifferent to 2 (continuity); and independence, or for any arbitrary distribution 3 a convex combination of 1 and 3 is preferred to a convex combination of 2 and 3 when 1 is preferred to 2.

Among the empirical results that seem important are: (1) the relative invariance of a person's gambling and insurance purchasing behavior to changes in wealth and the sensitivity of choice to the problem context (framing effects); (2) violation of the independence axiom as illustrated by the Allais paradox; (3) violation of the independence axiom by being oversensitive to changes in small probability events (i.e., individuals even when presented with objective probabilities act as if they transform these probabilities in a systematic way); and (4) decision makers violate transitivity. Others could be added. Schoemaker (1982) recently reviews much of this evidence.

In addition, there are attacks on orthodoxy that come indirectly from information theory. Bayesian learning may not describe how learning takes place (Viscusi 1985). Secondly, Heiner (1985) argues that uncertainty brings into play errors in decisions. These errors lead to more rigid behavior (rules of thumb) than is implied by expected utility maximization.[9] Further, free information may be discarded if it reduces reliability of behavior.[10]

These challenges to the new orthodoxy have spawned recent research aimed at generalizing expected utility. These include eliminating the independence axiom of expected utility (Machina 1982); eliminating the independence plus transitivity axiom (Fishburn 1982; 1983); less formalized methods of dealing with the above objections (e.g., prospect theory, Kahneman and Tversky 1979); considering more carefully how errors in decision making affect behavior and proposing a way to evaluate reliability (Heiner 1985); and considering ways to coherently consider certain and uncertain multiattribute preferences (Selden 1978).

Though in my opinion none of these theories has demonstrated great empirical promise, I believe that some will. Machina's theory provides a coherent explanation of the troubling facts with expected utility being a local approximation to his more general expected utility analysis. Fishburn finds a new skew-symmetric bilinear functional representation of preferences when independence and transitivity are relaxed but a new reasonable symmetry axiom is inserted. Heiner develops a condition based upon marginal costs and benefits that leads to reliable behavior but has only provided anecdotal evidence of its relevance.

How does this research impact on agricultural economics? Since risk is inherent to many decisions by producers and consumers involving natural resources and food and fiber, it seems incumbent upon the profession to lead the way in testing propositions about behavior. Normative risk analysis will have little impact if the tenets of some of the theories outlined here are more descriptive. For example, do we know very much about the production possibility for responding to information or do we as economists continue to ignore the wealth of information that psychologists have generated on this matter?

Some of the information on the relevance of these theories will no doubt come from experimental economics, an area in which I predict agricultural economists will become more interested. Yet, I believe that the research of Knez et al. (1985) is very relevant here. Markets may behave essentially as the theory predicts even though a group (perhaps large) behaves in a systematic way contrary to the theory. This can occur because it is the marginal decision makers that dictate market changes. In this respect Knez et al. found experimental evidence to support expected utility theory. Further, Viscusi (1985) has presented some evidence that some of the troublesome violations of expected utility are consistent with Bayesian learning theory. In any case, these issues can only be understood clearly with empirical research about how people respond.

GAMES. Game theory has been with us for several decades, but it has had minimal impact on agricultural economics. According to Schotter and Schwodiauer (1980), it has met with cyclical interest. During the 1950s, it was used extensively to study oligopolies and duopolies. Interest waned until game theory was revitalized as economists studied general equilibrium adjustments. Competitive and Pareto outcomes could be modeled in a game theoretic way (Scarf and Hansen 1973). Since this brought a new way of viewing general equilibrium results, but few new results, interest again waned during the 1960s and 1970s.[11] Finally, beginning in the 1970s, a large body of literature developed inquiring about the role of institutions in allocation mechanisms. Thus, the new theory of institutions is based heavily on game theoretic notions. This is in marked contrast to traditional economics, which for the most part has presumed institutional arrangements.

To illustrate, consider one example drawn from public choice. Green and Laffont (1977) and others have shown that allocation mechanisms do not exist for public goods that satisfy the balance condition of a Lindahl equilibrium (taxes = benefits for each individual) such that telling the truth about benefits is a dominant strategy. That is, there is a strong tendency to underreport benefits. Groves and Ledyard (1977) and others have developed cost share allocation rules that lead to the truthful revelation of preferences. This rule essentially internalizes the externality of being untruthful. However, as the above impossibility result shows, the resulting mechanism cannot be balanced. Thus, bankruptcy is a possibility.

One such application, which is by now standard in graduate training, is the possibility of strategic behavior of firms (Varian 1984a). Consider a conjectured impact of a firm's behavior on output price, $dp\,(Y)/dy$, where Y is industry output, y is a firm's output, and p is market price. The firm will maximize profit by choosing y so that

$$p(Y) + (dP/dY)(2dY/dy)y = \text{marginal cost} \qquad (6)$$

For a competitive firm, $dp/dy = 0$. For a Nash-Cournot firm, the firm takes other firms' output as given (see the contestable market discussion) and thus dY/dy is one. For a monopolistic firm dY/dy is Y/y and marginal revenue equals marginal cost. Finally, for the general case of Stackelberg equilibrium behavior, dY/dy is any correct prediction (conjectural variation) of how the industry responds as the firm's output increases. All of the above can be appropriately changed if price is the initial decision variable.

The above game theoretic notions not only provide a taxonomy but have important policy implications. Recently, in the *Journal of Political Economy,* Sullivan (1985), building on Sumner (1981), used the conjectural variations framework to analyze the degree of monopoly power in the cigarette industry. He found that the industry is characterized by a substantial degree of competition. Thus, one can attempt to measure social costs without resorting to concentration ratios or other measures of firm shares.

As one views applications in public choice and other areas, it is clear that an impressive revolution is under way. Not only is the traditional bargaining problem dealt with, but a host of IO and agency applications are apparent. Thus, it seems that it is not so much that new equilibrium solutions have been discovered as that new applications of fairly old notions have been skillfully used (e.g., Milgrom and Roberts 1984; Bell and Zussman 1976).

Concluding Remarks

Empirical applications of nearly all economic concepts can be found in the literature in journals in each field and in general applied journals like the *Review of Economics and Statistics.* Any explanation of the future use of economic concepts must model the reduced form for such knowledge. It seems to me that an induced innovation hypothesis about the generation and use of such information is descriptive in the long run. That is, behavioral issues and policy will drive the reduced form. Much of the literature here reviewed deals directly with attempting to understand economic behavior, behavior which may extend beyond traditional agricultural economic studies of the rural economy, food, and resources. As indicated in Table 10.1, economics may be drifting further away from microbusiness related topics and moving more toward the functioning of markets that may imply only rudimentary knowledge of such micro topics. Thus, areas like demography only become important to agricultural economists when social science is allowed to have its head without the ever present bridling implied by the short-run need for improved market efficiency, policy relevance, and clientele satisfaction. I believe that this will happen and that is why I have not forecast that more sophisticated versions of standard commodity models will rule the day. Just as natural resource economics may be viewed as an important extension of the traditional field of agricultural economics, I predict, for example, that regulation (political economy), labor, and demographic economics will similarly become important as we deal with understanding rural behavior and issues germane to the sector.

Notes

1. Analysis of other time periods revealed similar differences. The reason that a single month was used was to avoid some of the double counting that occurs throughout a year.
2. This may mean that many disciplinary issues are investigated in the short run and received or discarded. However, the trends in Table 10.1 seem to me a clear indication that interesting social science problems are not on the whole internally defined.
3. All variables are generally thought to be logs so that changes are percents.
4. I am struck by the irony that rational expectations is to replace time-series or ARIMA-type forecasts of price but virtually requires these procedures to forecast exogenous variables in agricultural applications since there are almost always contemporaneous exogenous variables.
5. I attempted to deal with this problem poorly in my dissertation. The basic issues regarding managerial attention and related inputs seem crucial for much behavior.
6. It is interesting to me that Dr. Ivan Lee suggested to me the innovation of modeling multiproduct agriculture using public inputs. Thus, the rather extensive development of scope economies in my Ph.D. thesis (prior to Panzar and Willig 1981) is due to Dr. Lee.
7. Chambers (1985) suggests this line of argument but a thorough treatment with regard to agricultural policy seems lacking in the literature. Since stabilization is an important rationale of policy, it would seem that a Ramsey-type analysis must include risk.
8. Rausser (1982) has mentioned some of the literature on the economics of regulation and political economy in general. It seems to me that many of the issues about how policy is formed are second-order small to the literature on rent seeking at this time. My position is that rent seeking is a good place to start. This literature is quite undeveloped and certainly future work will sharpen the measurements of societal losses and distributional effects of policy.
9. This work is not without criticism; see Bookstaber and Langsam (1985). Heiner's (1985) most recent work seems to have solved many unclear features of his theory.

10. This is called the informational overload paradigm in some marketing and psychology literature.

11. An exception might be the Scarf algorithm for computing the core of an economy.

References

Allen, B. 1981. Generic Existence of Completely Revealing Equilibria for Economies with Uncertainty When Prices Convey Information. *Econometrica* 49:1173–99.

Askari, H., and J. T. Cummings. 1977. Estimating Agricultural Supply Response with the Nerlove Model: A Survey. *Int. Econ. Rev.* 18:257–92.

Atkinson, A., and J. Stiglitz. 1980. *Lectures on Public Economics.* New York: McGraw-Hill.

Bailey, E., and A. Friedlander. 1982. Market Structure and Multiproduct Industries. *J. Econ. Lit.* 20:1024–48.

Baumol, W. J., J. C. Panzar, and R. D. Willig. 1982. *Contestable Markets and the Theory of Industry Structure.* Chicago: Harcourt Brace Jovanovich.

Becker, G. 1982. *A Treatise on the Family.* Cambridge: Harvard Univ. Press.

Bell, C., and P. Zussman. 1976. A Bargaining Theoretic Approach to Crop Sharing Contracts. *Am. Econ. Rev.* 66:528–88.

Ben-Porath, Y. 1982. Economics and the Family-Match or Mismatch. *J. Econ. Lit.* 20:52–64.

Bookstaber, R., and J. Langsam. 1985. Predictable Behavior: Comment. *Am. Econ. Rev.* 75:751–55.

Chambers, R. 1985. Least-cost Subsidization Alternatives. *Am. J. Agric. Econ.* 67:251–56.

Eckstein, Z. 1984. A Rational Expectation Model of Agricultural Supply. *J. Polit. Econ.* 92:1–19.

Fama, E. 1980. Efficient Capital Markets: A Review of Theory and Empirical Work. *J. Financ.* 25:383–423.

Fischer, S. 1977. Long-term Contracts, Rational Expectations, and the Optimal Money Supply Rule. *J. Polit. Econ.* 85:191–205.

Fishburn, P. 1982. Nontransitive Measurable Utility. *J. Math. Psych.* 26:31–67.

———. 1983. Transitive Utility. *J. Econ. Theory* 31:293–317.

Green, J., and S. Laffont. 1977. Characterization of Satisfactory Mechanisms for the Revelation of Preferences for Public Goods. *Econometrica* 45:427–38.

Grossman, S. 1978. Further Results on the Informational Efficiency of Competitive Stock Markets. *J. Econ. Theory* 18:81–101.

Grossman, S., and J. Stiglitz. 1980. The Impossibility of Informationally Efficient Markets. *Am. Econ. Rev.* 70:393–408.

Groves, T., and J. Ledyard. 1977. Optimal Allocation of Public Goods: A Solution to the Free Rider Problem. *Econometrica* 45:783–810.

Hall, R. 1978. Stochastic Implications of the Life-cycle Permanent Income Hypothesis: Theory and Evidence. *J. Polit. Econ.* 86:971–87.

Hannan, M. 1982. Families, Markets, and Social Structures. *J. Econ. Lit.* 20:67–72.

Heiner, R. 1985. Origin of Predictable Behavior: Further Modeling and Applications. *Am. Econ. Rev.* 75:391–96.

Hey, J. 1979. *Uncertainty in Microeconomics.* New York: New York Univ. Press.

Kahneman, D., and A. Tversky. 1979. Prospect Theory: An Analysis of Decision Under Risk. *Econometrica* 47:263–91.

Knez, P., Y. Smith, and A. Williams. 1985. Individual Rationality, Market Rationality, and Value Estimation. *Am. Econ. Rev.* 75:397–402.

Lucas, R., Jr. 1981. *Studies in Business Cycle Theory.* Cambridge: MIT Press.

Machina, M. 1982. Expected Utility Analysis Without the Independence Axiom. *Econometrica* 50:227–323.

Milgrom, P., and J. Roberts. 1984. Price and Advertising Signals of Product Quality. Yale University. Unpublished paper.

Mueller, D. 1979. *Public Choice.* Cambridge: Cambridge Univ. Press.

Muth, J. 1961. Rational Expectations and the Theory of Price Movements. *Econometrica* 29:315–35.

Nerlove, M. 1958. *The Dynamics of Supply: Estimation of Farmers' Response to Price.* Baltimore: Johns Hopkins Univ. Press.

Panzar, J., and R. Willig. 1981. Economies of Scope. *Am. Econ. Rev.* 71:268–72.

Peltzman, S. 1976. Toward a More General Theory of Regulation. *J. Law and Econ.* 19:211–40.

Pitt, M., and M. Rosenzweig. 1985. Health and Nutrient Consumption Across and Within Farm Households. *Rev. Econ. Stat.* 67:212–23.

Posner, R. 1975. The Social Costs of Monopoly and Regulation. *J. Polit. Econ.* 83:807–27.

Ramsey, F. 1927. A Contribution to the Theory of Taxation. *Econ. J.* 37:47–61.

Rausser, G. 1982. Political Economic Markets: PERTs and PESTs in Food and Agriculture. *Am. J. Agric. Econ.* 64:821–83.

Roll, R. 1984. Orange Juice and Weather. *Am. Econ. Rev.* 74:861–80.

Scarf, A., and T. Hansen. 1973. *The Computation of Economic Equilibria.* New Haven: Yale Univ. Press.

Schoemaker, P. 1982. The Expected Utility Model: Its Variants, Purposes, Evidence and Limitations. *J. Econ. Lit.* 20:529–63.

Schotter, A., and G. Schwodiauer. 1980. Economics and the Theory of Games. *J. Econ. Lit.* 18:479–527.

Selden, L. 1978. A New Representation of Preferences Over 'Certain Uncertain' Consumption Pairs: The Ordinal Certainty Equivalent Hypothesis. *Econometrica* 46:1045–60.

Sheffrin, S. 1983. *Rational Expectations.* Cambridge: Cambridge Univ. Press.

Singh, N. 1985. Monitoring and Hierarchies: The Marginal Value of Information in a Principal-Agent Model. *J. Polit. Econ.* 93:599–609.

Stigler, G. 1971. The Theory of Economic Regulation. *Bell J. Econ.* 2:3–21.

Sullivan, D. 1985. Testing Hypotheses about Firm Behavior in the Cigarette Industry. *J. Polit. Econ.* 93:586–98.

Sumner, D. 1981. A Measurement of Monopoly Behavior: An Application to the Cigarette Industry. *J. Polit. Econ.* 89:1010–19.

Tobin, J. 1981. The Monetarist Counter-Revolution Today—An Appraisal. *Econ. J.* 91:29–42.

Varian, H. 1984a. *Microeconomic Analysis.* 2d ed. New York: W. W. Norton.

_____. 1984b. The Non-parametric Approach to Production Analysis. *Econometrica* 52:579–97.

Viscusi, W. K. 1985. Are Individuals Bayesian Decision Makers? *Am. Econ. Rev.* 75:381–85.

Wallis, K. 1980. Econometric Implications of the Rational Expectations Hypothesis. *Econometrica* 48:49–73.

Developments in Economics of Importance to Agricultural Economics: **A Discussion**

GORDON C. RAUSSER

Professor Pope has undertaken an almost impossible task of determining what developments in economics will lead to significant applications in agricultural economics. One development that reappears throughout the paper is the concept of rational expectations. In the extreme, this concept can be used to explain why no one should read the Pope paper or, for that matter, that Pope should not have written this paper. On the one hand, as Pope notes, "my own rent-seeking behavior would prevent my telling you the truth free. Thus, my own behavior and the perfect markets literature might suggest that my forecast has little value." Hence, if Pope provides the profession with any real insights, this framework would regard him as a "stupid" agent. On the other hand, the perfect markets literature also tells us that, if readers believe that Pope will provide some real insights, they are stupid. The unequivocal inference of rational expectations and the perfect markets literature is that either Pope is stupid for writing the paper or the reader is stupid for reading the paper. This dilemma also makes it clear that agents cannot behave rationally if other agents are irrational. In a strict sense, the concept of rational expectations requires that agents take into account the potential irrationalities of other agents.

Fortunately, we have an alternative theory based upon asymmetric information and imperfect markets. This literature suggests that neither Pope nor any reader of this particular paper is stupid. In fact, Pope should be congratulated on the preparation of a very fine discussion of developments in economics. His approach in assessing changes in economic knowledge is to utilize data reported from the *Journal of Economic Literature* (*JEL*) for two years, 1974 and 1984. Given his approach, Professor Pope extracts as much as could be expected. A number of criticisms could be offered regarding his interpretation of the data, but most would be insignificant. The selection of the first year, 1974, is meaningful in the sense that it

Gordon C. Rausser is the Robert Gordon Sproul Chair Professor of Agricultural and Resource Economics, University of California, Berkeley, and Chairman of The Giannini Foundation of Agricultural Economics. In the preparation of this paper, he benefited from discussions with four colleagues: Professors Peter Berck, Larry S. Karp, Jeffrey M. Perloff, and David Zilberman. Professor Zilberman's insights were particularly valuable.

is toward the beginning of one of the most rapid inflation periods for the U.S. economy. Similarly, 1984 comes after the end of one of the worst recessions in the post-World War II U.S. economy. A natural question that arises is: How robust are the results reported by Pope to this interval selection?

During the post-World War II era, general economics has gone through a period of formalization and extended use of mathematical and statistical tools. Economics has aspired to become a rigorous discipline, along the lines of engineering and physics, and it has attempted to shake the reputation in many academic circles as the "dismal science." The 1950s witnessed the emergence and wide application of econometrics as a major tool of analysis; similar experiences occurred with mathematical programming in the 1960s; and the 1970s witnessed the diffusion of optimal control and topology as major analytical tools. Unlike the earlier periods, no major new mathematical techniques emerged during the late 1970s and the early 1980s. To be sure, important refinements have occurred, many of which have focused on econometrics (e.g., the work on unobservable and latent variables, on specification analysis, on measurement errors, on qualitative and disequilibrium estimators, on sample selection, on new models of technological change, and on new admissible estimators). Aside from these refinements, the major emphasis within the general discipline of economics seems to have been directed to the analysis of behavioral patterns resulting from human frailty and the role of imperfect information. There is also an emerging interest in the economics of institutions. There appears to be a movement afoot to return to the core of economics a number of concepts that have emerged in other disciplines (e.g., political science, psychology, sociology, and law).

From the standpoint of value to the agricultural economics profession, other approaches could have been employed in lieu of the JEL data utilized by Pope. One approach would be to identify the major leaders in each area of economics and examine the stream of citations to their work. Another and, perhaps, a more attractive approach would be to define the major problems (both recurrent and emerging) and those paradigms and associated analytical frameworks that can effectively address these problems. This approach would not restrict the examination to just the economics discipline but, instead, to all disciplines that would assist in addressing the identified problems. This, in fact, underlies much of the recent development in the new industrial organization, which in a large part has resulted from a merger of law, organization theory, and economics.

The directional change within economics (viz., away from methods to theoretical and conceptual developments) should provide much impetus in our attempt to address a number of long-standing issues that have eluded solution for some time. The first is public policy in food and agriculture.

Here a number of different perspectives can be taken, but the major concerns are to both explain and design the forces and processes that shape agricultural policies and their implications. From an explanatory perspective, the new economics of regulation, rent-seeking behavior, and the notion of political economic markets are natural frameworks in which to address these issues.[1] From an evaluative perspective, the comparative static analysis that is frequently used to trace through the impacts of public policies is grossly inadequate. What is required here and in the analysis of many other problems is comparative dynamic analysis. These methods have not been developed within economics but, instead, in electrical engineering. Here again, we see that we must look not only to what Pope describes as the "mother discipline" but to other fields to determine where the major advancements are likely to come within agricultural economics.

In the normative or prescriptive design of public policy, the so-called Lucas critique raises its ugly head. Prior to the Lucas critique, the standard approach to normative policy analysis was to set up an optimization problem where the policy process is viewed as a game against nature. The substance of the Lucas challenge is that policymaking is a game involving conscious players. It rejects the notion that the atomistic nature of the constituents of "the public" implies that public behavior can be modeled by a mechanical rule. To be sure, the Lucas critique does not imply that "policy" is ineffective even if all agents in the private sector form their expectations rationally. A more accurate statement is that it is unreasonable to expect most of the people to be fooled most of the time; a policy that counts on such foolish behavior is doomed to failure. Private agents' decisions are contingent on the state of the world; the rules that determine the decisions as functions of the state of the world are products of agents' optimization problems; a change in policy not only changes the state of the world but it also changes the agents' optimization problems and, hence, their decision rules. This means that the reduced-form estimation of behavioral relationships is inadequate for policy analysis. In any event, the Lucas critique has performed a valuable service in drawing our attention to the fact that the effectiveness of a policy today depends, in part, on expectations of that policy in the future. This has led to important insights regarding the constraints under which governments operate. Specifically, governments must be concerned with their credibility. For example, it does no good to announce that farm subsidies will be phased out if most farmers believe otherwise. If their beliefs are proven correct, the announcement weakens the government's ability to reduce subsidies in the future. This result also suggests the importance of studying bargaining problems and other games to properly investigate public policies in food and agriculture.

A second major set of issues relates to the demystification of agribusiness. Much remains to be accomplished in assessing the structure, conduct, and performance as we move along the vertical commodity marketing chain beginning with input suppliers and ending with ultimate consumers. The new industrial organization has much to offer in addressing this issue, focusing as it does on information (Diamond 1971, Salop 1977, Spence 1973, and Stiglitz 1979); tests of monopoly power and conjectural variation (Gollop and Roberts 1979, Porter 1983); product differentiation and monopolistic competition (Spence 1976, Dixit and Stiglitz 1977, Salop 1976); advertising and strategic behavior (Friedman 1977, Fudenberg and Levine 1983, Dixit and Norman 1978); vertical integration; and transaction costs and institutional models.

There are, clearly, numerous mechanisms or institutions that coordinate the exchange of food products. These alternative coordinating mechanisms (cooperatives, vertical integration, horizontal integration, commodity associations, marketing orders and agreements, spot markets, futures markets, forward contracts, governmental intervention, etc.) will influence transaction costs, technology, the quality and quantity of output in a particular economic system, the size and distribution of gains and losses, and, equally as important, the sharing of risk among various components of the food marketing system. At the heart of any analytical framework designed to evaluate the performance of alternative coordinating mechanisms must be the notion of a contract. Such a perspective can be traced back to the conception of a firm adopted long ago by Coase and recently accepted and employed by students of economic organizations. Contracting and limited information force us into a second-best world where first-best solutions are not achievable. Unless the conventional Pareto norm established in general economics is replaced by some other norm, we are, generally, left with ambiguous efficiency evaluations of food and agricultural systems.

The work in the theory of economic organizations has much to offer agricultural economics. Markets in food and agriculture comprise a great variety of contractual arrangements that have generally been ignored in the literature. For example, in agricultural credit markets, contractual arrangements exist that allocate capital and risk bearing among the economic agents. These contracts ordinarily involve sizable transaction costs and significant externalities that emanate from principal/agent relationships. The transaction costs cover such items as monitoring, enforcement, bargaining, agency cost, and contract formulation and documentation. In this setting, a "second-best" solution is one that minimizes the overall social cost under the imposed constraints. The upshot is that much more needs to be learned about the world of second best and the evaluation of performance, conduct, and structure under other norms or criteria.

The notion of sufficient statistics and under what conditions market prices are fully revealing must be explored in the context of the institutional coordinating mechanisms that exist for various commodity systems. We now know that costless information is both a necessary and sufficient condition for market efficiency, but we have only begun to realize what this implies in terms of the information content of market signals. The work in finance and on commodity futures markets has examined efficiency in a world of limited and asymmetric information. This work will ultimately define the market characteristics needed to achieve different types of informational efficiency. In this setting, the stochastic calculus (Rausser and Hochman 1979), has not been fully exploited. Much the same could be said for the recent literature on arbitrage pricing.

The previous arguments suggest that rational expectations and perfect markets are ideals that will not be duplicated in the real world. Rational expectations must take into account the benefits and costs of collecting information in a world in which various agents are only partially and unequally informed. The data available to those in agricultural economics provide us with a comparative advantage in developing empirical frameworks that recognize how rational expectations might be formed in a world of costly information. At Berkeley, we have developed a model that allows us to infer from the price dynamics in futures and spot markets the weightings across groups defined in accordance with their information set and the pattern by which they form expectations. In periods of significant market instability, a larger number of agents fall in the group that form their expectations rationally under costly information while, during periods of more stable prices, a larger share falls into "naive" expectation groups. This simply reflects the difference in benefits and costs of collecting information to form more precise conditional price expectations.

Finally, I do not share Professor Pope's enthusiasm for the contestable market theory. It would seem to me that this theory has done nothing more than formalize what was already known in the "old" industrial organization literature. Quasi-public inputs and scope economics, however, have much to offer agricultural economists. I was delighted to learn that Ivan Lee suggested this to Professor Pope when he was writing his dissertation at Berkeley. I only wish the two of them had realized the importance of what they had stumbled upon prior to its popularization in general economics.

Another set of issues relates to farm family and consumer choices including the labor/leisure trade-off. Theories of product quality choice, dynamic changes in preferences, and family production functions show real promise in explaining the behavior of consumers as well as farm families. In the former context, such understanding is especially important because sagging demands are a major constraint currently facing agriculture. For farm families, the work in demographic economics, eloquently outlined by Professor Pope, should prove to be particularly relevant. Very recently, agricultural economists have made major contributions to the theory of implicit markets and the separation of consumer taste from the demand for food nutrients. In a more general demographic context, the merger of economics with sociology and psychology will, indeed, entail large transaction costs but may also reap significant benefits as suggested by Professor Pope.

Another major set of issues relates to the forces behind the shifts in production capacities and market shares of agricultural products across nations and regions. Here, much can be accomplished in the evaluation of comparative advantage, competitive advantage, and effective protection. Once again, comparative dynamic methods will prove to be of much greater value than comparative statics. Research in this area should also benefit immensely from the merger of rent-seeking behavioral theories with the recent developments in international economics on trade under imperfect competition. Computable general equilibrium models, which have been applied to LDCs, could and should be applied to evaluate comparative advantage as well as competitive advantage. Moreover, such models will prove useful in examining the hypothesis that the only way to significantly increase the export demand for agricultural products from the United States is by designing policies for LDCs that lead to rapid rates of economic growth.

In his analysis, Pope chooses to neglect macroeconomics and thus focuses on new developments in microeconomics. This separation would make sense if the classical macroeconomic model held in the real world and if money was, in fact, neutral. Unfortunately, as I and others have shown, the U.S. economy is composed of both fixed- and flex-price markets and, as a result, money is at a minimum nonneutral in the short run. As a direct result of the nonneutrality of money, overshooting occurs in agricultural commodity markets. This means that three sets of causal forces must be identified and estimated in attempts to empirically explain the price dynamics of a particular (storable) commodity market. These sets of forces include internal demand and supply, the influence of governmental interventions, and the overshooting resulting from the nonneutrality of money and the equilibrium that must arise in the short run among asset markets. The linkages between agricultural markets and the macroeconomy, along with the international economy, cannot be treated by exogenous income, interest rates, exchange rates, and so on. To do so is to miss one of the three major causal forces that defines the dynamic path of storable commodity prices.

Few would argue with the observation that we need a better understanding of what determines the behavior of farmers. In this respect, the blending of psychology and economics shows much promise. Both the new approaches to decision making under uncertainty (cited by Pope) and the work on cognitive dissonance (Akerlof 1970) should prove of much value. The challenges to the conventional expected utility framework are exciting and could result in useful empirical formulations. In this respect, it is my belief that Professor Pope has underestimated the potential value of prospect theory which originated in the field of psychology.

Much more could and should be said regarding the new developments in economics, as well as in other fields, that might be of direct potential value to agricultural economists. In evaluating the potential contribution of such developments to our profession, we are well advised to continue to focus on applied, well-articulated problems. This is where our comparative advantage lies; it is also the ultimate gauge by which all new theories, concepts, and methods should be assessed.

Note

1. Pope, in his examination, incorrectly associates the theory of rent seeking with Stigler (1971) and Peltzman (1976). This theory is actually more correctly associated with Downs (1957), Buchanan et al. (1981), Krueger (1974), Tullock (1967), and others. In fact, Gordon Tullock wrote the first paper on this particular topic to correct some conceptual flaws in standard welfare economics and the measurement of deadweight losses.

References

Akerlof, G. 1970. The Market of Lemons: Qualitative Uncertainty and the Market Mechanism. *Q. J. Econ.* 84:488–500.

Buchanan, James, Gordon Tullock, and Robert D. Tollison, eds. 1981. Towards a General Theory of the Rent-Seeking Society. College Station: Texas A&M Univ. Press.

Diamond, P. 1971. A Model of Price Adjustment. *J. Econ. Theory* 3:156–68.

Dixit, Avinash and Victor Norman. 1978. Advertising and Welfare. *Bell J. Econ.* 9:1–14.

Dixit, Avinash and Joseph E. Stiglitz. 1977. Monopolistic Competition and Optimum Product Diversity. *Am. Econ. Rev.* 64:297–308.

Downs, A. 1957. *An Economic Theory of Democracy.* New York: Harper and Row.

Friedman, James. 1977. *Oligopoly and the Theory of Games.* Amsterdam: North Holland.

Fudenberg, D. and D. Levine. 1983. Subgame Perfect Equilibria of Finite and Infinite Horizon Games. *J. Econ. Theory* 31:251–68.

Gollop, Frank M. and Mark J. Roberts. 1979. Firm Interdependence in Oligopolistic Markets, *J. Econ.* 10:313–31.

Krueger, Anne O. 1974. The Political Economy of the Rent-Seeking Society. *Am. Econ. Rev.* 64:291–303.

Peltzman, Sam. 1976. Toward a More General Theory of Regulation. *J. Law Econ.* 19:211–40.

Porter, R. 1983. Optimal Cartel Trigger Price Strategies. *J. Econ. Theory* 15:313–38.

Rausser, Gordon C. and E. Hochman. 1979. *Dynamics of Agricultural Systems: Economic Predictions and Control.* Amsterdam: North Holland.

Salop, Steven C. 1976. The Noisy Monopolist: Imperfect Information, Price Dispersion and Price Discrimination. *Rev. Econ. Stud.* 44:393–406.

_____. 1977. Second-Best Policies in Imperfect Competition: How Improved Information May Lower Welfare. Center for the Study of Organization Innovation Discussion Paper 11.

Spence, A. M. 1973. Job Market Signalling. *Q. J. Econ.* 87:355–74.

_____ 1976. Product Selection, Fixed Costs, and Monopolistic Competition. *Rev. Econ. Stud.* 43:217–36.

Stigler, George J. 1971. The Theory of Economic Regulation. *Bell J. Econ.* 2:3–21.

Stiglitz, J. 1979. Equilibrium in Product Markets with Imperfect Information. *Am. Econ. Rev.* 69:339–45.

Tullock, Gordon C. 1967. The Welfare Costs of Tariffs, Monopolies, and Theft. *West. Econ. J.* 5:244–32.

Developments in Economics of Importance to Agricultural Economics: **A Discussion**

JEAN-PAUL CHAVAS

The paper by Pope had the difficult task of pointing out some promising avenues where developments in economics are likely to stimulate future agricultural economics research. For the most part, I agree with his evaluation. Here, I would like to pursue briefly some of the issues he raised.

It appears logical to argue that agricultural economics would greatly benefit from a refinement of conceptual tools used in the analysis of economic behavior. As an example, our past experience with the use of economic theory in the modeling of market supply-demand relationships is rather impressive. This indicates that the potential payoff from further improving our theoretical tools may be substantial. However, the theory is useful only if it helps describe and explain economic behavior. And it is only to the extent that economic decision-making processes are well understood and that economic tools can reliably be used in a normative or policy

Jean-Paul Chavas is Associate Professor of Agricultural Economics at the University of Wisconsin, Madison.

context. The difficult challenge is therefore to try to identify the developments of economic theory that are most likely to impact on the future of the agricultural economics profession.

Here, I would like to emphasize two topics mentioned by Pope that seem particularly promising: the economics of information and the analysis of multiperson decision-making processes. First, it seems clear that economic decision making under imperfect information is the rule rather than the exception. This is due to the complexity of a changing world, the absence of complete contingent claim markets, and the cost of acquiring information, as well as the limited ability of the human mind to process a large number of signals. This has stimulated considerable interest in the economics of uncertainty, as discussed by Pope. Also, improvements in the quality of human capital (leading to better economic choices) may be closely associated with improvements in the processing of information by decision makers; this suggests that the analysis of investment in human capital could benefit from the economics of information. Similarly, the rational expectations hypothesis has refocused attention on the processing of information by economic agents. Although forward-looking expectations are usually seen as an improvement over the backward-looking adaptive expectations, they leave some questions unanswered. First, if information is costly, it may be optimal for agents *not* to use some information. Second, the rate of information flow can influence the timing of economic decisions (e.g., investment). This suggests that Muth's hypothesis may need to be modified in order to address more directly the costs and benefits of information processed by economic agents. The existence of well-known cycles in agricultural markets (e.g., the pork cycle) should provide an excellent basis for agricultural economists to investigate such issues.

Second, the potential for a better understanding of multiperson decision making seems considerable. For example, since most households and firms involve more than one person, the allocation of tasks and rewards among individuals is of great interest. This requires analyzing altruism, incentives, preference-revealing mechanisms, moral hazard, adverse selection, monitoring, etc., as they affect the allocation of resources. Also, by outlining the incentives for sharing resources or wealth, this should allow economists to discuss distribution issues more objectively. It would stimulate a more thorough analysis of the comparative advantage of various market and nonmarket institutions. It would also sharpen our analytical tools in the investigation of property rights, contracts, and government policies. In that context, the development of new approaches in the analysis of the motivations and performance of farm policy may be quite promising.

Developments in Economics of Importance to Agricultural Economics: **A Discussion**

DANIEL A. SUMNER

Every economist has a list of "developments" that he or she thinks are unusually interesting or useful. Rulon Pope has had the fun of preparing such a list but also the difficult task of explaining his choices. He did a fine job. I have only to add a few clarifying comments and a few additional developments that might be added to the list. But first I point out that my preferred title for these comments would be different from the conference session title, and suggest some ways to improve our link to other fields in economics.

Improving the Economics of Agricultural Economists

To explore "developments in economics" from the point of view of agricultural economics (as implied by the official title) is to suggest that agricultural economists do not contribute to economics. This suggestion is not only wrong but dangerous. The error in the title is that many of the developments in economics "of importance to agricultural economics" were, in fact, the work of agricultural economists; but those contributions are *not* the ones we are to talk about in this session. Instead, Rulon Pope and the discussion openers focus on how developments in the other fields of economics can help our work in agricultural economics. The danger in the session title is that it encourages agricultural economists to think of ourselves as removed from other economists whom we then think of as a homogeneous group.

On this theme, I want to stress the importance of maintaining and improving our economics skills and training in order to better our work in extension, teaching, and research. The following suggestions are made to the AAEA, departments or other administrative units, and individual agricultural economists.

Daniel A. Sumner is Associate Professor, Department of Economics and Business, North Carolina State University, Raleigh.

1. It is important to encourage improved professional interaction with all economists, not just those working in government departments of agriculture, agribusiness, or university schools of agriculture. Joint courses or seminar series between agricultural economics and other fields help improve communications. The basis for useful communication is enhanced, however, if agricultural economists demonstrate their active interests and potential contributions to more than just their own narrow area of study.

2. We must continue to recognize and reward agricultural economists who publish in journals other than the agricultural economics field journals such as the *AJAE*. That means many of us need to read these other journals. This includes not only "general" economics journals such as the *American Economic Review* or the *Journal of Political Economy,* but also "field" journals such as the *Journal of Labor Economics* or the *Journal of Monetary Economics.*

3. Most agricultural economists are really "hyphenated" economists. We are agriculture-labor economists, agriculture-trade economists, agricultural-macroeconomists, etc. This dual alignment means we must keep up with — and contribute to — our other field in addition to agricultural economics. A good study, for instance, on futures market behavior for an agricultural commodity will contribute to the fields of finance or industrial organization as well as to agricultural economics. It also means that an agricultural trade economist may benefit more from interactions with other international trade specialists than with an agricultural labor economist. To get good research, teaching, and extension in agricultural trade may require opportunities for all trade economists to discuss their work.

4. To further the quality of our agricultural economics extension, research, and teaching, we need to draw into agricultural economics young economists who may *not* have specialized in agricultural economics in school. Ph.D. course work or dissertations are often more methodological than later work, and we can enrich agricultural economics by attracting, for example, good trade economists into agricultural trade.

5. We must also encourage research and teaching by agricultural economists on topics that may not be strictly agricultural. A good agricultural economist who works on farm finance issues will likely contribute occasionally to the finance literature itself. Such contributions may not be a direct agricultural application but will further the field of finance. Such work is important and is required to build the reputation of agricultural economics.

I believe that attention to the issues listed will help us insure that "developments in other areas of economics" will not be overlooked in our own field. Understanding of the economics of agriculture will improve as a result.

Additional Important Developments

Rulon Pope has focused on information and expectations, which is entirely appropriate. Both in theoretical models and in empirical studies, economists have recently expended much effort exploring implications of the endogenization of expectations and information gathering and processing. Pope has rightly called attention to the important contributions of Robert Lucus as an intellectual leader in these areas. In addition, I would encourage agricultural economists to study work in the area of implicit-contracts and the principle-agent problem. Much of the recent research takes as a starting point the sharecropping literature with which we are familiar to explore implications for labor, finance, and other business relationships.

I enjoyed Pope's section on demographic economics and liked that name for the collection of studies usually associated with Gary Becker and T. W. Schultz. Agricultural economists have contributed directly to this area, especially in applications to less-developed countries. In further work we should recognize the importance of understanding the family to understand the family farm. Treating the household as a firm leads to insights about family behavior. Recognizing the interactions between family and farm decisions will help in modeling both the farm and the family. This is true especially for our understanding of the economics of agriculture in less-developed countries.

Among the contributions in demographic or labor economics I would add the work growing out of MaCurdy's 1981 *Journal of Political Economy* paper. MaCurdy focuses on intertemporal substitution and the use of fixed effects in panel data to help estimate the parameters that we may really be interested in. He notes that in dynamic life-cycle models the marginal utility of income may be treated as a constant that is different across individuals. This leads to a specification of marginal-utility constant demand functions. But marginal utility cannot be measured, so MaCurdy uses a fixed constant for each individual in a panel data set to allow him to estimate the other parameters conditional on marginal utility. The result in his labor supply is estimation of the trade-off between leisure in different periods of the life-cycle. Some of these ideas go back to Mundlak's 1961 *Journal of Farm Economics* paper and have recently been followed up by Browning, Deaton, and Irish in a 1985 *Econometrica* paper. The general area of the econometrics of limited dependent variables and panel data (most notably associated with Heckman) are a topic for the quantitative methods session even though the economic interpretations have been important. Applications of these ideas to general demand systems and to the theory of the firm are to be expected.

The economics of regulation and industrial organization has moved towards asking about how policies come to be established. Endogenous policy models are also a major topic in agricultural economics, but we can continue to profit by reading the broader literature associated especially with Stigler (1981), Becker (1983), and Peltzman (1985).

Finally, I will mention the area of hedonic pricing and the literature following Sherwin Rosen's 1974 *Journal of Political Economy* paper. There are both theoretical and econometric contributions to how we deal with markets for commodities that have bundles of attributes. Of course, this characteristic applies to most agricultural commodities as well as to land markets. We have yet to incorporate quality variation carefully into our market models. There is an expanding literature that may help.

Rulon Pope was asked to do the impossible, and he made a very useful contribution with his paper. No one can read all of economics, and as *agricultural* economists we will read mostly in our own areas of specialization. My plea is that agricultural economists continue to read (and write) at least selectively in other areas of economics as well. We will be better *agricultural* economists if we do.

References

Becker, G. S. 1983. A Theory of Competition Among Pressure Groups for Political Influence. *Q. J. Econ.* 97:371–400.

Browning, M., A. Deaton, and M. Irish. 1985. A Profitable Approach to Labor Supply and Commodity Demands Over the Life-cycle. *Econometrica* 53:503–43.

MaCurdy, T. E. 1981. An Empirical Model of Labor Supply in a Life-cycle Setting. *J. Polit. Econ.* 89:1059–85.

Mundlak, Y. 1961. Empirical Production Function Free of Management Bias. *J. Farm Econ.* 43:44–56.

Peltzman, S. 1985. An Economic Interpretation of the History of Congressional Voting in the Twentieth Century. *Am. Econ. Rev.* 75:656–75.

Rosen, S. 1974. Hedonic Prices and Implicit Markets. *J. Polit. Econ.* 82:34–55.

Stigler, G. J. 1981. Theory of Regulation. *Bell J. Econ.* 12:3–21.

11

Management Problems of Farms and Agricultural Firms

R. P. KING and S. T. SONKA

Management issues have been a central focus of research, teaching, and extension efforts in agricultural economics throughout the history of our profession. Describing the profession's early years, Cochrane (1983, 63–66) notes that prior to 1910, nearly all work in agricultural economics was in the area of farm management. In the years that followed, a second strand of development in the profession concentrated on problems related to the marketing and distribution of agricultural products. This led to increased involvement by agricultural economists in the analysis of market structure and agricultural policy alternatives. Efforts to develop solutions to management problems encountered by farm supply and product processing and marketing firms were also, however, an important aspect of the work in this tradition. Today, farm and agribusiness management are strongly emphasized in most undergraduate teaching and state extension programs, and agricultural economists continue to be active in a wide range of management research efforts.

This paper examines the potential for agricultural economists to contribute to the future development and implementation of concepts, practices, and tools designed to make the managers of farm and agriculture-related firms more effective. In this discussion, the term *farm* refers to farms and ranches directly involved in agricultural production. The term *agriculture-related firm* refers to those firms that supply farm inputs and

Robert P. King is Associate Professor of Agricultural and Applied Economics at the University of Minnesota, St. Paul. He holds the E. Fred Koller Chair in Agricultural Management Information Systems and is Associate Director of the Strategic Management Research Center. Steven T. Sonka is Professor of Agricultural Economics at the University of Illinois at Champaign-Urbana. Seniority of authorship is not assigned.

process farm outputs. In one sense, the focus of this paper is unusually broad, since the firms considered range from small, part-time farms to very large corporations that operate on an international scale. On the other hand, two factors help narrow this focus and make it more manageable. First, the managers of all these firms operate in the same broad economic, technical, and political environment, and that environment has an increasingly important impact on the problems they face and the choices they can make. Although individual responses to changes in this environment may be different, the problems posed by it are often quite similar. Second, managerial work across this wide range of firms is being profoundly affected by changes in the need for and access to information. Again, responses to these changes are likely to differ, but the issues facing managers and the opportunities agricultural economists will have for improving managerial effectiveness are not firm-specific. Therefore, in the discussion that follows, differences across firms will be recognized, but common problems, issues, and opportunities will be emphasized.

This paper is divided into three major sections. The first outlines the current situation and suggests that a dominant current and future concern of the managers of rural firms will be to define strategies and procedures that will allow them to respond more effectively to change. Information is viewed as a key element in such strategies. The second major section describes five broad problem areas of critical importance to the managers of rural firms. The paper's final major section evaluates the potential for agricultural economists to contribute to the solution of management-related problems. In this discussion, the separate functions of research, extension, and resident instruction are considered.

Response to Instability and Change as a Central Theme

Management is the process by which decisions about allocating a firm's resources to meet desired ends are analyzed, made, and implemented. To perform these functions, a manager must consider the resources available to the firm and the technical possibilities for combining them, the opportunities offered and constraints imposed by the firm's environment, and the goals and objectives of the firm.

The importance of environment-based opportunities and constraints has, in recent years, gained increased attention in the general management literature. Tracing the evolution of managerial concerns and responses in American business firms, for example, Ansoff (1979) notes an increased preoccupation by managers with the problem of responding to uncertainty and rapid change in technology, market conditions, and socio-political forces. Ansoff attributes this to a marked increase in the turbulence of the economic environment. He notes (1979, 33), "From the mid-1950's accelerating and cumulating events began to change the boundaries, the structure, and the dynamics of the business environment. Firms were increasingly confronted with novel unexpected challenges which were so far-reaching that Peter Drucker called the new era an Age of Discontinuity."

Ansoff goes on to note that this was in marked contrast to conditions in the first half of the century, when the environment was more stable and manageable. In those years, problems related to exchange rates, inflation, government policies, and rapid technological change were secondary to "the business of business," technical efficiency and effective marketing.

The experience of rural firms closely parallels that of other businesses. In his historical analysis of American agriculture, Cochrane (1979) describes the period from 1933 to 1970 as one of technical revolution in an environment characterized by relatively stable market conditions and a steady stream of mechanical and biological innovations. At the farm level, management concerns centered around the adoption of new technologies, efficient resource use, and the expansion of farm size to take advantage of scale economies associated with increased mechanization. Managers of agriculture-related firms focused their attention on growth strategies designed to allow them to take advantage of rapid increases in the use of purchased inputs and significant expansion in the demand for processing and distribution services in the expanding food marketing industry.

Cochrane characterizes the period since the 1970s as one of world integration, instability, and uncertainty. During this period, the managers of farm firms have shifted the focus of their attention to risk management, adaptation to sudden changes in technology and industry structure, and financial management and control. Some farm operators have pursued aggressive growth strategies, while others have chosen to diversify their operations through off-farm investment and employment. Managers of agriculture-related firms have been forced to devote more attention to responses to structural shifts in the farm firms they serve, product innovation opportunities afforded by new technological developments, and problems stemming from monetary, fiscal, and trade policy decisions. Growth rates for the nonfarm segment of the agricultural sector have slowed somewhat, but individual firms have become larger as a result of mergers and consolidations.

EVIDENCE OF THE INCREASED IMPORTANCE OF INSTABILITY AND CHANGE.
Evidence of the importance of instability and change in the contemporary agricultural sector is broad-based, as are the sources of instability and change. Numerous reports and articles have described the changing structure of farming (e.g., Schertz 1979; U.S. Senate 1980; Tweeten 1984) and the effects these changes will have in agriculture-related firms (e.g., Dahl

1969; Hamm 1979; Minden 1970). Other studies have documented increases in price and income instability (e.g., Sonka and Patrick 1984) and have explored the forces underlying that instability (e.g., Firch 1977; Tweeten 1983). The causes of rapid change and increased instability are numerous and often interrelated. However, three broad categories of contributing factors are: (1) changes in weather patterns, (2) increased integration of the agricultural sector into the national and world economy, and (3) technological change.

Weather is a fundamental source of uncertainty in agricultural production. The importance of climate events for agricultural production was dramatically illustrated by the unexpected crop shortfalls and resulting worldwide food scarcities of the early 1970s. Since then several episodes have occurred in which climatic extremes have had a marked impact on domestic and international levels of agricultural output. The agricultural/climate relationship has been extensively studied in recent years (National Defense University 1978; Parry and Carter 1985). Resulting predictions of future climate patterns are controversial and sometimes contradictory. However, analysts have documented that summer weather conditions during much of the 1950s and 1960s in this country were unusual because of the relative absence of extreme weather events (Oram 1985). As climatic patterns have returned to normal in recent years, then, climate-induced shocks to agricultural markets have become more frequent and pronounced.

Today's U.S. agriculture is tightly integrated within the national and international economies (Dorner 1980). For farm firms, this has made the problem of understanding the economic and political environment much more important. Commodity markets are affected by a much wider range of forces, making price levels more volatile and difficult to forecast. In addition, public policies that materially affect agricultural firms are no longer limited to traditional price and income support programs. International relations, domestic monetary and fiscal policies, and trade initiatives all can have profound effects on the economic performance of farm firms. For example, the high real-interest rates stemming from recent monetary and fiscal policy have been a major factor in the current farm financial crisis. Finally, new participants, such as those who represent environmental concerns and consumer interests, have recently entered into farm policy debates.

Because their performance is intertwined with the financial well being of farm firms, increased integration of agriculture into the national and world economies has had similar impacts on agriculture-related firms. In addition to the problems caused by rapid structural change and greater instability in both farm input and agricultural commodity markets, however, higher degrees of economic integration have also broadened the scope of opportunities and competition these firms face. Agriculture-related firms are moving into new markets for traditional products and so must compete in an increasingly international setting. In addition, as agriculture-related firms develop new products, such as financial and information services, they face unfamiliar domestic competition. For example, agriculture-related firms offering on-line information services face competition from television networks, publishers, retail merchandisers, computer manufacturers, and telecommunications companies. Clearly, the boundaries of the farm supply industry are changing rapidly.

Technological change is a third major source of instability and change for farm and rural firms (Swanson and Sonka 1980). Over the past 50 years, the agricultural system has had to adapt to massive changes in production and processing technology. Particularly significant have been technical advances in farm machinery design, fertilizer-responsive plant varieties, livestock breeding, pesticides and animal health products, grain storage and handling technology, and food-processing technology. At the farm level these changes have resulted in considerable increases in physical productivity and in the scale of individual operations. They have also led to a marked increase in the importance of agriculture-related firms in the overall food system.

Although predictions of technological progress are often faulty, the potential for future biotechnological advances to markedly affect agricultural production seems high (Johnson and Wittwer 1984). For example, a recent analysis considered potential for growth hormones in dairy cattle (Office of Technology Assessment 1985). This innovation was estimated to increase production by 23 percent per cow for those dairy farms able to adopt it. Such an increase would significantly alter supply/demand relationships if widely adopted. Information technology is another area where significant advances are being made. New developments in computer hardware and software, storage technology, and telecommunications systems are altering the economics of acquiring and using information.

Innovations in biotechnology and information technology have yet to be implemented on a wide scale in agriculture. Their impacts are likely to be far reaching but are difficult to predict. In part, this stems from the fact that these technologies have different characteristics from other recent innovations in agriculture. Innovations based on biotechnology and information technology often have value primarily because of the information embodied in them. Because of the public good characteristics of such products and the resulting confusion over public and private sector roles in their development, markets for these innovations may fail without public intervention. In addition, patent and copyright protection for such products is often poorly defined and difficult to enforce. As a result, the uncertainty associated with further developments in information technology and biotechnology is considerable.

INFORMATION AS A RESPONSE TO INSTABILITY AND CHANGE. Managerial methods, organizational structures, and the problems that demand a manager's attention have all evolved in response to these changes in the economic, technological, and institutional environment of the agricultural sector. Sonka (1985b) has identified three historical stages of management practices in agriculture that help characterize these changes: the preindustrial stage, the industrial stage, and the information stage. This typology emphasizes differences in the role of information as the basis for understanding the evolution of management problems and practices. As such, it is also useful for gaining insights into the changing role of agricultural economists whose work focuses on management issues.

During the preindustrial stage, which extended into the early 1930s, the availability of labor was the critical determinant of farm-firm success. Information networks were simple. Experiences of family and neighbors were primary sources of information. Reliance on products and services provided by agriculture-related firms was relatively limited, and these firms tended to be small and locally based. Agricultural economists working with both farm and nonfarm firms during this period emphasized basic management skills, such as record keeping and comparative analysis.

The period during which the industrial-stage management style evolved roughly corresponds to Cochrane's period of technical revolution. Throughout this period, capital was being substituted for labor, and the adoption of technological innovations was a key determinant of success. Information networks expanded rapidly, as extension agency, farm media, input suppliers, and lenders became increasingly important sources of information. Thus, the importance of agriculture-related firms increased as farm managers became more dependent upon them. These firms grew rapidly in both size and scope, and their managers began to face a new set of problems associated with planning and control in large organizations and marketing over a wide geographic area.

Agricultural economists played an increasingly important role during this period. Working with both farm and nonfarm firms, they emphasized technical and economic efficiency and enjoyed considerable success. Their research and outreach activities were important in the development and implementation of new technological inputs and new management strategies. Because of the often clear-cut dominance of the new technologies and the relative stability of the operating environment, recommendations based on static production economic analyses were often both widely applicable and quite durable.

As the agricultural sector entered Cochrane's period of world integration, instability, and uncertainty, the information stage of management practices began to emerge. In the face of rapid structural change, increased instability, and rising costs for labor, capital equipment, and energy, the effective use of information has become a key to success for both farm and agriculture-related firms. Facilitated by developments in information technology and by new market linkages with firms outside the traditional agricultural sector, farmers' information networks are continuing to grow. They now include on-line data services, financial service firms, and production consultants, as well as extension agents, lenders, input suppliers, and the farm press. The demand for more comprehensive and complex internal information systems is intensifying as flexible management strategies, which allow for repeated reevaluation of plans as the decision environment changes, come into more widespread use. Such strategies rely on information to document and/or predict changing conditions. In the midst of these changes, managers of agriculture-related firms face a number of new challenges associated with managing still larger, more geographically dispersed organizations and with innovating into new markets and product areas. For these firms, too, effective information management is a major determinant of success.

Agricultural economists also face a new set of challenges. In part, this stems from the fact that the transition from industrial to information stage management processes is a gradual one. Therefore, the needs of both farm and nonfarm client groups are and will continue to be quite diverse. In addition, instability and rapid change in the environment increase the need for flexible management strategies based on dynamic analyses, while structural changes in both farm and nonfarm firms are creating new problems related to organizational design and human resource management. In the sections that follow, these new problems and issues are described in greater detail, and future directions for management research, teaching, and extension are explored.

Key Issues and Problems for Managers of Rural Firms

In an environment characterized by instability and rapid change, the particular issues and problems that confront managers may differ considerably across firms and from one year to the next. In general, however, we believe the following five broad problem areas will demand increased attention from the future managers of both farms and agriculture-related firms: (1) managing innovation and change; (2) managing risk; (3) organizational design; (4) information system design; and (5) human resource management.

In this section, critical dimensions of these problem areas are explored and major challenges for the agricultural economics profession are identified.

MANAGING INNOVATION AND CHANGE. As agriculture moves into the last years of this century, the increased rate of technical, economic, and institutional change makes it important for rural firms to innovate and evolve if they are to perform successfully and survive. This need is not unique to rural firms. Drawing on his experience with large industrial corporations, Ansoff (1979) notes an increase in managerial preoccupation with the need to adapt and change in a turbulent environment. More recently, managing innovation and change has been a central theme of books such as *In Search of Excellence* by Peters and Waterman (1982) and *The Change Masters* by Kanter (1983). From a market rather than a managerial perspective, innovation has also been a central theme in works by Arrow (1983), Kamien and Schwartz (1982), Mansfield (1984), and Ruttan (1984).

Based on a cross-industry study of innovation, Van de Ven (1986) has identified four central problems in the management of innovation: (1) the human problem of managing attention; (2) the process problem of managing ideas into good currency; (3) the structural problem of managing part-whole relationships; and (4) the strategic problem of institutional leadership.

Regarding the first of these problems, it is human nature to make activities routine, ignoring fluctuations in the environment until conditions have changed dramatically. Often this tendency puts managers in the position of being forced to react to crises when they should be developing emerging opportunities. To overcome this, managers need to improve their ability to scan the environment to distinguish between significant trends and short-term changes. This issue is critical for the managers of both farm and agriculture-related firms.

Gaining acceptance for innovative ideas—managing ideas into good currency—is a second central problem in the management of innovation. Managers must evaluate new ideas when organizational goals are complex, relevant data are costly or nonexistent, and resources for doing feasibility analyses are scarce. In addition, as organizational structures in both farm and nonfarm firms become increasingly complex, managers must often overcome considerable internal resistance to change. This can be an important problem for a farming operation managed by several members of the same family as well as for a large regional cooperative or an equipment manufacturing company.

Managing transitions in production technology, markets served, and organizational structures is an often-overlooked problem closely related to Van de Ven's final two central problems. It is, for example, a key issue for agricultural managers responding to the problems and opportunities created by the current financial crisis in agriculture. Managers must determine an appropriate path along which to move their organization from its existing state to that which is desired in the future, and they must deal with the task of integrating new people and processes into an existing system.

This set of problems poses a number of challenges for agricultural economists working on management issues. First it points to the importance of efforts to understand and predict structural changes in the sector and in the overall economy, as exemplified in the USDA (1979) report on Structure Issues of American Agriculture and the Project 1995 study by the Farm Credit System (1984). Understanding the forces that drive change is, however, only one aspect of managing change. Delineating the methods managers actually use and the difficulties they encounter as innovations are introduced is also essential. This requires research on less familiar issues, such as the design of more effective environmental monitoring systems and incentive structures that encourage and channel innovative activity.

MANAGING RISK. The forces leading to increased environmental turbulence have exposed the agricultural sector to increasing levels of market, financial, and institutional risk. At the same time, the range of risk management options available to managers of both farm and nonfarm firms has expanded dramatically. Risk transfer mechanisms such as contractual marketing arrangements, commodity options and futures instruments, and new, more widely available forms of insurance, combined with choices about the pattern of internal resource allocation, give firms the opportunity to substantially alter their risk exposure.

Managers can also respond to uncertainty by working actively to overcome it (Hirschleifer and Riley 1979). On the one hand, resources may be allocated to learning more about the system being managed and about future environmental conditions. Investments in irrigation scheduling, crop scouting, and commodity market forecasting services are examples of actions that combine information and flexible management strategies to overcome risk. Alternatively, risk management strategies may incorporate efforts designed to influence future environmental conditions. The organization of farmer bargaining cooperatives and the merger of agribusiness firms to gain increased market power are two examples of this type of active risk management strategy.

Managers face two broad sets of problems as they analyze risk management alternatives. First, while risks should, ideally, be assessed globally for the organization, actual decisions are usually made one at a time in piecemeal fashion (Cohen et al. 1972). Farm-level production and marketing decisions, for example, appear to be made separately, despite considerable theoretical and empirical evidence for the importance of making them jointly. One response to this problem is to make larger, more comprehensive models for analyzing managerial decisions. Given the limited information-processing capacity of human problem solvers (Miller 1956; Newell and Simon 1972), however, it may be more fruitful to identify conditions under which decisions can be decomposed (March and Simon 1958) and to formulate models that are robust even when key features of the choice problem are misspecified (Cohen and Axelrod 1984).

A second set of problems arises as flexibility and more extensive use of frequently updated information become more widely recognized as key features of risk management strategies. Although the more intensive use of information can improve performance dramatically (e.g., King and Lybecker 1976), this improvement comes at a cost. Managers must attempt to balance the benefits of more intensive information use against these costs. This problem has long been recognized among agricultural economists working on management-oriented problems (e.g., Johnson and Lard 1961). Despite some noticeable recent progress in this area (e.g., Bosch 1984; Chavas and Pope 1984; Antonovitz and Roe 1984), however, workable tools for analyzing investments in information and information-processing capacity are almost nonexistent.

Looking to the future, both of these broad sets of problems suggest that the challenge of agricultural economists will be to develop usable and effective analytical methods. Considerable progress has been made in this area over the past decade, but few of the tools and techniques developed are widely used. Advances in information technology are rapidly making widespread use of risk management models technically feasible, but it is not clear if these models actually meet the needs of the managers.

ORGANIZATIONAL DESIGN. Profound structural changes in the agricultural sector are having an impact on the organizational structure of both farm and nonfarm firms. Farm firms are growing larger and often involve multiple families. New financing arrangements involving outside equity interests differ considerably from the traditional relationship between an owner-operator and a lender. Among nonfarm firms, deregulation of the financial industry, consolidation and mergers in both the farm supply and grain marketing sectors, changes in the farm machinery industry, and new information technology–based products are all straining existing organizational structures. Changes in the sector and its environment are changing our view of the organizational boundaries of rural firms.

In essence, the problem of organizational design is one of deciding how work and decision-making responsibilities will be divided and how information will flow within an organization. This view of the problem emphasizes the managerial aspects of organizational design rather than the legal and tax implications associated with the alternative organizational structures. Although important, legal and tax issues have received considerably more attention and are less broadly applicable across firms, locales, and time than are managerial issues related to organizational design.

The emergence of larger, multiple family production units and the increased complexity of both production and managerial tasks in farming are creating a number of new organizational design problems. The adoption of specialized roles and responsibilities can be an effective response to increased size and complexity of operation. For the manager of a farm operation, however, specialization means giving up direct monitoring and control of factors that may have a key impact on overall business performance. These problems are compounded when no individual has clear decision-making authority for the firm as a whole. A further complication arises when nonfarm individuals share some of the decision-making responsibility. Managers facing these problems need insights about the design of organizational structures that promote communication, provide appropriate incentives and responsibility bearing, and encourage effective group decision making in a family setting. Simply borrowing organizational structures from corporate settings is not likely to provide adequate solutions to this problem. Rather, synthesis of concepts from areas as diverse as organization theory, family social science, and behavioral decision theory is needed.

For agriculture-related firms, choosing an appropriate level of centralized authority and decision making is becoming an increasingly important organizational design issue. Mergers, acquisitions, and consolidations are increasing the size and geographic scope of farm supply and grain marketing firms. Financial deregulation is allowing large urban banks to compare with, and in some cases gain control over, rural banks. These changes seem to encourage an increase in the centralization of authority and decision making. Other factors, such as the need to respond quickly to an unstable economic environment that may vary considerably across locales and the need to innovate, may make decentralized organizational structures more efficient, however. In the future, information technology is likely to have important impacts on the organizational structures these firms choose, and design strategies may need to allow for a relatively flexible mix of centralization and decentralization in decision making. Galbraith's (1974) information-processing approach to organizational design, for example, allows for decentralization and reduction in the need for information processing through the creation of slack resources and self-contained tasks. At the same time, he notes that centralized control and the ability to process information across units are facilitated through investments in vertical information systems and the creation of more extensive lateral relations. Although a firm need not adopt all of these strategies, they are by no means mutually exclusive.

In the area of organizational design, perhaps the most important challenge for our profession will be to extend our view of decision making beyond an almost exclusive focus on the individual. Throughout the sector, in both farm and nonfarm firms, decision making will increasingly be a shared activity. In this setting, research and educational activities will be useful if they provide an improved understanding of group decision processes and of the economic issues and options open to managers as they design and manage larger, more complex operations.

INFORMATION SYSTEM DESIGN. Recent advances in computer hardware and software and in telecommunications technology have made it feasible for even relatively small rural firms to have computer-based information systems (Holt 1985). At the same time, changes in the economic environment are making it increasingly important for managers to use information effectively. Despite lower costs and apparently greater need, however, the adoption rate of computer-based information systems has been much slower than expected. Important shortcomings in information systems design may be making it difficult for managers to fully exploit the potential of this new management technology.

A management information system (MIS) serves three important functions in an organization. First, it is a mechanism for collecting, organizing, storing, and retrieving data about the firm and its environment. Second, it is a medium for communication and the facilitation of information flows within and across organizational units. Finally, it provides support for the decision-making activities of managers. Problems associated with information system design for rural firms can be explored in relation to these three functions.

Recent advances in storage technology and data-base management software are making it easier and less costly to capture, organize, and use data. These developments make it possible for data to be managed as a separate resource (King 1985). As Everest (1974) notes, sharing data resources across users and applications and cooperating in the maintenance of these shared resources are key features of the "data-base approach." Despite these technical and conceptual advances, data collection and entry continue to be costly activities for small rural firms. Furthermore, considerable expertise is needed to organize a firm's data base so that data can be easily retrieved and used. Most accounting and record systems available to small farm and nonfarm firms are designed to generate standard statements and reports rather than to create a data resource for managerial use. As a result, managers often lack reliable data about their own firms. In contrast, data about the physical, economic, and political environment in which rural firms operate are becoming much more readily available through online data services. In this regard, managers face the problem of deciding how much to invest in and how to most effectively use this data resource.

In addition to being a mechanism for data capture, storage, and retrieval, an MIS is also a medium for communication within an organization. As rural firms become larger and more complex, the problem of matching information system and organizational design is likely to increase in importance. The key issues involve determining what information should flow within and across units of an organization. In a family farm operation in which specialized roles follow functional lines, for example, it is essential to determine what the person in charge of commodity marketing needs to know about production and financial activities within the business. If all information is shared, a major benefit of specialization is lost. If no information is shared, serious coordination problems may arise. The importance of the MIS as a mechanism for communication is still greater for farm supply, commodity marketing, and banking firms that have local outlets spread over a wide geographic area. For these firms, the flow of information can be influenced as strongly by changes in the rural telecommunications systems as by choices regarding organizational design.

Finally, from a managerial perspective, the support of analysis for planning and control is perhaps the most important function of a MIS. Often, however, formal management information systems provide little actual support for these key managerial tasks. As Mintzberg (1975) notes, this stems in part from the way managers work. Managerial activity is typically characterized by brevity, variety, and fragmentation, and managers are oriented toward action rather than reflection and analysis. They typically rely on verbal communication and ad hoc queries for information and analysis rather than on the regularly updated, aggregated information provided by most formal management information systems. Mintzberg further states that focusing attention on key issues and making effective use of analytic inputs represent a major challenge for managers.

The effective support of managerial work is the central theme of the emerging literature on decision support systems (DSS). Sprague and Carlson (1982, 4) define DSS as "interactive, computer-based systems that help decision makers use data and models to solve unstructured problems." An ideal DSS provides a flexible, easily used set of tools and data resources that a decision maker can use to identify problems and explore the consequences of potential solutions. The emphasis is on support of decision making rather than its automation. Effective DSS design often requires a synthesis of insights and tools from operations research, statistics, economic theory, and behavioral decision theory.

Rural businesses that provide products and services to farmers are also faced with difficult strategic decisions related to the design and provision of information technology–based products and services. Markets for on-line data services, accounting and management software, and computer-supported consulting services appear to have considerable potential (King 1984). These are also highly uncertain markets, however, that are drawing in new competitors and are blurring distinctions between public- and private-sector activity. In the area of on-line data services, for example, competing products are being offered by banks, farm supply cooperatives, publishing companies, land-grant universities, farm organizations, and communications companies.

For agricultural economists, the primary challenge will be to extend our understanding of the decision-making process and our ability to design workable tools to support managerial activities. Understanding the processes by which managers make decisions will be necessary and will require a synthesis of insights from the economic and behavioral sciences. Efforts to rigorously value information as it is used by agricultural managers must also be part of the process (Chavas and Pope 1984; Sonka, 1985a).

HUMAN RESOURCE MANAGEMENT. Economic, social, and political changes in rural areas are having an impact on the human resource pool from which rural firms draw labor and management services. Reduction in farm numbers and the demise of many "main street" businesses in rural areas have resulted in significant reductions in job opportunities and an attendant loss of skilled members of the work force. Conversely, trends toward exurban migration and the location of nonagricultural businesses in rural areas that began in the 1970s seem likely to remain a factor, especially near urban centers. Overall, the impacts of demographic and structural changes are difficult to predict. Regardless of the direction of these shifts, however, it seems likely that rural and urban labor markets will become more thoroughly integrated and that the managers of agriculture-related firms will be challenged to develop effective compensation schemes to attract and retain skilled personnel.

At the same time these structural changes are affecting the size and composition of the rural labor force, the increased rate of technological change in agriculture is posing a second broad challenge to agricultural managers. The use of more complex and specialized technology that changes rapidly over time requires more effective strategies for continuing training and education. This is a difficult problem if training and education programs are delivered by traditional means, because geographic dispersion of participants makes programs requiring direct contact considerably more expensive to deliver in rural areas. Just as information technology is changing the economics of firm location, however, it is also changing the economics of educational program delivery. In the future, more of these programs are likely to be delivered through media such as interactive video, video disk, and computer assisted instruction.

More effective strategies for training and education are not the only response to the problems posed by increased rates of technological change and more specialization. Often small firms, both farm and nonfarm, are not large enough to internalize certain types of specialized expertise. For example, it may be economically infeasible for the manager of a farm firm to invest the time and funds required to develop technical expertise in integrated pest management or financial planning. Markets for specialized consulting services are developing rapidly, however. In the future, agricultural managers will need to address the strategic problem of deciding when to internalize expertise and when to make use of consultants. The need to evaluate consultation services delivered partly or totally through computerized means (e.g., through expert systems) may be a particularly unusual challenge.

A final human resource problem stems from the fact that more farm enterprises are relying on off-farm work as a supplemental source of income. If the labor market for seasonal, part-time work is to function effectively, the managers of both farm and nonfarm firms may need to adjust patterns of labor utilization so that overall labor demands are relatively stable. This is by no means a new problem, nor is it one confined to the United States. As the agricultural sector undergoes major structural changes, however, these are issues that will demand renewed and continuing attention.

For agricultural economists, the challenges posed by these human resource management problems are twofold. First, we need to continue to improve our understanding of the structure of rural labor markets and of effective managerial responses to human resource issues. Efforts to design responses to changes in the human resource base must be closely related to organizational design issues, because these solutions to many human resource management problems are manifested in the boundaries and structure of the organization. Second, but equally important, we need to contribute further to the development of training and education programs that meet the needs of agricultural managers and their employees and the needs of the growing number of consultants who provide services to rural firms. This will be a difficult but exciting challenge as both the needs of program participants and the economics of program delivery evolve.

Implications for Future Directions in Management Research, Extension, and Teaching

As Jensen (1977) notes there was a major shift in management research, extension, and teaching efforts by agricultural economists during the years following World War II. Largely inspired by Heady's (1948, 1952) writings, farm management work shifted away from the empirical, comparative focus of the prewar years to an emphasis on results and models drawn from static neoclassical production theory. This new focus was well suited for the environmental conditions of the period, a time of relatively stable markets and steady technological change. It was made possible by significant developments in microeconomic theory, econometrics and statistics, and operations research. The development of computer technology was also instrumental in making the shift possible, and agricultural economists were leaders in the early use of computers as tools for the analysis of economic and managerial problems. This paradigm shift made work on management problems more analytical and more disciplinary. Although this has resulted in important progress in basic knowledge, it has also shifted the focus of management research, teaching, and extension away from an emphasis on problem solving and from the concerns of general managers (Johnson 1963; Schuh 1984).

If management scholarship will experience another paradigm shift in the next few years, in what direction will it take us? First, it is likely to be shaped by the new problems and concerns managers face in the more complex economic, social, and political environment. New knowledge and theories in disciplines related to management—dynamic economic theory, strategic management, organization theory, cognitive psychology, artificial intelligence, and management information systems—will also shape the direction of change. A key feature of these changes is likely to be an increase in work with other disciplines, not only with other agricultural disciplines but also with scholars in the behavioral sciences and in business schools. In addition, researchers will need to work more directly with agricultural managers, whose problems should be the focus of management research. Finally, just as the availability of mainframe computers had an important influence on management work from the late 1950s through the 1970s, advances in information technology are likely to have an important impact on future management scholarship. In the following sections the implications of these changes for research, extension, and teaching are explored.

MANAGEMENT RESEARCH. If the impacts of a possible shift in management research in the agricultural economics profession are to be examined, the domain of management research must first be defined. Since the early 1950s, farm management and production economics research, on the one hand, and nonfarm firm management and marketing research, on the other hand, have come to be closely associated in the agricultural economics profession. This development has helped focus attention on some key problems and has channeled insights from two areas of economic theory into management research. However, this trend also may have created a false dichotomy in management research and contributed to a lack of emphasis on research related to the emerging managerial problems identified in the preceding section.

Under a more integrated view of management research, which takes the manager and management problems as its starting point rather than production technology and market structure, three general areas of focus emerge. First, management research may be directed toward gaining a better understanding of managerial behavior. This is useful for identifying problems managers face and opportunities for improving managerial performance. Cross-sectional surveys designed to identify management practices, longitudinal case studies, studies of organizational behavior, and efforts to measure risk preferences are all examples of this type of research. Except in the area of risk preference measurement, however, relatively little work of this kind has been done since the Interstate Managerial Study (Johnson et al. 1961).

The development of analytical tools and problem-solving procedures designed to support managerial work is a second general area of focus for management research. Analytical tools, often computer based, may be designed to organize, process, and summarize data and information (e.g., accounting and management control systems) or they may be designed to assist in the evaluation of alternatives (e.g., optimization and simulation models). Research organizational design, competitive strategy formulation, and processes for managing innovation and change are also included in this category, because they are directed toward the development of general methods for solving managerial problems.

A third area of focus for management research is on the generation of information used by managers. Market forecasts, analyses of market structure, and estimation of industry financial and production performance standards are all examples of research activities directed toward the generation of management information. Efforts in this area are usually guided by analytical models and general problem-solving procedures.

Finally, representative firm and econometric studies designed to improve understanding of sector performance and to analyze the impacts of policy changes are often classified as management research. Research of this kind may influence policy decisions that have a major impact on the environment rural firms face. Although such efforts have recently become increasingly prevalent in the professional literature, their results do not focus directly on managerial problems and activities. Therefore, these efforts will not be considered further in this discussion.

In recent years, research in each of these areas has become increasingly disciplinary. This is not unique to the agricultural economics profession. Referring to professional schools in engineering, medicine, and business, for example, Simon (1981, 130) notes an increased emphasis on disciplinary research:

> In terms of the prevailing norms, academic respectability calls for subject matter that is intellectually tough, analytic, formalizable, and teachable. In the past much, if not most, of what we know about design and about the artificial sciences was intellectually soft, intuitive, informal, and cookbooky. Why would anyone in a university stoop to teach or learn about designing machines or planning market strategies when he could concern himself with solid-state physics? The answer has been clear: he usually wouldn't.

In Simon's terminology, the sciences of the artificial focus on designing tools (be they objects, methods, or institutions) to help people achieve desired ends. This should be, of course, a central focus of management research. For management researchers, a key question is whether our increased emphasis on disciplinary work has moved us away from or closer to an effective science of design.

One of the positive results of the emphasis on management research rooted in neoclassical theory is that increasingly powerful tools for designing optimal management strategies have been developed. At the same time, this research has helped identify and organize the data and information needed to support these strategies. The emphasis on deductive methods and optimizing models has also had adverse consequences, however. First, it has led to a deemphasis on work with decision makers. Models and methods tend to be tested either by logical argument or through simulation, and the reliability of such tests is highly sensitive to the validity of underlying assumptions. Therefore, the focus of empirical research relating to managerial behavior has shifted to an emphasis on verifying assumptions for populations rather than on describing the behavior of individuals and identifying key problems they face. Second, the cost of information and analysis has often been ignored in model building and testing efforts. As a result, many seemingly optimal strategies are actually unworkable. Finally, managerial research has often been model driven rather than user driven. Therefore, managers often find the information generated difficult to use.

This may be an overly critical view of the shortcomings of discipline-oriented management research. Nevertheless, these arguments are at the root of the perception that management research has lost its problem-solving focus (Johnson 1984; Swanson 1984). If, in the future, management research returns to that focus, what will be the likely characteristics of that research?

Considering research methods first, a broader range of modes of inquiry will be needed and direct interaction with managers will be increased. For example, case study methods will allow for more direct contact with managers and organizations. Prototyping is also likely to be used more widely in testing new analytical tools and institutional designs. Although sometimes not considered as research, prototyping can be an effective, highly interactive mode of inquiry, well suited for helping users formulate and articulate their needs (Keen and Gambino 1983; Moore and Chang 1983). Finally, experimental methods, often based on computer gaming models, are also likely to be used more widely in the future. This broadening of research methods is consistent with the pluralism advocated in contemporary views of the philosophy of science (e.g., Rorty 1982; Caldwell 1982). It will encourage increased attention to the normative and prescriptive knowledge that are necessary complements to positive knowledge in problem-solving research (Johnson 1984).

In addition to relying more on methods that encourage interaction with managers and organizations, agricultural economists are also likely to broaden the scope of their efforts by working more with other disciplines. Bioeconomic modeling projects are promoting increased collaborative research involving agricultural economists and agricultural production scientists (e.g., Mapp and Eidman 1976; Boggess and Amerling 1983). In parallel fashion, research in the emerging area of expert systems may facilitate interdisciplinary work with computer scientists and cognitive psychologists (Brachman et al. 1985). Interdisciplinary research need not always center around computer models, however. Work with other disciplines will also be beneficial in studies of organizational design, strategic management, and information system design. Such a reemergence of interdisciplinary efforts is quite consistent with the historic orientation of management research in agricultural economics. Here, however, interaction with a broader set of disciplines is proposed.

Finally, there will continue to be an important place for disciplinary efforts in future management research. New developments in organization theory, information economics, and game theory, for example, are likely to have important management applications. Similarly, continued development of quantitative methods will be needed. Advances in computing capabilities will change the economics of information acquisition and analysis and may make currently unworkable models feasible in the future.

As the mode of inquiry, scope, and disciplinary content of management research change, one of the most challenging problems for the profession will be to define and recognize "good science" in a problem-solving context. The reliance on economics as the sole behavioral discipline will be questioned. This questioning will challenge researchers trained primarily in economics. This problem will be resolved, in part, through debates about research methods and the philosophy of science. More importantly, we will also learn by doing. We believe a science of design is both possible and worth pursuing. In fact, it is essential if research is to contribute to solving the problems of agricultural managers.

A second, equally important, challenge for the future of management research is that of ensuring adequate funding. There is a trend in agricultural economics research toward increased reliance on competitive grants rather than on formula funding. At the same time, it appears that the USDA is placing less emphasis on funding management research. The small scale of farms and many agriculture-related firms makes it unlikely that needed research can be funded directly by the private sector. These trends suggest a decline in funds and associated professional emphasis for such research at a time when additional work on new issues and problems is critically needed.

EXTENSION ACTIVITIES. Implementation of results from this new research agenda will require transmission of findings to decision makers. A strong focus on preparing future managers through resident instruction and on updating and expanding the skills of current managers through extension programs is essential to an efficient and dynamic agriculture. Particularly in the management area, the successful conduct of these educational activities is every bit as challenging as are research investigations.

Current management-related extension efforts can be grouped in many ways. However, three broad categories are:

1. The generation of information defining the current and future status of the operating environment. Efforts include programs on new technologies, likely policy or legislative actions, and supply/demand conditions for the coming year.

2. Educational thrusts relating to use of management tools. Efforts to improve managers' capability to analyze alternatives are a major contribution. Tools presented in these efforts include budgeting, financial statements, and investment analysis. Recently major emphasis has been focused on utilizing computerized versions of these tools.

3. Problem diagnosis and evaluation of alternatives. Agricultural managers have often relied on extension specialists to aid in identifying and solving problems. In some cases, a publication with an illustrative example has been sufficient to clarify outcomes and justify general recommendations. Analysis of government program participation is an example. Alternatively, producers may desire firm-specific evaluations. Clarification of key issues as a second generation enters the firm and, recently, individual review for financially stressed producers are examples of such activities.

Extension activities in each of these areas have been valued in the past, and they will continue to be desired in the future. The following remarks will focus on the implications of the emerging trends identified earlier on activities and delivery mechanisms in extension education. Implicit throughout this discussion is the recognition that difficult choices of emphasis will continually be forced by resource constraints. The challenge is to continue to initiate those activities that utilize the unique strengths of the public sector.

If change and decision making in an environment of surprise are concerns of the future, how can extension management specialists have the opportunity to make essential educational contributions related to these concerns? Many of the important events affecting the agricultural manager in the last 15 years have occurred outside the agricultural arena. Decisions relating to domestic and international monetary policy, international relations, and artificially induced resource shortages have greatly affected agriculture. Extension educators often have responded to these events with effective analyses of the impact of specific events on producers in general.

In the future, there will be a need for educational programs that teach individual managers the skills needed to identify and interpret these impacts relative to their individual circumstances. Included in such efforts would be basic education on general economic forces and their interrelation with agriculture. Also needed is instruction in concepts of strategic planning and the formulation of flexible organizational structures.

Organizational design and information system design were identified previously as key future problem areas. Both topics are unfamiliar to agricultural producers and managers of small nonfarm firms. A challenge to extension educators will be to develop programs that are beneficial even though solutions to these problems tend to be highly firm specific. Programs that discuss these problems and general types of solutions have value in heightening manager awareness. Delivery mechanisms and tools that aid managers in better evaluating their individual situations will have considerably greater value.

Much has been written about the effects of computers on decision making and on the delivery of information to agricultural managers. Although computer literacy, both for managers and extension educators, is important as new management styles emerge, it is not the most critical management skill needed to exploit computer and information use. Instead, the basic management skills of goal formation, problem recognition, analysis, and decision making will continue to be key elements of successful management. The new information technologies, however, should allow extension educators to more successfully provide instruction and should help managers to more efficiently implement those skills.

How might the ongoing advances in computer technology affect extension delivery systems? The likely answer is that this technology will be implemented in diverse ways based on the resources and opportunities of individual states. A number of electronic communication systems will allow direct access by managers. The development of microcomputer-based software will continue. Some of these programs will be designed for end-user application and supported by public institutions. Others will be generated to illustrate concepts. Although possibly available for end-user application, such concept-oriented efforts can have significant impacts through their effect on private sector efforts.

The computer revolution should allow significant strides to be made in extension education for agricultural managers. Possibilities include:

1. Allowing producers to test risk response strategies or to experience the effect of new technologies for a range of economic conditions.

2. Synthesis of knowledge from multiple disciplines in a decision-relevant form. In a sense, the manager is the ultimate multidisciplinary researcher and, as noted by Swanson (1979), quantitative models are an

effective means to integrate multidisciplinary knowledge. Bioeconomic-simulation models can be particularly useful as educational tools.

3. Availability of expert systems that deliver sophisticated expertise to the firm manager in the form of consultation for specific problems.

4. Delivery of data that can be directly analyzed through complex quantitative algorithms and then reported in manager-usable terms.

5. Provision of time-sensitive data such as prices or weather-related pest infestations.

The developmental role of agricultural economists will be vital in the first three possibilities noted. Model building, for the development of tools that will become integral parts of larger educational thrusts, should be an exciting opportunity for the extension educator. For the latter two possibilities, extension specialists have much to contribute to the definition of needed data items and their form.

The one-hour to one–half day lecture and written publications have been vital components of the extension delivery system. Although these delivery mechanisms are likely to persist, sole reliance on these methods is unlikely to be effective if managers are to truly assimilate many of the educational topics noted. Instead, experiences that are more like educational courses will be needed. For many of these, student access to computers will allow simulation techniques and interaction with expert systems to be implemented. Management-oriented courses, if effective, can be a means for agricultural managers to accomplish the continual retraining likely to be needed in tomorrow's agriculture.

In this paper's first section, it was suggested that new management styles are emerging in agriculture. The distinguishing attribute noted was the orientation towards flexible, information-based strategies versus more rigid, recommendation-oriented approaches. The development and likely coexistence of these management approaches further complicates the extension educator's problem of serving a diverse management clientele. No easy solution presents itself and a multiplicity of responses is likely to evolve. Probably the most important point is the recognition that this new source of audience diversity exists and that no single extension product or delivery mechanism will satisfy the system's farm and nonfarm clientele.

An issue related to the development of a diverse audience is the emergence of private sector providers of management consultation and/or education. One attitude is to view such private-sector initiatives as strictly competitive to public-sector efforts. Another view is to consider private-sector efforts as a means to enhance the level of expertise available to agricultural managers. Historically, extension educators have had positive impacts through interactions with lenders, legal professionals, and government officials. Management consultants may well be another means to provide expertise to agricultural managers, particularly given the limited resources available relative to the needs that will exist.

RESIDENT INSTRUCTION ACTIVITIES. The implications of the emerging trends and key problem areas defined previously for resident instruction are similar to those just discussed for extension activities. Therefore, only a brief discussion of these topics will be provided. An area of significant similarity is that much of what is currently done in undergraduate resident instruction relating to management is useful. These efforts have, in general, contributed to improvements in economic efficiency by agricultural managers.

For many students, introductory farm management courses are valued because they present the farm firm as a single entity rather than as a set of individual physical processes. As students take additional coursework, instruction tends to divide the business management process into specialized activities, such as marketing, accounting, labor management, and operational and strategic planning. An unfortunate result may be that students lose sight of management as a holistic process and the interrelations of the individual firm with the larger economic system. An area that needs strengthening in management-related resident instruction is the concept of the agricultural firm, both farm and nonfarm, as it operates within a larger system.

An increased emphasis on strategic management, particularly in upper-level courses, would serve to counteract the tendencies just noted. The orientation of such efforts should include strategic thinking as well as numeric analysis and calculations. Concentrating on the questions an agricultural manager needs to ask to anticipate surprises can often be more useful than instruction on how to calculate quantitative solutions. Stressing problem formulation and information sources will be of significant value even though students may tend to appreciate precise formulas and rules amenable to memorization. In addition, curricula that encourage students to gain an appreciation of broader national and international forces will lead to a better understanding of the future workplace.

As noted for extension activities, the enhanced capabilities and expanded availability of computer resources should alter the resident instruction process. Computer models can enable students to experience a range of economic situations. Agriculture's experiences of the last 15 years provides ample illustrations of a wide array of economic situations. Embedding those relationships (in current dollars) into interactive firm models will encourage student users to experience and test differing management strategies.

The range of computer applications available for management instruction is exciting not because powerful technology is being used, but because it poses a challenging opportunity for students to better identify causal forces and interrelationships affecting firm performance. Several applications appear promising, including relatively simplistic operational and strategic planning tools, sophisticated expert systems, bioeconomic simulators, and computerized programs for internal control.

Finally, management-related graduate education, particularly at the doctoral level, presents a difficult challenge. By its nature, training at this level tends to be narrow and highly specialized. Conversely, the management process is broad and general in nature. Balancing the need for disciplinary rigor versus problem-solving relevance will require flexible degree-granting programs and a consensus within the profession that such flexibility is desirable.

Summary

The managerial problems of farm and agriculture-related firms are likely to intensify and change in character in the future. The environment within which these firms operate is likely to be one characterized by uncertainty and the potential for marked and sudden change. The continued evolution of commercial farms and the firms that serve them implies the need for increasingly complex organizational structures, information utilization, and human resource management.

Faced with these changes, the approaches and tools of management scholars must also evolve. Research efforts focused on the role of the manager as an integrator of information and a decision maker will be required. To realistically model the decision-making process, input from several disciplines will be essential. Those efforts should lead to an improved understanding of the manner in which various types of information affect manager behavior. Research results will need to be transmitted to agricultural managers. Extension and resident instruction activities will need to illustrate the manager's integrative function and improve the abilities of current and future decision makers in agriculture.

In several respects, the prospects are extremely promising for researchers and educators to understand and improve the agricultural management process. This opportunity appears potentially as rewarding as was the introduction of production economics into farm management shortly after World War II.

Future scholarly efforts should place greater emphasis on the integrative role of the manager. An uncertain agricultural environment, interdependent with the national and international economies, and the increasing complexity of the agricultural firm imply a need for significant improvements in management procedures and strategies. In addition, advances in the computer technologies available to researchers and managers are occurring at the same time that substantial strides are being made in several of the sciences related to decision making. Finally increasing our understanding of the manager's integrative role will require much less reliance on secondary rather than primary data and the recognition that economic theory is only one of the tools necessary for effective investigations in this area.

The effective use of information will become more important in determining the success of agricultural managers. The rigid management approach of industrial-stage farms was predicated on the availability of inexpensive raw materials and energy inputs. The role of information in the management process will evolve as more flexible management strategies, which strive to continually reevaluate plans as the decision environment changes, are developed. The role of the management scholar is critical in developing more flexible strategies, as well as in serving as a vital link in the information network available to the agricultural manager.

Five key problem areas are likely to be increasingly important to managers of farms and agricultural firms. This list is not all-inclusive, but the areas listed are likely to be common to a broad range of managers. The five areas are: (1) managing innovation and change; (2) managing risk; (3) organizational design; (4) information system design; and (5) human resource management.

Consideration of the issues relating to each of these problem areas suggests an exciting agenda of activities for agricultural economists concerned with management problems. This agenda includes major contributions in each of the functional areas of research, extension, and resident instruction.

References

Ansoff, I. 1979. The Changing Shape of the Strategic Problem. In *Strategic Management,* ed. D. Schendel and C. Hofer, 30–43. Boston: Little, Brown.

Antonovitz, F., and T. Roe. 1984. The Value of a Rational Expectations Forecast in a Risky Market: A Theoretical and Empirical Approach. *Am. J. Agric. Econ.* 66:717–23.

Arrow, K. J. 1983. Innovation in Large and Small Firms. In *Entrepreneurship,* J. Roren, 15–28. Lexington, Mass.: Lexington Books.

Boggess, W. G., and C. B. Amerling. 1983. A Bioeconomic Simulation Analysis of Irrigation Investments. *South. J. Agric. Econ.* 15:85–92.

Bosch, D. J. 1984. The Value of Soil, Water, and Weather Information in Increasing Irrigation Efficiency. Ph.D. diss., Univ. of Minnesota.

Brachman, R. J., S. Amarel, C. Engelman, R. S. Engelmore, E. A. Feigenbaum, and D. E. Wilkins. 1985. What Is an Expert System? In *Building Expert Systems,* ed. F. Hayes-Roth, et al., 31–57. Reading: Addison-Wesley.

Caldwell, B. 1982. *Beyond Positivism: Economic Methodology in the Twentieth Century.* London: George Allen & Unwin.

Chavas, J. P., and R. D. Pope. 1984. Information: Its Measurement and Valuation. *Am. J. Agric. Econ.* 66:705–10.

Cochrane, W. W. 1979. The Development of American Agriculture: A Historical Analysis. Minneapolis: Univ. of Minnesota Press.

_____. 1983. Agricultural Economics at the University of Minnesota, 1886–1979. Misc. Pub. 21-1983. Minneapolis: Univ. of Minnesota.

Cohen, M. D., J. G. March, and J. P. Olsen. 1972. A Garbage Can Model of Organizational Choice. *Adm. Sci. Q.* 17:1–25.

Cohen, M. D., and R. Axelrod. 1984. Coping with Complexity: The Adaptive Value of Changing Utility. *Am. Econ. Rev.* 74:30–42.

Dahl, D. C. 1969. Structure of Input Supplying Industries and Techniques of Analysis. *Am. J. Agric. Econ.* 51:1046–54.

Dorner, P. 1980. Agriculture Within the U.S. Economy: Integration and Interdependence. In *Farm Structure,* 51–61. Washington, D.C.: U.S. Senate Committee on Agriculture, Nutrition, and Forestry.

Everest, G. C. 1974. Database Management Systems Tutorial. In *Fifth Annual Midwest AIDS Conference Proceedings,* vol. 1, Al-Al2. Minneapolis: Univ. of Minnesota Press.

Firch, R. 1977. Sources of Commodity Market Instability in U.S. Agriculture. *Am. J. Agric. Econ.* 59:164–69.

Galbraith, J. R. 1974. Organization Design: An Information Processing View. *TIMS Interfaces.* 4:28–36.

Hamm, L. G. 1979. Farm Inputs Industries and Farm Structure. In *Structure Issues in American Agriculture,* 218–25. Agric. Econ. Rep. 438. Washington, D.C.: USDA, ESCS.

Heady, E. O. 1948. Elementary Models in Farm Production Economics Research. *J. Farm Econ.* 30:201–25.

_____. 1952. *Economics of Agricultural Production and Resource Use.* Englewood Cliffs: Prentice-Hall.

Hirschleifer, J., and J. G. Riley. 1979. The Analytics of Uncertainty and Information—An Expository Survey. *J. Econ. Lit.* 17:1375–1421.

Holt, D. A. 1985. Computers in Production Agriculture. *Science* 228:422–27.

Jensen, H. F. 1977. Farm Management and Production Economics. In *A Survey of Agricultural Economics Literature,* ed. L. R. Martin, vol. 1, 1–89. Minneapolis: Univ. of Minnesota Press.

Johnson, G. L. 1963. Stress on Production Economics. *Aust. J. Agric. Econ.* 7:12–27.

_____. 1984. Academia Needs a New Covenant for Serving Agriculture. Mississippi State: Mississippi Agricultural & Forestry Experiment Station Special Publication.

Johnson, G. L., A. N. Halter, H. R. Jensen, and D. W. Thomas, eds. 1961. *A Study of Managerial Processes of Midwestern Farmers.* Ames: Iowa State Univ. Press.

Johnson, G. L., and C. F. Lard. 1961. Knowledge Situations. In *A Study of Managerial Processes of Midwestern Farmers,* ed. G. L. Johnson et al. 41–54. Ames: Iowa State Univ. Press.

Johnson, G. L., and S. H. Wittwer. 1984. Agricultural Technology Until 2030: Prospects, Priorities, and Policies. Special Report 12. East Lansing: Michigan State Univ.

Kamien, M. I., and N. L. Schwartz. 1982. *Market Structure and Innovation.* Cambridge: Cambridge Univ. Press.

Kanter, R. M. 1983. *The Change Masters.* New York: Simon and Schuster.

Keen, P. G. W., and T. J. Gambino. 1983. Building a Decision Support System: The Mythical Man-Month Revisited. In *Building Decision Support Systems,* ed. J. L. Bennett, 133–72. Reading: Addison-Wesley.

King, R. P. 1984. Technical and Institutional Innovation in North American Grain Production: The New Information Technology. Strategic Management Research Center Discussion Paper 16. Minneapolis: Univ. of Minnesota.

———. 1985. Farm Information Systems: Needs, Methods, and Responsibilities. Paper presented at the North Central Farm Management Extension Workshop, Urbana, Illinois, May 7–9.

King, R. P., and D. W. Lybecker. 1976. Flexible, Risk-oriented Marketing Strategies for Pinto Bean Producers. *West. J. Agric. Econ.* 58:124–33.

Mansfield, E. 1984. R & D and Innovation: Some Empirical Findings. In *R & D, Patents, and Productivity,* ed. Z. Griliches, 127–48. Chicago: Univ. of Chicago Press.

Mapp, H. P., and V. R. Eidman. 1976. A Bioeconomic Simulation Analysis of Regulatory Groundwater Irrigation. *Am. J. Agric. Econ.* 58:391–402.

March, J. G., and H. A. Simon. 1958. *Organizations.* New York: John Wiley & Sons.

Miller, G. A. 1956. The Magical Number Seven, Plus or Minus Two: Some Limits on Our Capacity for Processing Information. *Psych. Rev.* 63:81–97.

Minden, A. J. 1970. Changing Structure of the Farm Input Industry: Organization, Scale, Ownership. *Am. J. Agric. Econ.* 52:678–86.

Mintzberg, H. 1975. The Manager's Job: Folklore and Fact. *Harvard Bus. Rev.* 53:49–61.

Moore, J. H., and M. G. Chang. 1983. Meta-design Considerations in Building DSS. In *Building Decision Support Systems,* ed. J. L. Bennett, 173–204. Reading: Addison-Wesley.

National Defense University. 1978. Climate Change to the Year 2000. Joint Study of the U.S. Department of Agriculture, the Defense Advanced Research Project Agency, the National Oceanic and Atmospheric Administration, and the Institute for the Future. Washington, D.C.

Newell, A., and H. A. Simon. 1972. *Human Problem Solving.* Englewood Cliffs: Prentice-Hall.

Oram, P. A. 1985. Sensitivity of Agricultural Production to Climate Change. *Clim. Change.* 7:129–51.

Parry, M. L., and T. R. Carter. 1985. The Effect of Climatic Variations on Agricultural Risk. *Clim. Change.* 7:95–110.

Peters, R. J., and R. H. Waterman, Jr. 1982. *In Search of Excellence.* New York: Harper & Row.

Rorty, R. 1982. *Consequences of Pragmatism.* Minneapolis: Univ. of Minnesota Press.

Ruttan, V. W. 1984. Social Science Knowledge and Institutional Change. *Am. J. Agric. Econ.* 66:549–59.

Schertz, L. P., ed. 1979. Another Revolution in U.S. Farming? Agric. Econ. Rep. 441. Washington, D.C.: USDA, ESCS.

Schuh, G. E. 1984. Revitalizing the Land Grant University. Strategic Management Research Center Discussion Paper 36. Minneapolis: Univ. of Minnesota.

Simon, H. A. 1981. *The Sciences of the Artificial.* 2d ed. Cambridge, Mass.: MIT Press.

Sonka, S. T. 1985a. Computer-aided Farm Management Systems: Will the Promise Be Fulfilled? Paper presented at the XIX International Conference of Agricultural Economics, Malaga, Spain.

_____. 1985b. Information Management in Farm Production. *J. Comput. Electron. in Agric.* 1:75–85.

Sonka, S. T., and G. F. Patrick. 1984. Risk Management and Decision Making in Agricultural Firms. In *Risk Management in Agriculture,* ed. P. J. Barry, 95–115. Ames: Iowa State Univ. Press.

Sprague, R. J., and E. D. Carlson. 1982. *Building Effective Decision Support Systems.* Englewood Cliffs: Prentice-Hall.

Swanson, E. R. 1979. Working with Other Disciplines. *Am. J. Agric. Econ.* 6l:849–59.

_____. 1984. The Mainstream in Agricultural Economics Research. *Am. J. Agric. Econ.* 66:782–91.

Swanson, E. R., and S. T. Sonka. 1980. Technology and the Structure of U.S. Agriculture. In *Farm Structure,* 62–73. Washington, D.C.: U.S. Senate Committee on Agriculture, Nutrition, and Forestry.

Tweeten, L. 1983. Economic Instability in Agriculture: The Contributions of Prices, Government Programs, and Exports. *Am. J. Agric. Econ.* 65:922–3l.

_____. 1984. Causes and Consequences of Structural Change in the Farming Industry. NPA Report No. 207. Washington, D.C.: National Planning Association.

U.S. Congress Office of Technology Assessment. 1985. Technology, Public Policy and the Changing Structure of American Agriculture. OTA-F-272. Washington, D.C.: GPO.

U.S. Department of Agriculture. 1979. Structure Issues of American Agriculture. Agric. Econ. Rep. No. 438. Washington, D.C.: USDA, ESCS.

U.S. Farm Credit System. 1984. *Project 1995.* Denver: Farmbank Services.

U.S. Senate. 1980. *Farm Structure.* Washington, D.C.: Committee on Agriculture, Nutrition, and Forestry.

Van de Ven, A. H. 1986. Central Problems in the Management of Innovation. *Manage. Sci.* 32:590–607.

Management Problems of Farms and Agricultural Firms: A Discussion

LUDWIG M. EISGRUBER

The authors should be commended for preparing a paper on an important, albeit difficult topic. The paper is well written and well reasoned. The first, and perhaps lasting, impression is that the scope of the paper is too broad, with the result that much of the discussion is at a very general level.

Once one accepts this approach (i.e., broad scope and general treatment), the paper has reasonable balance and no significant flaws. Nevertheless, a few comments about what is written in the paper are appropriate. A number of additional points not discussed in the paper will be raised.

The entire first half of the paper, which discusses this change in management environment, documents what the authors view to be major changes in the challenges facing managers. The case may be overstated. Certainly, conditions in agriculture markets have changed substantially in the last 10 years, but they have changed substantially in the 10 years prior to that and probably the 10 years prior to that. Every era has had its own unique characteristics in terms of agricultural markets and management challenges. The one we are now passing through, while seemingly quite profound, may indeed be no different than many other changes we have faced in the past. For instance, King and Sonka argue that greater price variability and market instability have created new risks and, therefore, demand new management approaches. Certainly prices are more variable in the last 15 years than they were in the 15 years prior to that, but they were also quite variable in the era immediately following World War I, and this instability was compounded by much greater yield variability than we have today. Thus, it may well be that managers of that era faced risks and uncertainties at least equal to those of managers today. The situation may, then, not be as unique as the paper seems to convey.

In some instances, the authors make recommendations or forecasts that simply cannot be disputed because of their very obvious nature. For instance, the authors state that, "looking to the future, both of these broad sets of problems suggest that the challenge for agricultural economists working in risk management is to develop analytical tools that will be

Ludwig M. Eisgruber is Professor of International Agriculture, College of Agricultural Sciences, Oregon State University, Corvallis.

useful and effective." No one ever argues for analytical tools that are useless or ineffective.

In the middle section of the paper, the authors argue for a new approach to management research. Basically, they suggest what is needed is an interdisciplinary approach which combines paradigms from a number of sciences and disciplines. They argue that the advent of computer technology may well make such interdisciplinary work more easily done. But in one sense this paper is an example of why it is difficult to effectively do interdisciplinary research and publish the results. The authors rely on a good deal of jargon and terminology that is unique to agricultural economics. It is written in a very discipline-specific language and, as a consequence, would be difficult for someone outside the profession to usefully contribute to or discuss.

The discussion of implications for future direction of extension activities is not as provocative as it might be. The authors state that and the paper seems to suggest that the extension educator becomes at best a computer operator who does occasional (computer) model building; at worst he is merely a computer operator. While it is reasonably certain that the computer will, if it is not already so, become a most prevalent and important tool, it is also reasonably clear that the mix of skills present in the pool of extension educators must be broader than is implied in the "Extension Activities" section of the paper. That much follows from the discussion earlier in the paper. What this mix of skills should be, how extension educators should be trained, and what the appropriate delivery system should be is less clear. What is furthermore missing from the discussion of extension activities is an assessment of the increasing role the private sector is playing in adult education.

As with extension, the major new thrust to develop tomorrow's agricultural graduates seems to be more of the same: more of the same curriculum and more computer modeling. While this is the recommendation of the paper, it neither follows from the earlier discussion nor is it in accord with what is happening and being discussed by employees and educators alike. If discussion earlier in the paper is sound, should students not take more political science, sociology, and psychology? A recently established agricultural high school in Chicago requires two years of foreign language because with "our shrinking world, it would be pretty silly not to have some foreign language as preparation for an agricultural career" (Smith 1985). Should agricultural managers of the future be trained to process information in another language?

Environmental management, a very important area, is not mentioned at all. I have examined the paper from the point of view of whether this issue can be reframed under one of the existing subheadings, but concluded that this issue is sufficiently different and sufficiently important to justify separate treatment. This issue, which includes the difficult topics of water rights, water quality, land use, erosion, food safety, management of public lands, etc., is of increasing importance to the agricultural manager, both present and future. It poses unique economic, legal, political, and biological problems. It also raises questions about the somewhat narrow definition of agricultural manager early in the paper. That is to say, is the Forest Service Manager who is involved in managing public lands for timber, forage, wildlife, water, and recreation an agricultural manager?

If human resource management is separately treated as one of the key problem areas of management, financial resource management should probably also receive such treatment. A large number of farmers are presently finding their business in jeopardy not because of inability to manage human resources but because of inability to manage financial resources. At the same time, the entire farm credit system is in a critical if not disastrous situation. These as well as other signs suggest that currently available financial management schemes and strategies are inadequate and that "financial resource management" (including legal and institutional arrangements) should be one of the "key problem areas."

Much has been said in the paper about the potential benefits and expected increasing importance of information systems. Missing is a discussion, or at least mention, of whether information and information systems are "size neutral." In view of the fact that a significant amount of the paper deals with public sector activities (extension, publicly funded research, and education), and that litigation is underway against a public research institution (University of California) for conducting research on mechanization that is judged not to be size neutral (and in addition reduces the number of jobs available), it would appear relevant, if not important, to ask this question. I propose that the kind of information systems discussed in or alluded to by the paper are not "size neutral." More specifically, they favor the better-educated manager and larger firms. Whether this is indeed so will need to be investigated, and publicly funded research and education will need to be planned accordingly.

Finally, it appears appropriate to raise the question of whether we are not proposing, at least implicating, that agricultural (firm) managers acquire knowledge and process information at levels far higher than can realistically be accomplished by one individual. If this is so, then agricultural management research, extension, and teaching must concern itself with questions of what new organizational firms could be useful in overcoming what otherwise would comprise an "information overload."

Reference

Smith, D. 1985. Chicago Launches All-ag High School. *Farm J.* 109:7.

Management Problems of Farms and Agricultural Firms: **A Discussion**

DUANE G. HARRIS

One of the key themes of the King and Sonka paper is that managers of farms and agricultural firms will face an increasingly uncertain operating environment during the remainder of the twentieth century. They also document that post–World War II conditions in the agricultural sector created incentives for structural changes that led farm firms to become less resilient. Substitution of capital for labor and debt for equity reduced the farm firm's ability to survive adverse economic periods. Thus, if agricultural firms are to successfully manage into the twenty-first century, they must develop (or restore) their ability to cope with this increasingly unstable operating environment.

The purpose of this review is to present a simple model that identifies the key structural and environmental sources of the uncertainty facing agricultural managers. Management responses suggested by the model will be identified, and the implications for teaching, extension, and research will be discussed.

Framework for Analysis

The agricultural firm is assumed to be a business unit that faces uncertain revenue incomes. Because revenue is a random variable, after-tax income is also a random variable. The important issue for examining the ability of agricultural firms to survive in an uncertain world is the nature of earnings volatility. Thus, the linkage between revenue and after-tax income is critical to a resolution of the management problem of an uncertain environment.

A standard concept that measures the impact of revenue volatility on earnings volatility is that of leverage. Specifically, the degree of total leverage (DTL) is defined as the percent change in after-tax earnings divided by the percent change in revenue. Or equivalently, the degree of total leverage is defined as the coefficient of variation of after-tax earnings divided by the coefficient of variation of revenue. Specifically,

Duane Harris is Manager of Business Analysis, Corporate Growth and Planning Department, General Mills, Inc., Minneapolis, Minnesota.

$$DTL = \frac{CV(ATE)}{CV(R)} = \frac{(1 - v)E(R)}{(1 - v)E(R) - F - rD} ; \tag{1}$$

where DTL is the degree of total leverage; ATE is after-tax earnings; R is revenue; $(1 - v)$ is the gross profit margin of the firm; F is the fixed cost of production; and rD is the fixed finance charge derived by the product of the interest rate, r, and the dollar level of debt, D. The terms $E(\ )$ and $CV(\ )$ denote the expected value operator and coefficient of variation, respectively.

The degree of total leverage measures the relative response of after-tax earnings to changes in revenue and is a direct function of both fixed operating and fixed financial costs. Thus, for a given level of volatility in revenue, the resulting relative volatility in ATE is increased by both increases in fixed operating costs and fixed finance charges. Equation (1) can be rewritten as

$$CV(ATE) - \frac{(1 - v)E(R)}{(1 - v)E(R) - F - rD} \times CV(R) \tag{2}$$

Thus, the variability of after-tax earnings is a function of the degree of total leverage and the variability of revenues.

Figure 11.1 assists in breaking down net-income volatility into structural and environmental sources. If, to operate successfully in the agricultural sector, it is necessary for agricultural firms to control the volatility of their after-tax earnings, then firms must pursue structural policies (F and

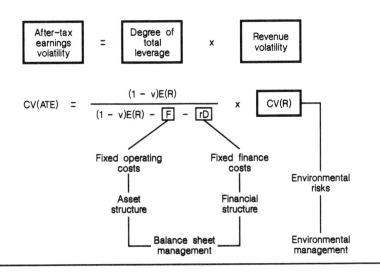

Fig. 11.1. Sources of earnings volatility

D) that reduce the degree of total leverage or adopt programs that reduce the volatility [$CV(R)$] of the environment in which they operate or both.

Management Programs for Survival

BALANCE SHEET MANAGEMENT. Structural policies that control the degree of total leverage are accomplished through balance sheet management. The selection of the level of fixed assets used in production is reflected in the make-up of the asset side of the balance sheet. The selection of the level of fixed financial obligations used to support the asset structure is reflected in the capital side of the balance sheet. To minimize the degree of total leverage and thus minimize the impact of revenue volatility on the net earnings of the firm, policies should be pursued that minimize the fixed assets committed to production and the amount of debt used to fund operations.

Jolly (1983) identifies such structural policies as "controlling risk impacts" and recognizes that those policies have no direct effect on underlying probability distributions, but rather influence the capacity of the firm to "withstand adverse or exploit favorable events." Unfortunately, balance sheet management, especially asset management, has not received its due attention from educators, lenders, and managers, and as a result, managers have abdicated an important source of control over their own destiny.

As an example, in a study of 288 Illinois farmers, Garcia et al. (1983) discovered that 197 or 68.4 percent of the farmers prepared balance sheets. Of those, 131 (66.5 percent) used the balance sheet for credit acquisition, while only 30 (15.2 percent) used it to compute any financial ratios. Thus, only about 10 percent of the total sample of 288 used balance sheet information to measure elements of performance or evaluate financial conditions.

If agricultural managers wish to lessen the impact on their business of a potentially hostile environment, they should think seriously about reducing the level of fixed assets necessary to generate each dollar of revenue. Fortunately, farmers have one of the best contractual vehicles available for controlling assets without incurring fixed charges — the crop-share lease. In addition, investments in used machinery and/or smaller machinery can reduce fixed operating costs as can increased use of custom or contract farming.

Farmers may also need to consider lower levels of financial leverage as necessary for business survival. Clearly, working capital is required for the operation of any firm, but the use of debt can be controlled by limiting growth and expansion to that which can be supported out of retained earnings.

Unfortunately, over time, as King and Sonka point out, farmers have subjected themselves to higher levels of both operating and financial leverage. Higher and higher levels of fixed assets (both land and machinery) have been assumed by using higher and higher levels of debt. That is the essence of financial vulnerability.

NEUTRALIZING THE ENVIRONMENT. The other approach to facing uncertainty in the agricultural sector is to, as Jolly (1983) says, "control risk exposure." In terms of the simple model, that means reducing the volatility of revenue. Management options to control or reduce variability in revenue include diversification, marketing programs, and insurance programs. Or the farmer can continue to rely on government programs to produce the desired environmental stability.

However, such efforts to "change the underlying probability distribution" can be at best incomplete and at worst totally ineffective, but costly. Unfortunately, a large share of our teaching and research efforts go into these "risk management" programs. Consider, for example, the amount of resources that have been devoted to the single topic of "portfolio management."

Special mention needs to be made regarding the role of information in controlling risk exposure. Management Information Systems (MIS) are expected to provide increased ability to successfully perform in an uncertain environment. Most MIS programs, however, require substantial overhead and demand time-consuming attention. Many do not provide a payoff to management that is commensurate with their costs, and some provide volumes of information that managers do not know how to use.

In fact, for many managers, the key problem is not a lack of information, but too much information. What are often needed are information management systems to effectively utilize management information systems. Information systems can only provide important answers if managers are capable of asking important questions. Successful managers are ones who can cut through the information "noise" to key on that which is critical to important strategic and operating decisions.

Implications for Resident and Extension Education

The fundamental leverage relationships previously discussed highlight the need for managers to be able to understand and adopt appropriate balance sheet structures to create resilient businesses. And, successful managers need to be able to understand and modify, where possible, the increasingly complex environment in which they operate. If our resident and extension education programs are to play a role in the area of management development, programs must address these two general educational needs.

The ability of educational programs to meet these needs will depend on the nature of programs offered for both general education and management education. To provide the educational foundation for successful understanding of the complex environment of agriculture, greater emphasis must be placed on broadly based educational programs. Education, beginning at the primary and secondary level, extending through college, and supplemented by extension education should concentrate on developing decision-making capabilities, not on providing answers. Educational programs should help people develop an intellectual framework for identifying issues, investigating alternatives, and making choices.

This emphasis on the decision process means that we must move away from the utilitarian approach to education that has resulted in such programs as vocational agriculture at the secondary level and specialized undergraduate business curricula at the college level. To develop effective managers, we must replace training with education. We must develop education programs that prepare individuals for an entire career, not just for a first job.

To cope with increasing levels of uncertainty and rapid change, management education should concentrate more on the importance of theoretical constructs (such as leverage) that are relevant to many situations and less on special topics that are useful now but may be irrelevant later. Managers must have the conceptual background to be able to internalize qualitative results that produce a comfort level for decision making. Analytical education and development are critical for providing that conceptual capability.

To develop educational programs that are responsive to this need for more broadly based management capabilities, it will be necessary to substantially modify course content and curricula in management programs. From my experience, meaningful changes in courses and curricula will come only with a zero-based approach to course and curriculum development. New educational objectives must be identified and then courses and curricula developed to meet those objectives. Little progress will be made if courses and curricula are changed on an iterative basis from the status quo.

Extension education should also concentrate on developing clientele that are broadly educated, conceptually adaptable, and ultimately self-sufficient. Programs should concentrate on the decision-making process with emphasis on the conceptual first and the computer later. Extension programs should be designed to eliminate the network of "extension addicts" who need answers or quick fixes to fundamental management problems.

In sum, all of our instructional programs must be linked to develop a well-educated rather than a well-trained manager. Training implies the need for external sources of retraining as the world changes. Education implies the internal capability to learn anew and adapt to a changing environment.

Implications for Research

With a more broadly educated management clientele, publicly funded management research could concentrate on those issues that are truly a public good in nature. Research with the potential for broadly based applications could be emphasized with less need for research that provides answers to specific management questions. Research users could be counted on to make their own applications or hire consultants to do so. Thus, with an increased capability to do applied research at the management level, few public resources would have to be devoted to what is currently regarded as management research.

Summary

The need to develop managers who can succeed in an increasingly complex and rapidly changing operating environment places emphasis on educational programs that develop learning and decision-making capabilities. Programs at all levels must move away from the long-term trend of utilitarianism. Public research programs to support management should focus on improving the decision-making process, not on providing specific answers to particular questions. This back-to-basics approach to education and research can help develop management capabilities and institutional structures that are much more resilient and capable of succeeding in an uncertain agricultural world.

References

Garcia, P., S. T. Sonka, and M. A. Mazzacco. 1983. A Multivariate Logic Analysis of Farmers' Use of Financial Information. *Am. J. Agric. Econ.* 65:136–41.
Jolly, R. J. 1983. Risk Management in Agricultural Production. *Am. J. Agric. Econ.* 65:1107–13.

Management Problems of Farms and Agricultural Firms: **A Discussion**

M. EDWARD RISTER

King and Sonka are to be commended for their insightful remarks regarding our current agricultural management environment. Their perception of key issues that will confront agricultural managers in future years is worthy of thought and will be inspirational, both for the remaining discussion segment of this conference and during the days thereafter. They challenge all members of the agricultural economics profession with respect to future directions in research, extension, and resident instruction activities.

The theme of "response to instability and change" is particularly suitable for consideration as we attempt to fulfill our professional responsibilities. Such a focal point accentuates the need to speed the shift from static analyses toward dynamic evaluations, explicitly accounting for uncertainty. Agricultural firms today are more dependent on capital inputs than firms of the past. Accordingly, firms have greater fixed cash obligations today and an associated weakened resiliency during adverse financial periods. Many agriculturalists perceive a need for managers to improve their abilities to look ahead and evaluate emerging opportunities on a discriminatory basis, while considering production, market, and financial risks, among other factors. Successful agricultural managers must be proactive; that is, they must anticipate change rather than merely respond to it. The fact that many of today's agriculturalists acquired their management skills during a period when the farm economy was relatively stable poses a problem to be dealt with while we attempt to improve the managerial capabilities within agriculture.

In a paper presented earlier, Hughes et al. (1986) discussed the range of firm-level impacts associated with two different possible versions of the 1985 Farm Bill. Three potential 1985–1990 macroeconomic scenarios for representative farms in four different regions of the United States were considered. The wide diversity of projected annual net farm incomes and

M. Edward Rister is an Assistant Professor in the Department of Agricultural Economics, Texas A & M University and Texas Agricultural Experiment Station, College Station. Review comments by several of the Texas A & M University Department of Agricultural Economics faculty and graduate students, including Richard Conner, Jesse Grady, Tom Knight, James McGrann, Chris McIntosh, James Richardson, and Paul Teague, are gratefully acknowledged.

changes in financial position over the planning period among the respective situations demonstrate the importance of considering the full range of future occurrences prior to executing decisions. This "forecasting" should be diligently pursued by producers and by persons in agribusiness and policymaking positions, among others. In an earlier draft of their paper, King and Sonka noted, "Because long term debt and variable interest rates are often used to gain control of assets, managers need to consider the viability of a specific decision for several policy scenarios in addition to the current policy."

While our research annals have recently reflected a prolific output of analyses similar to those previously suggested, the persistence and scope of the current "financial crisis" suggests agricultural producers, their advisors and creditors, and policymakers may have been negligent during prior years in anticipating the full range of possible economic scenarios. Certainly the credibility of our profession has been tarnished by the poor predictability of our "science." Our own abilities to improve on management efficiency within agriculture are hampered by the wealth of uncontrollable variables that determine the principal direction and magnitude of future events. As noted by Mark Twain, "Prophesy is an exceedingly difficult task, especially with regard to the future." Future management efforts should emphasize careful consideration of the full range of possible outcomes and involve wise and prudent use of risk management tools that either eliminate or minimize the dire economic consequences of unfavorable events.

As we move into the twenty-first century, agriculture will continue to be confronted with a turbulent economic environment. Anticipated technological innovations in agriculture have the potential of radically altering existing supply/demand situations for many agricultural commodities. Personal experiences in evaluating the economic impact of widespread adoption of Lemont (a new semidwarf long-grain rice variety) across the southern rice-producing states indicate substantial downside price risk would be present during the next several years if it were not for the existing rice loan rate, rice target prices, and deficiency-payment provisions associated with the 1981 Farm Bill (Rister and Grant 1984). Prospects for technologically induced yield increases, the general inelastic nature of agricultural demand (Tweeten 1983), and prospects for reduced government loan rates and income protection in association with the 1985 Farm Bill (Knutson 1985; Tweeten 1985), could materially hasten the transformation in American agriculture structure.

Central themes throughout my remaining comments are: (1) a need for an evolutionary incentive structure to foster an increase in the types of activities promoted by King and Sonka; (2) a perceived urgency for more cooperative extension/research efforts; and (3) a recommendation for heightened awareness of the subtle complexities of decision-making situations confronting agricultural managers.

While tomorrow's agricultural managers are a "captive audience" in our classrooms, we should strive to achieve the highest quality of instruction possible. Attention to curricula needs both in agricultural economics and other disciplines within our Colleges of Agriculture is appropriate. Empirical observations suggest a majority of agricultural professionals receive a minimal amount of business (e.g., economics and finance) training. Great need exists today for higher educational institutions to produce astute, business-oriented graduates. The infrastructure existing within agriculture is such that technical expertise is much more easily (and most often at an economical rate) acquired than economic management skills. While superior, competent agricultural management–consulting businesses do exist, the personal nature of decision-making processes and the uniqueness of firm situations mean that agricultural managers need more than an elementary introduction to economics, accounting, finance, and other management training.

Departments are operating with scarce resources, most notably our professional time, which must be allocated across resident instruction, extension, and research activities. It is my perception that, in many cases, the agricultural economics profession is not adhering to the Equal Marginal Principle, with emphasis on (and resulting quality of) resident instruction at less than optimal levels. Factors responsible for this are many and varied across institutions, but our profession's and the academic community's glorification of published research is partially responsible. Quality of instruction is hard to measure; numbers of journal articles are quite easy to count. Granted, many of today's journal articles eventually serve as teaching instruments in the classroom. Unfortunately, only a few such writings are well suited for use in undergraduate and/or managerial-related classes. In addition, the discounted present value, with a somewhat high risk premium given the low probability of future applications, does not justify the seemingly inordinate attention toward research at the expense of teaching activities.

With respect to more timely monitoring of the quality of our instructional programs, the implementation of pretest and exit examinations for our undergraduate and graduate students could serve as useful feedback. Such an evaluation process would encourage us to focus on meaningful objectives within our respective programs and also provide us with a standard of measurement in terms of our achieving such goals. Professional producer and agribusiness associations should be solicited to aid in developing such a set of evaluation standards. I encourage our profession's Economic Education Committee to consider the endorsement and development of such examinations for use in our resident instruction programs. Resident instruction should be increased in stature within our profession, with the intent of enhancing the quality of our graduates. Innovative teaching techniques aimed at introducing new ideas and materials into the classroom should be encouraged. More rewards for quality resident instruction efforts are necessary. Without intending to step on any toes, rigor in the classroom should supplant popularity as a major evaluation criterion of teaching effectiveness.

As inferred by King and Sonka, the emphasis of educational programs should shift away from general prescriptions and towards identifying concepts, principles, and analytical techniques that agriculturalists can effectively utilize in their businesses. The extension segment of our profession, by virtue of its applied orientation, is, in many cases, "leading the pack" in management scholarship. Government farm program participation, marketing strategies, and microcomputer software development and applications education are among the many program areas well supported by extension. Nonetheless, there is room for improvement. Extension must be innovative and inspiring in extending information and decision-support strategies to its clientele; methods must be identified to encourage agriculturalists to regard management activities as being just as exciting as driving a new tractor or going to the county fair. Individual reflections on our personal experiences, in attempting to keep current with respect to developments and advancements throughout the agricultural economics profession, provides a perspective of how many agricultural managers must approach our continuing educational programs. Twenty-minute "song and dances" are not (and never have been) an appropriate method of transmitting useful information and decision-making techniques to agricultural producers. Targeted audiences, new delivery methods, extended subject matter workshops, and in-depth follow-up programs are each feasible components of an appealing, comprehensive management-educational program.

In seeking to augment the value of their own programs, as well as to improve the application of subject-matter and disciplinary aspects of research, Extension economists should be much more aggressive in embracing the problem-solving aspects of management research. This includes being more willing to submit applied manuscripts to our professional journals. The repeated rhetoric that "the journals are worthless" is old and trite—low acceptance rates, caustic reviewers, and fragile egos are all obstacles that must be overcome. Peer review is a valuable ingredient in the success of any activity.

The areas identified by King and Sonka for future research are of significant importance in terms of enhancing the future viability of individual firms within the agricultural sector. One of the stiffest challenges confronting our profession, however, concerns the availability of suitably trained economists to pursue such research (Harl 1983; Conner 1985). I perceive a need to achieve a greater balance among disciplinary, subject matter, and problem-solving research efforts. Much of the disciplinary research reported today has little prospect for being integrated into a functional decision-support system. Neither is it appropriate for the use in developing components of such a system.

There is a tendency within our profession for researchers to lay the blame on extension specialists for their failure to be creative while, simultaneously, extension specialists chastise researchers for their inattention to reality. As a result, more balanced, cooperative extension/research efforts are needed throughout the country. Simply providing joint appointments to a few individuals in a department is not adequate. Truly integrated efforts are called for, with mutual benefits forthcoming to both aspects of our discipline's responsibilities. Extension's insights regarding the strategic and tactical management issues confronting the agricultural sector are an important (and often neglected) input into research activities. Similarly, research can lend support toward interpreting economic consequences of complex decision situations via development of expert systems, long-run evaluation of managerial processes, etc. As noted by Black et al. (1980), "A long-term integrated extension/applied research program is necessary for good performance. Neither 'publish and run' or 'spit over the fence' will 'cut it' in tomorrow's environment."

A wealth of 1970s and early 1980s research directed toward managerial activities lies dormant on reference shelves across the country, awaiting refinement for problem-solving applications. Meanwhile, our current literature appears to be leaning further away from managerial-type manuscripts.

A primary factor responsible for this apparent imbalance in our professional research activities may be associated with our graduate training. Many of our graduate students today are not interested in the types of research being discussed in this session. In part, this is because they perceive a reluctance on the part of our journal editors to publish such research. Provided that obstacle is either unfounded or can be overcome with management research fully aligned with the scientific process, at least one additional hindrance remains to achieving the challenges set forth by King and Sonka. Our profession's production economists are not adequately trained in the management-related disciplines (e.g., Management and Industrial Engineering) nor attuned to the contents of their journals. For the most part, our graduate programs emphasize economics, econometrics, quantitative methods, production economics, etc., with limited attention directed toward management. Swanson (1979) provides a brief review of others' perceptions along these lines.

Another possible explanation for the perceived deficiency in management scholarship may be associated with the profession's inability to identify with the complexity of decision processes confronting agriculturalists. The virtues of our theories are unquestionable (I think!); however, the profession's value to society is, at least in part, embodied in its ability to enhance the efficiency of the agricultural sector. This requires the application of some of our theories and methods, which is often either inappropriate or impossible given our data bases. We, accordingly, must be more willing to interact with managers and incorporate into our research the intricacies of their decision-making situations and the time frame within which they must evaluate and execute a decision. Well-defined research efforts ascribing to the scientific process are invaluable. Simultaneously, we should strengthen our interdisciplinary research linkages. The usefulness of both our own research and that of the other disciplines can be enhanced by such cooperative efforts (e.g., CIPM) (Jones 1985).

Anticipating the twenty-first century is exciting, to say the least. A review of the past indicates rapid technological developments in production and management have transpired. There is no reason to envision the future will be any different. Accordingly, the challenges confronting agricultural managers will seriously test the abilities of both our profession and managers to contribute to an efficient agricultural sector.

References

Black, J. R., J. Waller, and R. Brook. 1980. The Development of Software for Agricultural Decision-Making. Staff Paper 80-24. East Lansing: Dept. of Agric. Econ., Michigan State Univ.

Conner, R. 1985. Observations on Changes in Factors Influencing Agricultural Economics and Some Implications for the Profession. *South. J. Agric. Econ.* 17:1–6.

Harl, N. E. 1983. Agricultural Economics: Challenges to the Profession. *Am. J. Agric. Econ.* 65:845–54.

Hughes, D. W., J. W. Richardson, and M. E. Rister. 1986. Effects of Sustained Financial Stress on the Financial Structure and Performance of the Farm Sector. *Am. J. Agric. Econ.* 67:1116–22.

Jones, J. W. 1985. New Research Opportunities – Integrated Farm Systems. Paper presented at ESCOP Symposium: Research Planning for the State Agricultural Experiment Stations. Washington, D.C., June 16–19.

Knutson, R. D. 1985. Are Current U. S. Farm Programs Outdated? Arguments in the Negative. Paper presented at the Western Agricultural Economics Association Annual Meetings, Saskatoon, Saskatchewan, July 9.

Rister, M. E., and W. R. Grant. 1984. Economic Impact of Lemont. The Semidwarfs – A New Era in Rice Production. College Station: Texas Agricultural Experiment Station.

Swanson, E. R. 1979. Working With Other Disciplines. *Am. J. Agric. Econ.* 61:849–59.

Tweeten, L. 1983. Economic Instability in Agriculture: The Contributions of Price, Government Programs, and Exports. *Am. J. Agric. Econ.* 65:922–31.

_____. 1985. Are Current U.S. Farm Programs Outdated? Arguments in the Positive. Paper presented at the Western Agricultural Economics Association Annual Meetings, Saskatoon, Saskatchewan, July 9.

12

Institutions, Institutionalism, and Agricultural Economics in the Twenty-first Century

PAUL W. BARKLEY

Agriculture, like all industries in the U.S. economy, is governed by institutions. While the price system and the nation's broad system of property rights exert the most pervasive control over agricultural inputs, processes, and outputs, they are joined by tax codes, price and income policies, production quotas, bans on pesticides, special credit rules, immigrant labor laws, green-belt legislation, traditional and often local lease arrangements, conservation incentives, transportation regulations, information systems, and scores of other formal and informal rules that dictate or influence the terms of conduct and performance of the industry and each firm in it. Agricultural economists have sometimes become involved with the study of one or more of the institutions that affect the industry, but this research has, except in rare instances, been incomplete or has made up only a part of a research scholar's contribution to the profession.

The effects of institutions are likely to become more pervasive as the twentieth century comes to an end. The U.S. economy is more complex than ever before; the industry is experiencing both endogenous and exogenous shocks; and a worldwide agricultural economy is gradually coming into being. Each of these requires more formal arrangements within the industry as well as more rules or guiding principles that impinge on the industry from outside. Agricultural economists will be required to sharpen their skills in dealing with and researching the creation of institutions, the

Paul W. Barkley is Professor of Agricultural Economics at Washington State University, Pullman. The scope and content of this paper have benefited from comments by or discussions with Theodore R. Alter, Emery N. Castle, R. J. Hildreth, Ronald Powers, Philip Raup, and Philip Wandschneider. Remaining errors in fact or interpretation reside with the author.

obsolescence or demise of institutional forms, and the effects that institutions have on the use of resources, the distribution of the product of these resources, and the perpetuation of a viable agriculture. Although variously defined, institutions are generally thought of as sanctioned, well ordered, and reasonably stable relationships that affect people's behavior. They occur because problems grow beyond the point of being mere hindrances, or because one group wishes to absorb or eliminate the externalities that have been engendered by another group. Davis and North (1971), Hayami and Ruttan (1971), North and Thomas (1969, 1971), Schmid (1973), Georgescu-Roegen (1976), and Olson (1982) have all written extensively about the creation of institutions or the circumstances under which institutional change will occur.

Most authors stress technological change or massive social disruption. The change or disruption can extend over centuries, like the Enlightenment. It may be cataclysmic like the worldwide depression of the 1930s. It might be a one-time event like the consummation of the United States–Russia Wheat Deal in 1972. All of these have been viewed by one or more authors as social or economic forces that were strong enough to bring changes in the way things are done and in the rules that govern allocation and exchange. Such forces are always at work making new institutions and modifying or eliminating old ones.

The institutions that affect agriculture range from being very trivial to being highly important and almost global in origin and/or effect. A local sharing arrangement for a particular kind of lease has importance to those who enter into it, but it is of limited concern to the national economy. Changes in the GATT provisions can alter the way in which the international trade in agricultural commodities is conducted. In aggregate, the institutions that affect agriculture remain somewhat venerable ways of determining how people will behave. This last feature makes institutions a proper and necessary part of economic inquiry. Lionel Robbins (1932) wrote that economics deals with the allocation of scarce resources among alternative and competing ends. In so writing, Robbins insured that economists must consider institutions because institutions not only define resource sets, but they also have the capacity to place upper and lower bounds on how resource sets can be used. Institutions as well as prices are allocators of land, labor, capital, and entrepreneurial skill.

Since institutions themselves affect the allocation of resources, any institutional change reorders benefits and costs, benefactors and beneficiaries, and the distribution of compensated and uncompensated effects of human endeavor. Given the pervasiveness of these possible consequences, it is surprising that economists have spent so little time systematically studying the formation of institutions and institutional change. This is especially surprising among agricultural economists, since few productive enterprises or contemporary industries have been the direct object of more institutions or institutionalized interventions than agriculture.

It is unlikely that this will change.[1] Most agricultural economists will continue to research problems as if the problems existed in a given and fixed institutional framework. Those researchers who inquire into changes in institutions will likely work on limited themes—the changes in a taxing scheme, a change in the loan rate for a specified crop, or a move toward strict enforcement of rules to protect some aspect of the environment. In doing this, they will be making a correct application of the traditional rules, assumptions, and methods of neoclassical economics; they will be studying the effects of institutional change rather than the circumstances that brought about the change itself.

This paper argues that agricultural economists cannot ignore the changing institutions that impinge upon agriculture and rural areas. It starts with a modest list of some institutions that are likely to change demonstrably or that might have a demonstrably different effect on agriculture and rural areas as the twenty-first century approaches. It then strays from the effects of institutional change and asks a broader question about the causes of the growth and decline of institutions themselves. The paper ends where it well could have started: a discussion of Institutionalism, an ungraceful corner in the history of economic thought.

A caution is in order. The price system itself is undeniably an institution. It evolved gradually along with specialization and exchange to accommodate the need for easy and relatively sure ways of consummating trades without the cumbersome necessities that accompany bartering. At this time, the price system, and the relative prices that it engenders, are often taken as given. This is especially true in a study of or related to economics. Many of the institutions in the following discussion are designed specifically to regulate or modify the price system in order to assist it in overcoming its failures or to achieve some non-price-related goal for economic activity. Because of its pervasive characteristics, specific references to the price system as an institution will be infrequent.

Some Contemporary Institutional Issues Affecting Agriculture

It is impossible to know how many institutional issues will affect agriculture and rural areas in the coming years, and it is impossible to know the intensity of the effect that institutional changes will have on the industry or on rural America. A simple listing does not do justice to the problem, so the following list is offered only as a possible starting place in examining the breadth, depth, and ubiquitousness of institutions and institution-related problems. The items in the list are not ordered with respect to importance.

1. The structure of factor and product markets faced by farm operators is changing so that the traditional assumptions of atomistic competition are no longer effective in delineating a framework for agricultural economics research. Vertical integration continues to transfer decision-making powers from production firms to processing firms just as the formation of farmer-owned cooperatives transfers decision-making opportunities and obligations in the opposite direction. Each of these kinds of changes in structure means that the agricultural industry is less one of competitive firms and more one of oligopoly and monopolistic competition. The terms of exchange between and among factor owners, productive farm enterprises, and product markets will be determined by new and sometimes little-understood forms of bargaining institutions and practices that deviate harshly from those in the competitive model. Crocker (1971) has pointed this out with respect to group bargaining between apple producers and the owners (managers) of cedar trees that are host for an apple-damaging fungus. However, the general case for agriculture has yet to be elaborated with any degree of sophistication. The prospect of adapting models that do not rely on competition to agriculture and its problems offers a great challenge. The task will accommodate as well as require the skills of both the traditional neoclassical economist and the avant-garde, evolutionary economist.

2. The traditional "bundle-of-rights" approach to the exclusive ownership of land and other natural resources will continue to change. After decades of advocating the collection of the various sticks into a fee-simple bundle, agricultural economists, planners, and lawyers are among the leaders of movements designed to redefine, break, disaggregate, and scatter the rights that have been so collected. The sale of development rights and hunting rights, as well as the acceptance of terms dictated by use-value taxation schemes, dilutes the decision-making power of the farmer and adds limits or imperfections to land titles. This institutional evolution will likely continue. It could be carried to an extreme in which markets develop for very particular kinds of rights to use or not use real property now associated with agriculture. In an extreme case, a farmer-producer may have to begin many months in advance to search for land on which to grow a particular crop in a future time period (Guither et al. 1985).

3. Institutions surrounding water rights and water use will increase in complexity and number. With few exceptions, water law is state law, but water problems are always tied in unique ways to natural watercourses—surface, underground, and atmospheric—that show contemptuous disrespect for political boundaries. Market institutions may provide the best (most efficient in a Pareto sense) allocative devices in local areas, but some supramarket, large-area entity may be needed to generate the most desirable wide area, national, or even international approach to the proper

relationships among water, populations, and the conduct of economic activity.

4. The current national predilection toward deregulation is surely precursor to a similar period of reregulation. Soon after the recent haste to deregulate the economy began, Jesse et al. (1982, 912) wrote:

> . . . (T)he current administration, which generally views regulatory programs as being antithetical to "free competition," has taken steps it hopes will lead to less regulation of the agricultural sector. Whether this objective is based on the belief that the net public benefits to regulation are negative, or that deregulation will yield larger net positive benefits is not clear—nor is clarification necessary. The simple, direct question is whether deregulation will yield larger net public benefits than regulation.

The complete answer to the question posed by Jesse et al. (1982) is not yet clear. However, society is learning from the deregulation of the airlines, trucking, rails, telecommunications, and banking that instability and uncertainty are the incalculable costs of allowing some powerful and/or oligopolistic industries to operate without nonmarket rules (regulations).

This is an especially important topic for agricultural economists since there is currently more than the usual amount of talk in favor of abandoning many of the traditional programs (regulations) that affect farming. While agriculture has responded to the deregulation of many industries that provide its inputs, it is questionable how production agriculture would be structured if the major commodity programs were to be abandoned as part of a general policy of restoring the market as an arbiter of all issues relating to resource allocation.

5. Even though the population of many rural areas continues to grow, farmers continue to diminish as a proportion of the rural population. Rural nonfarm residents will increase their interest in the way agricultural resources are used and will have increased political power to invoke sanctions on farmers and farming (Elo and Beale 1983; Hite 1983). In some cases, the sanctions will give rise to increased costs of production for farm products; in other cases, the type and structure of local/regional agriculture may be changed. In the end, the results may bring conflicts among at least four groups: (1) producers who are committed to the status quo; (2) nonfarm competitors for the productive use of resources now in agriculture; (3) rural nonfarm residents who consume both rural amenities as well as agricultural products; and (4) the urban population that is interested primarily in low food costs.[2]

6. Many rural communities in areas highly dependent on agriculture will face rapidly escalating public costs and diminishing nonland tax bases. A large number of these communities are in a perilous circumstance

(Barkley 1974; Eddleman 1969; Hirsch 1968; Hushak 1983). Their public and private infrastructures have deteriorated and their ability to provide services has diminished. The communities are in a curious dilemma. If their populations grow, they have no choice but to revitalize their schools, hospitals, water systems, and waste disposal systems. The revitalization will be doubly expensive because development and redevelopment in the 1990s will have to meet state and federal building and safety codes, a problem that was less stringent during the original construction period. If, however, population continues to decline, the deterioration of the antiquated infrastructure may, in so doing, contribute to the demise of the community. In either case, the pressure for added public revenue will be on agriculture and agricultural resources. This pressure is sure to increase as federal revenue sharing is phased out and states, facing their own financial traumas, can do little to help.

7. Technical change will continue to reduce the unit price and/or expand output per acre of many agricultural commodities (Johnson and Wittwer 1984). This, coupled with the inelastic demand for agricultural products and the uncertainty of international markets, will put downward pressure on farm incomes. In the absence of adequate government-sponsored price and income programs, farm families will have little opportunity to maintain their total family incomes without turning to nonfarm sources of labor income.[3] If nonfarm income sources are to increase, institutions such as job retraining, skill grants, flex-time, job-sharing, and other workplace innovations will have to be introduced in rural areas. Concurrently, the profession's attitude about income from nonfarm sources will have to change away from one that assumes that all increases in off-farm income occur because of needed supplements to marginal family income from farming. Off-farm income can as easily represent successful farm operation that allows the farm family to engage in off-farm, professional work.

8. Schertz and Wunderlich (1982) have pointed out that the existing, broadly defined agricultural data system does not provide information in enough detail to allow thorough analysis of the ownership and use of farm land in the United States. It seems clear, however, that the process of parcellization will continue to change the structure of land ownership. More agricultural land will be held by nonfarmers. Whole farms that remain whole will become the exception rather than the rule. In consequence, farmers will have to spend an increasing proportion of their time gathering and processing information on land that may be available to buy, rent, or lease. A small farmstead may be the headquarters for a large farm, but the large farm may change from year to year in location, size, number of parcels, crops grown, and relative profitabilty. Moreover, the nonfarming owners (individuals, corporations, financial institutions, distant relatives, and the like) may take a more active role in managing their properties by dictating what can and cannot be done on a particular land parcel. Non-

farming owners may not interfere with agricultural production, but they may keep hunting rights for themselves (Kuhn 1985). Similarly, the nonfarming owners may be attracted by several of the newer and increasingly limiting rules relating to cross-compliance, commodity programs, and conservation. In either case, and especially the second, sorting out the total effect of institutional change will become a burden not just for researcher, but for farm operators as well. The transactions costs of institutional compliance or noncompliance may be very high.

9. The methods of transferring the ownership of land and nonland agricultural resources will continue to change. Various tax reforms at the state and federal levels have made new organizational forms and methods of intergenerational transfer popular and profitable among farm families. It is not clear that these kinds of changes have ended. Until they do, the ownership patterns of land and other durable resources will be clouded. Existing and anticipated imperfections will lend a degree of uncertainty and inflexibility to farm adjustments (Suter 1978; 1979).

10. It is increasingly clear that there is persistent redundancy among all classes of inputs used in agricultural production (Ericksen and Collins 1985; Harris 1983). Although attempts to remove some resources from the industry have been in place and institutionalized for 50 years, these efforts have been offset by equally institutionalized efforts to increase the number or productivity of the resources that remain in agriculture. Both institutional resource removal and resource enhancement have been heavily subsidized by and centered in the USDA/Land-Grant College complex. While there are good reasons for both classes of activities, they are clearly in conflict. Few attempts at coordinating the programs have been attempted; fewer still have been successful. It appears that, with only occasional aberrations over time, resource redundancy and overproduction will continue to be present through the professional lives of most living and trained agricultural economists. If this is so, more inventive genius will need to be devoted to perfecting institutions that coordinate programs, initiate research, release information, and/or remove resources from the industry.[4]

11. Rapid changes in the number of economic forces that impinge upon agriculture have caused the price of farm land to become uncertain and volatile. Since equity in farmland has always formed an important base for farm borrowing, this volatility has had drastic and deleterious effects on farming. It is one of the contributors to the financial stress currently being felt by the production industry and its supporting industries. A possible solution to this price-equity-debt problem is for individuals in the industry to divest themselves of the offending resource—land. U.S. agriculture, long based on the Jeffersonian and Populist ideal of owner operatorship, could allay this source of instability somewhat by selling land. Such land, being best suited for agricultural production, could then be rented back from its new, nonfarming owners and used for traditional productive purposes.

Given creative leasing instruments, there is no reason to believe that the absolute size or stability of the food supply would be jeopardized by such a change. Distribution of the rents would be negotiated and very difficult to predict until the lease-back system was in place. The system would require a shift to borrowing based on cash flow rather than on equity, a shift that is already underway in many parts of the nation.

These represent only the short list of all possible examples. Other authors would have selected a different 11 and may have established a hierarchy among them. Nonetheless, the list does indicate that agriculture is surrounded by institutions that affect the acquisition of factors, the production process, and the disposal of finished products. Moreover, there is no subarea, specialty, division, or region within agriculture or agricultural economics that is exempt from institutions or institutional change.

In some regards, the institutions affecting agriculture are so pervasive that they could be described as factors of production in much the same manner as land, labor, capital, and entrepreneurship. Such designation would require a major shift in the method of calculating the functional distribution of income. While this would be awkward, it does not seem either impossible or entirely arbitrary. The use of the factor-of-production nomenclatures is little more than a way of grouping resources that make an identifiable contribution to production (Barkley 1976). Surely, the naming scheme is flexible enough to accommodate the rules and regulations that give direct access to income streams. The designation would give credence or at least technical respectability to the notion that farmers, and other actors in the agricultural industry, might find it more profitable to "farm the institutions" than to plant traditional crops.

Farming the institutions also has direct implications on the things agricultural economists do in their capacities as researchers and purveyors of information. The institutions that affect agriculture have technical requirements, relative costs, relative rewards, and (within limits) ascertainable risks. Research tools stemming from classical and neoclassical economics are quite suitable and quite sufficient to enable discovery of the correct combination or selective involvement with institutions. The correct combination would, of course, change as the relative rewards among institutions changed, so knowledge and information about the direction and rate of institutional change would become highly valuable to producers as well as to researchers and planners.

The Demand and Supply of Institutions[5]

Institutions are created. The creation can be swift, like the drafting of agricultural and industrial policy during the first hundred days of the New

Deal; or it can be very slow like the gradual evolution of the land tenure system in the United States (Piore and Sabel 1984; Harris 1953). Regardless of the rate of formation, institutions are formed, changed, become obsolete, and are removed in response to pressure, agitation, or need. These attributes, while defying complete specification, are familiar in the literature of economics because they are precisely the attributes that cause disequilibrium and change in the markets for goods and services. Since these attributes can appear on either the demand side or the supply side of the market, the traditional supply and demand mechanism of microeconomics can be reconstructed with only slight modifications to show the circumstances under which institutions may be formed, changed, removed, or replaced.[6]

Figure 12.1 is a caricature of the supply and demand mechanisms for institutions. The figure is familiar and needs no explanation as long as it pertains to the prices and quantities of known goods and services. However, the world under discussion is broader. It includes both price and nonprice ways of affecting the quantity of institutions that will be available. This broadening of context requires a redefinition of the axes in the diagram.

The horizontal axis is now a complex measure of the quantity or numbers of institutions. Since many rules, habits, and conventions that can be defined as institutions are not additive, this axis is not merely a counting device. It is better described as a scale that shows the increasing intensity with which institutions, regardless of their number, affect human affairs. Under this scheme, increased effort to enforce a rule would not increase the

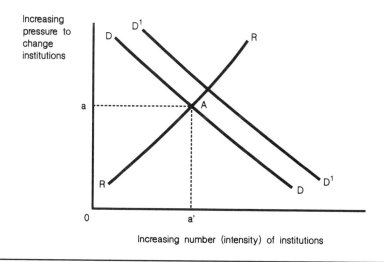

Fig. 12.1. The supply and demand for institutions

number of institutions, but it would cause a movement to the right along the horizontal axis.

The vertical axis must be treated similarly. There is no well-defined scale that measures "pressure." This is especially true when it is unclear whether the pressure is on an economic entity, a political body, an informal organization, or the public as a whole. It is known that increased restlessness, more sophisticated lobbying, a surge in righteous indignation, brute force, or a new morality puts noticeable pressure on groups responsible for developing or changing institutions. Following the arguments commonly associated with North and Thomas (1969), it is also known that the gradual obsolescence or decay of the effectiveness of institutions can lead to breakdowns in either the social or economic achievements of society. Such circumstance invites institutional innovation. The vertical axis in Figure 12.1 is intended to reflect the generation and notice of such increased pressure.

The supply or response curve, RR, shows how those who create or modify institutions will respond to the pressures that are brought against them. Response is shown as a positively sloped curve, indicating that as pressure for institutional change increases the rule-making body will be more and more likely to respond with new sets of rules in a struggle to eliminate or lessen the pressure being placed on it. The demand curves, DD and D^1D^1, have an analogous interpretation. As the number or intensity of rules increases, the pressure to generate more of them diminishes, reflecting a kind of diminishing marginal utility of institutions.

The system can be described as being in equilibrium in point A. No new institutions are being created and no old ones are being destroyed or replaced.[7] It is crucial to note that the equilibrium created by collection A does not remove the pressure to change. At this point, Oa pressure remains, but this is insufficient to force the governing body to change the stock of rules.

Once point A has been achieved, society has the stock of institutions indicated by Oa'. In a capitalistic economy, the distance Oa' will include the price mechanism, the system of property rights, and all other specific rules that determine or affect how resources will be allocated and how factor rewards and rents will be distributed. There is no way to tell, however, whether efficiency and equity are best served with this collection of institutions, or whether a change in Oa' would bring an improvement. Proponents of deregulation argue with some conviction that reducing the stock of institutions will improve the performance of the economy. At the same time, farmers are mixed in their dispositions about land and commodity programs. Some feel that increased rules relating to conservation or cross-compliance will improve the condition of agriculture. It is unclear whether these advocates of increasing institutional interference are basing their notions on favoritism toward agriculture or moving the entire economic system closer to a global optimum.

Discussion should not end without mention of demand shifters and supply shifters. Most authors who write about the creation of institutions take the long view. North and his co-authors talk about institutional change and the emergence of Western Europe over a period of centuries. Olson (1982) touches several geographic areas, but, like North, concentrates on long periods of time. Piore and Sabel (1984), although writing on a broader topic, consider many of the institutional changes that occurred in the United States between the Civil War and the present. These authors, as well as others, emphasize and imply that a long series of events is often responsible for changing the demand for institutions: social and technical changes need new rules before or after adoption. Harris (1985) similarly describes the long period of time after the Norman Conquest as one in which modern property institutions developed in response to needs for personal protection and political order. In all cases, an accumulation of events serves to shape the changing demand for institutions. The relevant research question is the frequency or pace of the events that engender change.

Changes in the supply of institutions are harder to grasp. Since most institutions have some public-good characteristics, they are put in place by groups or governments. If the governments are representative democracies, the demanders and the suppliers are conceptually the same. Some caution must be exercised in using this interpretation. While a constitutional or representative democracy may have a single population that is covered by the public good aspects of property rights, the price system, and the system of criminal justice, that same population may divide into groups when new rules are needed to encourage or discourage behavior. A group may be grazing sheep in the public park. An offended group (demanders of institutions) may petition the city council (suppliers of institutions) and an anti-sheep rule may emerge. While having many characteristics of public goods, institutions frequently arise because of divergences of views within a broad public. The notable increase in laws related to environmental protection in the United States in the 1970s was, for example, a people's legislative response to a people's problem, but the people were different people. In a despotic or autocratic government, those who supply the institutions may develop the supply mechanism without regard for the needs or desires of their constituents.

Described another way, there does not seem to be a "Say's Law of Institution Making." If there is, the details of its operation are not entirely clear. It may be that the Say's-Law–type mechanism is bifurcated with the supply of institutions eventually creating its own demand, and the demand for institutions eventually creating its own supply. The modifier "eventually" is needed because the response time is likely to be unique to each institution. In either case, the process of adjusting to institutional change itself may trigger additional demand shifters or supply shifters. In terms of

Figure 12.1, the equilibrium designated by point A is likely to be highly unstable because of both demand and supply forces.[8]

Others suggest that the long view is not an essential ingredient of institution building, removal, or change. Schlesinger (1960) argues that the cataclysmic economic events of the early 1930s called for immediate action to " . . . rebuild America through the reconstruction of economic institutions in accordance with technological imperatives." He continues, citing the AAA as an (eventually) successful effort to restructure the way in which agricultural production and marketing was carried out. Whether this came as a result of demand-side phenomena through beleaguered farmers or supply-side phenomena through Roosevelt's pragmatic advisers is a moot point. The recent mood for deregulation is similarly moot since it is not clear whether deregulation is a demand-side phenomenon in which the public has diminished the intensity of its desire for nonprice allocative mechanisms, or a supply-side phenomenon in which the rule-making elite has decided to replace a large number of market-affecting rules with a return to the relatively simple mechanisms of the market.

Quite clearly, the demand and supply mechanisms that affect institutions are not settled. It is known, however, that the quantity (or intensity) and object of institutions changes constantly. No one can make precise predictions of how quantity or intensity will change, but the suspicion is that more institutions are required as an economic society matures. Although evidence is sketchy, development of institutions was essentially halted during the Dark Ages, when economic and social progress suffered a major hiatus. Institution building emerged with the Enlightenment and the succeeding decades brought the perfection of the price system with new rules on coinage, contracts, and the control of money, as well as major changes in the ways in which private property was defined.

Although the contention would be hard to document, the pace of institution creation has seemed to increase in the nineteenth and twentieth centuries. The reason may not be hard to find: as technology has altered the way in which factors of production are combined, the relationships among factor owners, factor users, and factor controllers have become more complex. The complexity has led to real or potential instances in which one individual or group has had an adverse impact on another. These possibilities have entered the literature of economics as "market failures," "externalities," or "third party effects." Social and governing groups at all levels (public and private, local, state, national, and international) have intervened in these instances to protect individuals and groups from the (sometimes unwitting) harm that can come from the actions of others. The intervention has been explosive in terms of numbers and ranges of institutions. It has led to building codes, zoning, speed limits, preferential taxes, bans, mandates, inspections, limits, and a host of other mechanisms. The end of this era of institution building is surely not in sight. It is a part of a quickening struggle to reallocate resources and redistribute rewards to eliminate negative externalities, capture selected unearned rents for public use, and redistribute income. The idealist's hope is that such rules and rearrangements will either make the total behavior of society fit more closely with the Utilitarian's goal of "the greatest good for the greatest number," or move society closer to the neoclassical goal of Pareto optimality.[9]

Agriculture, an industry that is heavily affected by institutions and rules, will continue to feel pressure to expand or change many of the institutions that affect it. Agricultural economists will continue to be asked to define the form and intensity of expected changes; they will be asked to predict (or anticipate) when such changes will occur; and they will be requested to estimate the effects the prospective changes will have on the industry. Admittedly, the traditional supply/demand diagram is overly naive as an instrument of analysis, but some indicators of the imminence of change will be necessary in understanding and coping with the continual adjustment process faced by the industry. It is likely that traditional neoclassical tools will be used by virtually all agricultural economists who struggle to analyze the effects of institutional change. The hope is that more sophisticated tools and more reasoned approaches will lead to a greater understanding of institutions, their creation, and their effects.

INSTITUTIONS, INSTITUTIONALISM, AND AGRICULTURAL ECONOMICS. It is taken as given that institutions are an important attribute of the agricultural economy and that agricultural economists have important contributions to make in understanding and predicting the occurrence and effects of institutional change. Many within the profession are already engaged in this kind of activity and are making notable contributions to theory and empirical knowledge. Although hard to document, it seems that the major agricultural economist-contributors are concentrated in studies of natural resources. A growing subset may be developing in the broad area of marketing. The typical agricultural economist is, however, usually content to study aspects of the farm economy within a context that assumes most institutions to be fixed. The same can be said for most of economics—the parent profession. It has always been this way even though there is a subset of economists whose members claim to be "Institutionalists."

The books that deal with the history of economic thought invariably include a chapter on Institutionalism and treat it as a distinct school of economic thought. The school is described as uniquely American in its origins and is most frequently described as a product of the last 30 years of the nineteenth century—a time of widespread economic turmoil in the U.S. economy. During this time there were persistent depressions, labor unrest, monetary crises, the emergence of dominant monopolies and oligopolies, widespread corruption in business and government, and reckless abandonment of parts of the public's land and mineral domain.

The logic of Ricardo, even when combined with the rise of marginalism and presented through the synthesizing skills of Alfred Marshall, did not seem to provide an analytic framework that could explain the behavior of either microunits or, increasingly, the economy as a whole (Oser and Blanchfield 1975; Dorfman et al. 1963; Gruchy 1972). These conditions fostered the growth of discontent with the tradition of theoretical economics and led to a number of critics, both in the profession and out, who vitiated the ongoing body of thought. Some attempted reformulations of certain aspects of economic theory. These "reformers" or "revisionists" were the Institutionalists, who, even though they did not set out to do so, formed a school of economic thought. The school has no strong central theme and the proponents of the school were never in close correspondence. As a result, the school never coalesced. If Institutionalism is taught at all to contemporary graduate students in agricultural economics, it is taught through biography rather than analytics, and it is often considered to be a casual diversion from the main thrust of microeconomics, quantitative methods, and the exacting applications of neoclassical models to the problems of agricultural economics.

Chief among the original dissenters were Thorstein B. Veblen (1857–1929), Wesley Clair Mitchell (1874–1948), and John R. Commons (1862–1945). They decried the narrowness of economic theory and sought answers to economic problems in a much broader context. These three and their intellectual descendants are the progenitors of "The Institutional School" of economic thought. The name "School" is hardly apt since there is only one common theme to which they all ascribed: the conventional teaching of mainstream economics fails to explain the economic phenomena of a modern, industrial world. Put another way, the main body of neoclassical economic theory and its analytical apparatus is not sufficient to explain all the decisions and choices that affect the efficiency of production or the distribution of rewards. Beyond that, there is little to unify the Institutionalists. To be sure, they did not study institutions at all! They had a vision that assumed that artifacts other than relative prices helped people to make "economic" decisions. Habits, rules, cultural imperatives, social pressure, laws, and the like all exerted force on choices. It was for later economists to define these as "institutions" and to gather Veblen, Commons, Mitchell, and others into the Institutional School.

Even though only a slim thread holds the Institutionalists together, their individual experiences and commentaries provide some lessons for contemporary agricultural economists. Discussion of the Institutionalists must be entered with some care since the unifying contention of the School was (and is) negative or desultory. In spite of this, some positive elements can be identified that will aid in the understanding of agricultural and rural problems. Here, they are attributed to their authors and are restricted to the contributions of the founding three: Veblen, Commons, and Mitchell.

Veblen is sometimes dismissed from economics and called a social philosopher, sociologist, or cultural anthropologist. Even within economics, he is best known for his knowledgeable critiques of the basic assumptions of economic theory and analysis. The critiques center on the notion that much of choice, allocation, and distribution stems from cultural or social behavior and that conventional economic theories fail to include these. His notions were written in exceedingly turgid prose, but they gained wide readership because of their provocative titles and an element of truth that appealed both to the technical and semitechnical audiences. Veblen's secondary theme, and one that was persistent in his writings, was the notion that the United States is a technological society that has been and is condemned to chronic social and economic disequilibrium because the pace of technological change will always outstrip society's ability to adjust to the technology that it has produced for itself.

Nowhere is this more evident than in agriculture. Since 1887, the year the original Hatch Act was passed, the federal government has maintained institutionalized support for improving agriculture. The public monies coupled with private and corporate research funds have improved almost every dimension of the way in which the industry converts factors into products and makes products available to consumers. Since the turn of the century, agricultural productivity in the United States has consistently outstripped domestic demand. Frequently, it has outstripped both domestic and foreign demand. Even in the face of chronic overproduction, neither agriculture nor society have been able to adjust to the stream of changes. Veblen's observations about the creation of technology and the adjustment to it has proven to be correct. In terms of an earlier section, agriculture's demand for adjustment mechanisms has shifted the demand for institutions upward and to the right. Attempts to satisfy this demand have been made by manipulating the role of the price mechanism, expanding the number of rules that affect resource use, and expanding nonfarm opportunities for farm-family adjustment. None has been effective, and, one suspects, that the traditional approaches to finding equilibrium of the industry will not increase in effectiveness as the twenty-first century approaches.

Commons was more disciplined than Veblen. His concern centered on the multiple influences than impinge upon a transaction. He championed collective action and the way in which tastes, demands, and concerns of an individual are eventually subjugated to the concerns of a group. His wish was that the old, conventional rules and assumptions of economic logic could be made adequate to the task of studying group subjugation, group behavior, and group choice. His writing is difficult and sometimes contradictory, but he attracted a wide following and had an important, although sometimes indirect, influence on agricultural economics – especially the group that was growing in size and stature at the University of Wisconsin in the 1920s and 1930s.[10] [11]

A large proportion of today's natural resource economists who study and/or advocate changes to perfect systems of property rights are, knowingly or not, following in the tradition and teaching of John R. Commons. Although he did not totally ignore agriculture, Commons turned the force of his intellectual genius toward labor economics, labor relations, and industrial organization. If the labor market was not behaving well, Commons suggested remedies. He was an activist in the economic affairs of his times. If his major interest had been agriculture, and if he had been properly situated, he would likely have been invited into the policy deliberations held by Rexford Tugwell, John D. Black, M. L. Wilson, G. F. Warren, and other early architects of today's agricultural policies. If this had taken place, it is possible that the whole structure of agricultural policy might have been different today. The man's pragmatism and eclecticism have become important attributes in the descriptions of the Institutional School of Thought.

Wesley Clair Mitchell abjured the deductive logic of price theory. He could not accept the basic deductive requirements of hedonism or the Utilitarians. His views on the logic of pleasure and pain can be simply put: Individuals have good, broad ideas of what actions (purchases, allocations of time, investments in things and people, etc.) will make a marginal contribution to their own happiness or well-being, but they cannot translate the broad notions into reasoning that allows tightly defined, rational choice in the supermarket. Alternatively, the broad thrusts of consumers are perfectly understandable; the fine adjustments to choice situations are beyond the analytic capacities of economics, and economists ought not to bother with these topics until the discipline is broadened and sophisticated (Mitchell 1912, 1914).

Mitchell is the easiest of the early institutionalists to discuss in a paper that is directed to agricultural economists, not because his contribution was less, but because it was more. Although Mitchell chose to turn away from the mainstream, he did not attempt to change the discipline (as Veblen may have been doing), nor did he become an advocate or a rule maker (as Commons was). He was an empiricist and began empirical observations that led to major theoretical and empirical breakthroughs in economists' understanding of business cycles and the measurement of aggregate output. The message has no unique importance to agricultural economists except insofar as agricultural economists are becoming increasingly oriented toward macroeconomics, cycles, and the distribution of income.

The institutionalism of Veblen, Commons, Mitchell, and their many followers does not provide automatic entree or even substantial clues to the systematic study of the institutions, rules, or regulations that affect agriculture. Their institutionalism is limited to agreement (sometimes conditional) that the most powerful analytic tools of mainstream economics are sometimes unable to sort out the causal factors that effect change in the relationships among economic variables. This is unfortunate because the time has come when it appears essential that members of this profession say more about the well-ordered group relationships that help define resources, determine the way resources are allocated, have impacts on efficiency, and, in some cases, determine the way in which income will be distributed. Explicitly, agricultural economists need to know or seek to know (1) the forces that cause changes or the desire for changes in institutions; (2) the effects individual institutions have on resource collections, production, distribution, and people; (3) the measures and methods that can be used to predict when institutional change will occur; and (4) how these aspects of institutions and research on institutions can be superimposed over (or rationalized with) the kinds of things that agricultural economists are ordinarily trained to do.

There is little doubt that both the quantitative and logical tools of analysis presently available to agricultural economists can help them effectively research a known or suggested change in rules. The fine points of the neoclassical model can be used with complete authority and assurance to analyze the extension of the minimum wage laws to agricultural labor, a change in a state's preferential tax treatment for agricultural land, or the switch from permit-allocated to market-allocated grazing rights. Many agricultural economists have done these kinds of studies. There is no defensible reason why either the number of agricultural economists or the proportion of agricultural economists involved in this type of work should decrease.

To go beyond this is, however, another question. The object of continued research in institutions or institutionalism should be to predict the need for change, the timing of change, and the intensity of change. No analytical model exists in economics or in any of the social sciences to meet this objective. One must start as Mitchell did in his early attempts to understand business fluctuations. He arranged and rearranged lengthy sets of time-series data that had not been used together in earlier research. The requirement for vast amounts of data is not new since all empirical work depends on data and measurement. What is new is the fact that the nature of the data that are needed is not known.

Moreover, headway in the study of institutional change may be stymied because the data needed for this work do not, and probably cannot, resemble the data required for other empirical work done by researchers in the profession. The problem is more severe. Two highly qualified, empirically oriented economists, one following the path broken by Mitchell, while the second worked at Commons' involvement in the creation of rules and laws, would likely require data of two different types. Those who study institutions, then, are separated from the main body of theorists and researchers by evidence (or the lack of evidence) as well as by disposition.

The enormity of the task can be emphasized by recalling Veblen's lasting concern: The society in which we work is superb at arranging for technological change, but must suffer continually from institutional obsolescence, stagnation, or decay. Part of this fundamental problem stems from the fact that those who conduct research related to technological change have a tremendous advantage—disaggregation. They employ many disciplines, but depend on the fact that technical processes can be disaggregated into many subprocesses and each subprocess can be examined separately for ways in which it can be improved. Wheel pulls belt; belt turns axle; axle turns gear; gear engages lever in a Rube Goldberg sequence that can invariably be favorably modified. At its end, the modification process yields a sophisticated, high-technology product. Any subsequence can be the candidate for improvement, and, if it is improved, similar subsequences in other processes can be similarly treated. Reaggregating the subsequence into a whole mechanism always increases performance by a minimum of one measure (such as output per unit of input).

At this time, it appears that no parallel disaggregating process is possible in the study of institutional change. The process of forming a market for a good that had previously been considered a public good cannot be usefully disaggregated to find what can be modified. Moreover, even if such disaggregation were possible it is doubtful that knowledge of the subsequence could be transferred from one institution to another. Until such disaggregations, subsequences, and transfers are possible or until general principles and premises can be found within studies of institutions, investigators will have to proceed on an ad hoc or case-by-case basis. The systematic study of institutional change will be so severely circumscribed as to make the process of inquiry frustrating to the point of intractability.

A Brief Summary

In many ways, this has been an impossible task. Any ten agricultural economists asked to comment on the institutions likely to affect farming and rural areas in the twenty-first century could have approached the problem in at least ten different ways. The present way has been to talk about a small number of institutions and institutional changes that are or will be affecting agriculture, then to comment on how institutions are formed and how they might be analyzed. All this was done within a framework that mentioned, but could not elaborate on, the Institutional School and its relationship to the ongoing body of economic thought and to the present paucity of understanding of the institutions that affect and effect change in U.S. agriculture and rural areas.

From any perspective, the task is only partially complete. Some other, fundamentally institution-based problems are now facing agriculture. Among them are redundancy of agricultural labor; the institution of the family farm; the historical importance of inflation as a means of coping with farm indebtedness; the inability of the social safety net to reach farm and rural people; the false but widespread idea that the world cannot, in the short run, feed its populations; and the increasing number of international regulations designed to cope with the increasing complexity of foreign trade in agricultural commodities. All these and dozens more could fill additional papers, pamphlets, and books with stories and analyses that tie agricultural economists to institutions. One major point remains: Vast numbers of institutions now impinge upon agriculture and rural areas. The number is so vast and their collective consequence is so great that agricultural economists could well describe institutions as a factor of production side by side with land, labor, capital, and entrepreneurial skill. If institutions are defined in this way, agricultural economists can use existing skills to research existing institutions or institutional changes that have identifiable dimensions. The present generation of agricultural economists or economic analysts cannot, however, understand or predict the formation of new institutions or the demise of those that are obsolete. This remains a major challenge to all agricultural economists. Those that accept the risks of the challenge can make phenomenal strides in helping this and the parent profession understand more about economics, agriculture, rules, and the factors of production.

Notes

1. In all fairness, it must be noted that the number of agricultural economists showing interest in institutions seems to be increasing. The inability of classical and neoclassical economics to cope with or explain the problems of the post–World War II industrial world and the inability of all economists to bridge the gap between microeconomics and macroeconomics brought foment among a group of young economists in the 1960s. The group evolved into the Association for Evolutionary Economists. Few issues of its quarterly publication, the *Journal of Economic Issues,* are devoid of articles by agricultural economists.

2. The Sagebrush Rebellion is a recurrent example of the kinds of problems that arise when several parties have interests in the same resources. The most recent rebellion (1979–1981) pitted environmentalists, agriculturalists, and mineral developers against the government in a see-saw battle of power, influence, and precedent. One suspects that nonfarm users will continue to dominate the controversy but will win only continuation of present rules (Nelson 1984a).

3. It is not clear that the income earned off the farm would have to come from labor. A farm family that had invested prudently in a successful portfolio could find this nonfarm, nonlabor source of income sufficient to sustain it. The point remains that farming must accommodate to contemporary trends and expect that large parts of the family's income need not come from the farm enterprise or labor of a designated head-of-household. Agricultural economists have been dismayingly obdurate in their dispositions about nonfarm contributions to family income.

4. An alternative is to make efforts to render existing agricultural resources less productive. In the past, this kind of policy has proved to be philosophically repugnant to most U.S. citizens who continue to be appalled by the memory of the AAA's killing animals and plowing down mature crops while more than 25 percent of the nation's labor force was unemployed. Intentional reductions in productivity seem to gain wide public acceptance only if they can be disguised as programs related to conservation.

5. Reviewers of early drafts had divergent views on this section of the paper. Some felt it should be discarded because Ruttan (1984) and Ruttan and Hayami (1984), Myrdal (1969), Olson (1982), Gruchy (1972), and others have already covered much of this ground and used much of this language in doing so. Other reviewers felt that this section did provide a useful framework for those in the profession who have lived apart from the study of institutions and/ or institutional change. One reviewer went so far as to comment with some vehemence that the supply and demand diagrams that economists are wont to draw are of little use in any context, especially the present one. A private conversation between the author and the commentator led to the commentator's admitting that the diagram that is now shown as Figure 12.1 had forced him to think out some relationships that prior to that time had been vague or without special importance. It is with this spirit in mind that I have elected to retain this section and its (perhaps overworked) pedagogical devices.

6. The removal or rescinding of institutions is a moot point. While a specific rule or institution may be summarily stricken from the books (as when, for example, the Supreme Court struck down major portions of the Agricultural Adjustment Act of 1933), the void left by its going is quickly filled with new sets of rules, themselves institutions. The Reagan Administration's efforts at deregulation is a major effort aimed at eliminating institutions that have governed the market-place behavior of railways, airlines, labor unions, stock (commodity) exchanges, and many other industries. The institutions that have been cast aside, however, are quickly replaced by the institutions of the price system or other allocative mechanisms. No one can say for sure if deregulation has brought a decrease or an increase in institutions.

7. The vague measuring system along the horizontal axis reduces the incisiveness and accuracy of knowledge about the combination of institutions defined by point A. Institutional change around point A could be of a compensating fashion that leaves the system in mock-equilibrium. This seems to be an unlikely and perhaps nonresearchable possibility.

8. Ottoson (1962), in an extremely perceptive article that compares institutional economics with neoclassical economics (production-distribution economics), stresses that there is no place for equilibrium in the Institutionalist scheme. It is quite possible that his observation carries over and describes the process of creating and removing institutions as well.

9. It will be noted that the mood of this paper is decidedly positive and egalitarian. Institutions are viewed as mechanisms to correct injustices and remove certain evils that accompany large social and economic organizations. This tone is, of course, naive. Institutions can be, and frequently are, designed to be self-serving and protectionist. Moreover, they frequently act as impediments to progress as that term is commonly understood.

10. Commons is one of the few institutionalists who touched on methods or on the ways economists should form problems. His interest and depth of knowledge of collective bargaining led him to conclude that one should study the transactions conducted in bilateral monopolies when a powerful union bargains with a powerful industry. These transactions,

rather than those consummated in the perfectly competitive wheat market, for example, would provide instruction on the correct performance of a pure transaction, and, when aggregated, would provide insight into a pure market.

11. Commons' major arguments appear in the several books he wrote on the relationships between law and economics and on, simply, institutional economics. The development of his interests and thought processes is chronicled in his sometimes mystical autobiography, *Myself,* which was commissioned by a group of his former students in 1932 and published in 1934 when Commons was 72.

References

Barkley, P. W. 1974. Public Goods in Rural Areas: Problems, Policies, and Population. *Am. J. Agric. Econ.* 56:1135–42.

———. 1976. A Contemporary Political Economy of Family Farming. *Am. J. Agric. Econ.* 58:812–19.

Commons, J. R. 1934. *Myself.* New York: Macmillan.

Crocker, T. D. 1971. Externalities, Property Rights, and Transaction Costs: An Empirical Study. *J. Law and Econ.* 14:451–64.

Davis, L., and D. C. North. 1971. Institutional Change and American Economic Growth: A First Step Towards a Theory of Institutional Innovation. *J. Econ. Hist.* 30:131–49.

Dorfman, J., C. Ayres, N. Chamberlain, S. Kuznets, and R. Gordon. 1963. *Institutional Economics: Veblen, Commons, and Mitchell Reconsidered.* Berkeley: Univ. of California Press.

Eddleman, B. R. 1969. Financing Public Service in Rural Areas: A Synthesis. *Am. J. Econ.* 56:959–63.

Elo, I. J., and C. L. Beale. 1983. *Natural Resources and Rural Poverty: An Overview.* Washington, D.C.: National Center for Food and Agricultural Policy, Resources for the Future, Inc.

Ericksen, M. H., and K. Collins. 1985. Effectiveness of Acreage Reduction Programs. In *Agricultural-Food Policy Review: Commodity Program Perspectives,* AER-530, 166–84. Washington, D.C.: USDA.

Georgescu-Roegen, N. 1976. *Energy and Economic Myths: Institutional and Analytic Essays.* Elmsford, N.Y.: Pergamon.

Gruchy, A. G. 1972. *Contemporary Economic Thought: The Contribution of Neo-Institutional Economics.* Clifton, N.J.: August M. Kelley.

Guither, H. D., J. P. Marshall, and P. W. Barkley. 1985. Adjustment Strategies to Reduce Resource Redundancies: Land and Labor. Credit Crisis Task Force Working Paper. Mimeo.

Harris, H. M., Jr. 1983. Milestones of U.S. Agricultural Policy. In *Agriculture in the Twenty-First Century,* ed. John W. Rosenblum. New York: John Wiley & Sons.

Harris, M. 1953. *Origin of the Land Tenure System in the United States.* Ames: Iowa State College Press.

Harris, P. E. 1985. A Legal View of the U.S. Property System. In *Transfer of Land Rights,* ed. D. D. Moyer and G. Wunderlich. Madison: Department of Agricultural Economics, Univ. of Wisconsin.

Hayami, Y., and V. W. Ruttan. 1971. *Agricultural Development: An International Perspective.* Baltimore: Johns Hopkins Univ. Press.

Hirsch, W. Z. 1968. The Supply of Urban Public Service. In *Issues in Urban Economics,* ed. H. S. Perloff and L. Wingo, Jr., 477–525. Baltimore: John Hopkins Univ. Press.

Hite, J. C. 1983. Resource Policy and American Agriculture. In *Agriculture in the Twenty-first Century,* ed. J. W. Rosenblum, 81–82. New York: John Wiley & Sons.

Hushak, L. J. 1983. Advantages and Limitations of Using Traditional Methods to Provide Local Public Services in a New Federalism Era. *Am. J. Agric. Econ.* 65:1118–23.

Jesse, E. G., A. C. Johnson, and A. B. Paul. 1982. User Fees, Deregulation, and Marketing Efficiency. *Am. J. Agric. Econ.* 64:909–15.

Johnson, G. L., and S. H. Wittwer. 1984. Agricultural Technology Until 2030: Prospects, Priorities, & Policies. Agricultural Experiment Station Special Report No. 12. East Lansing: Michigan State Univ.

Kuhn, T. S. 1985. Farmer Management of Hunting Opportunities on Private Farmlands in the Columbia Basin Project. Master's thesis, Washington State Univ.

Mitchell, W. C. 1912. The Backward Art of Spending Money. *Am. Econ. Rev.* 2:269–81.

_____. 1914. Human Behavior and Economics: A Review Article. *Q. J. Econ.* 29:1–27.

Myrdal, G. 1969. *Objectivity in Science Research.* New York: Pantheon Books.

Nelson, R. H. 1984a. Why the Sagebrush Revolt Burned Out. *Regulation* 8:27–35.

_____. 1984b. The Subsidized Sagebrush: Why the Privatization Movement Failed. *Regulation* 8:20–26.

North, D. C., and R. P. Thomas. 1969. An Economic Theory of Growth in the Western World. *Econ. Hist. Rev.* 23:1–17.

_____. 1971. The Rise and Fall of the Manorial System: A Theoretical Model. *J. Econ. Hist.* 31:777–803.

Olson, M. 1982. *The Rise and Decline of Nations.* New Haven: Yale Univ. Press.

Oser, J., and W. C. Blanchfield. 1975. *The Evaluation of Economic Thought.* 3rd ed. New York: Harcourt Brace Jovanovich.

Ottoson, H. R. 1962. Synthesis and Differentiation of Economic Theories. In *Land Economics Research,* ed. Joseph Ackerman et al. Baltimore: Johns Hopkins Univ. Press.

Piore, M. J., and C. F. Sabel. 1984. *The Second Industrial Divide: Possibilities for Prosperity.* New York: Basic Books.

Robbins, L. 1932. *An Essay on the Nature and Significance of Economic Science.* London: Macmillan.

Ruttan, V. R. 1984. Social Science Knowledge and Institutional Change. *Am. J. Agric. Econ.* 66:549–59.

Ruttan, V., and Y. Hayami. 1984. Toward a Theory of Induced Institutional Innovation. *J. Devel. Stud.* 20:203–23.

Schertz, L. P., and G. Wunderlich. 1982. Structure of Farming and Landownership in the Future: Implications for the Future. In *Soil Conservation Policies, Institutions, and Incentives,* ed. H. G. Halcrow et al. Ankeny, Iowa: Soil Conservation Society of America.

Schlesinger, A. M., Jr. 1960. *The Politics of Upheaval.* Boston: Houghton Mifflin.

Schmid, A. A. 1973. Analytical Institutional Economics: Challenging Problems in the Economics for a New Environment. *Am. J. Agric. Econ.* 54:893–900.

Suter, R. C. 1978. Estate Planning and Farm Property Transfer. Agricultural Experiment Station Bulletin 250. Lafayette: Purdue Univ.
_____. 1979. Estate Planning and Farm Property Transfer. Agricultural Experiment Station Bulletin 261. Lafayette: Purdue Univ.

Institutions and Agricultural Economics in the Twenty-first Century: A Discussion

THEODORE R. ALTER

Professor Barkley correctly argues that institutions play an important role in the evolution of the agricultural and rural economy. He outlines numerous emerging institutional issues likely to be significant for agricultural and rural areas. Barkley contends that, despite the pervasiveness and importance of institutions and institutional change, agricultural economists have devoted relatively little professional energy, expertise, and resources to studying the causes and consequences of alternative institutional arrangements. Furthermore, he observes that analytical frameworks for studying institutions emerging from the tradition of Institutionalism in economics are, for the most part, not well developed. His response to this situation is "Agricultural economists will be required to sharpen their skills in dealing with and researching the creation of institutions, the obsolescence or demise of institutional forms, and the effects that institutions have on the use of resources, the distribution of the product of these resources, and the perpetuation of a viable agriculture."

The main themes of Professor Barkley's assessment are on target. Agricultural economists have a long and rich history in the design and analysis of agricultural price and income policy (Brandow 1977) and of credit (Brake and Melichar 1977), marketing (Helmberger et al. 1981), and

Theodore R. Alter is Associate Professor of Agricultural Economics in the Department of Agricultural Economics and Rural Sociology, the Pennsylvania State University, University Park. Don Epp, Jim Hildreth, Patrick Madden, and Dan Moore provided helpful comments on post-conference versions of this paper.

natural resource (Castle et al. 1981) institutions affecting agricultural and rural areas. Agricultural economists have also done extensive work linking advances in natural science knowledge, technical change, and economic growth. On the other hand, the profession has made less progress in its "attempts to understand the contributions of advances in social science knowledge to institutional innovation or of the contributions of institutional innovation to economic, political, or social change" (Ruttan 1984, 549).

Beyond the challenges posed by Barkley's list of emerging issues, two additional important challenges must be addressed before agricultural economists can deal effectively with many of these issues. These challenges are noted in Barkley's assessment, but they deserve further elaboration. These two challenges involve giving increased emphasis to (1) theory and methods for studying institutions and institutional change; and (2) institutions and institutional change in research programs and in undergraduate and graduate curricula. Logically, meeting the first challenge is at least a partial precondition for meeting the second challenge.

Theory and Methods

Before one can study institutions and institutional change, it is necessary to have a conceptual or theoretical framework and an appropriate set of methodological tools. Perhaps some of our reluctance as a profession to study nonmarket institutions (specifically institutions other than the price system and those designed especially to modify the price system) is based on disenchantment with the theory and methods that have been used to study such institutions. Another possible explanation is the perceived inadequacy of orthodox economic theory for dealing with these nonmarket institutions.

Understanding the causes and consequences of various institutional arrangements (market and nonmarket) is obviously important for dealing effectively with many agricultural and rural nonfarm issues likely to be important in the future. Agricultural economists must devote increased resources to learning how to study nonmarket institutions and institutional change. We must make additional investment in advancing the development of appropriate and useful concepts, theories, research methods, and data bases.

Where do we look to get started on this task? First, we should look inward to our own profession. Historically, many agricultural economists working in the land economics tradition dealt with the causes and consequences of nonmarket institutions (Castle et al. 1981). Agricultural economists have continued to devote considerable effort to developing concepts, theories, and research methods and applying them to the study of nonmarket institutions. The work of A. Allan Schmid (1972, 1978), for example, provides an analytical framework that complements and supplements neoclassical economics; Schmid's work also suggests methods for conducting institutional analysis. To repeat, agricultural economists interested in learning more about how to study nonmarket institutions should look first to the traditions and experience of their own profession. (See also Bromley 1982; Kelso 1977; Parsons 1974; Ruttan 1984; Storey 1978; and Shaffer 1969).

Second, we must look beyond our own discipline. We can learn much about studying institutions and institutional change from scholarship in political science, sociology, psychology, law, anthropology, philosophy, history, and other humanities and social science disciplines. The suggestion does not mean we should necessarily become political scientists, psychologists, or anthropologists as well as economists. Rather, we should become students of these disciplines. By casting our inquiry beyond the bounds of economics we may well discover concepts, theories, and research methods that we can adapt and incorporate with those of economics to help us better study the political economy of nonmarket institutions and institutional change. Such a multidisciplinary strategy may pose professional risks for some agricultural economists in some institutional circumstances. But, the risks must be carefully weighed against three kinds of potential benefits: (1) more penetrating insight into the multidisciplinary complexities of institutions and institutional change, (2) advances in institutional theory and analysis, and (3) improved ability to assist decision makers in clarifying and resolving institutional issues.

Research and Teaching Programs

As Professor Barkley has pointed out previously, skills in problem recognition may be the most neglected part of the training of contemporary agricultural economists (Barkley 1984, 801). The holistic perspective and multidisciplinary orientation required for studying nonmarket institutions and institutional change in a rapidly evolving political economy may very well have its greatest payoff in imparting to researchers and students greater skills in problem identification and definition. Improved problem identification and definition can provide more fruitful hypotheses regarding market as well as nonmarket issues important in agricultural and rural areas.

The issues outlined by Barkley provide a starting point as to what should be studied, but they do not go far enough. The following list of topics and questions is suggestive of other important areas of study.

1. Descriptive analyses of past as well as current nonmarket institutions and institutional change would provide the evolutionary context and

experiential base for studying the causes and consequences of emerging institutional innovations.

2. Study of the evolution of institutional analysis would provide a means for examining theory and methods for analyzing institutions and institutional change from the perspective of agricultural economics and other disciplines. It would also provide the context for further improvements in theory and methods for institutional analysis.

3. Through what institutional arrangements is demand for institutional innovation articulated?

4. What factors foster institutional innovation in different institutional settings? Conversely, what factors inhibit such innovation?

5. How do existing institutional arrangements distribute power, authority, and opportunity among individuals, families, groups, and communities?

6. How would proposed alternatives to existing institutional arrangements change the distributions of power, authority, and opportunity?

Summary

While agricultural economists have given primary attention to analysis of market institutions, the profession also has a tradition of interest and experience in analyzing nonmarket institutions and institutional change affecting agricultural and rural areas. This tradition provides a foundation for increasing agricultural economists' capability to understand and analyze nonmarket institutions and to contribute to the problem-solving needs of decision makers in both the public and private sectors. A first step in building on this foundation involves looking within agricultural economics and reaching out to other disciplines to learn more about studying institutions. A second important step involves incorporating this enhanced analytical capability in research programs and making nonmarket institutions a focal point in undergraduate and graduate teaching. These steps will help agricultural economists deal more effectively with institutional issues that will shape the future of agriculture, natural resources, and rural areas.

References

Barkley, P. W. 1984. Rethinking the Mainstream. *Am. J. Agric. Econ.* 65:798–801.

Brake, J. R., and E. Melichar. 1977. Agricultural Finance and Capital Markets. In *A Survey of Agricultural Economics Literature,* ed. L. R. Martin, vol. 1, 416–94. Minneapolis: Univ. of Minnesota Press.

Brandow, G. E. 1977. Policy for Commercial Agriculture, 1945–1971. In *A Survey of Agricultural Economics Literature,* ed. L. R. Martin, vol. 1, 209–92. Minneapolis: Univ. of Minnesota Press.

Bromley, D. W. 1982. Land and Water Problems: An Institutional Perspective. *Am. J. Agric. Econ.* 64:834–44.

Castle, E. N., M. M. Kelso, J. B. Stevens, and H. H. Stoevenor. 1981. Natural Resource Economics, 1946–1975. In *A Survey of Agricultural Economics Literature,* ed. L. R. Martin, vol. 3, 393–500. Minneapolis: Univ. of Minnesota Press.

Helmberger, P. G., G. R. Campbell, and W. D. Dobson. 1981. Organization and Performance of Agricultural Markets. In *A Survey of Agricultural Economics Literature,* ed. L. R. Martin, vol. 3, 503–652. Minneapolis: Univ. of Minnesota Press.

Kelso, M. M. 1977. Natural Resource Economics: The Upsetting Discipline. *Am. J. Agric. Econ.* 59:814–23.

Parsons, K. H. 1974. The Institutional Basis of an Agricultural Market Economy. *J. Econ. Issues* 13:737–57.

Ruttan, V. W. 1984. Social Science Knowledge and Institutional Change. *Am. J. Agric. Econ.* 65:549–59.

Schmid, A. A. 1972. Analytical Institutional Economics: Challenging Problems in the Economics of Resources for a New Environment. *Am. J. Agric. Econ.* 54:893–901.

_____. 1978. *Property, Power, and Public Choice: An Inquiry Into Law and Economics.* New York: Praeger.

Shaffer, J. 1969. On Institutional Obsolescence and Innovation—Background for Professional Dialogue on Public Policy. *Am. J. Agric. Econ.* 51:245–67.

Storey, G. 1978. Institutional Economics and Political Economy Revisited: Implications for Agricultural Economics. *Am. J. Agric. Econ.* 60:749–58.

Institutions and Agricultural Economics in the Twenty-first Century: **A Discussion**

RONALD C. POWERS

The original program indicated that we would be discussing "Changes in Agricultural and Rural Institutions." I would have preferred that Professor Barkley bring his considerable skill and capacity to bear on such changes and focus less on the lackluster history of institutionalism in the profession of agricultural economics. I would have liked to see attention focused on institutional failures and successes in addressing the many problems facing agriculture and rural America. I believe, however, that Professor Barkley may have done what was possible, namely, an examination of the central role of institutions in agriculture and rural areas, and thus the need for the profession of agricultural economics to be more attentive to institutions as "allocators of land, labor, capital, and entrepreneurial skill." I concur with Barkley's argument, "that agricultural economists cannot continue to ignore the changing institutions that impinge upon farming and rural areas," yet his paper only briefly considers those changing institutions.

Barkley's list of eleven contemporary issues affecting agriculture is very worthwhile in my judgment, and it holds the seeds of several important research priorities that should be pursued immediately. He points to the institutional impacts on factor and product markets, bundles of property rights, water rights and uses, marketization of regulated industries, public services, separation of land ownership from operation, conflicting institutional objectives in promoting increased and reduced production and the like. This is an excellent starter list of institutional phenomena that should be studied.

I would add to that list the following items: (1) the impact of the urban mind-set on institutions derived to serve the needs of rural people (such as the training programs, Job Services, and determination of unemployment rates and eligibility criteria); (2) the impact of the "sudden shift" by financial institutions from *asset-based* financing of agriculture to *cash flow* financing; and (3) the impact of the entire milieu of institutions related to environmental quality and safety (i.e., air pollution, water pollution, erosion controls, use of pesticides and insecticides, drinking water standards, solid waste disposal, etc.).

Ronald C. Powers is Associate Dean and Director, University Extension, and Professor of Sociology at Iowa State University, Ames.

I found little of intellectual substance in the effort to conceptualize the supply and demand of institutions in the usual supply/demand framework. The two axes are both so ambiguous as to be basically worthless. The analytical techniques used by Robert Paarlberg (as discussed in Chapter 3) to discover institutional changes are more to my liking. One could also profitably follow the "social power" model central to the Weberian tradition. The extension of the framework to hypothesizing the relationships between institutions and GNP is fraught with the same problems. The concept of optional level in institutional supply and demand is a graphic artifact. It is not real, it cannot be known, and if theoretically possible, it would last only momentarily because the cause of institutional arrangements is people. Perhaps the most important limitation is the separation of institutionally induced versus market induced changes. The market is after all, as Barkley observes, an aggregate of institutions.

Barkley's review and discussion of Veblen, Commons, and Mitchell was interesting and I benefited from the review. However, its relevance to future research, teaching, and extension programming in agricultural economics seems problematic at best. I find myself not entirely consistent on this point, however, because I firmly believe that today's agricultural economists are too narrowly trained and too oriented to quantitative analysis. One wonders why more effort is not devoted to achieving such breadth. However, a quick review of what departmental peers do during the tenure review process explains much of the fascination with highly quantitative work.

My second, third, and fourth impulse is to support Barkley's call for more research resources for the institutional aspects of problems in agriculture and rural America. As a person responsible for managing extension programs, I continue to be disturbed by the minimal number of agricultural economists interested in and prepared to conduct research, and eventually extension programs, on agricultural and rural community institutions. It is said that more dollars from experiment stations and/or extension services would solve this problem. I do not believe it. I believe that more agricultural economists would propose to do research in these areas if resources were added, but I am not convinced that the research would be conceptualized and carried out in a way that would avoid the major limitations of *ceteris paribus,* that analytic trap that is the bane of those involved with making decisions based on economic research.

My first impulse is to question the continued institutional linkages of research and extension rural development programs to agricultural economics. Researchers in public administration, business administration, and the like are not bound by the traditions and models (institutions, if you please) of the agricultural economist. So, while the historical institutional context of agricultural economics would seem to suggest a very strong commitment to examine the impact of the institutional mix and development on the well-being of rural areas, the question is whether the potential will be realized. The need is there. The rhetoric is there among a small set of practicing agricultural economists—or is it economists in agricultural economics departments? The "pull" is there among extension and experiment station administrators. The "push" is not widespread within the profession. Professor Barkley has taken an unusually kind and circumspect way to say the latter. Relevance is the elixer for determining the standing of academic departments within the body politic. The current difficulties in agricultural and rural areas call out for agricultural economics to be relevant for the farm, the firm, and the institutional milieu within which farms, firms, families, and communities strive to realize well-being. It is not too early for agricultural economics to move in that direction.

Institutions and Agricultural Economics in the Twenty-first Century: A Discussion

PHILIP M. RAUP

A point of departure for any projection of the role of institutions in agricultural economics is provided by the increasing acceptance of the perception that institutions are man-made and malleable—"susceptible of being fashioned or molded."

One of the most durable articles of faith in the economics literature traces from Adam Smith's conclusion over two centuries ago that an individual seeking his own gain "necessarily labours to render the annual revenue of the society as great as he can . . . he is in this, and in many other cases, led by an invisible hand to promote an end that was no part of his intention" (Smith 1937, 423).

In the mainstream of western economic thought, the nonvolitional nature of Smith's observation reenforced the tendency to accept institutions as given and to leave the explanation of their origins and functions to other disciplines. Almost two centuries later, Frederich von Hayek echoed Smith's point by referring to "spontaneously grown institutions," conclud-

Philip M. Raup is Professor Emeritus with the Department of Agricultural and Applied Economics, University of Minnesota, St. Paul.

ing that "the independent actions of individuals will produce an order which is no part of their intentions" (von Hayek 1955, 40). Note here that Adam Smith was referring to the social revenue, von Hayek to the social order (i.e., to the institutional structure).

This mainstream view of institutions as exogenous to the proper study of economics persisted into the second half of the twentieth century. This is changing. An increasing body of contemporary economic analysis seeks to include institutions within the framework of variables to be studied. Institutions governing economic behavior are being endogenized (Davis and North 1971; Ruttan and Hayami 1984). In tailoring a view of institutions appropriate to the twenty-first century, the dominant fact is that institutions are no longer regarded as "spontaneously grown." They now must be included among tools of the economist that are capable of being tested for fitness by functional tests.

Paul Barkley has given us an able summary of the background to this transformation, as it concerns agricultural economics. The comments that follow should be read as an elaboration of points raised in his paper that merit our specific attention.

What happened to affect our view of the role of institutions in economic life? There are no simple answers to this question. We can begin by noting the changing nature of production. It once had a direct connotation of material goods. It can no longer have this meaning. Economists always did presume that production included services, but analysis of the service economy simply was not a focus of interest in the classical and neoclassical economics tradition. The analytical tools of the economist, and the theory and data bases that make possible their use, were developed primarily to serve the goods economy. They function uncomfortably when confronting the service economy. This is reflected in and reenforced by a neglect of the role of institutions.

Many of the basic assumptions underlying the nature of prices, markets, capital stocks, transaction costs, and consumer preferences are difficult to apply to the production and exchange of services. In measuring supply and demand, the role of institutional arrangements in conditioning the demand side is of much greater importance for services than for goods. On the supply side, measurements of productivity and efficiency can be adapted to production of services, but performance tests developed by economists have been designed primarily with tangible goods in mind. With 74 percent of the U.S. labor force employed in the service sector, and over 25 percent of total GNP accounted for by expenditures on education, training, and health care alone, it is not surprising that the importance of institutions in economic analysis is increasing.

A second reason why the role of institutions in economic affairs is receiving renewed attention traces from the growing concern about environmental protection. A modern society has a greatly increased capacity to modify (and damage) environments that are dependent upon land, water, and air. The effects fall largely outside the immediate decision-making framework of individuals and firms using these resources. Any corrective measures involve the creation of new institutions to enable individuals and firms to cope with new problems. The outstanding example is the change that has taken place in the interpretation of private property rights in land and water.

The pressure for institutional change generated by environment concerns is in turn a reflection of a third reason why the study of institutional structures has expanded in recent decades: An unprecedented proportion of the population in highly developed countries now lives in rural areas but is not primarily involved in agriculture. This creates one of the most powerful reasons why the study of institutions is of particular importance to agricultural economics. Rural can no longer be equated with agricultural in any demographic analysis. Rural nonfarm populations are in the ascendancy.

Environmental concerns suggest that much of any cutback in the volume of agricultural output may occur in areas that depend heavily on agricultural chemicals and that have a large proportion of nonfarm rural residents. Land-use controls in these areas are likely to be insistently demanded by nonfarm residents, not only to protect their rural residential land values from competing nonfarm land uses, but to restrain agricultural land uses.

In Minnesota in 1980, the rural non-farm population outnumbered the farm population in every county. This was also true in Iowa in all but five counties. This relationship exists in all but a few counties of the corn-soybean and wheat belts of the Midwest, the dairy belts of the Northeast and the Great Lakes states, and the agricultural counties of the Gulf and Pacific Coast states. Farmers are becoming a minority group in their own communities even in traditional farming regions.

This has increased the demand for institutional change in rural areas to accommodate residents for whom natural resources are consumer goods, not producer goods. Significant components of rural resources of land and water are being transferred from the goods economy to the service economy. An inescapable consequence is that institutions once adequate for the needs of a farming community are no longer functional for the emerging suburbanized, commuter, and rural-residential communities.

A fourth reason lies in the revolution in communication that is now well under way. It is instructive to note that the major changes in rules and procedures governing rights in land in the nineteenth and first three-quarters of the twentieth centuries were the consequence of a transport revolution, first in rail, then in road and air transport. Modern concepts of eminent domain, or the right of the state to exercise its sovereignty over private land, were shaped by the need to acquire rights-of-way for railroads. This was as true in Europe as it was in the United States. In the twentieth century this process was repeated, and the power of the state expanded to affect a much larger proportion of agricultural land in acquiring right-of-way for big highways.

The erosion of core urban areas has been primarily a consequence of good roads and the private motor car. The resultant demand for urban renewal, coupled in the United States with the massive program of right-of-way acquisition for the interstate highway system, led to historic redefinition of the boundary between public and private rights in land. Until the 1950s, a taking of private land through eminent domain was confined to its acquisition for a public *use*. In the 1980s, the Supreme Court, in a case involving Hawaiian land has confirmed the taking of private lands for a public *purpose* (467 U.S. 229, 1984).

This shift in one of the most basic rules regulating rights in land is a milestone in the history of the evolution of an institution. It has many roots, but it seems valid to conclude that it was triggered by a revolution in transportation.

What subsequent shifts in basic institutions of property rights will be triggered by the communications revolution? It is unquestionably a major driving force in the growth of the service economy. It is opening new possibilities for the decentralization of economic activity into previously rural areas. It promises to introduce new dimensions to the phenomenon of part-time farming. In agriculture, it is redefining market areas and institutions for both input supply and product markets. If any single force can be identified as most likely to shape institutional structures in the twenty-first century, it is the revolution in communications and the falling real cost of information.

This prospect acquires special poignancy for those agricultural economists interested in the role of institutions. Historically in the United States, one of the most distinctive assets of the agricultural economics discipline has been its unmatched data base. This has conditioned the discipline, stimulated the development of analytical tools, and enabled it to retain contact with contemporary economic affairs while much of the larger discipline of general economics has devoted its best talent to increasingly abstract analysis.

It must now be acknowledged that there is a danger that the process of capital renewal of this data base is being neglected. One of Paul Barkley's most telling observations is his conclusion that, "Sadly, the data needed by the institutionalists do not resemble the data required for other empirical work in the profession." To this must be added the observation that the collection and analysis of data on the institutional structure of agriculture is currently in eclipse in the U.S. Department of Agriculture. This is occurring at a time when the potential for structural change in American agriculture is perhaps at its highest point since the Civil War.

Already enmeshed in a communication revolution, facing the prospect of massive land-use conflicts in rural areas, and standing at the threshold of a biochemical transformation of agricultural production, this is a strange time to be underinvesting in our institutional base. The comparative advantage of agricultural economics is threatened with internal decay.

The evidence supporting this conclusion lies in the fact that we are increasingly unable to measure the degree of functional specialization and concentration of economic power in agriculture. Farms classified by gross value of products sold yield meaningless measures at both the upper and lower ends of the size distribution, if the data are not corrected to show value added in production. Generalized data to permit this correction are not available.

While the number of farms and farm operators has steadily been declining since 1940, the number of farm landowners, and especially of nonfarm landlords, had more than doubled by 1978 (Boxley 1985). We lack a continuing data series to track this trend and, thus, to distinguish between farm program benefits that accrue to farm operators and those that benefit primarily landowners. With a major restructuring of federal farm policy in 1985, we do not really know how the benefits of current policies are shared, and who in fact are the ultimate beneficiaries.

This is a measure of lack of concern about the importance of the institutional structure in determining patterns of equity in distribution of the gains from investment in agriculture. If the goal is to mobilize national support for a farm policy that can credibly be claimed to be in the public interest, then greater attention will need to be given to the effect of the institutional structure. It can support or defeat farm policy goals. As agriculture sheds its aura of atomistic competition, the capacity of its institutions to yield benefits or harm increases. This alone should be sufficient reason for agricultural economists to incorporate institutional change into their research agenda for the twenty-first century.

References

Boxley, R. F. 1985. Farmland Ownership and the Distribution of Land Earnings. Washington, D.C.: USDA, ERS-NRED, May 31.

Davis, L. E., and D. C. North. 1971. *Institutional Change and American Economic Growth*. New York: Cambridge Univ. Press.

Hawaii Housing Authority et al. v. *Midkiff et al.* 1984. 467 *U.S.* 229.

Ruttan, V., and Y. Hayami. 1984. Toward a Theory of Induced Institutional Innovation. *J. Devel. Stud.* 20:203–23.

Smith, A. 1937. *An Inquiry Into the Nature and Causes of the Wealth of Nations*. New York: Modern Library.

von Hayek, F. 1952. *The Counter-revolution of Science*. Glencoe, Ill.: The Free Press.

13

The Macroeconomics of Agriculture and Rural America

G. EDWARD SCHUH and DAVID ORDEN

This paper addresses some challenges we face as we seek to understand the development of U.S. agriculture in an increasingly interdependent world economy, and as we seek to formulate appropriate policies for this sector. These are challenges in the macroeconomics of agriculture and related macroeconomic effects on rural communities.

As we undertake the task of addressing these challenges, it has become commonplace at the university where we recently resided to argue that macroeconomics occupies an interesting chapter in the history of economic doctrine, but it is of little value beyond that. From this perspective, what matters are the microeconomics of markets, the theory of the business cycle, and/or the theory of money. For the senior author, this cycle has gone full term. When he was a graduate student at the University of Chicago, he too studied microeconomics and the theory of money, wrote a preliminary examination in each field, and diligently studied *The General Theory* by Keynes to know why Mr. Keynes got it wrong. Keynesian economics, of course, is what in this lexicon is macroeconomics.

Despite these considerations, we have kept "macroeconomics" in our title for two rather simple reasons. First, there is still considerable debate about whether neoKeynesian macroeconomics is in fact discredited. Second, we want to give the concept a more general, and not so uncommon, interpretation to refer to the aggregate aspects of the economy. As our

G. Edward Schuh is Director, Agriculture and Rural Development, The World Bank, Washington, D.C. David Orden is Assistant Professor of Agricultural Economics, Virginia Polytechnic Institute and State University, Blacksburg. The authors wish to thank their reviewers for comments on an earlier draft of this paper.

point of departure, we take agriculture as a whole and think about it in the context of the economy as a whole, with the emphasis on how such things as monetary, fiscal, exchange rate, and trade policy affect the sector.

A major challenge facing our profession is that contemporary thinking on these issues is in a state of considerable flux. Moreover, much of the new classical or rational expectations perspective central to this discussion has not yet penetrated either the thinking about U.S. agriculture or the empirical work on the agricultural sector.[1] We have tried to resolve the many dilemmas that arise in addressing the macroeconomics of agriculture under these circumstances by examining the pragmatic implications of recent changes in the international economy and the institutional challenges posed by its management without ignoring some of the theoretical and econometric controversies that arise in contemporary analysis of these issues.

The general outline of our paper is as follows. First, we provide a general equilibrium perspective on agriculture and discuss some of its obvious implications. Second, we discuss the rather dramatic integration that has taken place in the world economy over the past 20 years and the role of the United States in the economic setting that has emerged. This is followed by a brief discussion of modern macroeconomic theory and of some controversial issues in the evaluation of macroeconomic policy. We then posit a conceptual analysis of the effects of macroeconomic policy on trade sectors in an integrated world economy and review recent empirical estimates of the magnitude of these impacts on agriculture. Last we consider some policy issues and needed institutional reforms. As we proceed, we attempt to identify some of the challenges raised for our profession by the issues that are addressed.

A General Equilibrium Perspective on Agriculture

The agricultural economics literature is replete with studies of this important sector of the U.S. economy. Unfortunately, a disappointingly large share of these studies are cast in a partial equilibrium, closed economy model. Such a perspective was probably not all that inappropriate as long as trade was not very important to agriculture or to the economy as a whole and as long as an international capital market was also relatively insignificant. In today's world, however, where trade is important to both agriculture and the rest of the economy, and where there have been other changes in how the United States relates to the international economy, that perspective can be dangerously misleading. Changes in the world economy and agriculture's role in it have greatly enhanced the relevance of general equilibrium considerations when evaluating the agricultural sector.

RELATIVE PROTECTION. Perhaps the best way to gain insight into the consequences of these two different perspectives is to consider a number of important issues where the distinction between partial and general equilibrium analysis is important. An obviously relevant issue in contemporary policy is whether policy is protective of agriculture or discriminatory towards it. If agriculture or a subsector of it constitutes a traded-good sector, a useful way to analyze this question is to evaluate the protection provided. A naive approach to this analysis would consider the nominal protection created by either tariffs or direct subsidies. A more sophisticated perspective, which would take account of some general equilibrium implications, would recognize the need to study *effective* protection and take into account the impacts of tariffs and taxes (both positive and negative) on inputs as well as the product market. Distortions in the value of the nation's currency would also be taken into consideration.

For many analysts, measurement of effective protection would convey the full policy impact on agriculture. But by focusing on only one sector, even this more sophisticated perspective tells only one part of the story. In general, there will be some degree of protection or taxation of other sectors in the economy as well. And, the *relative* protection or taxation is what matters in the final analysis, not the protection or taxation of one sector alone. It is the relative protection that determines relative social profitability. Thus, even though there is positive effective protection of the agricultural sector, the relative social profitability of agriculture may be weak if the rest of the economy has an even greater level of protection. It is relative social profitability that determines relative prosperity among sectors and the direction of investment flows.

Such issues are implicit in contemporary discussions of farm policies, but they are seldom brought out.[2] These issues come to the fore when the theory of second best is applied. The naive perspective is that establishing a free-market policy for U.S. agriculture would lead to a more efficient allocation of resources in the aggregate compared to the present distorted situation. This is piecemeal policy analysis, and, in general, the recommended policy is wrong. As long as there are other distortions in the economy, the second-best policy may be to provide agriculture with the same degree of "protection" as prevails elsewhere. Since agriculture is an export sector and there is apparently net tariff protection of about 10 percent on the rest of the U.S. economy, the ideal policy for agriculture, at least from the perspective of national resource allocation, may be an equivalent export subsidy.[3]

This reasoning points to other general equilibrium dimensions of agricultural policy. In particular, an overvalued currency is both an export tax and import subsidy and thus discriminates against trade sectors. When one recognizes that the U.S. dollar was overvalued during most of the 1950s and 1960s, the interpretation of the past history of U.S. agriculture and its policy is quite different from generally accepted versions.[4] In general, contemporary discussions of U.S. agriculture have been misguided for their failure to recognize this important issue.

Still another sense in which a general equilibrium perspective contributes to a more enlightened policy discussion is in terms of the measurement of relative social profitability. Historically, the index used to evaluate the relative economic condition of U.S agriculture is the agricultural parity index: the ratio of product prices to input prices. Among the many deficiencies associated with this concept, a serious problem is that it is based on a partial equilibrium, sectoral perspective and thus is too narrow. More relevant are the domestic terms of trade (namely, the price of agricultural goods and services relative to the prices of all other final products and services in the economy). In general, the domestic terms of trade may be quite different from the parity index.

OUTPUT AND FACTOR MARKETS. A general equilibrium approach centers policy considerations on linkages of the agricultural sector to other sectors of the economy. Perhaps the most important of these linkages is addressed by the notion of food as a wage good. As a wage good, the price of food is an important determinant of real wage rates. Real wage rates, in turn, are an important determinant of relative profitability of nonfarm sectors of the economy. If the price of food declines steadily, wage earners can experience a rise in their real wage with no rise in the nominal wage. This will enable export sectors to compete more effectively in international markets, other things being equal. It will also influence relative profitability among nonfarm sectors, depending on the relative intensity with which they use labor. In addition, as a wage good, the price of food can be quite a sensitive political issue, as experience has demonstrated time and again.

To fully appreciate the significance of the intersectoral wage-good linkage one needs only to go back to the community price boom of the early 1970s. The significance of food as a wage good became readily apparent at that time and macroeconomists and general policymakers became concerned about the price of food after a long period of ..eglect. Their concern was briefly translated into an export embargo and later into interest in whether increased agricultural exports were good or bad for the economy as a whole.[5]

In the United States, the expansion of the food stamp program probably attenuated some of the wage-good effects of food prices during the 1970s. However, as support for the food stamp program declines, if food prices rise sharply these issues may surface again, especially in light of the general increase in United States dependence on trade.

The implicit wage-good effect also probably explains why there was such strong support for agricultural research from almost all sectors of the economy as long as U.S. agricultural exports were relatively small and agriculture was essentially a closed economy. It may also explain why there has been a decline in support for such research as agriculture has become increasingly dependent on trade. With dependence on trade, a larger share of the benefits of agricultural research are passed on to foreign customers or captured by producers as economic rents, either to the relatively fixed supply of land or to entrepreneurial-innovative skills in limited supply.

A second important linkage between agriculture and other sectors of the economy arises among factor markets. This linkage works two ways, and again a general equilibrium approach provides an interesting perspective. In one direction, wage rates, nonfarm employment opportunities, the cost of borrowing and of using capital, and the cost of purchased inputs are important determinants of resource use in agriculture and the composition and level of output from the sector. A broad array of monetary, tax, fiscal, trade, and industrial policies impact on agriculture through their effects on these factors. In the other direction, agriculture provides resources for other sectors, and agricultural policy is an important determinant of this resource flow. Production control programs provide an interesting case in point. These programs release land, labor, and other resources to the non-farm sector, thereby lowering the price of these factors in the general economy.[6] This tendency reinforces the wage-good effect. Again, this may have contributed to the willingness of the nonfarm sector to accept such programs in the past. The absence of effective production controls in recent years, together with relatively high target and loan levels for export crops, is working in the opposite direction. One consequence may be erosion of the political support for agriculture.

Changes in the International Economy

The international economy and the way that individual economies relate to it have undergone drastic changes in the last 20 years. These changes have dramatically altered the economics of agriculture and how one must think about the agricultural sector.

INCREASED DEPENDENCE ON TRADE. Contrary to the trade-pessimistic mentality that prevailed at the end of World War II, since the war international trade has grown at a faster rate than world GNP in all but three years. The growth trend in world trade accelerated in the 1970s and the United States became increasingly related to the rest of the world through trade. The dependence of U.S. agriculture on exports doubled during the decade, as did the dependence on trade of many other sectors of the economy. By the 1980s, the American economy as a whole was essentially as open to trade as the economies of Western Europe as a whole or Japan.[7]

The economy's becoming more open has important policy implications for both the general economy of the United States and its agricultural sector. Perhaps of most significance is that the domestic economy becomes increasingly beyond the reach of domestic policies. This has been a major source of frustration in the U.S. where policymakers and the public expect much more direct control. In the case of agriculture, the problem is not that the government has not been doing anything. The problem is that the impacts of governmental policies designed for the domestic economy are literally swamped by forces from the international economy.

EMERGENCE OF A WELL INTEGRATED INTERNATIONAL CAPITAL MARKET. At the end of World War II, there was virtually no such thing as an international capital market. There were transfers of capital from one country to another, but these were largely on a government-to-government basis in the form of foreign aid.

By the early 1960s an international capital market began to emerge. A Eurodollar market developed as European banks discovered they could loan the dollars they had on deposit. This market grew very rapidly, eventually expanding into a Eurocurrency market as the banks discovered they could lend other currencies as well. The international capital market continued to expand through the 1960s; then it was propelled forward by the OPEC-induced petroleum crisis of 1973, which generated petrodollars in hugh amounts. We seem to forget today that the banking community in the 1970s was enjoined to recycle these dollars to keep the international economy from collapsing. This they did to a fault, to the current chagrin of the banks and of many less developed countries now burdened with excessive debt.

The important fact about the Eurocurrency market is that it is now huge. Although it is difficult to measure precisely, a widely accepted estimate is that the total amount of credit this market had outstanding at the beginning of the 1980s was about $1.7 trillion. That is approximately commensurate with the total annual value of international trade at that time.

Since 1980, the international capital market has continued to burgeon. The total amount of international financial flows was approximately $40 trillion by 1984, while the total value of international trade was approximately $2 trillion. Moreover, almost all countries use the international capital market in one form or another. Hence, the international capital market has become as important in tying the economies of the world together as international trade itself. In addition, as we will describe, it ties economic policies together in ways they were not tied together before.

THE SHIFT TO FLEXIBLE EXCHANGE RATES. At the Bretton Woods meeting after World War II, it was agreed that countries would fix the value of their currencies in terms of currencies of other countries and change them only under dire circumstances. The objective was to keep individual countries from "dumping" their domestic problems abroad. The expectation was that disequilibrium in the external accounts, or problems of unemployment, would be managed by changes in domestic monetary and fiscal policy, not by competitive devaluations.

This system of fixed exchange rates served the industrialized countries reasonably well for almost 30 years. For a variety of reasons, including inappropriate U.S. monetary and fiscal policies, this system came under a great deal of stress in the late 1960s and early 1970s. President Nixon devalued the dollar in 1971 to alleviate this stress, then devalued it again in 1973, eventually letting the dollar float to an exchange value determined in international markets.

The flexible exchange rate monetary system that has emerged since 1973 is essentially a system of bloc-floating. Many individual countries tie the value of their currency to the value of a major currency such as the U.S. dollar, the British pound, the French franc, or the German deutsch mark. While this may give the appearance of a great deal of fixity in the system, as the major currencies float against one another, most countries experience realignment of their currency values. Recent estimates suggest that approximately 85 percent of international trade takes place across such flexible exchange rates. This shift to an essentially flexible exchange rate regime is de facto recognition that in light of the large volume of international trade and financial flows, governments can no longer fix the value of national currencies.

INCREASED MONETARY INSTABILITY. International monetary conditions were quite stable during the 1950s and 1960s. Starting about 1968, however, this desirable situation changed, for reasons that no one seems to fully understand. Monetary policy in the United States, in particular, has been quite unstable during this period, being variously classified as stop-and-go, erratic, or zig-zag. Monetary instability in the United States has been exacerbated by conditions in other countries, resulting in large fluctuations in world monetary aggregates.

The significance of increased monetary instability for the agricultural sector is that it has occurred when agriculture has become increasingly vulnerable to changes in monetary conditions. As a result, an important part of the instability of U.S. agriculture over the 1970s and 1980s has been due to monetary instability, and not to the weather as is frequently argued.

Theoretical Issues in Macroeconomics

In addition to changes in the international economy, there are some controversies in macroeconomic theory that are also central to our concerns with the macroeconomics of agriculture and rural America. In this section we briefly examine the modern classical and the neoKeynesian fixed-price/flex-price macroeconomic models and discuss some issues in the definition and measurement of macroeconomic policy.

THE MODERN CLASSICAL MODEL: THE CRUCIAL ROLE OF EXPECTATIONS.

Recognizing the role of expectations in determining the outcomes of specific real shocks or government actions has been a critical insight of modern macroeconomics. Rather than being viewed as an application of policy measures to a passive public, the effects of government policy are seen to arise in a fluid context in which the public responds to policy measures in a fashion determined by its own optimizing logic. As a result, the public's perceptions affect policy impacts.

With this insight, it becomes important to evaluate the effects of anticipated versus unanticipated movements in policy variables. One basis for such an evaluation is provided by a stochastic equilibrium model in which participants in different markets have imperfect information about economywide variables (e.g., Lucas 1972; Barro 1976; Cukierman 1984).[8]

Briefly, the policy implications of such an equilibrium model arise as follows. Anticipated changes such as an expected increase in the money supply have known effects on nominal income and proportionate effects on individual prices and the general price level; hence, real economic activity is not affected—the traditional classical assertion. An unanticipated monetary shock, in contrast, is partly confused with shifts in relative demand and induces output responses. If price elasticities of supply and demand differ across markets, a monetary shock may affect relative prices and have very different impacts among sectors.

The distinction between anticipated and unanticipated monetary policy in the stochastic equilibrium model plays a crucial role in the modern classical view of macroeconomics. This distinction provides a basis on which to reconcile the "monetarist" view that monetary policy has no real effects (i.e., when it is anticipated), with the "monetarist" view that changes in money supply historically have been the principal cause of fluctuations in output levels (i.e., when these changes are not anticipated). Further, the stochastic equilibrium model provides a modern foundation for the recommendation that a stable money growth rate is the optimal monetary policy.[9]

The proposition that only unanticipated monetary policy has real effects has substantive implications as well for evaluation of macroeconomic impacts on agriculture. The proposition that systematically "tight" monetary growth dampens agricultural exports must rest upon real impacts of anticipated policy, or on such a policy embedding a sequence of realized monetary growth rates below expectations. If only unanticipated shocks matter, then the stability of monetary policy is of concern to agriculture, but the level at which stability is attained is of less consequence.

Equivalent questions can also be raised with respect to fiscal policy: Does the public respond to anticipated government deficits with offsetting increases in private savings so that the level of real interest rates and real output remain constant, while unanticipated fiscal shocks augment real demand, raise real interest rates, and shift the composition of production? In the case of fiscal policy the outcome depends not on whether nominal and relative price signals are confused, but rather on whether private agents optimize with respect to anticipated government dissaving with neutralizing increases in private savings.[10]

More generally, consideration of the public's expectations blurs the distinction between monetary and fiscal policy as private agents recognize that government expenditures must be paid for by taxes, borrowing, or creation of money. Recognizing this simple identity leads the public to question the permanence of incompatible monetary and fiscal policies. For example, a large deficit might lead to inflationary expectations despite temporary monetary restraint. If this induces high real interest rates for some interim period, whether one attributed this effect to unanticipated monetary policy (not as inflationary as expected during this period) or to fiscal policy would be quite arbitrary.

THE FIXED-PRICE/FLEX-PRICE MODEL. The policy inferences derived from a stochastic equilibrium model may be moderated, without abandoning the expectations concept, when price stickiness, varying costs of price adjustment, or staggered multiperiod contracting among markets are considered (e.g., Dornbusch 1976; Mussa 1981; Phelps and Taylor 1977). In these cases less than perfect price flexibility is realized in some markets for some medium-length time horizon, and both anticipated policy and policy shocks may affect relative prices and real output. In such a fixed-price/flex-price model, these impacts exist only as interim effects. Over time, as fixed prices adjust, prices and output are assumed to return to long-term equilibrium. Consequently, in the fixed-price/flex-price model the distinction between the short run and the long run is crucial. In contrast to the stochastic equilibrium model, which emphasizes the optimality of policy stability, the fixed-price/flex-price model may provide a rationale for policy intervention to achieve short-term macroeconomic goals.

The differences among theoretical models concerning whether anticipated versus unanticipated macroeconomic policies have real effects has generated an extensive, but not conclusive, empirical literature. This literature has focused on testing the proposition that only unanticipated monetary policy affect aggregate output or employment. Barro (1977; 1978), Barro and Rush (1980), and Leiderman (1980) find evidence favoring these propositions. Mishkin (1983), on the other hand, finds evidence that monetary shocks have real impacts while anticipated monetary policy does not only when empirical models constrain monetary impacts to short lags. Over longer lag periods (20 quarters), Mishkin finds that impacts of anticipated monetary growth exceed those of unanticipated monetary shocks. McGee and Stasiak (1985) also report evidence favoring real impacts of both anticipated and unanticipated money growth.

In the analysis of macroeconomic issues in U.S. agriculture, the application of fixed-price/flex-price models has been pioneered by Rausser and his colleagues at the University of California, Berkeley (Frankel 1984; Rausser 1985; Stamoulis et al. 1985; Rausser et al. 1985). In their models, asset markets and some sectors of the economy (in particular agriculture) have flexible prices while other sectors have fixed or sticky prices. This dichotomy results in nonneutrality of monetary policy as prices overshoot long-run equilibrium among flex-price sectors where the bulk of the short-run impact of monetary policy is absorbed.[11] Rausser and his colleagues thus link monetary disturbances to commodity markets. Whatever the broad objective motivating monetary policy, an intervention affects relative prices creating a source of short-term macroeconomic externalities. Expansionary monetary policy creates a subsidy for flex-price sectors; contractionary policy creates a tax.

THE DEFINITION AND INTERPRETATION OF POLICY. Closely related to the issue of the impact of anticipated versus unanticipated policy are questions about the appropriate definition of a policy action. In an influential paper, Lucas (1976) argued that traditional econometric models do not provide a valid basis for evaluating the impact of government policy alternatives. Underlying his critique is the assertion that the parameters of fixed, well understood rules of government behavior comprise part of the environment in which economic decisions are made by rational participants in an uncertain and dynamic world. Thus, the parameters of decision rules of private agents (i.e., such behavioral equations as supply and demand functions) depend on the parameters of the government's policy. As a result, the effects of a policy intervention cannot be computed simply as the impact of an exogenous change given fixed behavioral coefficients—essentially the usual econometric approach. Rather, to assess the impact of a change in government policy, the impact of the intervention on the private agents' decision rules must be evaluated.

Usual econometric analysis of the effects of alternative government policies has also been questioned on the basis that such analysis imposes "incredible" restrictions on the magnitude and, more importantly, the causal direction of relationships among economic variables (Sims 1980). The alternative, this reasoning holds, is to capture the essential stochastic characteristics of the economy in loosely structured time-series representations. Once coefficients of these representations are estimated, impacts on the economy of unanticipated shocks to each variable can be evaluated. The merit of alternative theories may then be tested as restrictions on the unstructured model. Vector autoregressive econometric models come into their own when this perspective is taken.

At first glance, it may appear that the Lucas (1976) and Sims (1980) critiques raise similar questions about policy inferences derived from the coefficients of standard econometric models. But the two critiques are actually quite distinct. The Lucas critique places emphasis on well-defined policy rules. In this context, meaningful policy analysis can be applied only to changes in such rules. Of course, such rules have a stochastic element, but effects of specific shocks (i.e., unanticipated realized outcomes given a particular rule) do not have a well-posed interpretation for policy. The choice of the policymaker is among rules, not to specify one rule and then consistently affect the economy by following deviations from that rule.

Loosely structured representation of the stochastic characteristics of the economy takes quite a different approach than the Lucas critique. The emphasis in this case is precisely on the impacts of the type of shocks that Lucas asserts have no policy interpretation. That is, unanticipated government decisions (such as an intervention decision arising from a contentious meeting at the Federal Reserve) are government policy. The challenge the loosely structured approach raises is to determine, first, what characteristics of the evolution of the economy lead to such policy decisions and, second, how and in what order these decisions are reflected as stochastic shocks in various economic variables. If these questions are resolved then policy analysis may proceed without reference to changes in fixed policy rules.

Macroeconomic Policy Effects on Agriculture in an Integrated World Economy

That differences in basic perceptions of the nature of the aggregate economy between the classical and fixed-price/flex-price models continue to underlie differences in macroeconomic analysis does not imply that nothing has been learned from past management of the economy or the policy debates it has generated. To the contrary, a great deal has been learned. To illustrate, recognition of the importance of inflation expectations (as they might shift the Phillips curve, for example) now precludes acceptance of a naive assessment of expansionary effects of short-run monetary policy. Likewise, the critical lesson from the oil shocks and stagflation of the 1970s has been that governments can do little good with a monetary response to real shocks.

Despite these experiences, an assertion that no government actions have real impacts seems inconsistent with the recession and recovery, and the overwhelming appreciation of the dollar, that have accompanied monetary and fiscal policy in the United States and elsewhere since 1980. Either reasoning that unexpectedly tight monetary policy and expansionary fiscal policy have created a sequence of shocks with real effects or that rigidities in the economy have caused macroeconomic policies to have real impacts even though they were anticipated seems more consistent with these observations. In either case, the changes in the world economy described above have important implications for the magnitude and incidence of macroeconomic policy impacts.

Of particular importance in this regard is that the shift to flexible exchange rates be understood in the context of the emergence of integrated world capital markets. Under a system of fixed exchange rates and an absence of international capital flows, the impact of monetary policy is widely diffused in the economy. Agriculture, in particular, may be almost completely isolated from changes in monetary and fiscal policy, especially if agricultural credit markets are insulated from monetary impacts. That, of course, was the historical, post-World War II experience of U.S. agriculture through the end of the 1960s. Except for the sensitivity of labor outmigration to the aggregate level of unemployment, changes in macroeconomic policy, in particular monetary policy, had very little effect on agriculture. In part, of course, this was due to the fact that monetary and fiscal policies were relatively stable during this period.

With a well-integrated international capital market and flexible exchange rates, however, the situation is changed dramatically.[12] When the Federal Reserve adopts a restrictive monetary stance, tight monetary policy (i.e., an unanticipated reduction in the rate of growth of money in the stochastic equilibrium framework) includes an incipient rise in the domestic interest rate together with reduced aggregate demand. Downward price movement reduces overall output. The potential increase in interest rates also attracts foreign investment. As a result, the value of the dollar rises, inhibiting exports and stimulating imports. The resulting trade deficit provides foreigners with the revenue to sustain their investment decisions.

The important point to recognize is that international capital mobility releases upward pressure on domestic interest rates arising from tight monetary policy and shifts some of the adjustment burden from interest rate–sensitive industries to trade sectors. Hence, the impact of the monetary policy falls heavily on these sectors. Under this circumstance, the problems of U.S. agriculture and of many of its traditional manufacturing industries are cut from the same cloth, as has been the case during the past four years. Of course, the converse also applies. Easy monetary policies stimulate output and induce lower interest rates, a capital outflow, and an improvement in the trade account. Again, the "burden" falls largely on export- and import-competing industries, but in this case policy favors these sectors.

A capital inflow induced by restrictive monetary policy (and/or expansionary fiscal policy) also shifts the relative burden of that policy from dampening aggregate consumption to dampening aggregate production. International borrowing reduces the increase in the interest rate necessary in equilibrium and allows short-term consumption within the domestic economy to temporarily exceed income.

When expansionary fiscal policy accompanies monetary restraint, as has been the case recently, upward pressure on interest rates arising from either policy on its own is exacerbated and an even greater influx of foreign capital is induced. Again the burden is shifted to trade sectors. Tight monetary and expansionary fiscal policies are not compatible in the long term, an inconsistency brought to the fore when expectations of private agents are recognized to affect policy impacts. By shifting the burden of adjustment to these policies from interest-sensitive activities and consumption to trade sectors, their impact is concentrated on a narrower component of the economy. This allows some short-term latitude to policymakers and temporarily postpones the point at which reconciliation of policy inconsistencies becomes necessary.

Thus, when fiscal as well as monetary policies are considered, the emergence of international capital markets and the shift to flexible exchange rates again have important implications for U.S. agriculture and agricultural policy. The crucial point is that U.S. agriculture has shifted from a situation in which it was almost totally isolated from the effects of monetary and fiscal policies to a situation in which it bears the burden of adjustment to changes in such policies. A key conduit of these impacts is the exchange rate. This is quite likely the most important sense in which changes in the international economy have changed the economics of U.S. agriculture.

The Magnitude of Macroeconomic Impacts on U.S. Agriculture

Substantial evidence of macroeconomic impacts on agriculture has accumulated since the move to flexible exchange rates in 1973. Nevertheless, the relative importance of these impacts remains controversial. In this section we review some of the empirical evidence linking macroeconomic factors to agricultural prices, trade, and income.

PRIMA FACIE EVIDENCE OF MACROECONOMIC IMPACTS. Central to our conceptual model of macroeconomic effects on agriculture is the impact of monetary instability on agricultural commodity prices. Some evidence suggestive of the destabilizing price effects of monetary policy is shown in Figure 13.1. Movements in farm prices (measured by the rate of change in the index of crop prices received by U.S. farmers deflated by the consumer price index) and movements in the U.S. money supply (measured by the rate of change in M1) are shown.[13] These variables exhibit a clear correlation. Moreover, since prices are expressed in real terms, the observed relationship between the money and price variables reflects nonneutral monetary impacts on the agricultural sector. Of course, not all price movements are associated with changes in money growth rates. Deviations from a close association of these variables are explained by the many other factors that affect agricultural prices.

Further prima facie evidence of the importance of macroeconomic factors to agriculture is derived from the historic time paths of realized real interest rates, the real value of the dollar, and the real value of U.S. agri-

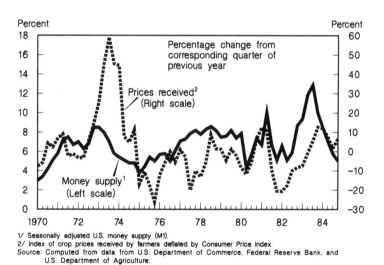

1/ Seasonally adjusted U.S. money supply (M1).
2/ Index of crop prices received by farmers deflated by Consumer Price Index.
Source: Computed from data from U.S. Department of Commerce, Federal Reserve Bank, and
    U.S. Department of Agriculture.

Fig. 13.1. Trends in the U.S. money supply and the real prices of agricultural commodities, 1970–1984

cultural exports, shown in Figure 13.2. Expressed in real terms, these variables account for the effects of inflation on nominal interest rates and the value of exports, and for the effects of inflation differentials among countries on exchange rates.[14]

During the period between 1972 and 1980, real interest rates fell below their average over previous years and tended to be negative. The value of the dollar was also generally low and agricultural exports increased throughout the period. The value of the dollar fell sharply in 1971 and 1972 and again in 1977 and 1978. Large increases in the value of agricultural exports accompanied both of these sharp currency declines; in 1972 through 1973 the value of agricultural exports rose 76.8 percent in real terms, while in 1977 through 1979 the real value of agriculture exports rose 22.9 percent.

Since 1980, the conditions of the 1970s have reversed, but the pattern of comovements among the interest rate, the exchange rate, and the value of agricultural exports has remained the same. Real interest rates have risen to unusually high levels, and the U.S. dollar has appreciated rapidly. The real value of agricultural exports that peaked in 1980 fell 27.2 percent by 1984, from $41.2 billion to $30.0 billion (in 1980 dollars).

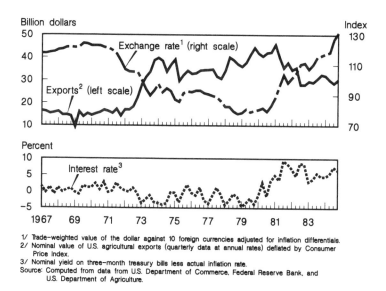

1/ Trade-weighted value of the dollar against 10 foreign currencies adjusted for inflation differentials.
2/ Nominal value of U.S. agricultural exports (quarterly data at annual rates) deflated by Consumer Price Index.
3/ Nominal yield on three-month treasury bills less actual inflation rate.
Source: Computed from data from U.S. Department of Commerce, Federal Reserve Bank, and U.S. Department of Agriculture.

Fig. 13.2. Trends in the realized real interest rate, the real exchange value of the dollar, and the real value of U.S. agricultural exports, 1967–1984

Another aspect of the prima facie evidence of macroeconomic impacts on agriculture arises when the growth of U.S. agricultural and nonagricultural exports are compared. Changes in these broad categories follow quite similar patterns, as shown in Table 13.1. Similarity of these patterns would be expected to the extent that macroeconomic phenomena impinge on both sectors, less so to the extent that exports of each sector are influenced primarily by sector-specific factors.

Table 13.1. Trends in the value of U.S. exports, 1970–1984

	Agricultural	Nonagricultural
	(percentage change in nominal value)	
1970–1980	+468.0	+396.0
1980–1981	+5.1	+5.8
1981–1982	−15.5	−18.2
1982–1983	−1.4	−6.3
1983–1984	+4.7	+8.9

Source: Computed from data reported in USDA, Foreign Agricultural Trade Statistical Report (Washington, D.C., 1984).

Finally, and closely related to the impact of the interest rate and the exchange rate, has been the increased proportion of world agricultural trade that involves middle-income developing countries. These countries accounted for fully 45 percent of the increased value of U.S. agricultural exports from 1976 to 1981. They also accounted for almost half of the decline in agricultural exports in 1982.[15] There is a substantial macroeconomic dimension to these fluctuations. When world credit conditions are easy, the monetary and fiscal policies adopted by many of these countries induce an inflow of capital, so that consumption is expanded through a deficit in goods and services trade. When world credit conditions tighten, trade-deficit inducing macroeconomic policies are less viable and imports are constrained.

EMPIRICAL STUDIES OF MACROECONOMIC IMPACTS

EXCHANGE RATE IMPACTS ON PRICES AND EXPORTS. Our analysis of the impacts of monetary and fiscal policy suggests that under flexible exchange rates currency realignments play a crucial role in shifting the burden of policy adjustment onto trade sectors of the economy. This reasoning has led many empirical studies of macroeconomic impacts on agriculture to focus on the impact of the exchange rate on agricultural exports and prices.[16]

Analysis along this line is illustrated by a recent simulation study by Longmire and Morey (1983) in which the effects of appreciation of the dollar from 1980 through 1982 on U.S. prices, exports, and stocks of wheat, corn, and soybeans were evaluated. In this study, domestic and foreign supply responses were carefully considered under various assumptions about price expectations. The impacts of cross-price effects among the three commodities and the possibility of less than perfect transmission to foreign prices of changes in dollar prices or exchange rates were also taken into account.

Longmire and Morey conclude that real appreciation of the dollar of approximately 20 percent between 1980 and 1982 caused the real value of U.S. wheat, corn, and soybean exports to drop by about $3 billion (or 16 percent). This exchange-rate effect accounted for close to 70 percent of the total decline in the value of exports of these commodities that occurred during this period—a rather sizable exchange rate impact.

The Longmire and Morey study also demonstrates an important interrelationship between exchange-rate fluctuations and U.S. farm commodity programs. Loan rates were approximately stable in real terms from 1980 and 1982, setting a floor under dollar prices of supported commodities. With appreciation of the dollar, the stable loan rates caused world prices of these commodities to be higher than they would otherwise have been. Foreign demand for U.S. grains was choked off, while other countries were given an incentive to increase their grain supply. As a direct consequence, an estimated 20 million tons of grain entered U.S. farm program stocks at a cost of some $2 billion. This was one-fourth of the total increase in program stocks (80.8 million tons) during this period.

Though the Longmire and Morey study and other similar studies provide useful estimates of exchange-rate impacts, measurement of these impacts in a partial equilibrium framework that focuses solely on the prices and quantities traded of one or more closely related products raises a number of concerns. First, such studies depend on imposed partial elasticities of foreign demand with respect to prices and the exchange rate. Unfortunately, the state of our knowledge about these critical parameters can only be described as still somewhat muddled.

A second concern arises because our conceptual model suggests that fiscal and monetary policies induce an association of the real exchange rate and capital flows that shifts consumption expenditures from countries with a trade surplus to those with a trade deficit. The impact of these income transfers on the prices and trade of specific commodities is not considered in a partial equilibrium analysis. When these income transfers are taken into account, exchange-rate effects can exceed constraints imposed by focusing only on a small group of closely substitutable goods.[17]

A third concern arises from the linkages among commodity markets and other asset markets. These linkages are not incorporated in static equilibrium analysis (either partial or general) and remain poorly understood. Yet, there are reasons to expect asset substitution to affect markets for storable farm products. That monetary phenomena may cause exaggerated short-run movements in prices of some storable commodities (price overshooting) has been illustrated in the fixed-price/flex-price models discussed previously. In the model of Rausser et al. (1985), the effects of monetary and fiscal policies are significant in this respect, and the linkages from macroeconomic policy to the agricultural markets are by means of the exchange rate and financial markets. Evidence of overshooting of agricultural prices in response to monetary policy is also reported by Frankel and Hardouvelis (1984).

A final concern raised by studies such as Longmire and Morey's arises from treatment of the exchange rate as the primary exogenous macroeconomic variable and subsequent comparison of impacts attributed to the exchange rate to actual observations. The differences between these measures may be explained by a variety of factors. If these factors have had counteracting effects, the impact of the exchange rate relative to that of other factors could easily be misstated.

Some of our own historical analysis provides insights into the magnitude of these concerns. Using the moving average representation of a 12-variable autoregressive model, we have investigated reasons for divergence between forecast and realized values of U.S. corn exports and prices for the 1970 to 1980 period. In our analysis these differences are attributed to the dynamic effects of shocks to each of the variables in the model. Aggregating the effects of shocks to individual variables into exchange-rate effects, income-transfer effects, domestic-income effects, and corn-sector effects, we find that over the entire 11-year period exchange-rate shocks explain 19.8 percent of the differences between forecast and realized export quantities, compared to 24.6 percent for income-transfer shocks, 14.6 percent for domestic-income shocks, and 33.6 percent for shocks specific to the corn sector. Effects of the exchange-rate on corn prices are more dominant, explaining 33.6 percent of the difference between forecast and actual values, compared to 24.6, 14.6, and 27.2 percent, respectively, for the other variables. These results suggest macroeconomic factors are a major source of instability in the world corn market and that income transfers (associated with trade imbalances and the OPEC oil cartel) have had substantial impacts. The price volatility associated with exchange-rate shocks is also consistent with the monetary overshooting hypothesis.[18]

INTEREST RATE EFFECTS. Though empirical studies of macroeconomic impacts on agriculture have focused largely on the exchange rate, our conceptual model associates macroeconomic policy with simultaneous impacts on the exchange rate and the real interest rate. Agriculture bears both adjustment burdens, being an exports industry with a high value of physical capital and land investment per worker and unit of output. This explains why, squeezed between the effects of declining exports and rising interest rates, real net farm income has declined to historically low levels since 1981. This decline has continued through a recession and, more recently, a period of quite rapid growth of the aggregate domestic economy.

In assessing the various effects on agriculture that can be attributed to the exchange rate or the interest rate, it is important to recognize that blaming the high value of the dollar on high interest rates is not quite appropriate. Were it not for the high value of the dollar, and the associated trade deficit and investment by foreigners in dollar-denominated assets, real interest rates in the United States would be even higher than they are, to reduce credit demand and induce more domestic savings. Policies to lower the value of the dollar without changing underlying credit conditions would have to suppress foreign investment and would cause real interest rates to rise. It is not clear that this would be to the advantage of agriculture.

One might also expect that the emergence of a well-integrated international capital market would cause interest rates to be more stable, though not necessarily lower, than they would otherwise be, with the response to alternative monetary and fiscal policy among countries reflected in international capital flows rather than changes in interest rates. However, monetary disturbances have been so large under the flexible exchange-rate system that such conditions have not yet prevailed. Moreover, there is an inherent relationship between the exchange rate and interest rates, reflected in uncovered interest rate parity.

So long as interest rates vary, related impacts on agriculture will occur. These include significant impacts on livestock sectors because of the effects of the interest rate on the cost of carrying livestock inventories. There are similar effects on the cost of production and the cost of carrying grain stocks. These effects are reflected in asset values, particularly land prices, as the interest rate affects the discounted value of future earnings from these assets. Of course, in addition to the effect of the interest rate as a discount factor, land prices reflect changes in expectations about future prices, and thus a wide array of sectoral and macroeconomic developments.

We have not reviewed all of the empirical studies that trace the net implications of a rise in the interest rate through its impacts on production costs, supply and storage decisions, prices, income, and farm asset values.[19] But there is no question that the rise in real interest rates during the 1980s has resulted in an unparalleled farm financial crisis. With farm debt over $200 billion, each 1 percent rise in the interest rate, if applied to the entire debt, would raise interest costs by over $2 billion. With nominal net farm income estimated to be from $23 to $27 billion in 1985, the interest rate impacts are clearly substantial. Further, interest rate impacts have had enormous distributional consequences among classes and types of farms.

OTHER MACROECONOMIC EFFECTS. In addition to the macroeconomic effects associated directly with the exchange rate or the interest rate, there is a range of related indirect impacts of macroeconomic factors. Often it is incorrectly argued that these interrelated factors do not reflect macroeconomic policy. For example, the effects of the exchange rate on U.S. exports have been contrasted in a reduced-form equation with the effect of changes in national incomes, as if the former but not the latter carried implications of macroeconomic policy influences (Batten and Belongia 1984).

Further, and though it is somewhat off the theme of our paper, there are other effects of fiscal policy as it is reflected as tax, rather than spending, policy. An important macroeconomic effect is associated with accelerated depreciation for agricultural machinery and livestock herds that builds excess capacity in agriculture and causes the sector to be more capital intensive than it would otherwise be, to the disadvantage of agricultural labor. Tax policy also has important microeconomic effects. Hanson and Eidman (1985) have shown, for example, that U.S. tax policy is not size neutral; it benefits large farms relative to small farms.

Despite these latter considerations, it is our view that as long as the international economy and the U.S. role in it stay in their present configuration the major effects of monetary and fiscal policy on agriculture will be reflected in their impacts through international capital and commodity markets, with a principal transmission mechanism being the exchange rate. International capital movements will play a crucial role in determining the value of the dollar, and hence the level of foreign demand for U.S. agricultural (and other) exports. Foreign demand is a key determinant of what happens to the income of those subsectors of agriculture that depend on trade and, thus, to U.S. agriculture as a whole. International capital movements will also play a crucial role in determining the levels of domestic interest rates, and hence the impact of monetary and fiscal policy on agriculture through asset values and financial markets.

MEASUREMENT OF MACROECONOMIC POLICY IMPACTS. Studies that focus on a reduced form conveying the impact on agriculture of the exchange rate, the interest rate, or some other variable are adequate as measures of macroeconomic impacts on the sector only if any movement in such economywide variables is treated as "macroeconomic." The more focused interpretation suggested by our conceptual model, however, would center on the impacts of government's monetary and fiscal policies, both in the United States and abroad. To address these policy questions, empirical models treating the exchange rate (or the interest rate or other factor) as exogenous provide only part of the requisite information. In addition, it is necessary to identify policy-induced movements in these variables.

One approach to such an evaluation is based on large-scale econometric models in which the agricultural sector is modeled in detail. We have already discussed the fixed-price/flex-price model developed by Rausser and his colleagues. A second econometric model, one that focuses on financial flows and balances, is the COMGEM model of Texas A & M University and Texas Tech University. Using COMGEM, Hughes and Penson (1986) have considered the likely impacts on agriculture through 1990 of three alternative scenarios for U.S. macroeconomic policy: (1) a real government budget deficit continuing at about $100 billion with monetary policy that brings the inflation rate to zero; (2) a real deficit continuing at about $100 billion with monetary policy that causes the rate of inflation to rise by one percent each year; (3) and a 15-percent budget deficit reduction each year with a policy of modest monetary growth. Over the 1984 to 1990 period, forecasts of aggregate GNP under these three scenarios are: (1) for a recession followed by annual real growth of less than 3 percent; (2) no recession and 4–6 percent annual real growth; and (3) no recession and 3–4 percent annual real growth. The real interest rate and value of the dollar rise under the first scenario and fall under the third, while under the second scenario they fall briefly then rise. Agriculture fares best with reduction of the government budget deficit. Real net farm income rises to $35 billion (in 1980 dollars) and farm asset values climb steadily under the third scenario. Real farm income remains under $25 billion and asset values decline steadily under either of the high-deficit scenarios, with faster growth of the money supply leading to higher income in the short run.

An alternative approach to evaluating the linkages of macroeconomic policy to variables such as the interest or the exchange rate, and hence to agriculture, is to focus more narrowly on development of the theory, such as that of exchange-rate determination. The literature is truly enormous. We have already noted the controversy in the economics literature concerning the aggregate impacts of anticipated versus unanticipated monetary policy, a controversy that is now spilling over into assessment of monetary impacts on agriculture.[20] Similar controversies surround theories of interest rate and exchange-rate determination and the empirical evidence brought to bear to resolve these theoretical issues.[21] [22]

Regardless of the approach undertaken to evaluate the linkages from monetary and fiscal policy to agriculture, it is important to recognize that linkages of policies among countries should be, but often are not, taken into consideration. The strong dollar of the 1980s is not just a consequence of U.S. monetary and fiscal policies, misguided as they might be. Where the United States has been pursuing a highly stimulative fiscal policy and a restrictive monetary policy, European countries have collectively been pursuing a restrictive fiscal policy and an expansionary monetary policy. The net effect has been a sluggish European economy and relative low European interest rates. The flow of capital into the United States that would have been induced by U.S. policy has been exacerbated by policies of the Europeans. This suggests that looking at U.S. macroeconomic policies alone is not adequate as a basis for assessing macroeconomic impacts on agriculture. Rather, the policies of U.S. trade partners also have to be taken into account.[23]

MACROECONOMICS AND RURAL AMERICA. A somewhat different dimension to our concerns with the identification and measurement of macroeconomic impacts involves extending our analysis from agriculture per se to rural commodities more generally. We have purposefully kept the phrase "and rural America" in our title to focus attention on this issue. This concern is shared by our colleagues Deaton and Weber (1985) who identify internationalization of the economy as one of the principal forces shaping the future of rural areas.

From a theoretical perspective, the issues with respect to the macroeconomics of rural areas are similar to those we have raised with respect to agriculture. These center on the relative protection provided to rural economies and the effects of narrowing of the burden of adjustment to changes in monetary and fiscal policy onto trade sectors.

A number of issues arise. First, rural America is based in large part on agriculture. A depressed agriculture contributes to a depressed rural America; small towns in the Corn Belt are linked directly to the international economy through the impact of monetary and fiscal policy on trade sectors. That many of the traditional smokestack industries are located in states dependent on agriculture, and are affected by the same policy linkages as agriculture, has exacerbated the adjustment problems. Adjustment through nonfarm employment for agricultural operators is not easy in these cases, since the very industries where such employment might be found are depressed as well.

Second, the massive decline in asset values in agriculture due to the combination of high interest rates and low commodity prices has seriously weakened rural banks and the private and public capital base of many rural communities. If macroeconomic policy should reverse direction, the effects on rural areas would reverse as well. There might be significant "overshooting" in resource adjustment since import-competing industries that have expelled workers with the 1980s' policy configuration would have to attract them back if they are to recover.

Third, not all rural areas are primarily dependent on agriculture. For these non-agriculturally dependent areas mining, forestry, manufacturing, or transfer payments undergird the local economy. Macroeconomic impacts on these sources of income will have important local implications.

At a national level, certain rural areas, particularly largely agricultural areas, are highly disprotected and susceptible to macroeconomic policy impacts. But when rural areas overall are compared to urban areas, we have little evidence about the relative protection each receives. Similarly, at this juncture we have little evidence about the impacts of monetary or fiscal policies on rural versus urban areas overall, though one might anticipate that social adjustment costs may well be higher when the impacts are borne by rural communities. These are important issues with local and national implications; yet, we simply do not have the empirical evidence we need to address these questions.

THE CHALLENGE FOR THEORETICAL AND EMPIRICAL RESEARCH. Concerning the evaluation of macroeconomic impacts, our profession now stands in somewhat of a quandary. By and large, our theories are consistent with real impacts of some, at least unanticipated, policy actions and prima facie evidence supports such a perspective. Yet, our brief review suggests that difficult analytic and statistical issues confront efforts to clarify points of theoretical controversy and explain actual macroeconomic developments. Past studies provide theoretical outcomes or empirical evidence that seem regrettably specification specific.

In our view, therein lies the challenge facing our profession, at least with respect to understanding the effects of macroeconomic forces on agriculture and rural communities. There are two aspects to this challenge. The first challenge is to incorporate theoretical developments emerging from the broad fields of macroeconomics and international economics into our conceptual analysis and to make contributions to the theory of macroeconomic relationships where we can. The second challenge is to model the impact of macroeconomic factors on the agricultural sector and other rural industries, and to quantify these impacts in a cohesive empirical framework.[24] This work is really still in its infancy. Economic policy, as a consequence, continues to be ineffective and misguided.

Policy Issues and Institutional Reform

It should now be apparent that changes in the international economy, in the U.S. economy, and in how the U.S. relates to the international economy have changed the way we have to think about U.S. agriculture. Thinking about the sector as a closed economy and using a partial equilibrium framework to consider narrow sectoral issues is no longer relevant. Instead, it is imperative that we take an international perspective to agriculture, and view it through the prism of an open economy model. When we do that, of course, it becomes necessary to consider a far wider policy agenda: an agenda that includes monetary, fiscal, exchange rate, and trade policy. Moreover, agricultural commodity policy also has to be viewed from a quite different perspective.

THE DUAL CONSTRAINTS ON NATIONAL POLICY. The general failure to recognize the significance of international capital markets has caused us to think about international economic relations primarily in terms of real trade. We tend to think about the balance of payments in terms of the balance of trade and to assume that is our primary external constraint. Perhaps the best example of the popularity of such a perspective is the frequency with which observers of the contemporary scene expect each new report on the U.S. trade deficit to bring the dollar crashing down.

In point of fact, each country has both a trade account and a capital account. In today's world, the capital account tends to be dominant. To understand what has been driving exchange rates one need not look to international trade flows as much as to international capital flows. Thus, the United States has a large trade deficit *because* the dollar is strong. And the dollar is strong because of events happening on the capital account. The dollar may eventually also fall because of what happens on the capital account.

These dual accounts impose a dual constraint on both the economy and on what policymakers can do. It seldom seems to be recognized in contemporary discussions of economic policy, but these dual constraints are imposing very real limitations on the choices policymakers face in today's world.

Consider simultaneously the less-developed countries of the world (LDCs), with their large foreign debt, and the developed countries of the world such as the United States, which have extended them that credit. To a certain level, the LDCs could go on borrowing additional capital if their economies are growing, and the developed countries can go on lending to them. If such a situation prevails, the borrowing countries will need to run a trade deficit, the parallel of being a net capital importer, and the developed countries will need to run a trade surplus, the parallel of their net export of capital.

Suppose instead that the developing countries need to scale back their net borrowing from abroad. To service this debt and to amortize part of it, they will have to become net exporters on the trade account. But a net exporter requires someone else who will be a net importer. Typically that role must fall on those countries that loaned capital in the first place; hence, a country like the United States would need to be a net importer, as we have been recently. But that also means the United States is a net importer of capital. The developing countries may view this outcome as draining much-needed investment funds away from them. Yet it is just the obverse of their need to have a trade surplus. The constraints on U.S. policy in this situation are no less than those on the developing countries, with the caveat that the United States has a special role in the international economy due to the size of our domestic economy and the unique role we play as essentially the central banker for the world.

The dual constraints arising from the symmetry of the balance of trade and capital accounts explain a great deal about current pressures for trade, trade access, and the need for international finance. One of the important aspects of the international scene today is the pressure for the debtor countries to become export-oriented. In fact, both the United States and international agencies, such as the World Bank, often press hard on the debtor countries to change their policies to favor the export objective. Less often is any question raised about who is going to take those exports. Burden sharing and symmetry require that the United States and other creditor countries remain open to exports from the debtor nations. If we do not, policy-induced inconsistencies are inevitable.

It turns out that in today's world there are considerable vested interests in favor of trade liberalization that come about, for the first time, through the international capital market. Bankers in the United States, for example, know full well that if the loans they have extended to the developing countries are to be serviced and repaid, the United States will have to accept an ever-growing flow of imports. Hence, their lobbying efforts (and they are not insignificant) lean against protectionist measures.

Because of the perversity of its macroeconomic policies in recent years, the United States may face an even more severe shock and challenge in the years ahead. Because we have borrowed so much abroad we have now become the world's largest debtor nation, and we are importing additional capital at an annual rate of about $150 billion. At some point, we too may have to repay some of that debt, just as the developing countries are at present. That would require that we shift from a large trade deficit to a trade surplus. The fall in the value of the dollar required to bring that about would be quite large. Such a fall would provide a positive stimulus to agriculture, but it would also require another massive reallocation of labor in the rest of the economy, as well as a reduction of consumption relative to output.[25] One wonders how long such major adjustments can be imposed on the populace without major political dissatisfaction.

MACROECONOMIC POLICY AND COMPETITIVE ADVANTAGE. It is just such pressures as those described above that have caused major realignments of economic policy in many developing countries. Brazil is an important example. From having one of the most closed economies in the world a few short years ago, Brazil has turned outward and launched a major export drive. To do that, it has undertaken a draconian realignment in the value of its currency. The result is that its latent comparative advantage in crops such as soybeans has been brought to the fore as a competitive advantage, after many years in which policy discriminated against potential export crops. If Brazil persists with current policy it may well take away the U.S. soybean market, and may even have the potential to export soybeans to the United States.

The point this example underscores is that the implications of international capital flows for agricultural trade are great. U.S. policies are not the only policies that affect U.S. export potential; nor are the exports of any other country determined solely by its own policies. Rather, competitive advantage, and hence trade flows, will be determined by the joint effects of each country's policies on one another. Again it is the dual nature of the capital and trade accounts that is relevant.

DOMESTIC COMMODITY PROGRAMS. Commodity programs that operated by intervening in domestic markets could be sustained in a world of fixed exchanged rates and no international capital market. In today's world, however, that no longer seems possible. Monetary and fiscal policies, as well as conditions in international financial markets, can cause those programs to be counterproductive and costly.

Consider again the recent experience with U.S. commodity programs. The dramatic rise in the value of the dollar in the early 1980s translated international prices to the domestic economy at lower and lower levels. At some point U.S. market prices settled on the support rates provided by farm programs, and they could decline no further. As the value of the dollar continued to rise, U.S. prices were translated abroad as increasingly higher foreign-currency prices. Thus, rigid U.S. loan rates provided an underpinning to the world market, with the result that we could easily be undersold by foreign competitors. If we had set out to design a policy to lose market shares, we could not have designed a better one.

With present program arrangements, excess U.S. production is diverted into government program stocks or reserves. When these reserves burgeoned out of control in 1982 and 1983, the result was the costly PIK program. The final costs of PIK are still not tallied.[26] Furthermore, it appears likely that farm support costs at unprecedented levels will continue to be incurred if current programs are maintained.

Therefore, it is questionable whether commodity programs as we have known them in the past can be sustained under present economic arrangements. They will be very costly while doing little to improve the welfare of farmers. A great deal of flexibility is now needed in domestic farm programs, since agriculture has to adjust to changes in both the international economy and domestic monetary and fiscal policy. Failure to adjust can be very costly both to agriculture and the economy as a whole.

Similar comments apply, incidentally, to the potential for international commodity agreements. The problem is that realignments in exchange rates bring about implicit changes in relative domestic prices. Hence, fixing prices in nominal terms will bring about significant pressures for an agreement to break down. To fix them in any other way would appear to be an impossible task.

SAVINGS RATES AND U.S. COMPETITIVENESS ABROAD. By international standards, U.S. savings rates are notoriously low. That may give rise to a new version of the Dutch disease.[27] If the United States has a highly productive economy, the marginal productivity of capital will be high. Under certain circumstances that will cause the real rate of return on capital and the demand for investment to also be high. If U.S. savings rates are too low to provide the aggregate level of savings needed to fill investment demand, a net inflow of capital will be induced. That in turn will cause the value of the dollar to rise, making U.S. export goods less competitive abroad.

By way of contrast, consider the case of Japan, which has one of the highest savings rates in the world. It consequently finds itself in the position of being a capital exporter. This acts to keep the yen weak (other things being equal), which is an incentive to a strong export performance.

Hence, one of the serious contradictions the United States faces is that our investments in research and development together with its relatively unregulated economy may give us a higher productivity on capital investment than many, if not most, other countries of the world, but we have a savings rate that is not consistent with that high-productivity economy. Consequently, the United States may have shifted into a capital-importing status for the longer term. This can be a chronic problem unless something is done to raise the savings rate. There are things that can be done. Greater use of consumption taxes, reduction in fiscal incentives to borrow for consumption goods, and stronger incentives to save could be among the measures used to raise the U.S. savings rate and reduce pressures attracting foreign capital inflows. These are options the United States has. In the meantime, however, the low savings rate will be a factor affecting export and import performance.

TRADE DISTORTIONS IN A FLEXIBLE EXCHANGE-RATE SYSTEM. Current thinking about the effects of tariffs, export subsidies, and other trade interventions in the United States is heavily influenced by past experience under a fixed exchange-rate system. Under such a system many of the potential second-order or general equilibrium effects could be ignored. Moreover, many domestic problems could be "dumped" abroad, despite the original intention of the Bretton Woods Convention that national governments would adjust their domestic policies to restore balance in their external accounts when they got out of order.

These issues need considerable rethinking. For example, by keeping imports at a lower level, tariffs may cause the value of the nation's currency to rise. This makes all imports enter at a lower price, so the tariff's effects are spread across the economy. Clearly, there may well still be some relief to the immediate sector, but other trade sectors bear more of a burden than under fixed exchange rates.

Export subsidies have similar counterproductive second-order effects. By increasing exports, such policies also increase the value of the national currency (other things being equal), and thus again spread the effects of the subsidy through the economy, to the detriment of other sectors. Political leaders interested in promoting trade liberalization can and should capitalize on these distributional effects of trade intervention by emphasizing that domestic problems cannot be dumped abroad, and that instead they will be shifted to other trade sectors. They should also recognize that the cost effectiveness of such interventions in today's world is probably in general quite low.

THE NEED FOR REFORM OF INTERNATIONAL MONETARY AND TRADE INSTITUTIONS. Existing international institutional arrangements, such as the General Agreement on Tariffs and Trade (GATT), the International Monetary Fund (IMF), and other institutions, were designed on the premise that a fixed exchange-rate system would prevail in the post-World War II period. There was little perception that technological developments in the communication and information sectors would make possible the kind of international capital market we now have. Given the changes that have taken place in the international economy, the existing institutions are largely irrelevant. We need to rethink these institutions and help to put a new system in place.

Unfortunately, the United States seems to have little stomach for taking on this arduous task and, paradoxically, appears to be retreating from an international involvement at the very time our economy is becoming increasingly internationalized. Nothing could be more counterproductive to our own best interests.

We need to recognize that many present problems of agriculture and the rest of the economy are rooted in deficiencies in the international system. We also need to recognize that as our economy becomes increasingly open, it is increasingly beyond the reach of domestic policies. Wishing it to be otherwise will not cause it to be so.

High on the agenda for institutional reform should be our international monetary arrangements. Many Bretton Woods' conventions were swept away when the world moved to a system of bloc-floating exchange rates in 1973. But nothing has been put in their place, so we limp along, handling each crisis on an ad hoc basis. Failure to deal with the problems of international monetary instability is giving rise to strong protectionist pressures and creating disillusionment among those who were originally supportive of a flexible exchange-rate system. Failure to take action in this area can cause us to slip back into a destructive spiral of declining trade and negative economic growth approximating that of the 1930s.

The paradoxes in the international monetary arena are legion. For example, the United States and other industrialized countries have starved the IMF for resources almost since its creation, because these countries feared the IMF would go on an inflationary binge. But when the international capital market emerged and petrodollars flowed rapidly, it was the commercial banks that went on a lending binge, as the experience of the last decade documents. Moreover, the commercial banks were unable to impose any conditionality that the IMF would have attached to its lending program. As a result we have the worst of all possible worlds.

Similarly, the United States is essentially the central banker for the world since the world is for all intents and purposes on a dollar standard.[28] But we refuse to accept this unique role, while at the same time opposing any initiative either to strengthen the IMF or to create a new institution. Instead of managing our money supply as if we were central banker for the world, we manage it primarily as if only domestic conditions were relevant. The exception, of course, is when there is crisis such as Brazil and Mexico experienced in 1982. In those crisis situations, the Federal Reserve has acted like a banker of last resort.

Reform of international monetary arrangements should be at the top of our agricultural policy agenda. We are playing Russian roulette with an issue that is of the greatest importance to this nation. A continuation of the instability of the last decade, with wide swings in currency values and large shocks to trade conditions, will cause a loss of confidence in the system and a breakdown of both international trade and international monetary arrangements. It is better to work to strengthen the existing system before we see its collapse.

The United States has two options in attempting to reform the system. First, we can accept our responsibilities as international banker and manage our money supply accordingly. That is a feasible approach, and it certainly would be an improvement over present arrangements. The problem with this option is that U.S. trade sectors, including agriculture, would remain quite vulnerable to monetary disturbances, although probably less so than in recent years.

Alternatively, the United States can work to reform and strengthen the IMF. This can be done on a gradual basis.[29] The first step would be to strengthen the Standard Drawing Right (SDR) so that it becomes a more attractive reserve asset to hold. This could be done by providing for a market-determined rate of interest. Then, the IMF should be given a mandate to create new SDRs and, consistent with the notion of stable monetary policy being optimal, a mandate to keep the stock of SDRs growing at a constant rate commensurate with the growth in international trade and finance. Such modest reforms would see the SDR gradually replace the U.S. dollar as an international reserve asset. At the same time, these reforms would free United States monetary policy to be managed primarily on domestic considerations. The dollar would be free to circulate or to be held in reserve, and all nations would retain their domestic currencies and be free to manage their domestic monetary policy independently.

Concluding Comments

In this paper we have argued that in today's world, U.S. agriculture and agricultural policy must be viewed through the prism of an open economy model. From this perspective, the macroeconomics of agriculture encompass the relative degree of protection provided to the sector and a shift of the burden of adjustment to monetary and fiscal policy onto trade sectors. This shift results from the emergence of a large international capital market that ties national economic policies to one another in a world of flexible currency exchange rates.

It is now clear that the opening of the U.S. economy, and of its agricultural sector in particular, has created a new setting for agriculture. An important challenge to emerge for our profession is to quantify the net impact of macroeconomic factors on agriculture and other rural industries in an open economy. The dilemmas we face in addressing this challenge arise in part as a consequence of the considerable debate within contemporary economics over the theoretical and econometric foundations upon which the assessment of these impacts should rest.

Despite these analytic issues, the extent to which our international economic integration has proceeded remains the outstanding characteristic of today's economy. Indeed, our economic integration has far outpaced our social and political integration. Economically, we are in each other's hair at every twist and turn. But the institutional and political means to deal with that growing economic integration are deteriorating rather than improving. This is potentially a very explosive situation with serious consequences. This nation needs to address these issues and to collaborate with other nations in strengthening existing institutional arrangements and designing new ones. Our profession has a role to play in this pressing task.

As the economics of agriculture have changed, so too the basis for agricultural policy should have changed. Unfortunately, our institutional arrangements on the domestic side are as out-of-date as they are on the international scene. Herein lies part of the challenge we face. In today's world it is monetary, fiscal, exchange-rate, and trade policy that really matter for agriculture. However, our domestic political arrangements link agriculture to House and Senate agricultural committees that have little or no responsibility, or perhaps even understanding, of these broader policies. The consequence is that we will continue to tinker with domestic commodity programs that have little potential to do anything for agriculture, despite its serious plight. Out of such conditions there arises a political disillusionment and a general lack of confidence in political arrangements. This nation desperately needs to get its domestic political arrangements up to speed with the kind of economy we now have and to work for a strengthening of international institutions consistent with the increasingly well-integrated international economy that has emerged.

Notes

1. Among the recent exceptions are Eckstein (1984), Fischer (1982), Goodwin and Sheffrin (1982), Huntzinger (1979), and Todd (1983). While these studies model agricultural supply in a rational expectations framework, none utilizes that framework to address macroeconomic issues.

2. For further discussion of the measurement of relative protection and its policy implications, see Schuh (1984).

3. Strictly speaking, this argument requires that a uniform level of protection applies to all sectors so that no relative prices are distorted. If tariff levels vary among sectors, raising the protection afforded to any one sector to the average among sectors will not necessarily improve resource allocation. The argument for uniform protection also ignores any gains the United States might acquire by adoption of optimal tariff policies, and the negative effects of export subsidies on world prices. Identifying these impacts may be problematic in a multisector economy, but there is little doubt that any U.S. gains would come at the expense of export sectors such as agriculture.

4. See Schuh (1974) for a preliminary attempt to reinterpret the post–World War II history of U.S. agriculture and agricultural policy in light of distortions in the value of the dollar.

5. See Bosworth and Lawrence (1982) or Fischer (1981) for discussion of macroeconomic impacts arising from agriculture and Doering et al. (1982) for one view of the social costs and benefits of agricultural exports.

6. This analysis is developed further by Rodgers (1985).

7. For the period 1980–1982, for example, the proportion of GDP attributed to trade (an average of exports and imports as a percentage of GDP) was 8.5 percent for the United States, compared to 12.8 percent for Japan.

8. To illustrate the stochastic equilibrium model, consider a case in which supply and demand functions in the jth market at time t are given, in log-linear form, by:

$$y_t^s(j) = a(j)\{p_t(j) - E[P_t|I_t(j)]\} + e_t^s(j) \tag{1}$$

$$y_t^s(j) = -b(j)\{p_t(j) - E[P_t|I_t(j)]\} + c\{Y_t - E[Y_t|I_t(j)]\} + e_t^d \tag{2}$$

where, at time t, $y_t^s(j)$, $y_t^d(j)$, $e_t^s(j)$, and $e_t^d(j)$ are, respectively, quantities supplied and demanded in market j and random market-specific shocks to supply and demand, $p_t(j)$ is the price in market j, P_t is the general price level, Y_t is nominal income, and $I_t(j)$ is the information available to participants in the jth market. The notation E is the expectations operator. The coefficients $a(j)$ and $b(j)$ measure the impact on supply and demand, respectively, of the price of the jth good relative to the expected overall price level, and the coefficient c measures the impact on demand of actual nominal income relative to expected income. In the above model, information discrepancies arise when it is assumed that participants in a particular market observe the current price in their market $[p_t(j)]$ but only observe the general price level with a one-period lag [i.e., $I_t(j)$ includes P_{t-1} but not P_t]. Price determination arises from setting supply and demand in equilibrium:

$$P_t(j) = E[P_t | I_t(j) + \{c/[a(j) + b(j)]\} . Y_t - E[_t | I_t(j)]\} + \{1/[a(j) + B(j)]\}e_t^d - e_t^s)(3)$$

If nominal income is equal to expected nominal income plus an error term, say e_t^y, and is driven by monetary policy, then actual price in market j depends on the expected price level and an error term that includes both market-specific shocks and an aggregate demand shock. An observation on $pl_t(j)$ carries information on a linear combination of these shocks, thus affecting $E[P_t | I_t(j)]$ and leading to some confusion between relative and aggregate phenomena. Deriving an equilibrium solution to the model (1)–(3) entails solving simultaneously for market price, $p_t(j)$, and the price level, P_t, assuming agents forecast rationally given the information available to them. For brevity, this solution is not pursued herein. The general method of solution is discussed in Cukierman (1984). Stochastic equilibrium models may also be extended to consideration of intertemporal problems, in which case the real interest rate becomes an important relative price. For one such approach, see Barro (1981b).

   9. Given the confusion element associated with unanticipated monetary shocks, it can be shown that a perfectly anticipated monetary policy is optimal in the above model, in the sense that the variance of economic output around its full information level is minimized by such a policy. The full information output level is derived from optimizing decisions of agents whose information set includes observation of the current price level so confusion between relative and nominal price changes is avoided. In a stochastic environment this does not mean output is constant; rather prices and outputs in the economy respond naturally to real supply and demand disturbances.

   10. For alternative views, see Barro (1981a) and Feldstein (1982).

   11. Price overshooting may also arise in equilibrium models that do not impose the fixed-price/flex-price distinction. For an illustration in which changes in portfolio preferences induce transitory overshooting even when all prices are flexible, see Lawrence and Lawrence (1981).

   12. Reasoning that monetary policy has important implications for U.S. agriculture under a regime of flexible exchange rates and well-integrated international capital markets has been pursued consistently by Schuh (e.g., 1976, 1981, 1983, 1986a).

   13. Evaluation of monetary impacts on agriculture in terms of world money supply and international prices, rather than U.S. money and price variables, may be more appropriate. Analysts at the Australian Bureau of Agricultural Economics (BAE) have compiled evidence of a remarkably strong correlation of movements in OECD money growth and an index of world commodity prices during recent years (1975–1981). These results are reported in Rae (1984).

   14. The results displayed in Figure 13.2 are invariant to a simple respecification of the real interest rate variable as the nominal interest rate less inflation that is anticipated on the basis of a univariate autoregressive equation. Since the evidence in the figure is only suggestive, we did not pursue more sophisticated specification of inflation expectations.

15. Agricultural exports to the developing countries rebounded in 1983 and have continued to increase modestly, while agricultural exports to the developed countries have continued to decline. In part, the recovery of agricultural exports to the developing countries despite macroeconomic conditions is due to a variety of direct and credit subsidies — nonagricultural exports to these countries have continued to fall badly.

16. The studies we review do not address the critique of econometric analysis posed by Lucas (1976). While we recognize that Lucas's concern with policy variance of economic decision rules may be quite important (particularly when the impacts of "large" changes in policy are being considered), we believe that in many cases much can be learned from empirical analysis of how the economy responds to specific monetary and fiscal shocks. Policy rules are not, and perhaps cannot, be so well known that the economy does not respond to modifications of policy implementation.

17. For further discussion of general equilibrium exchange-rate effects, see Orden (1984b). In particular, in a general equilibrium analysis the percentage change in equilibrium price need not be less than the percentage change in the exchange rate. Further, even if foreign price of an agricultural commodity is constant, the income transfer associated with a real appreciation of the dollar may contract foreign demand. Assuming constant foreign supply, U.S. exports then fall.

18. In this historical analysis, each factor may have either a positive or negative effect on actual versus forecast exports or price. Thus, the percentages of these differences reported are the proportion of the absolute values of all impacts attributed to each factor. See Orden (1984a) for further discussion of these sources of instability in the world corn market. Commodity price instability is also examined in Fischer (1981) and Stockton (1983), as well as in the references to "overshooting" cited in the text.

19. See Rausser (1985) for one discussion of the effects of the interest rate among subsectors of agriculture.

20. To date, there has been little research to differentiate between the impact on agriculture of anticipated versus unanticipated money, and those few studies that have been undertaken vary widely in methodology and focus. Bond et al. (1983) find evidence that both anticipated world money supply and monetary shocks have positive effects on the real price of traded food commodities over the period from first quarter 1975 through third quarter 1982. Enders and Falk (1984), using a distinction between anticipated and unanticipated money attributed to Barro and Rush (1980), present evidence that only monetary shocks affect pork output. Belongia (1985) also reports preliminary estimates suggesting no effect of anticipated money growth on the real price of farm products and only very brief impacts of monetary surprises. Azzam and Pagoulatos (1985) find the Enders and Falk results quite sensitive to the sampling period. Rausser (1985) also makes a distinction between anticipated and unanticipated changes in monetary aggregates.

21. The literature is narrowed somewhat by focusing solely on papers addressing the high level of real interest rates or the value of the dollar in the 1980s. Clearly, a model such as COMGEM works upon real impacts of fiscal policy, but there remains a diversity opinion. See Evans (1985), and Blanchard and Summers (1984).

22. One of the problems with many of these latter studies is that regression estimates of one or several essentially reduced-form equations (with a few macroeconomic variables treated as dependent while a group of others are treated as independent) seem less than convincing, since the right-hand-side variables are clearly not necessarily independent or exogenous. The vector autoregressive (VAR) models offer an alternative approach. Association of interest rate shocks with changes in the value of the dollar are quite robust in such unstructured time-series representations, but often neither of these variables appears responsive to money-supply or fiscal variables. Based on statistical tests using restricted and unrestricted VAR models, Litterman and Weiss (1985) go so far as to suggest that one cannot reject exogeneity of the real

interest rate in a four-variable system with money, the nominal interest rate, prices, and income.

23. See Blanchard and Summers (1984) for an evaluation of the effects of monetary and fiscal policies of the major OECD countries on real interest rates and the value of the dollar. Also, see Marris (1984) for discussion of the inconsistent mix of policies being pursued by the United States and its trading partners.

24. A research problem one has in evaluating macroeconomic impacts, especially when trade sectors are crucial, is that there has been only a short history with a flexible exchange-rate regime. The exchange rate became flexible in nominal terms only in 1973, and the nominal interest rate became flexible in one sense only in 1979. The resulting data series are thus quite short if an analysis is based on nominal terms. In real terms, of course, adjustments in the exchange rate and interest rate have always been possible, but impacts of particular monetary or fiscal policies may differ under alternative regimes. See Schuh et al. (1984) for a comprehensive evaluation of the new open-economy situation of U.S. agriculture and a careful look at the research priorities that have emerged.

25. See Krugman (1985) for one view of whether the recent high value of the dollar is sustainable. This issue is also discussed by Marris (1984).

26. See Kinney (1985) for a summary of the costs of the PIK program. In addition to the direct costs, the reduction in output associated with the program may have caused a loss of as many as 200,000 jobs nationwide.

27. Traditionally, the term Dutch disease has described the phenomena of a new and productive export sector (such as oil) causing a country's currency to appreciate, thus crowding out sales from its traditional export sectors.

28. The extent to which the world economy operates on a dollar standard and some implications of this situation for macroeconomic policy are discussed in McKinnon (1982). See also Blanchard and Summers (1984).

29. Strengthening the IMF to reduce world dependence on the U.S. dollar is discussed by Schuh (1986b).

References

Azzam, A., and E. Pagoulatos. 1985. Unanticipated Money Growth and Agricultural Supply Decisions. Paper presented at the meeting of the American Agricultural Economics Association, Ames, Iowa, August.

Barro, R. J. 1976. Rational Expectations and the Role of Monetary Policy. *J. Monetary Econ.* 2:1–32.

_____. 1977. Unanticipated Money Growth and Unemployment in the United States. *Am. Econ. Rev.* 67:101–15.

_____. 1978. Unanticipated Money, Output, and the Price Level in the United States. *J. Polit. Econ.* 86:549–80.

_____. 1981a. Output Effects of Government Purchases. *J. Polit. Econ.* 89:1086–121.

_____. 1981b. International Substitution in the Business Cycle. In *Supply Shocks, Incentives, and National Wealth,* ed. K. Brunner and A. H. Meltzer. Amsterdam: North Holland.

Barro, R. J., and M. Rush. 1980. Unanticipated Money and Economic Activity. In *Rational Expectations and Economic Policy,* ed. S. Fischer. Chicago: Univ. of Chicago Press.

Batten, D. S., and M. T. Belongia. 1984. The Recent Decline in Agricultural Exports: Is the Exchange Rate the Culprit? *The Federal Reserve Bank of St. Louis Rev.* 66:5-14.

Belongia, M. 1985. Relative Farm Prices and the Long-run Neutrality of Monetary 'Surprises'. St. Louis: Federal Reserve Bank. Mimeo.

Blanchard, O. J., and L. H. Summers. 1984. Perspectives on High World Real Interest Rates. In *Brookings Papers on Economic Activity,* ed. W. C. Brainard and G. L. Perry, 273-324. Washington, D.C.: The Brookings Institution.

Bond, G., C. Vlastuin, and P. Crowley. 1983. Money and Primary Commodity Prices: A Global Perspective. Paper presented at a conference of the Economics Society of Australia, August.

Bosworth, B. P., and R. Z. Lawrence. 1982. *Commodity Prices and Inflation.* Washington, D.C.: The Brookings Institution.

Cukierman, A. 1984. *Inflation, Stagflation, Relative Prices, and Imperfect Information.* New York: Cambridge Univ. Press.

Deaton, B. J., and B. A. Weber. 1985. Economics of Rural Areas. Paper presented at the AAEA Conference on Agriculture and Rural Areas Approaching the 21st Century: Challenges for Agricultural Economics, Iowa State University, Ames, August.

Doering, O., A. Schmitz, and J. Miranowski. 1982. The Full Cost of Farm Exports. Giannini Foundation Working Paper No. 206. Berkeley: Univ. of California.

Dornbusch, R. 1976. Expectations and Exchange Rate Dynamics. *J. Polit. Econ.* 84:1161-76.

Eckstein, Z. 1984. A Rational Expectations Model of Agricultural Supply. *J. Polit. Econ.* 92:1-19.

Enders, W., and B. Falk. 1984. A Microeconomic Test of Money Neutrality. *Rev. Econ. and Stat.* 66:666-69.

Evans, P. 1985. Do Large Deficits Produce High Interest Rates? *Am. Econ. Rev.* 75:68-87.

Feldstein, M. 1982. Government Deficits and Aggregate Demand. *J. Monetary Econ.* 9:1-20.

Fischer, B. S. 1982. Rational Expectations in Agricultural Economics Research and Policy Analysis. *Am. J. Agric. Econ.* 64:260-65.

Fischer, S. 1981. Relative Shocks, Relative Price Variability, and Inflation. In *Brookings Papers on Economic Activity,* ed. W. C. Brainard and G. L. Perry, 381-441. Washington D.C.: The Brookings Institution.

Frankel, J. A. 1984. Commodity Prices and Money: Lessons from International Finance. *Am. J. Agric. Econ.* 66:560-66.

Frankel, J. A., and G. A. Hardouvelis. 1984. Commodity Prices, Overshooting, Money Surprises, and Fed Credibility. Working Paper No. 1121. Cambridge, Mass.: NBER.

Goodwin, T. H., and S. M. Sheffrin. 1982. Testing the Rational Expectations Hypothesis in an Agricultural Market. *Rev. Econ. Stat.* 64:658-67.

Hanson, G. D., and V. R. Eidman. 1985. Agricultural Income Tax Expenditures—A Microeconomic Analysis. *Am. J. Agric. Econ.* 67:271-78.

Hughes, D. W., and J. B. Penson, Jr. 1986. Effects of Selected Macroeconomic Policies on Agriculture: 1984-1990. *Agric. Finance Rev.* 45:81-91.

Huntzinger, R. L. 1979. Market Analysis with Rational Expectations. *J. Econ.* 10:127-45.

Kinney, J. A. 1985. For Full Production on the Farm. *Wall Street Journal,* June 17.

Krugman, P. R. 1985. Is the Strong Dollar Sustainable? Working Paper No. 1644. Cambridge, Mass.: NBER.

Lawrence, C., and R. Z. Lawrence. 1981. Global Commodity Prices and Financial Markets: Theory and Evidence. New York: Dept. of Economics, Columbia Univ. Mimeo.

Leiderman, L. 1980. Macroeconomic Testing of the Rational Expectations and Structural Neutrality Hypotheses for the United States. *J. Monetary Econ.* 6:69–82.

Litterman, R. B., and L. M. Weiss. 1985. Money, Real Interest Rates, and Output: A Reinterpretation of Postwar U.S. Data. *Econometrica* 53:129–56.

Longmire, J., and A. Morey. 1983. Strong Dollar Dampens Demand for U.S. Farm Exports. Foreign Agricultural Economics Report No. 193. Washington, D.C.: USDA, ERS.

Lucas, R. E., Jr. 1972. Expectations and the Neutrality of Money. *J. Econ. Theory* 4:103–24.

_____. 1976. Econometric Policy Evaluation: A Critique. In *The Phillips Curve and Labor Markets,* ed. K. Brunner and A. H. Meltzer. Amsterdam: North Holland.

McGee, R. T., and R. T. Stasiak. 1985. Does Anticipated Monetary Policy Matter? Another Look. *J. Money, Credit, and Banking* 17:16–27.

McKinnon, R. J. 1982. Currency Substitution and Instability in the World Dollar Standard. *Am. Econ. Rev.* 72:320–33.

Marris, S. 1984. Why the Dollar Won't Come Down. *Challenge* 27:19–25.

Mishkin, F. S. 1983. *A Rational Expectations Approach to Macroeconometrics.* Chicago: Univ. of Chicago Press.

Mussa, M. 1981. Sticky Prices and Disequilibrium Adjustment in a Rational Model of the Inflationary Process. *Am. Econ. Rev.* 71:1020–27.

Orden, D. 1984a. The Exchange Rate and the International Corn Market. Paper presented at the AAEA Short Course on the Macroeconomics of Agriculture, Cornell University, Ithaca, August.

_____. 1984b. The Exchange Rate and Agricultural Commodity Markets: A General Equilibrium Perspective. Blacksburg: Dept. of Agric. Econ., Virginia Polytechnic Inst. and State Univ. Mimeo.

Phelps, E. S., and J. B. Taylor. 1977. Stabilizing Powers of Monetary Policy Under Rational Expectations. *J. Polit. Econ.* 85:164–90.

Rae, J. 1984. Major Impacts on Agricultural Trade: A View From the South. Paper presented at the Annual Outlook Conference, USDA, December.

Rausser, G. C. 1985. Macroeconomics and U.S. Agricultural Policy. Giannini Foundation Working Paper No. 385. Berkeley: Univ. of California.

Rausser, G. C., J. A. Chalfant, and K. Stamoulis. 1985. Instability in Agricultural Markets: The U.S. Experience. Paper presented at the meeting of the International Association of Agricultural Economics, August.

Rodgers, J. 1985. General Equilibrium Effects of an Agricultural Land Retirement Scheme in a Large, Open Economy. P85-16. St. Paul: Dept. of Agric. and Appl. Econ., Univ. of Minnesota.

Schuh, G. E. 1974. The Exchange Rate and U.S. Agriculture. *Am. J. Agric. Econ.* 56:1–13.

_____. 1976. The New Macroeconomics of Agriculture. *Am. J. Agric. Econ.* 58:802–11.

_____. 1981. Floating Exchange Rates, International Interdependence, and Agricultural Policy. In *Rural Change: The Challenges for Agricultural Economists,* ed. D. G. Johnson and A. Maunder. Westmead, England: Grover.

_____. 1983. U.S. Agricultural Policy in an Open World Economy. Testimony presented before the Joint Economic Committee of the U.S. Congress, Washington, D.C., May.

_____. 1984. Trade and Macroeconomic Dimensions of Agricultural Policies. In *Alternative Agricultural and Food Policies and the 1985 Farm Bill,* ed. G. C. Rausser and K. R. Farrell. Berkeley: Giannini Foundation of Agricultural Economics, Univ. of California.

_____. 1986a. Policy Options for Improving the Trade Performance of U.S. Agriculture. Paper prepared for the Trade Policy Task Force of the National Agricultural Forum.

_____. 1986b. The U.S. and the Developing Countries. Paper prepared for the National Planning Association.

Schuh, G. E., D. G. Johnson, A. F. McCalla, V. L. Sorensen, and R. L. Thompson. 1984. Research and Agricultural Trade. Washington, D.C.: USDA, ESCOP.

Sims, C. A. 1980. Macroeconomics and Reality. *Econometrica* 48:1–48.

Stamoulis, K., J. A. Chalfant, and G. C. Rausser. 1985. Monetary Policy and the Overshooting of Flexible Prices: Implications for Agricultural Policy. Paper presented at the meeting of the American Agricultural Economics Association, August.

Stockton, D. 1983. Relative Price Dispersion and Aggregate Price Movement. Ph.D. diss., Yale Univ.

Todd, R. M. 1983. A Dynamic Equilibrium Model of Seasonal and Cyclical Fluctuations in the Corn-Soybeans-Hog Sector. Ph.D. diss., Univ. of Minnesota.

The Macroeconomics of Agriculture and Rural America: **A Discussion**

GORDON C. RAUSSER

Edward Schuh and David Orden have advanced a "call to arms" for the agricultural economics profession. Consistent with the previous work of these authors, it is argued that macroeconomics should be studied and that it matters. Given the recent experience of U.S. agriculture, this argument is easy to accept.

Schuh and Orden outline a number of possible channels by which the macroeconomy can impact on the U.S. agricultural sector. Unfortunately, no attempt has been made to distinguish between the various channels of interaction between the macroeconomy and the U.S. agricultural sector. Theoretical and empirical evidence on the relative ranking of importance among the various channels is not provided; nor is any attempt made to structure an analysis to determine the relative importance of the various channels. In essence, much of the paper is devoted to a survey of the reasons why macroeconomic and international factors affect agriculture.

On the whole, the discussion is primarily a review of well-accepted factors. There are, however, some concerns expressed in the paper that have not been articulated in the agricultural economics literature. These include, inter alia, the dual constraints on national policy, the export orientation of debtor countries, and the relative importance of capital mobility.

The major issues addressed can be assessed and evaluated from a large number of perspectives. In what follows, I will collect and summarize my views on their paper in terms of (1) the state of the world facing U.S. agriculture, (2) alternative macroeconomic paradigms, (3) the relative importance of sector-specific versus macroeconomic policies on U.S. agriculture, (4) second-best policies, (5) capital flows, (6) partial versus general equilibrium analysis, and (7) the empirical results and concluding remarks.

State of the World

Schuh and Orden place less emphasis on the inherent instability in commodity markets and more emphasis on the external linkages with other

Gordon C. Rausser is the Robert Gordon Sproul Chair Professor of Agricultural and Resource Economics, Department of Agricultural and Resource Economics, University of California, Berkeley, and Chairman of the Giannini Foundation of Agricultural Economics.

markets. The deregulation of the credit and banking system has resulted in greater exposure of agriculture to conditions in domestic money markets. Also, because of the shift from fixed exchange rates to flexible rates, commodity markets have become more exposed to international money markets and real trade among countries. Since the 1970s, the emergence of a well-integrated international financial market has meant that agriculture, through domestic and foreign money and exchange-rate markets, has become increasingly more dependent on capital flows among countries.

Greater dependence on trade since the early 1970s has exposed U.S. agriculture to more shocks from foreign markets. Consistent with increased dependence on trade for the world economy as a whole, U.S. agriculture is heavily dependent on exports. To be sure, this increased dependence has made the demand structure facing U.S. agriculture less stable due, in part, to the emergence of the Soviet Union, with its unstable agriculture, as a major importer and due to barriers to trade which cause changes in foreign markets to be borne by the United States and other exporting countries that practice relatively free trade.

The linkages of commodity markets with U.S. money markets are indeed pervasive. Since agricultural production is extremely capital intensive and debt equity ratios have risen dramatically over the last 10 years, movements and real interest rates have significant effects on the cost structure facing agricultural production. Stock-carrying and storable commodity systems are sensitive to changes in real interest rates; and for nonstorable commodities (e.g., live cattle and hogs), breeding stocks are interest-rate sensitive. These effects, combined with the influence of interest rates and the value of the dollar, exert pressure on grain products from both the demand side (export demand, domestic livestock, grain demand, and stock-holding demand) and the cost side. The especially sensitive nature of agriculture to interest rates suggests that this sector is vulnerable to monetary and fiscal policy changes. Our empirical work at Berkeley has shown that since 1972 the instabilities in monetary and fiscal policies have contributed importantly to the instabilities of commodity markets (Rausser et al. 1986).

The effects of U.S. fiscal and monetary policies on interest rates, exchange rates, and inflation must be placed in the context of world economic conditions. The trend in world agricultural trade is toward dependence among nations, more competition among suppliers, and lower export prices. The world recession and associated international credit problem brought about a shifting back of demand for U.S. exports at any price, exacerbating the effects of high domestic support prices and exchange rates. In the minds of many, the continuing world recession will be the most important obstacle to revived growth in world agricultural markets. In addition to these conditions, high interest rates and a strong dollar have the indirect effect of encouraging foreign governments to contract their own money supplies. This, in turn, to the extent that money is nonneutral in the short run, leads to lower aggregate foreign income and a lower demand for U.S. farm goods (Rausser 1985).

It must be emphasized that the heightened importance of macroeconomic factors on U.S. agriculture does not represent a structural change in long-term patterns. To argue that the linkages with the macroeconomic and international sectors emerged in the early 1970s and were not previously witnessed is to ignore the historical record. Macroeconomic disturbances and their links to the agricultural sector are central to any historical account of policy developments in the agriculture sector. For example, the organized agricultural interest groups that emerged during the populist protest of the late nineteenth century were motivated, in part, by monetary restrictions associated with the greenback period and the return to fixed exchange rates under the gold standard in 1879. Continued price deflation into the middle 1890s and real interest rates that are estimated to have averaged 8.5 percent in the period 1870 through 1889 proved particularly burdensome to debt-ridden farmers. The demands of various farmer movements thus consisted of easy money created by government action, government funds for farm mortgages, and the scheme for the creation of government paper money with stored crops as collateral.

The discontent voiced by farmers over the macroeconomic policies of the nineteenth century explain, in part, the later institutional changes that organized the Federal Reserve in 1913 and led to creation of Federal Land Banks in 1916. The introduction of sector-specific policies in 1933 followed a farm crisis that had its origins in macroeconomic adjustments after World War I.

After the Depression and World War II, the set of macroeconomic policies implemented through the 1950s and 1960s afforded the U.S. economy a period of unprecedented macroeconomic stability. During this period, in essence, the macroeconomic linkages with agriculture were dormant. When the important aspects of the macroeconomic policy structure began to change in the late 1960s, the linkages with the macroeconomic environment returned as a prime factor influencing the U.S. agricultural sector and, thus, complicating agricultural policy.

Alternative Macroeconomic Paradigms

Our perspective on the state of the world quite obviously depends critically upon the paradigms we employ to interpret and explain economic events. In the case of the macroeconomic environment and its linkages with agriculture, a number of paradigms have been advanced in the literature.

These include the monetarist, the new classical, Keynesian, neo-Keynesian and post-Keynesian. Among these paradigms, as implied by Schuh and Orden, there are two major contending paradigms—the new classical and the neo-Keynesian.

A fundamental aspect of the new classical school is the belief that nonadjusting prices and wages implicit in the traditional Keynesian framework are inconsistent with the optimizing behavior of microeconomic theory. The rational expectation hypothesis provides an alternate behavioral assumption that describes how agents form expectations in a manner that is stochastically consistent. The basic assumptions of this paradigm imply that money is neutral (i.e., if information about money stock changes is widely available, there should be no effect of monetary factors on real variables). Likewise, real interest rates are not affected by monetary policy and nominal interest rates will respond to changes in expected inflation rates quickly according to the Fisher equation. A related implication, the "Lucas critique" or the "policy ineffectiveness proposition," is that accurately anticipated changes in monetary or fiscal policy will be rapidly incorporated into expectations about inflation and, therefore, will have no effects on output and employment.

With regard to exchange-rate determination, the ideas for the new classical school are consistent with what has been referred to as "global monetarism"; that is, under a flexible exchange-rate system, international arbitrage forces exchange rates toward purchasing-power parity levels reflecting the "law of one price." With rational expectations, it is further implied that changes in money stock will also be quickly reflected in exchange rates.

With the new classical paradigm, all the unanticipated changes in monetary policy can be expected to have significant effects on the agricultural sector. The long wave of steadily increasing asset values in agriculture during the 1970s and the long wave of downward movements in asset values over the 1980s cannot be readily explained by the new classical paradigm. These long waves, however, can be generated within the confines of the neo-Keynesian paradigm. The critical factor that differentiates the neo-Keynesian school is its contention that all markets do not behave like Walrasian auction markets. Rather, the economy can be broadly categorized into sectors where prices adjust sluggishly to demand and supply shocks (fixed price) and a group of markets that exhibit rapid adjustments. Okun (1975) has justified this differential pattern by pointing out that, unlike those goods that are actually traded on auction markets, fixed-price goods are more heterogeneous in quality and need to be inspected prior to purchase. As a result, search costs can be prohibitively large if prices are allowed to vary frequently.[1]

Under this paradigm, differential effects of monetary policy between agricultural and nonagricultural markets are admitted. If agricultural commodity markets behave as "flex price" while other markets behave as "fixed price," "macro externalities" will be imposed on the agricultural sector. Differential speeds of adjustment in the two types of prices following changes in monetary policy mean that overshooting in agricultural prices will occur even if expectations are formed rationally.[2] As Frankel and Hardouvelis (1985, 4) point out, "This overshooting phenomenon can be thought of as a macroeconomic example of the Le Chatelier principle. Because one variable in the system (manufactured good prices) is not free to adjust, the other variable in the system (commodity prices) must jump correspondingly further in order to compensate."

The nonneutrality of money lasts as long as prices fail to adjust to reflect demand and supply forces. Empirical evidence has also been accumulated that strongly suggests fiscal policy is nonneutral. During the 1980s, these two sets of policies have resulted in high and volatile interest and exchange rates, which have worked together with corresponding contractions in world income and agricultural export demand. This combination of forces strongly suggests that resources should come out of agricultural production. Due to agriculture being capital intensive and its dependence on international trade, however, farmers are faced with a painful adjustment tax resulting from these forces. Over the period from 1980 to 1983, this tax took the form of higher interest payments and lower commodity prices in cases where the supply of goods did not shrink sufficiently fast. An additional tax was imposed in the form of a significant drop in farmers' stock of wealth. With government intervention, of course, much of the burden of adjustment appears as increases in the cost of agricultural programs. Precisely the opposite situation occurred during much of the 1970s. Government policies, the accumulation of wealth through large increases in land values, and the increasing production capacity left the agricultural sector ripe for the shocks of the 1980s.

It is interesting to note that the two alternative paradigms (new classical and neo-Keynesian) merge under rational expectations with imperfect and significant costs for information. The new classical model concerns itself largely with the benefits of forming rational expectations and not with the cost of collecting the information base that is needed to form rational expectations. New developments in industrial organization provide much theoretical justification and empirical evidence in support of Okun's fixed-price or customer markets. In the case of the differential response of agricultural and nonagricultural markets to monetary shocks, the empirical evidence weighs in favor of the neo-Keynesian paradigm (Rausser et al. 1985). Finally, "overshooting waves" on agricultural commodity markets can last as long as the nonneutral period of changes in monetary and fiscal policies lasts. The length of such waves can be expected empirically to be much longer than unanticipated monetary effects on agriculture admitted by the new classical paradigm.

The implications of the above discussion for teaching, research, extension, and policy analysis are rather dramatic. In each of these major activities of our profession, we can no longer focus on only the internal demand and supply forces for a particular agricultural commodity and the implications of various coordinating mechanisms, especially governmental intervention. The experience in the United States, as well as numerous other countries, makes it clear that the conventional microeconomic analysis of agricultural markets is inadequate. Students, researchers, extension agents, and policymakers must recognize that the dynamic path of agricultural commodity markets cannot be explained on the basis of private market demand and supply functions alone. In fact, the appropriate characterization of such dynamics can only be obtained by specifying (1) the real demand and supply forces for a particular market; (2) the influence of coordinating mechanisms, especially governmental intervention; and (3) the linkage among domestic agricultural markets, exchange rates, and domestic as well as international money markets.

Sector-Specific versus Macroeconomic Policies

It would have been useful if Schuh and Orden had distinguished more clearly between sector-specific and macroeconomic policies. Throughout the paper, they seem to view sector policies, at least those beyond export subsidies, as ineffective and unimportant. For example, they state that "the problem is that the impacts of policies designed for the domestic economy are literally swamped by forces from the international economy." They also state, "In today's world, it is monetary, fiscal, exchange-rate, and trade policy that really matter for agriculture." These views are consistent with the perspective that Professor Schuh has advocated for some time. In an earlier paper, Schuh (1984, 122–23) states that "the evidence is both abundant and painful that modern agriculture is an inseparable part of the overall economy and that macroeconomic problems are at the core of commercial agriculture's present problems."

In contrast to the above view, Bruce Gardner lays the current problems in U.S. agriculture at the doorstep of sector-specific policies. Gardner (1984, 131–32) states that "the fundamental reason for current policy problems is that the incentive prices in the grain programs are too high, causing a tendency to overproduce that no perspective weakening of the dollar or worldwide recovery is likely to offset for long."

The empirical work that we have conducted at the University of California, Berkeley, strongly suggests that the extreme positions that only sector policies matter or that only macroeconomic exchange-rate and trade policies matter are foolish. Our empirical results demonstrate quite clearly that monetary and fiscal policies can have substantial effects on prices and incomes in the agricultural sector. Due to the nature of current sector-specific policies, however, there is an asymmetry in the effects of monetary policy. This asymmetry results from price supports that limit downward trajectory of prices but have little, if any, influence on price increases. For nonneutral monetary and fiscal policies that result in commodity price increases, many if not all of the benefits accrue to the private sector. However, for nonneutral policies that result in price decreases, much of the costs are borne by the public sector.

In the long run, sector-specific policies are likely to have more significant influence on resource allocation to the U.S. agriculture sector than do macroeconomic policies and external events. This is especially true since neither of the two major paradigms admit nonneutrality of money in the long run. To the extent that money is neutral in the long run and the effects of fiscal policies are also neutralized, sector-specific policies will dominate in the long run. The sector policies that provide incentives for overallocation of resources to agricultural production, however, leave the sector especially vulnerable to macroeconomic policies that impose adjustment costs. Such policies must, almost by definition, lead to a financial crisis and many of the current problems that have been witnessed by rural banks and governmental agencies.

Second-Best Policies

As Schuh and Orden imply, the optimal choice of a distortion of a particular market, given fixed distortions in other markets, is a problem in the theory of second best. For a modern treatment of this problem, Dixit and Norman (1980) should be consulted. For an application of this treatment, another useful reference is Dixit and Newbery (1985). In these works, it is formally demonstrated that the optimal distortion in a particular market is a weighted average of the fixed distortions in other markets; the weights sum to one but need not all be positive. Hence, if some weight is negative, it is possible that all sectors with fixed proportions are subsidized; yet, it is optimal to tax the remaining sector.[3]

The theory of second best, advanced by Schuh and Orden, most certainly does not call for the same degree of intervention in all sectors of the economy. In fact, just the opposite can be true depending upon the policy objectives. More than just the relative rate of protection matters. The "optimal protection" depends, in accordance with a Ramsey optimal tax scheme, on the relative price-marginal cost differences. Such a scheme does not imply equiproportional intervention.

On one hand Schuh and Orden argue for an equivalent export subsidy based on a faulty interpretation of second-best theory; but on the other, they argue strongly for trade liberalization. Their equivalent export subsidy policy will also be nonneutral with respect to the exchange rate. As a result, the effects of the subsidy can be spread throughout the economy to the detriment of other sectors. These potential counterproductive second-order effects can and should be recognized in our assessments of second-best policies. Moreover, some consideration must be given to the predictable retaliation of other countries in the export subsidy policies that might be pursued by the United States.

Capital Flows

Schuh and Orden emphasize the importance of capital flows. Unfortunately, little success has been achieved in explaining capital flows in a general equilibrium context. One framework of monetary policy/interest rates and capital flows/income has been developed in Nishiyama and Rausser (1985). The theoretical framework incorporates assets into a portfolio balance model. In one version of their framework, it is shown in a two-country model that U.S. interest rates decline and foreign interest rates rise as a direct result of portfolio adjustments that follow a negative change in the U.S. current account balance. As a result of this change, foreigners who receive dollar-denominated assets as payments adjust their portfolios (some are kept in dollars, some switch to interest-bearing assets denominated in their own currencies, etc.), and U.S. citizens also adjust their portfolios after the wealth transfer. All of these adjustments culminate in investment demand increasing in the United States with corresponding increases in future outputs and incomes.

In the context of a traditional partial equilibrium model with exchange rate and income given exogenously, Nishiyama and Rausser (1985) demonstrate that exchange-rate effects on import demands occur through the own-price, cross-price, and policy distortions. These effects are called direct or first-round effects. Relaxing the assumption that income is given, four additional secondary effects can be identified. The first can be defined as the wealth-transfer effect associated with capital flows outlined above. Another secondary effect stems from the systematic official intervention in foreign exchange markets that are pursued by central banks to bound the erratic movements of exchange rates. When these activities are unsterilized, such official responses change money supplies of the intervening countries;

and to the extent that money is nonneutral, this results in changes in income levels. Another secondary effect emanates directly from the trade balance, which in turn stimulates or dampens aggregate demand. Finally, a secondary effect results from changes in foreign incomes due to the direct effects and the wealth-transfer effect. These forces affect the aggregate demand for domestic goods through trade and will influence domestic income.

Partial versus General Equilibrium Analysis

Throughout the Schuh and Orden paper, emphasis is placed on general equilibrium analysis to the neglect of partial equilibrium frameworks. Although Schuh and Orden outline a number of limitations of partial equilibrium models, their legitimate concerns are never crystallized. In the context of exchange-rate effects, are they concerned about better measurement, prediction, or explanation? Their position on these matters should be clarified because it has important implications for the research, teaching, and extension activities of our profession. Largely for purposes of simplicity, most of our efforts have focused on partial equilibrium rather than general equilibrium analysis.

A number of quibbles could be raised with regard to Schuh and Orden's application of general equilibrium analysis to agriculture. For example, they correctly argue that the domestic terms of trade ideally should determine relative social profitability. However, the index they suggest has one of the same limitations as the parity index. In particular, both ignore relative productivity (cost) effects.

From a research strategy standpoint, the Schuh and Orden analysis should be extended to evaluate when partial equilibrium versus general equilibrium models should be utilized to analyze the effects of trade and macroeconomics on U.S. agriculture. There is clearly a trade-off between complexity and accuracy, and this trade-off should be taken into account in advocating a partial versus a general equilibrium approach to consider issues addressed by Schuh and Orden.[4]

Empirical Results and Concluding Remarks

The empirical analysis conducted by Schuh and Orden is most peculiar. In their section entitled "Prima Facie Evidence of Macroeconomic Evidence on Agriculture," all they offer is simple graphical comparisons and qualitative remarks regarding correlation analysis. In Figure 13.1, the U.S. money supply is compared with the real prices of agricultural commodities. They argue that the variables exhibit a clear correlation and that deviations from a very close association of these two variables are explained by the many other factors that affect agricultural prices. Similar conclusions are drawn from trends of real interest rates, real exchange values of the dollar, and real values of agricultural exports. In the former case, they report data from 1970 to 1984, while in the latter case data from 1967 to 1984 are recorded.

If general equilibrium analysis is the correct vehicle to evaluate the issues addressed by Schuh and Orden, it is rather surprising that the only empirical analysis they are prepared to advance is simple correlation analysis. For the periods over which they report data in Figures 13.1 and 13.2, many of the causal forces that influence agricultural real prices and agricultural exports all pointed in the same direction. For example, through much of the 1980s, the relatively tight monetary policy, particularly in 1981 and 1982, came in conjunction with (1) record crops, (2) a significant decline in the rate of export growth from less-developed industrialized and Communist countries, and (3) increased competition from a large number of competing suppliers on world markets. In the early 1970s, production shortfalls occurred in conjunction with expansions in money supply and declines in the real exchange value of the dollar. Moreover, during this period, huge governmental stocks had been eliminated as a result of the Soviet grain deal. In contrast, during the early 1980s, public stock holding increased dramatically due to the record crops of 1981 and 1982. Also, in the early 1970s, real export demand growth occurred, in part, because of countries upgrading their diets and some Communist countries deciding to maintain their livestock populations regardless of real prices or the real exchange value of the dollar. These additional influences do not detract but, instead, enhance the apparent degree of simple correlation. Obviously, what is required is a complete model representation involving the system of relationships, both real and monetary, which can separate out the relative importance of different causal influences.

Even with the clarification offered in the section on capital mobility, it should be noted that empirically no formal link has been established between capital flows and consumption, investment, or income in the United States. This is simply a hypothesis that has yet to be formally tested. Some leading authorities in international trade have argued that it is not possible to model capital mobility on the basis of economic influences. In other words, the systematic variations in capital mobility that can be explained by economic forces are unacceptably small.[5]

Finally, it is unfortunate that Schuh and Orden leave the reader with the responsibility of drawing the implications of fiscal and monetary policies for rural America. Professor Schuh was the first to articulate the significance of exchange rates on U.S. agriculture. I am sure if he had chosen to do so, he could have provided the same clarity in assessing the implications of monetary and fiscal policies on rural America. In this sense, the title of the Schuh and Orden paper is grossly misleading. They choose, instead, to focus on an open economy, capital mobility, international factors, and the exchange rate. The common theme throughout the paper is that macroeconomic effects on agriculture are important, but they work mainly through the effects of macroeconomic policies on exchange rates and the demand for agricultural exports. The preoccupation with trade is such that, even in discussing the issues of whether policy subsidizes or taxes agriculture, the discussion is cast in terms of nominal or effective protection. In tracing through the dynamic impacts of monetary, fiscal, and exchange-rate policies on rural America, such a focus is far too constraining.

Notes

1. An alternative justification for differential price adjustments across sectors has been advanced by Hicks (1974). His justification emphasizes the management of inventories; producers in fixed-price sectors hold inventory stocks for the purpose of meeting fluctuations and sale orders, and output adjusts to obtain the desired inventory-sales ratio. However, in fixed-price sectors, inventory shocks are traded speculatively. Large price fluctuations thus result in a market process that balances demands for stocks with available supplies.

2. This overshooting is analogous to the exchange-rate overshooting studied by Dornbusch (1976) and amounts to either a tax or a subsidy for agriculture through relative price changes.

3. To illustrate this point, as in Dixit and Newbery (1985), suppose there is a small country with three sectors. Let sectors 2 and 3 be subsidized; if a net output of sector 2 increases as a result of an increase in the price of good 1, it may be optimal to tax good 1. The calculation of optimal distortions, holding other distortions fixed, provides the type of empirical evidence necessary to support or refute the argument that agriculture should be subsidized to offset the distortions resulting from heavy subsidization of the nonagricultural sector. Of course, in the world of two goods, such a subsidy will bring the relative price between nonagricultural and agricultural goods closer to a free-market equilibrium relative price. However, in a world of many goods, such an outcome cannot be inferred.

4. Along these lines, the earlier work of Rausser and Just (1982) should prove useful.

5. Along similar lines, Schuh and Orden focus on the importance of capital flows from small countries to the United States, especially for the oil-producing countries of OPEC. The importance they place on capital flows from these countries to the United States and its implications from income transfers is rather surprising. Given the capital controls imposed by many of these countries, it is difficult to believe that such impacts are significant.

References

Dixit, A., and D. Newbery. 1985. Setting the Price of Oil in a Distorted Economy. *Econ J. Supplement* 95:71–82.

Dixit, A., and V. Norman. 1980. *Theory of the International Trade.* London: Cambridge Univ. Press.

Dornbusch, R. 1976. Expectations and Exchange Rate Dynamics. *J. Polit. Econ.* 84:1161–76.

Frankel, J. A,. and G. A. Hardouvelis. 1985. Commodity Prices, Monetary Surprises, and Fed Credibility. *J. Money, Credit, and Banking* 17:425–38.

Gardner, B. L. 1984. Agricultural Policy. In *National Resources and the Environment: The Reagan Approach,* ed. P. Portney, 111–40. Washington, D.C.: Urban Inst. Press.

Hicks, J. R. 1974. *The Crisis in Keynesian Economics.* Oxford: Basil Blackwell.

Nishiyama, Y., and G. C. Rausser. 1985. Exchange Rates: Backward Linkage on U.S. Agriculture: The Case of Japan. Working Paper No. 389. Berkeley: Univ. of California, Dept. of Agric. and Resource Econ.

Okun, A. M. 1975. Inflation: Its Mechanics and Welfare Cost. *Brookings Papers on Economic Activity* 2: 351–401.

Rausser, G. C. 1985. Macroeconomics and U.S. Agricultural Policy. In *U.S. Agricultural Policy: 1985 Farm Legislation,* ed. B. L. Gardner, 207–252. Washington, D.C.: American Enterprise Inst. for Public Policy Research.

Rausser, G. C., J. A. Chalfant, and K. G. Stamoulis. 1985. Instability in Agricultural Markets. In *The U.S. Experience.* Proceedings of the Nineteenth International Conference of Agricultural Economics. Oxford: Oxford Univ. Press.

Rausser, G. C., J. A. Chalfant, H. A. Love, and K. G. Stamoulis. 1986. Macroeconomic Linkages, Taxes, and Subsidies in the U.S. Agricultural Sector. *Am. J. Agric. Econ.* 68:399–412.

Rausser, G. C., and R. E. Just. 1982. Principles of Policy Modeling in Agriculture. In *New Directions in Econometeric Modeling and Forecasting in U.S. Agriculture,* ed. G. C. Rausser and R. E. Just, 763–800. New York: Elsevier North-Holland.

Schuh, G. E. 1984. Trade and Macroeconomic Dimensions of Agricultural Policies. In *Alternative Agricultural and Food Policies and the 1985 Farm Bill,* ed. G. C. Rausser and Kenneth R. Farrell. San Leandro, Calif.: Blaco.

Tobin, J., and J. D. de Macedo. 1979. The Short-run Macroeconomics of Floating Exchange Rates: An Exposition. Cowles Commission Discussion Paper No. 522: Yale Univ.

The Macroeconomics of Agriculture and Rural America: **A Discussion**

WILLIAM D. DOBSON

After making a few observations about the broader contributions of the paper to our understanding of the macroeconomics of agriculture, I will attempt to identify implications arising from it for extension programs.

Contributions of the Paper

Overall, the paper makes contributions that help us to focus our thinking about the impact of macroeconomic forces on agriculture and rural America. The authors make a particularly strong case for taking an international perspective regarding agriculture and for viewing the sector through an open economy model. In addition, the reader will find useful and generally well-developed reminders in the paper of the:

1. Importance of food in the United States as a wage good and the implications of this characteristic of food for real wages, competitiveness of different sectors of the United States economy in international markets, and support for agricultural research in the United States.

2. Increased openness of the U.S. economy, which places many problems of the economy beyond the reach of domestic policies. As a result of the increased openness, we witness phenomena such as the swamping of large federal expenditures for farm price supports by international economic developments.

3. Numerous instances in which painful economic adjustments have been shifted to the traded-goods sector of the U.S. economy (especially agriculture) by recent macroeconomic developments.

4. Shifts in the political and economic positions of different groups regarding trade liberalization. A noteworthy change is the emergence of certain U.S. bankers, specifically those with large loans outstanding in South America, as proponents of open international markets.

5. Potential importance of monetary instability as a determinant of

William D. Dobson is Professor and Head of the Department of Agricultural Economics at Purdue University, Lafayette, Indiana.

instability in world commodity prices. Hypotheses relating to this problem were suggested by the figures and arguments presented by the authors.

6. Major influence of the emergence of a well-integrated international capital market and large international capital flows on the level and stability of exchange rates, international trade flows, and interest rates. These findings also suggest that there is a need to better understand the determinants of international capital flows, in effect to learn much more about who holds what assets and why.

Perhaps equally as important, the authors identified major areas of disagreement in the macroeconomic literature. We are given glimpses of how the ideas of those using the Keynesian fixed-flex price model, modern classical economists, monetarists, the rational expectations groups, and others are vying for ascendency and/or legitimacy in a disorderly fashion that may do little to restore confidence in macroeconomics. The authors discussed mostly mainstream ideas and major controversies. Accordingly, they mercifully subjected the reader to only a short examination of the frequently discussed, but apparently barren, hypothesis that suggests the public responds to anticipated government deficits with increases in private saving, leaving the level and composition of real output unchanged in the face of larger government deficits.

The authors argue that the correlations observed between interest rates, the value of the dollar, and the value of agricultural exports are strongly suggestive of the importance of macroeconomic factors to agriculture. Among other things, their comments identify a debate that is taking place among economists, bureaucrats, farmers, business officials, policymakers, and others about the relative strength of the different forces that affect U.S. agricultural exports (including USDA commodity loan rates, export subsidies of competing countries, the supply response in the United States and abroad to the high commodity prices of the 1970s, and macroeconomic developments). The evidence offered in this debate has made it apparent that U.S. agricultural exports are influenced by complex forces and that the quality of the discussion on farm and export policy could be elevated by careful efforts by economists to disentangle the effects of the different forces on these exports.

Implications for Extension Programs

Implications arising for extension programs can be obtained by examining changes in extension clientele and the changing needs of the clientele groups for macroeconomic information. Many extension economists now have a diverse clientele that includes farmers, officials of farm organizations, business officials, legislators, legislative staff people, and employees of lending agencies, university officials, and a host of others. Because of efforts of educators such as G. Edward Schuh and the emphasis given to macroeconomics by the mass media, many customers of the extension economist have acquired an improved general knowledge of the impact of macroeconomic developments on their businesses and organizations. Thus, many of those customers now have less need for general information on the impact of macroeconomic developments on commodity prices or general information relating to the more obvious effects of the strong dollar. Rather, they often need specific information on macroeconomic forces that can be used for planning and decision making. When searching for such information, they often ask extension specialists and others questions such as: Can Brazil, through currency realignments and other measures, really take away the U.S. soybean export market? How much would a 20 to 25 percent reduction in the value of the dollar increase corn exports over a three-year period? What is the probability that federal budget deficits will be heavily monetized during the next five years? How much inflation would such monetization of the deficits produce? Are changes in prospect that could significantly improve economic conditions in U.S. agriculture during the next two to three years? The last question has become important to agricultural lenders since the conclusion they reach regarding it often determines whether they will encourage certain financially strapped farm borrowers to "hang on" for additional years or, alternatively, to sell their assets in the near future. Business officials often ask complex "what if" questions that include macroeconomic considerations.

Among the more apparent implications of these developments are: (1) the needs of extension clientele for economic intelligence relating to macroeconomics have become more sophisticated; (2) many extension economists will need to acquire a more complete knowledge of macroeconomics if they are to do an adequate job of answering questions such as those mentioned above; and (3) if the extension economists fail to acquire an increased knowledge of macroeconomics, they are likely to abdicate more of the job of providing economic intelligence to others, especially to others in the private sector.

Some questions that extension economists now receive relating to macroeconomics are so complex as to be nearly impossible to answer with any assurance that the information supplied will be even approximately correct. In my opinion, forecasts of interest rates for more than a few months into the future fall in this category. Forecasts of when the value of the dollar will increase or decrease substantially in value also seem to fall in this class. My skepticism regarding the ability of economists to forecast such variables reflects opinions formed during several years of experience as a business forecast watcher.

How can extension economists acquire the knowledge needed to deal with the changes in clientele and the problems of those clientele groups?

1. A stronger research base will be needed for extension work relating to the macroeconomics of agriculture. I believe that the recommendations of the authors calling for the modeling of the impacts of macroeconomic factors on the agricultural sector and the quantification of these impacts in a cohesive empirical framework would help to establish such an improved research base.

2. Extension personnel will require more training in macroeconomics. This will include training acquired through formal course work. It also will mean gaining practical knowledge of the type acquired by business economists about exchange rates, economic growth rates, interest rates, money supply figures, and other macroeconomic variables as a normal part of their work.

3. Extension economists will need access to sophisticated forecasting and policy analysis models that take into account the impact of macroeconomic developments on agriculture. This does not mean that every agricultural economics department will need to develop and maintain such models. In some cases, extension specialists may choose to "retail" macroeconomic information generated from models operating in the USDA, in departments other than their own, or in the private sector. In other cases, agricultural economics departments might share the cost of developing and maintaining such models.

4. In some instances, the most useful contribution to be made by the extension economist may be to acknowledge that economists are unable to offer useful answers on some complex questions. As suggested earlier, requests for forecasts of interest rates for more than a few months into the future might be treated this way. Such an admission might help to redirect efforts of the questioner away from efforts to obtain forecasts of questionable value to the potentially more useful business of managing risks in the face of largely unpredictable values for interest rates. By exhibiting such candor, the extension economist also could help in a small way to restore the credibility of economists on macroeconomic matters.

Concluding Note

In summary, the Schuh-Orden paper is a comprehensive piece that suggests how macroeconomic considerations might be taken into account as research, extension, and teaching priorities in agricultural economics are reassessed. My comments suggest that a larger investment of human capital in the study of the macroeconomics of agriculture and an expansion of the research base for extension programs relating to the macroeconomics of agriculture would improve extension programs in the United States.

The Macroeconomics of Agriculture and Rural America: **A Discussion**

MICHAEL D. BOEHLJE

This review of the Schuh and Orden paper will be structured in two parts. The first part will focus on content; the second part will emphasize, as requested, the implications for the profession from the perspective of a college-level administrator.

The paper focuses on an important topic, but the discussion is much narrower than the title. A more descriptive title of the paper might be "International Commodity and Financial Markets and Production Agriculture." The arguments on this more limited topic are developed logically and in detail; the broader topic requires more development and discussion than provided here. More specifically, macroeconomics is broader than the issues of international commodity and financial markets, and rural America encompasses much more than production agriculture. Issues related to domestic fiscal and monetary policy as it impacts on the agricultural sector deserve more emphasis. Such issues include, for example, the impacts of interest rates on capital investment and debt financing in the agricultural sector; tax policy including the implications of tax sheltering and the differential impact of taxes on agriculture compared to other sectors of the economy; the net aggregate income enhancement and redistribution effects of changes in government expenditures for farm programs such as price and income supports; and the net effect of changes in tax and expenditure policy on budget deficits, interest rates, capital investment in agriculture, agricultural output, commodity prices, and food prices. Clearly, an analysis of the effects of macroeconomic policies on individual farms and decision makers will be required to obtain a thorough understanding of the impacts of these policies. Such analyses may be microeconomic in nature, but they are essential to determine how a sector of the economy will respond to macro policy. A missing link in past assessments of the impacts of changes in macro policy is this micro-macro linkage; policymakers had only limited information on the actual responses of individual decision makers to policy changes.

The implications of macro policy on other segments of agriculture beyond the farm gate is also given little emphasis by Schuh and Orden.

Michael D. Boehlje is Dean of the College of Agriculture, University of Minnesota.

Macro policy including international trade dimensions have significant implications for input supply firms, particularly those that are raw-material based. The product-processing, grain-merchandising, transportation, and service sectors also are impacted by macro policy. And clearly rural communities are directly influenced by the expenditure dimension of fiscal policy. Discussion in recent years of an industrial policy to target specific government expenditure and tax incentives to particular industries to stimulate expansion and employment opportunities is important to rural communities as they evaluate rural industrialization and community viability. Again, the response of individual firms and decision makers to macro policies, although not considered as part of macroeconomics by some, is essential to understand the implications of various policy options.

Although the authors did respond to earlier review comments concerning the important broader dimensions of macroeconomics in agriculture, the discussion of these broader issues is not parallel to that of the implications of international financial and commodity markets on production agriculture.

The Schuh and Orden paper raises a number of challenging issues from the perspective of a college-level administrator. First, with respect to the teaching program, a basic question is how to make macroeconomic concepts relevant to undergraduate students in agricultural curriculums. Quite possibly one of the reasons that macroeconomics is so hard to teach is that the theoretical underpinnings of the field seem currently to be in slight disarray. A more concise and accepted set of theoretical constructs could possibly make it easier to teach and illustrate the practical usefulness of macroeconomic theory. The strong microproduction orientation of the typical student in the college of agriculture provides an additional challenge to the teacher of macroeconomic concepts. Allowing the "economics department" to take responsibility for instruction in applied macro theory is probably not appropriate, because the applications will most likely focus on nonagricultural industries. To be understood, the concepts of macro theory must be integrated in the specific courses in agricultural finance, marketing, policy, and management. Similar issues are encountered in extension programming.

Possibly a more fundamental problem agricultural economists currently face in colleges of agriculture is that many administrators do not understand what economists can and cannot do. This is particularly the case with respect to predictions and forecasts of future events. Like the students in colleges of agriculture, many college-level administrators are micro-oriented, with a technical rather than a social science focus. For example, their perspective is that we will produce our way out of the current financial stress problem in agriculture. As to macroeconomics, the viewpoint seems to be that with the limited direct influence that individuals and farmers can have on macro policy combined with the disagreement as to what is the appropriate policy to implement, the topic just does not merit much time or emphasis.

Undoubtedly, part of the challenge we face as economists, whether macro- or micro-oriented, is to improve our professional credibility. Our predictions have been wrong in many cases, and we have not been willing to be appropriately cautious in making predictions or in stating them in probabilistic rather than deterministic terms. In some cases, the precision of our analysis and our ability to evaluate complex problems has been oversold. And to some degree our concepts have been judged to be unneeded and possibly irrelevant; during the 1970s, individual producers could be successful without applying the concepts of economics, and the problems of the 1980s are sufficiently complex and severe that economists cannot seem to solve what would appear to be economic problems at both the micro and macro levels. Our response as economists must be to accept the challenge and strive to solve real-world problems with the appropriate combination of technical data, economic theory, and common sense.

14

The Economics of Rural Areas

BRADY J. DEATON and BRUCE A. WEBER

> It is . . . the social enthusiasm which revolts from the sordidness
> of mean streets and the joylessness of withered lives, that is the begin-
> ning of economic science. Here, if in no other field, Comte's great
> phrase holds good: "It is for the heart to suggest our problems; it is for
> the intellect to solve them . . . " [Pigou 1920, 51.]

Since the founding of the discipline, agricultural economists have been
concerned with the interrelationships between the agricultural economy and
the communities affected by agricultural and other natural resource economic bases.

The purpose of this paper is to analyze critical issues that either
emerge from or impinge directly on these interrelationships and to assess
the theoretical and analytical foundations that the profession will require to
effectively address these issues. The first section summarizes six social and
economic trends that are shaping the rural economic environment. The
second section provides an interpretation of the changing policy context to
establish a framework for interpreting the trends, the issues, and the professional role of agricultural economists. A third section addresses three
selected issues. The first issue is the interrelationship between farm and
nonfarm economic activity in rural areas. Particular emphasis is given to
the effect of expanding nonfarm employment opportunities on farmers'
perceptions of risk and thereby, the choice of products, techniques of production, and capital intensity of farming.

The second issue regards the functioning of rural capital markets in a

---

Brady J. Deaton is Professor of Agricultural Economics at Virginia Polytechnic Institute and
State University, Blacksburg. Bruce A. Weber is Professor of Agricultural and Resource Economics at Oregon State University, Corvallis. We are indebted to the formal reviewers of our
paper Kenneth Farrell, Thomas Hady, and Gerald Klonglan for their perceptive reviews. We
are also grateful to Paxton Marshall, Wes Musser, Glenn Nelson, and Dave Orden for reviewing an early draft of this paper and providing some very insightful suggestions.

403

deregulated financial environment. It is hypothesized that the demand for capital in rural areas stimulates new institutional change to provide capital to both the public and private sectors of rural areas.

The third issue is the continued high levels of poverty and inequality in rural areas and the rural poverty consequences of current social and economic forces. The inadequacy of our information base and our theories in this area for providing useful policy guidance is stressed.

A final section of the paper provides interpretation of the implications of these issues for the research, teaching, and extension missions of our profession.

Trends Affecting Rural America

The principal forces that we see shaping the social, political, and economic framework are encompassed in six trends.

INTERNATIONALIZATION OF THE ECONOMY. Growing global interdependence in patterns of trade is now having major impacts on the domestic economy. One quarter of our GNP is now attributable to our international trade and our borrowing from abroad has reached an annual rate of $80–100 billion (Schuh 1984). Foreign capital investments are currently the principal source of manufacturing investment for some states (e.g., South Carolina) and are becoming more dominant in a number of other states and regions of the United States. At the same time a "product cycle" unfettered by national boundaries is partly responsible for a significant number of manufacturing jobs moving abroad. That is, as the production process for goods becomes routinized, firms will move to areas where labor is relatively unskilled and inexpensive. In the absence of strong restrictions, some firms move to low-wage regions of the world. Combined with relatively more centralized capital markets and international aid, there has been a massive restructuring of world economic interrelationships.

CHANGING DEMOGRAPHIC STRUCTURE. Four major demographic changes have shaped and will continue to affect rural areas in this country: (1) migration from the North to the South and West and between metropolitan and nonmetropolitan areas; (2) the changing age structure of the population; (3) increases in single-parent families and single-person households; and (4) increases in female labor-force participation.

Migration to seek employment, to search out more acceptable living environments, and to return to home culture all continue to reshape rural society, invigorating some communities and depressing others. While migration to the South and West is a continuation of a decades-old trend, metro-nonmetro shifts are in a state of flux. Rural areas grew much more rapidly than metro areas in the 1970s, a sharp reversal of earlier trends. Data from the early 1980s, however, suggest a return to the earlier pattern of relatively greater metropolitan growth (Weber and Deaton 1984).

Increasing life expectancy has resulted in both relative and absolute growth in the elderly population. Bureau of the Census projections suggest that one in five Americans will be 65 years old or older by the year 2030. Improved health, greater mobility, and a willingness of the elderly to live apart from their adult children are factors that have helped create a greater proportion of elderly population in rural areas. The elderly are more concentrated in the South and their numbers are growing there disproportionately due principally to growth in retirement-related communities.

Although the increase in the "over 65" population during the 1980s will be large, the age cohort that will increase the most is the early middle-aged (35–44) population. This group will account for three-fifths of the net increase in population during the current decade. Expected female labor-force participation of this and the younger cohorts combined with their large numerical increases will keep the labor force growing faster than population.

Household composition is also expected to change dramatically. Non-family households (mostly single-person households) and single-parent families are expected to be the fastest growing household types, accounting for almost two-thirds of the increase in households over the 1980s. This change has implications for the distribution of income and demands for public and private goods and services.

CHANGING ECONOMIC STRUCTURE. Differences in income, employment, and cultures between the city and the country in past years have been altered by technological advances in communications and transportation and by the increasing integration of these different areas. Yet, the continuing heterogeneity of rural America has been well documented by Deavers and Brown (1983) and even their attempt to find some common groupings underscores the persistence of diversity, a point that contains important economic ramifications. The terms rural and urban are now end points on a continuum rather than separable categories, and rural and urban areas are interlinked in a pattern of spatial interactions that require the simultaneous consideration of activities in both areas. Yet, their cultural heritages, spatial relationships, and institutional characteristics make rural communities the continuing subject of literary and scientific inquiry.

Rural economies are more complex today than in the past. Four aspects of the changing economic structure merit attention: (1) the increased dependence of farm households on off-farm income and the implications of this for the farm sector, (2) the sectoral employment shifts, (3) the shift in income structure from earnings to transfer and investment incomes, and (4) changes in the size distribution of income and poverty.

The agricultural sector has been moved by technological advances, market forces, and government policy toward greater interdependence with both the global economy and the local nonfarm sector. For farms in value-of-sales classes below $40,000 (representing three-quarters of farms in the United States), net farm income was negative in 1981; nonfarm income provided all the family income and subsidized farm losses in the aggregate. Nonfarm income was 69 percent of family income for the $40,000–99,000 sales groups, and it dropped to 17 percent for farms in the $100,000 and above category.

The structural changes in the nonfarm sector have been even more pronounced. Service-sector employment is of growing importance nationally and now represents an essential part of the export base of rural communities. This reflects improvements in transportation and communications that have altered spatial interdependencies. By historical standards, a massive shift has occurred in the spatial distribution of manufacturing locations over the past two-and-a-half decades. The relative contribution of manufacturing to total employment has grown most rapidly in the South and West while declining in the Northeast and North Central states. Smaller towns and rural areas have experienced a disproportionate share of this growth, except in the Southwest where metropolitan areas have remained predominant. Most rural communities are now linked strategically to urban centers in terms of job markets and service dependency. In this sense, rural communities have become more differentiated, specialized, and autonomous.

Between 1962 and 1982, transfer payments nearly doubled as a percent of total personal income, increasing from 7.7 to 14.6 percent; investment incomes increased their share from 13.5 to 18.8 percent. Transfer payments and investment incomes are relatively more important in nonmetro than in metro counties, accounting for 18.1 and 20.1 percent of nonmetro county income in 1982. The relative increase in transfer payment and investment incomes and the relative decrease in earnings (labor and proprietor income) represents a major shift in our income structure, reflecting both changes in age structure and government policy decisions affecting transfers (principally Social Security) and interest rates.

Trends in poverty and the structure of income distribution are not so clear. Poverty incidence in both metro and nonmetro areas declined between 1959 and 1979 rather steadily. With the severe post-1980 downturn in the economy, poverty incidence increased and remains in the mid-1980s at higher than late 1970 levels. Income distribution patterns are much more stable and appear not to have changed much between 1950 and 1970 (Reynolds and Smolensky 1977). There is some dispute about whether there has been a major shift in income distribution over the past five years.

DECENTRALIZATION OF GOVERNMENT. The authority and fiscal responsibility for governmental functions is shifting from the national to the state level under New Federalism. In turn, state governments have thrust greater responsibility back to local units of government. In fact, perhaps the major realignments are occurring between state and local governments as a new sense of local autonomy creates new demands for redefining local taxing and spending authority. Economic development activities at the local level have increased as a consequence of new demands for job provision being placed on rural, local governments.

Government deconcentration, or devolution, is occurring throughout the Western democracies and has been characterized as a fundamental realignment in governmental power by Jequier (1984). The pervasiveness of the trend suggests fundamental causes that have not been well established by any research. Dissatisfaction with the ability of central governments to manage local affairs appears to be a contributing factor.

DEREGULATION OF KEY ECONOMIC SECTORS. Spatial linkages between certain rural communities and urban centers have been affected by changes in rail and airline regulations. Population centers may not be as well served in the aftermath due to the lack of effective demand and the absence of competitive suppliers of services, airlines in particular. To some degree, potential economic disadvantages are offset by expanded interstate highway systems and by improved communication links.

A more pervasive set of changes may come from deregulation of the banking system and other financial institutions. Consolidated banking operations within states, interstate banking, the expansion of banklike activities by retail stores and credit card suppliers have altered the spatial flows of capital. While the net level and rate of capital flows from these changes have not been determined, it is clear that for any given rural community capital flows can be altered rapidly in either direction.

Capital flight from rural areas has been a foundation of modernization processes around the world. Ultimately, however, both agriculture and rural communities depend on reinvestment for survival. Current deregulations appear to have reduced support for long-term fixed investments in rural areas (Markley 1984; Barkley 1984b). Whether rural business and industry and rural governments will be able to take advantage of a more complex world financial market to sustain their economic growth must still be determined.

EVOLVING CONCEPTION OF JUSTICE AND HUMAN RIGHTS. A society's sense of justice is to some extent embodied in its laws and other institutions. As society's norms change and become embodied in legal institutions, markets adapt to the new rules of the game. Since *Brown v. Board of Education* in 1954 and the Civil Rights Act of 1964, our society has undergone significant social change that has realigned expectations for economic opportunity among almost every segment of American life. Perceptions of the likelihood of obtaining a given job are altered, potential mobility is reconsidered, and a broader view of family labor-force participation emerges with multiple job holders in each family unit. OSHA regulations and environmental protection activities further constrain the forces of business and industry vis-a-vis more broadly conceived human needs.

Public education is particularly affected by these changes. Its responsibilities are continually being redefined, and its support broadened as the public shapes the foundations of its own future by creating the human capital and basic values deemed essential to society (Deaton 1983). Through a myriad of equalization rules at the state level, combined with federal support, access to a publicly prescribed minimum level of education is being guaranteed. Minimum wage legislation as well as movements such as that associated with "comparable worth" attest to the conviction held by broad segments of the population that labor markets are simply inadequate and/or unacceptable for establishing wage rates. Many such rules already in place represent society's attempt to modify the rate of social change created by market forces.

These changes do not affect all areas of the country evenly. The adjustments to these changing social norms may be more disruptive in rural areas than in urban areas to the extent that rural demographic and job mixes and culture are different.

The Changing Policy Context

Rural communities are shaped by both exogenous and endogenous forces and interactions among them. The past few decades of economic change have resulted in the ascendancy of the exogenous forces as compared to the endogenous ones. Among the former, particular attention is called to the growing internationalization of the rural economy and the rapid penetration of technological change into rural communities because of enhanced communications networks and deregulations of important economic sectors. National and state economic policies contribute significantly to the evolution of economic affairs. This section briefly summarizes three important eras of policy and discusses their significance to rural economic change.

RURAL ECONOMIES IN A NEOMERCANTILIST AGE. The sectoral and spatial structures of rural economies respond to corresponding evolutionary changes in national policy. From this perspective, it is instructive to interpret changes in rural economies within the context of national economic policy orientations as they have evolved since 1950. The current rural scene is reminiscent of an earlier age of mercantilism under which nation-states sought to reorganize their internal economies to enable the economy of the nation to compete most effectively in the international arena. Building and preserving national power were principal objectives. Internal social structures that impeded the accumulation of national wealth were modified or eliminated in the process. The enclosure movement that displaced rural residents and created an ownership pattern that maximized the flow of raw materials into the national and, subsequently, international market is perhaps the clearest illustration. The social costs of displacing rural residents were realized only as an afterthought (Polanyi 1944).

Today, international competition is marked by the pursuit of national economic and political power. The political and economic enterprises of some national economies are so intermeshed that they are almost indistinguishable, as in the cases of Japan, and both Eastern and Western Europe. Similarly, in the United States public policy is called on to engage in sufficient tax and subsidy action so as to match the mercantilist tendencies of our competitors. Yet, financial, transportation, and communication deregulations are pursued in attempts to realign local economies to enhance national competitiveness. And, once again, the social costs of the growing social instability generated in this process are being relegated to a state of secondary consideration.

The evolution of neomercantilism can be seen most clearly by interpreting postwar policy changes. The postwar period can be divided into roughly three time periods of relatively different structural adjustments. These periods can be characterized as: (1) Technological Ascendency, 1950–1960; (2) Balanced Growth, 1960–1972; (3) New Internationalism, 1972 to the present.

Each period will be briefly discussed to establish the roots of the current structural conditions in rural America. The influence of public policy toward rural areas, including the role of agricultural policy, will be assessed in each period.

TECHNOLOGICAL ASCENDENCY AND UNANTICIPATED POLICY OUTCOMES: THE 1950S.[1] Through the 1950s, the rural economy became more fully shaped by technological, social, and economic processes set in motion by the industrial revolution that began in the previous century and that created the major agricultural transformation of this century. The scientific and technological achievements of the twentieth century flourished in the 1950s, particularly in the form of a cost-reducing technological treadmill that displaced over a million people a year from U.S. farm production for several years. The major active policies toward rural areas were the farm programs. The implication that such programs geared to commodities would alleviate low-income conditions among a sizable portion of the farm sector was a misleading aspect of the policy debate during the 1950s and 1960s. In fact, these policies created sufficient stability of expected income to provide incentives for the rapid adoption of cost-saving machinery, which in turn displaced labor from the farm sector in greater numbers than would have occurred in the absence of farm programs. Smaller-sized farms were particularly affected by these changes, although their rate of demise may have been slower under the minimal income floors provided by price and income support programs. Small farm operators tended to survive more effectively than farm laborers per se. Fortunately, strong kinship ties in urban centers and income floors provided by commodity programs enabled rural residents to search for better jobs and higher incomes at a more leisurely pace than would be possible later.

Many changes in the structure and function of rural communities occurred over the 1940 to 1970 period due to technology, marketing, economies of size, and competitive factors unique to each sector of the economy. In spite of the massive exodus of people from rural communities and a 70-percent decline in farm employment, the total population of rural communities and small towns remained more or less constant (Jordan and Hady 1979). To some extent then, increased employment in both the private and public sector helped offset reduced employment on the farm.

During this period, the business sector of rural communities realized a degree of benefit from the stable flow of funds derived from commodity programs. For both agriculturally linked and consumer-oriented businesses, orderly adjustments were possible. Both the relative stability of farm income, which increased the rate of mechanization, and the greater intensity of inputs that substituted for land (such as fertilizers, seeds, pesticides, and insecticides) led to a thriving agribusiness sector through the 1960s.

By the end of the decade, the seeds of fundamental change had been sown. The dislocation of such large numbers of rural workers during the 1950s undoubtedly contributed to the urban crises of the 1960s, the growing disaffection with life in our major metropolitan areas, and the so-called "population turnaround" of the 1970s. The rural-urban migration process was related directly to the mechanization of American agriculture. In turn, the urban-to-rural movement of people and industry of the 1970s was made easier by the residual strength of the rural economy, which had been buoyed by a combination of farm commodity programs and transfer payments to the disproportionate numbers of the rural poor and elderly.

BALANCED GROWTH AND POLICY CONFLICTS: 1960–1972. The distinctive aspect of this period was the policy attention given to "balanced" economic growth and a societal focus on distributive justice. These themes characterized major policy initiatives on both the domestic and international front. Significant steps were taken through the Kennedy Round of GATT negotiations to significantly reduce trade barriers. Domestically, attention focused on some of the most severely depressed areas of the country, and innovative programs were launched to address the problems of poverty, malnutrition, and regional growth. For example, the Economic Development Administration was initiated in 1965, and regional programs such as the Appalachian Regional Commission and the Title V Regional Commissions, as well as a renewed regional development focus within TVA also appeared during this time period. Unfortunately, the targeted approaches for addressing many critical issues became diverted later in the period as political interests forced more widespread distribution, blurring the intent of many programs.

Efforts at the state and local level followed the federal lead in establishing institutional mechanisms to encourage economic growth in relatively depressed rural areas and to encourage job creation designed to employ the unemployed. Also, tax concessions given to industry by local authorities had been substantial (Mulkey and Dillman 1976). How effective these policies were in altering the settlement patterns of the United States is not clear. A number of major factors contributed to the changes.

The decentralization of manufacturing was accentuated in the 1960s in part due to the abundance of relatively cheap labor in small towns and rural areas. The labor market adjustments out of rural areas that were predicted by standard general equilibrium theory appeared to lag so severely as to bring the theory itself into question. An unexpectedly high elasticity of labor supply in many rural areas kept wages relatively low. The labor supply response increased as a result of growing participation of women in the work force, returning migrants from urban centers, and expanding commuter fields made possible by improved transportation and communication systems.

Farm programs of price and income supports in the 1960s changed in form but continued to be based on an overriding concern for commercial farmers. Their effects on the structure of rural areas continued to be secondary considerations. On the other hand, urban social costs were a frightening reality that commanded public attention.

NEW INTERNATIONALISM: 1972 TO THE PRESENT. Rural communities experienced significant structural changes in the decade of the 1970s as consequences of both the rapid outmigration of the 1950s and the balanced growth focus of the 1960s. While these structural changes were first observed in the 1970s and associated with a historical reversal in population trends, the so-called population turnaround, the rural economy was already under the influence of more powerful international forces. These forces were accentuated as a result of the Russian Wheat Deal of 1972 and the OPEC embargo of 1973. A gradual opening up of the rural economy to international market influences has characterized our policy orientation since 1972. Our purpose is to call attention to the pervasive penetration of the international economy into the rural economies of the United States, both in agriculture and manufacturing. The choice of which sectors to expose to international competition remains very much a national policy decision. Rural areas have suffered because their economic base is largely agricultural, mining, and low-wage manufacturing. These sectors face stiff competition in international markets and/or are inordinately affected by the overvalued U.S. currency, particularly in the case of major export sectors such as agriculture.

International competition in both manufacturing and agriculture has varying consequences for the rural economies of different regions of the country, depending on their sectoral composition of enterprises. The international linkages may either compound or offset cyclical economic changes driven by domestic competition, capital investment, and monetary and fiscal policies. Almost all facets of rural economies have become acutely aware of the strength of international forces. Low-wage industries, particularly shoe and textile manufacturing, face stiff competition from abroad. Many low-wage firms have moved to Third World countries. Small-town banks engage regularly in international transactions, and the strength of the U.S. dollar has become the subject of their daily discourse. In addition, direct foreign investment in the United States is now a major source of new job creation for some states. Neither agricultural nor general economic policy has addressed the unique consequences of these uneven impacts.

Selected Critical Issues

The above trends and policy orientations have significantly altered the sectoral and spatial organization of rural economies. Yet, the secondary effects of this internationalism have been essentially ignored by public policy. Among the many reasons behind ineffectual public policy, the slow response of research and education programs must bear some of the blame. For example, there has been almost no research linking international factors with domestic changes outside their effects on commodity prices and trade flows. Research and education programs must be aware of the positive and negative consequences of such changes and help design policies to preserve the social advantages and offset the social disadvantages. Public policy simply has not had an appropriate knowledge base for dealing with some of these critical issues.

FARM AND NONFARM INTERACTIONS. The importance of nonfarm income sources for farm families was described earlier under "Changing Economic Structure." Nonfarm employment helps determine family income in important ways, and it further influences economic development through its impacts on both capital and labor markets by reducing family income risk, by generating savings, and through services provided by rural communities to the farm population. These interrelationships have not been given the research attention deserved by an issue that is so significantly shaping resource allocation in rural economies. Two aspects of this issue will be briefly discussed: (1) the farm-level implications posed by the changing risk environment created by growing nonfarm employment; and (2) public-sector involvement in shaping the level and pattern of nonfarm job creation in rural areas.

NONFARM EMPLOYMENT AND RISK. By drawing on concepts of risk analysis, farm/nonfarm interactions provide an important example of the need to rethink basic approaches about interpreting sectoral interaction. Agricultural economists have almost exclusively addressed the issue of farm risk from the perspective of the farmer as an entrepreneur whose principal focus is on farm markets, farm prices, credit, and technologies.

A recent analysis by Just and Zilberman (1984,4) classified farmers on the basis of "several important regimes of behavior" to interpret their risk-oriented behavior. They argued that small and part-time farmers may tend to fall into a group of technologically lagging farms that do not readily adopt new technologies. Young, expanding farmers were expected to be highly leveraged but to lack sufficient capital for needed farm investments. Older farmers with large farms were more likely to be risk diversifiers, and large aggressive operators or corporate farms were expected to be the risk takers.

Their classification scheme was used to illustrate the distributional implications of agricultural policies between producers and consumers. The response of supply to increased price supports, the stability of consumer prices and government costs, and the income distribution effects will vary by the relative structure of the agricultural sector. They argue that policies designed to simultaneously achieve growth and equity must be based on the joint distribution of farm size, risk preferences, and credit availability.

Our intent is not to argue with these essential aspects of their classification, but to recognize their limitations for a wide spectrum of farm families where one or more members of the household works off the farm. Risk analysis must recognize household labor allocation between the farm and nonfarm sectors. Farm size, risk preferences, and farm credit availability almost certainly alter the household members' desires to participate in nonfarm employment. For example, risk averse farmers may be more likely to participate in nonfarm employment. They create a more elastic labor supply for the nonfarm sector at relatively low wages. Risk analysis ought to focus also on farm household capital allocation between farm and nonfarm sectors. Nonfarm investments of farm families are also affected by farm size, risk preference, and credit availability. Risk averse farmers may be more likely to make off-farm investments, once size economies in farming operations have been exploited.

At the same time, a more secure nonfarm income stream should create a more conducive environment for adopting relatively more capital intensive on-farm technologies. This could be particularly important for the roughly 80 percent of the U.S. farmers in sales classes below $100,000 who depend on nonfarm income to a very significant degree. In the face of growing uncertainties facing agriculture and growing nonfarm employment opportunities, greater diversity of farming technologies is likely to emerge in the farming sector. Farm families will be more innovative in exploring new cropping systems. Specifically, it is likely that transitions from traditional to alternative technological enterprises are occurring more rapidly and smoothly in those parts of the country where nonfarm job opportunities are more prevalent.

EXTENSION IMPLICATIONS. The emerging structural changes in agriculture pose some difficult choices for extension with regard to program emphasis. On one hand, extension could emphasize highly sophisticated technology to serve a relatively few commercial farms, most of whom probably do not need much extension help because they are already in constant touch with private sector technology producers. On the other hand, and more in keeping with its historical mission, extension could emphasize assistance to the majority of American farmers who will be making significant economic adjustments in both farm and nonfarm enterprises. It is our opinion that technical support from research and extension services should emphasize assistance to the latter group. Broad-based research and extension support from our land grant colleges and universities should be directed to developing multipronged programs addressing infrastructure and financial support for small businesses and industry as well as agricultural production and marketing strategies. The transition into new crops that may provide more optimal resource use may be impeded unless nonfarm opportunities are available to reduce the income risk associated with the new farm practices, marketing systems, and technologies that will be involved.

Extension programs must be broad enough to address household needs. Farm household units will depend increasingly on nonfarm jobs for employment. Their farming operations will be modified to meet the new demands for less intensive labor inputs and more capital intensive technologies. The income security provided by nonfarm jobs will lead to a more innovative, experimental approach to agricultural production. Agriculture will become even more information-based. The distinction between farm and nonfarm extension programs will become increasingly blurred, and the appropriate technologies for most farms will not be the same as those for the largest commercial farm operations.

Extension programs should be coordinated with state programs of economic development. Their common clientele are the many small towns and rural communities that require balanced economic growth based on entrepreneurship, venture capital, and interdependencies between farm and nonfarm sectors. Rural-based economic development will draw on the same information bases that drive the larger economy. Rural people will be "left behind" only if extension programs and the policies of federal and state governments fail to recognize that their needs require immediate, concerted attention.

RESEARCH AND POLICY IMPLICATIONS FOR RURAL DEVELOPMENT. Public-sector subsidies, grants, loans, and administrative regulations have been used as tools for addressing the needs of low-income families and for stimulating lagging economic regions of the country. The expansion of occupational choice through strategies of economic diversification helps provide ladders of opportunity for farm and nonfarm rural residents. It also creates a broader "safety net" that draws on a wider range of job skills, thereby reducing the probability of being unemployed. Public participation can also help guarantee that low-income families and minorities are targeted for job training and that their communities benefit from public investment decisions that stimulate job creation. These objectives cannot be readily achieved unless public policy encourages spatially balanced job opportunities. Most likely such a strategy will result in the development of value-added industries that strengthen the farm sector as well.

Continuing research must be devoted to the relative effectiveness of alternative public-sector approaches such as infrastructure investments, capital subsidies, and other economic development incentives. Adam Smith notwithstanding, our empirical knowledge of public-sector investments provides no basis for asserting that they are any less productive than private-sector investments. In fact, the high rates of return on publicly funded agricultural research (Ruttan 1982) and public education (Becker 1975) are greater on the average than private-sector investments. Empirical attempts to separate public- from private-sector influences may miss the more important synergistic effects of the interaction between sectors.

Empirical research on the rates of return to local infrastructure investments has been limited. Convincing evidence has accumulated that infrastructure investments such as water, sewerage, education, fire and police protection, and others have statistically significant relationships with new manufacturing locations and employment expansions. Barrows and Bromley (1975) found that U.S. Department of Commerce's Economic Development Administration's (EDA) investments had the most significant employment effect in the smallest population centers and in the communities farthest from Standard Metropolitan Statistical Areas (SMSAs), implying that these investments compensated for other locational disadvantages. Likewise, Smith et al. (1978) reported that even the most locationally disadvantaged communities could overcome their disadvantages by undertaking significant investments in industrial sites. Kriesel's (1984) work further supported this observation.

Research to determine an optimal mix of infrastructure investments has not been undertaken. A great deal of conceptual attention is needed to develop operational measures of public sector output to enable rates of return to be calculated for alternative investment patterns. The lagged nature of the benefits derived from public investments and the importance of local leadership, social structure, and perceptions of private business investors make this a knotty set of issues.

The effects of capital subsidies on business location and expansion have been analyzed more thoroughly by Stober and Falk (1967), Moes (1961), Bridges (1965), Dewar (1981), and Heckman (1982). While these results are mixed, most point to the effectiveness of capital subsidies in guiding the location of manufacturing plants. Research on a wider variety of service-oriented firms has not been undertaken, though they have become critical components of the export base of rural communities.

The research on the question of the relative effectiveness of public sector activity suffers from a number of problems:

1. The influence of exogenous factors such as foreign competition, the international transfer of technology, and windfall gains due to market-windows opening up either domestically or internationally have not been included in most analyses.

2. Changes in the rate of job creation due to the business cycle, product cycles of specific types of industry, and the interrelationships between these cycles and international competition have not been well documented.

3. Endogenous influences that vary by geographic region are not well understood. Chief among these are the issues of variation in efficiency wages (money wages adjusted for productivity differentials) and the effects of economies of size and agglomeration economies.

CAPITAL FORMATION. Understanding the process of capital formation is essential to understanding how rural economies work. Both public- and private-sector processes and the interaction between the two must be recognized. Our intent here is to emphasize the changing nature of capital formation in an international capital market. International market forces and deregulations reduce local control over capital flows. State and local governments have been forced to respond in unprecedented fashion to reassert an element of social control over the market. A classic illustration of an historical struggle is being reenacted, presenting a new environment for rural economic affairs. The institutional bases of capital formation are being affected by the economic forces delineated earlier.

Kendrick (1976) estimates that U.S. capital stock is roughly one-fourth in the form of government capital, one-fourth in the form of business capital, and one-half in the form of individually owned capital, both human and tangible (Stinson 1985). To understand the economics of rural areas, it is essential that the relative productivity of each type of capital be known along with its rate of accumulation, complementaries among types, and factors that determine variation in the growth and utilization of each type. Unfortunately, this task is severely impeded by both our conceptual approach and data availability.

PUBLIC CAPITAL INVESTMENTS. Stinson (1985) has advanced a life-cycle theory of household savings to help interpret infrastructure investment decisions in rural areas. Drawing on the work of Ghez and Becker (1975), he suggests that time paths of market-wage rates and consumption preferences produce a pattern of net borrowing, then net saving, followed by dissaving in the elderly life stage. Such life-cycle behavior by the postwar baby-boom generation may be sufficiently strong to explain the current lag in rural infrastructure investments. That is, the current outcry about deteriorating public infrastructure may simply reflect utility-maximizing behavior on the part of a dominant cohort of younger voters who are now emphasizing current consumption until peak earning years are reached. A later period, when this dominant cohort enters the net-investor stage, should result in renewed support for public investments in infrastructure as well as greater private investment.

Additional insight into rural capital formation is provided by Stinson's introduction of risk concepts into both private and public investment decisions. For example, he defines "community risk" as "a systematic risk attached only to the public sector investments in each community caused by unanticipated population changes" (1985, 12). Sudden decreases in population common to boom towns near energy developments (such as the historical cycles in the Appalachian coal fields), may reduce local public revenues, driving up per capita costs and reducing the value of the claims on local public services for any given individual. Such local risks drive up the capital return required by local investors in public-sector capital (p. 13).

Uncertainty associated with international market fluctuations interact with public- and private-sector investments to add complexity to Stinson's arguments. More risky public-sector investments drive up the risk for private investments for both businesses and households. Reduced value of claims on local public services will result in relatively less investment in fixed capital by homeowners and by businesses. If these processes persist in given regions of the country or in particular communities affected by sudden shifts in population, then conditions of downward-spiraling levels of public and private investments may occur in such communities.

This argument could help explain the reduced levels of housing investments for given income levels in such regions as the central Appalachian coal fields where mobile homes have constituted over 90 percent of new housing starts for the past decade. Reduced private and public investments feed on each other creating the setting for intergenerational deterioration of public and private capital. This may be particularly onerous for low-income groups who may be less able to migrate out of the region or commute long distances to other communities. Human capital would deteriorate as well under these conditions, as the local emphasis on school expenditures would decline due to the greater risk factor and the reduced certainty of reaping local returns on human capital investments because of outmigration.

Attempts on the part of local taxpayers to reduce community risk most likely explain efforts to establish industrial parks and to provide incentives to attract new private investment. This may be a major rationale behind what has been labeled as wasteful local spending in what is a near zero-sum game from the national perspective. The analogy with national mercantilist policies is inescapable. Actions that may maximize local social welfare may be wasteful from a national perspective. National programs may play a useful role in minimizing local risk, thereby leading to local decisions that are more optimal from a national perspective.

The implication of these alternative perspectives is illustrated by a more recent study of the cost-effectiveness of economic development incentives (Rasmussen et al. 1982, 25). They argue that "Industrial Revenue Bonds are a highly efficient way to subsidize loans from a state's perspective but are, by far, the least efficient method when the costs of the state and federal governments are combined." This study concluded that direct grants should be made from the federal to the state level and that subsequent programs at the state and local levels be directed toward loan guarantees, equity investments, and limited land acquisition assistance (p. 28).

PRIVATE CAPITAL INVESTMENT. The banking system has traditionally played a significant role in channeling local savings into support for residentiary businesses that enhance the equity position of local investors and entrepreneurs. Banks have also been the principal purchasers of local revenue bonds. With the rapid deregulation of the banking system, relatively larger capital funds can be drawn on to support a given community's bond issue, though the aggregate funds available may have diminished with the growth of international market transactions. Offsetting capital infusions from abroad compensate to some extent for reduced local savings and capital outflows, but these accrue primarily to the private sector.

Research is needed to analyze the net effects of these flows on rural economies. The relative slowdown in manufacturing movement into rural areas may portend a weaker position for rural economies. Markley's (1984) analysis of rural banks concludes that the effects of banking deregulations may vary significantly even among sub regions of a state depending on the composition of the local economy and the behavior of the particular bank's decision makers. Markley argues that institutional innovations occur in response to the marginal gains to be derived by the principal action group. As she points out, "Institutional change will likely create costs and/or benefits in rural areas that are external to the decision-making process of the primary action group and represent a source of externality" (p. 692).

The differential impact of institutional change on rural areas is generally recognized ex post and haphazardly. Institutional change generally and banking deregulation specifically hold both promise and pitfalls for rural economies. Whenever such changes are generated by national and international principal actors, reactionary elements may arise at the state and local level. Following the basic institutional change model of Davis and North (1971) and the modifications suggested by Markley (1984) provides insight into changes in the capital formation process of the past three-and-a-half decades.

CAPITAL FORMATION UNDER BALANCED GROWTH POLICIES. The period from 1960 to 1972 was characterized by an active pursuit of alternative organizational approaches to channeling capital into rural economies. The capital flows through organizations such as ARC, EDA, SBA, FmHA, undoubtedly contributed to the infrastructure that undergirded the movement of manufacturing and business into small towns and rural areas during the next decade. Many local community efforts were initiated to take advantage of federal largesse; most of these were stimulated by federal activity. A mix of local public and private capital was usually marshalled through nonprofit or limited profit local development corporations to attract private capital investment principally from outside the local economy. The locally generated capital was basically sold to outside bidders who then controlled the equity of local firms and, if successful, increased the value of their equity through the public largesse at all levels. This model is still the rule.

A great deal of organizational and intellectual effort was given to reshaping the institutional base of capital in rural and urban areas (Deaton et al. 1985). A major aim was to broaden the base of capital ownership through equity accumulation by individuals and by community organizations. Supported by a national commitment to address the special needs of the rural poor, these activities attempted to alter the institutional form of savings generation and capital channeling. The Special Impact Program of the Office of Economic Opportunity and the Community Action Agencies stimulated the development of cooperatives and community development corporations that promised a new grip on life for many depressed rural areas. They resulted in relatively few significant alterations, though some projects have continued to be quite successful. The limited success appears to stem from their failure to marshall the support of primary action groups that controlled the financial network undergirding local development efforts. The capital resources and political power of this group at either the state or local level simply overwhelmed the meager funds provided through the Special Impact Program, private foundations, churches, and individuals. The major thrust of federal activity was to alter the spatial pattern of investments through credit provisions that served to strengthen the equity position of the principal action group.

CAPITAL FORMATION UNDER NEW INTERNATIONALISM. Changes in state and local activity in response to the openness of rural economies and financial deregulations stand in sharp contrast to earlier periods. As private financial capital has become more concentrated nationally, political power has become less concentrated. The New Federalism has served notice to state and local governments that their actions will become the primary factors guiding future public investment activity. Rural areas are receiving far less special attention as primary concern has focused on the ability of the states to develop new partnership arrangements with the private sector, on one hand, to maintain a competitive flow of private capital into the state. On the other hand, states have been caught up with the process of redesigning the rules and regulations governing their relationships with local governments. Because of the greater openness of the local economies, state governments can shrug off demands from local governments while simultaneously eliciting broad public support to address public policy matters, particularly state economic policy.

As this process has evolved, alternative approaches to capital formation are emerging, mostly in the form of credit subsidies to industry with relatively greater emphasis on high-technology industries. Several states have also provided stronger incentives for private venture capital funds. Tax credits to private investors and access to state retirement funds to support equity capital investments have been initiated in Illinois, Michigan, and a few other states. Relatively less attention has been paid to directing these capital formation efforts toward rural communities, though Iowa, Alaska, and Virginia have initiated legislation with this expressed intent (Deaton et al. 1985).

The major shift that has occurred as compared to previous time periods is that primary action groups at the state level have coalesced to take advantage of a more open financial market and to protect their accrued position from eroding under the more powerful influences of international market forces. In other words, new forms of state controls over financial markets are being created using creative incentive programs and public subsidies. These state reactions may be much stronger than expected and may ultimately reshape national institutions to afford relatively more protection against international influences. This is now being seen in the protectionist arguments being posited by a number of special interest groups and principal Congressional committees. Whether rural areas receive net gains in this process remains to be determined.

IMPLICATIONS. Each of these later time periods stand in sharp contrast to the 1950s when capital formation at the local level was determined principally by local savings and manufacturing locations driven by technological adjustments. Bosworth (1982, 317) concluded that increased savings can no longer be "relied upon to increase domestic capital formation." The international flow of capital renders obsolete the view that domestic savings serve as a major constraint on domestic investment. Banking deregulations establish the basis for similar conclusions regarding the contribution of household savings in rural communities to local capital formation. They simply may not matter either in agriculture or in business and industry. On the other hand, local savings can matter a great deal if capital institutions are consciously designed to achieve public objectives.

At the same time, rural communities face a far more competitive environment for maintaining an appropriate mix of capital investment at the local level. National and international factors may serve to draw local savings away without compensating reinvestment. Technological change and the product cycle create greater uncertainty for rural areas. The uncertainty drives up the necessary rate of return to elicit private and public investments. Local banks may no longer support local bond issues for public capital investments. The future appears to be far more uncertain.

Successful rural communities will be those that (1) design institutions to marshall and channel capital in support of local investments; (2) successfully broaden the base of equity participation in the local economy; (3) create effective partnerships with state governments and with the broader private sector of the state; and (4) effectively use traditional industrial incentives to broaden their economic base. At the same time, attention to increasing the local share of human capital will significantly alter the competitiveness of rural areas in the information-based economy toward which the United States is moving (Black 1985). Research attention should shift toward the macroperspective provided by Stinson (1985) to determine the strength of demographic changes, risk and public/private complementaries in determining the rate and level of capital formation.

Increasingly, rural economies will be caught up in cyclical changes that stem from international and national forces. Determinations should be made of the importance of economic diversity, local factor productivity, and local and state institutions in protecting rural economies against the vicissitudes of such uncontrollable events. This would appear to be a significant future challenge for rural leaders, researchers, and educators alike.

POVERTY AND INCOME DISTRIBUTION. The notion that poverty and income distribution are central to the study of economics has been around a long time. Alfred Marshall (1920,4), in the introductory chapter of his famous *Principles of Economics,* asserts that it is elimination of "the pains of poverty and the stagnating influences of excessive mechanical toil" that "gives to economic studies their chief and their highest interest."

Yet several forces have kept the study of this question from occupying a central place in agricultural economics research.

First, while the neoclassical paradigm that has served as a foundation for our disciplinary research explains the distribution of income among factors of production, it does not yield insights into income distribution among income classes. We have tended to avoid areas of research in which we have no strong theoretical foundation. Second, economists are faced with serious conceptual and measurement issues in the study of income distribution and poverty (see Atkinson 1975; U.S. Department of Health, Education, and Welfare 1976). Thirdly, data that describe relevant distributions of income or poverty populations are often difficult to obtain (Danzinger and Gottschalk 1983). Finally, given the observed improvement in living standards of the vast majority of people in this country during the twentieth century as the nation's economy grew, there was some basis for a belief that poverty could be most effectively reduced by merely ensuring continued economic growth.

Several things happened during the 1950s and 1960s that changed the focus of agricultural economics research toward increased attention to personal income distribution issues. First there was an increased awareness about poverty in the midst of plenty in the early 1960s, which riveted the attention of policymakers and economists on the plight of the poor and the rural poor (President's National Advisory Commission on Rural Poverty

1968). This awareness was complemented by a growing skepticism within the economics profession about the effectiveness of growth in reducing poverty. "The most certain thing about modern poverty," observed John Kenneth Galbraith in 1958, "is that it is not efficiently remedied by a general and tolerably well-distributed advance in income." The development of a poverty index by Molly Orshansky in 1965 allowed the collection of empirical data that could be used to track progress in the war on poverty in both rural and urban areas and to test various hypotheses about factors affecting poverty incidence.

These factors led to a period of intense research on poverty-related issues in both rural and urban America in the 1960s and early 1970s. Although this concern and the funding support for it dropped off in the late 1970s, we sense a renewed interest in this question in the 1980s (although no new funding) as a result of both the 1982 recession and the current problems experienced by the farm sector.

These recent trends suggest the need to refocus attention on poverty and inequality issues in agricultural economics. The internationalization of the economy, the neomercantilist response of the federal government, and the resultant shifts in employment structure have major implications for poverty and income distribution. While the evidence is not conclusive, some have suggested the emergence of a "two-tier" economy, with low-wage jobs expanding faster than high-wage jobs. The overall effects of the changing job structure on poverty and income distribution will depend in part on how labor demand shifts interact with increases in the labor supply caused by the maturing of the baby boom and projected increases in female labor-force participation. Poverty trends will also depend on household composition (i.e., the extent to which rapid growth in single-parent families and single-person households continues). The "decentralization" of government, with attendant cuts in certain social programs, has increased poverty incidence particularly among the young.

On the other hand, increases in social security payments and investment incomes have led to a decrease in poverty incidence among the increasing elderly population. Since transfer payments tend to equalize and investment incomes disequalize the overall income distribution, the net effect of this change in income structure on the overall income distribution is unclear.

A major recent shift in social perceptions about economic justice could dramatically alter poverty and income distribution. Equal opportunity concerns of the 1960s focused on inequalities among races, and between urban and rural areas. Attention has shifted to inequalities between women and men. The idea that this shift is warranted is strengthened by the recognition that there is a large area of overlap between income-class inequalities and male-female inequalities; the poor are disproportionately female. The implications of this changed social perception for social policy and, ultimately, income distribution warrant further research attention.

EXPLAINING POVERTY AND INCOME DISTRIBUTION. Economists have tended to approach the study of rural poverty and income distribution by drawing from both neoclassical economic theory (Schuh 1981) and structuralist hypotheses such as Kuznets' (1955) "inverted U" hypothesis about intersectoral employment shifts and income distribution and Anderson's (1964) "trickle down" hypothesis about aggregate growth and poverty incidence.

As economists formulated and tested models of poverty incidence and income distribution, they looked at four different sets of variables to explain these phenomena: (1) aggregate income and income growth (in an attempt to test the "trickle down" hypothesis); (2) variables related to the structure of the economy, particularly the export base of the region; (3) characteristics of household members, particularly those associated with human capital, such as age or education; and (4) characteristics of the community or region within which the individual lived, particularly those identified as critical in central place and location theory. Empirical studies either examine the effects of these variables on aggregate measures of poverty and income distribution or focus on changes in income and poverty status of families and individuals with household data. Examples of a rural-oriented study that focused on aggregate measures are West (1978) and McGranahan (1980). Examples of the latter kind of study are Weber (1973), and Deaton and Landes (1978).

IMPLICATIONS. Major economic and social changes in the coming decades will affect the extent of poverty and inequality in urban and rural areas of this country and the policy response to these changes. At least four types of research would help us to monitor and understand poverty and inequality changes and to design effective policy.

1. We need to continue to monitor how rural families earn their income and receive unearned income in the form of transfer payments and investment income. While aggregate data are useful for describing overall trends in the distribution of income and in the sources of income, it is generally not adequate for answering specific questions about factors that affect changes in family income, movement out of poverty, and a family's place in the overall income distribution. This requires household survey data of the very basic kind that has long been part of the tradition of agricultural economics. With survey data, for example, we can learn the extent to which transfer incomes equalize the overall income distribution, or the effect of farm income on the overall income distribution of farm

families. It appears, for example, that between 1968 and 1982, farm income may have become a more disequalizing force in the farm family income distribution (Saupe and Weber 1974; Shaffer et al. 1985).

Perhaps more importantly, answering questions about income dynamics requires the kind of panel data on income dynamics that has been collected at the University of Michigan Institute for Social Research (Duncan 1984). We have known for a long time that a large share of families and individuals who are poor one year have incomes above the poverty line the next year (Smith and Morgan 1970). Yet without panel data, we cannot distinguish the "persistent poor" (in poverty for extended periods) from the "transitory poor" and cannot design policy appropriate for their respective needs. With panel data we could better understand the dynamics of poverty in rural areas: What proportion of poor families and individuals is persistently poor and what are the characteristics of this population and their environment? It could permit us not only to understand movements of families and individuals within the income distribution and into and out of poverty, but also to relate those movements to changes in personal characteristics, community characteristics, and health of the overall economy.

2. After 20 years of debate about the definition of poverty, some progress has been made. Poverty can be defined as the condition of not having enough income to meet ones basic needs. Yet, there is no accepted standard of "basic needs." The University of Wisconsin Institute for Research on Poverty recently undertook a study in Wisconsin that attempted to define basic needs and estimate income levels necessary to purchase these basic needs. This kind of research can help us to measure the extent of poverty and to assess the extent to which our transfer programs provide for basic needs. Replication of this kind of research in other places would allow us to answer the questions about whether basic needs are different in different parts of the country, and whether it costs more to provide for basic needs in a small town than in a large city. We do not presently know.

3. We do not merely need information, however, about the sources of income for families in different situations and about the definition of poverty. We also need models that help us understand what affects poverty and income changes in ways that are helpful to policymakers. Several kinds of research could be useful in helping policymakers in the design of poverty-reducing strategies. At the aggregate level, following the lead of Gottschalk and Danziger (1985) we could profit from models that enable us to separate the effects of changes in employment and earnings on poverty from changes in transfer payments. It is only in this way that we will be able to separate out the effects of macroeconomic policies on poverty incidence from those of strictly transfer payments policies. It would be interesting to use this framework to analyze possible differences between regions and between urban and rural areas in their responsiveness to these different kinds of policies.

Williamson and Lindert (1980) analyze long-term trends in inequality in this country in a neoclassical, general equilibrium framework. They attempt to explain patterns of inequality over time in terms of capital accumulation, growth in labor supply and sector-specific technological progress. While they conclude that government policy has not been a major factor in historical trends in inequality, their analysis does not cover the period of major growth in transfer payments. It would be useful to expand their framework by incorporating more recent data on earnings and on investment and transfer incomes and by looking for rural, urban, or regional differences in patterns. Such regional disaggregation would allow the dramatic differences in settlement patterns, natural resources, and cultural history to emerge as explanatory factors.

Williamson and Lindert claim their neoclassical, general equilibrium framework gives them access to certain insights that would not be available without that model. It is also possible, however, that the restrictive neoclassical model precludes consideration of important factors identified in alternative models.

The development economics literature provides some alternatives such as models of "cumulative causation," which draw on ideas of Myrdal (1957) and Kaldor (1970). These models, which formalize the idea that increasing returns activities in which there are increasing returns to size will become concentrated geographically to the benefit of certain regions and the detriment of others, can be expanded to address poverty and income distribution concerns (Weber and Deaton 1984).

"Rural" and "urban" are increasingly viewed as a "continuous, integrated system, rather than as a sharp dichotomy" (Hoch 1979, 959). This implies that the study of rural economies must deal with the spatial location and position in the urban hierarchy, issues central to the theoretical foundations of regional economics (location theory, central-place theory, export-base theory). Although it has become standard procedure for agricultural economists to call for the integration of spatial relationships into our rural models (see, for example, Edwards 1979, 71), a satisfactory way of doing this has not been forthcoming. We may be able to learn something about this in designing rural growth models by looking at the approach of Richardson (1973) and, for a rather unorthodox view, of Dunn (1980). Neither of them is attempting to explain poverty or distribution of income. Incorporation of spatial dimensions into the study of poverty incidence and inequality would allow the study of regional and rural-urban differences in poverty associated with location and position in the central-place hierarchy.

As global economic interdependence becomes more of a reality, our search for factors explaining domestic income distributions will need to include international factors. The outlines of a conceptual framework proposed by Schuh (1981) can guide the selection of these factors. In addition to studies of aggregate behavior, we need to study behavior of individual economic units. Particularly important is the need to pursue the understanding of the dynamics of poverty over the life cycle and between generations and the effect of changing incentive structures on economic participation of low-income people.

4. With this understanding, it would be possible to do better policy research and to better analyze the effects of alternative policies on the extent of poverty and inequality in this country and for specific areas and demographic groups. It would be possible not only to assess the impacts of transfer payments or employment creation strategies, but also the effects of macroeconomic fiscal and monetary policies and trade policies on poverty and inequality as well. By being better able to anticipate negative distributional consequences of international economic forces and domestic policy, it would be possible to determine the need for and general outlines of institutional innovations to modify any socially unacceptable outcomes.

Challenges for Rural Economists

As we look to the challenges facing the discipline as we approach the twenty-first century, it is important also to look at our history. In this concluding section, we will examine the historical roots of our discipline, reflect briefly on some elements of the tradition we should seek to recapture, and conclude with some challenges to the profession growing out of our history and out of the emerging social and economic context.

HISTORICAL CONTEXT OF AGRICULTURAL ECONOMICS. Agricultural economics developed during a period when higher education was in transition from the dominant model of the college to that of the research university (Bellah et al. 1985). The American college of the nineteenth century did not emphasize disciplinary divisions. Higher learning was assumed to be a "single unified culture" encompassing literature, the arts, and science and unified by moral philosophy. In the late nineteenth century the research university (with graduate education, research, and specialized departments) came into ascendency and the "unity and ethical meaning" of higher education was obscured. This transition affected the development of the early social sciences.

> While they [the early social sciences] were concerned with establishing professional specialties providing useful knowledge about an increasingly complex society, many social scientists still felt the older obligations of moral philosophy to speak to the major ethical questions of the society as a whole. This tradition has never died, but it has been driven to the periphery by an ever more specialized social science (Bellah et al. 1985, 299).

Agricultural economics departments also developed within land grant universities, which had an orientation to applied problem solving. As Schuh (1984, 3) reminds us, "In addition to the notion of providing mass education for society, the essence of the Land Grant university was traditionally a strong institutional mission orientation. The idea was that the university had a major responsibility to address the problems of society and to apply the tools of science and technology to the solution of those problems."

Both this mission orientation and the emergence of the science-oriented research university greatly shaped the discipline of agricultural economics as it evolved in the first two decades of the twentieth century.

Some idea of what the founders of agricultural economics had as their vision of the discipline can be obtained by looking at an early report of a committee charged with defining the boundaries of the discipline. Shortly after the founding of the American Farm Management Association (forerunner of the American Agricultural Economics Association) in 1910, the Committee on Instruction in Agriculture of the American Association of Agricultural Colleges and Experiment Stations created a Subcommittee on Rural Economics and Farm Management to "study the relationship between rural economics and farm management and, if possible, to define the subjects and determine their lines of cleavage" (Taylor and Taylor 1952, 90). In its report the committee presented its rationale for recommending that the term "rural economics" be used as the general reference for the profession:

> Rural economics is preferable to agricultural economics because the former term indicates that the affairs of the community, as well as of the individual farmer, are to be considered under this head. Rural economics or economy has for a long time been used in this sense in this country and abroad.
>
> Your committee is deeply impressed with the importance of developing strong courses in rural economics and sociology and the other subjects just referred to. These all involve the human element in agriculture and country life. They tend to raise the college courses in agriculture above the materialistic plane, to emphasize broadly the human interest that properly inheres in agricultural studies, and thus to inspire both faculties and students in our agricultural colleges with a higher sense of the wide responsibilities attaching to leadership in agricultural affairs. Pedagogically they serve to show that agriculture, when broadly treated, is to be enrolled among the humanities, as well as the sciences; ethically, they point out the vital connection between agricultural science and the welfare of rural people and even of all mankind (Taylor and Taylor 1952, 95).

An important thing to note here is the breadth of scope of what they called "rural economics," placing the discipline among the humanities and viewing it as having major ethical concerns. It is interesting to note also that the founders of the discipline recommended using the term rural economics rather than agricultural economics to highlight that the discipline encompassed "the affairs of the community, as well as of the individual farmer."

A major overall challenge facing agricultural economics (and indeed all the social sciences) as we adapt our discipline to the changing economic and policy context is to hold in creative tension both the focus on problem solving, model building, and institution building and concern for the ethical dimensions of our pursuit.

CHALLENGES IN RESEARCH, EXTENSION AND TEACHING. Earlier we noted some fundamental changes affecting rural areas as we approach the twenty-first century. Foremost among these were the neomercantilist orientation to the internationalization of the economy, the changing demographic and economic structure of the United States, and the new philosophical cross currents in social ethics. These changes viewed in the context of the intellectual tradition of agricultural economics pose some challenges to the profession. We are challenged by these trends and traditions to redirect our professional energies in research, extension, and teaching.

RESEARCH: TOWARD A RURAL DEVELOPMENT PARADIGM? Paul Barkley (1984a, 798) has recently suggested that the "total social product of the profession could be increased by increasing the amount of time spent in formulating problems, generating hypotheses, and selecting appropriate theories." He argues that our facility with quantitative techniques may have blurred our ability to recognize problems and reassemble our research results in a meaningful way (p. 801). What Barkley views as critical for the entire agricultural economic discipline, we view as particularly important for rural development economics. Perhaps this problem is accentuated for rural development research since such problems have broad social consequences, but the supporting theoretical paradigms are severely limited in scope.

Recent attempts to identify the conceptual or theoretical bases of rural development economics have drawn eclectically from various theoretical paradigms. If the purposes of economic study are to understand, predict, and shape economic events, a discussion of the theoretical basis of rural development economics ought to be placed in the context of a framework useful for all three purposes. Such a framework exists in Jan Tinbergen's *Theory of Economic Policy* (1952) applied most recently to rural development questions by Glenn Nelson (1984). One can use this framework to examine the relationship between policy instruments and policy target variables after specifying links between instruments, the structure of the economy, and target variables. In this framework target variables are selected with reference to some notion of society's goals. Development economists focusing on international development often do this explicitly. Todaro (1977, 70), for example, borrowing from Goulet (1971, 23), bases his definition of development on three explicit core values: "life-sustenance, self-esteem, and freedom from servitude representing common goals sought by all individuals and societies." Using these values as guidelines, he identifies the target variables of development economics as the level and growth of income, and the levels of unemployment, poverty, and inequality in the distribution of income (p. 68).

Domestic rural development studies have tended to focus on changes in income or employment and to implicitly define development in these terms.[2] Recently, there have been attempts to ground the selection of target variables in explicit ethical systems. Nelson (1984) used Rawl's Theory of Justice as the basis for his arguments that the most important target variable for rural development studies is poverty and that, in addition to poverty, economists ought to study income levels and distribution, employment, and public sector "productivity." For us these variables ought to be supplemented with target variables relating to level of unemployment (requiring attention to labor-force participation as well as jobs) and income stability.

Agricultural economists have devoted a fair amount of attention to policy-oriented research in rural development. Policy research has been oriented toward those policies affecting growth of income and employment. Analysts have looked, for example, at the effect of industrial parks, extension of water and sewer lines, the level of support for public education, taxes, and other variables on industrial location (Smith et al. 1978; Kriesel 1984). Much, if not most, of this work is oriented toward local policy instruments. With regard to poverty incidence, there was some important work done on national policy alternatives for reducing poverty in rural areas in the early 1970s.

The lack of an underlying comprehensive conceptual model for rural development that links policy instruments and target variables has been a source of frustration for economists for a number of years (See, for example, Edwards 1976, 1979, 1981; Jansma et al. 1981; Nelson 1984). There have been three attempts in recent years to identify the components of a comprehensive framework for rural development research (Edwards 1981; Jansma and Goode 1976; Schuh 1981).[3] While these reviews have focused generally on growth and did not attempt to incorporate within a single framework elements that would explain growth, unemployment, poverty, and income stability, many of the elements used in models of growth almost certainly have relevance for the understanding of these other target variables as well.

Four bodies of theory were identified in these three papers as bases for a comprehensive framework for rural development: (1) supply-oriented neoclassical theory and its developmental variants dealing with human capital and the Baumol (1967) hypothesis; (2) demand-oriented export base and trade theory, including the insights of Keynes and the "Structuralists"; (3) regional economics and central-place theory, to incorporate spatial dimensions of rural development; and (4) institutional economics to capture the interrelationships between institutions (laws, working rules, etc.) and economic activity. Schuh would include within this category theories of induced institutional innovation and theories of endogenous government behavior drawing on the work of Downs (1957), O'Connor (1973), and Stigler (1971). We would add and emphasize the important theoretical developments of Olson (1965).

While arguing that these four bodies of theory will provide the elements upon which a "theory of rural development" can draw, we also note that each of these bodies has its limitations. The foundations of neoclassical economics, for example, have been challenged by three ideas that came into prominence in the 1960s: the concept of uncertainty, the theory of the second best, and theories of social choice (Fusfeld 1982). Uncertainty, for example, seems to be playing a larger role in the economic affairs of rural areas. This uncertainty, generated by the internationalization of the world economy, deregulation, and technological change calls into question conclusions about optimal resource allocation out of general equilibrium theory. And Breimyer (1984), discussing rail and trucking deregulation impacts on rural areas, notes the inconclusive nature of analysis based on neoclassical assumptions. Breimyer has often noted that a preponderance of solutions are, at best, second best or even third best. We can no longer claim that the results obtained from the free operations of self-adjusting markets are necessarily desirable. These challenges imply that, in our attempts to draw from neoclassical theory and the other bodies of theory, we need to give more explicit attention to the limits of the theories and not extend them beyond their limits.

Shaffer (1979, 976) has commented on the need to recognize the limits of current theory and at the same time pursue further development of an integrated rural development paradigm: "It may be that we need to remind people of the uses and limitations of our theories and caution them about the conditions that make their use appropriate or inappropriate. The synthesis of a comprehensive theory can remain as our long-run goal, and more appropriate use of existing theories and tools remain a legitimate short-run goal."

A general rural development paradigm should explain regional differentials in output growth, unemployment, poverty and inequality, and employment instability. In an earlier paper, we argued that the Kaldorian cumulative causation model provides a more adequate starting point than the standard neoclassical framework (Weber and Deaton 1984). This perspective recognizes the powerful influences of price adjustments, the spatial forces of market organization, and the forces of demand that drive the export-base model of regional growth. The Kaldorian model can be adapted to incorporate the cumulative aspects of interregional (or international) change that can be generated by differential rates of adjustments to technological change, wage differentials, and economies of size. Any one or a combination of these factors creates regional differences in the prevailing efficiency wage (i.e., money wages divided by an index of productivity). This view incorporates the potential equilibrating effects of price adjustments, but it suggests that technological externalities in the form of agglomeration economies and social amenity values may stimulate continuous disequilibrium. Disequilibrium becomes the rule, not the exception. Anticipated market adjustments along neoclassical lines actually create continuing disequilibrium adjustments among regions.

We feel that the arguments can be extended to incorporate the supply-side influence of human capital, savings, invention and innovations, and the differentials in wage adjustments created by psychic preferences for cultural, social, and amenity values. Further elaboration of the "Verdoorn effect" was provided in a tentative model developed by Weber and Deaton (1984), principally incorporating the economies of size and human capital improvement effects created by government spending.

The disequilibrium perspective suggested by the Kaldorian approach is sufficiently robust to include both the supply-oriented factors of growth and development and variants of demand-oriented, export-base, and trade theory. In addition, it lends itself to easier accommodation to institutional changes and the disequilibrating influence that these set in motion, particularly induced institutional innovations. Yet, it remains vulnerable to many of the limitations of existing theory, such as the challenges identified by Fusfeld (1982).

How important a prerequisite for relevant research is an integrated paradigm for rural development? Nelson (1984) makes a strong case for the need for an integrated framework for rural development research. Without an understanding of the structural relationships between target variables and policy instruments, he argues, agricultural economists are not able to provide rural policy analysts with information to help them design appropriate public policies. Nelson argues an underlying paradigm would help us determine what data to collect and what relationships to analyze in a way that would help our information to be more relevant to policymakers.

A second reason for attempting to develop a rural development paradigm is that it would increase the intellectual excitement of those working in the area by giving researchers a sense of "contributing to a larger whole or of attacking a critical gap in understanding" (Nelson 1984, 695). We see value in attempts to develop a model of rural development that integrates the four bodies of theory into a comprehensive framework not merely because of the increased policy relevance and intellectual stimulation of researchers, but because it would also help us to put our own disciplinary insights in a broader perspective and would perhaps facilitate links between economics and other disciplines.

Even the development of an adequate conceptual model for rural development, however, would not insure the relevance of our research without attention to what Bonnen (1975) has called "operationalization and measurement issues." Jansma and Goode (1976) offer some suggestions about how this operationalization and measurement of relevant concepts in rural development might proceed.

EXTENSION. "Extension was launched to deliver new applied knowledge to farm and rural people in the United States and to transmit their interests to the land grant university research community" (Hildreth and Armbruster 1981, 853). The challenge to agricultural economists in extension is to adapt this role to fit a new environment in which the demands for information and education are changing, the resources for program delivery are shrinking, and the technology for extending information is changing, while at the same time applying the traditional principles of extension programming identified by Hildreth and Armbruster: "involving students in program development, presenting education in an informal setting, and focusing on practical information" (p. 854).

The trends identified earlier provide some indicators of new demands for informal education as we approach the twenty-first century. As the age structure "grays" and the family structure and labor-force participation patterns of men and women change, we are seeing an increasing demand for education over the life span. Education is not something that ceases at high school and college graduation, as the tremendous growth in community college, nondegree programs attests. While much of this demand is for leisure skills and midcareer and career-change education, there is also a desire to better understand the increasingly complex world within which we live and to more effectively participate in public affairs.

The decentralization of governmental authority provides the opportunity for more effective participation by citizens in local affairs and, consequently, a potential demand for information that enables people to understand the complex issues, and for leadership skills to make their input more effective.

Internationalization, deregulation, and the changing economic structure are dramatically affecting the conduct of business in rural areas. Local business leaders and local government officials often do not have time to keep up with the trends and think through their implications for local economies or local business opportunities. Extension can take advantage of the opportunity by both explaining the larger social and economic trends and by showing community leaders and citizens how local community changes either reflect or can take advantage of these trends.

The same forces that affect nonfarm businesses also affect farms and farm families. Perhaps the most important thing for agricultural economists to do is to recognize in their extension programs the increasing interdependence of farm and nonfarm economic activities. Rural development specialists need to pay more attention to "farm" issues, and farm management specialists need to pay more attention to the off-farm economic activities and opportunities of farm households in analyzing farm enterprise decisions.

Extension can also keep new opportunities and trends in perspective by providing information on the local and national social costs of economic change. While extension has done this in the past for local areas in its impact modeling, it has often not put the local and national perspectives together.

As the program needs and potential clientele for extension education change, so also may the needed delivery mechanisms. Some demographic trends like the aging of the population allow some people to have more time for education. Other trends, like the trend toward two-earner families, decreases the amount of leisure time for education. These shifts may dramatically affect the kinds of educational formats demanded. There may be less demand for public meetings by the family audiences and more demand for written materials, correspondence courses, video cassettes, and computer-assisted learning packages to be used at home. This suggests a need to better target education programs about rural development issues and to involve these target audiences in the traditional program design mechanisms to insure effectiveness.

TEACHING. A major challenge is to broaden the students' conception of social science to enable them to cross the boundaries between economics and the humanities and to help them understand the value implications embedded in the selection of research and extension projects. To this end we see the importance particularly of reorienting graduate instruction to include more emphasis on the history of economic thought and on the philosophy of science. We would echo Barkley's (1984a) call for more training in "problem recognition," and Wunderlich's (1984) call for more attention to the ethical underpinnings of economic analyses in our graduate teaching programs. Adequate preparation for analyzing economic events in an increasingly interdependent world will also require more attention in training all agricultural economists to international development economics, international trade, macroeconomics, and income distribution.

Following Arthur Lewis (1984), we also believe that more attention to economic history would give students a better appreciation of the evolution of the market system and of the economic institutions that exist today. This is particularly important in development because of the long-term and dynamic processes that development economists study.

We believe that teaching has a critical role in the development of a comprehensive rural development framework. Because our work in research and to a lesser extent extension tends to be rather narrowly focused, and because the only time many of us are forced to attempt a comprehensive view of the rural economy is in the classroom, it is our opinion that the outlines of a comprehensive rural development economics framework are most likely to be developed in teaching development economics in a classroom. We are particularly impressed with the potential of development models spawned in a third world context to provide the intellectual groundwork for advances in domestic rural development models.

Summary

We are guardedly optimistic as we approach the twenty-first century. We see the world undergoing fundamental change, and we see a growing relevance of the discipline of agricultural economics with its broad philosophical base and deep concern for public issues and the role of public institutions in shaping the economic context. We understand some of the incredible complexity in the economic and social systems, and we are aware of the narrow professional social science orientation that has tended to dominate our discipline. We sense, however, a reawakening of interest in broad issues of social ethics and their economic dimensions, and we see active interest in the relationship between institutional change and economic behavior. We are confident that by appropriating out of our own and other traditions that which is useful, and by maintaining dialogue with society about issues of common concern, agricultural economists will be able to match the discipline's greatest strengths with society's greatest needs.

Notes

1. This section has been revised in response to a reviewer's observation that we implied that "technological ascendency . . . ran its course in the 1950s." The language in the conference draft of this paper did seem to imply this kind of interpretation. In the revised section, we have chosen words that more clearly reflect our original intent.

2. Indeed, in the 1976 session of the American Agricultural Economics Association

meetings entitled "Rural Development, Poverty, and Regional Growth," poverty was mentioned only once in passing in one of the four papers. (Edwards 1976, 914).

3. Schuh's (1981,767) paper is actually an attempt to develop a conceptual framework to help us to understand the world economic system and "to design a more orderly, efficient and equitable international economic system." Because of the increasing importance of international economic developments to rural America and because of the richness of Schuh's discussion, we have included it here.

References

Anderson, W. H. L. 1964. Trickling Down: The Relationship Between Economic Growth and the Extent of Poverty Among American Families. *Q. J. Econ.* 78:511–24.

Atkinson, A. B. 1975. *The Economics of Inequality.* Oxford: Oxford Univ. Press.

Barkley, P. W. 1984a. Rethinking the Mainstream: Discussion. *Am. J. Agric. Econ.* 66:798–802.

———. 1984b. Using Policy to Increase Access to Capital Services in Rural Areas. In *Restructuring Policy for Agriculture: Some Alternatives,* ed. S. S. Batie and J. P. Marshall, 23–40. Blacksburg: College of Agricultural and Life Sciences, Virginia Polytechnic Inst. and State Univ.

Barrows, R. L., and D. W. Bromley. 1975. Employment Impacts of the Economic Development Administration's Public Works Program. *Am. J. Agric. Econ.* 57:46–54.

Baumol, W. J. 1967. Macroeconomics of Unbalanced Growth: The Anatomy of Urban Crisis. *Am. Econ. Rev.* 57:415–26.

Becker, G. 1975. *Human Capital.* New York: Columbia Univ. Press.

Bellah, R., N. R. Madsen, W. M. Sullivan, A. Swidler, S. M. Tipton. 1985. *Habits of the Heart.* Berkeley: Univ. of California Press.

Black, S. H. 1985. From the Industrial to the Information Economy Policy Implications for the South. Paper prepared for the 1985 Committee on Southern Trends, Southern Growth Policies Board, Research Triangle Park, N.C.

Bonnen, J. T. 1975. Improving Information on Agriculture and Rural Life. *Am. J. Agric. Econ.* 57:753-64.

Bosworth, B. P. 1982. Capital Formation and Economic Policy. In *Brookings Papers on Economic Activity,* 273–326. Washington D.C.: The Brookings Institution.

Breimyer, H. F. 1984. Consequences of Transportation Regulatory Reform on Agriculture and Rural Areas: Discussion. *Am. J. Agric. Econ.* 66:663–65.

Bridges, B. Jr. 1965. State and Local Inducements for Industry: Part I. *Natl. Tax J.* 18:1–14.

Danziger, S., and P. Gottschalk. 1983. The Measurement of Poverty: Implications for Antipoverty Policy. *Am. Behav. Sci.* 26:739–56.

Davis, L. E., and D. C. North. 1971. *Institutional Change and American Economic Growth.* Cambridge: Cambridge Univ. Press.

Deaton, B. J. 1983. New Institutional Arrangements for Supplying Local Public Services Under New Federalism with Special Reference to Education. *Am. J. Agric. Econ.* 65:1124–30.

Deaton, B. J., T. G. Johnson, B. Farmer, and P. Schwartz. 1985. Rural Virginia

Development Foundation: The Making of an Institution. Virginia Cooperative Extension Service, Publication 302-002.

Deaton, B. J., and M. R. Landes. 1978. Rural Industrialization and the Changing Distribution of Family Incomes. *Am. J. Agric. Econ.* 60:950–54.

Deavers, K. L., and D. L. Brown. 1983. Sociodemographic and Economic Changes in Rural America. Rural Development, Poverty, and Natural Resources Workshop Paper Series. Washington, D.C.: Resources for the Future.

Dewar, M. E. 1981. The Usefulness of Industrial Revenue Bond Programs for State Economic Development: Some Evidence from Massachusetts. *New Engl. J. Bus. and Econ.* 7:23–34.

Downs, A. 1957. *An Economic Theory of Democracy.* New York: Harper & Row.

Duncan, G. J. 1984. *Years of Poverty, Years of Plenty.* Ann Arbor: Univ. of Michigan, Inst. for Social Research.

Dunn, E. S., Jr. 1980. *The Development of the U.S. Urban System.* vol. 1, *Concepts, Structures, Regional Shifts.* Baltimore: Johns Hopkins Univ. Press.

Edwards, C. 1976. The Political Economy of Rural Development: Theoretical Perspectives. *Am. J. Agric. Econ.* 58:914–22.

———. 1979. Modeling Rural Growth. *Am. J. Agric. Econ.* 61:967–73.

———. 1981. The Bases for Regional Growth: A Review. In *A Survey of Agricultural Economics Literature.* ed. L. K. Martin, vol. 3, 159–284. Minneapolis: Univ. of Minnesota Press.

Fusfeld, D. R. 1982. *Age of the Economist.* Glenview: Scott, Foresman.

Ghez, G. R., and G. S. Becker. 1975. *The Allocation of Time and Goods Over the Life Cycle.* New York: Columbia Univ. Press.

Gottschalk, P., and S. Danziger. 1985. A Framework for Evaluating the Effects of Economic Growth and Transfers on Poverty. *Am. Econ. Rev.* 75:153–61.

Goulet, D. 1971. *The Cruel Choice: A New Concept in the Theory of Development.* New York: Atheneum.

Heckman, J. S. 1982. Survey of Location Decisions in the South. Federal Reserve Bank of Atlanta. *Econ. Rev.* 6:16–19.

Hildreth, R. J., and W. J. Armbruster. 1981. Extension Program—Past, Present, and Future: An Overview. *Am. J. Agric. Econ.* 63:853–59.

Hoch, I. 1979. Settlement Size, Real Income, and the Rural Turnaround. *Am. J. Agric. Econ.* 61:953–59.

Jansma, J. D., and F. M. Goode. 1976. Rural Development Research: Conceptualizing and Measuring Key Concepts. *Am. J. Agric. Econ.* 58:922–28.

Jansma, J., H. B. Gamble, J. P. Madden, and R. H. Warland. 1981. Rural Development: A Review of Conceptual and Empirical Studies. In *A Survey of Agricultural Economics Literature,* ed. L. K. Martin, vol. 3, 285–392. Minneapolis: Univ. of Minnesota Press.

Jequier, N. 1984. Appropriate Technology for Rural Governments. In *Local Leadership and Rural Development, Implications for Research and Extension.* Organization for Economic Cooperation and Development, USDA and Virginia Cooperative Extension Service.

Jordan, M., and T. Hady. 1976. Agriculture and the Changing Structure of the Rural Economy. Structural Issues of American Agriculture. Agric. Econ. Rep. 438. Washington, D.C.: USDA, ESCS.

Just, R. and D. Zilberman. 1984. Risk Aversion, Technology Choice, and Equity Effects of Agricultural Policy. Berkeley: California Agricultural Experiment Station, Giannini Foundation of Agricultural Economics.

Kaldor, N. 1970. The Case for Regional Policies. *Scott. J. Polit. Econ.* 17:337–48.

Kendrick, J. W. 1976. *The Formation and Stocks of Total Capital.* New York: Columbia Univ. Press.

Kriesel, W. 1984. The Estimation of Benefits, Costs, and Probabilities of Manufacturing Plant Location in Rural Virginia. Master's thesis, Dept. of Agric. Econ., Virginia Polytechnic Inst. and State Univ.

Kuznets, S. S. 1955. Economic Growth and Income Inequality. *Am. Econ. Rev.* 45:1–28.

Lewis, W. A. 1984. The State of Development Theory. *Am. Econ. Rev.* 74:1–10.

McGranahan, D. A. 1980. The Spatial Structure of Income Distribution in Rural Regions. *Am. Sociol. Rev.* 45:313–24.

Markley, D. M. 1984. The Impact of Institutional Change in the Financial Services Industry on Capital Markets in Rural Virginia. *Am. J. Agric. Econ.* 66:686–93.

Marshall, A. 1920. *Principles of Economics.* 8th ed. London: Macmillan.

Moes, J. E. 1961. The Subsidization of Industry by Local Communities in the South. *South. Econ. J.* 28:187–93.

Mulkey, D., and B. L. Dillman. 1976. Location Effects of State and Local Industrial Development Subsidies. *J. Growth and Change.* 7:37–43.

Myrdal, G. 1957. *Economic Theory and the Underdeveloped Regions.* London: Duckworth.

Nelson, G. L. 1984. Elements of a Paradigm for Rural Development. *Am. J. Agric. Econ.* 66:694–701.

O'Connor, J. 1973. *The Fiscal Crisis of the State.* New York: St. Martin's Press.

Olson, M. 1965. *The Logic of Collective Action.* Cambridge: Harvard Univ. Press.

Pigou, A. C. 1920. *The Economics of Welfare.* London: Macmillan.

Polanyi, K. 1944. *The Great Transformation.* Boston: Beacon Press.

President's National Advisory Commission on Rural Poverty. 1968. Rural Poverty in the United States. Washington, D.C.: GPO.

Rasmussen, D. W., M. Bendick, Jr. and L. C. Ledebur. 1982. *The Cost-Effectiveness of Economic Development Incentives.* Washington, D.C.: The Urban Inst.

Reynolds, M., and E. Smolensky. 1977. Post-fisc Distributions of Income in 1950, 1961, and 1970. *Pub. Fin. Q.* 5:419–38.

Richardson, H. W. 1973. *Regional Growth Theory.* London: Macmillan.

Ruttan, V. W. 1982. *Agricultural Research Policy.* Minneapolis: Univ. of Minnesota Press.

Saupe, W. E., and B. Weber. 1974. Rural Family Income in Wisconsin. Research Report R2634. Madison: Univ. of Wisconsin.

Schuh, G. E. 1981. Economics and International Relations: A Conceptual Framework. *Am. J. Agric. Econ.* 63:767–79.

_____. 1984. Revitalizing the Land Grant University. Paper presented at Colloquim, Strategic Management Research Center, Univ. of Minnesota, September 28.

Shaffer, R. E. 1979. Rural Employment and Rural-Urban Population Shifts: Discussion. *Am. J. Agric. Econ.* 61:975–77.

Shaffer, R., P. Salant, and W. Saupe. 1985. Rural Economics and Farming: A Synergistic Link. Paper presented at North Central Regional Conference on Interdependences of Agriculture and Rural Communities in the 21st Century, Zion, Ill., Feb. 12–14.

Smith, E. D., B. J. Deaton, and D. R. Kelch. 1978. Location Determinants of Manufacturing Industries in Rural Areas. *South. J. Agric. Econ.* 10:23–32.

Smith, J. D., and J. N. Morgan. 1970. Variability of Economic Well-being and Its Determinants. *Am. Econ. Rev.* 60:286–95.

Stigler, G. J. 1971. The Theory of Economic Regulation. *Bell J. Econ.* 2:3–21.

Stinson, T. F. 1985. Life Cycle Behavior, Uncertainty, and the Demand for Infrastructure. Paper presented to the National Symposium on Local Infrastructure Investment Decisions, Arlington, Va., April 17–19.

Stober, W. J., and L. H. Falk. 1967. Property Tax Exemption: An Inefficient Subsidy to Industry. *Natl. Tax J.* 20:386–94.

Taylor, H. C., and A. D. Taylor. 1952. *The Story of Agricultural Economics in the United States, 1840–1932.* Ames: Iowa State College Press.

Tinbergen, J. 1952. *On the Theory of Economic Policy.* Amsterdam: North Holland.

Todaro, M. P. 1977. Economic Development in the Third World. 2d ed. New York: Longman.

U.S. Department of Health, Education and Welfare. 1976. The Measure of Poverty. A Report to Congress as mandated by the Education Amendments of 1974. Washington, D.C.

Weber, B. A. 1973. Trickling Down: The Responsiveness of Rural and Rural Poor Family Income and Labor Supply to Regional Economic Growth. Unpublished Ph.D. diss., Univ. of Wisconsin, Madison.

Weber, B. A., and B. J. Deaton. 1984. U.S. Regional and Rural-Urban Growth Differentials: An Examination of the Cumulative Causation Hypothesis. Agricultural Economics Staff Paper SB-85-1. Blacksburg: Virginia Polytechnic Inst. and State Univ.

West, J. G. 1978. Consequences of Rural Industrialization in Terms of Income Distribution. *Growth and Change.* 9:15–21.

Williamson, J. C., and P. H. Lindert. 1980. *American Inequality.* New York: Academic Press.

Wunderlich, G. 1984. Fairness in Land Ownership. *Am. J. Agric. Econ.* 66:802–7.

The Economics of Rural Areas: **A Discussion**

KENNETH R. FARRELL

Deaton and Weber have prepared a comprehensive, insightful paper on selected aspects of the economics of rural areas. The paper itself and the appended references provide a useful foundation for considering design of future research, extension, and resident teaching programs and for the discussions to begin shortly.

Although implicit in some of the trends identified by the authors, I would be inclined to give much greater emphasis than they to the development and adoption of technology as a factor affecting patterns of rural economic development and social and economic issues related there to. I allude not merely to technologies affecting the economic organization and performance of agriculture, but to the externalities, second and tertiary effects of the technologies on resource use, quality of the natural environment, income and wealth distribution. I also would give more emphasis to the development and deployment of communication, transportation, and information-processing technologies and their effects on both the supply of and demand for social services within and among rural communities.

I do not agree with the authors' inference that technological ascendancy as a driving force shaping public policies ran its course in the 1950s; on the contrary, I would argue that technological determinism will continue as a powerful force in the remainder of the century and well beyond, with major implications for agriculture and rural areas including employment, demand for labor skills, capital requirements, and, consequently, on the economic structure of rural communities.

I quibble with little in regard to the three major issues identified by the authors: (1) farm and nonfarm interaction, (2) capital formation, (3) poverty and income distribution. I am, however, surprised that issues related to human capital development were not singled out for attention. If the adjustments in rural America continue to be as far-reaching as the authors imply, the needs for training and retraining of human capital would seem to have very important implications at all levels of education and for extension programs.

If I have one major disappointment with the paper for the purposes at

Kenneth R. Farrell is Vice President of Agriculture and Natural Resources, University of California, Davis.

hand in this conference, it is the failure of the authors to identify a coherent conceptual framework within which to examine research, extension, and resident teaching needs for the future.

While in general agreement with the authors' identification and diagnosis of the issues and the needs and many of their particular recommendations for research, I am left with an uncomfortable feeling of the lack of objective (function) criteria for selecting among the many needs or opportunities for research. I agree with the need for more research on such matters as the relative effectiveness of alternative public-sector investments in infrastructure, research to improve our understanding of the process of capital formation, research to determine what affects poverty and income, and many of their other recommendations. However, I would like some means of knowing how important such research might be relative to many other research avenues and how important the payoff from such research might be relative to the research and some objective function(s) concerning rural economic development.

The authors recognize the need for a rural development paradigm and indeed touch lightly on several possible approaches to development of a paradigm. It might have been more useful for our purposes had they chosen to develop the merits and shortcomings of such approaches in greater detail before their subjective selection of particular topics.

The absence of a comprehensive framework or paradigm within which to view and study rural development plagues much of our research and the formulation and implementation of public policies and programs. That is not to argue that we have not conducted much useful research or that public policies and programs have not been entirely ineffectual in attaining some development-related objectives. But it is to argue that the absence of a suitable theory or paradigm of rural development may explain why our research appears to be in many respects nonadditive and incapable of yielding an integrated, cohesive body of knowledge, and why our public policies and programs appear fragmented and sometimes inconsistent.

I would urge the authors and those in the small discussion groups to think further about needs for improved extension programs in rural development. I like the authors' recommendation of coordinating extension programs with state economic development programs. It seems that much could be done through applied research and extension programs to provide better information and analysis to assist not only states, but also local and regional development agencies concerning the selective use of taxing authorities and capital investments for development.

Finally, it seems that as agricultural economists, we may not yet have fully grasped the significance of the "deagriculturalization" of rural areas and the increased diversity of rural America. If we are serious about *rural* development as distinct from *agricultural* development, we must reach out to work with other disciplines and clientele and to go well beyond neoclassical Marshallian economics, which has driven much of what agricultural economists have done in the past 75 years. In turn, that means a searching reexamination of curricula on which agricultural economists are reared.

The Economics of Rural Areas: A Discussion

GERALD KLONGLAN

Deaton and Weber have packed a lot of ideas into a very few pages. In general it was easy to follow the authors' logic and arguments. I especially liked its futuristic orientation. Some ideas in the paper were well integrated across the four sections of the paper; others were not as explicitly integrated as they might have been.

Two major themes — the need to focus on rural rather than agricultural economics and the need to adjust to the internationalization of the world economies — are prominent throughout, and there are many suggestions for new research, extension, and teaching initiatives throughout the paper. Most of my comments will focus on ways to extend some of the suggestions made by the authors.

Section I is a very good, brief description of six major trends affecting rural America. (Three of them: demographic changes, decentralization of government, and evolving conceptions of justice and human rights are major topics of research for sociologists.) Section II presents an interesting three-period conceptualization of domestic economic policy thrusts since 1950. Section III clearly identifies three critical issues (of which I will highlight the first on farm and nonfarm interactions). Section IV has many good suggestions for needed research as well as for needed changes in extension programming and graduate education for economists.

The authors' brief historical context for the agriculture economics discipline was very illuminating, especially the 1911 USDA report on Instruction Needs in Agriculture. In that report, the subcommittee on Rural

Gerald Klonglan is Professor, Department of Sociology and Anthropology, Iowa State University, Ames.

Economics and Farm Management recommended that the term "rural economics" be used as the general term for the profession rather than "agricultural economics."

It seems that while economists did not take the committees' advice, the sociologists did. We have always been rural sociologists. And so now we have several departments of Agricultural Economics and Rural Sociology around the United States. In Rural Sociology, one of our major areas of study is agricultural sociology or, as we call it, the sociology of agriculture. We also have major thrusts in demography, organization, community, natural resources, technological and social change, and so on. In this historical light, it is of interest to note that the newest division in the Economic Research Service has been named the Agriculture and Rural Economics Division.

The next step in coming up with an appropriate name for our field of study, following the authors' argument, would be to focus on "rural social science," a term more widely used in developing countries than the United States (which would also be in keeping with the authors' interest in borrowing ideas from other countries to help our own domestic programs). For example, the Agriculture Development Council (ADC) is using the term "rural social science" in its new human capital and institution building thrust in Africa, in contrast to ADC's earlier agricultural economics thrust in Asia. "Rural social science" captures the need for greater interdisciplinary collaboration among economists, sociologists, political scientists, psychologists, communication experts, historians, and so on. Maybe someday the Economic Research Service in the USDA will be renamed the Rural Social Science Research Service.

The authors might strengthen their arguments for a rural rather than an agricultural perspective by referring to the current crisis in rural America. I believe the current crisis gives social scientists a chance to point out the need for a major thrust (high research, extension, and teaching priority) in the rural social sciences. The solution to today's problems are social, political, and economic. The solutions will not be found in the models of biology used in animal science, agronomy, and horticulture, nor in the physical science models of agricultural engineering. We need some reallocation of scientific resources to focus on solutions to existing problems. One could make a good argument that the research thrust in biotechnology should be put on the back burner for a while as we try to eliminate the potential for revolution in the rural United States.

I agree with the authors' suggestion to focus more on farm and nonfarm interaction in rural development. I believe they could have strengthened their argument by more explicitly illustrating their general point by referring to the recent USDA Payment-in-Kind (PIK) program that was designed to help farmers (and did), but which severely affected many farm-supply organizations and rural communities. The same social phenomena occurred with the soil bank program in the 1950s, but we did not have a good enough recall system in the agriculture community to avoid doing the same thing twice. The PIK experience is still very real to many people who were adversely affected by the program, which is now an advantage in selling the importance of farm-nonfarm interaction to the general rural populace.

I was somewhat surprised to see the suggestion that Jan Tinbergen's Theory of Economic Policy was suggested as a possible "guiding light" to use as a framework to develop a rural development paradigm. The suggestion sent me scurrying to my bookshelf to dust off Tinbergen's book, which I had as a text in a 1961 socioeconomic development course taught by an energetic young assistant professor originally from the Netherlands, Eric Thorbecke, and former USDA economist Karl Fox. A set of ideas that helped earn the first Nobel Prize in economics should provide some help to students of rural development.

The authors are seeking an integrative model for rural development combined with a concern for human values in general and the values of rural economists in particular. Such an effort might be strengthened by including concepts such as "human greed" and "exploitation." Some would argue that much of America's "development" has been motivated by extreme personal self-interest (greed) and exploitation of natural resources (land, water, timber, etc.) and labor (blacks in the South). Can Tinbergen's theoretical perspective incorporate these "Marxian" ideas? Can it include the idea that many rural communities should never have been created in the first place? Many railroads received free land on the line of rail and sold it to speculators who started new communities. Many of the rural towns were never really needed. Most, at least in the Midwest, are not needed now.

I really liked several of their suggestions for changing the content of the graduate education for rural economists. There is a need for more emphasis in the history of economic thought. I further suggest they expand the focus to the history of social thought.

There is also a need for more emphasis on the philosophy of science. It is my opinion, based on my participation on economics Ph.D. committees over the past 20 years, that economics graduate students know less and less about science. They are not doing as well as they used to when asked questions such as: What are the characteristics of science? How does deduction in mathematics differ from deduction in science? What is your unit of analysis? How do levels of abstraction differ from abstract-empirical levels?

I agree with the authors that economists in general have given too much attention to mathematics and logical consistency, while giving less attention to how to make meaningful observations (measurements) of the contemporary social-economic scene. (The obverse may be true in sociology!) Too many economists have been concerned with logical proof rather than empirical proof. I am not sure how many economists discuss the idea that mathematics per se is not science. It can be a useful part of science, but is not required to do science; it is not, in principle, required to do good economic science.

I also liked the authors' suggestion that more time should be spent teaching economists how to identify problems. You need to be sure that you train them to identify problems both in economics and outside (e.g., problems in the real world, which is the authors' focus). It is hoped that research the rural economists do will be double barrelled; it should first help solve rural social problems and secondly help advance the discipline. I sometimes get the impression that faculty (at least in sociology) believe their salary comes from the American Sociological Association (discipline orientation) rather than from state taxpayers or students who are paying tuition and who want problems solved and want to learn skills.

I believe the authors' arguments for new graduate training would be strengthened if they pointed out that the problems of today are too big to be solved by one discipline; students should be taught that it is good (indeed necessary) to be able to work in interdisciplinary settings, rather than spending time staking out the boundaries of one's discipline. Knowledge knows no bounds. It creeps everywhere. Universities, foundations, and government agencies should probably require project teams to be composed of different disciplines and also people from research, extension, and teaching roles. Extension and teaching staff can help clarify problems to be studied and research utilization strategies.

I agree with the authors that rural economists need more training in international understanding. This probably means many current faculty need more international experience. It also means economics departments will need to change criteria for promotion and tenure. To assure understanding of international settings we probably need to require each faculty member to have an international experience before they can be granted tenure and promoted to associate professor, with another significant international experience before an associate professor can be promoted to full professor, and then significant international experience every five years as a full professor if they are to continue receiving salary increases.

We probably need to have the same requirements on the domestic side before each promotion decision (e.g., a significant experience living in rural poverty areas in the United States, working in a rural business, etc.). The goal is to get people out of their logical models and into the real world.

The current trend in evaluating faculty by the number of refereed journal articles is creating a wall between the university and people with many years of nonacademic economic experience. It is very difficult to get the latter hired into university discipline-oriented departments because they do not have the publication record. Everyone loses!

One thing about the paper that concerned me a bit was the implication that government decentralization is good. This is not necessarily so. The Civil Rights movement to give blacks the right to vote needed external thrusts to achieve social change. Local control is not always good.

The implication that federal decentralization gets problem solution closer to the people is not necessarily so either. The federal government may decentralize "problems" and their "solutions" to the states, but states often do not have the money to deliver the same services. It then becomes necessary for states to close out county and district offices and consolidate at the regional (within state) or state level. So the result of federal decentralization is less "local service" to people.

In closing, I would like to reiterate my hope that agricultural economists will implement many of the suggestions the authors have made. Maybe someday I will attend a meeting of the American Rural Economics Association! Or, heaven forbid, a meeting of an American Rural Social Science Association! ARSSA, here we come!

The Economics of Rural Areas: **A Discussion**

THOMAS F. HADY

In the 1960s, the development of rural areas suddenly became a national priority. Those who experienced the period remember how sparse was the research to guide us, and how long it took to get a more adequate research base. If this symposium is successful, it will help to prevent that from happening again. It seems what really is needed is a long-range estimate of the problems of the first part of the next century, so we can begin now to weave the underlying research to understand those problems. We cannot predict what the policy issues of the early 2000s will be, but we ought to try to predict the major changes we face and start some research on the forces underlying them.

Deaton and Weber point out what is to me one of the most important trends affecting rural America: its increasing integration with the world and the national economy, as well as the increasing degree to which agriculture is no longer the dominant force in rural economies. While this is a commentary on the Deaton and Weber paper, I find myself in agreement with most of what they say. Hence, this short discussion is devoted primarily to highlighting some of the changes in rural America and discussing some of the research implications of those changes.

I am not convinced, however, of the utility of tying our research to Deaton and Weber's theme of increasing mercantilism, either in our foreign interactions or our domestic ones. First, I view increasing mercantilism as a problem of the 1990s; I have to hope that saner heads will prevail by the early 2000s. Moreover, while Deaton and Weber certainly are correct that "Today, international competition is marked by the pursuit of national economic and political power," it is important to understand that this is nothing new. What is new is the environment in which the United States pursues its own interests. During the 1950s and the 1960s, the United States dominated world trade and had little need for mercantilist measures. By the 1980s, we find our industry out competed in many markets. Understanding the reasons for these changes seems to me to be near the top of the list of needed research. Even within the United States, a chauvinistic approach of

---

Thomas F. Hady is Chief of the Aggregate Analysis and Macroeconomics Branch of the Agriculture and Rural Economics Division, Economic Research Service, USDA.

"let's keep our jobs in our hometown" has hampered efficient rural development for many years.

Deaton and Weber are correct, however, that America in the last 20 years has rejoined the world. Decisions that once would be made with little attention to their international implications now are heavily influenced by world considerations. Agricultural economists in general have recognized this fact, but those who specialize in rural development problems are only beginning to explore its relevance.

World integration gets a lot of attention, but it may be less significant than the integration on our own doorstep. Rural America has changed. When Congress passed the Agricultural Adjustment Act of 1933, farming was still the predominant way of life in rural areas. By 1980, only seven percent of total earnings in nonmetropolitan areas came from agriculture (U.S. Department of Agriculture 1984, 17). What these figures depict is not, primarily, the decline of agriculture; they show the increasing integration of rural areas into the national economy. Two related trends can be identified. First, the economies of nonmetropolitan areas are becoming much more diversified. There were 678 nonmetropolitan counties in 1979 with more than 30 percent of their labor and proprietors' income from manufacturing, and only 702 in which farming contributed as much as 20 percent on average in 1975 to 1979 (Bender et al. 1985, 2–4). Second, agriculture itself is more closely integrated in the economy. Farmers purchase more inputs than formerly, and many farmers or family members have off-farm jobs. Farmers are beginning to realize that their welfare may be affected more by the actions Congress takes on the general economy than by the actions it takes on the Farm Bill. With the growth of our population, improved transportation and communications, and prospects of continued improvements in production technology, I see no reason to expect those trends to abate.

This integration has raised a whole set of policy issues with which social scientists have been asked to deal over the last two or three decades. Analysts have been asked to provide an increasing flow of information to help communities attract and nurture firms manufacturing everything from baseball gloves to computers. Legislators continually want to know whether a particular subsidy program or some new credit institution will help promote job development in rural areas. Even when we are considering farm policy, people increasingly ask about the impacts of the farm programs on the rest of the rural economy. In the old days, the farm economy and the rural economy were regarded as synonymous.

The research implications of these changes are legion. An overriding one, in my opinion, is that we need a far more detailed and accurate understanding of the way in which agriculture fits into the rural economy and of the way the rural economy interacts with the remainder of the U.S. and world economies. To cite a current example, several different arguments have surfaced in the last year or so purporting to show that farmers bore a special burden in stopping the recent inflation, either because they own a lot of land or because they are somehow especially sensitive to borrowing costs. While that particular issue is gone for the moment, we still need to know much more about the mechanisms that govern the distribution of the burdens of national economic policy among sectors of the economy and among firms and individuals within those sectors.

Another whole set of research needs revolve around the effects on nonfarm economies of the "overvalued" dollar. Deaton and Weber argue that the businesses that moved to rural America in the 1960s and early 1970s are the labor-intensive factories most vulnerable to foreign competition, and this means rural areas are especially disadvantaged by the strength of the dollar. They may be right; however, we need to explore the relationships between exchange rates and domestic output of specific industries more fully.

Further, the low-wage rural industry argument raises another fundamental issue. Development is a dynamic process. Labor in particular does not simply move into a job and stay there. What happens to the resources that were in the low-wage domestic industries when those industries close because they can no longer compete? To cite a current example, to what extent did the previous existence of low-wage industries contribute to training and socializing the labor force that is now making rural Tennessee an auto and truck manufacturing center?

Recent theoretical developments make the picture even more complicated. The rational expectations hypothesis suggests that some of what we thought we knew about rural impacts may be wrong. Our analyses of rural impacts have typically proceeded from some assumed national impact. The proponents of rational expectations are encouraging us to question our assumptions about those national impacts. For example, changes in monetary policy may not affect output; perhaps only unforeseen shocks have any output effects. Even if the rational expectations advocates are wrong, they have reminded us of what economists long have known but frequently have ignored in their theories: if people believe your predictions, they will often confound you by taking actions that make your predictions wrong. Whether or not the formal requirements of the rational expectations hypothesis are valid, I think there is a lesson for analyses of other policy changes—tax changes, PIK programs, credit programs, or rural development programs.

Once we correctly identify the national impacts, however, we are not home free. In a seminal paper in 1984, Glenn Nelson suggested that rural development was seriously hampered by the lack of a paradigm that would enable us to analyze the local consequences of a proposed change in policy. The existing models tend to be either too limited in the scope of problems they address or too aggregate in their geographic detail. Further, interactions between agriculture and the rest of the rural economy are inadequately treated in most of the models with which I am familiar.

As Deaton and Weber point out, we need an adequate conceptual model. More than that, though, we need to make that model operational. For rural development analyses, perhaps what is really needed is not a single, gigantic econometric model, but a series of integrated models, probably run by different organizations, which are able to work with one another. Thus, some organization might maintain a national model capable of predicting consequences of various policy alternatives down to the level of the five census regions, for example. Each census region would have its own organization which could take those results and break them down to the state level or perhaps to major substate regions.[1] Further, of course, there is no monopoly on the truth at the national level. The state and regional models should iterate with the national model, to refine the estimates.

That is only one of the aspects of the rural-national relationship that needs better delineation. A second, already mentioned, is the international economy and its impacts. A third important area is to develop models that will help to classify rural areas in manageable subaggregates: models akin to the type-of-farming classifications. These models should classify rural areas in ways that take account both of the characteristics of their local economies and of the policy questions we need to answer. ERS has recently completed an initial study along these lines, but much more work is needed. (Bender et al. 1985; Ross and Green 1985)

Finally, there is a responsibility to our profession to develop better tools. It has been argued that economics is a science waiting for the breakthrough in mathematics, a breakthrough that will do for economics what discovery of the calculus did for physics. Whether or not that is true, gravity models, economic base analyses, and local input-output models often leave us with as many questions as they answer. Some of our best minds need to take time to develop better theory for the study of the rural economy.

Our rural economy has become considerably more complicated in the last thirty years, and it is likely to become still more so in the next thirty. Economists who specialize in rural areas need to adapt to those new realities.

Note

1. To try to predict consequences of federal (or even state) rural development actions at the local level seems to me to be going too far. There is a large random element in local development, depending among other things on the personalities (and political connections) of the local leadership and of the officers of businesses that might locate there. We need to aggregate to average out these influences.

References

Bender, L. D., B. L. Green, T. F. Hady, J. A. Kuehn, M. K. Nelson, L. B. Perkinson, and P. J. Ross. 1985. The Diverse Social and Economic Structure of Nonmetropolitan America. Washington, D.C.: USDA, ERS-EDD.

Nelson, G. L. 1984. Elements of a Paradigm for Rural Development. *Am. J. Agric. Econ.* 66:694–700.

Ross, P. J. and B. L. Green. 1985. Procedures for Developing a Policy-oriented Classification of Nonmetropolitan Counties. Washington, D.C.: USDA, ERS-EDD.

U.S. Department of Agriculture. 1984. *Chartbook of Nonmetro-Metro Trends.* Washington, D.C.: USDA, ERS-EDD.

15

Improving the Socioeconomic Data Base

JAMES T. BONNEN

> Facts do not cease to exist because they are ignored.
>
> ALDOUS HUXLEY
> *A Note on Dogma*

This paper first explores the causes and implications of the profession's growing flight from the empirical. If we do not surmount this problem, the profession will not be capable of dealing with the data issues subsequently discussed here. The second part of this paper deals with the economic nature of data, its demand and supply. Since the Reagan administration has been acting on the belief that data are or should be private goods, the third section provides a brief summary of the current state of the federal statistical system and describes the administration's efforts to modify the nation's policies on data collection, processing, and dissemination. Finally, some conclusions are drawn about the responsibilities of our profession in academia, the government, and the private sector for dealing with issues discussed here.

A Flight from the Empirical

Data, I assert, are important. This was once obvious to agricultural economists, but no longer. Today, many agricultural economists act as if empirical measurement of the real world were not important. This behavior flies in the face of the experience of the profession. It also ignores what has

---

James T. Bonnen is Professor of Agricultural Economics at Michigan State University, East Lansing.

been known about the epistemology of knowledge since Immanuel Kant. If an inquiry does not include both the inductive and deductive, there can be no validated knowledge and, absent continuing iterations between both, no accumulation of that knowledge. Until theory is tested with empirical evidence designed for that test, and until empirical measurement is designed around an appropriate theoretical construct, you do not have valid scientific knowledge (Churchman 1971). You do not know anything about the real world, even in the conditional manner in which all scientific knowledge must be held.

Agricultural economics made its reputation as an empirical science. Any claim to scientific validity in agricultural economics depends on its capacity as an empirical science. The intellectual tradition upon which our profession's reputation and capacity stands is based on an equal or balanced emphasis on theory (including disciplines other than economics), statistical measurement techniques, and data (i.e., the three-legged stool of the empirical tradition).

Given this tradition and its accomplishments, why do so many agricultural economists today act as if data were not important? We are experiencing a drift toward an antiempirical outlook. We are moving away from the tradition we inherited toward the celebration of theory and statistical methods while ignoring data. Any profession becomes what it celebrates and rewards.

Part of the problem lies in academic economics and it is not new. Fifteen years ago in his presidential address to the American Economic Association, Professor Wassily Leontief (1971) described this part of our problem very clearly. On economic theory he observes:

> The weak and all too slowly growing empirical foundation clearly cannot support the proliferating superstructure of pure, or should I say, speculative economic theory. . . . Uncritical enthusiasm for mathematical formulation tends often to conceal the ephemeral substantive content of the argument behind the formidable front of algebraic signs . . . the assumptions on which the model has been based are easily forgotten. But it is precisely the empirical validity of these *assumptions* on which the usefulness of the entire exercise depends.

> What is really needed, in most cases, is a very difficult and seldom very neat assessment and verification of these assumptions in terms of observed facts. Here mathematics cannot help . . .

> To sum up with the words of a recent president of the Econometric Society, " . . . the achievements of economic theory in the last two decades are both impressive and in many ways beautiful. But it cannot be denied that there is something scandalous in the spectacle of so

many people refining the analysis of economic states which they give no reason to suppose will ever, or have ever, come about. . . . It is an unsatisfactory and slightly dishonest state of affairs" (Hahn 1970).

Then on statistical techniques he notes that econometrics,

. . . can be in general characterized as an attempt to compensate for the glaring weakness of the data base available to us by the widest possible use of more and more sophisticated statistical techniques. Alongside the mounting pile of elaborate theoretical models we see a fast-growing stock of equally intricate statistical tools. These are intended to stretch to the limit the meager supply of facts.

Since. . . referees do a competent job, most model-testing kits described in professional journals are internally consistent. However, like the economic models they are supposed to implement, the validity of these statistical tools depends itself on the acceptance of certain convenient assumptions pertaining to stochastic properties of the phenomena which the particular models are intended to explain; assumptions that can be seldom verified.

In no other field of empirical inquiry has so massive and sophisticated a statistical machinery been used with such indifferent results. Nevertheless, theorists continue to turn out model after model and mathematical statisticians to devise complicated procedures one after another. Most of these are relegated to the stockpile without any practical application or after only a perfunctory demonstration exercise.

In the same address Leontief went on to applaud agricultural economics as an ideal empirical science.

An exceptional example of a healthy balance between theoretical and empirical analysis and of the readiness of professional economists to cooperate with experts in the neighboring disciplines is offered by agricultural economics as it developed in this country over the last 50 years. A unique combination of social and political forces has secured for this area unusually strong organizational and generous financial support. Official agricultural statistics are more complete, reliable, and systematic than those pertaining to any other major sector of our economy. Close collaboration with agronomists provides agricultural economists with direct access to information of a technological kind. When they speak of crop rotation, fertilizers, or alternative harvesting techniques, they usually know, sometimes from personal experience, what they are talking about. Preoccupation with the standard of living of the rural population has led agricultural economists into collaboration with home economists and sociologists, that is, with social scientists of the "softer" kind. While centering their interest on only one part of the economic system, agricultural economists demonstrated the effectiveness of a systematic combination of theoretical approach with detailed factual analysis. They also were the first among economists to make use of the advanced methods of mathematical statistics. However, in their lands, statistical inference became a complement to, not a substitute for empirical research.

We have not fully deserved this praise for some time. Even as Leontief spoke, agricultural economics was already abandoning its empirical tradition.

Why should such self-destructive behavior become so dominant in agricultural economics? There are at least two sources. First, we are emulating academic economics, which, with some distinguished exceptions, now exhibits little commitment to the empirical.[1] I believe another source of the problem is the modern search for "academic excellence" in agricultural economics that places its emphasis on, and rewards, the development of axiomatic disciplinary knowledge. When pursued as an exclusive ideal, this neglects empirical work and the development of subject matter and problem-solving knowledge, all of which are essential outputs of an effective agricultural economics department.[2] Economics departments can achieve distinction through contributions to disciplinary knowledge alone.[3] Agricultural economics cannot. Thus, a badly flawed notion of what agricultural economics is about has led to incentive structures for tenure and promotion penalizing those who emphasize empirical work or who spend their lives at problem solving and subject matter expertise without a major commitment to disciplinary contribution. It is not surprising that many of these same departments now have some difficulty sustaining a vital extension activity and are losing public support because their clientele perceive them as not very useful. When departments devote themselves solely to pleasing disciplinary peers, they eventually lose their grasp of and relevance to the real world and its problems. This pathology is not limited to agricultural economics, but afflicts entire colleges. Colleges of agriculture that become no more than a collection of disciplinary researchers cannot effectively address the problems of agriculture and are not likely to survive in the long run. Not only will clientele desert them, but their rationale for an independent existence will disappear. One observes a reverse pathology as well. Some departments and colleges have retreated into such an exclusive focus on problems and applied research that vital linkages to the disciplines and the command of science are eventually lost. As a consequence, even the capacity for problem solving slowly erodes into mediocrity. The problem is one of balance.

Perhaps a third source of the antiempirical drift can be traced to the rapid increase in the cost of well-designed data since World War II. The collection of data has remained a labor-intensive activity in a period of rapidly rising labor costs. In data processing, capital invested in computers has been substituted for large pools of comptometer operators and long rows of file cabinets, causing labor costs and unit costs of processing to fall. However, the increasing costs of data collection have more than offset cost savings in data processing and dissemination. The rising value of time may have also had some impact on the profession's attitude toward data via the substitution effects of the greatly increased cost of graduate education on university-sponsored data collection.

The empirical tradition in agricultural economics is withering away, especially in graduate training, research, and those activities we celebrate as central to the profession. A colleague characterized the problem:

> The whole process is terribly perverse. Once a (data) gap appears, the methodologists and quantitative jocks will build models to "make do" without the numbers. This then breeds a cohort of students and assistant professors who are willing, accustomed to, and eager to do without data. In fact, our younger people are appalled by the thought of going after primary data, knocking on doors, chasing down farmers, etc. They, in turn, exacerbate the problem of doing without or making do with less (data) and tell the next generation that data are "O.K." but not all that important. And so it goes. I have no quarrel with rationalism, but my training says that the data-based empiricism that got us where we are is terribly important (Barkley 1985).

Pioneers as disparate in their views as John D. Black, George Warren, and O. C. Stine would rise in common wrath at the spectacle.

The effect of this drift toward nonempirical, axiomatic theory as the ideal of the profession is a withdrawal from effective problem solving. We see ourselves as economists with economic theory and mathematical and statistical tools and at best we go out and apply them. We resist multidisciplinary and empirical involvement. We are less and less focused on or motivated by empirical work and problem solving. Consequently, we do not really learn very much about problems, usually only the minimum needed to fit a model. Even then we often view the model through a data set collected by someone else for another purpose. Sometimes we do not even do that but rather program a computer to squint at the data for us. Or we use no data at all. So, we are less and less able to help people solve their problems. This undermines the social value of agricultural economics and the capabilities that brought the profession to where it is. It leaves agricultural economics without a culture capable of sustaining extension or many types of applied research.

Improved disciplinary rigor and capacity are necessary and needed, but not sufficient. In research and graduate training, we must achieve and maintain a current mastery of economic theory. This requires a faculty well trained in economics. But not every faculty member must be devoted entirely to theory, econometrics, or even economics. Indeed, to be successful in achieving their multidisciplinary, problem-solving purposes, agricultural economics departments must be staffed with an eye to the appropriate mix of diverse skills and knowledge. We cannot surrender the goals and culture of agricultural economics to that of economics. If we do, we will have become at best second-rate economics departments, of which there is already a sufficiency. A chasm is opening between this profession's potential and its performance.

If we are to improve the profession's data base to meet today's needs, we must face and resolve this issue. The profession has great capacities and opportunities. I am sure we shall surmount this difficulty as well as others.

SEVERAL CHALLENGES. The profession must face other challenges in its environment in recovering its balance as an empirical science. One is the ideological, antiempirical, "don't confuse me with facts" drift in political and social discourse. The processes that sustain and dominate society's decisions are increasingly ideological and antiempirical. The reasons for this are not entirely clear. One is the problem of coping with growing information overload. More and quicker communication of more facts by itself never ordered the world. Another influence is the growing complexity and interdependence in the economy and society, where far less existed before. The optimistic belief in the inevitability of progress and the confidence in rationalism and science have eroded. A sense of having lost sovereignty and control over one's future pervades society. There is a general disillusionment with government and a decline in the legitimacy and authority conceded to most public institutions. The response has been increasing resort to ideology.[4]

The precursors of this response could be seen in politics as early as a decade ago. They were clearly present in the Carter administration. Excessive dependence on ideology leads to distorted perceptions of reality and to a failure to define problems adequately. Instead of throwing dollars at problems (other than defense) today, we weave comforting media images around them so that they do not disturb us unduly. To a greater extent than in the past, supposedly responsible officials hide problems and disturbing effects of policy behind disingenuous or self-serving uses of statistics. The test of inductive reasoning is not brought to bear or even thought legitimate by many. Many professions neglect, and the government is now permitting to erode, the public data base in social and economic statistics.

This is not say that ideology is unimportant or avoidable. Indeed it is ideology that moves the world and from which many of our values are drawn. However, sole dependence on faith or ideology unchecked by positive knowledge of the world is dangerous in a dangerous world, misleads, and will inevitably produce disasters of one scale or another. The philosophy of knowledge, the epistemology from which individuals and society proceed, is important.

In the private sector there is a contrasting trend. Firms are increasingly dependent on and place a growing value on data and analysis. They have an ex post balance sheet test of market success and failure that is now being reinforced with ex ante statistical and economic analysis. The private-sector movement toward greater dependence on empirical analysis arises out of the growing complexity and market interdependence that firms face, combined with the improved capacity for quantitative analysis and more informed decision making.

The information revolution is here. We have analytical capability today based on computer and communication technologies and advances in statistical and quantitative methods that were not available even a decade ago.

What are the implications of all this for the profession? We are entering a period in which agricultural economics exhibits declining empirical capacity and thus declining social value. We run a risk of losing public support if we do not recover our sense of purpose. Some formulate that purpose as applied economics, which they confuse with problem solving. Applied economics is not problem solving but the development and application of disciplinary tools. Applied economists are applied disciplinarians. Problem solving is multidisciplinary and prescriptive. Some applied economists do proceed on to problem solving. When they do, however, they become more than applied disciplinarians, they become collaborators in a multidisciplinary, problem-solving process. They have to learn something about other disciplines and far more about the problems and become pragmatic and teleological in their approach to do so (Johnson 1984).

If agricultural economics departments do not move back toward their original philosophy and problem-solving capability, they will in some substantial degree be replaced by the private sector. One may not doubt that capability. Many profit and nonprofit corporations are already in the education business. A few such as the Rand Corporation even grant degrees (Eurich 1985). Private-sector agricultural R & D is growing. More importantly, private-sector information firms are now providing a growing proportion of the input of data and analysis for public and private decisions. Some of this growing information industry's output is excellent; some is of very poor quality. Agricultural economics along with other professions is responsible for defining society's problems for social and political discourse, and setting the standards for data collection and analysis. Together with government they are also responsible for the social investments in the public good aspects of society's problem solving, which the private sector will never voluntarily make.

The political process is increasingly ideological and less capable of accurately defining society's problems today. Politics is dominated by media and communication strategies of image making that promote individual politicians like toothpaste and try to make everyone feel good. However, this confuses the issues, if it does not hide them, while some problems grow intractable and evolve into crises. The potential value of what the profession has to offer in defining and in helping to solve problems is much greater today, because the public sector and the political process are increasingly fragmented and ideological in orientation (Bonnen 1984b). Some quite effective problem definition and problem solving continue in the government sector, but overall capability is declining. Over the past decade, much of the federal government's human capital and professionalism has been allowed to depreciate, and its institutional capability and capacity are eroding. The situation among state governments varies.

Today the role of the public sector itself is under assault. Indeed, the inquiry process in the federal government is increasingly dominated by people who believe that the public sector is not necessary.[5] This belief is self-fulfilling. We are dismantling much of the problem-solving and analytical capability in the federal government under the twin pressures of an antigovernment, antibureaucratic ideology and unprecedented budget and trade deficits, created by that same ideology unrestrained by little if any apparent macroeconomic understanding.[6] Only a little of this can be attributed to the intellectual disarray in the economics profession. The federal government is with greater frequency limited in its perception of reality by the growing dominance of ideology. If it continues, this lack of pragmatism assures a high incidence of policy failure and even greater disillusionment with government. Appeals to empirical or, for that matter, validated conceptual knowledge appear to have less and less bearing on policy. The decline of the federal role seems assured by these events. Indeed, such is a stated goal of the administration.

For the private sector and for society as a whole, one of the dangers in what is happening is that the public-good nature of many of the necessary investments for growth, productivity, and equity is being depreciated or ignored and the public investment has not been made. The private sector cannot operate effectively without complementary public-sector investments. That is, the private sector can operate, but it will not operate at optimal resource combinations, and other social goals will not be well served. Therefore, potential productivity, growth, and equity are forfeited. The productivity of the private sector is, in part, the product of complementary public-good investments in research, human capital, and institutions. The social performance of the private sector itself is at stake in the failure to understand and sustain necessary public-sector investment, for example, in maintaining an adequate data base and related analysis capacity. The argument over whether government is too large has obscured the need for and the nature of the long-term, public-good investments that explain much of the success of any society's development. Many private- and public-sector leaders appreciate this and are disquieted by what is happening. The movement of the private sector toward greater investment in data and analysis and its support for similar public investment reflects this growing concern (U.S. Congress 1982a).

Agriculture is in the middle of a fundamental transformation. The industrial revolution in agriculture has already changed its nature and structure. Rural social and economic structure has and continues to change. The data base finds its roots in concepts and in measurements that range from 50 to 75 years old. While some data series have been improved, others are eroding in meaning and accuracy as a result of changes in the nature of agriculture and rural life and related policy agendas (Bonnen 1977). Equally fundamental changes still face us in the new genetic technologies of molecular biology, the impact of computer and electronic communication, and robotics and sensing technologies. Current macroeconomic policies and the deregulation of transportation, communication, and banking and finance are irrevocably affecting the institutional conditions of productivity, welfare, and equity in both rural communities and agriculture. The same forces are making some human capital obsolete while creating demand for new human skills and knowledge, which in turn affects the institutional conditions of productivity, welfare, and equity.

Some of these challenges are inherently public issues; others are private, and many are mixed. The administration, however, wants to believe that government has no role in any domestic issue. This includes the provision of data where, except to support public policymakers, the administration believes the expanding private-sector information industry should be responsible. Their view is driven by ideology without any effort at conceptual argument or empirical evidence. They quite misunderstand the economic nature of data and information.

The Economic Nature of Data

The demand for data as a commodity is derived from its value in reducing uncertainty in the decision processes of private individuals and firms or government.[7] Its value, then, cannot be known with any certainty until it is obtained and used. Consequently, problems arise in estimating the demand for data or the demand for data and analysis combined to form an information product. Data users who are risk adverse will tend to demand less data than is socially optimal because of the uncertainty of their returns, a priori, to investments in data. On the other hand, if its value were known with certainty, a priori, that value, paradoxically, would have to be zero because data only becomes an economically valuable commodity under conditions of uncertainty. Nevertheless, OMB rules for clearance of new federal data collections now require prior proof of their value.

Data, viewed as a commodity, have some of the characteristics of a public good, no matter who produces it. Thus, its production and consumption involve allocative inefficiencies compared to private goods in competitive markets. The existence of uncertainty is inherent in our definition of information and data. Data generally refer to the direct product of measurement or counting (i.e., of a collection process). Information is a decision input that usually integrates data from different collection processes and subject matters with analytic interpretation. That interpretation may range from little more than formatting of data for presentation, to encoding in an index or scale, or to complex economic modeling. Information is data interpreted and analyzed to provide utility in a specific decision or subject matter context. On the other hand, epistemologically data and information are identical. In all cases, the inductive content implies a deductive prior and vice versa.

Not only does data inherently involve uncertainty, it is also by definition indivisible. In addition, the producer of data cannot fully appropriate the returns to data production, since it is not possible for them to charge for further uses of the same data once it is disseminated. The attributes of uncertainty, indivisibility, and nonappropriability all violate the classical properties of purely private goods. Yet OMB's early efforts to impose user fees on federal statistical output were accompanied by rhetoric that treated data as if it were a private good.

If an individual or firm possesses information about a commodity traded in a market, they must trade in that market to earn a return on the information. But by trading one exposes the general nature of the information to other participants. Patents and copyrights will not prevent others from using the information. User fees charged for information must be set very low if the producer wishes to avoid creating an incentive for resale. Full cost recovery of original collection and processing is impossible in the case of most basic data series.[8]

When examined, what appears to be a private-sector sale or resale of basic data is a transaction valued for the convenience of format or access and the continual, timely updating of a data base by a merchandiser, or for some associated analysis that adapts the data to specialized uses. In most cases, large, continuing private markets for information depend on the public sector for a significant part of the basic data base necessary to maintain that private market.

Some market data have such a brief life that the recovery of even resale cost depends on developing a sufficiently large initial market. For example, several dozen private firms sell crop forecasts a week to ten days ahead of USDA monthly estimates. They are really selling "advance" information on markets, a commodity that has no value by the time the USDA releases its estimates. These firms are piggybacking on the USDA base and are quite dependent on the USDA data to keep their forecasts "trued-up" from month to month.

The market for resale of data and information is often dominated by the phenomenon of increasing net returns. Increasing net returns result from the indivisibility of information when combined with the high fixed costs involved in producing data relative to the costs of transmitting the same information once acquired. The initial user is able to resell the information to other users at a cost lower than that incurred by the original producer. Increasing returns prevail only as long as the value of the information remains relatively constant for each subsequent use. Incomplete appropriability only exacerbates the difficulties brought on by increasing returns in use, since it prevents the original producer from charging for subsequent uses of data once it is disseminated. This means that the producer's high fixed costs cannot be spread over all users and full cost recovery is impossible. Yet the question of recovery of the full costs of large collections was raised repeatedly in the Reagan administration's first term.

CHANGED NATURE OF DEMAND FOR DATA. Fundamental and often unrecognized change is taking place in the demand for data and statistical data bases. The growing complexity of industrial societies has changed the agenda and processes of policymaking and, thus, also changed the value of existing data. Since World War II, the society and economy of the United States have become very much more complex, specialized, and interdependent. Various sectors interact, each sector creating many kinds of conflicts and effects external to itself. In responding to these growing conflicts and externalities, government has intervened in society in a pervasive manner and with immense impact. Federal policymaking has become far more extensive, interactive, and complex. The distinction between public and private sectors has become blurred. Try as it may, the Reagan administration will not get this genie back in the bottle. As a result of greater complexity and interdependence, national policy decisions today are much more dependent on quantitative measures to identify and understand complex problems that have gotten beyond the capacity of "seat-of-the-pants" decision making. Aggregate demand for data, thus, has increased.

In addition, since many problems now interact with one another, policy decisions more frequently involve choices that cut across present departments, government policy decision structures, and their data bases. Growing numbers of these crosscutting issues involve so many diverse, conflicting participants that more and more executive branch decisions are being forced to the White House for resolution. Crosscutting issues that reach the White House for decision involve trade-offs between conflicting goals and interests. Examples include conflicts among agricultural resource use, environmental protection, and resource conservation, or between agricultural trade and national security. The secretary of agriculture has almost no control today over the agricultural policy agenda and only limited influence over the outcome of crosscutting issues. He also needs more information and more highly processed, specific data and analysis to hold his own in these policy conflicts. The same is true for other participants.

This means that the nature of the demand for data and information is changing. Several decades ago most of the statistics used by both public and private decision makers were descriptive data drawn from single, general subject matters (e.g., housing, agriculture, energy, or subsets thereof); this data was combined with a modest amount of staff analysis before use by decision makers. Today, in a far more complex, interdependent economy and society, some information needs are still served reasonably well by subject matter data, but a much larger and growing part of decision makers' information needs requires more specific, more highly processed information products combining complex analysis with data that are integrated from multiple subject matters. These are not subject matter but problem-solving data designed to address a specific problem and to serve a specific decision maker, rather than to serve some general class of problems and decision makers (Johnson 1984). Government statistical agencies usually provide subject matter information for general classes of decision makers, but in many cases they do not have the mandate or resources to provide highly specialized problem-solving information, even for public policymakers.

The growing interaction between areas of policy represents a significant change in the public decision-making process. Increased interaction between policy areas automatically increases the number of participants in any policy decision. As the number of actors increases, conflict increases and decisions get pushed to ever-higher levels in the policy process. This overloads the decision processes of the office of the chief executive. It changes the locus of decision and the nature of the decision process with which analysis and the provision of data must be coordinated. The shift in locus of decisions to the top of a hierarchical decision structure increases the risk of technical or factual error in decision. The decisions made at lower levels in a policy process are usually well informed on the facts, even of quite complex subject matters, but more frequently will be poorly informed on trade-offs involved in crosscutting issues and will often err in judgment about political purpose and current top-level policy. The reverse is true of top-level decisions, where political generalists prevail and lack of understanding of complex technical matters will more often flaw decisions.

Thus, the technically complex decisions now increasingly pushed to the White House, if they are to be well informed, create a demand for much greater integration of diverse data bases to deal with the trade-offs between the subject matter areas that are at issue. It creates an even greater need for relevant analysis and interpretation of that data.

Changing economic policy practices are also changing the nature of the demand for data. Decisions and analysis for macroeconomic policy in the 1960s and early 1970s were generally conducted separate from those for microeconomic policy. Today various types of sectoral models are combined with macro variables in macroeconomic policy simulation analyses. This appears to be an empirical response to the increasing interdependence in the economy as well as the perceived (and perhaps related) inadequacies of macroeconomic theory in predicting economic behavior. This is a new and growing data-base phenomenon that requires not only new data but larger samples for accuracy of more detailed economic subsector collections. It also requires greater accompanying effort in conceptual development, standards, and integration of data. It should be noted that these are some of the same pressures generated by the growth of state and local government data needs.

Despite popular impressions to the contrary, the greatest expansion in public-sector activity has occurred not at the federal, but the subnational level. Growing social and economic interdependence and complexity have many of the same effects on all levels and sectors of the society. We reach for quantification to deal with greater complexity and more variables, and for more specialized, integrated data sets combined with equally specialized analysis to handle a specific problem in a more complex context. Thus, there is a growing public and private interest in local area data today and a need, not always backed by dollars, for greater detail. This makes the USDA's National Agricultural Statistics Service federal-state system and other detailed, local area statistical products more important to society.

As if this were not enough, another challenging and fundamental change in the nature of the decision process arises out of the technological and institutional innovations in transportation, communication, and data processing. Before World War II, there often was time for reflection, thoughtful analysis, and even data collection, when faced with a policy issue. Today, the technological and institutional compression of time and space turns a higher proportion of national decisions into immediate crises of varying importance, simply because all the policy variables interact much more quickly, whether the problem is economic, political, or military. This places a premium on having in place flexible, integrated, and accessible data bases as well as the relevant analytical capability.

STRUCTURE AND DISTRIBUTIONAL CONSEQUENCES OF DATA AND ANALYSIS. Economists generally assume information will reduce inequality in power, wealth, and income. However, differences in the ability to use or act on information can cause effects quite the opposite of those expected. The ability to capture returns on data is dependent on the ability to use data, which in turn is related to the analytical capabilities of the user. Data usually require combination with analysis applied to a specific decision to become information useful in problem solving. So a more equal distribution of data does not always assure greater equality in information among individual users, since analytical capabilities will differ between individuals and firms. Education and training of individuals and the development of specialized analytical units in larger firms provide superior capacity to interpret data (Thurow 1970).

When new information becomes available to both concentrated buyers and dispersed sellers, the buyers have a substantial advantage. Not only do the buyers usually have greater analytical capabilities and capacity to use information, but they also have a greater capacity to take action on that information. The actions of oligopsonistic buyers of agricultural commodities often affect the market price, giving them far more capacity to act on information. The two comments most frequently given by farmers for their refusal to respond to government surveys are that the surveys benefit others more than farmers and that the surveys hurt farmers. The truth of these statements is debatable, but they do suggest the possibility of data being used against the more dispersed traders in a market. Large oligopsonists, especially in grains, maintain their own worldwide market intelligence systems, so elimination of public market information would only create an even greater advantage for the large firms.

These insights have important implications for the relationship of information to income distribution. First, since the value of information arises only in its use, the capacity to use or act on information will have a significant effect on income distribution. Secondly, economic structure influences the distributional consequences of information. In so far as the size of firms is related to market structure (e.g., firms in oligopolistic industries are assumed large enough that their decisions will influence the market), large firms probably have both superior analytic capability and a greater capacity to use or act on information than do small firms. These larger firms can be expected to use their superior information to influence in their favor transactions with smaller, less informed firms, so the subsequent income distribution will favor larger, more concentrated firms.

There is a less obvious effect in the opposite direction (i.e., information affects economic structure). The attribute of increasing returns in use of information affects industrial organization. Radner (1970, 457) states that "the acquisition of information often involves a 'set-up cost'; i.e., the resources needed to obtain information may be independent of the scale of the production process in which the information is used." Wilson (1975) calls this same phenomenon "information economies of scale," and suggests that it is self-reinforcing, since a greater scale of operation justifies better information acquisition and more information will in turn justify a larger scale of operation. Following this logic, economies in acquiring information can contribute substantially to the incentive for firms to increase in size to the point of monopoly. Both Wilson and Radner limit their discussion to the horizontal structure of firms, but Williamson (1975) goes further and argues that this also applies to vertical integration. Hence, increasing returns in use of information can affect the vertical structure of an industry by yielding an incentive for vertical integration solely to reduce uncertainty.

It should be clear now why governments collect more data and perform more analyses for highly competitive industries, such as agriculture, than for more concentrated industries such as steel or the automotive industry. Government-collected data for private decisions was a significant factor in the increases in agricultural productivity in the United States in both the nineteenth and twentieth centuries. The returns to improved resource allocation in agriculture due to improved information have been captured by society in the form of lower food costs and the availability of excess farm labor and other resources for nonagricultural production. The returns to improved resource allocation from public information on atomistic industries, when compared to concentrated industries, creates an economic incentive for public spending on statistical systems. Thus, the logic for allocation of public revenues to statistics for different industrial sectors follows in part from the structural characteristics of those industries.

At the other extreme in structure, another motivation for data collection comes into play. If concentration grows to the point that it results in regulation of the industry, mandatory collection of data by government to support regulation will usually result.

Weisbrod (1969) indicates a number of ways to redistribute income in society. One of the most important of these is the use of the redistributional "side effects" of policies aimed primarily at efficient resource allocation. Even though government information systems in agriculture, for the most part, seem to be directed at resource allocation problems arising from uncertainty, it is possible to argue that programs in this area have had substantial income redistribution effects. The redistribution in all cases may not have led to greater equality because of the market structure of agriculture. The superior analytical capability and capacity to use information by the concentrated buyers as opposed to the dispersed sellers can lead to redistributions of income in favor of buyers. On the other hand, the distribution of income will become more equal to the extent that government data collection and analysis equalize the information among traders of agricultural commodities. Equality of access to analysis is as important as access to data.

Movement toward a more equal income distribution has probably been aided in the United States by the land-grant college system and extension education programs, by cooperative marketing, and more recently by private advisory services, since these have probably lessened the disparity in analytical capabilities between farmers and the concentrated buyers of agricultural commodities. The farmer's capacity to use information has also been enhanced by such actions as the establishment of commodity and market standards and government regulation of futures markets. Supplying price information on agricultural commodities is a government activity in many countries of the world. The justification for government price reporting in agriculture follows from the general reasoning behind the role of government in supplying information presented above. The specific rationale for public price data collection and dissemination has a somewhat broader, more complex basis.

In his classic article on the economics of information, Stigler (1961) suggests that as more information on prices is available, ceteris paribus, the amount of price dispersion in the market will decrease. Since commodity prices in agriculture are a principal determinant of farm income, price dispersion can affect the distribution of income in the farming sector. Farm price dispersion might have adverse effects on the distribution of income in farming, which could be inconsistent with the goals of society. Hence, the redistributional side effects of price reporting can justify government price reporting in agriculture. This important aspect is not often considered.

Government can also affect the income distribution of farmers by reducing the costs of price information. Problems of asymmetrical access to information in trading between large firms and small firms can be alleviated through government price reporting. The normal expectation would be for large firms to have more price information when the costs of obtaining information are relatively fixed. In agriculture this arises because commodity buyers tend to make purchases from more than one farmer. Thus, buyers will have a lower cost of obtaining information per unit sold than will an individual farmer.

The lack of information on market conditions (i.e., uncertainty) can lead to the substitution of internal organization, such as vertical integration, for market exchange mechanisms (Williamson 1975; Arrow 1975). If this relationship between vertical integration and insufficient price information holds, then government price reporting can enhance competition in a given market and thus can help prevent concentration and its subsequent detrimental effects on consumer well-being. In addition to impeding concentration, government price reporting can also remove barriers to entry in an industry by providing outside investors with price information for decisions on potential entry into a market.

The role of government as a mediator of conflicts between individuals also provides a justification for public price data collection and dissemination. When government plays the role of an objective price reporter, it supplies a routine means for the resolution of disputes concerning the value of a given commodity. Finally, in more recent times the evaluation of government farm-income support programs has been a critical justification for agricultural price reporting.

RISE OF THE INFORMATION INDUSTRY. Business has long been a respondent and user of public statistics. Today it is increasingly a producer of statistics and various types of analysis. Many other institutions have gotten into the business of analyzing, presenting, and even sometimes collecting statistics. These include research institutes, public and private interest groups, quasi-public bodies, universities, and some foundations, to name only a few. The data and information supply scene is growing quite complex.

We have entered the information age, in which the coordination of society's functions depends critically upon appropriate subject matter and problem-solving knowledge and upon the information process itself. Every decision system is built upon an information system foundation, which must be consciously managed for institutional effectiveness and survival. Information is the ubiquitous straw in the bricks from which today's major institutions are constructed.

A private-sector information industry has evolved in response to the need for highly specialized, decision-specific information, which neither the public sector nor the typical commercial or manufacturing firm is prepared to provide for itself or others. As complexity and specialization have grown, government statistics are less frequently well adapted to specific decision needs since they are usually focused on general subject matters (e.g., housing, population, manufacturing, transportation, agriculture, etc.). When a private firm needs information that cannot be generated by its own internal information system, it is often faced with high costs and may have limited technical capacity for retrieval and analysis of data from external sources. Specialized information firms have found various niches in providing data and analysis to both public- and private-sector institutions. These range from provision of on-line, continuously updated data bases for modeling and forecasting, to specialized analysis by consulting, research, and management firms, to statistical organizations with substantial competence in design, collection, and analysis of data, and to various types of communications and publishing services.

A large number of information-industry firms specialize in the further processing and analysis of government statistics into specialized forms of information, which they then sell not just to private-sector firms but back to the government (even to the statistical agencies that collected some of the data). The program-related statistical agencies of the United States that were created or expanded greatly in the past decade, such as the Energy Information Administration, have been forced by government personnel ceilings to contract with the private sector for a very high percentage of their basic data collection and processing. Some of this is of good quality, but some is very poor. The fault is often both that of the agency as well as the private firm.

There is a growing tension and mutual interdependence between the public and private sectors in the collection, processing, and presentation of information. In the proliferation of information and its sources, government statistical organizations have lost the near monopoly they once had. They now face competition (and comparison) not only in data collection, but especially in processing, analysis, and presentation of statistics.

Some statistical activities that should remain a function of government will not, if public statistical organizations do not develop a greater capability and commitment to serve increasingly specialized, complex decision needs. This is most clearly so in the case of the obligation to provide relevant, accurate information to the general public and to government policymakers and program managers. Public provision of statistics to the private sector is a more complex question. For the general public, statistical agencies need to identify the appropriate areas of subject matter knowledge that should be maintained as public goods. As major societal problems or issues are identified, government statistical and research organizations should also develop accurate problem descriptions and objective analyses of alternative approaches to those problems. This becomes a broad information base, which not only serves to inform the public but also leaves the statistical agency much better prepared to develop the decision-specific type of analysis needed by public policymakers.

Due to large economies of scale in data collection and the fact that many types of data can only be collected with integrity by the federal government, the obligation of federal statistical agencies extends in some areas to state and local policymakers. This is a neglected area of major responsibility, which is filled with politically difficult management problems. For the same reasons, there are also obligations to collect data for the coordination of private markets, and for private-sector use where scale economies of data collection are substantial. In some of the latter instances, user fees would be appropriate. Except where users agree to pay for the information, the Reagan administration refuses to recognize these federal obligations.

There are difficult issues to be faced in achieving the right mix and balance in public and private roles in the provision of data and analysis. The rapid rate of technological and institutional change will continue to disturb this balance and to change what is appropriate or socially desirable. Both public and private groups need to collaborate in fashioning a broad, common philosophy and a strategy for the development of the entire information industry, public and private. Otherwise a continual, unproductive conflict will prevail over the location of this boundary. The approach of the Reagan administration, as manifest in OMB, is to impose on public agencies the full burden of proving that any data they propose to collect should be collected by a public agency. Their sole criterion is "practical utility" for federal program management. The only exceptions from this test are some existing, very visible, widely used statistical products that OMB calls "national base-line indicators."

The Current State of Federal Statistics

Libertarian ideology combined with the rapid growth and lobbying of the information industry leads the Reagan administration to the strong view that, short of a conclusive demonstration to the contrary, all of society's information needs (including government's) should be supplied by the private sector. OMB, in its role as the ideological enforcer of the Reagan administration, has been pounding this message home to the agencies in various forms since 1981. The goal appears to be the "privatization" of federal statistical and nonstatistical data collection, processing, analysis, and dissemination.

Most industrial nations have centralized statistical systems with a single large statistical agency responsible for all official statistics. The United States has a decentralized, if not fragmented, system that grew like Topsy, department by department, in response to needs and vision, or the lack thereof. Most older cabinet departments have one or more specialized statistical and analytical or research agencies with major statistical programs. There are 38 major statistical agencies or programs with identifiable lines in the budget, but attempts to identify all statistical programs will produce as many as 100 agencies with responsibility for producing official statistics (Duncan and Shelton 1978). This does not include administrative data produced to manage action programs. Official statistics generally serve multiple public and private purposes. When these purposes become sufficiently important, the data are designed and collected using modern statistical techniques. For all of its lack of order as a system, our statistical output has generally been considered the best in the world. Whether it will remain so now lies in the balance.

A DECADE OF NEGLECT AND INJURY. The net impact of the Carter and Reagan administrations on the federal statistical system has been quite unfortunate. Enthusiasm for reorganizations during the Carter administration disordered the environment of several statistical agencies. In the

USDA, the Economic Research Service (ERS), the Farmer Cooperative Service, and the Statistical Reporting Service were combined solely to simplify the table of organization. With no substantive goal, the impacts were negative. The central coordinating unit for the federal statistical system, OMB's Statistical Policy Division, was stripped of the clearance function (its only real source of bureaucratic and political clout) and sent into exile in the Commerce Department in the early Carter years.

Growing political support for reduction of government "paperwork burden" through the 1970s led to a joint Congressional–White House Commission on Federal Paperwork Reduction. The Commission's final report was sent to Congress and the White House in 1977. In late 1980 Congress finally enacted paperwork legislation revising the 1942 Federal Reports Act. This legislation assigned statistical policy authority and that for paperwork reduction to OMB. No attention was paid to any of the problems of the statistical system. Over the same period, Carter administration enthusiasm for deregulation of transportation, communications, and banking and finance and for increased regulation for environmental and health purposes led to the creation of an Office of Information and Regulatory Affairs in OMB, combining paperwork reduction and regulatory policy. The 1980 Paperwork Reduction Act transferred statistical policy into this highly political, regulatory policy unit in OMB. For statistical policy to succeed it must be managed as an objective, highly technical, and non partisan function. It is unlikely to be effective or survive in a highly politicized environment. Such has proven to be the case.

The Reagan administration arrived in 1981 and soon transferred the statistical policy unit to the Office of Information and Regulatory Affairs (OIRA) in OMB, as directed in the paperwork legislation. However, before doing so they stripped away most of the senior positions and many experienced personnel; total positions were reduced from 25 to 15. Subsequent resignation of the long-time director and several others left the unit with no more than ten professionals by early 1982. Finally, in April 1982 the unit itself was dissolved and personnel scattered across OIRA. When the smoke cleared, only 6 professionals or 4.5 full-time equivalents (3 were part-time employees) still worked on statistical policy.

The director of OIRA, a regulatory lawyer, took so much continuing flak for dismantling this battered remnant of statistical policy and for failing to replace its director that finally in 1984, after being instructed to do so by Congress, he announced the pro forma reconstitution of the unit and the hiring of a director. The new director has little experience in the federal statistical system and has had difficulty establishing the credibility necessary to make the statistical policy function effective. Counting the new director, six people are all that is left of a 69-person OMB unit created four and a half decades ago. We are supposed to believe that this ragged remnant coordinates all the statistical resource and policy decisions for 100 statistical programs and over a billion dollars in statistical budgets! I have recorded elsewhere the full story of the decline and fall of U.S. statistical policy and its coordination (Bonnen 1984a).

The acid test of OMB's capacity in statistical policy coordination occurred during development of the 1982 and 1983 fiscal year budgets when the real resources of federal statistics were cut by 20 percent, with consequent widespread reductions in sample size, detail, and frequency of collection. In almost every agency, long-standing programs were eliminated and much geographic detail was lost in other programs. Timeliness and quality of federal statistics declined not only because of reductions in sample size and frequency but also due to delays in sample redesign and reductions in quality control activities. The future has been mortgaged by elimination of statistical and survey research, delay of methodological improvements, and loss of highly qualified staff (Wallman 1982; U.S. Congress, House 1982a). Many agencies had recovered some of their real resource losses by fiscal 1985 (U.S. Congress, House 1984). But, fiscal 1986 budget cuts put statistical agencies back where they were in 1983, facing 20 percent fewer real resources than in fiscal 1980 (U.S. Congress 1985).

The National Agricultural Statistics Service (NASS) will command 18 percent fewer real resources in the 1986 budget than it did in 1980. The Energy Information Administration will have lost 54 percent of its resources, partly due to deregulation and the dismantling of much of the Energy Department. The National Center for Education Statistics will have lost a third of its 1980 resource base. Both of these latter agencies support functions in which the Reagan administration believes the federal government has no role. Only the Census Bureau has gained any resources since 1980, and this is due to Congress putting back resources the Reagan administration had removed in its proposed budgets, including the very large Survey of Income and Program Participation (SIPP) (Bureau of the Census 1984, 1985).

Many agency heads believe that to date personnel reductions have impaired statistical performance and capacity more than have budget cuts. Personnel levels were abruptly cut 19 percent between fiscal 1980 and 1982 in eight major statistical agencies reviewed by Congress in 1985. Since then personnel has recovered slowly to a level 11 percent below that of 1980. This is an average, however. Almost all of the increase since 1982 is found in the Census Bureau and the Bureau of Labor Statistics (BLS). Much of this increase is illusory, especially in BLS, since it involves programs transferred in from other agencies. Two other agencies had small gains, and four agencies continued to decline in personnel numbers, NASS among them. NASS is down 14 percent between 1980 and 1986. The Economic Research

Service was not included in these studies (U.S. Congress, House 1984, 1985).

A third and growing constraint on federal statistics is the paperwork burden budget established by the Paperwork Reduction Act of 1980. Over its first three years the volume of federal paperwork (measured by personnel time needed to fill out forms) was reduced by 29 percent. Subsequent congressional and OMB goals have reduced even further the annual burden budgets that agencies are allowed to impose on respondents. So far the priorities and performance of most statistical agencies have not been seriously impaired by the burden budget. But easily reduced burden has been eliminated, and the potential for distortion and constraint is now present.

If the Reagan administration had moved all of its proposed budgets through Congress without modification, I estimate that total real resources in federal statistics today would be 35 to 40 percent below 1980 levels, instead of 20 percent. Many Reagan cuts in statistical budgets never made it through Congress, and the recovery from 1983 levels is due to congressional concern and action. The level of activity and interest in Congress on statistical budgets and policy since 1981 has been nothing short of remarkable. In effect, the Congress has been performing the statistical policy priority-setting function abdicated by OMB, despite the fact that congressional oversight of statistics is too fragmented for Congress to manage this function well.

The president's fiscal 1983 budget eliminated the redesign of the federal household surveys. This is an especially egregious example of the failure of OMB to establish national statistical priorities when making budget decisions. The sample frame for these surveys, based on the 1970 census, was then over a decade old, and the 1980 census was in hand. Each year billions of dollars of federal expenditures and major policy decisions depend on the accuracy of five large household surveys. Another example was the attempt to eliminate the Survey of Income and Program Participation in which millions had already been invested to link participation in various welfare programs to income. The administration had vowed to clean up the "welfare mess" but apparently needed no facts to do it. Congress thought they should have a few numbers.

Congressional action on and concern for statistics took many forms ranging from hearings mostly of statistics users (U.S. Congress 1982a), reports to the Congress on the jeopardy in which reorganization and budget cuts placed the nation's statistical system (U.S. Congress 1982b), a Joint Economic Committee (1981) study of the impact of the president's proposed 1983 budget cuts on statistics, followed by a report to the Congress with recommendations to the appropriations committees (1982c) and a General Accounting Office report on OMB stewardship (1983). The House

Committee on Government Operations has subsequently had the Congressional Research Service of the Library of Congress contract or conduct studies of the state of the federal statistical system (U.S. Congress, House 1984, 1985). A description of the content of these hearings and the reports and actions taken can be seen in Bonnen (1984a) and Wallman (1982).

Much of the congressional interest and action in statistics has been generated by professional association activity, primarily through the Council of Professional Associations on Federal Statistics (COPAFS), which with substantial media coverage galvanized and focused the concerns not only of the professionals but also of statistics users in the private sector and in state and local government. We can be proud of the American Agricultural Economics Association's role as a founding member of COPAFS and the leadership our representatives on the council have provided and continue to provide in COPAFS.

NEW OMB RULES. OMB has consolidated all its earlier circulars setting forth rules for the management of information resources to bring these into a common focus for implementation "of the Paperwork Reduction Act of 1980 as well as other statutes, Executive Orders, and policies concerning general information policy, information technology, privacy and maintenance of Federal records." The proposed draft circular was posted in the *Federal Register* for public comment in March 1985 (General Services Administration 1985). While in large part a compilation of past practice and wisdom, this draft circular nevertheless reflects the very narrow view of the Reagan administration on information management. To wit: all collection must be justified by the agency's statutory mission and be collected only if it serves the agency's program managers; collection does not justify public dissemination, which must either be required by law or essential to the collecting agency's mission; by inference all costs for dissemination of data provided to nonfederal users should be recovered; and any federal collection, processing, analysis, or dissemination responsibility that can be abandoned to or contracted with the private sector should be (General Services Administration 1985, 10,739–40).

Excluded from any consideration are the information needs of the Congress. This encourages the dubious congressional practice of developing its own separate data base for policy. Since Watergate and Vietnam, the effort of Congress to maintain an independent policy capability has created a large congressional bureaucracy, which does its own staff analysis and in some cases commissions data collection as well. This expands the potential for conflict between the executive and legislative branches.

Also excluded from consideration in the proposed OMB circular are the information needs of state and local government and the public. In many matters of serious contest, the federal government is viewed in both the public and private sector as the only neutral, reliable, and authoritative source of information. Private sources would be viewed with suspicion by the contestants. In any case, it is unlikely that the private sector could or would fill many of the information gaps left by federal failure to collect multiple-purpose information needed outside or, for that matter, within the executive branch.

While the large statistical agencies have legislative mandates to collect information, the OMB circular raises a serious question about the authority to collect information in the more than 60 agencies that produce official statistics but have no clear statutory statistics responsibility. In fact, the OMB draft circular nowhere mentions statistics. Statistics are treated without distinction from other data collected without a shred of concern for statistical design or quality control. Nor are distinctions made between the purposes for which federal collections are made. For management purposes, such distinctions are critical, because without them paperwork burden control especially is a bludgeon, distorting priorities and imposing unjustified reductions in some areas, while others escape with a lighter burden relative to problems created, benefits to respondents, or the value of the collection. Thus, distinctions in information management decision criteria should be made, but are not, between such differing sources of data as tax records, regulatory records, action agency administrative records, statistical data collection, grant program records, and research data collections.

Finally, in the dissemination of information, the proposed OMB circular raises concerns well expressed in the April 1985 COPAFS newsletter: " . . . users of federal statistics have observed that the policies set forth in the circular would discourage distribution of federally produced information, and have voiced concern that access would be constrained either because agencies could choose (or be instructed) not to disseminate data, or because users could not afford information available only through private sector organizations" (Council of Professional Associations on Federal Statistics 1985). A hearing held April 29, 1985, by a subcommittee of the House Committee on Government Operations focused on some aspects of the proposed OMB rules. "Testifying for the American Library Association, Francis L. Buckley, Jr. indicated that the circular would lead to the commercialization and privatization of information, and that access would be provided in the future via Freedom of Information Act requests" (Council of Professional Associations on Federal Statistics 1985). He expressed the fear that "increased reliance on private organizations to publish government information will make the cost of such documents prohibitively high and thus curtail access to them" (Coughlin 1985). The executive director of the American Physical Society, Robert L. Park, " . . . said that, when the Paperwork Reduction Act was first passed, many critics charged that it could become a censorship tool. The proposed rules implementing the act are an example of that, . . . and could be construed as an attack on free speech" (Coughlin 1985).

Some government information functions are more amenable to contracts with the private sector such as data processing and electronic, on-line dissemination. Collection of data and its design present greater problems, as does analysis. These can be done by contract, but it impairs the government agency's understanding of their information needs and their ability to interpret and analyze the data, if it does not destroy it entirely. It also skews access toward those who can afford to pay for information and tends to skew collections toward information with proprietary value, leaving out that with only a social value. There are also potential threats to the perceived objectivity of the data process and to the integrity of the agency's promise to respondents of privacy and confidentiality.

The National Agricultural Statistics Service has long contracted for its national electronic network between the various state offices and its headquarters. This seems to work. The USDA has just implemented a privately contracted, electronic, on-line dissemination system for current data and information releases from the entire department. Badly needed is an on-line, U.S. data base of time series commonly used for agricultural analysis and research. Resources are now being invested in such data bases by many different commercial firms and universities, as well as various government agencies. Duplication is rampant and quality uneven. This is a clear example of the need for a public, on-line data base maintained by the USDA. If designed properly, net social gains in efficiency, quality of data, and equity of access would be substantial.

Both of the USDA examples above were initiatives taken independent of OMB pressures and for pragmatic problem-solving reasons. There are similar examples in recent years of departments and statistical agencies contracting with private firms for data processing and dissemination. They too were usually taken for pragmatic reasons and have improved capability. In fact, a major reason statistical agencies contract with private firms for data processing capacity is the greater ease and lower cost of keeping up with the rapid change in computer technology. The shift toward micro- and mini-computers could change this. The point is that pragmatism should rule such decisions. This is not a commodity in large supply at OMB and the White House these days.

The profession needs to be concerned and alert to the data issues arising from budget, personnel, and burden budget constraints. We must defend the nation's data base from the nearly random stew of ideology, ignorance, and indifference to statistical matters in OMB and elsewhere in the Reagan administration. Given all these current problems, there is also the question of our ability to contend with future needs for data. Will the

USDA and universities have the resources, conceptual ability, and political will to modify old data series or create new ones? The profession must be involved in and support USDA efforts to improve the public data base. Clearly the future holds great change for agriculture and for rural society. Data-base needs thus are changing, as is the research agenda that must lead and direct changes in our data base.

Conclusions

Assessing future data needs for all subject matters is an impossible task for any one scholar. The other papers in this volume constitute a rich resource base that should not be ignored for thinking about future data needs. One needs to keep in mind that all empirical measures involve prior conceptual knowledge and vice versa. Thus, all issues of needed knowledge in some degree raise both data and conceptual issues.

The issues of the profession's purpose and philosophic values are of preeminent importance to the future value of this profession to society. Half of the authors in this volume have raised these issues. We must in our research and teaching be concerned with achieving a proper balance in emphasis on the three components of the empirical tradition. We cannot afford the suicidal flight from empiricism with its overly rationalistic emphasis on induction at the expense of deduction. We must achieve a much more conscious command of methodology and philosophic values in research and graduate education if we are to avoid this and other epistemological dead ends.

The narrow, modern "search for academic excellence" is helping dissolve the land-grant tradition of problem solving and service to all people irrespective of wealth or position. Its near exclusive focus on basic disciplines and the depreciation of applied problem solving and the failure to admit problem solvers and prescriptive analysis to the academic pantheon turns good land-grant universities into second-rate private academies. In many states the land-grant covenant with society has been broken, not by the people or their legislature, but by land-grant leadership who, unable to sustain even the mildest populism, have turned toward a narrow intellectual and social elitism. The disciplinary excellence is absolutely necessary, but not sufficient.

Closely related, if not part of it, is another issue. Next to the flight from the empirical, the greatest disgrace in agriculture today is the loss of material and political support for and intellectual energy in the broader issues of rural welfare. Papers in this volume by Barkley, Deaton, and Weber point to this failure. Land-grant universities, colleges of agriculture, and the agricultural economics departments, with some distinguished exceptions, have abandoned this early broad commitment, allowing it to be narrowed not just to farmers but to commercial farmers. The changing structure of agriculture and declining urban political support for commercial agriculture prefigures an eventual decline of the associated public R & D and education role. If not broadened in their scope, the social relevance of the colleges of agriculture is likely to decline. This is both an issue of philosophic values and purpose as well as of survival. Rural welfare and human and community development have to become major emphases if we are to keep faith with the profession's founders and with the land-grant tradition.

An issue for the rest of the 1980s will be whether public policy in this decade has made the income distribution more unequal. Distributional questions are of growing political importance in a society with low and uneven rates of growth. One of the major macroeconomic policy issues is the differential effect of macro policies on various sectors of society and the political consequences. A rising tide no longer lifts all boats – if it ever did. In this context, the importance of equal access to information, of equalizing analytical capacity, and the public provision of analysis for those who otherwise are disadvantaged in market contests or politics is clear. It is important, not only to some contestants but also to the performance of the society, that the United States maintains the democratic values of an open society where opportunity is available to all to achieve on the basis of ability, rather than one where wealth and power, or their lack, dominate the fate of individuals. Rapid changes in world markets and in technology and institutions mean that this generation is faced with making many of those decisions over again.

Another issue is the threat to the availability and objectivity of the nation's current and future social and economic statistics. Indeed, the philosophic commitment to any public responsibility for an informed public in a democratic society is being challenged, especially by OMB and in some of the cabinet departments such as Education, Health and Human Services, Energy, and, to a lesser extent, Interior and Treasury. The current administration has not set out to destroy public statistics as such. It is just that they do not recognize what they are doing or, blinded by ideology, they do not care. The effect is the same. Increasingly, we have what Goethe described as the worst situation in governance of the state – ignorance in action. On this issue, I have tried to provide an overview of events with footnotes to all the major sources. The profession should be prepared to testify in Congress and to participate in development of any legislative remedy affecting the rural data base.

Improving the data base is not enough. We, along with other academic, government, and private-sector participants, need to devote ourselves to developing a public information policy for the information age. This requires first that we pound out a common philosophic foundation for such a policy. We need an agreed-upon set of criteria for guidance of the public and private roles to assure the complementarity of public and private investments in information. The Reagan administration's answer is to privatize everything politics allows. I question the intelligence of that position.

Finally, unspoken but implicit in this paper is the important question of what future role the USDA will be allowed to play in agricultural R & D and data development and maintenance. I have spoken before about the decades of progressively greater abuse of the department's research and statistical functions by political leadership in Congress and the executive branch (Bonnen 1977, 1983a). The effect has been a disordering of and a withdrawal from these functions and from crucial leadership the USDA historically has provided agriculture and relevant professions. Increased demands on ERS for policy analysis from the secretary's office, executive agencies, and Congress and for outlook analysis, especially international, at the same time that total real resources are decreasing, have over a decade or better reduced the resources available for research.

Some good things are happening despite an adverse environment. ERS has, for example, laid the foundation for major improvements in the farm financial data base. With NASS statistical design and collection help, the Farm Costs and Returns Survey will provide a continuing set of detailed national indicators linked to a microdata set on individual farms that has substantial potential for analysis and research on many welfare, equity, and structure issues. It is a very flexible instrument that represents a quantum jump in analytical power. To achieve this, the sample must be expanded to produce reliable state data as well as reliable disaggregated detail on farm costs, assets, debt, and components of the farm balance sheet, and the farm household accounts. Farm income accounts have been improved substantially over the last decade and work on them continues in ERS. NASS is moving toward an integrated survey system that will also expand the potential for integrated data sets and more powerful analysis. As a consequence of two years of the most comprehensive strategic planning I have ever seen in a U.S. statistical agency, NASS is revising its organization, methods, and procedures to accommodate changes in statistical theory and technology, and to reposition the agency to face a changing world. This will greatly improve its ability to produce high quality agricultural statistics. These are all exciting innovations that will expand the profession's basic capacity.

ERS and the USDA generally have slowly burned their bridges to the land-grant colleges. The colleges of agriculture have alternately treated the USDA as if it were a philanthophic foundation or the enemy with whom they compete for federal budget dollars. Yet these two institutions need each other, considering their limitations and the challenges they face in common.

The role of government as the conservator of the long-run interests of society, as the institution responsible for the larger public-good investments in productivity, equity, and human welfare, has clearly declined. After all, who today in government really cares that federal macroeconomic policy has created a deficit of more than $200 billion mortgaging our children's future? Congress? The president? Not if their actions mean anything. Besides ignorance of economics, this flows from the trivialization and fragmentation of our political institutions under the impact of single-interest groups and the unintended consequences of political reforms of party, electoral, and congressional rules (Polsby 1983; Bonnen 1984b; Shafer 1983). It is in this context that we have seen the USDA abandon or be forced to abandon much of its broader, longer-run view and responsibilities for society's interests in rural life. The commodity interests have narrowed agricultural policy, including research policy, to little more than a concern for a few commodities. Rural development and welfare are trivialized by confused populists with romantic delusions and by clear-eyed, commercial interests who see every dollar in the USDA budget that does not feed their greed as wasted. So who among political appointees is concerned about the welfare of rural communities and people? No one, as far as I can see.

There is little commitment to research as such in the national centers of agricultural power, except as individuals transcend the politics of agriculture. There is a growing belief that the provision of information, even for government use, belongs in the private sector. The situation is badly out of kilter with the real needs of agriculture and the nation. I can only believe that a reaction to current abuses and ignorance will set in, allowing something more sensible to prevail.

The USDA has an important role to play that neither the private sector nor the universities can assume. Foremost is the provision of an objective, public data base, analysis, and research to maintain a level playing field for participants in the market and in public policy for agriculture. No less important is long-term, fundamental research on the changing nature and problems of agriculture and rural life that allows the USDA and the society to anticipate and be prepared for major policy problems.

Notes

1. One should add that there is a growing body of self-critical literature in economics (e.g., McCloskey 1983) and quantitative methods (e.g., McAleer et al. 1985).
2. Glenn Johnson (1984, 155–57) distinguishes between types of knowledge (i.e., disci-

plinary, subject matter, and problem solving). Disciplinary knowledge is the theory, empirical measurements and/or measurement techniques, and methods explaining a fundamental class of phenomena such as physics, history, or economics. Subject matter knowledge is multidisciplinary knowledge useful to a set of decision makers facing a common set of problems. Problem-solving knowledge is multidisciplinary knowledge useful to a single decision maker facing a specific problem or to a set of decision makers facing the same specific problem. Problem solving requires that one reach a prescription for action.

3. Even the accumulation of disciplinary knowledge requires empirical validation.

4. By ideology I mean a system of beliefs, or a set of perceptions, about both positive knowledge and values, whose validity is so based on faith (and a set of decision rules) that no amount of conflicting positive knowledge is capable of directly altering the belief system of its adherents.

5. The Reagan administration has raised many legitimate questions about which activities should be public and which private, but it has confused these legitimate questions with a frontal assault on almost all government. Selective refusals to enforce existing laws without attempting to change the law have not helped.

6. One measure of this is that the Congressional Budget Office has far greater credibility today than does the president's Office of Management and Budget. OMB has been progressively politicized for some years and is now known more for its loyalty to the president than its intellectual capacity and integrity. The President's Council of Economic Advisers, when trapped by the same forces, chose to protect its integrity, but as a consequence it has had almost no influence on the White House in recent years. After some speculation in early 1985 that the council might be phased out, a new council has been appointed, but to what end remains to be seen.

7. For a more comprehensive treatment, see the article by Riemenschneider and Bonnen (1979, 145–52) and Bonnen (1983b) on which this section draws.

8. This is patently the case of the U.S. Census of Population. Yet the staff of one senator throughout a 1983 conference on the 1990 census (sponsored by the senator) persisted in efforts to get participants to identify ways for the government to recover the full cost of the census by selling parts of the output to the private sector and to state and local government. This it appears was the real purpose of the conference! For the conference report see U.S. Congress, Senate 1984.

References

Arrow, K. J. 1975. Vertical Integration and Communication. *Bell J. Econ.* 6:173–83.

Barkley, P. W. 1985. Personal correspondence, January.

Bonnen, J. T. 1969. The Decline of the Agricultural Establishment. In *Readings in the Economics of Agriculture,* 495–509. New York: R. D. Irwin Inc.

_____. 1977. Assessment of the Current Agricultural Data Base: An Information System Approach. In *A Survey of Agricultural Economics Literature,* ed. L. R. Martin, et al., vol. 2, 386–407. Minneapolis: Univ. of Minnesota Press.

_____. 1983a. Historical Sources of U.S. Agricultural Productivity: Implications for R & D Policy and Social Science Research. *Am. J. Agric. Econ.* 65:958–66.

_____. 1983b. Official Statistics in Troubled Times: The Changing Environment of Producers and Users. In *Proceedings of the 44th Session of the International Statistical Institute,* vol. 2, 836–51 Madrid.

_____. 1984a. Federal Statistical Coordination Today: A Disaster or a Disgrace? *Health and Society/Milbank Memorial Fund Quarterly* 62:1–41.

_____. 1984b. U.S. Agriculture, Instability, and National Political Institutions: The Shift from Representative to Participatory Democracy. In *United States Agricultural Policy for 1985 and Beyond*, 53–83. Tuscon: Dept. of Agric. Econ., Univ. of Arizona.

Bromley, D. W. 1985. Resource and Environmental Economics: Knowledge, Discipline, and Problems. Workshop on Agriculture and Rural Areas Approaching the 21st Century: Challenges for Agricultural Economics. Ames: Iowa State Univ. Mimeo.

Churchman, C. W. 1971. *The Design of Inquiring Systems*. New York: Basic Books.

Commission on Federal Paperwork. 1977. Final Summary Report. Washington, D.C. October 3. The Commission issued a total of 30 special reports including one on statistics.

Coughlin, E. K. 1985. Proposed Rules on Government Data Worry Librarians and Scholars. *Chronicle of Higher Education* 30:11.

Council of Professional Associations on Federal Statistics. 1985. News from COPAFS. Washington, D.C.

Duncan J. W., and W. C. Shelton. 1978. *Revolution in United States Government Statistics, 1926–1976*. Washington, D.C.: U.S. Dept. of Commerce.

Eurich, N. P. 1985. *Corporate Classrooms: The Learning Business*. New York: The Carnegie Foundation for the Advancement of Teaching.

Hahn, F. H. 1970. Some Adjustment Problems. *Econometrica* 38:1–2.

Johnson, G. L. 1984. Ethics, Economics, Energy, and Food Conversion Systems. In *Food and Energy Resources,* ed. D. Pimentel and C. Hall, 147–180. New York: Academic Press.

Leontief, W. W. 1971. Theoretical Assumptions and Non-Observed Facts. *Am. Econ. Rev.* 61:1–7.

McAleer, M., A. R. Pagan, and P. A. Volker. 1985. What Will Take the Con Out of Econometrics? *Am. Econ. Rev.* 75:293–307.

McCloskey, D. N. 1983. The Rhetoric of Economics. *J. Econ. Lit.* 25:481–517.

Polsby, N. 1983. *Consequences of Party Reform*. New York: Oxford Univ. Press.

Radner, N. 1970. Problems in the Theory of Markets Under Uncertainty. *Am. Econ. Rev.* 60:454–60.

Riemenschneider, C. H., and J. T. Bonnen. 1979. National Agricultural Information Systems: Design and Assessment. In *Information Systems for Agriculture,* ed. M. J. Blackie and J. B. Dent, 145–71. London: Applied Science Publishers.

Shafer, B. E. 1983. Reform and Alienation: The Decline of Intermediation in Politics of Presidential Selection. *J. Law and Pol.* 1:93–132.

Stigler, G. J. 1961. The Economics of Information. *J. Pol. Econ.* 69:213–25.

Thurow, L. C. 1970. Analyzing the American Income Distribution. *Am. Econ. Rev.* 60:261–69.

U.S. Bureau of the Census. 1984. Economic Characteristics of Households in the United States. Current Population Reports, Series P-70., No. 1–4. Washington, D.C.: U.S. Dept. of Commerce.

U.S. Congress. House. Committee on Post Office and Civil Service, Subcommittee on Census and Population. 1982a. *Impact of Budget Cuts on Federal Statistical Programs*. 97th Congr., 2nd sess., hearing.

U.S. Congress. House. Committee on Government Operations. 1982b. *Federal Government Statistics and Statistic Policy.* 97th Congr., 2nd sess., hearing.

U.S. Congress. House. Committee on Government Operations. 1982c. *Reorganization and Budget Cutbacks May Jeopardize the Future of the Nation's Statistical System.* 97th Congr., 2nd sess. H.R. 97-901.

U.S. Congress. House. Committee on Government Operations. 1984. *The Federal Statistical System, 1980 to 1985.* 98th Congr., 2nd sess.

U.S. Congress. House. Committee on Government Operations. 1985. *An Update on the Status of Major Federal Statistical Agencies, Fiscal Year 1986.* 99th Congr., 1st sess.

U.S. Congress. Joint Economic Committee. 1981. *Maintaining the Quality of Economic Data.* 97th Congr., 1st sess.

U.S. Congress. Senate. Committee on Governmental Affairs, Subcommittee on Energy, Nuclear Proliferation and Governmental Processes. 1984. *Federal Statistics and National Needs.* 98th Congr., 1st sess., Senate Print 98-191.

U.S. General Services Administration. 1985. *Federal Register* 50:51.

U.S. Government Accounting Office. 1983. Implementing the Paperwork Reduction Act: Some Progress, But Many Problems Remain. GAO/GCD 83-85.

Wallman, K. K. 1982. Federal Statistics: The Effects of Program Cuts on Availability, Utility, and Quality. *Review of Public Data Use* 10:241–59.

Weisbrod, B. A. 1969. Collective Action and the Distribution of Income: A Conceptual Approach. In *The Analysis and Evaluation of Public Expenditure: The PPB System,* 177–97. Washington, D.C.: GPO.

Williamson, O. E. 1975. *Markets and Hierarchies: Analysis and Antitrust Implications.* New York: The Free Press.

Wilson, R. 1975. Information Economies of Scale. *Bell J. Econ.* 6:184–95.

Improving the Socioeconomic Data Base: **A Discussion**

JAMES D. JOHNSON and KENNETH BAUM

The issue of data and statistical systems has been a topic of recurring and energetic discussion by the Association even before the AAEA Committee on Economic Statistics presented its seminal report on obsolescence in our food and agricultural data systems in 1972. A cursory review of the *American Journal of Agricultural Economics* indicates that since this report, the Association has sponsored at least nine additional sessions treating issues related to economic information systems and data. One can conclude that the Association's leadership has made a concerted effort to move a complex issue higher on the list of the profession's priorities. But, as Bonnen strongly suggests, little substantive progress apparently has occurred. Given the last 15 years of discussion, we thus wonder if there is a consensus by the profession that a serious data gap really does exist, and if so, for whom.

Bonnen's paper extends the existing literature and discussion by sounding a clear warning for the agricultural economics profession as he (and we) know it, summarizes current federal data collection activities, discusses federal government action toward data collection and dissemination, and highlights possible future data needs for various subdisciplines of the profession. In our view Bonnen's paper should be read carefully by every member of our profession more than once, because there are many points that he has cogently argued. Rather than trying to comment on each, we will confine our comments to a few main points.

First, it is clear to us that designing, locating, and accessing localized and national data are significant problems for the profession and need to be taken seriously. But, even given the limited amount of data presently available, Bonnen delivers a sobering indictment of agricultural economics as an empirical science, stating that "we are experiencing a drift toward an antiempirical outlook . . . and are moving away from the tradition we inherited toward the celebration of theory and statistical methods while ignoring data."

Several reasons are offered for this professional drift including the search for "academic excellence" and the cost of obtaining well-designed

James D. Johnson and Kenneth Baum are Chief and Leader of the Farm Cost and Returns Section, respectively, of the Economic Indicators Branch of the National Economics Division, Economic Research Service, USDA.

data sets. We would add that there are also large investments in research funds and human capital associated with specifying, designing, collecting, editing, and analyzing primary data, much of which may have been collected by agricultural scientists in other disciplines without any real thought to further economic analysis (Forster 1978, 906–7).

Such investments are necessarily made under uncertainty and with some risk for two reasons: (1) lack of assurance of success in obtaining high quality primary data, and (2) with the knowledge that data have properties of a public good, especially, as Bonnen noted, incomplete appropriability. Thus, an individual or institution may have to invest substantial resources without an immediate and obvious payoff in an era of declining budgets. Moreover, if the profession's incentive structure is in fact oriented toward rewarding disciplinary research, as has been argued, arguments proposing that individuals spend more time working with empirical issues and building primary data sets would not be consistent with rational behavior. Thus, change in the orientation of the profession to include more applied work, problem-solving research, and data analysis would likely occur only if the reward structure of the profession is itself revised. The decision criteria through which institutions make personnel decisions would need to include a heavier emphasis on applied, problem-oriented, and subject matter research. In addition, publication outlets for our profession, which act to set the tone and define the most important types of research, extension, teaching, and industry activities, may need to revisit the circular debate over what constitutes a "good paper."

Bonnen also argues that we as a profession "resist multidisciplinary and empirical involvement," "learn little about problems . . . usually only the minimum needed to fit a model," and "rarely go beyond squinting at it through a data set collected by someone else for another purpose. . . . Or . . . use no data at all." The result from Bonnen's perspective is that we have little to offer in helping people solve their problems. Although he may be correct, there are exceptions. For example, the current financial situation has demonstrated our profession's ability to respond to a widespread practical and empirical problem. True, relevant data were not available at either the state or federal level to provide early warning or analysis. But, in many states, the State Department of Agriculture, State Crop Reporting Board, and agricultural economics departments, along with other disciplines, have joined to collectively obtain relevant data, coordinate analyses, and develop recommendations. Some states have also extended their extension programs to work with financially pressed farm families.

We would agree with Bonnen that the cost of data collection is a major obstacle to the building of primary data sets to address specific problems, especially on a national basis and even on a regional or local area basis. Our experience is that the Economic Research Service (ERS) spends about $150 for each completed survey form obtained through direct enumeration. Conducting surveys large enough to yield statistically reliable estimates would be an overhead expense much too large for most institutions and certainly for an individual researcher. There are means other than enumeration to obtain data, but all are expensive in terms of time and money.

Since 1982, ERS has worked to obtain more relevant farm and household financial data. We have met considerable resistance. Some arguments put forth included: such data were felt to be highly sensitive, bordering on an invasion of privacy, would not be provided by farmers, and could cause unspecified problems with other USDA surveys. Our resulting experience suggests that rather than forgoing data to test theoretical constructs or tackling specific problems, agricultural economists must be fully prepared to explain and substantiate the need for economic or "atypical" data for their research program. This implies that we have a good grasp of problems being addressed, the underlying theory, and associated data needed for analysis. If data needs can be clearly specified, to those who fund data collection activities as well as to those people who respond to surveys, the odds of obtaining needed data are greatly improved.

Second, we agree with Bonnen that many problems have been treated theoretically or prescriptively with inadequate data, leaving an empirical void with regard to many policy decisions. For example, the profession still has prepared no substantive analysis relating to how public policies affect the distribution of farm and rural household income, a priority issue for many years. But part of our empirical shortcomings may be characteristic of the agricultural economy itself and the way that data are collected, maintained, and reported. Bonnen notes that the "demand for data . . . is derived from its value in reducing uncertainty in the decision processes of private individuals and firms or government . . . and that . . . decisions are becoming more interrelated and complex for agriculture. Changes in our industry, the problems it faces, and in rural economic and social systems create the need for new and perhaps nontraditional data." What we have found in practice, however, are data available only in highly aggregated forms and based on concepts that no longer reflect the reality of our industry. In many cases, new data series may not be available because agencies or persons responsible for data series are quite reluctant to change long-standing data collection or estimation practices. This is not altogether the fault of statistical agencies or other groups responsible for data series. Often there are political or institutional constraints that restrict, even prohibit, changes in the way data may be collected and/or reported. There are also user-group restrictions; objections are raised if long-standing series are changed or dropped and familiar numbers are no longer available. Many of us fall into this category.

Moreover, Gardner (1975, 895) has argued, "Since we cannot in general predict what hypotheses future social scientists will want to test, how can we say anything useful about long-term investment in social and economic statistics for rural areas? Thus, we shouldn't be totally surprised to find that data are not available to test economic hypotheses based on current theoretical constructs." He concluded, and we agree, "the main lesson is that the statistics generated should be adaptable to various treatments as the concepts that researchers and policymakers operate with change." Instead, our current statistical base has been pieced together like a patchwork quilt and at best is highly aggregated, inflexible, and largely unshared.

Third, Bonnen presents a useful discussion of the demand and supply characteristics of data and the attributes of uncertainty, indivisibility, and nonappropriability that are common to data and violate the classical properties of its being considered as a purely private good. This necessitates a continuing public role in the collection and dissemination of data. The supply/demand framework presented is developed from the viewpoint of users (the profession, private industry, government, etc.) and major competing suppliers such as government and private industry. We would add that the ultimate supplier of raw data is the farmer, the business person, or the household. The comments that we have heard over the past three years indicate that the individual's benefit/cost ratio is already less than one, or even negative. Our surveys take an average of an hour (and for many operations much longer) of an operator's time and for more complex operations, the operator actually pays his bookkeeper or accountant to provide us with information. Moreover, we are but one of many types of questioners seeking information. Unless we provide what is perceived as a useful information product, we will see the ultimate suppliers of data become less cooperative and primary data even less available.

Fourth, Bonnen provides a thorough discussion of budgetary, policy, and administrative decisions, which are affecting federal data collection, processing, analysis, and dissemination activities. We would just add that the budget and personnel constraints are real. For example, when Congress required the collection of cost of production statistics in 1974 and appropriated funds for this effort, additional funds were not added until 1985. To cope with rising costs, sample sizes were reduced, surveys were conducted over several years, and some commodities were eliminated. To help obtain an acceptable level of statistical reliability, ERS has recently combined cost-of-production and other surveys into one unified whole-farm survey. How well our survey efforts will fare in future years, given the present federal budgetary environment, remains to be seen.

As Bonnen indicates, "assessing future data needs for all subject matters is an impossible task for any one scholar." With the philosophical caveat that, "One needs to keep in mind that all the empirical issues involve prior conceptual knowledge and vice versa," he summarizes the data needs expressed in other workshop papers. In one sense, we strongly endorse each of our profession's subdisciplines' effort to acquire more cross-sectional or longitudinal data expressed as each author's needs list. Nevertheless, we are reminded of Upchurch's (1977, 305) remarks that "Despite the variety and quantity of data readily available to every agricultural economist, probably no economist ever had all the data he wanted, in exactly the form or at the time that he desired."

One important aspect of our stated needs as a profession for additional data is that collection and use of this data need to be justified to those providing resources for its collection. If so, two areas must be considered by us here. First, although "greater attention to data collection for outlook modeling and analysis and for basic research" has been recently recommended (U.S. Department of Agriculture 1985), perhaps greater use should also be made by our profession of farm record data bases already existing within the colleges of agriculture at many land-grant institutions, trade association data, and other agribusiness data currently available. Whenever we talk with producers, they express continual aggravation at the numerous requests for data that they receive daily. Where does this information go? To whom? For what purpose? Evidently, we know very little about these activities. Bonnen also suggests that the agricultural economics profession has little current involvement in data collection except either to observe it, comment upon it, or (more often) request it. From our viewpoint, the profession is comprised of many individuals with different interests, but it is you and I as individuals who make a difference in data collection and analysis.

Second, we are concerned with the statement that "many of our research and data needs can only be provided by the public sector," because several questions concerning implementation remain to be answered. First, who will design questionnaires, select the sample, train the enumerators, and collect the massive amount of data desired? Second, how large a survey should be run in each case and who will be willing to provide the necessary resources? That is, who are our clientele and do they know they are our clientele? Third, who will be granted access to the data and actually use this information system to provide socially relevant and perhaps even problem-solving empirical economic research? That is, if Bonnen is correct and the profession is not actively involved in applied problem-solving analysis, why is this data being collected? This is a classic catch-22 situation.

In conclusion, several emerging and future data needs are already becoming apparent including distributional information on farm finance, income, production practices, returns, wealth, program participation, etc. Bonnen's discussion of the data implications contained in the papers presented in sessions of this workshop underscores these needs. This data will become increasingly important as future administrations and Congresses begin to target farm programs to specific problems to reduce taxpayer costs and maximize social welfare. The basic questions will be: Who is in trouble? Why? Can the government do anything to solve the problem? Should the government do anything to solve the problem? In addition, if we are to be actors in the policy, program implementation, and decision process, we will need a flexible and comprehensive farm data base to develop micro/ disaggregated economic indicators of the agricultural sector. If agriculture is increasingly viewed as a set of heterogenous and often competing industries, we will be providing information on these behavioral interrelationships to both public and private decision makers.

References

Forster, D. L. 1978. Developments in the Economic Theory of Information: Discussion. *Am. J. Agric. Econ.* 60:906–7.
Gardner, B. 1975. Strategies for Long-run Investment in Rural, Social, and Economic Statistics. *Am. J. Agric. Econ.* 57:892–99.
Upchurch, M. L. 1977. Developments in Agricultural Economic Data. In *A Survey of Agricultural Economics Literature,* vol. 2, 305–72. Minneapolis: Univ. of Minnesota Press.
U.S. Department of Agriculture. 1985. *Report to Secretary of Agriculture John R. Block.* Economics and Statistics Review Panel.

Improving the Socioeconomic Data Base: **A Discussion**

PIERRE CROSSON

Jim Bonnen has written an interesting paper. In fact, he has written two interesting papers. One is in the first seven pages of the manuscript he has prepared, dealing with his perception that agricultural economics is undergoing "a flight from the empirical" that endangers the social value of the profession. The second paper is the rest of the manuscript and deals with the economic nature of data, the current state of federal statistics, and emerging data needs.

I see two papers in the manuscript because the discussion of the "flight from the empirical" is not well integrated with the subsequent discussion, and in fact the two parts could stand on their own. Bonnen does not document his assertion that agricultural economics is moving away from empirical research, and when I first read this portion I was not persuaded that he is right. This perhaps reflects my own professional background. I came to agricultural economics rather late, and my first contact was with the use of the discipline to study agricultural development in less developed countries (LDCs). There the work of Schultz, Hayami and Ruttan, Mellor, Johnston, Falcon, and others struck me as combining theory and empiricism in the best sense of scientific research. Their concern was with pressing real-world problems, and they used theory as a guide to frame researchable hypotheses and define data needs. I think it fair to say that their work and that of subsequent researchers greatly advanced our understanding of agricultural development and its role in the development process generally. And some shifts in LDC government policies, particularly toward giving freer play to markets, suggest that this understanding is having impact where it counts, outside the halls of academe and the covers of professional journals.

This said, Bonnen may nonetheless be right about the antiempirical drift of agricultural economics. After reading his paper I checked his argument with some of my colleagues at Resources for the Future, a group that included two former presidents and current fellows of this association. The consensus was that agricultural economics now shows an unhealthy preoccupation with technique and too little concern for the quality of the data that we pump through our models. There is an increasing tendency for

Pierre Crosson is a Senior Fellow, Resources for the Future, Washington, D.C.

research to be driven by what the models can do rather than by the problematics of the real world. One colleague summed up his comments by saying, "If Leontief made his speech today, and understood the situation, he would not exempt agricultural economics from his charge of antiempiricism."

So my empirical research points to the conclusion that Bonnen probably is right in the main thrust of his indictment of agricultural economics. But if he is, then the two papers in his manuscript stand in a curious relationship to one another. The second paper is a perceptive treatment of the nature and economic significance of data, the present status of data demand and supply, and some future data needs. But if the thrust of agricultural economics is inexorably antiempirical, these concerns about data would appear to put the cart before the horse. If agricultural economists are indifferent to the quality of data and their research agenda is set by the capabilities of their analytical apparatus, what benefit do we gain from better data and understanding of data needs? Priority should be given to rescuing agricultural economics from the intellectual and policy sterility that now seems to be its fate, if Bonnen is right. Yet Bonnen has little to say about how the rescue might be effected.

That he does not, and that his second paper occupies the major portion of his manuscript, suggests to me that Bonnen does not really believe the antiempirical drift of the profession to be as pronounced, or its consequences as grim, as the tone of the first paper suggests. Clearly he believes that better understanding of the issues discussed in the second paper will enhance the social value of agricultural economics, despite the antiempirical drift of the discipline.

In this, too, I think he is right. Space limitations preclude full discussion of the topics Bonnen treats in the second paper, but let the record show that in my judgment the treatment is an insightful review of issues of great importance to the profession. Here I touch on one issue I think especially deserves highlighting, discuss another Bonnen neglects, and point to some present data gaps he does not mention.

Bonnen notes that data, or more generally information, has economic value because it can reduce uncertainty about the future consequences of decisions taken today. But because some information of economic significance, and maybe some aspects of all such information, is a public good, private investment in supplying it may fall short of the socially optimal amount. This raises a host of important issues about the proper roles of public and private investment in information supply. And Bonnen gets in some hard licks on the present administration for abdicating its role in response to misguided ideology. Whether the blows are entirely deserved may be questioned. It is a fact that under this administration the Soil Conservation Service in 1982 conducted a National Resources Inventory

(NRI) that provided the richest supply of data ever available for analysis of soil conservation and nonpoint water quality issues. But Bonnen is far better informed than I about data collection activities of the federal government, generally, and the 1982 NRI may be an exception. If it is, it is a most important exception for those of us concerned about natural resource use in agriculture.

But for me the more interesting point Bonnen makes in this part of his discussion is that achieving socially optimal investment in information supply would not only increase the national income, it might also make its distribution more unequal. The reason is that those already with more income probably have more capacity to use additional information than those with less income. This, of course, is an empirical (and researchable!) proposition, but it is plausible. Indeed, it is likely that one of the reasons why the rich are richer is an innate or acquired capacity to make better use of information than the poor.

I take it most of us would be dubious about policies that increased existing income inequalities unless there were substantial gains in total income. How much additional income would be required to compensate for how much more inequality? What is the marginal income benefit of investment in data and information and what is the marginal impact on income inequality? The first question is outside the range of economic analysis, but the second is not. We need more research along that line if we are to push responsibly for more public investment in data and information. The research should examine the income and income distribution consequences of alternative patterns of investment. If we are lucky we will find an alternative that ranks highest by both income and income distribution criteria, but in any case we need alternatives if we are to devise wise policies in this area.

A question not addressed by Bonnen is how data and information may come to force changes in government policies. Any policy has a constituency or it would not be adopted. And over time the constituency can become a powerful vested interest resisting change in the policy. The massive special interest resistance to proposals for changes in tax policy is but a contemporary example of behavior that must be as old as government.

Yet policies do change, and sometimes new data and information have something to do with it. Indeed, if this were not true, or if we did not believe it to be true, probably most of us would not be in economics. But there are too many instances of policies being completely impervious to data and information showing them to be wrongheaded to pretend that the line from data to analysis to policy change is simple and direct. And where resistance persists, vested interests usually are the cause. Why is it that in some instances data and information succeed in breaking resistance and in others they do not?

I do not know the answer, but current experience with soil conservation policy provides some interesting, albeit anecdotal, evidence. Since its beginnings in the 1930s federal soil conservation policy has rested on two basic premises: (1) the main threat of soil erosion is to productivity of the soil, not off-farm sediment damage; and (2) soil conservation resources should be widely distributed around the country. Now both premises are under serious challenge, and there are signs that policy is beginning to shift in response. The challenge is based completely on data and analysis made possible by the National Resources Inventories (NRI) of 1977 and 1982 taken by the Soil Conservation Service. The 1977 NRI for the first time provided reliable information about the amount and location of erosion around the country. It demonstrated beyond any doubt that severe erosion is highly concentrated on a relatively small part of the nation's cropland. Knowledgeable people in the conservation community had always known this in some sense, but they had no solid evidence. Consequently there was no effective counter to the political pressures to spread soil conservation funding widely. The 1977 NRI, reinforced by the 1982 NRI, provided the hard data needed to mount a strong campaign to target soil conservation funding on the really severely affected areas. The vested interests, represented in this case by the National Association of Conservation Districts, have stoutly resisted targeting, and its adoption has been slow. Still, targeting now is the official policy of the U. S. Department of Agriculture, and I am convinced the shift would not have come without the data provided by the NRIs.

The 1977 NRI also provided the data for the first analyses of the impact of erosion on soil productivity in major crop-producing regions. These analyses were done at the USDA in connection with the 1980 appraisal of soil and water resources (U. S. Department of Agriculture 1981), by me at Resources for the Future (Crosson with Stout 1983), and by soil scientists at the University of Minnesota (Pierce et al. 1984). And the USDA now has a new model called the Erosion Productivity Impact Calculator (EPIC) to study erosion-productivity relationships in connection with the 1985 Resource Conservation Assessment.

Although differing substantially in methodology, all of these studies point to the same conclusion: the impact of erosion on soil productivity in the United States has been, and is likely to remain, small. Using the Minnesota model, which calculates impact on soil productivity over 100 years, I calculated the annualized value of the loss in crop output (with current crop prices and a 5 percent discount rate) at $550–$600 million (Crosson 1985).

Concurrently with this research, a study by analysts at the Conservation Foundation concluded that costs of off-farm erosion damages are between $3 billion and $13 billion annually (1980 prices), with a "best guess" estimate of $6 billion (Clark et al. 1985).

With all due allowance for wide margins of error, the estimates of costs of soil productivity damage and of off-farm damage leave little doubt that the off-farm costs are significantly higher. I have no direct evidence that this finding was instrumental in causing the USDA to shift priorities in erosion control policy, giving more attention to off-farm damage relative to soil productivity loss, but such a shift is now perceptible. And its timing closely followed the emergence of the research results concerning costs of the two kinds of damage.

I am sure that with some looking we could find other instances in which data and information turned up by research may have an impact on policy similar to that which the NRI data and associated analysis seem to have had on soil conservation policy. I submit that research comparing these instances with those in which equally good data and analysis were unsuccessful in moving policy would be of great professional interest and social value. Such research obviously would call for professional skills in addition to those of the economist. But economics would have an important role to play.

Drawing on other papers prepared for these special sessions, Bonnen gives us a most useful review of emerging data and information needs. I want to discuss briefly certain needs in the resources and environment area that Bonnen does not deal with specifically. At the Environmental Protection Agency (EPA) and in the environmental community generally, nonpoint pollution is getting increased attention. Sediment and agricultural chemicals carried from farmers' fields are major sources of water pollution. Indeed, by volume, sediment is easily the major pollutant. Nonpoint pollution policy is badly handicapped by the absence of reliable information about the behavior of costs of nonpoint damage and the costs of alternative systems of control. The Conservation Foundation estimates of total costs of damage are valuable, but they do not show the behavior of costs over a range of damage. We need functions both for costs of damage and costs of control, and we do not have them. Estimating these functions faces major difficulties. Off-farm erosion damages illustrate this. We poorly understand the processes by which sediment moves through a watershed from its place of origin on a farmer's field to the place downstream where it does damage, but we know the process is halting. The time it takes may vary from a year or two to more than a hundred. Consequently, we cannot reliably predict how damages we now observe may respond to changes in land management practices in the watershed, or where in the watershed we should effect changes. The problem is complicated by the tendency of streams to scour sediment from their banks and beds if the amount delivered overland is reduced (e.g., by erosion control measures on farmers' fields).

The result of all this is that even if we had functions for off-farm erosion costs and for erosion control (and we have nothing reliable for either) we could not use them to guide policy. The linkage between them is missing; providing it requires research by hydrologists and agricultural engineers, not economists. But economic research to determine cost functions for sediment damage and for control costs nonetheless would provide useful policy information. If nothing else it would identify those places around the country where the payoff to an incremental reduction in off-farm damage would be highest. I have no doubt that policy people in the USDA and maybe in the EPA would be delighted to have such information. Its availability likely would spur research on the costs of alternative measures to reduce damages in the high payoff areas.

References

Clark, E. H., II, J. A. Haverkamp, and W. Chapman. 1985. Eroding Soils: The Off-Farm Impacts. Washington, D. C.: The Conservation Foundation.

Crosson, P. 1985. National Costs of Erosion Effects on Productivity. In *Erosion and Soil Productivity*. St. Joseph, Michigan: American Society of Agricultural Engineers.

Crosson, P., with A. T. Stout. 1983. Productivity Effects of Cropland Erosion in the United States. Washington, D. C.: Resources for the Future.

Pierce, F. J., R. H. Dowdy, W. E. Larson, and W. A. P. Graham. 1984. Productivity of Soils in the Cornbelt: An Assessment of the Long-term Impact of Erosion. *J. of Soil and Water Conserv.* 39:131–36.

U.S. Department of Agriculture. 1981. *Soil Water and Related Resources in the United States: Analysis of Resource Trends, 1980 Appraisal,* part II. Washington, D.C.: GPO.

Improving the Socioeconomic Data Base: **A Discussion**

GEORGE HOFFMAN

Jim Bonnen's paper on data issues and the social value of agricultural economics is an excellent presentation of the most critical issues facing the profession today. I will not attempt to summarize it or to prioritize the main points, but I will begin by commenting on three topics discussed in the paper.

A Flight From the Empirical

Bonnen's concern about the profession's drift from empirical tradition is well founded. This problem, in my opinion, is a threat to the long-term viability of the agricultural economics profession and should receive high-level attention within the AAEA in the years ahead. I agree with the supposition that there is an increasing tendency to seek "academic excellence" while short-changing the development of subject matter and problem-solving knowledge. Within the profession, there seems to be greater interest in techniques and methodology than in addressing some of the more critical issues facing agriculture today. Agricultural economists have a tendency to write for each other, and in the process fail to address some fundamental questions. Why is this research being conducted? Who is the audience? How can this research be applied? Does this research really tell us anything new?

The current situation with the development of long-term agricultural policy clearly illustrates the extent of the problem. The agriculture sector is currently experiencing tremendous financial stress and fundamental structural change. This calls for new and innovative agricultural policies for the 1990s. Agricultural economists and agricultural economics research has had a role in the current debate, but the overall impact to date has been limited. Current policy proposals are not fundamentally different from past programs, only the level of support is being seriously debated. Agricultural economists should be in the midst of the current debate, analyzing the consequences of the various policy options. In fact, this role is being filled mostly by the legislative staff.

George Hoffman is Director of the Commodity Analysis Department, The Pillsbury Company, Minneapolis.

The availability of data may be a contributing factor in the "flight from the empirical," but not a major factor. More likely, new-generation agricultural economists in a university or a government research agency setting may not be exposed enough to "real-world" issues. New masters and Ph.D. graduates with no job experience outside the university system are not likely to have an intuitive understanding of problems and issues facing agriculture. This problem likely will worsen as fewer new graduates have an agricultural background.

Bonnen notes a contrasting trend in the private sector, which increasingly relies on data and analysis for business decisions. One reason for this contrast is that agricultural economists in a business environment are daily faced with "real" issues requiring answers on a very limited timetable. Also, there is the added incentive in that there is an audience for the research and the results will be a factor in a current decision. It is also interesting to note that the agricultural economist in a business environment is a minority and the results of analysis are rarely prepared for other agricultural economists.

Income Distribution

Agricultural economists tend to believe that more good quality data is better than less data for the efficient operation of markets. However, it should be recognized that not all market participants favor the increased availability of market data and information. Bonnen points out the income distribution aspects of market information and that the redistributional side effects can justify the government's role in price reporting. The general view is that more market data reduces the disadvantage of many small, highly dispersed farmers in a market with a few large buyers of agricultural products. It should be emphasized that increased market data can also affect the distribution of income among farmers. Redistribution means some market participants benefit while others lose. Those market participants that benefit from the lack of information will resist increased availability of new data. A current example may be the collection and reporting of more data concerning the distribution of farm income by type, size, and location. The wide variation in income by farm has already led to policy proposals to further limit program payments to certain farmers and to question the level of support from one commodity to another. Generally, large, high-income farmers may not benefit from the availability of this new data to the extent it results in policy changes reducing their benefits. It will be increasingly difficult to convince these farmers to voluntarily provide the government extensive data concerning their financial conditions.

We, as agricultural economists, also need to recognize that not all policymakers are anxious for additional data and analyses concerning the structure and financial condition of agriculture. Many policymakers prefer to preserve the myth of the small, homogeneous family farm struggling to preserve a way of life. This perception makes it easier to sell farm programs to nonfarm legislators in Congress. Additional information regarding the distribution of farm income and farm program benefits also greatly complicates the legislative process and farm programs.

Unlimited Data Needs

Economics is basically the study of how to balance unlimited demand with limited resources. As Bonnen points out, data might be viewed as a commodity with a supply, demand, and price. However, when we as agricultural economists, begin discussing our unlimited data needs, we do not spend much time discussing the costs or the value of the data other than to say it is all urgently needed. The shopping list of data needs resulting from this conference would cost many millions of dollars. Realistically, those dollars will have to come from taxpayers. Who determines the balance between unlimited data needs and the limited availability of funds, and how is this done? Perhaps this responsibility should rest with some statistical policy unit within the Office of Management and Budget. But how would they decide on the allocation process?

At least part of the responsibility for determining the "value" of data must rest with the profession, particularly those who cite data needs. We, as economists, are hesitant to attach a value to data because there is no simple analysis that tells us the value of a survey or other data collection effort. But, if an economist is unable to somehow quantify the value of a proposed survey effort, how can we expect a noneconomist political appointee to judge? What is the value of the data needs outlined in these conference proceedings? How much would you allocate from the limited USDA budget? Is the data worth $1 million, or $10 million, or $100 million? Who will benefit? When will they benefit? What is the discounted net present value of those benefits? These are not trivial questions because of the trade-offs required in the budget allocation process. Adding funds for data collection often means reducing funds for some other program. Presumably those other programs also have public value. Bonnen expresses great concern that the current and recent past administrations have failed to recognize the need for developing and maintaining the federal statistical system. Perhaps the profession is partly to blame for putting forth a convincing enough argument for maintaining the system. This suggests the profession must do more to prioritize and value our data needs instead of simply lengthening the shopping list.

16

Human Capital for Agriculture

WALLACE E. HUFFMAN

Agriculture, the food system, and rural communities face a rapidly changing array of problems. The profession may be able to establish a set of priorities that helps society understand and adjust to these changes. The objective of this paper is to help define issues and priorities for the subject of human-capital for agriculture.

The human-capital field owes a major debt to T. W. Schultz and Gary Becker. The rapid recovery of Europe and Japan after World War II impressed upon Schultz that expenditures on education, health, and information were investments in people rather than consumption expenditures. In his 1960 address to the American Economics Association, Schultz (1961) put forth the bold propositions that people deliberately invest in skills, knowledge, health, and human migration; that this is a form of human capital; and that these investments in human capital account for much of the rise in real earnings per worker over time. Gary Becker (1975) formalized the basic framework for considering investments in human capital. Advances in theories of human time allocation (Becker 1965; Michael and Becker 1973) and the new home economics (Nerlove 1974; Becker 1981) have been complementary to the rapidly expanding human-capital literature.

From the myriad of topics that could be emphasized in this paper, I have chosen four: (1) farmers' decision making; (2) off-farm income, (3) farm labor; and (4) food, nutrition, and health. For each topic, I describe significant new events, summarize the state of current research, and suggest

Wallace E. Huffman is Professor of Economics, Iowa State University, Ames. Robert Emerson, Loran Ihnen, Glenn Nelson, William Saupe, T. W. Schultz, Marta Tienda, J. Peter Mattila, Philip Martin, and Helen Jensen provided helpful comments on an earlier draft of this paper.

important unresolved issues.[1] The final section of the paper concludes with a few critical remarks.

Farmers' Decision Making

The markets and technologies facing agriculture promise to be dynamic in the future. Likely sources of changes in market prices include changes in international exchange rates, world markets for agricultural products, U.S. price and income programs for agriculture, and domestic business cycles (Schuh 1984). Likely sources of new technologies include biotechnology, which greatly expands the genetic potential of plants and animals, robotics, which use computer technology for advanced mechanization (and control) of agriculture, and microcomputers, which have dramatically reduced the cost of information storage and analyses (Johnson and Wittwer 1984). Thus, farmers and agribusiness can expect to continue to need skills to process information and to operate in a dynamic agricultural environment.

SOME CONCEPTS. The ability to adapt efficiently to an economic environment that has been altered in a specific way may be a scarce resource in agriculture (Schultz 1975; Huffman 1985). In particular, adaptive ability may be scarce relative to the ability to produce maximum output from a bundle of inputs. The setting is one in which farmers face uncertainty about the future course of events (production, technologies, prices, and governmental policies) and production is dynamic. A large share of inputs is purchased from the nonfarm sector, and a significant share of output is exported. Information is available, but acquiring, storing, and analyzing information is costly. Farmers are assumed to differ in their adaptive ability, which is viewed as a form of human capital.

Adaptive ability seems unlikely to be important when the processes generating the variables, which farmers take as exogenous, are stationary and unaltered. However, when these processes undergo structural change, adaptive ability is expected to affect the quality of production, marketing, and investment decisions.[2] Farmers who have superior adaptive skills are expected on average to make and implement better decisions. Furthermore, successfully adapting to structural change seems to be selective. Farmers possessing poor adaptive skills can be expected to constitute a relatively large share of the persons forced to seek alternative employment or retirement, provided governmental intervention does not completely neutralize this selection process.[3]

PREVIOUS FINDINGS. Farmers' schooling and agricultural extension have been shown to increase the efficiency or productivity of agriculture. Previous empirical studies have found it useful to distinguish between technical and allocative effects (Welch 1970, 1978). A firm is technically efficient if it is on the production possibility frontier or transformation function. Technical inefficiency occurs when the firm faces the opportunity of, but does not choose, an activity vector containing more of some outputs and less of some inputs, holding other quantities unchanged. A firm is allocatively efficient if it is technically efficient and if it meets all the marginal conditions for optimization (e.g., profit maximization). Thus, allocative efficiency requires that the appropriate mix of inputs and outputs be chosen.

Farmers' schooling and information may enhance both the technical and allocative efficiency of agricultural production. The potential efficiency gains are conditioned by the nature of the economic environment. A dynamic technical environment, created by the introduction of new technologies, provides greater potential than a static environment. [4]

A considerable amount of evidence has accumulated on the contribution of education to agricultural production since Griliches' early studies (1963, 1964). Much of this later evidence has been compiled and summarized by Schultz (1975), Welch (1978), and Jamison and Lau (1982). Their summaries indicate that a number of different methodological approaches within a production framework have been applied.

Griliches and some of the other early researchers have fitted aggregate production functions to state- or county-level data. For U.S. data, this procedure has been quite successful in finding positive and statistically significant effects of farmers' schooling on farm sales or agricultural productivity (e.g., Griliches 1963, 1964; Fane 1975; Khaldi 1975; Huffman 1976). Although these might be taken as estimates of technical efficiency effects of schooling (and extension), they most likely include technical and allocative efficiency effects.

New and creative approaches have been developed for direct tests of allocative efficiency. Khaldi (1975) and Fane (1975) investigate allocative efficiency by contrasting minimum hypothetical cost of realized output with actual cost. Using aggregate average data for U.S. farms, each finds that the proportional difference between actual cost and minimum cost declines as farmers' average schooling level increases. Huffman (1974, 1977) and Petzel (1978) consider allocative efficiency in a different way by focusing on the rate of adjustment over time by farmers to new technology and changes in relative prices. Both find that farmers adjust their resource use faster as their average schooling level increases. Huffman's studies also show a positive effect of agricultural extension on allocative efficiency. Wozniak (1984) and Rahm and Huffman (1984), using micro- or farm-level data, also find a positive effect of farmers' schooling on the adoption of new technology.

Jamison and Lau (1982) have summarized much of the evidence for developing countries. They reached the conclusion that farmers' schooling enhanced the efficiency of agricultural production when there was a technically dynamic environment. Several studies cited by them suggest that a threshold number of years of schooling (4–6 years) must be attained before farmers' education has a consistent, persistent, and statistically significant effect on agricultural production in developing countries.

UNRESOLVED ISSUES. The markets and technologies facing agriculture promise to be dynamic in the future. A major challenge for agricultural researchers is to identify types of human capital that enhance adaptive ability of farmers (and those in agribusiness). This includes the relative importance of formal schooling (of different types), experience (OJT), information processing ability, and public and private information sources. We know very little about how the content of education and extension translates into human capital that affects the probability of surviving in agriculture. The government sector is reducing real expenditures on data collection and distribution, but we know very little about how this has affected the demand for private information sources. Furthermore, what are the distributional consequences for farm sizes and types of different mixes of publicly and privately supplied agricultural information? What should be the relative role of private- and public-sector information collection of U.S. and world business conditions?

For the dynamic agriculture of the future, farmers and those in agribusiness seem likely to need additional training in biological sciences, business, economics, finance, and personal computer use. At what level of technical sophistication is this training needed? How will the private-sector firms and public educational institutions (universities, community colleges, high schools, and extension services) share these training needs? How should public programs be organized, or what groups should be targeted to have the largest social benefit? What role should the extension service have in supplying this information?

More research is needed on the economics of occupational entry to and exit from farming, including the retirement decisions of farmers. How is human capital accumulation related to these decisions? What role does human capital play in the greater specialization within agriculture? When individuals leave farming for other occupations, which skills are most useful?

Off-farm Income

The nonfarm income of U.S. farm operator families has exceeded their net farm income during every year except for 1973 and 1975 since 1969. More than 70 percent of this income is off-farm wage and salary income (U.S. Department of Agriculture 1984). Off-farm wage income is a result of dual jobholding by farm operators and nonfarm labor-force participation of their wives. Off-farm income is a relatively more important source of income for families operating small- and medium-sized farms than for families operating very large farms.[5]

The relative frequency of small and large farms is increasing in the United States at the expense of medium-sized farms (U.S. Department of Agriculture 1984). For the large number of small farms, off-farm employment of household members is generally the primary source of income. For some of these households, the negative net farm income is the price of a life-style that they desire. If the families who operate these small farms do not have off-farm income, poverty is almost assured.

SOME CONCEPTS. The human resource endowment of farm families, especially of adults, and its allocation among farm, off-farm, and household work are important determinants of family income and welfare. Off-farm labor- supply decisions of farm household members can be viewed as the result of household utility maximization subject to constraints on human time, income, and farm technology (Rosenzweig 1980; Huffman 1980; Sumner 1982). Adults are permitted to have dual employment, on-farm and off-farm. Household members' welfare is assumed to be summarized in a single household utility function and to depend on a vector of members' home or leisure time and goods purchased for direct or indirect consumption.[6] The household is assumed to face constraints. First, a vector of human time endowments of members is allocated between farm work, off-farm work, and leisure or home time. To simplify the analysis, the time allocation of only one or two adult household members (e.g., husband and wife) is considered. Because men and women generally acquire different skills, their time is indexed separately. Second, households receive income from members' off-farm wage work, net farm income, and other sources, and they spend this income largely on goods for consumption. (Because these are one-period models, saving does not generally have a key role.)[7] Third, the transformation of farm inputs into farm outputs is constrained by the technology employed. Farm output is produced by a vector of labor inputs, a vector of purchased inputs, and environmental inputs.

In this model, the off-farm labor-supply decisions are made jointly with household consumption and farm production decisions. Thus, the off-farm labor supply functions have as determinants the off-farm wage rate, prices of purchased consumption goods, prices of variable farm inputs, prices of farm output(s), and environmental variables, including the schooling level of adult household members. The expected marginal effects of these variables on off-farm labor supply are, however, generally indeterminant.

The off-farm labor demand or wage-offer equations of adult household members are assumed to depend on their marketable human capital, local labor market characteristics, and possibly job characteristics (Rosenzweig 1980; Sumner 1982). Marketable skills may be proxied by the amount of formal schooling, vocational training, and experience of an individual; each of these variables is expected to increase the wage. Local labor-market conditions are expected to affect labor demand functions when workers and firms are immobile and when local labor markets for particular skills are thin. Land rental and ownership opportunities, location of cities and towns, and tied spouses are expected to be a source of reduced labor mobility in rural labor markets. Thin labor markets are due to a small local labor market for many specialized skills in nonmetropolitan areas. As a simplification, the wage rate faced by individuals is generally assumed to be independent of hours of off-farm work.

Within this framework of off-farm labor supply and labor demand functions, which has been derived from modern labor economics, the effects of human-capital variables on off-farm hours can be investigated. Although the conceptual model suggests that all household consumption and farm production decisions should be considered jointly, data availability considerations have generally caused these studies to consider off-farm hours in isolation from other decisions on production and consumption. Sometimes production decisions are separable from consumption decisions (Barnum and Squire 1979).

PREVIOUS RESULTS. Empirical studies of off-farm work have focused almost exclusively upon male farmers. This includes Ph.D. dissertations by Barros (1976), Schaub (1979), and Sexton (1975), and articles by Huffman (1980) and Sumner (1982). Exceptions are Lange (1979); Huffman and Lange (1984); Rosenzweig (1980); and Evenson (1978), where decisions of males and females are considered.

For U.S. farmers, off-farm wage rates have been shown to increase with farmers' schooling and age (or experience). The effect of age (or experience) is quadratic (inverted U). However, vocational training has frequently had a negative effect on off-farm wage rates (Sumner 1982; Huffman and Lange 1984). The reason for this surprising result is that completing vocational training evidently represents an adjustment for an individual's ability. Individuals who have obtained vocational training may be less able and earn a lower wage, other things being equal.[8]

Off-farm work decisions include participation and hours components. In reduced-form equations, farmers' schooling and nonfarm vocational training tend to increase the probability of their participating in off-farm work. Being raised on a farm or having past farming experience reduces the probability of off-farm work among farmers.

In quasistructural off-farm hours equations fitted to data for off-farm work participants (those with zeros are excluded), the coefficient of the farmers' wage rate is sometimes positive (e.g., Sumner 1982) and sometimes negative (e.g., Huffman and Lange 1984). Being raised on a farm or having past farming experience reduces off-farm hours supplied. Farmers' schooling has had mixed effects on their hours of off-farm work.

UNRESOLVED ISSUES. With large structural changes in agriculture, changes in rural communities, and changes in family composition, many of the researchable issues associated with off-farm employment of farm household members are unexplored. We know very little about the life-cycle aspects of dual jobholding at farm and off-farm work and how this relates to farm investment decisions. Also, to what extent is off-farm participation affected by business and farm income cycles? What role does off-farm income play in stabilizing farm household incomes over farm business cycles and how does it compare with other income sources (e.g., government farm program payments). How are husband's and wife's off-farm work decisions interrelated? What share of the nonfarm income is due to the off-farm work of women? How serious are tied-spouse and thin labor-market effects on wage rates and on off-farm participation? How have diffused rural development strategies of the 1960s and 1970s affected off-farm participation rates and income levels of farm household members (Marshall 1974, 73–76)? What skills provide the highest expected return for dual jobholders? Skills that have a dual purpose of raising the productivity of time at both farm and off-farm work promise higher returns than other skills. This may be general (e.g., math and science) as opposed to vocational schooling (e.g., vocational agriculture).

For households that operate small farms, the theory of the household as a combined producing and consuming unit is a promising framework for evaluating their welfare. Time spent working on their farm- and home-produced food may be a significant direct source of household utility. This should be taken into account in considering the distribution of income or welfare of households.

Farm Labor

Farm work is performed by farmers, their spouses and children, and hired (nonfamily) workers. The total amount of labor input and average labor intensity of agricultural production have shown long-term declines since about 1910 because of the rising value of human time and mechanization. Fruit, vegetable, and nursery crop production continue to be labor intensive relative to other agricultural products because of significant hand labor, especially at harvest time. Overall, hired and contract farm labor expenses make up about 13 percent of all production expenses, but they average about 56 percent of all production expenses on fruit, vegetable, and nursery crop farms (Coltrane 1984, 11). Although these vegetable and horticultural crop farms compose about 6.4 percent of all farms, they incur about 35 percent of all expenses on hired and contract labor (Coltrane 1984, 14). Geographically, these expenses are highly concentrated in two states, California and Florida. Currently, most hired farm workers are relatively young (less than 25 years of age) and work only a few weeks on average per year. Immigrant farm laborers are concentrated in the labor intensive fruit and vegetable production areas (Coltrane 1984).

Important human-capital topics associated with farm labor are the low economic returns to schooling and worker mobility, including migration and immigration. Except for farm operators, formal schooling levels of farm workers are on average low. The U.S. Department of Labor has, however, sponsored training programs targeted to nonimmigrant seasonal farm workers (Rochin 1984; Martin 1985).

MODELS AND PREVIOUS RESULTS. Much of the farm labor research has focused upon aggregate labor supply and demand, aggregate labor demand, and disaggregate labor demand. The aggregate farm labor market analyses by Schuh (1962) and Tyrchniewicz and Schuh (1966, 1969) are well known. Schuh (1962) considers a two-equation simultaneous equation model of the national market for hired farm labor, where labor is defined as the number of workers. The quantity supplied of hired labor is considered to be a function of the agricultural wage rate, expected nonfarm income foregone, and the size of the civilian labor force. The quantity demanded of hired labor is a function of the price of farm labor, the price of other farm inputs, and the price of farm output. The equations have a partial adjustment mechanism of the Nerlovian type. For the national labor market fitted (1927–1957), Schuh obtains estimates of supply elasticity of .25 for the short run and .76 for the long run. The estimates of the demand elasticities were −.12 for the short run and −.40 for the long run. When Tyrchniewicz and Schuh (1969) expanded the farm labor market model by adding four equations for the demand and supply functions of operator labor and family labor, the size of the estimates of the supply elasticities for hired farm labor more than doubled.

The aggregate demand for farm labor has been considered within a multiple-input production framework in which the labor demand function is one of several input demand functions. These equations have been fitted to U.S. data for a national aggregate (Antle 1984), state aggregates for pooled states (Binswanger 1974), and one or two states (Shumway 1983; Weaver 1983). In these studies, all types of labor are aggregated together, and generally, labor is adjusted for quality by employing some type of schooling index. Although all these studies report estimates of the elasticity of demand for farm labor, I am focusing on Antle's results obtained for 1910 to 1978. His results suggest that the wage elasticity of farm labor demand is much smaller in the post–World War II than in the pre-war years. The estimate of the wage elasticity of labor demand is −1.31 for 1910 to 1946, but it is near zero (−.008) for 1947 to 1978. This suggests that the demand for farm labor, where all components are aggregated together, is not currently wage responsive.

The labor demand functions that individual hired farm workers face are undoubtedly affected by a number of economic and other factors. For example, a small share of the hired farm workers (perhaps 5 percent) are migratory, and others are illegal aliens. For individuals employed at nonfarm jobs, hedonic wage equations have been fairly successful in explaining wage rates (e.g., DaVanzo et al. 1976). For hired farm workers, earnings functions have been fitted by Emerson (1984) and Matta (1984) that include human-capital variables. Emerson (1984), using a 1970 to 1971 sample of male, hired farm workers in Florida found that for nonmigrants, one year of schooling increases earnings by 1.9 percent and one year of experience increased earnings by 1.5 percent. (In obtaining these estimates, the share of time allocated to different occupational categories and total weeks worked are being held constant.) Matta (1984), using hired farm working force microdata for 1975, has also fitted earnings functions. For male, hired farm workers, who worked primarily on farms, one year of schooling increased earnings by 1.6 percent and age had a positive but diminishing marginal effect on earnings. Earnings seem to peak at age 24, holding days worked constant. These results suggest that schooling of farm workers may affect their wage, but the size of this coefficient is smaller than estimates obtained for males that are employed at nonfarm jobs (DaVanzo et al. 1976).[9]

Wage rates for seasonal field workers are frequently set on a piece-rate basis. Martin (1985) indicated that the employer sometimes records individual's accomplishments, and in others, a work crew (of 20–40 individuals) divides a piece-rate wage. In both cases, the daily rate of pay is determined by the speed per hour and number of hours worked per day. When individuals share a piece rate, the crew can be expected to consist of individuals who work at a similar, generally fast, pace.[10] Formal schooling seems unlikely to be important for determining a worker's daily wage in a piece-rate system, but experience, physical endurance, and strength seem likely to be quite important. Martin (1985) indicates that daily earnings of piece-rate workers tend to peak when they are relatively young. This is common when little formal training is required and physical strength and endurance peak at a relatively young age. Earnings peak close to the age of peak physical endurance.

Although concerns have been expressed about wage rates and employee benefits paid by U.S. employers of seasonal farm labor, these employers are frequently engaged in intense international competition (e.g., fresh fruit and vegetable producers). Because labor, especially harvest labor, is a relatively large share of the cost of production, producers may try to find lower-cost mechanization or labor (Coltrane 1984). Martin (1985) describes labor-saving harvest mechanization and labor-using field packing that have been adopted in California to reduce labor costs. Immigrant farm labor is frequently a lower-cost source of field workers than domestic workers. Some of these workers have been admitted under special work permits (e.g., H-2 Temporary Foreign Worker Program), but since the end of the Bracero program in 1964, a large majority of the immigrant workers in U.S. agriculture are illegal Mexican aliens (Coltrane 1984).

Most of the aliens come to the United States because wage employment opportunities are much better here than in their home countries. For example, the daily wage rate for low-skilled agricultural labor in the United States is more than five times higher than in Mexico (Huffman 1982). Analyses of the effects of illegal aliens on the farm labor market (and other labor markets) are impeded by the absence of statistical information on the number of illegal aliens employed in U.S. agriculture, the amount of time they work, and the location of their work. Torok and Huffman (1986) have, however, made some progress. New and stricter immigration legislation may significantly change the supply of immigrant labor to agriculture in the future.

UNRESOLVED ISSUES. The labor intensity of agricultural production seems likely to continue to decline. Biogenic research has the potential for developing new fruit and vegetable varieties that ripen uniformly, and robotic-type technology has the potential for the development of new fruit and vegetable harvesting technology. Computer technology can also control and monitor machinery, crop irrigation, and livestock feeding systems.

Empirical measures of the incentive effects of alternative pay schemes for seasonal agricultural workers (e.g., hourly wages, individual and group piece rates, salaries, and bonuses) are not currently available. This is important information for farmers and growers.

Many of the unsettled issues associated with farm labor seem to be associated with immigrant labor.[11] What effects do illegal immigrants have on wage rates for agricultural labor and availability of dependable harvest labor? To what extent would a strict immigrant labor program shift the comparative advantage of fruit and vegetable production to foreign producers and away from U.S. producers? How price responsive is the development of new labor-saving technologies for fruit and vegetable production? Can computer information systems be employed to help the seasonal farm labor market function more efficiently?[12]

U.S. Department of Labor CETA 303 and JTPA 402 programs are specifically targeted to nonimmigrant migratory and seasonal farm workers. These are primarily training programs to enhance job skills of farm workers either for farm work, especially in machinery mechanics and welding, or for nonfarm jobs, mainly clerical. Given the substantial funding of these programs, they need to be evaluated for impact. Have they been a good social investment? Recently, these programs have promoted skills for full-time employment of workers in agriculture rather than leaving agriculture for nonfarm jobs. Have they had a significant effect on the supply (total or specific skills) of farm labor?

New personnel management programs have been suggested for employers of significant numbers of farm workers. The basic idea is that employers can increase worker productivity by providing improved work conditions and worker benefits. The key question is whether workers and employers can both be made better off by altering the total compensation package to include a larger share of nonwage benefits. These programs need careful evaluation because, in our highly competitive agriculture, firms are likely to have small margins for adjusting employees' total compensation.

Much of the general research and extension activities dealing with farm labor are impeded by an absence of good quality and regularly collected data on hours worked and wage rates. This includes data that accurately measure characteristics of agricultural labor and show some of the heterogeneity. There is also a need to calculate hypothetical wage rates in H-2 areas and under the California Agricultural Labor Relations Acts. A higher priority should be placed on obtaining and preserving this data.

Food, Nutrition, and Health

Significant increases in the life spans of people in developed and developing countries have occurred during the past 30 years (Fuchs 1979; Ram and Schultz 1979; Schultz 1984). These changes are unmistakably linked to the production of good health and are important for how households allocate their resources over a lifetime. Agricultural economists have made their main contribution to this area through consumer demand studies, which have a long history. These include the estimates of income and price effects and food program effects on households' demand for food and nutrients. The demand for food and nutrients are derived from the demand for good health (a form of human capital) and other considerations.[13]

SOME CONCEPTS. The new home economics provides a rich new framework for considering the production and consumption of good health by households. The early theories of consumer choice, however, considered the household to be a pure consuming unit. Goods purchased in the market were considered to be direct sources of welfare (utility). Furthermore, households purchased these consumption goods from exogenously determined income. Thus, the quantity demanded of goods depended on their prices and household income. Unfortunately, this methodology is being perpetuated in a number of studies today.

First, these studies ignore the basic labor supply decision, which in most households is made jointly with consumption decisions (Keeley 1981; Barnum and Squire 1979). In its simplest form, leisure of adult household members is a consumption good. Leisure and purchased goods enter the household utility function. Households also face a time constraint on adult household members' time. Their time is allocated between leisure and work for a wage (and possibly farm work). The household receives income from wage work and assets (and possibly a farm business). When households choose the quantity of labor and market goods that maximizes utility subject to the human time and income constraints, the demand functions for purchased goods are altered. They now include the prices of the purchased goods and the wage rate. The wage rate is the price of leisure. Also, asset income enters these demand functions rather than total household income. Earnings from work are the product of hours of work, which is endogenous, and the wage rate, which is the price of leisure. Thus, different sources of income are expected to have different effects on household choices of food, nutrients, and other goods.

Second, food and nutrients are not really an end in themselves. They are one input into the production of (good) health and other commodities (e.g., life-styles) that household members consume. Household production is an innovation of the "new home economics." (See Becker 1981; Michael and Becker 1973; Nerlove 1974; Becker 1965.) In this model, the inputs of human time of one or more household members, food, and other inputs are transformed by the technology of household production into commodities for final consumption (e.g., good health, life-style, children, meals, vacations) or to energy and skills. Environmental variables (e.g., genetic potential, education, and age of household members; availability of health facilities; ingredient and nutrient labeling of food; hazardous substances) may affect the efficiency of household production. A key relationship is how food and nutrients map into health (and work).

Third, individuals' participation in food programs (e.g., school lunch and health programs) is the result of a joint set of food and other household choices (Heckman 1979).

PREVIOUS FINDINGS. Much of the recent research on household demand for food and nutrients in U.S. households is summarized in a paper by Davis (1982). He points out that the useful implications of the new home economics have been ignored in most studies. Nutrient demand studies have considered "available" nutrients in food, based upon standard nutrient-food tables, rather than actual nutrients consumed. Households can be expected to differ in their efficiency of converting available nutrients into consumed nutrients. Nutrients may be lost in the storage and preparation of food, and the amount of this loss may be related to education and information. He also shows that most studies have not made a distinction between asset and labor income or included a wage variable in food or nutrient demand functions.

Studies by Adrian and Daniel (1976), Price et al. (1978), and Basiotis et al. (1983) are examples of U.S. demand studies and nutrients. Adrian and Daniel consider the annual intake of eight nutrients. Their income variable is annual disposable household income, and they find a positive but diminishing marginal income effect on all nutrients except for carbohydrates. They employ the suspect practice of including a dummy variable for wife's employment.

Price et al. (1978) consider the demand for food nutrients by school children and participation in school food programs. The per child demand for total energy and 11 food nutrients is assumed to depend on a fairly large set of variables. Some of these variables are really jointly determined with nutrient intake (e.g., frequency of participation in school lunch programs and frequency with which particular types of food are served at home). In four of the ten nutrient demand equations, assets (liquid or total) have a positive effect on nutrient consumption. No wage variable is, however, included in the demand functions. Although the coefficients of dummy variables for participation in school food programs have positive signs, this is an unsatisfactory modeling strategy.

Basiotis et al. (1983) consider the nutrient consumption patterns of low-income households using data from the special low income component of the 1977 to 1978 Nationwide Food Consumption Survey. They propose and fit a system of simultaneous equations for estimating total food cost and diet component availability in home consumed food. Although they do not test for sample-selection bias or consider Food Stamp Program participation as being a household choice, they find that actual Food Stamp Program participation has a small positive impact on diet-component availability levels. They obtain estimates of positive but small income elasticities of demand for the eight nutrients considered in their study, ranging from 0.1 to 0.3. They, however, commit the sin of aggregating all household income together, thereby confusing price and income effects of an increase in household income.

For farm households in developing countries, Strauss (1984) and Pitt and Rosenzweig (1985) have investigated the effects of better nutrition. Strauss, using data for farm households in Sierra Leone, finds that calories consumed have a positive marginal product in an estimated farm production function. Pitt and Rosenzweig, using a productive household model and Indonesian data on individual nutrients and health, investigate how changes in commodity prices and health program interventions alter household nutrient intake and health status of individuals and how changes in the composition of nutrients directly alter health.

UNRESOLVED ISSUES. We know relatively little about the life-span revolution. It does, however, seem to be the result of long-term processes of health production that are centered in the household and affected by the environment. Preventive health or health maintenance seems to be much more important than acute or emergency medical care (Fuchs 1979). We need more research on the link between food or nutrient consumption and good health, including energy, work days, and life expectancy.[14] Also, how is the production of good health being affected by the generally rising value of human time over time, by increased labor force participation of women, by nutrient education programs, and by food programs? What is the relationship between good health, life expectancy, and education? These are largely unresolved but researchable issues.

Although there has been a relative abundance of household foods and nutrient demand studies, we do not have very good estimates of the pure income and wage effects. Agricultural economists should incorporate the recent advances in modeling pioneered in labor economics and the new home economics.

Useful consumer information is a form of human capital. Both public and private sectors are engaged in distributing food and nutrient information relating to good health. Consumer groups have been influential in adding ingredient and nutrient labels to food. What have been the effects on food demand and good health of these labels? The Extension Service has a long history of supplying food and nutrient information. What effect have these programs had on food demand and good health? Have the content and emphasis of extension food and nutrition programs been changed because of activities of farm commodity pressure groups? If they have, how might we alter our institutional framework to protect the social good?

Concluding Remarks

The view that I have presented is one in which investments in human capital make an individual more productive. An alternative view is the screening or signaling hypothesis. It is most closely tied to the relationship between schooling and wage rates, when information on workers' potential performance is imperfect. According to this view, schooling has no direct effect on workers' useful skills. Schooling is a certification system used to identify preexisting (might be innate) skills. Completion of a certain level of schooling is a signal to employers that workers have certain desirable characteristics for which the employer is willing to pay a particular wage. If schooling were primarily a screening device, cheaper screening methods seem likely to have been developed and to have replaced it. Also, schooling as a screen has no meaningful role in self-employed occupations.

In the human-capital framework, investments in useful skills increase a workers' productivity. The value of these skills as a source of income is, however, determined largely by market conditions. In a system of well-functioning labor markets that are in equilibrium, compensating differentials for higher levels of training would be expected to provide a normal rate of return. Labor market conditions sometimes change or are different from expected, and wage rates may become depressed for particular labor services and in particular geographic areas until individuals can make adjustments. With tied spouses and thin labor markets for many skills in rural areas and small towns, some skills may not be fully employed or may not increase wage rates much over those received for skills requiring less training.

Notes

1. I have undoubtedly excluded some topics and issues that are important to the agricultural economics profession.

2. Differences in the institutional environment seem likely to be quite important in determining the available options that farmers have for adjusting to technological change (Hayami and Ruttan 1985, chap. 4). At this point, it is useful to think of the institutional structure as being imposed by events that are outside the direct control of farmers. Farmers and others may, however, form interest groups, which lobby for governmental policies that affect the size of gains and losses from other institutional structural changes (i.e., institutional structures may be endogenous at the aggregate level).

3. Given the random nature of weather, biological, and economic events and heterogeneity of agriculture, some farmers who have considerable adaptive ability will also be unsuccessful. Some of the uncertainty associated with farming is, however, insurable.

4. The speed of the technology treadmill that faces U.S. farmers may be unusually fast compared with the one facing managers in the nonfarm sector.

5. The number and share of farm households that report off-farm wage income is clearly conditioned by the definition of a farm. The U.S. Department of Agriculture and Census of Agriculture have chosen a farm definition that is not very restrictive (i.e., a place that has annual sales of farm products in excess of $1,000 after 1974). Under this definition, we would expect a significant amount of off-farm work.

6. The model can be extended to permit households to receive utility directly from the work of its members.

7. A multiple-period farm-household model could be used to investigate life-cycle patterns in work, consumption, and investment. In this model type, it may be useful to distinguish between permanent and transitory income. Allocating more time to off-farm work and less time to farm work is one way that farm households can reduce the variance of household income.

8. If most of the vocational training is obtained in high school, the negative coefficient could also imply that a year of vocational courses has less effect on wage rates than a year of general schooling.

9. One of the main effects of additional schooling is to change an individual's occupation. Thus, estimates of returns to schooling that hold occupation constant seem likely to contain sizable selection bias.

10. If the crew consists of a family, more variation in the pace of work by crew members would be expected.

11. Tienda and Jensen (1985) have shown that immigrants are considerably less likely than native U.S. citizens to participate in government welfare programs, other things equal. Immigrants do, however, have a slightly higher actual participation rate in public welfare programs than natives.

12. The combination of piece-rate wage rates and the labor contractor system, which provides the market coordinating function between employers and workers, seems to function relatively efficiently. Thus, it is not obvious that a computer information system would be superior to existing networks that have been built up over time.

13. Some advances in food production and processing that have lowered the price of food may have also lowered food quality and have implications for good health. During the past 15 years, there have been large increases in easily available nutrient information on food packages and containers in the United States.

14. As with other human-capital concepts, obtaining an adequate measure of good health is difficult.

References

Adrian, J., and R. Daniel. 1976. Impact of Socioeconomic Factors on Consumption of Selected Food Nutrients in the United States. *Am. J. Agric. Econ.* 58:31–38.

Antle, J. M. 1984. The Structure of U.S. Agricultural Technology, 1910–1978. *Am. J. Agric. Econ.* 66:414–21.

Barnum, H. N., and L. Squire. 1979. An Econometric Application of the Theory of Farm Household. *J. Dev. Econ.* 6:79–102.

Barros, G. S. D. C. 1976. Asking Wages, Market Wages, and the Off-Farm Labor Supply by Farm Operators. Ph.D. diss., North Carolina State Univ.

Basiotis, P., M. Brown, S. R. Johnson, and K. J. Morgan. 1983. Nutrient Availability, Food Costs, and Food Stamps. *Am. J. Agric. Econ.* 65:683–702.

Becker, G. S. 1965. A Theory of the Allocation of Time. *Econ. J.* 75:493–517.

――――. 1975. *Human Capital.* 2d ed. New York: National Bureau of Economic Research.

――――. 1981. *A Treatise on the Family.* Cambridge: Harvard Univ. Press.

Binswanger, H. P. 1974. The Measurement of Technical Change Biases with Many Factors of Production. *Am. Econ. Rev.* 64:964–76.

Coltrane, R. 1984. Immigration Reform and Agricultural Labor. Washington, D.C.: USDA, ERS.

DaVanzo, J., D. N. DeTray, D. H. Greenberg. 1976. The Sensitivity of Male Labor Supply Estimates to Choice of Assumptions. *Rev. Econ. and Stat.* 58:313–25.

Davis, C. G. 1982. Linkages Between Socioeconomic Characteristics, Food Expenditure Patterns, and Nutritional Status of Low Income Households: A Critical Review. *Am. J. Agric. Econ.* 64:1017–25.

Emerson, R. D. 1984. Migration in Farm Labor Markets. In *Seasonal Agricultural Labor Markets in the United States,* ed. R. D. Emerson, 104–35. Ames: Iowa State Univ. Press.

Evenson, R. E. 1978. Time Allocation in Rural Philippine Households. *Am. J. Agric. Econ.* 60:322–30.

Fane, G. 1975. Education and the Managerial Efficiency of Farmers. *Rev. Econ. Stat.* 57:452–61.

Fuchs, V. R. 1979. The Economics of Health in a Post-Industrial Society. *The Public Interest* 56:3–20.

Griliches, Z. 1963. The Sources of Measured Productivity Growth: United States Agriculture, 1940–1960. *J. Polit. Econ.* 71:331–46.

———. 1964. Research Expenditures, Education, and the Aggregate Agricultural Production Function. *Am. Econ. Rev.* 54:961–74.

Hayami, Y., and V. W. Ruttan. 1985. *Agricultural Development: An International Perspective.* Baltimore: Johns Hopkins Univ. Press.

Heckman, J. J. 1979. Sample Selection Bias as a Specification Error. *Econometrica* 47:153–62.

Huffman, W. E. 1974. Decision Making: The Role of Education. *Am. J. Agric. Econ.* 56:85–97.

———. 1976. The Productive Value of the Human Time in U.S. Agriculture. *Am. J. Agric. Econ.* 58:672–83.

———. 1977. Allocative Efficiency: The Role of Human Capital. *Q. J. Econ.* 91:59–79.

——— 1980. Farm and Off-Farm Work Decisions: The Role of Human Capital. *Rev. Econ. Stat.* 62:14–23.

———. 1982. International Trade in Labor versus Commodities: U.S.-Mexican Agriculture. *Am. J. Agric. Econ.* 64:989–98.

———. 1985. Human Capital, Adaptive Ability, and the Distributional Implications of Agricultural Policy. *Am. J. Agric. Econ.* 67:429–34.

Huffman, W. E., and M. D. Lange. 1984. Off-Farm Work Decisions of Husbands and Wives: Joint Decision Making. Ames: Iowa State Univ. Unpublished paper.

Jamison, D. T., and L. J. Lau. 1982. *Farmer Education and Farm Efficiency.* Baltimore: Johns Hopkins Univ. Press.

Johnson, G. L., and S. H. Wittwer. 1984. Agricultural Technology Until 2030: Prospects, Priorities and Policies. Agricultural Experiment Station Special Report 12. Lansing: Michigan State Univ.

Keeley, M. C. 1981. *Labor Supply and Public Policy.* New York: Academic Press.

Khaldi, N. 1975. Education and Allocative Efficiency in U.S. Agriculture. *Am. J. Agric. Econ.* 57:650–57.

Lange, M. D. 1979. An Economic Analysis of Time Allocation and Capital Labor Ratios in Household Production of Farm Families in Iowa. Ph.D. diss., Iowa State Univ.

Marshall, R. 1974. *Rural Workers in Rural Labor Markets.* Salt Lake City: Olympus.

Martin, P. L. 1985. Seasonal Workers in American Agriculture: Background and

Issues. Research Report Series RR-85-04. Washington, D.C.: National Commission for Employment Policy.

Matta, B. N. 1984. The Off-Farm Work of Hired Farm Workers. In *Seasonal Agricultural Labor Markets in the United States,* ed. R. D. Emerson, 140–64. Ames: Iowa State Univ. Press.

Michael, R. T., and G. S. Becker. 1973. On the New Theory of Consumer Behavior. *Swed. J. Econ.* 75:378–96.

Nerlove, M. 1974. Economic Growth and Population: Perspectives of the 'New Home Economics.' New York: Agricultural Development Council.

Petzel, T. E. 1978. The Role of Education in the Dynamics of Supply. *Am. J. Agric. Econ.* 60:445–51.

Pitt, M. M., and M. R. Rosenzweig. 1985. Health and Nutrient Consumption across and within Farm Households. *Rev. Econ. Stat.* 67:212–23.

Price, D. W., D. A. West, G. E. Scheier, and D. Z. Price. 1978. Food Delivery Programs and Other Factors Affecting Nutrient Intake of Children. *Am. J. Agric. Econ.* 60:609–18.

Rahm, M. R., and W. E. Huffman. 1984. The Adoption of Reduced Tillage: The Role of Human Capital and Other Variables. *Am. J. Agric. Econ.* 66:405–13.

Ram, R., and T. W. Schultz. 1979. Life Span, Health, Savings and Productivity. *Econ. Dev. and Cultural Change* 27:399–422.

Rochin, R. I. 1984. Farm Worker Service and Employment Programs. In *Seasonal Agricultural Labor Markets in the United States,* ed. R. D. Emerson, 412–46. Ames: Iowa State Univ. Press.

Rosenzweig, M. R. 1980. Neoclassical Theory and the Optimizing Peasant: An Econometric Analysis of Market Family Labor Supply in a Developing Country. *Q. J. Econ.* 94:31–56.

Schaub, J. D. 1979. A Simultaneous Equations Model of Multiple Job Holding Farmers with Endogenous Farm Inputs. Ph.D. diss., North Carolina State Univ.

Schuh, G. E. 1962. An Econometric Investigation of the Market for Hired Labor in Agriculture. *J. Farm Econ.* 44:307–21.

_____. 1984. U.S. Agriculture in the World Economy. In *Farm Policy Perspectives: Setting the Stage for 1985 Agricultural Legislation.* Washington, D.C.: GPO.

Schultz, T. W. 1961. Investment in Human Capital. *Am. Econ. Rev.* 51:1–17.

_____. 1975. The Value of the Ability to Deal with Disequilibria. *J. Econ. Lit.* 13:827–46.

_____. 1984. The Changing Economy and the Family. Human Capital Paper No. 84. Chicago: University of Chicago, Dept. of Econ.

Sexton, R. N. 1975. Determinants of Multiple Job Holding by Farm Operators. Ph.D. diss., North Carolina State Univ.

Shumway, C. R. 1983. Supply, Demand, and Technology in a Multiproduct Industry: Texas Field Crops. *Am. J. Agric. Econ.* 65:748–60.

Strauss, J. 1984. Does Better Nutrition Raise Farm Production? New Haven: Yale Univ. Economic Growth Center. Unpublished paper.

Sumner, D. A. 1982. The Off-Farm Labor Supply of Farmers. *Am. J. Agric. Econ.* 64:499–509.

Tienda, M., and L. Jensen. 1985. Immigration and Public Assistance Participation: Dispelling the Myth of Dependence. Discussion Paper No. 777–85. Madison: Univ. of Wisconsin, Inst. for Research on Poverty.

Torok, S. J., and W. E. Huffman. 1986. U.S.-Mexican Trade in Winter Vegetables and Illegal Immigration. *Am. J. Agric. Econ.* 68:246–59.

Tyrchniewicz, E. E., and G. E. Schuh. 1966. Regional Supply of Hired Labor to Agriculture. *J. Farm Econ.* 48:537–56.

———. 1969. Econometric Analysis of the Agricultural Labor Market. *Am. J. Agric. Econ.* 51:770–87.

U.S. Department of Agriculture. 1984. *Economic Indicators of the Farm Sector.* Washington, D.C.: USDA, ERS.

Weaver, R. D. 1983. Multiple Input, Multiple Output Production Choices and Technology in the U.S. Wheat Region. *Am. J. Agric. Econ.* 65:45–56.

Welch, F. 1970. Education in Production. *J. Polit. Econ.* 78:35–39.

———. 1978. The Role of Investments in Human Capital in Agriculture. In *Distortions of Agricultural Incentives,* ed. T. W. Schultz, 259–81. Bloomington: Indiana Univ. Press.

Wozniak, G. D. 1984. The Adoption of Interrelated Innovations: A Human Capital Approach. *Rev. Econ. Stat.* 66:70–79.

Human Capital for Agriculture: A Discussion

MARTA TIENDA

Professor Huffman has addressed a number of provocative and challenging research and policy questions that can benefit from interdisciplinary dialogue. Although it is much easier to raise questions than to find the answers, asking the "right" set of questions is as great a challenge as providing their solutions. Fruitful interdisciplinary dialogue requires a common understanding of the issues, and their implications for policy and research. It is in this spirit that my comments should be taken.

I limit my commentary to two of the four issues discussed by Professor Huffman: (1) farmers' decision making and (2) farm labor. This decision does not reflect the lesser importance of the other two topics, but instead my preference to dwell on subjects most akin to my own research interests in labor processes and structural change.

Farmers' Decision Making

Professor Huffman stated: "A dynamic technical environment, created by the introduction of new technologies, provides greater *potential*

Marta Tienda is a Professor of Rural Sociology at the University of Wisconsin, Madison.

than a static environment." At first blush, who could disagree? On second thought, it is not clear that technological change is always beneficial for all those affected. To wit, consider the social consequences of mechanization for farmers and farm laborers, changes promoted in the interest of production and efficiency. Thus, before assuming the great potential of technological change, it is essential to determine *who* stands to benefit and lose from the introduction of new technology.

From a sociological perspective, addressing and prioritizing human-capital issues for agriculture requires a clear understanding of the recent changes in occupational specialization within the industry. Such questioning also should comprehend how these changing opportunities translate into unequal opportunities for various segments of labor. A few concrete examples can illustrate this point.

Since World War II, declining agricultural employment has been the primary motor of industrial transformation, making possible the shift from a goods-oriented economy to a service economy. In this process, the agricultural industry itself experienced extensive occupational restructuring, as shown in Table 16.1. Between 1960 and 1980, when total agricultural employment declined from 7 percent to 3 percent, the share which farmers comprised of the total industry declined from 57 to 43 percent. Also, employment in farm laborer occupations fell from 33 percent in 1960 to 31 percent in 1980. As the prevalence of farm-related jobs in agriculture declined, the industry became more occupationally diverse due to a more complex division of labor and the growing specialization of economic tasks. During the period from 1960 to 1980, the size of the professional, semiprofessional, and managerial work force engaged in agriculture almost quadrupled, rising from 1.8 to 6.8 percent.

Concurrently, most occupations within the agricultural industry became much more feminized during the period. Whereas women comprised 5 percent of all farmers in 1970, their presence in this occupation had almost doubled by 1980. The sex composition of farm laborers increased from 15 to 23 percent between 1970 and 1980. Overall, women's employment share of the agricultural industry increased from 22 percent in 1970 to 28 percent in 1980. This proportion is lower than the percent female of total employment in 1980 of approximately 34 percent.

Not only are men and women differentially allocated among occupations within the agricultural industry, but an inspection of their educational attainments shows considerable diversity by occupation, with women exhibiting higher schooling levels than men in the lower prestige (farmer, laborer, and farm laborer) occupations. Why this is so is unclear, but it is an issue worthy of further investigation in searching for explanations about the persistence and possible redefinition of gender boundaries in agricultural employment, and their implications for economic returns on edu-

Table 16.1.   Selected characteristics of the agriculture industry by occupation, 1960–1980

Occupation	Allocation of total agriculture labor force			Percent female		Educational composition		Mean earnings	
	1960	1970	1980	1970	1980	Men 1980	Women 1980	Men 1980	Women 1980
Professional	1.2	2.3	3.5	8.3	18.6	15.2	14.4	12,858	7,218
Semiprofessional	.1	.5	.9	16.4	39.8	12.7	13.1	9,448	5,422
Farmers	57.4	50.1	43.8	5.1	9.8	11.8	12.4	2,888	1,106
Managers	.5	.9	2.4	11.6	19.6	13.0	13.1	14,409	7,064
Clerical	.7	1.9	3.2	80.0	87.4	13.0	12.6	10,532	5,561
Sales	.2	.5	.6	32.2	31.0	13.0	11.8	12,323	3,836
Crafts	.7	1.8	1.2	5.0	3.9	10.4	10.7	10,006	4,371
Operatives	2.5	2.1	2.6	17.1	20.8	9.9	9.6	9,195	4,939
Service	.3	.6	.9	38.9	31.1	11.0	10.3	8,328	3,687
Laborers	2.9	6.9	10.1	9.8	17.5	10.5	11.9	5,637	3,176
Farm laborers	33.4	32.4	30.7	14.7	22.9	9.4	10.0	6,286	3,066
Total	99.9	100.0	99.9	21.8	27.5	11.8	11.8	5,208	3,365

Source: 1960, 1970, and 1980. Public Use Microdata Sample of U.S. Census of Population and Housing.

cation. Note, for example, that women's average earnings were consistently lower than those of men in every occupation, including those where the education gap was quite small (e.g., clerical and managerial jobs), and where women had the average schooling advantage (e.g., semiprofessional jobs).

An examination of the entries and exits from and into jobs within the agricultural industry could provide fruitful insights about the transferability of general and specific skills within the agricultural industry and in the context of a high-tech production strategy. This type of analysis, familiar to sociologists, also could promote interdisciplinary dialogue with economists. The data in Table 16.1 suggest a critical need to factor gender into the research and policy agenda addressed to issues of human-capital requirements of modern agriculture.

That differentials in occupational placement and educational requirements of men and women become translated into earnings disparities by gender suggests that we need to ask not only how much education and what kind of education is needed for a more productive agriculture, but also who benefits from such investments. Policies targeted to specific segments of the agricultural labor force—women, immigrants, minorities—must include enforceable provisions to ensure equitable returns for similar investments. This is as much a research and policy challenge for the 1980s and 1990s as the thorny question of determining how the content of education enhances decision making in agriculture. Perhaps our interest in human capital should focus less on productivity and more on the way human-capital investments can erode the deep contours of inequity within the industry.

Finally, a discussion of the human capital needs for agriculture should be sensitive to the process of occupational restructuring that has gained momentum during the past two to three decades. Such dialogue could profit from posing questions about human-capital requirements for agriculture in structural as well as individual terms. In light of the extensive change in the occupational mix of the agricultural industry, we should include within the priority research agenda studies which document how the skills requirements of the increasingly diverse array of occupational tasks in agriculture have changed. We should ask ourselves whether our conceptual categories to analyze structural changes are sensitive to the nuances of technology and its revolutionizing impact on the nature of work.

Farm Labor

On the topic of farm labor, and in light of econometric evidence showing that "the demand for farm labor . . . is not currently wage responsive," I was encouraged by the immediate acknowledgement that "other factors" may influence labor demand functions faced by hired farm workers. However, I was disappointed that political factors were not accorded the prominence they deserve in the discussion of the role of immigrant labor in U.S. agriculture.

That immigrant workers comprise an increasing share of the work force engaged in farm laborer jobs is not primarily a matter of human capital. It is, instead, a matter of political economy. Why else would immigrant labor cost less than domestic labor? If productivity of foreign workers were lower, they would be inferior inputs in production and would generate labor market inefficiencies. Foreign workers in agriculture cost less, not because of their lower quality, or lower stocks of human capital, but because as a labor input, these workers are politically and economically vulnerable.

Foreign workers are attractive to growers involved in perishable commodities because they seldom challenge wage rates or attempt to unionize or organize work stoppages — strategies which could devastate the perishable commodities. Preferred workers in the perishable commodity crops must be responsive to a highly variable demand function and be able and willing to work irregular schedules. The attractiveness of foreign laborers for the farm sector is that, in addition to these characteristics, they "willingly" accept lower wages than domestic workers. This is not because they are less productive; this is because they are powerless.

By posing the very revealing question: To what extent would a strict immigrant labor program shift the comparative advantage of fruit and vegetable production to foreign producers and away from U.S. producers?

Professor Huffman exposed the political, rather than economic factors at play in ensuring the availability of a pool of low-skilled workers that serve to protect profit margins of growers. For them, wage rates are not determined on the basis of productivity (i.e., output per a specified unit of labor input), but rather on an ascribed criterion, immigrant status, which renders growers fuller control of the labor process. That is what power is all about.

Raising questions about human-capital requirements to increase the productivity of the farm laborers without first acknowledging the importance of political factors governing their presence (either through legitimate contract labor programs or through clandestine means) is to beg the question about whose interests are served by the involvement of immigrant laborers in U.S. agriculture, and how past and present training programs can solve the problem. Nowhere is this better illustrated than in the current immigration legislation which protects growers who hire illegal aliens but makes it a felony to harbor or be an illegal alien.

I take issue with the view that the Job Training Partnership Act (JTPA) is designed to update the human capital of the farm work force. In my judgment, the JTPA legislation is largely irrelevant for foreign-born workers engaged in farm laborer occupations not as legislated, but as implemented. Under the decentralized structure of JTPA, identifying farm laborers and workers with low levels of education as special target groups means nothing if the local authorities entrusted to establish training programs ignore the needs of these workers. If it is true that immigrants comprise a low-wage, unprotected labor supply that is particularly attractive to the agricultural industry precisely because of these characteristics, why should Private Industry Councils (PICS) representing local grower interests seek to upgrade the educational certification of these workers? Certainly it is not in their interests to do so.

Moreover, given the extensive human-capital literature showing the positive effect of education on earnings, the training provisions of the JTPA legislation, if extended to agricultural workers, would certainly drive up the wage bill and decrease the profit margins of an already fragile industry. In a real sense, the JTPA legislation, with its decentralized implementation strategy, asks local service providers to train a work force that is employed largely because it is untrained. My interpretation is consistent with empirical literature cited by Professor Huffman which shows the effects of education to be much weaker for farm as compared to nonfarm workers. Hence, by training farm workers, a growing share of whom are foreign born, private industry representatives essentially would consent to upgrade a labor pool that conveys significant economic advantages to agricultural industries in their area because it is untrained. This poses an irreconcilable clash of interests that cannot be addressed with a human-capital policy.

In theory, JTPA may be an appropriate legislative instrument to increase the skill levels and productivity of farm workers, but because of political realities, in practice it is not. That most agricultural laborers and especially immigrant farm laborers lack the political clout or institutional participation to make local service agencies take the initiative to represent their interests makes JTPA largely irrelevant as a vehicle to promote human-capital enhancement in agriculture. JTPA means an increase in the power of certain groups to determine which clients are served and what types of programs are offered. Until farm workers are represented among these groups, their training needs are not likely to become a priority, much less an issue of human-capital policy in agriculture.

Human Capital for Agriculture: **A Discussion**

ROBERT D. EMERSON

Professor Huffman has given us a comprehensive statement of the contributions of the human-capital literature to economic problems in agriculture. The four areas that he has chosen to focus on are farmers' decision making; off-farm income; farm labor; and food, nutrition, and health. The first two relate to problems of the farm family, the third to other persons employed in agriculture, and the last to agriculture through the effect on the demand for agricultural products by the general population. The four areas provide a good overview of human capital research in agricultural economics. I will first briefly address each of the areas, and then consider an aspect of human capital that is not treated in detail in the paper and has not received much attention by agricultural economists.

The theory of human capital has made significant contributions to the role of the decision-making process in agriculture. This has been evaluated primarily through the contributions of education, research, and extension activities to allocative and technical efficiency. While we have considerable evidence that extension activities improve allocative decision making, our

Robert D. Emerson is Associate Professor of Food and Resource Economics, University of Florida, Gainesville.

evidence for different types of extension activities (e.g., economic versus varietal information) is sketchy. We also do not know very much about the optimal institutional structure for providing extension services under alternative economic structures. We know that extension services have provided positive benefits, but we do not know if it is a result of direct contact or through various information services or other agribusinesses that are actually synthesizing the information for producers. As we move further into the electronic age, an important question within the land-grant system is what type of clients should be targeted by extension programs.

The household time allocation model has contributed significantly to understanding the off-farm work decision. The notion of off-farm work has become closely aligned with the "small farms issue." However, off-farm work is observed across all sizes of farms. I agree with the agenda outlined by Huffman, and I would reemphasize the notion that the household model has additional potential for interpreting problems related to small farms. From a policy perspective, we need to be able to distinguish between the consumptive and productive components of small farm households in order to distinguish between production activities and merely purchasing a way of life. The household model may offer some additional insights on this issue.

The focus by the profession on farm labor issues has been largely in the context of labor markets rather than a human-capital framework, and this is borne out by Huffman's discussion. Perhaps because of the perceived low stock of human capital by this segment of the labor force, human capital has been viewed as having little to contribute. Nevertheless, there have been extensive manpower training programs (CETA 303 and JTPA 402) directed toward farm labor that have not received much attention by economists. Likewise, other community service and health programs are devoted to farm workers and have received little attention by economists. A particularly significant problem to be addressed is human-capital issues related to the children of farm workers, particularly of migratory farm workers.

A large component of the farm labor market consists of highly casual workers. Do these workers merely work in agriculture for a short period while developing job skills and then move on to more lucrative forms of work? Longitudinal data sources would help sort out what happens to the casual workers. Is the farm worker population a rotating group or a continuing group over the generations? Our information base is not very good on this.

My observation with respect to the food, nutrition, and health section is that it is the area of agricultural economics that has most regularly utilized concepts from human-capital theory. Nevertheless, this points out a potential deficiency in the way we present our graduate theory courses. Too much of the applied work utilizes human-capital "variables" in a rather ad hoc fashion rather than recognizing the way in which the household model modifies demand theory. Perhaps this suggests that the theory of human capital deserves more attention in our graduate training programs.

The one area I would like to expand upon from Huffman's paper is the personal distribution of income. Most of the human capital research in the areas of decision making and off-farm work activities is concerned with the contribution of human capital to improved decisions and to increased efficiency of resource allocation. The presumption is that the contribution of human capital is increased growth and per-capita income. To the extent that differences in human-capital stock are reduced this should presumably reduce income inequality among farm households. Yet the size distribution or the personal distribution of income of farm households has received little attention.

T. W. Schultz (1962, 2) stated as one of three hypotheses regarding investment in human capital:

> With respect to the distribution of personal income, based on the assumption that the rise in the investment in human capital relative to that invested in non-human capital increases earnings relative to property income and that the more equal distribution of investments in man equalizes earnings among human agents, the hypothesis here proposed is that these changes in the investment in human capital are the basic factors reducing the inequality in the distribution of personal income.

One study clearly falling within this area is Gardner's (1969) study of the variance of farm family incomes based on 1949 and 1959 census data. Other studies addressing the inequality issue with respect to persons living in rural areas or employed in agriculture are by Huffman (1981) and Welch (1967) focusing on black-white differences in human-capital investment. The latter two, however, are not directly concerned with the size distribution of income.

The presumption is that the level of human capital has been rising among farm households and that inequities in human-capital investments have been narrowing. If this is true, we should expect a more equal distribution of income. Empirical work on both the changes in the distribution of human-capital attributes and the distribution of personal income would be worthwhile here. A useful question is the extent to which increased off-farm work has reduced income inequality. At a more fundamental level, it would be useful to relate changes in the distribution of human-capital attributes to changes in the distribution of income.

Comparisons of farm incomes are often made with the overall economy. Average incomes of farm families have risen substantially over the past two decades. In 1960, the average farm operator family income was $5,047 as compared to a 1982 level of $25,728 (U.S. Department of

Agriculture 1985). Over the same time period, U.S. median family income rose from $5,620 to $23,433 (U.S. Department of Commerce 1984). The corresponding ratios of farm family to U.S. family income are 0.90 and 1.10 for 1960 and 1982, respectively. While this comparison suggests that farm family households have gained on average relative to the rest of the economy, it says nothing about changes in the distribution of income. Much of the debate over small farms in recent years would suggest that the distribution of income in agriculture has worsened. However, the latter conclusion is generally drawn on the basis of incomes by sales class rather than the size distribution of income.

In closing I would like to add that information on the personal distribution of income would be useful information for agricultural policy. Not only does the size distribution give more information than just the means or the medians, but it places the focus directly on the households rather than a consideration of the distribution by sales class of farms.

References

Gardner, B. L. 1969. Determinants of Farm Family Income Inequality. *Am. J. Agric. Econ.* 51:753–69.

Huffman, W. E. 1981. Black-White Human Capital Differences: Impact on Agricultural Productivity in the U.S. South. *Am. Econ. Rev.* 71:94–107.

Schultz, T. W. 1962. Reflections on Investment in Man. *J. Polit. Econ.* 70:1–8.

U.S. Department of Agriculture. 1985. *Economic Indicators of the Farm Sector: Income and Balance Sheets, 1983.* Washington, D.C.: USDA, ERS.

U.S. Department of Commerce. 1984. *Statistical Abstract of the United States.* Washington, D.C.: GPO.

Welch, F. 1967. Labor-Market Discrimination: An Interpretation of Income Differences in the Rural South. *J. Polit. Econ.* 75:225–40.

17

A Synthesis of Teaching Issues

HOY F. CARMAN

Participants in this conference have tended to focus on research issues in the papers and in the discussions. I was not surprised by the emphasis, since it is consistent with our system of professional rewards and recognition. Despite the emphasis on research issues, the papers and discussion sessions raised very important questions and issues related to teaching. The strong ties between our teaching and research programs insure that calls for a change in research direction or emphasis will have an impact on our curriculum and courses. I should also note, however, that courses and curriculum changes tend to be a continuing and very incremental process.

I was uncertain about what would be involved in a synthesis of teaching issues and implications for action but decided that serious reactions to issues would likely involve proposals for changes in courses and curriculum at both the undergraduate and graduate levels. As a basis for evaluating suggestions for changes in undergraduate courses and curriculums, we conducted a survey of agricultural economics and agricultural business management curriculums throughout the United States. These programs provide the academic foundation for students who will pursue agricultural careers as well as those entering our graduate programs. We did not survey graduate programs since most offer the student considerable flexibility in pursuing fields of study and developing a research area. Suggestions for change can more easily be accommodated in existing graduate programs than in existing undergraduate programs.

In this synthesis of teaching issues, I will provide some background on recent trends in student enrollment. Then I will present some preliminary results of our survey of undergraduate agricultural economics and

Hoy F. Carman is Professor of Agricultural Economics at the University of California, Davis.

agricultural business management curriculums. This will be followed by conference recommendations related to courses and curriculum. The paper will conclude with some of the major issues related to teaching, particularly at the undergraduate level.

Enrollment Trends

Blank (1985) has reported a survey of enrollment trends in agricultural economics programs for the 1975 to 1984 decade. He found that undergraduate enrollment increased significantly and, while average graduate enrollment was unchanged, there were regional differences. Average undergraduate enrollment increased from 136 per program in 1975–1976 to 219 in 1983–1984, a 61 percent increase. Average graduate enrollment was 39 at the beginning and end of the period, with decreases in the Northeast, North Central, and Central regions offset by increases in the South, the West, and Canada. Combining undergraduate and graduate enrollments gives a net increase of 47 percent for agricultural economics for the decade while average college of agriculture enrollments were decreasing 11 percent overall. As a result, agricultural economics departments increased their share of agricultural college enrollments from 11 to 18 percent.

Blank found that about 54 percent of agricultural economics departments' undergraduate students were enrolled in an agricultural business management option or major program. Our survey results were similar with 55 percent of total enrollment in agricultural business programs. Over 60 percent of the departments replying to Blank's survey indicated that they expect agricultural business to be the area of greatest growth during the next decade.

The changing composition of our student body is an important consideration in any discussion of curriculum. As forecast by Beck et al. (1977), an increasing proportion of our students come from a nonfarm background. In 1975, 54 percent of the departments indicated that more than half of their students had a farm background. The similar figure for 1984 was only 34 percent (Blank 1985). Now we find that the majority of students in the majority of agricultural economics departments are from a nonagricultural background. More women are entering agricultural economics and agricultural business programs. In Blank's survey, 39 percent of the departments indicated that women account for 25 to 50 percent of undergraduate enrollment; 32 percent of the departments indicated that women account for 26 to 50 percent of graduate enrollment. Women will likely continue to increase their share of graduate enrollment and faculty representation as the agricultural economics profession approaches the twenty-first century.

Curriculum Survey

We recently surveyed U.S. agricultural economics departments concerning their undergraduate curriculums (Carman and Pick 1985). Questionnaires were sent to all of the U.S. agricultural economics departments listed in the *AAEA Handbook Directory*. We received a total of 53 responses from land-grant, 1890s, and other universities. These 53 departments have 42 major programs in agricultural economics and 33 major programs in agricultural business management. The major programs in agricultural business management tend to be significantly larger than those in agricultural economics with average enrollments being 213 and 136, respectively.

Average quarter unit requirements in selected academic areas for agricultural economics and agricultural business management majors are shown in Table 17.1. These data indicate that the average agricultural economics major has more calculus, more statistics, more intermediate micro and macroeconomic theory, less computer science, and less accounting than does the average agricultural business management major.

As one would expect, there are substantial differences in program requirements from school to school. Thus, the distribution of course requirements, which we will present for five of the course areas, is more revealing than are the averages. There are also some important similarities. For example, English writing and oral communications requirements account for an average of 14.53 and 14.40 quarter units respectively in agricultural economics and agricultural business programs (see Table 17.1). The typical undergraduate program for either major includes two or three writing courses and one course in oral communications (speech/rhetoric). Several schools have recently increased their writing course requirements and others indicated they are considering increased writing requirements.

Table 17.1. Average quarter unit requirements for agricultural economics and agricultural business programs, 1984–1985

Course Area	Agricultural Economics	Agricultural Business
	Average quarter units[1]	
English Writing	10.35	10.02
Speech/Rhetoric	4.18	4.38
Computer Science	3.80	4.08
Calculus	5.21	3.80
Intermediate Micro	4.31	3.86
Intermediate Macro	3.40	2.38
Statistics	5.45	4.70
Natural Science	16.83	16.65
Social Science/Humanities	18.31	19.23
Agriculture	16.19	17.48
Agricultural Economics	34.13	34.36
Accounting	6.62	8.68

Source: Carman and Pick (1985).
[1]All responses were converted to a quarter-unit basis.

The quantitative orientation of the undergraduate programs is reflected by requirements in computer science, calculus, and statistics. Computer science requirements are rather recent for most programs and the agricultural business programs require slightly more units on average than do the agricultural economics programs. Average calculus and statistics requirements, however, are higher for the agricultural economics programs (see Table 17.1).

Calculus requirements for the two programs are illustrated by the distributions in Figure 17.1. As shown, 12 percent of the agricultural economics and 36 percent of the agricultural business management programs have no calculus requirement. The majority of the agricultural economics programs require one calculus course and some 30 percent require two or more calculus courses.

A statistics requirement is almost universal for the two major programs (Figure 17.2). All of the agricultural economics programs have a statistics requirement, and only three agricultural business programs do not require at least one statistics course.

As one might expect, the intermediate micro and macroeconomic theory requirements are higher for the agricultural economics than for the agricultural business programs. All but four of the agricultural economics programs require at least one course in intermediate microeconomic theory, but 6 of 33 (18 percent) of the agricultural business programs have no intermediate microeconomic theory requirement. The relative emphasis of

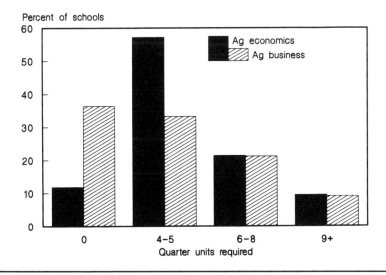

Fig. 17.1. Calculus requirement

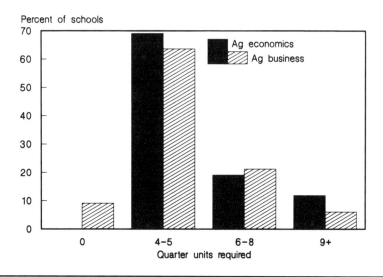

Fig. 17.2. **Statistics requirement**

the programs of micro versus macroeconomic topics is reflected in macroeconomic theory requirements. The distribution of requirements by program in Figure 17.3 shows that some 48 percent of the agricultural business and 29 percent of the agricultural economics programs do not require an intermediate macroeconomic theory course. In a way, the greater emphasis of agricultural economics programs on macroeconomic theory, when compared to agricultural business programs, is surprising. Students who obtain jobs with agricultural business firms are required to deal with macroeconomic topics such as interest rates, level of growth, taxation, consumption, national income, money supply, etc., on a daily basis. Several programs have recently added an intermediate macrotheory requirement and others are considering adding it as a requirement.

Emphasis on accounting in the agricultural business programs is not surprising. Figure 17.4 shows the distribution of accounting requirements for both programs. Only one of the agricultural business programs and only four of the agricultural economics programs do not have an accounting requirement. Note that approximately a quarter of the agricultural business programs require more than nine units of accounting, while only one of the agricultural economics programs has such a heavy requirement.

There are at least two approaches that the increasing portion of students who do not have a farm background can use to become familiar with the agricultural industry. They can enroll in agricultural courses and they

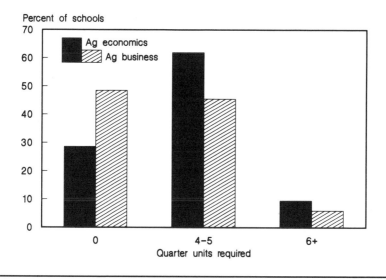

Fig. 17.3. Intermediate macroeconomic theory requirement

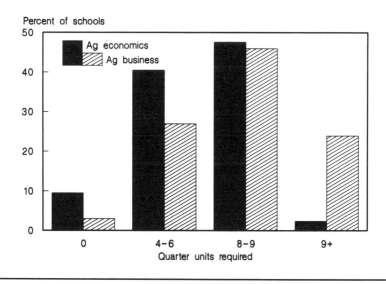

Fig. 17.4. Accounting requirement

can participate in work experience or internship programs available in many universities. Requirements for agricultural courses demonstrate considerable variation by school, region, and program. The agriculture requirement averaged 1.29 quarter units more for the agricultural business than for the agricultural economics programs in the survey. This difference is evident in the distribution of unit requirements shown in Figure 17.5. Internship programs are available in most of the agricultural economics (71 percent) and agricultural business (85 percent) programs but student participation in internships is relatively low. The percentage of students participating in internships tend to be an inverse function of the enrollment in the program. Our survey indicates that approximately 8 percent of all agricultural economics and 13 percent of all agricultural business students participated in an internship program.

A question asking about recent changes in major requirements found that 21 percent of the departments had increased writing requirements; 13 percent had increased intermediate macroeconomic theory requirements, and another 7 percent plan to add a course requirement in international agriculture; 28 percent had added a computer science course, and 10 percent plan to add a requirement in computer science. Only 15 percent of the programs do not now have a computer science requirement. Almost 19 percent of the departments have added a calculus requirement in the last six years and 12 percent had added another mathematical or quantitative requirement.

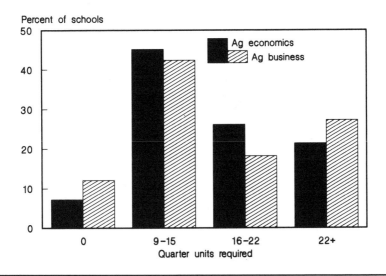

Fig. 17.5. Agriculture requirement

Needs and Issues

Conference participants discussed a number of aspects of teaching related to courses, curriculum, and students. The focus of the comments was usually not explicit and, thus, I assume that the general comments relate to both undergraduate and graduate programs. Group discussion related to both course requirements and course content.

Several groups listed needs or made recommendations related to broadening course requirements and moving away from a "traditional agricultural" curriculum. A "traditional agricultural" curriculum was not defined, and we can only infer what might have been meant from the tone of the suggestions. Specific recommendations related to course requirements were to

1. Include more history and history of economic thought courses in the curriculum. Students need to gain an understanding of institutions and institutional arrangements important to agricultural economics.

2. Teach students about world agriculture with courses in comparative government, international politics, and geography.

3. Expose students to multidisciplinary approaches through a broad selection of courses.

4. Improve the empirical training of all of our students. Minutes of the discussion groups indicated a diversity of opinion on how this could be accomplished. There were no specific recommendations, but the discussions did emphasize the need to consider the trade-offs between mathematical, computer, statistical, and subject matter skills. Participants emphasized the need to teach students problem identification skills together with an understanding of appropriate quantitative tools. Some questions related to quantitative training for our students included

   — the need to determine the proper mix of quantitative courses and the methods which should be taught in these courses, and

   — the possible need for post-doctoral training in quantitative methods.

5. Several of the discussion groups considered the need to increase the macroeconomic theory requirements in our curriculums. None of the groups recommended specific course requirements or the topics that should be covered in the course(s). Some participants suggested that undergraduate majors should include at least an intermediate macroeconomic theory requirement and that graduate programs should include formal coursework covering macroeconomic theory topics.

Conference participants discussed several of the formal presentations in terms of implications for topics covered in present coursework. Recommendations relative to course content were to

1. Teach process as well as content.

2. Teach ethical considerations of economic theories and value presumptions in benefit-cost analysis.

3. Teach interactions between entitlements and economic conditions.

4. Work harder in our courses to bridge the gap between theory and applications.

5. Devote more attention to macroeconomic concepts and their applications in finance, farm management, agribusiness, and agricultural development courses. Macroeconomic concepts should be integrated in present courses whenever possible, especially as they apply to agricultural economic problems.

6. Do a better job of keeping up-to-date on important developments in economics.

The AAEA last sponsored a major workshop on curriculum development and teaching at the University of Florida, August 23–25, 1972. Given developments since then, it is probably time to plan for another session devoted to courses and curriculum for agricultural economics and agricultural business management. Conference participants suggested that course and curriculum revisions might be developed in response to a perceived need: (1) for increased training related to institutional analysis; (2) to develop educational programs related to organizational and information system design; (3) to expand educational efforts to nontraditional groups; and (4) to train graduate students (especially foreign students) to return to managerial roles in their countries.

Summary of Issues

The challenges for agricultural economics discussed at this conference have important long-run implications for our undergraduate and graduate courses, curriculum, and teaching. A number of issues were raised that will affect our teaching programs, and there were some suggestions for changes in courses and curriculum. Our survey of undergraduate programs found that considerable diversity exists; whether suggested changes will increase or decrease diversity is unclear.

There are perceived needs for changes in courses and curriculum. Given the range of present requirements, these comments may or may not be universally applicable. Agricultural economics majors have traditionally been quite flexible, but recent additions to course requirements and proposed changes that tend to increase requirements will reduce its flexibility.

A comparison of existing curriculum and conference recommendations indicates that we must do more in the area of macroeconomics, through new course requirements and the integration of macroeconomic concepts in existing courses. There were several questions related to quantitative requirements with recommendations to examine the mix of quantitative courses and the proper methods to be taught.

Most academic agricultural economists have both teaching and research responsibilities. Given existing procedures for resource allocation in our colleges of agriculture, it is doubtful that the significant growth in undergraduate enrollment in agricultural economics and agricultural business majors has been matched by increased teaching resources. Increased teaching work load adversely affects research productivity and can influence faculty advancement. While there may be some economies of size, more teaching and more research can only be done with more resources.

The rapid growth in agricultural business enrollment has implications that were discussed only briefly by conference participants. Questions that will have to be addressed include

1. Who will teach management-type courses? A cursory review of recent Ph.D. recipients in agricultural economics reveals very few with an obvious interest in management topics.

2. Do the agricultural business students have any interest in agriculture as a career or do our programs simply provide an opportunity for students who cannot gain admission to a business program?

3. Should agricultural economics departments teach management courses in areas separate from their research thrust?

There is a need to develop an appreciation for agricultural practices and institutions for students with no agricultural background. This can be done through coursework and internships. Approximately 10 percent of our students presently participate in internship programs. These programs are quite effective and probably should be expanded if sufficient resources are available.

Teaching programs change over time in response to a variety of factors and these changes will continue. The increasing integration of agriculture into the national and international economies will be reflected in courses and curriculum as will the continuing revolution in computers and information technology. Agricultural economics faces exciting opportunities as we move toward the twenty-first century. A continuing dialogue on curriculum and teaching issues will be required for our profession to make optimum adjustments to external forces.

References

Beck, R. L., A. F. Bordeaux, Jr., J. T. Davis, R. H. Brannon, and L. L. Mather. 1977. Undergraduate Programs in Agricultural Economics: Some Observations. *Am. J. Agric. Econ.* 59:766–68.

Blank, S. C. 1985. A Decade of Change in Agricultural Economics Programs, 1975–1984. Paper presented at the Annual Meeting of the Northeastern Agricultural and Resource Economics Association, Amherst, Mass.

Carman, H. F., and D. H. Pick. 1985. Undergraduate Curriculum in Agricultural Economics and Agricultural Business: Past, Present, and Future Developments. Working Paper 85-7. Davis: Univ. of California, Dept. of Agric. Econ.

18

A Synthesis of Extension Issues

JOHN E. IKERD

A synthesis is defined by Webster as the combination of diverse conceptions into a coherent whole. Thus, the task of this paper is to combine two days of diverse discussions of agricultural issues into a coherent picture of challenges confronting agricultural economists and to derive implications for extension programs. First, four major issues are synthesized from a wide variety of related issues discussed during the conference. Next, some implications of these issues for future agricultural economic extension programs are outlined and discussed. Finally, the paper concludes with a synopsis of conference discussions concerning future roles of cooperative extension, agricultural economists, and the land-grant university system.

Challenges to Agriculture Approaching the Twenty-first Century

The single most significant agricultural development of the last one-third of the twentieth century might well be the internationalization of markets for U.S. agricultural production capacity, higher land prices, greater reliance on debt financing and optimistic expectations among U.S. farmers. All these factors left American agriculture vulnerable to severe adverse economic impacts from a partial loss of those export markets during the 1980s.

However, any hope for restoring the profitability of U.S. agriculture, without returning to a significantly smaller agricultural sector, depends on holding, regaining, and expanding export markets for U.S. agricultural

John E. Ikerd is Professor and Head of the Department of Extension Agricultural Economics, University of Georgia, Athens.

commodities. A twenty-first century agriculture without significant export markets likely would bear little resemblance to the basically free, competitive, and independent decision-based agriculture of the past and present.

The farm financial crisis of the 1980s stems from factors largely beyond the control of individual farmers. An abrupt, unexpected change in U.S. and world economic conditions transformed the farming boom of the 1970s into the farm financial crisis of the 1980s. Farm land prices and farm wealth grew throughout the 1970s. However, farm cash-flow problems began to develop with the rising inflation rates of the late 1970s. Land prices turned down in 1981 and currently are 30 to 50 percent below peak levels in major north central agricultural states. American agriculture is confronted by a major recapitalization of its financial structure.

Many farmers now face negative cash flows and declining asset values with little prospect for improvement in either in the foreseeable future. This situation may have broad implications for U.S. agriculture. The competitive structure of twenty-first century agriculture may be shaped in large part by the financial crisis of the 1980s. New directions in agricultural policy eventually may result from realization of past policy failures reflected by the current farm problems. Dramatic changes in farm financial institutions and farm-community relationships may evolve before the twenty-first century as a consequence of the current financial crisis in agriculture.

Many family farmers have been forced to rely on nonfarm sources of income to supplement and subsidize their farming operations. In addition, many full-time job holders have become part-time farmers in the process, moving their families back to the country to live. Nonfarm income now accounts for more than two-thirds of all income of farm families. Part-time farming operations, in general, appear to be better able to survive the current financial crisis in agriculture than are most other types of farms.

Current trends toward part-time family farming may cement a growing interdependence between family farms and rural communities. Community development in terms of local off-farm jobs may become vital to survival of family farming. Available off-farm based employees or part-time farming opportunities may become a vital element in decisions of some industries to move to rural communities. Such interdependencies may become important considerations in local public policy issues, in environmental questions and concerns, and even in national policy issues related to structure and performance of the agricultural sector of the economy.

Emerging biotechnology may result in increased productive efficiency of the agricultural sector. Individual farmers will have strong incentives to adopt any new cost-reducing technologies during this time of depressed prices and profits. However, farmers still are facing basic inelastic markets for agricultural commodities. The ultimate impact of biotechnological innovation could be even greater overproduction and/or greater excess capacity for agriculture in the twenty-first century.

Emerging information technology will create opportunities for more efficient financial management and marketing for farmers through application of modern management practices and principles. Effective management decisions depend on accurate analysis of data relevant to logical decision alternatives. New information technology will facilitate development of better information, more efficient delivery of more up-to-date information, more accurate analysis of information, and consequently more effective decisions. The twenty-first-century family farmer will have access to more information and computing power than did the twentieth-century corporate business.

Implications for Extension Programs

Future profitability of agriculture in general will be determined largely by factors beyond the control of individual farmers. Farmers must learn to cope with things they cannot manage or control. They cannot cope effectively with forces they do not understand. Thus, farmers need to understand the factors that determine their economic environment.

Individual decisions of farmers can improve their odds for survival and long-run profitability in spite of their inability to control either their market prices or input costs. Farmers can make decisions that will minimize losses during unprofitable times and maximize gains during times of general profitability. Extension programs of the future must give farmers the understanding to cope with the things they cannot control, the information and ability to manage the things they can control, and the wisdom to know the difference between the two.

INTERNATIONALIZATION OF U.S. AGRICULTURE. Farmers must understand that the economic future of American agriculture is closely tied to development of international markets. They need to understand comparative advantage, floating exchange rates, trade treaties, and international policy issues. Farmers will need to be able to evaluate potential impacts of general economic developments and agricultural policies on trade and impacts of trade on their markets and prices.

Growing world population means growing markets for U.S. commodities only to the extent that developing countries increase their ability and willingness to buy U.S. commodities as their populations increase. An uneducated agriculture will not support policies of international economic development and competitive world pricing, both of which are necessary in development of international markets. Extension agricultural economists must respond to this challenge to educate if agriculture is to support its best future prospect for growing markets and restored profitability.

RECAPITALIZATION OF AGRICULTURE. Farmers need to understand also the factors underlying the current recapitalization of agriculture. They need to understand the basic nature of economic forces that have depressed demand for their commodities and thus are forcing their land prices downward. Farmers need to understand the long-term process by which resources have been shifted out of agriculture and into other uses. A primary benefit of this understanding will be a restored faith that agriculture will again be profitable once the recapitalization process is complete.

The financial crisis in agriculture presents a unique opportunity for extension agricultural economists to develop effective economic decision-making programs for farmers. These programs likely will focus on farm survival as long as the financial crisis persists. Economists cannot restore profitability to agriculture, but economists can assist farm families in assessing their economic resources, in setting reasonable financial goals, in analysis of their financial situations, and in choosing among logical alternatives for the future. Farm families can make their own decisions regarding their future in agriculture on the basis of such information and analysis, and farmers can be taught the basics of financial management in this process. Such programs should be designed to assist farmers in taking advantage of future periods of profitability as well as helping them cope with the current period of financial stress.

Risk management will be a key element in future decision-making programs for farmers. International markets tend to be less certain and more risky than are domestic-based markets. Also, a highly leveraged agriculture faces greater financial risks. Perceived failures of past decision-oriented programs, whether real or only perceived, will force economists to accept a change in basic farm management philosophy. Most farm decision programs have dealt with profits as an ex post facto concept and thus have tended to focus on the past rather than the future. Decision-risk analysis facilitates realistic, before-the-fact assessment of future uncertainty and risks in analysis of alternative decisions. Risk analysis facilitates integration of production, marketing, and financial considerations in the management process. But most important, risk analysis helps farmers look forward rather than backward to assess realistically the future risks and potential profits from logical decision alternatives.

SOCIOECONOMIC INTERDEPENDENCIES. Internationalization and recapitalization have made farmers increasingly interdependent with their socioeconomic environment. An increasingly important interdependency is reflected in the growing number of part-time farmers. Farmers are choosing off-farm employment as a strategy to cope with greater revenue uncertainty and increasing financial risks. A new breed of farmer, a hybrid, has emerged from this process. These hybrid farmers appear to have greater risk tolerance and are more financial-stress resistant than are full-time farmers. Thus, they may represent an increasingly important extension clientele of the future.

Effective county-level extension programs of the future may well be hybrid programs reflecting roughly equal emphasis on community economic development and production agriculture. Hybrid farmers may be at least as concerned with their off-farm employment alternatives as with their farming operation. Many of these hybrids may come into farming from full-time employment. These farmers will need basic production and management skills that have been the mainstay of past county agricultural extension programs.

Hybrid farmers will be a more receptive audience for extension programs dealing with social issues. They will have a more direct stake in local public policies affecting resource use, human-capital development, environmental impacts of population growth, and quality of life in their communities. This orientation will strengthen traditional extension programs with local agribusiness firms, local government agencies, and community leaders. New hybrid programs could easily replace commercial agriculture programs as a source of primary political support for continued county-level extension work.

EMERGING TECHNOLOGICAL INNOVATIONS. Emerging biotechnology will represent a continuing challenge to agricultural economics to develop more effective management strategies for choosing among ever-changing technological alternatives. With emerging technologies, county-based delivery of commercial agricultural extension programs may be increasingly difficult but possibly less necessary as well. With improved telecommunication systems, larger commercial farmers will get more information and educational assistance direct from area or state extension specialists or from those conducting applied research. This should not be seen as a threat to extension but rather as an opportunity to free extension resources for use in reaching new clientele.

The microcomputer represents potentially the most powerful tool ever developed for extension agricultural economics work with farmers. The microcomputer can make the "dead science" of economics come to life on the "little green screen." Computers facilitate storing, assembling, and processing of information for individualized decision making. Computers can receive and process up-to-date information needed to execute production and marketing strategies. Computers facilitate individualized, realistic decision-risk analysis. All these things have been possible for years through terminals connected to main-frame or minicomputers. The critical difference is that farmers have total control of their microcomputers. Microcomputers cannot make decisions for farmers, but computers can make decision making much easier for a farmer who knows how to make good decisions.

Emerging telecommunications technology represents a golden opportunity for extension to tailor program delivery to the needs of its clientele. Videotapes and disks, computerized information retrieval, audio and video teleconferencing, and electronic publishing can be used to target programs to specific needs of groups and individuals. Adult learners are self-directed in that they prefer to choose the time, place, and pace at which they receive information and learn. Emerging technologies make possible more self-directed programs, and thus more effective programs, if extension economists have the courage to break old habits and develop new skills needed to use new delivery technology.

The Work of Agricultural Economics Extension

The work of agricultural extension is to educate and to inform. Section 1 of the Smith-Lever Act charges extension with diffusing useful and practical information among the people and with encouraging its use. Section 2, however, defines extension work as giving instruction in agriculture and related subjects to persons not resident in land-grant colleges. Cooperative extension in the past has tended to put more emphasis on promoting use of practical information than on instructing or educating those involved in agriculture. The challenges for agriculture approaching the twenty-first century may require a change in this emphasis.

The extension workers creed states our belief in people and their "right to make their own plans and arrive at their own decisions" and "that education, of which extension is an essential part, is basic in stimulating individual initiative, self-determination, and leadership, and that people, when given facts they understand, will act not only in their self-interest but also in the interest of society."

Our future extension programs must be based on the faith that education will result in more rational world and national economic policies, more effective agricultural policies, more acceptable state and local regulations, and more profitable individual decisions. The benefits from education are ellusive and difficult to measure. But, we must have the courage to insist that evaluations of our programs be based on whether they "educate" and not on whether they "promote" some specific action.

Extension economists of the future will view themselves as agricultural economists working in extension rather than as extension workers in agricultural economics. Agricultural economics represents our unique contribution to the overall extension process. Extension economists will have an increasingly important role in shaping the agricultural economics profession. Extension economists are aware that agricultural economics is and should continue to be a profession rather than a discipline. Disciplines inquire and teach in order to advance the state of knowledge. Professions apply disciplines in fulfilling missions through solving problems and exploiting opportunities. Professions may advance their parent disciplines, but this is not their primary role or function.

Agricultural economics is one of the mission-oriented departments within a mission-oriented land-grant university system. The basic mission of land-grant agricultural research and extension programs has been to generate benefits for society in general through more efficient production of food and fiber. The results have been impressive with less than five cents of each consumer dollar currently going to pay farmers for raw commodities. The mission and thus the success of land-grant research and extension have not been well understood by farmers or by the general public.

Support for land-grant agricultural programs has come largely from innovative farmers who reap first-round benefits from efficiency-improving technology and methodology. But, farmers are becoming fewer in number and potential for further social gains becomes less as fewer total resources are devoted to agriculture. In the future publically supported agricultural research and extension will have to build a new support base. Agricultural economists are confronted with a unique challenge in building this support base for future programs of land-grant universities.

Future social gains from agricultural research and extension must come largely from exploitation of potential export markets for agricultural commodities. Successful exploitation of these markets will require continued efficiency gains for U.S. agriculture and development of greater demand for U.S. commodities. Exports will be competitive with domestic consumption and thus may support food prices at higher levels than would exist with domestic-oriented markets. Economic development of foreign countries may develop competition for producers of specific commodities even though it is essential in developing markets for U.S. agriculture in general. Thus, support for export-oriented programs may not be readily forthcoming from either domestic consumers or producers of agricultural commodities.

Neither consumers nor producers will support future research and extension programs for agriculture unless they understand the broad social benefits from exploiting our comparative advantage in producing food and fiber for world markets. Agricultural economists are unique among agricultural scientists in understanding the nature of social benefits from efficient allocation of our economic resources. Our profession has failed to communicate past social benefits from lower food prices. Our programs survived on support from first-round benefits to farmers, but, there will be no clearly defined first-round benefactors to support our future mission. We have no choice but to teach the concept of social benefits and social costs to all public support groups. The future of the land-grant university concept may well depend on our success or failure in this vital mission of the agricultural economics profession.

19

A Synthesis of Research Issues

PRESTON E. LA FERNEY and JOHN E. LEE, JR.

The purpose of this paper is to begin the process of synthesizing the papers and discussions of the past two days relative to research issues. This brief synthesis is based on limited participation in discussion papers, a quick review of the printed drafts of papers, review of summaries of discussions from the various groups, and personal views of state and a federal administrators.

The purpose of this conference is to help the agricultural economics profession better serve during a period of rapid transition, change, and uncertainty—in agriculture, in the U.S. economy, and in the world—both now and as we look to the twenty-first century. Alternately stated, our purpose is to help agricultural economists to improve and articulate the value or worth of their contributions in view of (1) overall total effectiveness and (2) allocation of scarce resources in their direction, both now and into the twenty-first century.

First, a few personal observations may be useful. This conference has been very concentrated, pointing up the complexity of our domain, the considerable uncertainties facing society and us as a profession serving that society, the wealth of issues bidding for our individual and collective attention, the extent and strength of our talents, and the need to better structure ourselves to develop a product and communicate it effectively to potential users. For any one individual, such a conference is almost overwhelming, and it is somewhat presumptuous to attempt to synthesize all that we said and learned into a short paper. Thus, this paper cannot be a summary; it can only serve as a guide to the broad thrusts and conclusions of the conference.

Preston E. La Ferney is Director, Arkansas Agricultural Experiment Station. John E. Lee is Administrator, Economic Research Service, USDA.

The conference is only a beginning. We are generating new materials that now must be organized, packaged into carefully selected top-priority issues for research, developed into a blueprint for action, and finally incorporated into the budget process for consideration for funding through both our regular programs and as specially funded areas such as special and competitive grants. Our lot as the initial synthesizers for the research function is to begin the process of pulling it all together into a blueprint for research activity. The easy way out would be to develop the proverbial "laundry list" of issues, but the extent and complexity of issues and the limits on resources available to fund agricultural economics research dictate a prioritizing of issues. In fact, three sets of actions are called for before we are ready to enter the budget process:

1. Selection and clear statement of top-priority, umbrella-type issues for research. (Each would likely have several top-priority subissues clearly defined.)
2. Brief statements on methodology or process for each issue or set of issues.
3. A strategy through which our message can be communicated to potential users of the research and incorporated into the budget process.

The Priority Research Issue

It should be emphasized that our list of issues discussed here is not a complete one, but one that includes some broad areas or issues likely to be at the top of almost any agricultural economist's list of priority issues. Reading the papers, listening and participating in these discussions, one begins to see some common threads or recurring issues running through much of the deliberations. There is also some overlap among the broad discussion topics that served as the framework of the conference. To a great extent, "everything is related to everything else."

As an example of the overlap, we cite the broad issue, Domestic Food and Agricultural Policy, which is very closely related to International Agricultural Development, Macroeconomic Issues in Agriculture, and Agricultural Economic Structure and Adjustment—each a major, important umbrella issue in its own right. While this overlap is useful in identifying broad priority issues, it also signals a need to breathe some order or organization into the maze. It is hoped, our discussion here will begin the thought process necessary to such a logical ordering of issues.

FOOD AND AGRICULTURAL POLICY. This clearly is the agricultural economists' domain, and there is a great need to better synthesize what we know and do not know as a means to better channel our knowledge and analyses into the policymaking process. There is also a great need to broaden the scope of traditional domestic agricultural policy to focus analysis on food, trade, monetary issues, credit issues, and perhaps other relevant subissues. If the profession is to push one broad area for special grant-funding consideration, this is one of two logical candidates; there simply is no greater need facing agriculture and our society as a whole today.

NATURAL RESOURCE AND ENVIRONMENTAL MANAGEMENT. The importance of water, land, timber, and quality of the environment all make this or a similar umbrella research issue a must for the profession. We sense, on the basis of these discussions, that a lot of theoretical and methodological issues need to be thrashed out among ourselves as we move the research effort forward in this area. These issues will need to be faced internally early on. But, for now, we need to flesh out this area, complete with identification of high priority subissues and some attention to how we will proceed. A special task force may be needed to further develop this area as a funding issue before entering the budget process. This is the second single research area that we deem of sufficient importance to articulate more effectively before those who allocate research resources.

APPLIED MANAGEMENT. This issue is related directly to the "profitability" issue Dr. Bentley mentioned in his paper. Again, this is an issue clearly within the agricultural economists' domain, yet one that offers great opportunity and challenge for interdisciplinary research (one of those process-type common threads that have run throughout the conference). This issue includes at least (1) both production and marketing technology simultaneously, (2) household management, (3) financial and risk management within a dynamic, changing economic environment, and (4) information management. It surely would involve teaching and extension activity as well as research activity. It calls for a systems approach to research/extension, another key thought that has permeated discussions at the conference.

TECHNICAL INNOVATIONS. This issue area is receiving much attention currently because biotechnology and associated information technology related to the biotechnologies are such prominent issues worldwide. The renewed emphasis is appropriate, even though this is one of our traditional priority areas within the profession. Agricultural economists likely do not need to go forging into basic laboratories in great numbers, but they should begin to get involved early and significantly in applied technology issues. The costs, efficiencies, social impacts, etc., of various new technologies must be assessed by agricultural economists. Our judgment is that much of this effort will best be done through interdisciplinary teams of researchers.

This is both a priority issue demanding economists' input and a currently hot area for research funding.

ECONOMICS OF RURAL AREAS. We are in the midst of significant trends in the demographics, structure, and governing of rural America. This is a large, complex issue area, with a potential to be a "catchall," "heterogenous" issue. The current subissues constitute a maze in need of clarification and organization so that we can set about building a more orderly and useful body of knowledge for rural decision makers and local, state, and federal policymakers. Farm/nonfarm interactions, capital formation, poverty and income distribution, rural infrastructure, and financing local governments and services are logical, priority subissues.

MAINTAINING AND IMPROVING THE SOCIOECONOMIC DATA BASE. This is a priority issue area, considering the perceived departure from empirical research by the profession, the need for education and/or information regarding available statistics, and statistics policy (state and federal roles, coordination of efforts, etc.). Surely, in our rapidly changing economy and society, there is a growing need to enhance our basic pool of data, reexamine how we collect and maintain data, and be more inventive and efficient in the development, maintenance and sharing of data bases. On the latter point our capacity for electronic manipulation and dissemination of data has moved well beyond our institutional infrastructure for building and providing access to efficient and high-quality data bases.

Lest this set of priority issues take on the appearance of yet another laundry list, it may be helpful to group research priorities another way: (1) research to define and assist needed *adjustments* for the agricultural, rural, and resource sectors; and (2) research to assist the *adjustors* within those sectors.

The first broad group may be thought of, loosely, as more macro or aggregate in nature. It includes research to help define agriculture's rightful place in the U.S. and world economies (something that should not be taken for granted that we know already); the policies (commodity, trade, resource, etc.) consistent with that "rightful place"; the adjustment paths to that end; the consequences and distributional effects of alternative adjustment paths; and the performance of the agricultural and rural sectors and markets and the relationships of that performance to current and alternative policies. This broad area of research is particularly important in light of contemporary uncertainty about both the proper role of U.S. agriculture in world markets and the proper role of public intervention in the performance of that role. Especially at the federal level, public policymakers (hence funders) should be able to relate to this broad thrust of research.

The second broad category of research relates to providing assistance to the individuals, firms, and institutions who actually have to do the adjusting. Given the overall policy environment, global and domestic markets, and likely trends and uncertainties, research is needed to assist the management decisions of farmers, farm families, farm workers, resource owners and managers, rural governments, and agribusiness firms. To the extent that agricultural economists doing this kind of research are public employees, attention should be given to the focus of their research to assure that the benefits are distributed as broadly as possible, rather than captured by a few individuals or firms.

Agricultural economists at the federal level probably have some comparative advantage and certainly are accountable for research on the broader adjustment processes and the more macro and aggregate issues, but they have no exclusive rights to that research territory. The research tilt for agricultural economists in universities and at state and local levels will likely be toward aiding those who must make the adjustment decisions and bear the consequences, as well as toward regional and local aspects of broader national and global adjustments. Again, these relative emphases among researchers in the various institutions will be matters of degree.

Process or Methodology

Again, our discussions were characterized by several common threads involving the way we do our research as agricultural economists — our methodologies and processes. We try here to highlight and capture the essence of these priority concerns of the profession.

INTERDISCIPLINARY RESEARCH. Agricultural economists should have an advantage here inasmuch as our training is interdisciplinary in nature. Furthermore, the state-of-the-art in agricultural research is such that problem-solving and subject matter issues are increasingly multidisciplinary in nature. In our own self-interest, as well as in the interest of the society we serve, we must give careful, serious attention to greater involvement in these efforts. This approach will lead us to new constituencies and new sources of support. Certainly, this approach is anticipatory of the twenty-first century, with the prospect of even greater emphasis on a systems approach in our agricultural research.

NEW MECHANISMS FOR SYNTHESIZING AND DELIVERING RESEARCH OUTPUT. We must forge better systems for delivering our research output into effective application and use. This need is particularly clear in the case of research support of the food and agricultural policy process. We must find a way to better synthesize and deliver objective research information. The same processes or institutions could simultaneously (1) improve our basic capability to generate research output and (2) be most helpful in articulating and demonstrating the value of our product and in accessing the all-important budget process.

COMMUNICATING OUR FINDINGS. This process issue has much in common with the previous one. It involves assessment and communication of the value or worth of our findings to policymakers and other economic decision makers. We must do a better job of communicating with constituents, legislators, secretaries of agriculture, and even colleagues in other disciplines and Experiment Station directors. We still have the traditional challenge to back away from our technical jargon and speak in terms our users and administrators and members of Congress understand. This challenge is complicated by new demands of the information age. This area is particularly important to us in our research/extension interrelationships.

IMPROVING TIES AMONG OUR SUBGROUPS. There is a great need to improve the effectiveness of interaction among various subgroups of the profession. Among the key interrelationships in need of our best attention and effort are

- Research/Extension;
- Research/Teaching;
- State/Federal;
- Public/Private (especially in the technology area); and
- Agricultural Economists/Economists.

USE OF ECONOMIC THEORY. Much attention has been given in this conference to the need to assure that our research is consistent with sound economic theory; the need for agricultural economists to contribute to improvements in theory; and the need to expand our acquaintance with areas of economic theory traditionally beyond our mainstream. Examples of the latter include macroeconomic theory and trade theory.

CONTINUED IMPROVEMENT IN QUANTITATIVE METHODS. There likely will be increasing need for attention to this issue as we approach the twenty-first century and an increasing complexity of issues. Johnson makes the point in his paper of the possible need for greater specialization by a few organizational units to be able to afford the intensive input required for significant development of quantitative methods. In any event, the quantitative methods, particularly the analytical/forecasting/policy models, should grow out of or follow on theoretical development and issue-oriented or policy-type research.

Some may well argue that "Quantitative Methods," as well as "Economic Theory" previously discussed are not only methodological issues but also research issues in their own right. We would agree that both areas need attention as research issues, even though they are method-oriented.

Strategy

By strategy, we refer to the development of the blueprint for action that can be used as an organizing mechanism among us for conducting research and delivering product to users as well as a means of effective entry into the budget process. The essence of the document required for any broad research area is envisioned to be a brief treatise laying out in a terse manner (1) a well-defined umbrella-type, broad research issue, stated with justification to be top priority with respect to society's needs, with subissues, also stated to be top priority, developed and related to each other; (2) a brief methodology, laying out what we propose to do, what it will do for society, and what it will cost to get the job done; and (3) presentation of the package to the budget process via the Experiment Station Committee on Policy, the Joint Council on Food and Agricultural Sciences, the National Association of State Universities and Land Grant Colleges, and other such bodies.

The kind of prototype document we have in mind for any one broad, umbrella-type issue is the "Silver Bullet" document cited by Dr. Hullar in his paper, which has been successful in attracting significant new, special grant funds earmarked for the biotechnology area of research.

We have many pluses going for us to make such an effort successful:

- Lots of talent;
- An established, respected profession;
- This conference and the wealth of raw product it has produced on issues and process, and the experience it has provided in working together to plan forward for agricultural economics research;
- An Assistant Secretary and an Administrator of CSRS who are eager to help and who have demonstrated effectiveness in getting important things done; and
- A world crying out for our help.

Conclusion

The bottom line, in our view, is whether we are truly useful to our society, not whether we score points with our presentations at this conference or impress those who fund us. To be useful in a world of growing need for economic understanding but with limited resources for economists, we must do the right things, do them well, do them efficiently, and effectively deliver the results to those who need them. If we do, the support we need will be there.

INDEX